1,001 Computer Hints & Tips

1,001 Computer Hints & Tips

An A-to-Z Guide to Making the Most of Your Computer and the Internet

Reader's Digest

The Reader's Digest Association (Canada) Ltd., Montreal

National Library of Canada Cataloguing in Publication Data:

Main entry under title:

    Reader's Digest 1001 computer hints & tips: an A-Z guide to
making the most of your computer and the Internet.

Includes index.
ISBN 0-88850-746-1

    1. Computer—Popular works. 2. Internet—Popular works.
I. Reader's Digest Association (Canada) II. Title: One thousand and one
computer hints & tips. III. Title: 1001 computer hints & tips.

QA76.5.R43 2001   004   C2001-901886-X

Address any comments about *1,001 Computer Hints and Tips* to:
Editor, Books and Home Entertainment,
c/o Customer Service, Reader's Digest,
1125 Stanley Street, Montreal, Quebec H3B 5H5

For information on this and other Reader's Digest products
or to request a catalogue, please call our 24-hour Customer Service hotline at 1-800-465-0780.

Visit us on our website at: www.readersdigest.ca.

Printed in Canada

01 02 03 / 5 4 3 2 1

PLANET THREE PUBLISHING NETWORK

Edited, designed, and produced by
Planet Three Publishing Network
Northburgh House, 10 Northburgh Street, London EC1V 0AT

EDITOR Gordon Torbet • **DEPUTY EDITOR** Clive Somerville
ASSOCIATE EDITORS Eva Lauer Mary Pickles
SUB-EDITORS Amie McKee Jane Donovan Lisa Dyer
ART DIRECTOR Paul Mitchell • **ART EDITOR** Darren Jordan
DESIGNERS Harj Ghundale Heather Dunleavy
STILLS ART DIRECTOR Darren Jordan
PHOTOGRAPHY Karl Adamson
ILLUSTRATORS Richard Elson Nigel Dobbyn Ian Ward
Willian McLean Kerr David Farris Matt Drew
INDEXER Laura Hicks

CONTRIBUTORS
Jillian Werb Kevin Wiltshire Mike Williams Clark Dunn Owain Bennallack
Paul Ricketts Kate Russell Tufan Unal Pete Connor Stephen Dunthorne
Raymond Dunthorne Gary Irwin Lewis Lyons Mike Williams Sandra Vogel
Lisa Magloff David Fox David Wright Andrew Hutchinson Clive Somerville
Consultant Barry Plows

Reader's Digest Project Staff

PROJECT EDITOR Andrew R. Byers
COPY EDITOR Gilles Humbert
DESIGNER Cécile Germain
PRODUCTION MANAGER Holger Lorenzen
PRODUCTION COORDINATOR Susan Wong

CONTRIBUTORS
Researcher Patricia Buchanan
Consultant Paul Schwartz

Books and Home Entertainment

VICE PRESIDENT Deirdre Gilbert
MANAGING EDITOR Philomena Rutherford
ART DIRECTOR John McGuffie
EDITORIAL ADMINISTRATOR Elizabeth Eastman

U.S. Staff

SENIOR EDITOR Don Earnest
DESIGNER George McKeon

ABOUT THIS BOOK

Whether you're a PC novice or you're already familar with certain aspects of your PC—perhaps you regularly type letters, send e-mail, or browse the Net—*1,001 Computer Hints and Tips* will help you get more from your PC. It's packed with simple, detailed explanations to help you expand your knowledge.

A-Z SECTIONS

The information in *1,001 Computer Hints and Tips* is clearly divided into four categories: Windows, Software, the Internet, and Hardware. Within each section, the subjects are arranged in alphabetical order, making it easy to locate topics when you're browsing through the book. Unlike conventional PC guides, you are positively encouraged/invited to dip into the pages of *1,001 Computer Hints and Tips* in any order.

SAMPLE DOUBLE-PAGE ▼

Like an encyclopedia, the first and last entry on each double-page is shown in the top left- and right-hand corners of the page for easy reference.

The title of each entry is shown in a different color, so you can quickly see what the entry is talking about.

WINDOWS

Learn about the world's most popular operating system and how to keep it running smoothly to make the most of your PC's power.

SOFTWARE

Discover quick tips and little known features of a wide range of practical programs, both familiar and new.

INTERNET

This category guides you through the often bewildering world of the Internet straight to the best websites, and explores the various features that are available.

HARDWARE

You don't need to know exactly how your printer, monitor, and other computer components and peripherals work to get the best out of them. This section shows you how.

Windows

Software

The Internet

Hardware

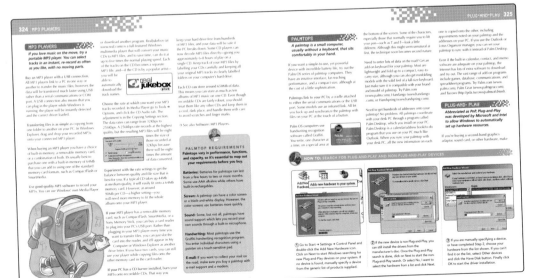

WHICH SOFTWARE? ▼

This book assumes that you're using a PC with either the latest edition of the Windows operating system—Windows Millennium— or Windows 98.

SPECIAL FEATURES ▶

Interspersed within the A–Z sections are 50 feature pages covering topics of special interest in greater depth. Subjects include optimizing your PC, desktop publishing, digital cameras, and printers as well as sports and travel planning on the Internet.

TEXT PANELS ▼

Check out the websites in the yellow text panels for the most up-to-date information as well as numerous sites that allow you to download useful and often free software.

Blue text panels provide instructions or additional tips, such as introductions to programs, explanations of terms and tools, and helpful keyboard shortcuts.

MAKERS OF HOME AND GARDEN SOFTWARE

The big boys in do-it-yourself design.

HomeStyles.com
(www.store.homestyles.com)
Steal a few ideas. HomeStyles publishes several CD-ROM libraries of home plans.

IMSI (www.imsisoft.com)
Look out for IMSI's comprehensive interior design program.

Macmillan U.S.A.
(www.macmillansoftware.com)
Macmillan U.S.A.'s gardening software includes 3D Garden Designer 3.0 Millenium Edition.

WORDS OF WISDOM

Learning the main terms used in the programs will help you understand Works better.

Task: Any activity you carry out in Works, from adding appointments to the calendar to creating a spreadsheet.

Template: A ready-made document that helps you get started and can be customized to your individual needs.

Wizard: A step-by-step guide that helps you create a document, such as a letter or fax.

Task Launcher: The home page of Works—
the area from which you can launch all your

GLOSSARY ▶

For clear, concise definitions of the computer terms used in *1,001 Computer Hints and Tips*—including instructions on navigating menus, dialog boxes, and toolbars and using your mouse—turn to the Glossary at the back of the book.

INDEX ▶

A comprehensive cross-referenced index of topics that will help you locate any subject of your choice.

HOW TO: ▶

The easy-to-follow step-by-step instructions help you to carry out a useful activity mentioned in one of the main entries. You are guided through each exercise by snapshots of the PC screen showing what you should be seeing on your own screen. Often more than one picture will be shown for each step.

The numbered instructions that accompany the snapshots sometimes show actions linked by an arrow (→). This means that you carry out the actions immediately after each other, often as options available in a drop-down or pop-up menu.

HOW TO: NAME A RANGE IN EXCEL

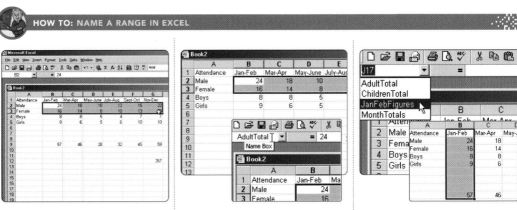

① Highlight the data cells you want to include in the range. First place the cursor in the top left-hand cell (B2). Hold down the left mouse button and drag the mouse to the far right-hand cell (G3), then release the button.

② Click in the Name Box below the main toolbar and type the name you want to use for your range. Do not include any spaces between characters. Press Enter to assign the name to the range. Name as many ranges as you wish for quick reference.

③ The named ranges can now be accessed by clicking on the down arrow at the side of the Name Box. To view a named range on your worksheet, select it from the list and the cells will be highlighted automatically.

CONTENTS

Entries in color are double-page special features.

SOFTWARE

THE INTERNET

HARDWARE

Windows

Open up the world's most popular operating system, and discover what makes your PC tick. Learn how to keep it running like clockwork, and make the most of your PC's power.

ACCESSIBILITY

Using a PC straight out of the box won't work for everyone especially if you have a disability.

Windows can help if your vision, hearing, or mobility is less than perfect. Windows Accessibility Options include HighContrast and Magnifier to aid readability. FilterKeys screens out inadvertent repeated keystrokes, and StickyKeys lets you press key combinations one key at a time. For more information, check the Microsoft website (www.microsoft.com/enable).

Have trouble maneuvering a mouse? Go to Start ➔ Settings ➔ Control Panel and double-click the Accessibility Options icon. Click on the Mouse tab in the Accessibility Properties

INSTALLING THE ACCESSIBILITY OPTIONS

The Accessibility Options aren't always loaded as standard so you'll need your Windows CD to install them.

1. To see if you have Accessibility Options installed on you computer, click on Start ➔ Programs ➔ Accessories. Look for an Accessibility choice on the drop-down Accessories menu.

2. If you don't see it, install it by choosing Start ➔ Settings ➔ Control Panel and selecting Add/Remove Programs, then the Windows Setup tab. Select Accessibility, choose the Details button, and add a check to both the Accessibility Options and Accessibility Tools options.

3. Click OK, then OK again to confirm. Windows then asks you to put the Windows CD in your disc drive and will install the Enhanced Accessibility feature automatically from the CD.

window and click the Use MouseKeys box. You can adjust the settings by clicking on Settings, or just click OK. Now you can use the numeric key pad numbers to move your mouse pointer.

Take a shortcut to turn Mouse Keys on and off. If you check the Use Shortcut box in the settings dialog box, you can switch Mouse Keys on and off: just hold down your left Shift key and left Alt key, and then press Num Lock.

Are you hard of hearing? Use SoundSentry to add visual clues to the audio warnings that your PC makes. Open Accessibility Options in the Control Panel,click on the Sound tab and check the Use SoundSentry box.

ACTIVE DESKTOP

Using Windows Active Desktop means that your computer is truly integrated with the Web.

Your Windows Desktop can be made to look and work like a web page so you can display web content directly on your Desktop and get the most from your Internet connection. Content is updated automatically.

Many popular portal sites—such as Yahoo! or Excite—feature customizable pages for registered users. Select one of these as your Active Desktop page for the latest news and weather—even horoscopes—right there on your Desktop.

Are you thinking about building a website of your own? Now you can create your own "personal admin" page, hide it behind publicly accessible pages, and even password-protect it. You can also make it your Active Desktop page and set up links to the files that you want access to—Word or Excel documents, pictures, contacts, and so on—stored on your web server. That way you can make any PC your very own by setting this page as an Active Desktop.

You can include all sorts of elements as part of the HTML code when you use your own web page as the Windows background. Try text in different fonts, colors, and sizes; tables, pictures, and clickable links to web pages, files on your hard drive or your company's network, and even specific locations—like a section of an Excel spreadsheet—within those files.

⇨ See also **Internet: HTML** and **Website Creation**

ADD/REMOVE PROGRAMS

The longer you have your computer, the more software you're likely to install on it. Use the Add/Remove Programs icon to upgrade.

To access the Add/Remove Programs function, just go to Start ➔ Settings ➔ Control Panel and double-click on the Add/Remove Programs icon. The Add/Remove Programs Properties dialog box opens. Click the Install/Uninstall tab, scroll through the list of programs in the main panel, select the one that you want to remove, and then click the Add/Remove button below it.

Some software may not be as useful as you thought and you'll need to remove it so your PC doesn't get filled up. Just deleting a program's folder from the Windows Explorer folder will leave traces of the program all over the place. Use Windows Add/Remove Programs feature to keep your computer functioning efficiently.

Even if you have upgraded to Windows Me, there are two entries in the Add/Remove Programs Properties dialog box on uninstalling Windows Me. These are Uninstall Windows Millennium and Delete Windows Millennium uninstall information. If you want to revert to your previous version of Windows, select Uninstall Windows Millennium and click on Add/Remove. Windows Me prompts you to confirm the uninstall operation. Click Yes. You are then prompted to run ScanDisk. Click Yes again. When

ScanDisk is finished, Windows Me prompts you to confirm uninstall again. Just click Yes again and Windows Me shuts down and restarts in DOS. It prompts you to confirm uninstall once more, then removes itself from your hard disk.

And while you may have upgraded, there's still a remote possibility that you could have hardware or software that doesn't work with it. The best thing to do in this situation is to go back to your previous version of Windows, and keep a look out for a fix or patch that will make Me work with your set up. One important point to remember: when you upgrade to Windows Me, make sure that you save existing files just in case anything doesn't go as planned!

Installed Windows Me without any problems? Free up some hard drive space by removing system files from your previous version of Windows. Access the Add/Remove Programs Properties dialog box, select the Delete Windows Millennium uninstall information item, and click on Add/Remove.

Don't use the Add/Remove Programs box to remove any unrecognizable names. This is

because removing the small but vital programs supplied with hardware—such as your video card—may adversely affect the way your computer works.

Even if a program that you have installed on your PC has its own uninstall routine, it's always best to use Add/Remove Programs to make sure that no traces are left on your PC.

Create a spare Windows Me Startup disk. To do this, place a blank floppy in your A:/ drive, click on the Startup Disk tab on the Add/Remove Programs Properties dialog box, and then click on Create Disk.

To add or remove different Windows features, click on the Windows Setup tab. You'll need to use your Windows CD, so make sure you have have it nearby.

 HOW TO: REMOVE A PROGRAM

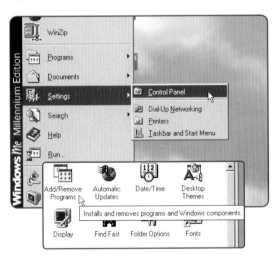

(1) First open the Add/Remove Programs Properties dialog box. Go to Start → Settings → Control Panel, and double-click the Add/Remove Programs icon.

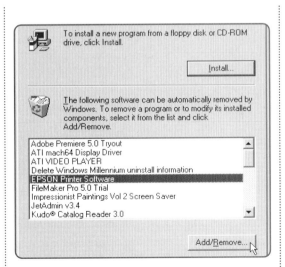

(2) Listed in the window are the programs you can remove. To view the whole list, scroll up or down with the scroll bar on the right and locate your program. Highlight it with the mouse cursor. The Add/Remove button is now active; click it to begin uninstalling.

(3) Now confirm whether you wish to continue the "uninstall" routine. Click Yes to continue. Your PC will now search through its files and folders, attempting to delete all the program components placed on your hard drive. Click OK to finish.

BACKING UP

Your PC is a great business tool, fantastic for browsing the Internet, sending e-mails, and matching the best consoles for game play. But sometimes you have to do a bit of work to make sure things don't go wrong. To avoid losing your favorite files, backup your system using a floppy disk, Zip drive, or hard drive.

WHAT IS A BACKUP?

A backup can be just one file that you've copied to a floppy disk, or it can be a compressed copy of the contents of your entire hard drive. If you only have a few important files, it may not seem necessary to go to the trouble of backing up other data. However, if your hard drive fails, your Word preferences, e-mail settings, and all your e-mails and Internet Favorites will be lost—not to mention programs you may have previously installed and any Windows settings.

Don't forget your backup. Although modern hard drives are superbly engineered, all your precious documents and files cannot be replaced if something goes wrong—unless you've backed up your data. Performing a backup is a task that can be mostly automated. Windows provides a Backup Wizard to help you, and there are a number of options for the safe storage of your files.

DATA STORAGE OPTIONS

If you only intend copying a few files onto a floppy disk, use a file-compression program to squeeze more data onto the disk. WinZip or WinRar will compress an Excel spreadsheet or Word document by as much as 85 percent without losing any data. Although images can't be compressed as much as text-based files, this is still a great way to maximize the number of documents you can fit onto a disk. Even if you're using a larger storage medium, compression gives you a more efficient use of space. You can download a free trial version of WinZip (www. winzip.com) from the Web.

When the number of files you want to backup exceeds the capacity of a floppy disk, there are better options. If you want to store up to 250Mb of data, an Iomega Zip drive is ideal. For data storage of up to 2Gb, consider a Jaz drive. Each of these comes with simple-to-use software to help you set up the device, and establish an automatic backup schedule. Whichever you buy, choose a USB version because it's fast and allows you to plug in the device while Windows is running.

To backup several gigabytes of data, use a tape streamer—a device which backs up data very fast onto a digital tape. There are several formats available from your local PC store. A popular one is DAT (digital audio tape), and this process normally runs overnight—despite the high speed, compressing and copying large amounts of data is time-consuming.

How regularly you backup data comes down to how often you update it. If you only use your PC to type an occasional letter, then once a month is adequate. However, if you store all your personal expenses in Excel or use your PC for a small business, then once a week or at the end of each work day is better. You can manually copy files or set up an automatic backup using either the Backup Wizard in Windows Me or Cibeo's Backup Scheduler (www. cibeo.com/ software_store/) or Datakeeper (www.power quest.com).

ARCHIVE OR BACKUP?

Archiving is when the data is to be kept intact rather than overwritten each time a backup is performed. If you need to keep a permanent record of changes in documents, then a CD writer is the ideal solution. You can install an internal unit, which takes up one slot on the front of your PC and plugs into a spare IDE port. Alternatively, you can get a USB external drive. A Recordable CD (CD-R) stores up to 650Mb of data but doesn't allow you to delete files, and thus will gradually fill up. To update information, consider a CD-RW (ReWritable), which allows you to treat the CD almost like a hard drive.

STORAGE ON THE WEB

With a fast Internet connection, you can store data for free on the Internet. Dedicated sites provide space for use as an Internet hard drive, and they're very secure—some will even appear in your Windows Explorer window as an extra hard drive, letting you drag and drop files to and from the server. While it's is not suitable for automated backups, it's a great way to store your data where it can't be affected by local conditions or accessed easily by others.

LOOK IN THE MIRROR

When the data on your hard drive is virtually irreplaceable, the solution is to install a second hard drive to "mirror" your main drive. This means whenever you write data to a drive, it is also written to a second hard drive, creating an exact copy in event of failure. Of course, this provides no recourse if your computer is struck by a virus, because it will simultaneously infect both drives. Another option is to use software such as Norton Ghost, which creates an exact compressed copy of your primary drive on the second drive. If the first drive fails, the compressed files can be restored.

To create a backup of your Word settings, use the Windows search utility to find a file called "normal.dot." This is the default Word template containing all your preferences. Make a note of its location and copy the file to a floppy disk. Another

important set of files are your Outlook Express e-mail folders. Search for "*.dbx"—you will find a series of files representing your e-mail folders called "inbox.dbx," "outbox.dbx," and so on. These are large files, so you'll need to compress them. Note their folder, and copy them to a suitable location. Make a manual note of your e-mail and Dial Up Networking settings.

If you have just bought your PC or have just performed a reformat, and reinstalled Windows, make a ghost copy of your entire hard drive onto a CD-R disc. This will be an exact mirror image of your initial set up. If something goes wrong or your hard drive fails, you can restore the image from the ghost disc and your system will be ready to run without you having to reinstall and reconfigure everything. This method only works if your PC has exactly the same hardware that it had when the ghost image was originally created. You can't just copy the data across because the data must be exactly as it is on your hard drive and must be restored that way to work.

HOW TO: USE WINDOWS' BACKUP WIZARD

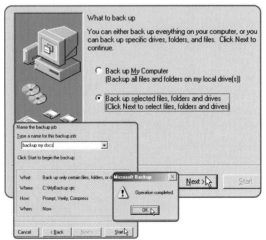

① With your Windows Me CD in the CD drive, browse to the MSBackup folder. Double-click on "msbexp.exe" to start installation. Click on Start → Programs → Accessories → System Tools → Backup. Select Create a new backup job option and click OK.

② Select Back up selected files, folders and drives and click Next. Check each file and folder you want backed up, and select the All selected files. Click Next again. Choose a destination, and choose a name for your backup. Click Start, then click OK.

③ Backup regularly. Go to Start → Programs → Accessories → System Tools → Scheduled Tasks. Double-click Add Scheduled Task. Click Next, then Browse. Double-click Program Files, then Accessories → Backup → MSBACKUP file. Select Weekly, choose a day, and click OK.

CD PLAYER

Play music while you work with Windows Me Media Player.

Use your CD-ROM drive to listen to music while you work. It can be a great way to keep you alert and increase your productivity. Insert your favorite CD into your PC and, as long as you have speakers or—for added privacy—a set of stereo headphones, you can hear your favorite music play automatically.

When you insert an audio CD into the CD-ROM drive, Windows Media Player pops up and starts playing. If you want to turn this Autorun function off, go to Start → Settings → Control Panel, and double-click on the System icon. Select the Device Manager tab, open the CD-ROM branch, and double-click the CD-ROM drive. Click Properties, choose the Settings tab, and uncheck the Auto insert notification box. Click OK, then Close, and restart Windows.

You can play your CDs in random or continuous modes. Go to Start → Programs → Accessories → Entertainment → Windows Media Player. In the CD Audio window, go to Play and click Shuffle or Repeat. To hear only the first few seconds of each track, use Ctrl+F to skip from one to the next, or Ctrl+B to skip backward through the CD tracks.

Media Player lets you place all the important information about a CD into its memory. If you enter the name of the artist, the title of the CD, and all the song titles, the next time you insert that CD, the information will reappear.

Media Player enters the track titles of many CD albums automatically, but if it doesn't, you can do it by clicking on View → Now Playing Tools → Show Playlist. In a panel to the right, you'll see tracks listed. Right-click on each track and select Edit, then simply type in the name of the track. Click anywhere outside the Playlist panel to deselect the track and right-click on the next track, and so on. Media Player will

then automatically remember all the track titles you have entered and be ready for the next time you want to play the CD.

To switch between tracks while a CD is playing, click the Next button (a right-facing arrow with a vertical bar) at the base of the Media Player window. Alternatively, double-click the track you want from the available tracks in the Playlist panel.

Don't like the Media player? There are plenty of other CD players on the Internet. Many shareware and commercial products, like

Winamp, have equally advanced features. You can locate and download them from a freeware site like Download.com (www.download.com).

⇨ See also **Windows: Windows 95 to Me; Internet: Downloading** and **Shareware.**

HOW TO: DOWNLOAD AND INSTALL THE WINAMP CD PLAYER

Saving:
winamp271_std.exe from download.nullsoft.com

Estimated time left: 4 min 27 sec (170 KB of 917 KB
Download to: C:\My Documents\winamp271_
Transfer rate: 2.79 KB/Sec

☐ Close this dialog box when download completes

Open   Open Fol

① Go to www.download.com where the free Winamp CD player download is located, and follow the on-screen instructions. When the download is complete, double-click the installation program called "winamp272_lite."

Winamp Setup: Installation Directory

Setup has determined the optimal location to install. If you wo like to change the directory, do so now.

Select the directory to install Winamp in:

C:\Program Files\Winamp   Bro

Space available: 2
Space required: 11

Winamp Setup: User information

Email address: a.nother@email
ZIP code (US) or Country: ZN2000

☐ Yes, sign me up for a Free 3GB Winamp Locker so that I c access my music from any PC (Recommended)
☐ Yes, send me Winamp announcements (Recommended)
☐ Yes, send me the latest news from trusted 3rd parties on special offers of interest to me
☑ Yes, allow anonymous usage statistics (Recommended)
   With this option checked, Winamp will occasionally sen basic usage statistics back to Winamp.com. The inform that is reported is simply how much Winamp is being use
   ☐ Stop buggi

② In the Installation Directory window make sure the program is installed in a suitable folder, such as C:\Program Files\Winamp. When you click Next the files will be installed. Click Next at the Settings window, and add your details in the User information window.

Winamp Setup: Winamp successfully installed

Winamp is now installed. Select 'Run Winamp' to begin.

New users should try our Winamp Walkthrough

Advanced users should check out Winamp.com for Winamp skins and plug-ins.

minibrowser

Welcome to the Winamp Minibrowser
Find artist information while listening with the Nullsoft Winamp Minibrowser

• Free Music, Live MP3 Radio - Tune into SHOUTcast
• Visit Winamp.com for News, Winamp Skins and Plug ins
• Store your music online in your Winamp Locker
• Search for music on Ebay
• Buy CDs from Amazon.com
• Artist Photos, Bios and Reviews on Rollingstone.com

Where Music Lives Online

③ Winamp then sends the details to its website. When this is done, click on Run Winamp to start the program. The interface is split into four elements—Main Window, Playlist Editor, Equalizer, and Minibrowser. You can close each separately without affecting the rest.

CLIPBOARD

Use this Windows feature to move data between documents.

Every time you copy or cut something from a document, the text, image, or file is kept on the Windows Clipboard until you decide where you want to paste it.

The Windows Clipboard helps you take pictures of the screen. To capture an active Window only, press Alt+Print Screen. Press Print Screen by itself to capture everything on the screen. Either of these actions sends the captured image to your Windows Clipboard. You can then launch Paint (go to Start ➜ Programs ➜ Accessories ➜ Paint) and choose Edit ➜ Paste to retrieve the image.

Windows provides Clipboard Viewer so that you can see the contents of the Clipboard— which contains the latest item you have copied or cut from a document. To access Clipboard Viewer, go to Start ➜ Programs ➜ Accessories ➜ System Tools, and click on Clipboard Viewer.

It's a good idea to use Clipboard Viewer if you have cut a large amount of text that you don't want to use it right away. Launch the Clipboard Viewer, click on File, select Save As, and save

the text or image as a .clp file. Make sure you save it into a logical place, such as a folder for all your .clp files.

CONTROL PANEL

Something you want to change about the way your PC works? The Control Panel is the place to do it.

You can access the Control Panel in two ways. Either go to Start ➜ Settings ➜ Control Panel, or simply double-click on My Computer on your Desktop, then double-click the Control Panel.

Adjust your audio and video functions exactly the way you want. Go to Start ➜ Settings ➜ Control Panel and double-click on Sounds and Multimedia to reveal the Multimedia Properties dialog box. From here you can set the audio devices you want to use for playback and recording. You can also select a preset sound scheme, such as the ones that are used by Windows Themes.

Adjust the standby times for your desktop PC. For advanced power management features, click on Power Options in the Control Panel and you can set different functions, such as when your monitor and hard drive will go into standby after inactivity. If this is set for 10 minutes, you may find it constantly interrupts your work, so try 30 minutes instead.

If your PC is set to standby or hibernate after a while, add a password that needs to be entered before it wakes up. Control Panel's Power Options is one of the places where you can add password protection. Click the Advanced tab and then check the box next to Prompt for password when computer goes off standby and hibernate. When someone presses a key or moves the mouse to bring the PC out of the standby mode, the Enter Password box will appear. In this case, it's the same password that you use for user or network log-in.

Keep an eye on your mouse. Go to Control Panel and double-click on Mouse. Select the Pointer Options tab. Check the Show pointer

trails box to initiate mouse trails. Set how much of a trail to leave by adjusting the slider.

You can add new programs, or remove any old ones that you no longer use. Go to Control Panel and double-click Add/Remove Programs. You can add new software, install additional components from your Windows installation CD, and even create a Startup Disk to help you, should you ever experience any problems with trying to boot up Windows.

➪ See also **Windows: Start Menu.**

CONTROL PANEL ICONS
There are over 20 Control Panel functions. Here are just a few of them.

 Add New Hardware: Essential for adding new gear, such as soundcards and modems.

 Gaming Options: Configure and test game controls, such as joysticks, joypads, and steering wheels.

 Internet Options: Great for taking care of your History folders and temporary Internet files. Also adjusts your security settings and ISP connections and specifies which programs Windows uses for each Internet service.

 Keyboard: Change the speed at which the text cursor blinks and switch between keyboard layouts.

 Sounds and Multimedia: You can use this to assign sounds and sound controls to various Windows tasks and actions, such as startup, shutdown, and warning messages.

COLORS

You can adjust the speed and performance of your computer by selecting different color settings for the monitor to display.

If your computer is a bit pokey, you can increase the speed—and make it work more smoothly at the same time—by decreasing the "color depth" of your display. This means reducing the amount of colors that are used to make up the picture on the screen. Be aware that you'll be sacrificing some screen detail.

To access the color depth settings for your display, right-click on the Desktop, select Properties, then select the Settings tab. Click the

COLOR SETTINGS

The color settings options you are likely to see on most computers.

16 Colors
Uses 16 different shades of color to make up your display. This is the lowest quality.

256 Colors
Uses 256 different shades of color in the visual display.

Hi Color (16-bit)
Uses more than 32,000 colors. A good setting for most average home PCs.

True Color (24-bit)
Uses 16 million colors in the display. Since the human eye can only distinguish a few million colors, this is more than enough to accurately represent any color image on your screen.

True Color (32-bit)
Theoretically capable of showing more than 16-million colors. In practice, it is identical to 24-bit True Color mode.

small black arrow inside the Colors section to reveal a pop-up menu of your options. Select a lower number of colors than you have currently to decrease your color depth.

Some modern graphics cards have additional features that enable you to optimize the color settings of your monitor. To access them, open the Display Properties dialog box, select the Settings tab, and then click Advanced. You can then adjust your specific graphics card settings.

Some PCs require you to restart before new color depth settings are put into effect. Make sure that you save any work and close any programs that might be open before selecting OK to make the adjustment.

For clearer, crisper, more realistic looking images, you should use a large number of colors. This is because color depth is categorized by the number of colors and the amount of bits that comprise each pixel. A bit is the smallest possible point that your graphics card and monitor can display— much like the tiny dots that make up a photo in a printed newspaper.

COPYING FILES

From time to time, you might want to copy files on your hard drive into a different folder or transfer them to a floppy or Zip disk.

The Move To and Copy To buttons on the toolbar at the top of each Windows Millenium window can be used instead of the right-click process (see How To opposite). Select the file you want to copy, then click the Copy To button. Finally, select the folder you want to copy the file to and click OK. The Move To button works in the same way—except that it

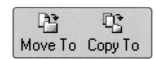

will delete the original file after copying it to the new folder.

If you want to use a file on another computer, place a formatted floppy disk in your A drive. Select the files and go to Edit → Send To → Floppy (A:). It will be copied onto the disk. The file can be transferred onto any PC that has a compatible drive.

To copy several files at the same time, hold the Ctrl key while clicking on the files to highlight them. Release the Ctrl key and click the Copy To icon. You can deselect any file in the group by clicking it while depressing the Ctrl key.

If you want to copy the entire contents of a folder, go to Edit → Select All. Pressing Ctrl+A together will also select all the files in the active window. Now copy them as usual.

The larger the file you are copying, the longer it takes to appear in the new folder window. In the case of very large files, or groups of files, you'll see a dialog box detailing the progress of the task your PC is performing. With such larger files, it's always advisable to let your computer finish copying these files before attempting another operation.

⇨ See also **Software: Cut and Paste; Hardware: Floppy Disks.**

DELETING FILES

If you don't delete unwanted files regularly, you could quickly run out of space for storing more information on your hard drive.

Multiple files can be deleted together by holding down the Ctrl key, and then clicking each file once to select it. When all the relevant files are highlighted, follow any one of the deletion procedures below.

After you have deleted a file, it will be stored inside the Recycle Bin. This is a safety precaution to help prevent any files from being deleted accidentally. Once you're positive you want to delete the files, you can empty the Recycle Bin by right-clicking it and selecting Empty Recycle Bin.

To delete a file without it appearing in the Recycle Bin, right-click the file then hold down the Shift key while clicking Delete. Do this only if you are sure that you want to delete the file.

If there are any deleted files in your Recycle Bin, the icon displayed on your Desktop will indicate this by showing it full of trash. To open and view the bin's contents, double-click on it.

If you delete a file accidentally, you can restore it to its original location. Open the Recycle Bin, select the file, and then click on File followed by Restore. The file you have selected will then be automatically restored to its previous location on your hard drive.

When you delete a file, you're only telling your operating system that you no longer need to use it—the information stays on the disk until your operating system overwrites the space it occupies with new data.

If you don't want anyone to access your deleted files, empty the Recycle Bin and defragment your hard drive. This causes the

data to be rearranged into neat blocks, thus covering up the ghost of your deleted files. Go to Start → Programs → Accessories → System Tools and select Disk Defragmenter.

Before giving away or disposing of any removable media—such as floppy disks, Zip disks, and tape drives—make sure you have deleted any sensitive or private files. The best way to ensure this is to perform a complete reformat (see Floppy Disks and Zip drives in the Hardware section for how to do this).

There are three ways to delete files. You can locate the file you want to remove on your hard drive, right-click it and select Delete. Or click on an unwanted file and hold the left mouse button down as you drag it over to the Recycle Bin icon. Or select the files to be removed and click the Delete button on the toolbar at the top of the window. Click Yes to confirm.

Find the confirmation message annoying? You can eliminate this message, which asks if you're sure you want to delete the file every time you put something in the bin. Right-click the Recycle Bin and select Properties from the pop-up menu. Now simply uncheck the box marked Display delete confirmation dialog.

HOW TO: TRANSFER FILES IN WINDOWS USING COPY AND PASTE

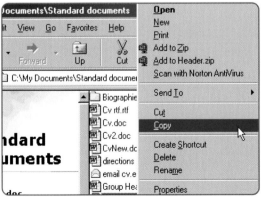

① First locate the file you want to copy on your computer's hard drive, right-click it, and then select Copy from the pop-up menu of options that appears.

② Now locate the particular folder you want to place the file into. Then right-click inside that folder and select Paste from the pop-up menu of options.

③ Finally, after a brief pause, the file you have just copied should appear in the new folder window, ready for you to continue working on.

DESKTOP

In the early days of computers, PC users had to type in every single command they wanted their machine to perform. But now—with Windows—you can accomplish tasks just by clicking on icons and objects on the Desktop. If you manage your Desktop effectively, your work experience will be much smoother.

THE DESKTOP FUNCTION

The Desktop is a full-screen display—or user interface—where all Windows activity takes place. It represents—in computer terms—a real desktop, where everything that you are currently working on is at hand. Using your Desktop toolbars, Taskbar, menus, and shortcut icons, you can access any item on your PC. If you notice that your screen is becoming a little overcrowded, save space by creating folders to store important files, so you can access them quickly. Creating shortcuts for your favorite programs is also a good idea, but it is best to arrange them in a useful order so that you can locate them without confusion and operate more efficiently.

BASIC FEATURES

At the foot of the Desktop is the Taskbar. On the far left is the Quick Launch toolbar, where you can click on program icons that you frequently use. Whenever you start up a program, you will see a button appear in the Taskbar in the center of the screen, indicating that the program is running. The Taskbar can be moved or resized on the Desktop.

Clicking on the Start button, located on the bottom left of the Desktop, will access the Start Menu. Here, you will find a list of your PC's contents. You can access files, programs, documents, and settings, and locate any item you want through the Search or Help menus.

The Start Menu is your entry to the working programs and settings in your computer. Use your mouse to scroll to the item you need, and click on it to open it.

DESKTOP ICONS

The My Computer icon is one of the regular icons found on any Desktop. If you double-click on it, you will open a folder containing other icons for the PC's main functions, such as the hard disk. From My Computer, you can customize the Desktop by double-clicking on the Control Panel icon and then selecting Display.

The My Documents Desktop icon is a folder that provides you with a convenient, easy-to-back-up place to store documents, pictures, and files you create. When you save a file in MS Office programs such as Word or Excel, they are automatically saved in the My Documents folder, unless you specify another folder.

Net results. The other icon generally present on the Desktop is Internet Explorer. Once you're connected to an ISP, click on the icon to connect to the World Wide Web. Internet Explorer has an address bar, where you type in the web address that you want to visit.

ICONOGRAPHY
A guide to icons on your Desktop and their functions.

My Computer
Gives access to your hard disk and the CD-ROM drive.

Internet Explorer
This icon gains entry to the World Wide Web.

Recycle Bin
The computer's wastebasket for throwing away files and folders.

My Documents
A storage folder for your files, pictures, and work documents.

Outlook Express
Double-click this icon to open the standard Windows e-mail program.

Connect to the Internet
The Wizard helps you configure your modem for Internet connection.

One icon that is slightly different from the rest is the Recycle Bin, which is not so much an icon as a wastebasket, where you throw away unwanted files and icons. To use the Recycle Bin, click and drag the item you want to delete to the Bin. If you accidentally remove a file, don't panic; just double-click on the Recycle Bin icon and—when the window opens—drag the file back onto your Desktop.

CUSTOMIZING YOUR DESKTOP

Change the way your Desktop looks by right-clicking in any empty space on the screen. In the pop-up menu, scroll to Active Desktop and click Customize My Desktop. The Display Properties dialog box appears, with options for changing the appearance of the Desktop. Click on Background, Settings, or Effects to adjust colors, background images, or icons.

Arrange your Desktop icons in groups to keep your work in order and help you avoid trashing a useful file by mistake. A useful location for the Recycle Bin is in the bottom-right corner of the Desktop. Make sure Auto Arrange is not checked, then put the My Documents, My Computer, and Internet Explorer icons in the top-left corner. Place the shortcuts for your

favorite programs in the top-right. Organizing the Desktop helps you find folders easily, and is useful as your collection of software and downloaded files increases.

If the number of icons on your Desktop starts to look like the rush-hour traffic, create some folders to store your programs in. To do this, right-click on an empty space on the Desktop. When the pop-up menu appears, go to New → Folder, and a new folder will appear on the Desktop. Now name the folder and then press the Enter key.

So much to do and so little time? If you are the kind of person who has too much to do and too little time, organize your icons into an

easy-to-find format in two steps. Right-click on the Desktop. In the pop-up menu that appears, click Arrange Icons. Now, you have several options to choose from. You can sort your icons by name, size, type, or date. If you scroll down and click Auto Arrange, the icons will be placed down the left side of the screen; if you try to relocate an icon, it automatically reverts to the left side.

Adding an icon to the Quick Start Taskbar is a simple process. To do this, first go to Start → Programs. Scroll through the programs and click on the one you want. In this case, it is Microsoft PowerPoint. Once you've located it, click and drag the icon to the Quick Launch Taskbar, then release it. The icon now appears on the Taskbar. Go to the icon and click it to start the program.

If you want to resize the Taskbar, then place the mouse pointer by its uppermost edge.

When the cursor changes to a double-headed arrow, click and drag the edge in towards the center of the Desktop. However, if you want to keep the Taskbar small, you can still access all the icons by clicking the double arrow at the edge of the Taskbar. A small menu reveals the hidden icons.

⇨ See also **Windows: Active Desktop, Recycle Bin, Shortcuts, Start Menu, Taskbar,** and **Wallpaper.**

HOW TO: CREATE A SHORTCUT ON THE DESKTOP

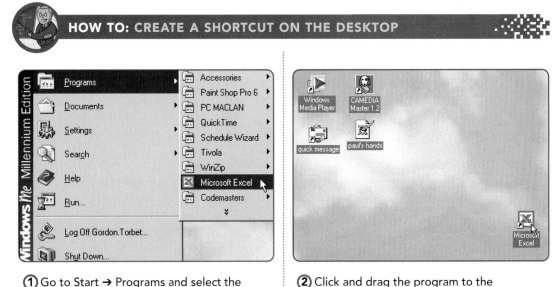

① Go to Start → Programs and select the program you want to place on the Desktop as a shortcut—in this case, Microsoft Excel.

② Click and drag the program to the Desktop. When you release the mouse button, a shortcut icon appears, denoted by the small arrow in the bottom-left corner.

DIALOG BOXES

Every time you use your computer, you will come across dialog boxes, whether it's to save a file, or shut down your PC.

Dialog boxes appear on your screen to request information about a certain task, prompting a dialog between you and the relevant program. So, if you want to print, the dialog box will appear with your options. You can make sure the right printer is selected, choose to print at draft quality, and so on. When you're ready to print, you simply click OK.

You can get help with some dialog boxes in the same way as with other features. With the dialog box open, click the question mark button near the upper right-hand corner of the box.

From the list that appears, click the item or button that you want to know more about.

A dialog box will appear if you click on a command button that has an ellipsis (...) after it. For example, if you go to the Insert menu and select Date and Time... or Field... a dialog box will pop up with your options.

Changed your mind? A quick way to close a dialog box is to press the Esc key. This will cancel the action you were performing. You can also close any dialog box by pressing Alt and F4 together or by clicking on the little square in the upper right-hand corner of the box.

You can move forward through the dialog box options by pressing the Tab key. Pressing the Shift key together with Tab will move you backward through the options.

If you're "saving as" or opening a file, there's an easy way to move up through the folder hierarchy. From within the dialog box, select a folder and press the Backspace key. The next folder up will magically appear.

⇨ See also **Software: Menus.**

DISK DRIVES

Get to know your PC's drives—these are the most common types.

Hard disk drive
Often called the "hard drive," it reads and writes onto your PC's main storage area. It's usually labeled as the C drive, with any secondary hard disks labeled D or E.

Floppy disk drive
Normally labeled A, this drive is used to read and write data onto a 3.5-inch magnetic media disk, holding up to 1.44Mb of data.

CD drive
This drive is used only to read data from music CDs and CD-ROMs, which can store 650Mb of data. The CD drive is generally labeled D.

CD-R drive
The "R" denotes a drive that can read and record up to 650Mb of data onto compact discs. Usually, it's installed instead of a CD drive so will probably be labeled D.

Zip drive
This is a special drive that allows you to use Zip disks with your PC. Zip disks are ideal for storing back-up versions of important files. They can hold up to 250Mb of data—the equivalent to almost 150 floppy disks. Once installed, this drive will appear on your PC as the next available letter in the alphabet.

Jaz drive
This is similar to a Zip drive, but packs an even bigger punch. Jaz disks can hold up to 2 Gb of data. That's more than 1,300 floppy disks' worth of information!

DVD drive
The DVD drive plays "digital versatile discs," also known as "digital video discs." If it replaces a CD drive, it's normally labeled D. Otherwise, it will take the next available letter. It holds at least 4.7Gb of data—enough to store a feature-length movie.

DISK DRIVES

Maximize the performance of your disk drives to give faster access to your hard drive, floppies, and CDs.

If you use one particular drive a lot, place a shortcut to it on your Desktop for quick and easy access. Open My Computer and drag the icon of the desired drive onto your Desktop. A dialog box appears telling you that you cannot move or copy the drive to the Desktop and asking if you want to create a shortcut to the item instead. Click Yes.

Get a quick read-out of how much space is available for storage on your hard disk by double-clicking on the My Computer icon on the Desktop, and then selecting the hard disk icon in the My Computer window. The panel in the status bar at the bottom of the window shows both the amount of free space available as well as the hard disk's overall capacity.

DISPLAY

Use the screen resolution settings on your computer to get the clearest, sharpest display possible.

Screen resolution refers to the number of dots per inch (or pixels) that make up the entire display area. The more pixels, the sharper the image on the screen. Selecting a screen resolution of 640x480 will instruct your monitor to display 640 distinct dots across 480

RAGE IIC AGP (English)

lines—307,200 individual pixels in total. At the top end of the scale, a screen resolution of 1,024x768 yields a million pixels with which to compose your screen.

For quick and easy access to your screen resolution settings, you can place the Display Properties icon on your Windows task bar. Go

to the Start menu ➔ Settings ➔ Control Panel and double-click the Display folder. In the window that appears, click the Settings tab, then Advanced. Under the General tab, check the box next to "Show settings icon on task bar," and click Apply. Next time you want to change the screen resolution, click the icon on the task bar and choose your settings from the pop-up menu.

If the text on your screen is too small at the resolution you've chosen, you can make the font size bigger. Go to Control Panel ➔ Display ➔ Settings. Select Advanced, then the tab marked General. Click the arrow in the box next to Font Size, select Large Fonts from the dropdown menu, and click OK. Restart your PC for the change in font size to take effect.

Monitor size matters when choosing your screen resolution. A high resolution (more pixels) on a small monitor could make the screen images too small to see. A low resolution on a large screen could make the images too blurred.

What's the ideal setting? Most computer monitors are 15 to 16 inches and work well with a 800x600 setting. For a smaller monitor of 13 inches or less, try 640x480. A resolution of 1,024x768 is ideal for monitors 17 inches and over, or for a laptop's LCD monitor.

Website pages are usually designed to be viewed at 800x600, because this produces the best results on most monitors. If you're having problems viewing a web page, try changing your resolution to this setting and clicking the Refresh or Reload button on your web browser's toolbar.

To apply new color settings without having to restart your PC, open Display and select the Settings tab. Click Advanced, followed by the General tab, then select the appropriate option under Compatibility.

 HOW TO: GET A SHARPER SCREEN IMAGE

① Open the Display Properties box by right-clicking with your mouse on a blank area of your Desktop and selecting Properties from the pop-up menu. When the dialog box appears, click on the Settings tab.

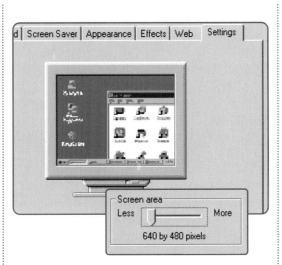

② Adjust the screen area using the sliding bar. Moving the bar to the left will reduce the value of the screen resolution, giving you a larger screen area but with less pixels and therefore a poorer quality image.

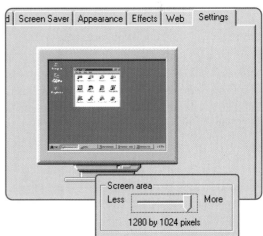

③ Slide the bar to the right for a higher resolution. Images will be sharper, but your screen area will be smaller—the display above the bar shows you how it will look. Click OK when you're happy with the setting.

DOS

By accessing DOS through Windows you can run older DOS programs.

DOS (Disk Operating System) is a predecessor to Windows that is still accessible through Windows (Start → Programs → MS-DOS Prompt). Although now almost obsolete, it is still used to run DOS-based programs and games. It's also used to alter the file system, but don't attempt this unless you know exactly what you're doing!

Access DOS easily through Windows. If you want to run a DOS program occasionally, you can create a shortcut to DOS on your Desktop. Right-click in the top right corner of the Desktop area. Select New → Shortcut and type "c:\command.com" in the Command line text window. Click Next, then Finish, and the shortcut icon will appear on your Desktop. Right-click it and select Properties. An Options window appears in which you can change the display properties of DOS. For instance, you can open it as a full screen or Desktop window.

Play games! If you have a DOS game or other DOS application on your PC that you want to use often, you can access it easily by creating another Desktop shortcut from the New → Shortcut facility (see above). Simply browse for the program and select the .exe file that activates it. The shortcut icon to this program will appear on your Desktop.

FINDING FILES

Recover lost files by name, location, content, or application.

Locate misplaced files or folders with the Search facility. Go to the Start menu and select Search → For Files or Folders. In the dialog box that appears, type in the file or folder name and click Search Now.

Know only part of a name? You may have forgotten a file name but remember that it had, for example "card" somewhere in the description. To locate all files that have that letter combination somewhere within their name, simply insert * before the word "card" and *.* after. The search string then becomes *card*.* and will locate files with names such as "buscard" or "cardoor."

Save time by searching one drive at a time. If you have more than one drive installed, a search for a particular file can take ages. So, if you're confident that the file is on hard drive C, it makes sense to look through just that one first. In the Search for Files and Folders window, there's an option called Look in. Click on the drop-down menu and select your chosen drive.

Forgotten the file name? If you don't know where a document is and can't remember what you called it either, you can always run a search on the contents. Maybe you know it was a letter to your accountant, or a list of car expenses. Go to Start → Search → Files or Folders and type your search word in the Containing Text box. For example, to find a letter you've written to Mr. Smith, enter

"Mr. Smith." Speed up your search by defining where you wish the computer to look, such as in your My Documents folder.

To review all the files worked on during a particular day or period of time, use the Search facility to collect them together. From the Search for Files and Folders box, click Search Options, check the Date box, and enter the relevant "between" dates.

Search for files for a particular application. This is a handy solution if you can't remember the file name or extension, but do know which program it was created in. As above, click Search Options, but this time check the Type box. Select an application from the pop-up menu. The search can be refined to certain file sizes, too, but unless you're sure about the minimum or maximum size of the file, leave these fields blank.

FOLDERS

Use a filing system of folders to keep your work organized and easy to find.

Create new folders in Windows Explorer. Either select File → New → Folder from the menu bar, or right-click on the right side of the Explorer window and select New → Folder from the pop-up options. Name the folder to suit its contents, such as "Music files" or "Games." Move any relevant files to the folder by holding down the Ctrl key to highlight all the files, and then drag them onto the new folder.

Build a virtual filing cabinet by grouping folders together inside other folders. For example, inside your "Holiday photos" folder you could store all the picture folders for holidays you've taken, such as "Banff '98 photos," "Florida '99 photos," and "Peggy's Cove 2000 photos." This system takes up less space in the Explorer window and makes finding your files quicker.

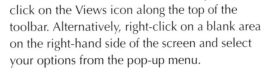

Install software where you can find it easily. Most programs give you the option to change the default installation settings, so you can install software directly into your own folders. It makes sense to group together similar programs in one easily accessible place. For example, the default installation for the game "c:\Physicus" can easily be changed to "c:\Personal\ Games\Physicus," thus directing the install procedure to put the software in the "Games" sub-folder of your "Personal" folder.

Customize the way you view files and folders by setting them to hide or highlight the information they contain. There are several ways of doing this in

Windows Explorer. The one you choose depends on how much information you want to see. To change your options,

select the View menu in Windows Explorer, or click on the Views icon along the top of the toolbar. Alternatively, right-click on a blank area on the right-hand side of the screen and select your options from the pop-up menu.

⇨ See also **Windows: Desktop, Startup Folder,** and **Windows Explorer.**

FONTS

There's more to life than Times New Roman. Liven up your letters with interesting new fonts.

The Web is a fantastic place for free fonts. To add to your collection, visit a font website (see below). In most cases, you can just click on the font of your choice to start the download process. The font will probably come as a Zip file, so you'll need to unzip it before you can use it (see Software: Zip files).

Install your new font. You've just downloaded a font onto your Desktop, but to use it you need to install it. No problem. Double-click the Control Panel in My Computer, then double-click the Fonts folder to open it. Select File → Install New Font from the menu bar. The Add Fonts dialog box will now appear. Browse through your folders until you locate your new font. Highlight it and click OK. Your font is now ready for action!

Want to see what a font looks like? Go to Start menu → Settings → Control Panel, and open your Fonts folder. Double-click on any of the fonts listed for a close-up view.

Spring clean your fonts folder. Of the thousands of fonts available, you may have several stored in your folder that are practically identical. It's a good idea to periodically go through them and delete the ones you're least likely to use. Just right-click on the ones you wish to discard and select Delete from the pop-up menu.

Fond of your fonts? Because fonts take up so little space you can store the least-used ones on floppies, rather than delete them. A standard 1.44Mb disk should hold at least 10 to 20 fonts. Copy them to the floppy disk and then delete the files from the Fonts folder. Label the disks clearly so that you can easily find any fonts you want to view or reinstall at a later date.

Create your own fonts. You can download shareware programs from the Web to do this. Font Creator (www.high-logic.com) is an easy-to-use program that enables you to create everything from symbols to signatures. Although creating a unique font from scratch can be quite an involved process, it's great fun to do and the results can be extremely satisfying. Alternatively, edit fonts you already possess to achieve a similar result. Type Tool (www.fontlab.com) is a useful font editing program aimed at the home computer user.

FONT SHAREWARE SITES
Find great fonts and font creation software on the Web.

**Blue Vinyl
(http://reflectdesign.com/bvfonts)**
Free fonts, and links to other free sites for all kinds of downloadable treats.

**DownLoad 32
(www.download32.com)**
Liven up your letters with 3D shareware fonts—they're compatible with MS Word.

FlatFont PI (www.fontfiles.com)
A resource with over 1,000 fonts that is well designed and easy to navigate.

GetFonts.com (www.getfonts.com)
Free fonts and font creation software, plus help with installation.

Jumbo! (www.jumbo.com)
Fonts, games, screensavers, and MP3 files.

**Online Business.com
(www.onlinebusiness.com/shops)**
Take advantage of dozens of links to sites offering free fonts.

Soft Seek (www.softseek.com)
Free script, fun and calligraphy fonts, plus some useful links to other font sites.

**1001 FreeFonts
(www.1001freefonts.com)**
An amazing array of fonts, screensavers, ClipArt, and other freebies, along with some helpful tutorials.

**tyworld.com
(http://max.tyworld.com/download)**
Choose from a good selection of over 500 free fonts, all thoughtfully arranged in alphabetical order.

HARD DRIVE

Windows Me does a fantastic job of keeping your PC running smoothly and efficiently behind the scenes. But taking preventative measures—and regularly setting aside time to clean up your hard drive, too—can make a huge difference to your PC's overall speed and reliability.

HARD-DRIVE HOUSEKEEPING

Each time you boot up, Windows Me takes a "snapshot" of your system, including all installed software and the hardware setup. If something goes wrong, you can roll back in time to a point prior to the problem. Coupled with the extensive System Tools and Task Scheduler, which automatically runs hard-drive diagnostics for you, Windows Me helps maintain and improve your PC dramatically better than previous versions of Windows.

Windows needs a certain amount of free disk space to manage its swap file, also known as "virtual memory." The size of file is managed automatically; however, if there is insufficient free disk space,

and you have limited RAM, you will experience a noticeable reduction in speed and increased hard-drive activity. Check how much hard-drive space is used by clicking on the C: icon in the My Computer window.

SYSTEM TOOLS

Many tasks that will help organize your PC automatically are found under the Start → Programs → Accessories → System Tools. Here you'll find Disk Defragmenter and Disk Cleanup, along with Scheduled Tasks, which allows you to set times for performing tasks.

Tidy up! When Windows saves data to your hard disk, it doesn't always put a file or piece of data all in one place. Over time, all the data— files and programs—becomes fragmented. To reorganize the data to keep related files together, run Disk Defragmenter—found under System Tools—regularly. The "defrag" process speeds up application and file-loading times and reduces the chances of data disruption.

Use ScanDisk to repair data areas. Each file and program on your hard disk is split into clusters (tiny chunks). Often these are split into several pieces when the file is stored on the hard disk. This isn't as drastic as it sounds—since Windows can retrieve and piece the file together at any time. But on rare occasions, some clusters can

be lost—through damage to the hard disk surface or a crash. ScanDisk checks the drive to repair lost clusters and to mark damaged areas so that Windows avoids using them.

To check the entire drive with ScanDisk, go to Start → Programs → Accessories → System Tools, select ScanDisk, and choose the Thorough option. (Don't use your PC while ScanDisk is operating.)

System Restore is a clever feature, new to Windows Me, that stores information about your computer's setup, software, and hardware each time that you turn on your machine, or every 10 hours after a short period of inactivity. It works like taking a snapshot of the computer. Windows, however, only stores a limited

FORMATTING CHECKLIST
Make sure you have the following before reformatting your hard drive.

- **A Windows Me startup floppy disk** from which to boot your computer. To create a disk, go to Start → Settings → Control Panel and double-click on the Add/Remove Programs icon. Select the Startup Disk tab and click Create Disk. (See Windows: Startup Disk).

- **All your original software CD-ROMs** or installation disks, including the registration keys (product codes).

- **Any disks or CD-ROMs** that came with your PC for the graphics card, soundcard, and modem.

- **A backup of all your data,** including templates, e-mails, addresses, Favorites, and notes of ISP connection details.

number of system snapshots because they occupy a lot of space.

The usual suspects? If you think some recently installed software or hardware has impeded your PC's performance, or caused it to crash, use System Restore. Go to Start ➔ Programs ➔ Accessories ➔ System Tools ➔ System Restore. Check the Restore my computer to an earlier time, and click Next to enter in the date or time.

If your PC crashes during work, or something goes wrong with an installation, temporary files (those with the .tmp suffix) may have been left on your hard drive. These are created while you work and during some software installation processes. Normally, files are deleted when no longer needed. To check your drive and delete unnecessary temporary files, select Disk Cleanup in System Tools.

MANAGING PROGRAMS AND FILES

If you want to get rid of a software program, make sure you uninstall it carefully. Correct removal of programs ensures that Registry entries (information stored by Windows about your PC settings) referring to the program are deleted, and program groups and menu entries are erased. If you simply delete the program files, you risk leaving associated files that will clutter up your hard drive and slow loading times, and performance. To remove a program correctly, go to Start ➔ Settings ➔ Control Panel and select Add/Remove Programs.

To check file or folder size, right-click on them and choose Properties. To find the largest files on your PC, do a search. Go to Start ➔ Find ➔ Files or Folders ➔ Advanced Tab and click on At Least. Use Search Options to specify a size of at least 20000Kb (20Mb). Sort the results by size. Go to View, select Details, and click on the Size column header in the main window. As you click, the sort order is reversed so you may need to click

twice to get the largest top file. If you see any files with the .tmp suffix, you can delete them.

MAKE THE MOST OF YOUR PC

If you only have 64Mb or even 32Mb RAM in your PC and are running Windows Me, your hard disk is working overtime. It has to swap some data normally in RAM to and from spare hard disk space to let Windows function as if it has more memory than it actually has.

Upgrading your memory improves your PC's speed and makes for less wear-and-tear since the hard-drive heads have to move back and forth less. With programs' high demands on memory and since you probably run several programs at the same time, upgrading to 128Mb RAM makes a big difference.

Some PC experts frequently reformat and reinstall Windows. This is usually because a large number of programs and extra hardware have been installed and uninstalled, and the PC has slowed down considerably. Sometimes it

may crash too frequently. Reformatting the hard disk and reinstalling Windows and all software should be safe so long as a few precautions are taken (see box opposite). But reinstallation can fail halfway through, so leave it to the experts.

➪ See also **Windows: Hard Disk Space; Hardware: Hard Drive** and **Memory.**

HOW TO: USE MAINTENANCE WIZARD

Maintenance Wizard

The Maintenance wizard adjusts your computer for top-notch performance. Setting up a regular maintenance schedule ensures that you get the most from your computer.

- Your programs run faster than ever.
- You get more free hard disk space.
- Your system performance is optimal.

What do you want to do?

⦿ Express - Use the most common maintenance settings
○ Custom - Select each maintenance setting myself.

When do you want Windows to run maintenance tasks?

○ Nights - Midnight to 3:00 AM
○ Days - Noon to 3:00 PM
⦿ Evenings - 8:00 PM to 11:00 PM

Wizard

Windows will perform the following tasks:

- Speed up your most frequently used programs.
- Check hard disk for errors.
- Delete unnecessary files from hard disk.

Remember to leave your computer on evenings from 8:00 P.M. to 11:00 P.M. so that maintenance can occur.

☑ When I click Finish, perform each scheduled task for the first time.

[< Back] [Finish] [Cancel]

1 First, go to Start ➔ Programs ➔ Accessories ➔ System Tools and select Maintenance Wizard. Select Express under What do you want to do? Click Next. Now choose a time and interval when you don't need to use your PC. Click Next.

2 Verify your task choices in the open box and check the When I finish, perform each scheduled task for the first time box. Click Finish. Windows will run all three tasks—Defragmenter, ScanDisk, and Disk Cleanup.

General | Sharing

Mary's bits

Type: File Folder
Location: C:\My Documents\old stuff - on the way
Size: 26.1 MB (27,387,805 bytes)
Size on disk: 26.7 MB (28,041,216 bytes)
Contains: 301 Files, 22 Folders

Created: 20 September 2000, 5:18:52 PM

HARD DISK SPACE

Check your PC's hard disk space to see how much memory is available.

Use your Desktop to check hard disk space. If you run out of disk space, you'll have nowhere to store new files and programs. Double-click the My Computer icon on your Desktop to call up information on your hard drive (or drives). If you view the information as Large Icons, Small Icons, or List, and then select the drive (usually C:), the capacity and free disk space available is displayed in the Status Bar along the bottom of the window. If you view it as Details, this information is displayed beside the drive letter.

Check hard disk space from Windows Explorer. Go to Start → Programs → Accessories → Windows Explorer, and click the letter of the drive you want to check. You'll then see details of available free space displayed in brackets at the bottom of the window. The figure outside the brackets shows the amount of space used by the visible files and folders on the drive, but not the total used space. If you have enabled Web content in folders in the Folder Options window under the Tools menu, you see a pie chart showing used and free space.

Check the total occupied space on a drive from Windows Explorer. After clicking on the drive concerned, go to Edit → Select All to view the file size for the current folder. Alternatively, use the keyboard shortcut Ctrl+A to highlight the contents of a hard drive. Right-click anywhere on the selected folders and select Properties from the pop-up menu. The total amount of occupied space on the drive will be displayed.

Here's another way to view a pie chart of your available drive space: go to Explorer or My Computer, right-click the drive letter you want to

check, and select Properties from the pop-up menu. A pie chart and a numeric readout of your used and free drive space will be displayed.

View the total free drive space from DOS. From either a DOS screen or a DOS window, change to the drive you want to check by typing its letter followed by a colon, such as C:, then press Enter. At the prompt, such as C:\>, type "chkdsk" and then press Enter. The command tells your PC to count the number of bytes used and the amount available for use. The chkdsk also counts a small part of the PC's memory.

View the amount of occupied space in a folder from Windows Explorer—right-click on any directory folder and choose Properties. This

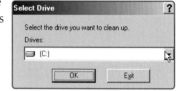

method of viewing information reveals the amount of space the folder is using, as well as the number of subfolders and files contained in that directory, and the date the folder was created.

Prevention is better than cure. It's a good idea to get into the habit of checking your drives for errors and deleting any unused files to free more drive space. The Disk Cleanup facility (see Windows: Hard Drive) will locate any unused files and temporary Internet files and give you the choice of deleting them. Rest assured that the deletion process will not affect any of your normal Internet settings.

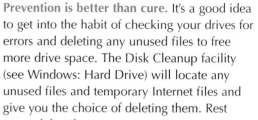

Most software installations have to spread their files across the hard disk, making them slower to access. Regularly running Defrag, a disk defragmentation program (see Windows: Hard Drive), will check the drive for errors, tidy up files, and bring files together on your hard disk for faster loading.

How long to defragment your hard disk? This depends on the size of the drive. A larger drive

---

ICON SITES

There are thousands of amazing icons that you can download from the Internet. These sites offer some of the best designs around.

Cool Archive
(www.coolarchive.com/icons.cfm)
4,000 icons in 125 categories, plus loads of graphics and clip art.

Free Graphics.Com
(www.free-graphics.com)
Choose from over 5,000 graphics images, plus links to other graphics sites and the option to download a trial version of an icon creator.

Free Search
(www.free-search.com/afil/index2.shtml)
The Free Search site includes 20 pages of cartoon .gif images, plus dozens of different links to other graphics pages.

A+Art.com
(www.aplusart.com)
A directory of a wide variety of icons, 3D animations and clip art images, all of which are free for personal use.

IconsPlus
(www.iconsplus.com)
Here, you'll find entertainment icons, plus a very good selection of comic books, science-fiction, movie, TV, and pop culture icons to decorate your Desktop.

Leo's Icon Archive
(www.silverpoint.com/leo/lia/)
Free popular comic strip icons, plus a .gif to .ico file converter program to download.

could take several hours. To set a regular time interval between Defragmentation and to preset a time to automatically perform the job, use the Task Scheduler facility. Go to Start ➔ Programs Accessories ➔ System Tools and click Scheduled Tasks. Then double-click the Add Scheduled Task entry and create a defrag task. Select the drives you wish to defrag and enter in the times you wish it to be done.

➪ See also **Windows: Hard Drive, Optimize Your PC,** and **Windows Explorer.**

HIDDEN FILES

You can choose which files you wish to be displayed, and which program you want to keep hidden from view.

Want to keep a secret? You can hide selected files and folders from view in Windows Explorer. Right-click on the file you want to hide, and choose Properties from the pop-up menu. In the box that appears, go to the Attributes section at the bottom and put a check beside Hidden.

Attributes: ☐ Read-only ☑ Hidden ☑ Archive

Files may be gone, but not forgotten! You might find that files you have set to be hidden are still visible in Windows Explorer and are only grayed out. To make these hidden files completely invisible, go to Explorer ➔ Tools ➔ Folder Options. Click the View tab and select the Do not show hidden files and folders option. Click on OK to confirm the change.

Don't be distracted. The purpose of hiding files is meant as a useful way of organizing them rather than as a secretive gesture. Removing selected files from normal lets you concentrate on those you look at on a regular basis without being distracted. All hidden files can be revealed again simply by opening the relevant folder window, going to the Folder Options window from the Tools menu, clicking on the View tab, and selecting the Show hidden files and folders option under Advanced settings.

ICONS

Download icons from the Web and create your own designer Desktop.

Why are icons used on the Desktop? The icons that appear on your Desktop and in your hard disk represent programs, folders, and files. Apart from enhancing the look of your Desktop by creating visual effects, they save you time—instead of typing in the file name to open it, you can double-click on the icon instead.

Search the Internet for icons. There are literally hundreds of websites where free graphics can be obtained. Use a search engine such as Yahoo! (www.yahoo.com) to track them down. If you specify "free icons," "free clip art," or "free graphics" in your search, you'll be given plenty to choose from.

Check the icon file is authentic. Although a website can use just about any graphic file as an icon, a PC needs to use an authentic icon file; most have the suffix .ico at the end of the file name but some may have .bmp. If you are downloading icons from the Internet for use on your Desktop, make sure they have one of these file extensions.

Many downloadable icons come in sets. These usually comprise 10 to 20 different icons, all based around a central theme, such as animals or cartoon characters, and stored as a Zip file. Download the complete set and unzip the file into a recognizable folder for easy access.

To change an existing Desktop icon, right-click on a blank area of the Desktop, and select Properties from the pop-up menu. Click the Effects tab in the Display Properties dialog box. In the Desktop icons area of the box, select the icon you wish to change. Click the Change Icon button below it. In the box that appears,

select a new icon and click OK. Click OK again on the Display Properties box to transfer the new

design to your Desktop. The Default Icon button reverts it back to the original icon.

Do-it-yourself icons! There are many icon-creation packages available for download from the Net. Bear in mind that Web versions may be shareware. This means that they only last a few weeks before you need to register and pay for them. This usually allows you enough time to create several icons and decide whether you want to buy or not. For a 30-day trial version, try searching for "icon cursor" at MalekTips (http://malektips.envprogramming.com).

Convert graphic files into icon images. With an icon creator you can not only design your own icons from scratch, but you also have the ability to convert other graphic files, such as JPEG and BMP formats, into .ico images.

Keep it simple. If you're familiar with using a particular graphics package, you can draw your icons in that package. Save the icon as a bitmap (.bmp) file and you can use it as is. Make sure to stick to icons of 32 x 32 pixels. For the best clarity, create images without too much detail and with uncluttered backgrounds. The golden rule to bear in mind when creating icons is "small and simple."

Check what formats the graphics package can save in before you start creating your icon.

Some may be limited in their selection of file formats. Otherwise, you may find all your labors have been in vain, having found your ideal image, only to find that you cannot save it in a usable format.

⇨ See also **Windows: Desktop; Internet: Downloading; Software: Zip Files.**

MANEUVERING FILES

Move files easily from one folder to another, or transfer them with a floppy disk to use on another PC.

Move files using drag-and-drop. Select the files for moving, then click and hold the mouse button as you drag them over and drop them in the appropriate folder.

Make haste with Cut and Paste. Transfer files from one place on your PC to another. Right-click on the file and choose Cut from the menu. Release the mouse button and move the pointer to the desired location. Right-click again and

choose Paste from the menu. The file appears in its new location. Select several files to move together in this way by holding down the Ctrl key as you select each one.

Make extra copies. If you have several files to copy to the same location, highlight them all and right-click your mouse. Choose Copy from the menu, then open the folder and paste the files. The files now exist in both locations. To erase the originals, drag them to the Recycle Bin.

If you want to move files to another computer, they can be copied straight to a floppy disk for transportation by highlighting and right-clicking the files, then selecting Send To → Floppy (A).

MAXIMIZE/MINIMIZE

Minimize and maximize the windows on your Desktop for a more manageable working environment.

The buttons in the top right-hand corner of a Desktop window can be used to minimize,

maximize, or close a window. To determine which icon is which, just rest your mouse over each one until a text box reveals its function.

To maximize using two monitors, move the window into the monitor you want to use, and click the Maximize button. If the window is split across the two monitors, the screen containing the larger portion of the window will be used to display it when fully maximized.

Open to order. Almost any program can be set to open as a minimized or maximized window when you first launch it. To achieve this, all you need to do is create a shortcut to the

application in question, then right-click it and select Properties. Click the Shortcut tab, and make your selection— Normal, Minimized, or Maximized— from the drop-down Run menu and click OK.

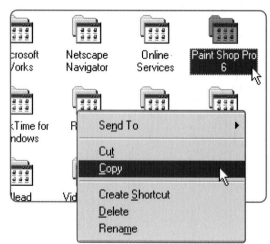

HOW TO: LAUNCH AN APPLICATION AT STARTUP

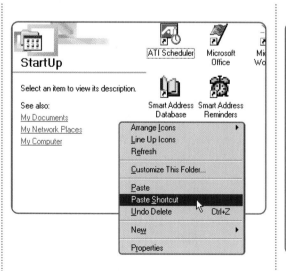

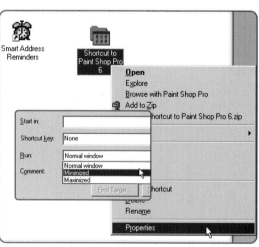

① Right-click the Start button and select Open. Double-click Programs, and locate the shortcut to the program you want to launch at startup. Now right-click the shortcut and select Copy.

② Go back to the Start Menu → Programs and double-click on the Startup folder. Right-click your mouse in the open window and select Paste Shortcut.

③ To start the program in a minimized window, right-click the shortcut you have just pasted, and select Properties. Under the Shortcut tab click the arrow beside Run. Choose Minimized, then OK.

Minimize all open windows at once by right-clicking the Taskbar and selecting Minimize All Windows. Right-click the Taskbar and select Undo Minimize All to restore the windows to their original position.

Need to hide a window in a hurry? You can minimize all the open windows instantly by pressing the Windows key and M together. To return your windows to their original state, press Windows, Shift, and M.

Maximization gone mad? If your Desktop has too many screens maximized at the same time, scroll through all of the maximized windows one at a time by holding down Alt and pressing Tab. And think about reorganizing the way you work in future!

MY DOCUMENTS

The My Documents folder on your Desktop provides a convenient filing cabinet for your documents.

Use the My Documents folder to store all the files you create—even if a program suggests otherwise. For example, some older programs offer their own folder as the default storage location when you save your files. But it's best

to create and use a folder within the My Documents folder. That way, it's easier to keep track of these files and easier to include them in your backups.

You can remove the My Documents folder from the Desktop by going to Start menu ➔ Settings ➔ Control Panel and then double-clicking on the Folder Options icon. Click on the View tab and scroll down the Advanced settings list. Remove the check from the Show My Documents on the Desktop option and click OK.

Give My Documents an individual look by customizing the background and colors. Open My Documents, and click View ➔ Customize This Folder. Click Next when the Wizard box appears. Check the Modify background picture option, and click Next. Choose a background template and click Next. Now choose a picture file name to view a thumbnail of the picture in the left-hand frame. To finish off the look, select a color for the text. Click the Text button, and choose from the color palette. Click Next and Finish.

Access recent documents from the Start menu. Windows keeps a list of the documents you have saved most recently on your PC. Go to Start ➔ Documents to see what's there.

Need easy access to the Web while you work? By pressing Ctrl+I when My Documents is open, you can display your Internet Favorites list from Internet Explorer (or Bookmarks, as they are called in Netscape Navigator) in the left-hand frame. Click a site to log onto the Internet and visit it. Once you've finished using your Favorites list, click the x in the top right of the frame to close the list and return to the My Documents view.

Can't find that important document? With the My Documents window selected, press Ctrl+F to initiate a search facility in the left-hand frame. You can use it to search My Documents for a file or folder name. Or, if you can't remember the file name, use the Containing text: box to search for files that have a particular word or phrase in them. Finally, if you can't find the relevant file in My Documents, you can click in the Look in: box. A drop-down list appears, allowing you to search elsewhere on your PC for the file.

➪ See also **Windows: Desktop, Finding Files,** and **Folders.**

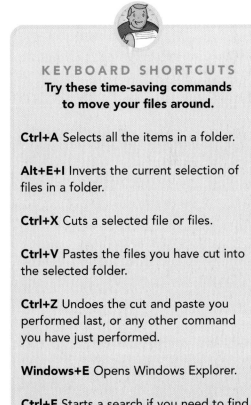

KEYBOARD SHORTCUTS

Try these time-saving commands to move your files around.

Ctrl+A Selects all the items in a folder.

Alt+E+I Inverts the current selection of files in a folder.

Ctrl+X Cuts a selected file or files.

Ctrl+V Pastes the files you have cut into the selected folder.

Ctrl+Z Undoes the cut and paste you performed last, or any other command you have just performed.

Windows+E Opens Windows Explorer.

Ctrl+F Starts a search if you need to find a file before you can move it.

Ctrl+S Saves any changes you've made to a document before you close and move it.

NETWORKS

Connecting several computers via a network allows you to share files and accessories with others.

Set up your home network with Windows Me Dial-Up Networking Wizard. All you need in each computer is a network or Ethernet card. You can choose one of two cable and connection options: the RJ45 connector needs a small network hub to connect all your PCs together in a star configuration. The other option is a BNC type connector, which uses coaxial cable like a TV and connects your PCs in a series, although the first and last PCs will need terminators.

GLOSSARY OF PRINTER FOLDER OPTIONS

Don't know your Print Pause from your Properties? Here's a list to help you.

File menu Gives most of the main features.

Add Printer Double-click to begin a wizard that will help you install a new printer.

Printer icons Double-click on the icons to view a list of the current print jobs, and check their status.

What's Wrong? Identifies and explains a problem when a print job fails to process.

Open Reveals current print job list.

Pause Printing Pause current printing.

Set as Default Selects a printer as default.

Purge Print Documents Clears all current print jobs from memory.

Printer specific properties Accesses controls specific to your printer type.

Network protocols are like languages. Each PC must speak the same tongue to understand each other, so make sure you choose the same protocol on every PC on your network. You must also all be on the same Workgroup. Right-click on My Network Places and choose Properties. Click on the Identity tab and make sure all your Workgroup names are identical. Choose NetBEUI for a small home network as it's the easiest to set up and the fastest protocol.

Before you can start sharing computers over a network, you need to enable file and printer sharing on all the computers concerned. Open My Computer, click on the Control Panel, and double-click Network to bring up the Network dialog box. Now click on the File and Print Sharing button, and tick the options you want before clicking OK.

Having turned on file and printer sharing, you must also indicate which folders you want to share with other computers on the Network. Open Windows Explorer by pressing Windows+ E, then locate the folder for sharing and click it once to select. Now click File → Properties, and select the Sharing tab. Click Shared As, then choose the Access Type you want—remember to add a password if you want to restrict access to this folder to authorized people only.

See what resources are being used by another PC on your network. Open My Network Places (Network Neighborhood in Windows 98), select the computer you want to check, and click File → Properties. Click the Tools tab, and then click Net Watcher. On the Net Watcher View menu, click the type of resource information you want to see.

My Network Places

This folder automatically displays the shared folders available on your home network.

To set up or view your modem connections, click Dial-Up Networking.

Set up or change your home networking settings using the Home Networking Wizard.

Select an item to view its description.

See also: Printers

Check which folders and printers are available for sharing on your network. Open My Network Places, select Entire Network, and then double-click the computer whose shared resources you want to investigate.

Share a single Internet connection across your networked computers. Use the Control Panel's Add/Remove Programs to install Internet Connection Sharing from the Windows CD-ROM.

Be careful not to break copyright law when setting up your network. This states that you must have a software license that covers every computer that a single set of software is installed or used on. The license normally comes as part of the software package. Contact the software company for further information.

⇨ See also **Hardware: Home Networking**.

PRINTERS FOLDER

The Printers Folder can be found in the Control Panel. It contains all the controls you need to manage your printer settings.

Access your printer properties. Open the Control Panel, double-click the Printers icon, and when the Printers Folder opens, right-click on your printer and select Properties. The options included here will vary, depending on which printer drivers are installed on your computer. Explore the tabs to see what features are available to you.

All for one and one for all. If you are networked, any printer settings you change in the Printer Folder will be applied to all of the networked computers. If you want to adjust the settings for a single job, you must access the printer properties from within the application you are using to print. For example, to change the printer settings for a single Word document, open the document, go to File → Print, and then click the Properties button.

The printer icon appears on your Taskbar any time you begin a print job. Double-click this icon to see a list of the jobs in progress.

All change. If you need a document printout in a hurry but you have other print jobs ahead of it, you can change the order of the print jobs in your list. Simply drag the relevant job to the top of the list and drop it.

Remember—you have no power over others! If you're using a network printer, you can only pause or cancel your own jobs—you don't have

the power to affect the printing schedule of the other computers on the network.

PROFILES

Personalize PC settings to give each family member their own Desktop design and to add passwords that keep settings personal.

Allow users to personalize their own settings on your PC. Go to Start menu → Settings → Control Panel. Double-click the Passwords icon and select the User Profiles tab in the Password Properties dialog box. Choose the option that says "Users can customize their preferences and desktop settings," then check the User profile settings you want to include.

Change your log-on password regularly. This can help protect your data from unauthorized access. Click on the start menu and then Control Panel and double-click Passwords. Click the Change Windows Password button.

Then type in your old password, followed by the new one twice— once to set the new password and again to confirm.

Switch between users without shutting down your PC. Click Start and select Log Off "user name." Click Yes to confirm, and, after a few moments, you'll be presented with a log-on screen containing the current list of users. Simply click on the one you want to use. Windows switches to your personal settings when you log on.

If you need to change the personal settings in a particular user profile, double-click Users within Control Panel, select a name from the list, and then click Change settings.

HOW TO: SET UP AND USE PROFILES

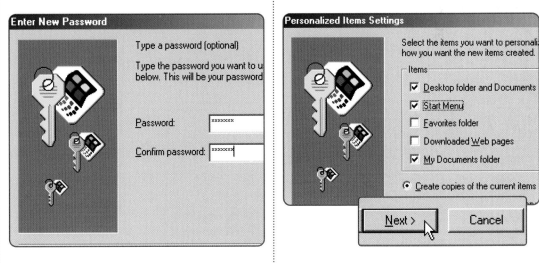

① Open the Control Panel and double-click Users. Clicking the New User button initiates a wizard that guides you through the process of setting up a new user profile. Click Next, enter the user's name, and click Next again.

② Entering a password on the next screen will protect this user's information from preying eyes. Clicking Next without entering a password will allow this profile to be started by anyone.

③ After entering a password, check the options you require, and choose the way you want the information stored. Click Next then Finish to complete. Now, every time you turn your PC on, a list of users will be displayed. Click your name to launch your own profile.

OPTIMIZE YOUR PC

Over time, you may have noticed your PC start to run down. As you install more software and new hardware, the Windows Registry, which keeps track of such things, gets bloated and corrupted. Optimizing and maintaining your PC's performance may seem like a boring job, but you'll reap countless rewards.

MEMORY CONSIDERATIONS

The single most significant component that affects the perceived speed of a PC is the amount of RAM (Random Access Memory —the memory used for active files). How you approach getting the most from your PC, and making sure it's healthy, depends on the type you have, and if it has 16Mb or 256Mb RAM.

If you have a relatively old PC, install as much RAM as you can. Changing from a Pentium to a Pentium III, but retaining only 16Mb RAM, will not have as much impact on performance as upgrading to 64 or 128Mb RAM. This means that more programs can run simultaneously without crashing.

If you can't afford to upgrade your memory, or your PC has no more slots for RAM, make sure you have enough free hard disk space for Windows virtual memory. This is disk space that Windows' uses as if it were memory. If there isn't enough space left on your hard disk, Windows will slow down and may even start to freeze up.

Keep at least 250Mb free on your hard disk, and if you're low on memory, only run one program at a time. This will let your PC focus on the task in hand and minimize swapping of data from RAM to virtual memory. Programs like Outlook require a large amount of memory to run. If you are using Outlook mostly just for e-mail, consider using Outlook Express instead.

If you want to try out new software, you may need to make more space available. You may have accumulated programs that load when you start Windows, and some may be seen as icons in the System Tray (the icons in the Taskbar next to the time). These programs may take up valuable memory, so only keep the ones you need. To remove the rest, go to Start → Settings → Control Panel. Double-click on Add/Remove Programs to uninstall them. Can't find a program? Open it from the System Tray and disable it from within the software.

DISPLAY

The more colors and the higher the resolution you choose, the more work your PC and graphics card are going to have to do to update the screen. If you have a graphics card with less than 4Mb built-in RAM, you may see the screen redrawing slowly from top to bottom. There are two solutions: either upgrade your graphics adaptor to one with 16Mb RAM or more, or reduce the number of colors and the resolution

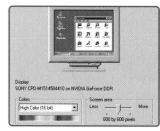

you use onscreen. To do this, go to Start → Settings → Control Panel, double-click the Display icon, and select the Settings tab.

If you opt to upgrade your graphics card and your motherboard has an AGP (Accelerated Graphics Port) slot, choose a 3D-accelerated AGP card. The AGP system is dedicated to graphics and provides a fast, direct connection.

A 16Mb or 32Mb graphics card will give you a high resolution, fast refresh rates, and true color depth. But make sure your monitor is up to the task before choosing a fast refresh rate—85Hz is ideal for avoiding flicker.

HARDWARE AND SOFTWARE

Check the Internet regularly for driver updates for all your hardware. The most important devices are your graphics and sound cards, modem, and BIOS. Each new release fixes earlier problems and upgrades performance.

Even if the previous drivers are fast and seem to work well, compatibility problems can arise if everything isn't up to date. Install new drivers using either the Device Manager or the manufacturer's installation program.

SYSTEM CHECKS

Windows Me comes with a System Information utility to provide in-depth information about your system, hardware, and hardware resources. To access it, go to Start → Programs → Acessories → System Tools and select System Information. A collection of useful tools (see box, opposite) helps optimize performance.

Run regular disk diagnostics (on the System Tools menu) to keep your PC healthy. Running ScanDisk and Disk Defragmenter at least once a month keeps your hard drive in order. Using special disk-maintenance software, like Norton Utilities, helps locate errors and problems and fix them—and it will monitor your system while you work.

A BIOS (Basic Input Output System) upgrade, often made available over the Internet, may

help resolve irritating glitches and speed up your PC. BIOS is the set of operating instructions built into your PC. Follow the instructions included with the download or on the website, and be sure to use the correct version for your specific BIOS and motherboard (see how to, below).

⇨ See also **Windows: Hard Drive; Hardware: Memory.**

HOW TO: RUN DISK DEFRAGMENTER

① To run Disk Defragmenter in Windows go to the Start menu → Programs → Accessories → Systems Tools, and then click on Disk Defragmenter. The Select Drive window will now pop up on your screen.

② Choose the drive that you wish to defragment— for example, the hard drive, C. Click on the settings tab, and check the relevant options. Click OK to return to the Select Drive window, and then choose OK to start the Disk Defragmenter.

③ The Defragmenting Drive C window will now appear. The blue bar shows the progress of defragmenting. When finished a new window will appear asking "Do you want to quit Disk Defragmenter?"click on Yes to quit.

READ-ONLY FILES

Making files read-only is the conventional way to protect them from being accidentally overwritten or amended.

You can check a file's read-only status by right-clicking on the file icon in Windows Explorer and selecting Properties. If the Read-only box is checked the file can be opened and viewed but not saved with the same name. Simply check or uncheck the box to change the file's read-only status.

Windows needs to be able to change the contents of a variety of key files—for instance, those in the Windows folder and any system files—so beware of making files read-only if you don't know what they are. If you do so, you might cause your PC to crash.

Making a file read-only doesn't prevent the file from being damaged, deleted, or even from being changed and saved with a new name, so it's not an alternative to proper security and back-up procedures. If a file is important enough for you to change its attribute to read-only, make sure it's also securely backed up and that only appropriate users have access to it.

Protect master copies, forms, and final drafts of documents with read-only status. This will keep your master copy clean and prevent anyone else who has access to your files from changing your documents.

Read-only status may not prevent files from being infected by computer viruses, so use a good antivirus program rather than relying on file attribute changes to protect your files.

Files copied from a CD-ROM are usually already set to Read-only, since CD-ROMs are read-only media anyway. So, if you need to edit a file from a CD, check the attribute properties before you make any changes or be prepared to save the file with a different name.

If you try to save a read-only file after making changes to it, you will get an error message. Simply give the file a different name, and you will be able to save it. The new file will not have read-only status.

RECYCLE BIN

The Recycle Bin is the Windows' trash can. It hides all the files you've deleted and keeps them safe—just in case you change your mind.

The amount of space set aside for the Recycle Bin can be adjusted. The default is 10 percent of your hard drive capacity, which is probably much more space than you need on drives over 10Gb in size. If you want to free up disk space, you can reduce the size of the Recycle Bin by right-clicking on the Recycle Bin and selecting Properties. Simply drag the slider to adjust the setting for the space allocated to the Bin.

Recycle Bin

If you have multiple hard drives on your PC, you can define the Recycle Bin space available for each drive. You will have a separate tab with its own slider setting for each drive. Select the Configure drives independently option on the Global tab of Recycle Bin Properties window to activate this.

WEB ADDRESSES FOR SCREENSAVERS
Here are a few sources of free, fun screensavers on the Internet.

FreeSaver.com (www.freesaver.com)
A site devoted to free screensavers. Choose from hundreds of files arranged by name or category. The best are given star ratings.

ScreenSaver.com (www.screensaver.com)
A large library of freeware and shareware screensavers. Also, how to create your own.

ThemeWorld.com (www.themeworld.com/savers)
Hosts thousands of screensavers as well as full Desktop themes, icons, and fonts.

Subloads (www.topdownloads.net/screensavers)
Includes hundreds of screensavers divided into all variety of different themes.

If you don't want to see the "Are you sure?" message every time you delete a file, you can turn it off by unchecking the Display delete confirmation dialog box option in the Recycle Bin Properties window. You will still be asked to confirm whenever you empty the Recycle Bin, because this is an irreversible action that you wouldn't want to do accidentally.

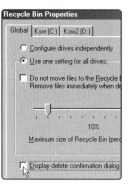

Floppy disks and other removable or network drives can't access the Recycle Bin, so you can't recover items deleted from these drives from the Recycle Bin. However, maintenance programs, such as Norton Utilities, are able to restore such files (see Software: Norton Utilities).

To delete a file permanently, hold down the Shift key at the same time as you press Delete or drag the file to the Recycle Bin. You'll be asked to confirm the deletion and, if you do so, the file will be erased rather than placed in the Recycle Bin. If you don't want any of your deleted files to be put in the Recycle Bin, check the Do not move files to the Recycle Bin option on the Recycle Bin Properties dialog box.

Empty the Recycle Bin regularly. Deleted files continue to take up hard drive space until they're removed from the Recycle Bin. The quickest way to empty the Bin is to right-click on the Recycle Bin icon and select Empty Recycle Bin. This will permanently delete all the files currently held by the Bin, so be sure there's nothing in there you might want again.

If you want to restore a deleted file to a location other than its original folder, right-click on the Recycle Bin icon and select Explore from the pop-up menu. This opens a standard Explorer window, which allows you drag and drop files to and from the Recycle Bin.

Always check out the Settings options for your screensaver. You'll be able to customize your screensaver to your personal taste. The 3D Flying Objects screensaver, for example, includes an option to add your own image as a texture when the Textured Flag style is selected. Another useful option is the ability to add your own text to the Scrolling Marquee screensaver.

Add a password and use your screensaver as a Desktop security tool. Check the Password protected box on the Screen Saver tab in the Display Properties dialog box and enter your password. This option will not protect your PC from determined intruders, who can get around the screensaver password obstacle by rebooting the PC.

Some system tools work better if you turn off your screensaver when you're running them, particularly if you have an older PC. This is because the screensaver program interrupts

other computer activity to check whether it should turn itself on or off. For instance, the Disk Defragmenter utility clashes with some screensavers, and modem communications may be hampered if a screensaver kicks in. To disable your screensaver, choose None from the drop-down selection list on the Screen Saver tab.

When you download a screensaver from the Internet it will be in one of two formats. Copy any files with the extension .scr into the directory C:\Windows on your computer. If your screensaver has the extension .exe, simply double-click on it to load it.

Virus alert! There are lots of screensavers available for download free from the Internet, but remember that many are executable files and can, therefore, easily hide viruses. Only download files from reputable sites, and check all files with an up-to-date virus scanner.

Create a unique screensaver of one of your own pictures or photographs, and add music or your own sound to accompany it. Use a screensaver program, such as Screen Saver Studio (www.screensaverstudio.com).

SCREENSAVERS

Screensavers were developed to protect old-fashioned monitors from screen burn, but today they're mostly used for fun.

Windows comes with its own collection of screensavers, and you can change between them easily by right-clicking on the Desktop and selecting Properties. The Screen Saver tab lists all the screensavers currently installed on your PC and allows you to preview them.

Your screensaver initiates when your keyboard and mouse have been inactive for a specified length of time—between 1 and 60 minutes. You can set how long your PC waits before launching your screensaver on the Screen Saver tab of the Display Properties dialog box.

HOW TO: RECOVER A DELETED FILE

① To recover a deleted file double-click on the Recycle Bin icon on your Desktop. A window will appear displaying all the files you have deleted since you last emptied the Bin. You can check the date you deleted the files by going to View → Details.

② Highlight the file you want to retrieve. Alternatively, hold down the Ctrl key while you click on several file names to select multiple files. Click the Restore button in the panel on the left to return the files to their original folders.

SHORTCUTS

Shortcuts are handy icons that allow you to launch programs or files directly from your Desktop—plus they're easy to create and delete.

If you don't like the look of your current Shortcut icon, you may be able to customize it. With some programs, including those in Microsoft Office, you can easily give it a new look—just right-click on the existing icon, scroll down to Properties, and then select the Shortcut tab. Now press the Change Icon button and select a fresh icon from those displayed.

You can create Shortcuts within folders as well as on the Desktop. This can be handy if you use a particular file or program while in a given folder—for example, if you want to use your household expenses spreadsheet when you're in a bank letters folder. To create a Shortcut in a folder, navigate to the folder

where you want to place the Shortcut. Go to File → New → Shortcut. In the Create Shortcut box that appears, click Browse and then navigate to the file to which you want to create the Shortcut. Double-click on the file and its path will appear in the Create Shortcut window. Click Next and, providing the name given to the file is the correct one, click Finish. The new Shortcut is now available within the folder.

Delete unwanted or rarely used Shortcuts to keep your Desktop free of clutter and easy to work on. Just click and drag the Shortcut folder to the Recycle Bin. Don't worry—you won't harm the associated file or program when you delete a Shortcut.

Change the type of window a program or file will open in to suit your Desktop and the way you wish to work. First, right-click on the Shortcut icon, select Properties from the pop-up menu, and then the Shortcut tab. Now use the drop-down menu beside Run to select a Normal, Minimized, or Maximized window when the program or file opens.

If you have a lot of loose Shortcuts, tidy up your Desktop by placing them all in a Shortcuts folder. Right-click on the Desktop, select New and then Folder and name the new folder Shortcuts. Now drag all your Desktop Shortcuts into this folder. It will take you one more click to get to the collated Shortcuts, but they're all in one place and not cluttering up the Desktop.

Remember that you don't usually need a Shortcut to both a document file and its associated program. Double-clicking on the file Shortcut will open it in its associated program, so keep just the file Shortcut on your Desktop.

HOW TO: CREATE A SHORTCUT

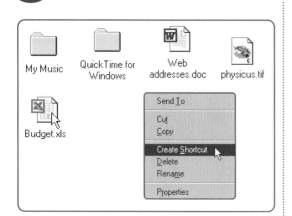

① Using Windows Explorer, navigate to the folder where the file or program file to which you want to create a Shortcut is stored—this can be any file or program. To create the shortcut, right-click on the file and select Create Shortcut from the pop-up menu.

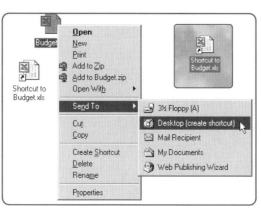

② The shortcut to the file appears in the same folder, but you may drag and drop it to another location. If you would prefer your shortcut to appear on the Desktop, select Send to → Desktop (create shortcut) from the pop-up menu instead.

SOUNDS

Learn how to manipulate and alter the sounds on your computer to get your machine truly wired for sound.

Enjoy the sound of silence—get rid of all event sounds on your computer. Go to Start menu → Settings → Control Panel and then double-click on the Sounds and Multimedia icon. In the Sounds and Multimedia Properties dialog box, click on the down arrow beside Scheme and, from the drop-down list that appears, select No Sounds. System events will now take place without any accompanying sound. Simply reverse the process to reactivate a sound.

If you alter the Sounds associated with various system events in the Sounds dialog box—accessible by going to Settings → Control Panel → Sounds and Multimedia—then save them as a Windows Scheme so that your special configuration is instantly available to you at a later date. Once you've made your Sound choices, just press the Save As button, type an appropriate name in the Save Scheme As pop-up box, and then click OK.

If you prefer a visual alert, use SoundSentry to provide you with a warning that you can see whenever a particular sound event is generated. You can choose from a variety of settings that flash different parts of your screen, depending on how you view files. Go to Settings → Control

Panel → Accessibility Options, and click the Sound tab. Check the box next to SoundSentry, then click Settings. Now use the drop-down menu to select the kind of warning you want to appear.

START MENU

The Start menu is the launch pad for much of what you do on your PC. Personalize and streamline this menu to speed up your computing.

If you have a lot of Start menu Shortcuts, you might find the menu colliding with the top of your screen. Make extra room by going to Start → Settings → Taskbar and Start Menu; then check the box next to Show small icons in Start menu. The icons will now be reduced in size, so you have room for more entries.

Change the order of an item on the Start menu by dragging it to a new position. A horizontal bar indicates where it will appear—when you're happy with the new position, release the mouse button and the item will be moved.

If you would like to display the contents of your My Documents and My Pictures folders in your Start menu, go to Start → Settings → Taskbar and Start Menu. Click the Advanced tab and check the boxes next to Expand My Documents and Expand My Pictures.

Program Shortcuts missing from the Start menu? This is probably because Windows Me has a feature that hides little-used program Shortcuts. You can see these Shortcuts if you click on the down arrow at the bottom of the list. If you want to see all program Shortcuts all of the time, go to Start → Settings → Taskbar and Start Menu. Select the General tab and uncheck the box next to Use personalized menus.

If you often work on the same file on your PC—modifying data in a spreadsheet, for example—put a shortcut to the file in the Start menu. Drag the file's icon to the Start button, wait a moment for the menu to pop up, and drop it in place there.

Get fast access to your favorite websites by adding them to the Start menu. Go to Start → Settings → Taskbar and Start Menu. Select the Advanced tab and check the box next to Display Favorites.

HOW TO: CHANGE YOUR START SOUND

① Go to Start → Settings → Control Panel. If you do not see the Sounds and Multimedia icon displayed, click on the "view all Control Panel options" link. Then, double-click on the Sounds and Multimedia icon.

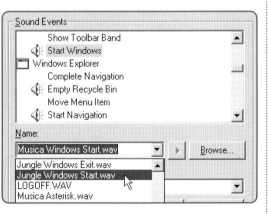

② Any Windows Default Events that have a sound are denoted by a loudspeaker icon. Scroll down the list and select Start Windows. Choose a new sound from the Name drop-down menu. To hear a sound, simply click the Play button (▶).

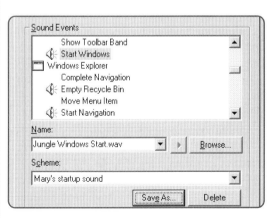

③ Save your sound as a new Sound Scheme that you can apply whenever you like. Click the Save As button, type in a name and click OK. Your new Scheme now appears as an option in the Scheme drop-down menu.

STARTUP DISK

Create a disk to backup vital system files to use in an emergency.

One of the cheapest but most vital insurance policies you can take out for your PC is to create a startup disk. This floppy disk will contain the few vital Windows files you need to start your computer in the event of a serious system crash. It can also help diagnose what caused the crash and reset your system to an earlier and healthier status.

If you are installing Window yourself, whether as an upgrade or on a new computer, you will be offered the opportunity to create a startup disk as part of the installation process. Accept this opportunity. This is absolutely the best time to take out this insurance.

A new PC with Windows pre-installed should come with a startup floppy disk as part of the computer package (it may be labeled "emergency disk" or "boot disk").

Use the startup disk to restart your PC if there's a serious problem and Windows fails to load. First make sure the the computer is switched off. Put the disk in the floppy drive and then switch on the computer. Follow the on-screen instructions to restore your machine.

Don't wait until something goes wrong before creating a startup disk; you must do it when the system is stable. You may not succeed in creating a startup disk if you wait until after the computer suffers a serious crash.

Protect your startup disk in a disk box and store it in a safe location, away from excessive heat and direct sunlight. But do not hide it somewhere so secret that you might forget it. If you ever need to use it, you are likely to need it in a hurry.

Make extra copies of your startup disk. If you use a notebook, it can be useful to have a startup disk tucked in your carrying case when traveling and other copies that stay in your office and at home.

Print out the Readme file on your startup disk and keep it safely with the disk; it contains important information about how to use the disk. To print the file, insert your startup disk in the drive and open it. Double-click on the Readme icon and select Print from the File menu.

HOW TO: CREATE A STARTUP DISK

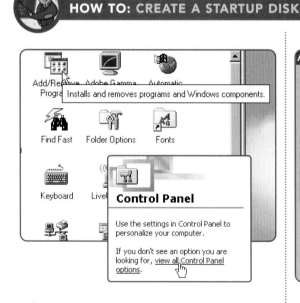

① Go to Start → Settings → Control Panel and double-click on the Add/Remove Programs icon. (If you can't see it, try clicking on the "view all Control Panel options" hyperlink to display all icons.)

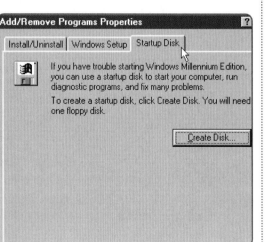

② Have a blank 1.4Mb floppy disk ready. Select the Startup Disk tab and click on Create Disk. Your computer then locates all the necessary files that need to be copied onto the floppy disk.

③ When prompted, label the floppy disk and insert it in drive A. Click OK. Windows now copies the necessary files to the startup disk, which can take a few minutes. Remove the disk, and store it in a safe place.

STARTUP FOLDER

Placing program or file shortcuts in the StartUp folder launches the programs and files automatically when you turn on your PC.

To put a program or file in the StartUp folder, drag the file or program from your Desktop to the Start button, wait for the menu to pop up, then go to Programs → StartUp, and drop the file in the StartUp submenu. A shortcut of the file is created there, and the next time you switch on your computer, the program or file will run. You can also drag programs to the StartUp folder from the Programs menu itself.

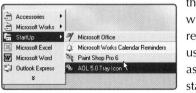

Resist the temptation to set lots of programs to launch at startup. Too many will give you a cluttered and confusing Desktop, make your PC take longer to start, and eat up vital system resources. To delete unwanted shortcuts in your StartUp folder, click Start → Programs → StartUp, right-click on a shortcut and select Delete from the pop-up menu.

Put shortcuts to files you use daily in your StartUp folder to get instant access them. Your contacts database is a good file to store like this.

If you perform variations on the same theme on your PC most of the time—writing letters to clients on your own letterhead stationery, for example—put a shortcut to the file template in the StartUp folder. Both the file template and the program will then be ready for use as soon as your PC starts up.

If you use a program often, but not every day, it's a good idea to put a shortcut to it on the taskbar, rather than in the StartUp folder. No matter how many windows are opened at one time, the program's icon will be visible on the taskbar, and you'll be able to launch it quickly and easily from that location.

⇨ See also Windows: Start Menu, Shortcuts, and Taskbar.

SWITCHING PROGRAMS

When two or more applications are running at the same time, your screen can seem a confusing mass of windows, but there are ways to bring order to the scene.

To quickly change between several active program windows, hold down the Alt key and press the Tab key. A small dialog box appears showing program icons for the applications you have running. Keep the Alt key held down and press Tab to move from one icon to the next until you reach the program you want. To go through the icons in reverse order, hold down the Shift key at the same time. When you release the Alt key that program window is brought to the front.

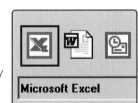

To reduce screen clutter, minimize a program window that you're not using right now to the taskbar. Just click on the Minimize button—the first of the three buttons at the top right of the window. Click once on a minimized taskbar program to get it back to its previous size.

If you need to see more than one program window on your desktop simultaneously, right-click on the taskbar, and in the pop-up menu, click on Cascade Windows. This will result in all the title bars of your windows becoming visible and being neatly stacked on your Desktop.

TASKBAR

The taskbar keeps the programs and files you are currently using within easy reach. You can modify it to suit the way you work.

Keep your most frequently used programs as shortcuts on the taskbar in the Quick Launch toolbar. To switch on the Quick Launch toolbar right-click on an empty area of the taskbar, go to Toolbars and make sure Quick Launch is selected. Now create a shortcut (see page 38) and simply drag it onto the Quick Launch part of the taskbar.

Regularly clean up the Quick Launch toolbar, to prevent it from getting crowded. Drag less frequently used shortcuts to the Recycle Bin;

YOUR TASKBAR OPTIONS EXPLAINED

For quick and easy access to popular programs and controls, get to know your taskbar a little better.

 Internet Explorer: One-click access to the Internet.

 Outlook Express: Check your e-mail with ease.

 Volume Control: Adjust your multimedia volume.

 Norton AntiVirus: Keep an eye on your virus checker.

 Mouse Controls: Customize your mouse activity.

 Media Player: Play audio, video, or animation files.

 Clock: Check the time, adjust it or change the display format.

they are quick and easy to create if you really need to have access to them again.

You do not have to position the taskbar at the bottom of the screen—you can put it on either side, or even at the top. Just click in an empty area of the taskbar and drag the whole panel to the side or top, releasing the button when it's in position.

Temporarily hide the taskbar if you want maximum Desktop space. Place your cursor over the top edge so that it becomes a double-headed vertical arrow. Now click and drag down until only a thin sliver of the taskbar is visible. To restore, click and drag it back.

If you have the space, why not give a busy taskbar a bit more room to breathe? Move your cursor over the top edge so that it changes to a double-headed vertical arrow, then click and drag the bar to expand it. You can even increase the taskbar to around half of the total screen if you wish.

Clear your screen instantly by reducing all open windows and dialog boxes to the Taskbar. To do this, click on the Show Desktop icon in the Quick Launch toolbar to hide the windows. When you want to restore any of them to their original size, simply click on it again.

If you want to close a program which has been minimized to the taskbar, you can close it without going to the trouble of reactivating the program window. All you need to do is right-click on the minimized program panel on the taskbar, and click on Close in the pop-up menu that appears.

Get easy access to websites by having a "floating" URL Address bar on your Desktop. Right-click on an empty area of the taskbar and select Toolbars ➜ Address. An Address bar will appear on the taskbar. You can now simply drag the Address bar onto your Desktop.

To delete unwanted toolbars, right-click on an empty area of the taskbar, select Toolbars from the menu, and uncheck the unwanted toolbar.

TIME

You can easily change your PC's time settings when you travel to a different time zone or if your clock gets out of sync.

The current time is displayed at the far right of the taskbar on the computer, in a special area called the System Tray. Icons for programs and utilities that easily alter aspects of your settings, such as the time setting, are stored here.

To reset the time, right-click on the clock in the taskbar and then select Adjust Date/Time. In the

---

HOW TO: ADD A FOLDER TO THE TASKBAR AS A TOOLBAR

① Placing a folder on the taskbar as a new toolbar enables quick access to the files within the folder. Right-click on an empty area of the taskbar, select Toolbars from the pop-up menu, and click the New Toolbar option.

② Locate the folder you want, for example, the My Pictures folder. Click the + next to any main folders to view other folders inside. Click on the appropriate folder—its name appears in the Folder box at the bottom of the window—and click OK.

③ The chosen folder appears as a toolbar on the taskbar, with its contents available for immediate use. Click on the double-headed arrow at the right of the toolbar to display the files (and folders) not currently shown, then click on a file to open it.

Date/Time Properties dialog box, click in the digital time display below the analog clock and delete and replace the numerals. Alternatively, select a numeral and use the up and down buttons to change the time. Click OK.

Need to know the exact day and date your retirement takes place, or when you started that job back in '86? The Date/Time Properties calendar can tell you days and dates as far back as 1980 and as far ahead as 2099. Just use the up and down buttons to change the month and year—but don't forget to click the Cancel button so that your PC reverts to today's date afterward!

Make sure your system updates itself when the clocks go forward or back an hour by checking the box that reads Automatically adjust clock for daylight saving changes at the bottom of the Date/Time Properties window.

Where do you go to get the right time? Canada's National Research Council is the federal agency responsible for official time. The NRC provides time services through the Frequency and Time Group of its Institute of National Measurement Standards. Visit the Institute's website (www.ncr.ca/inms/time/whatime.html), which has all sorts of details about time zones, daylight savings, and other time-related matters.

VOLUME

The Volume Control icon gives you quick control over all aspects of sound on your computer.

When you're playing pumping rock music and the phone rings, you need peace and quiet very quickly. So double-click on the yellow loudspeaker Volume Control icon on the taskbar, and check the Mute all box at the bottom left. The result is instant silence. Deselect the box to go back to your music.

Not getting any sounds at all through your speakers? Open Volume Control through the taskbar and make sure that you haven't inadvertently checked the Mute all box in the master Volume Control panel or that the volume level is not set to minimum.

Before altering any of the other sound options in Volume Control set the master Volume Control slider on the lefthand side to between 55 and 75 percent of maximum. This will increase or decrease the overall sound and give you a wide range of audio levels for multimedia programs.

Can't see the loudspeaker in the taskbar? Go to Settings → Control Panel and double-click on the Sounds and Multimedia icon. If you cannot see this option, click the View all Control Panel options link. Select the Sounds tab and check the box next to Show volume control on the taskbar. Click OK and the loudspeaker icon will appear.

Experiment with the Volume Control settings to find the overall levels that suit you or the particular kind of music you're playing. You can either choose to leave the Volume Control window open all the time, or minimize it, for easier access.

Can't get the right balance between music and Windows sound effects? Set the Wave volume slider as low as the second or third mark on the mixer panel and raise the Line-In volume to around three-quarters of the maximum. Control the overall volume from the master Volume Control slider.

Can't see the volume slider for the function you want? Click on Options and Properties. Check appropriate control in the Show the following volume controls panel, and click OK.

⇨ See also **Windows: Sounds.**

TAKE TIME OUT ON THE INTERNET
Set your PC to atomic time or check out the history of timepieces.

World Time Server (www.worldtimeserver.com)
Provides free atomic clock sync for your PC. It also has Time and Chaos management software for your appointments calendar.

How Stuff Works (www.howstuffworks. com/atomic-clock.htm)
A guide to atomic clocks and how they keep the world ticking! The effect of atomic time is felt by all of us in the form of alarm clocks, answering machines, and computers.

NIST Physics Laboratory (http://physics.nist.gov/lab.html)
See timekeeping through the ages with the U.S. National Institute of Standards and Technology's "A walk through time."

Horology (www.horology.com)
A comprehensive index with crosslinks information on horology—the science of time and timepieces. You can find out where you can have that antique clock repaired or set your computer time exactly over the Web.

VIRUSES

V iruses are programs that you unwittingly store on your hard disk, where they can open and cause havoc. They are self-replicating and may be passed from one PC to another. But you can take steps to minimize infection. Virus-protection programs will destroy most viruses and help shield you from future infection.

A GUIDE TO VIRUSES

Macro viruses are the most common, with names like Concept, Nuclear, and Laroux. They are written in a macro—a sequence of instructions—attached to a Word or Excel file. If you open an infected document, the macro virus writes itself into your copy of Word or Excel, and then infects all future documents created by you. Some strains of Word macro virus even propagate by e-mail, using Outlook Express to send copies of themselves to names randomly chosen from your address book. Versions of Word and Excel from Office 97 onward warn you of the possible presence of macros in files to be opened and offer to disable them.

Boot-sector viruses were best-known in the days of the Disk Operating System (DOS). They still exist in large numbers, surviving in your hard disk's boot sector—where the files used to start up your PC are stored. A boot sector virus becomes active each time you start up—or restart—your PC. Once active, it will copy itself onto every floppy disk inserted into your PC.

File-infecting viruses are also known as parasitic viruses. While they are more common under DOS, some Windows file viruses exist as well. They lurk inside a program. When you run it, the virus starts meddling with your RAM, and then infects the other programs that you run.

Viruses known as worms spread copies of themselves over networked computers. While they can replicate themselves and use memory, they can't spread by attaching themselves to other viruses. The notorious Internet Worm of 1988 spread to thousands of machines in a few days, and marked the first time that users were concerned about viruses over the Net.

A multipartite virus combines boot-sector and file-infecting viruses. It is found within an executable program. When the program is run, the virus infects the hard drive's boot sector.

Polymorphic viruses are viruses that attempt to escape detection by changing their form each time they spread.

Strictly speaking, Trojan horses are not viruses since they don't replicate. They tend to be hidden inside programs, usually games, and they display a message, erase files, or lose data. You can get rid of them just by deleting them.

VIRUS PROTECTION SOFTWARE
Special programs will protect your PC from vicious viruses.

Command Anti Virus (www.commandcom.com)
Set it to run scans during periods of inactivity. Scan files by right-clicking on them while working in Windows Explorer or on the Desktop. A 24-hour helpline is provided and the product may be purchased online.

McAfee VirusScan (www.mcafee.com)
The scanner component can be run from the Start menu, from Internet Explorer. Set it to run automatically at certain times or when your screensaver starts up. There's an automatic background virus checker and updates are available online or on disk.

Norton AntiVirus (www.symantec.com)
Tried-and-true product with disinfection and virus-scanning components. The program can perform checks at set times, and there are regular free updates. The Repair Wizard will guide you through removing any virus.

PC starts. Since a boot-sector virus mimics your real boot code, it will try to start up from the floppy. The virus copies itself to your hard drive and gets to work. You can be infected whether the attempt to boot from the floppy was successful, or not.

Script viruses are written in script programming languages, like Visual Basic Script and JavaScript. They can be caught by opening a .vbs or .js file, or they can be embedded into the HTML of a web page. In theory, just opening a web page could cause infection, though there are no confirmed reports of this happening—yet.

METHODS OF INFECTION

A floppy disk or other removable media remains a common source of infection, especially one given to you by a friend or co-worker. The person may not realize that it contains a virus, and you can't be sure it has been effectively virus-checked.

Opening an e-mail attachment could cause infection, although reading a plain text e-mail won't. You can never be sure what the attachment is. It might look like it's a .jpg file, or a harmless picture, but you never know…

Downloading software can mean downloading a virus. If you go to a reputable site like Download (www.download.com) and download a well-known program, you're unlikely to get a virus. But if someone sends you an e-mail with a new program attached, don't open it!

Office networks can spread viruses. Worms can operate over a network and work their way around several PCs.

HOW TO AVOID VIRUSES

Eject floppies from your disk drive before you start your PC. If the floppy has a boot-sector virus, it will infect your hard disk as soon as the

If you are opening an unknown Microsoft Word file, open it with another related program, such as WordPad. This is because Word macro viruses can only infect copies of files in Word, and WordPad cannot run macros.

```
Document - WordPad
File  Edit  View  Insert  F
  New...          Ctrl+N
  Open...         Ctrl+O
  Save            Ctrl+S
  Save As...

  Print...        Ctrl+P
  Print Preview
  Page Setup...
```

Set antivirus software to automatically scan all floppies you use, even new ones. Write-protect any floppies you give to others to prevent them passing on viruses inadvertently when they return them. Hold the floppy face down, with the metal cover toward you. Slide the tab on the upper left corner up to uncover the hole and write-protect the disk.

Create an emergency startup disk to boot up your PC if it crashes. If you have a diagnosis and repair program—like Norton Utilities—you can start up from the CD-ROM or a startup

floppy that the program creates for you. Or create a startup floppy. Go to Start → Settings → Control Panel, double-click on Add/Remove Programs, and select Startup Disk tab.

Use virus-protection software to safeguard your PC. An effective program has two components: disinfection and scanning. First, it finds viruses on your hard drive and destroys them, then runs in the background, scanning for viruses as you open and close files, insert floppy disks, or surf the Net. Download updates, called "definitions," from program manufacturers' websites, or subscribe to have updated software sent to you on CD-ROM so that you can identify and destroy the latest viruses.

Check warning sites for the latest news on viruses. Top Threats at Symantec's AntiVirus Research Center (www.symantec.com/avcenter) has stories on the latest viruses. Or see the Wild List (www.wildlist.org), a complete virus listing—updated monthly—currently out there "in the wild."

Top Threats		
Risk	**Threat**	**Dis**
✷	W95.MTX	8/
✷	W32.HLLW.QAZ.A	7/
✷	VBS.Stages.A	6/
✷	VBS.LoveLetter	5/
✷	VBS.Network	2/
✷	Wscript.KakWorm	12

TOP 10 WARNING SIGNS

Think you've got a virus? Not all these symptoms will appear, and some will conceal themselves or may be caused by other reasons. But they will provide a solid starting point for your diagnosis.

1. Your PC runs very slowly for no apparent reason.
2. Programs take longer to load.
3. Files disappear from your hard drive.
4. Program files expand in size.
5. You have trouble opening or saving Word documents.
6. Your PC often crashes or suddenly reboots itself.
7. Your hard drive is accessed more often.
8. Your screen colors change, or strange messages appear, such as "Your computer is now stoned."
9. Devices that once worked, now don't, even though you haven't changed your system configuration.
10. If you are on a network, you notice that the problems affecting your computer have started occurring on other PCs in your office.

WALLPAPER

The patterns or images you can use as a Desktop background are unlimited. Select from Windows' own range, or create your own.

Redecorate. To change your wallpaper, right-click in a clear space on your Desktop and select Properties. In the Display Properties box, select the Background tab. You can choose a background from one of the images listed, or if you have an image elsewhere on your PC that you'd like to use, click Browse and go through the folders to locate that image. You can choose to "stretch" the background image to fill the whole screen, or "center" it on your Desktop, or "tile" it, so that the image is repeated over and over across your monitor. When you're happy with your image, click OK and it will appear as your new background.

If you are using a sizable image as wallpaper, do not tile it. Instead, use the Center command to position the image so that the it falls exactly in the middle of the Desktop, or make it fit using the Stretch command.

Search the Web for images of your favorite star. For example, go to a search engine and type in "George Clooney .jpg." Now you will get pages containing .jpg files, the most widely used format for quality Web images.

Found a web page with a really cool image? Turn it into Desktop wallpaper by right-clicking on the image and selecting Set As Wallpaper. It will appear immediately on your Desktop.

Wallpaper saved using the Set As Wallpaper command will be replaced the next time you use that command. If you want to save this image rather than risk overwriting it, don't use the Set As Wallpaper option—right-click on the image, select Save Picture As and name it.

To make an image from a specialized wallpaper website fill the whole screen, download it at the maximum resolution offered, which is normally 1,024x768.

Give yourself a laugh—download humorous wallpaper from Joke Wallpaper (www.jokewallpaper.com) or Groovy Wallpaper (www.groovywallpaper.com). You'll find politicians, TV shows, movies, and celebrities lampooned.

If a web page has lots of small thumbnail images, first left-click on the image to enlarge it. Then right-click to select the Set As Wallpaper or Save Picture As options.

Manage extensive wallpaper collections with a free downloadable utility, such as WallMaster (www.tropicalwaves.com). These small programs sit on your Taskbar, allowing you to manage wallpaper files and to schedule automatic wallpaper changes.

WINDOWS

Ensure quick and easy access to all your computer's areas.

Arrange windows in a manageable sequence by right-clicking the taskbar and selecting Cascade Windows, Tile Windows Horizontally, or Tile Windows Vertically. Minimized windows will not be included.

Resize a window. Hold the mouse pointer over the edge of the window until it turns into a double-headed arrow. Now click and drag the edge of the window in or out. Clicking the corner of a window will allow you to resize both the horizontal and vertical edges at the same time.

If navigating folders through a single window

is inconvenient, set each folder you access to open in a separate window. To do this, go to Start → Settings → Control Panel and double-click the Folder

Options icon. Click on the General tab. Here you will see a number of options for controlling your folders. Select the option to open each folder in its own window, and click OK.

If you want the file icons within a window to appear larger or smaller, click on the Views button to the right-hand side of the toolbar and select an option by clicking on it. The thumbnails option is designed to show miniature representations of picture files.

Are you the creative type? Windows offers an alternative to drab Desktops. For a truly original look, customize each folder. Open the folder in question and click View, then Customize This Folder. This launches a wizard, which allows you to change the layout, text, and background colors, or add a background picture or image. You can even include a personal comment, which will be visible in the left panel of the window when the folder is open.

Windows may begin to slow down after a year or so of good use. Take a bit of the workload off your computer's processor by turning off the animated transitions that your operating system uses to bring up menus and minimize windows to the taskbar. Go to Settings → Control Panel

It sits on your Desktop and in a separate window displays the magnified portion of the screen which corresponds with the position of the mouse cursor.

⇨ See also **Windows: Accessibility, Hidden Files, Maximize/Minimize, Switching Programs.**

WINDOWS EXPLORER

Windows Explorer lists all the drives, files and folders on your PC. It's like a virtual filing cabinet.

To open Windows Explorer, right-click on any folder or disk and select Explore. If you prefer keyboard shortcuts, press Windows+E.

Control the way the files on your PC appear in Explorer. Select a folder in Windows Explorer, click View, and choose how you want the information displayed. For example, you can set your folder contents to display as thumbnails. Once you

have a folder view you like, you can apply the same design to every folder on your hard drive. Open Windows Explorer and select the appropriate folder. Click Tools ➔ Folder Options ➔ the View tab ➔ Like Current Folder.

Select various toolbar options for Explorer by going to View ➔ Toolbars and clicking on Customize. A dialog box opens, which lets you select the buttons you want to see on your toolbar. Choose a button in the lefthand panel and click Add or Remove as desired. Click the Reset button to restore the toolbar to its original state.

When you point to an option on a menu, the status bar at the bottom of the window displays a description of what that option does and how much space it takes up. If the status bar is not visible, go to View ➔ Status Bar.

⇨ See also **Windows: Finding Files, Folders,** and **Start Menu.**

and select Display. Click the Effects tab, and uncheck the Use transition effects for menus and tooltips box. Another way to speed your computer up is to uncheck the box next to Show window contents while dragging.

Use the magnifier, which is an extra window in Windows Millennium Edition, to enlarge selected text and specified on-screen areas.

HOW TO: USE THE WINDOWS MAGNIFIER

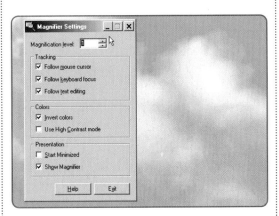

① The magnifier is an optional extra, found in the Accessibility section of your Windows CD-ROM, so you may need to install it before you can use it. Once installed, launch the magnifier by going to Start ➔ Programs ➔ Accessories ➔ Accessibility ➔ Magnifier.

② Choose the settings you want from the Magnifier's display options. For instance, you can set the magnifier to follow your mouse-pointer, keyboard, or text-editing activity. You can also invert the color settings to help the improved readability of text.

③ When you are happy with the Magnifier settings, minimize the dialog box and work as usual. The Magnifier will run at the top of your screen.

An operating system is an essential part of any computer, and Microsoft has been producing and developing operating systems for many years. Discover the various types available, find out whether to upgrade your system, and get some handy tips on how to resolve compatibility problems.

WHAT IS AN OPERATING SYSTEM?

An operating system (OS) is a collection of software that controls how your computer works. It saves you having to use—or write—programs to do every little task. For example, the operating system makes sure your printer is installed correctly and can be accessed by different programs, that your Internet connection is correctly set up and accessible by different programs, and that your programs themselves are able to talk to each other and share data if they need to. As hardware and software advance, operating systems have to advance, too, so that they can handle the latest, most complex equipment and programs.

Operating systems need to change as people's use of computers change. Ten years ago most people would not have dreamed of using computers to access the Web, five years ago creating and listening to music using a computer was not a popular idea and as recently as two years ago using them to network at home was a rarity. Operating systems need to reflect our changing computer usage and handle potential future developments, too. Microsoft, with operating systems like Windows 95, Windows 98, and most recently Windows Me, has done just that.

SMOOTH OPERATORS

Microsoft has more. Windows 95, 98, and Me are not the only operating systems from Microsoft. Others include Windows NT, Windows 2000, and Windows XP, and a special OS for handheld computers, PocketPC. Windows NT has been Microsoft's operating system for professional users, aimed at those wanting to run a network of computers. Windows 2000, launched at around the same time as Me, has many of the Windows NT features and looks set to replace it as the professional's choice. Windows XP is the most advanced system to date, aiming to combine programs, Internet services, and hardware devices in a far more user-friendly way.

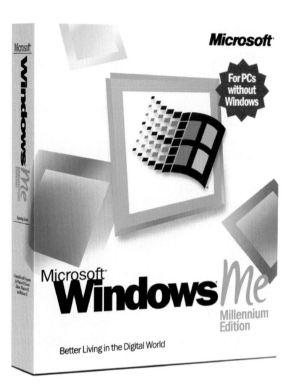

Microsoft doesn't have a monopoly on operating systems. Macs (made by The Apple Corporation) have their own MAC OS, and there are other PC operating systems, such as Linux. Most PC users, however, find it easiest to stick with a Microsoft operating system, because the alternatives can be rather technical.

Second time around. Along with the initial releases of its operating systems, Microsoft has issued second editions (SE) of Windows 95 and 98. In both cases these have additional features, such as support for new hardware, as well as fixed bugs. For example, Windows 98 has added full support for Universal Serial Bus (USB), some home networking tools, DVD, and multiple monitors connected to the same PC.

Besides completely new editions, there are also "plus packs" that add new software and utilities to your operating system. With Windows 98, the plus pack allows you to customize the look of your system, too.

SYSTEM REQUIREMENTS

Like all other software, operating systems have a certain set of minimum system requirements. Check that your computer meets them before installing an upgrade.

	Processor	RAM	Hard drive space
Windows 95	Intel 386DX*	4Mb	Up to 83Mb
Windows 98	Intel 486DX/66*	16Mb	Up to 355Mb
Windows Me	Intel Pentium 150*	32Mb	Up to 435Mb

*Or equivalent.

TO UPGRADE OR NOT TO UPGRADE?

Microsoft issues different versions of its operating systems, depending on what you are upgrading from initially. If you buy the correct version, then upgrading should be a simple matter of following the instructions on your screen. However, it is always advisable, whenever you make any major changes to your computer, to back up all data that you consider valuable before you begin the installation.

The cost of upgrading to a newer Windows version depends on which version of the operating system you're currently running. Check the website of a reputable online seller, such as Future Shop (www.futureshop.ca), or look in your local computer store for prices.

You don't have to upgrade your version if you don't want to. Microsoft supports Windows 95

and 98 through its website. Both have their own homepage (www.microsoft.com/ windows95 and www.microsoft. com/windows98),

from which you can obtain software updates, advice on using the software, and information on what's new.

Sometimes it's best to leave it alone! In certain cases you'd be well advised to continue with your current OS rather than upgrading it. If your PC doesn't have enough system resources to run the new OS, if you don't use any of the new hardware or software that a newer OS supports, and if you've never had any problems with your current setup, then why upgrade?

Unsure about your PC's specifications? If you want to check on your PC's processor or, perhaps, the amount of memory it has, it's easy to find out. Go to Start ➔ Settings ➔ Control Panel. Then double-click the System icon. The window that opens gives you at-a-glance information about the current version of your operating system and how much RAM (Random Access Memory) is in your computer. If you want to find out how much space is available on your hard drive, click the My Computer icon on your Desktop, right-click C: and choose Properties. The new window will show you how much space has been used on your hard

drive and similarly, how much you still have available to use.

WHAT'S NEW?

Windows Me has several new features that make using your PC more efficient and fun. These include video editing capabilities, easy importing of digital images from a digital camera (providing your camera has the required software built into it), Windows Media Player, the System Restore feature, and good support for networking so that you can link two or more computers together.

Need to install new features? If your computer came with Windows Me or earlier already installed, or if you have upgraded yourself and chosen a "typical" installation, then all the extra features of the software may not be

installed. To add more features in Windows Me, 98, or 95, go to My Computer ➔ Control Panel ➔ Add/Remove Programs. Click the Windows Setup tab, and wait

 HOW TO: SET UP A HOME NETWORK USING WINDOWS ME

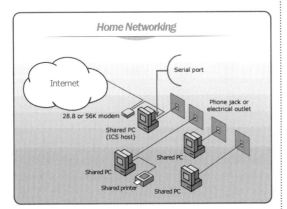

① First you need to determine what hardware you need. Every computer on the network will need a network adapter— probably in the form of a card to be installed internally. You may also need some cables unless you are using a wireless network.

② Run the Home Networking Wizard by clicking on Start ➔ Accessories ➔ Communication and finally clicking on Home Networking. Click through the Wizard's dialog boxes, answering any questions as you go. Click Finish on the final box.

Congratulations! Home Networking is set up on this computer.

1. Now run the Home Networking wizard on your other home computers.

   In Windows Me, click Start, point to Programs, point to Accessories, point to Communications, and then click Home Networking wizard.

   In Windows 98 and Windows 95, use the Home Networking Setup disk you created. Re-run the wizard if you need to make a Setup disk.

2. Restart the computers. Shortcuts to shared resources are found in My Network Places (Network Neighborhood in Windows 98 and Windows 95) on your desktop.

③ Restart your PC when prompted, and the Wizard will then inform you that home networking is set up on your computer. Click OK to confirm.

while Setup searches for installed components. Once the search is complete, you'll be able to select any new elements and simply add them individually.

WIZARD OF OS

Windows Me includes a tutorial to help get you started with the operating system. The tutorial is a good place to pick up the basics of using your computer and should help you understand more about the features that are built into Windows Me, including its many different programs. Along with screens of

ME GAMES

Windows Me is designed for home use, and many home users enjoy playing computer games.

Me comes with several games for you to play. To see the list, go to Start → Programs → Games, then click the desired game icon.

Hearts is just one of Windows' classic card games. You can play against the computer or other players on your network.

Minesweeper requires you to find the mines by clicking on cells in a grid. To make things tough, you play against the clock.

3D Pinball is a fast and furious game of virtual pinball—to remind you of the arcade classic.

Solitaire is the classic solo card game that's come with every version of Windows to date. Microsoft simply had to include it with Me.

information for you to read through, there are clearly illustrated tours with animated sequences aimed at helping you understand the additional functions of the new operating system more clearly.

If you're using Windows 98 as your operating system and want to understand more about how it works, you can use the Help feature. Go to Start → Help and select from the Help topics listed. Besides providing information on the use of various Windows 98 components, the Help section has several troubleshooters that cover a variety of technical problems.

If your computer runs Windows 95, you may not have enough system resources to upgrade to Windows Me. If this is the case, you could consider upgrading to the Second Edition of Windows 98, instead. This has a number of advantages over Windows 95. For example, it has support for USB built in, so you can use the many devices that now connect to your PC that way. USB is faster than serial connections and is also easier to set up and use, but you must make sure your PC has USB ports before upgrading. Windows 98 also has later versions of software such as Internet Explorer.

Even if you have installed add-ons and upgrades as they have become available, in order to bring your Windows 95 operating system up to near Windows 98 standard—or 98 up to Me—it may be worth considering completely upgrading your operating system. The components in Windows 98 will probably work together a lot better if they are installed as part of a single operating system rather than as separate elements, and the same applies to those in Windows Me.

COMPATIBILITY CONCERNS

Most of your software should work with Me, and all that work with Windows 95 should also work with 98. But to be on the safe side, it's always a good idea to check the packaging of new programs before you buy, and to be wary of software that states it works only with later versions of Windows, if you are currently using an older version.

Whatever OS you are using, you may find it useful to keep yourself up to date with new developments such as the publication of software updates. Take a look at the Microsoft website (www.microsoft. com) regularly for the latest information. This will help ensure that your current operating system can cope with the most up-to-date hardware and software available on the market.

Don't be too hard on your operating system! When you start up your PC, your operating system must read millions of lines of program code and work out how to get all your PC's components working both individually and together. It is then designed to present the results in a user-friendly fashion that you can understand. So it's not surprising if sometimes things don't go quite according to plan.

What's so different about Me? Windows Me (pronounced "me" rather than "em, ee") is really only Windows 98 with a few extras. The first things you'll notice are the Desktop icons—they have a hand-drawn "cartoon" look rather than the computerized appearance of 98. Other additions include the new Windows Media Player (see how to, opposite), video-editing software, and a program that restores your OS to its previous version if your present one

becomes corrupt. But it's behind the scenes that Windows Me has it's most useful improvements—it's far more stable than 95 or 98 and therefore much less likely to crash.

Do I need to upgrade? If you still have Windows 95, then it's definitely worth upgrading to Me—you'll find that it's much smoother to use and the new features are great fun, too. However, if you currently use Windows 98, an upgrade is perhaps not so urgent—many of Me's additional features are available as free downloads from the Microsoft website (www.microsoft.com).

The Big Freeze. Although Windows 98 and Me are less prone to crashes than Windows 95, screen freezes do inevitably occur. So, rather than reaching for the power button to solve this problem, simply close the program you are currently using by pressing Ctrl+Alt+Delete on your keyboard, selecting the program you want to close, then click on End Task.

Some freezes are deeper than others. You may find that the Ctrl+Alt+Delete keystroke has no effect. Wait for a few seconds—just to make sure that the system isn't busy doing something else—and then try one more time. If this still doesn't work, there's no alternative but to switch the PC off and then on again.

When hardware causes heartache! Sometimes a device—such as a printer—will fail to work with Windows 95 or 98, or a peripheral that has been working perfectly under an earlier operating system will fail to work under Windows Me. This is usually because the device drivers—the software that tells the

hardware how to operate—is incompatible with your computer's

operating system. To avoid this, check the hardware's compatibility with 98 or Me. You can do this at the Windows Hardware Compatibility List website (www.microsoft. com/hcl/default.asp).

Manage your devices. All versions of Windows come with a Device Manager to help solve your compatibility problems. You can use the Device Manager to update existing drivers, find out if a device is working, or turn them on and

off. To access the Device Manager, right-click on My Computer and select Properties. In the System Properties window, click the Device Manager tab, select the device and then click the Properties button.

If in doubt, use the drivers that came with the OS, rather than the hardware—just in case the drivers are already out of date.

If you have trouble with a laser printer in Windows 98 or Me, choose the HP Laserjet series II printer in the Add Printer Wizard. This works for most laser printers, because they comply with the HP standard for Printer Control Language (PCL) drivers and laser printers, regardless of the manufacturer.

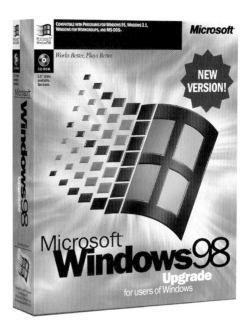

HOW TO: USE WINDOWS MEDIA PLAYER

① Media Player comes with the Windows Me operating system. To access it, click on the Media Player button in the Quick Launch area of the Taskbar. If you have a music CD in the CD drive, click on Now Playing to start listening to it.

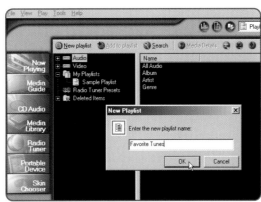

② Make your own music compilation by creating a playlist. Click the Media Library button and then choose New Playlist from the options. Now you can add new items as you choose, to create your perfect playlist.

③ Media Player also supports "skins," or different looks. To choose a new look for your Player, click the Skin Chooser on the left-hand menu and browse through the skins by clicking them. When you find one you like, click on Apply Skin to cover your Player.

Software

Discover the tricks of the trade with everything from Access to Zip files. Master menus, mail merge, and macros. Design newsletters and cards. Create your own images, and conquer spreadsheets.

ACCESS

Organize and summarize info on anything from wedding lists to record collections.

Microsoft Access is a database manager. Feed it a mass of related information, such as your record collection, or details of your household bills, and it will help you to organize it in any way you want. The database enables you to easily extract the specific information you need, such as which bills haven't been paid yet this month. You can choose from a variety of printed reports to summarize your data.

Don't be put off! Beginners to Access are often scared off by the apparent complexity of Queries, but you just need to get used to them. All the information in your database appears as a massive grid. To extract the information you want, you need to use the Query feature. For instance, if you have a database of your record collection, you can instruct Access to search it for all your 1960s Beatles recordings.

For simple tasks, such as finding one particular record, go to the Edit menu and select Find. Enter the details of the required search, and Access will locate the matching records for you.

Reorganize your data. You can sort the entire contents of your database alphabetically, by any

of your database's fields. For instance, in an address database, you can click on a last name entry, go to the Records menu and select Sort, then A-Z Ascending or Descending. To keep the new order, close the table. Click OK when the prompt asks if you want to save the changes.

Learning how to use Queries gives you much more power, enabling you to easily group and sort data. Queries run much faster when applied to indexed fields, so it helps to think about this when designing your table. Fields

that will often be used for sorting, such as "Last name" in an address book, should have their Indexed property set to "Yes" to give the best results.

Once you've seen how much faster a Query runs on an indexed field, it's tempting to turn indexes on everywhere—but don't! Each index you create must be rewritten every time you alter the database; too many can actually reduce your overall performance. Use indexes sparingly and only on frequently used fields where you'll see the most gain.

Automation saves time and typing. Create a macro group called AutoExec, and any commands it holds will be run every time you open that database. But beware of the downside to this. Access viruses may attempt to use this mechanism to infect your system. If someone sends you an MDB (Microsoft Database) file, make sure you scan it with an antivirus program, just as you would treat any other program or Internet download.

It's easy to edit data in Microsoft Access. But that's not always a good thing, especially if you're setting up a system where you want users to be able to view information, but not change it. In situations like this, one good solution is to design forms to display the information you need, and set the form's "Allow Edits" property to "No."

Tab	Moves to the next field.
Shift+Tab	Moves to the previous field.
Home	Moves to the first field of the current record.
End	Moves to the last field of the current record.
Ctrl+; (semicolon)	Inserts the current date.
Ctrl+: (colon)	Inserts the current time.
Ctrl+Alt+Space bar	Inserts the default value for the current field.
Ctrl+' (apostrophe)	Inserts the value from the same field in the previous record.
Ctrl++ (plus sign)	Adds a new record.
Ctrl+- (minus sign)	Deletes current record.
Ctrl+Z	Undoes typing.
Esc	Undoes changes in the current field, then the current record.

A tool like the Database Splitter can be useful if you have several people who want to access the same database, such as household finances. The splitter separates the data itself from the forms and queries, meaning that each user can work with the data in their own way. Database Splitters aren't installed unless you specifically select them, though, so it might be worth running Access setup again to see which add-ins are available.

Even if you install every option available on the Access installation disk, chances are your system won't be fully up to date. Microsoft occasionally makes bug fixes and new add-ins available, free of charge. Visit their website (http://officeupdate. microsoft.com) to check for updates.

If you have any technical problems, the Microsoft support site (http://support.microsoft.com/support/access/) should be the first place you look. But don't wait until things go wrong before you visit—it has lots of useful tutorials and articles. You'll find even more help at the Office page (www.microsoft.com/office).

There are plenty of other websites around that provide Access-related advice, tips, and tricks. The Microsoft Access web ring (www.iversonsoftware.com/accessring.htm) brings many of them together.

⇨ See also **Software: Databases.**

ALIGNING

Style your text quickly and easily with Word's alignment feature.

With Microsoft Word, as with most word processors, there are four options for horizontally aligning paragraphs of text—left,

center, right, and justified. All you have to do is

click one of the four Alignment buttons on the toolbar.

To realign text that you've already typed, highlight the relevant text, then choose your required alignment option from the toolbar. When aligning a single paragraph, there's a handy shortcut—click anywhere in the paragraph text, select the option you want, and that paragraph will be realigned accordingly.

If text doesn't align to the left or right margin as you expect, you may have set up the paragraph to be indented. To check this, click on the Format menu, then choose Paragraph and then Indents and Spacing. If you don't want text indented, set your indents to 0 inches.

Hate reaching for the mouse each time? Try a few keyboard shortcuts. In Microsoft Word, you can select text by holding down the Shift key as you move the arrow keys, then align with the relevant shortcut: Ctrl+L (left), Ctrl+E (center), Ctrl+R (right), or Ctrl+J (justified).

You can also align text vertically, either to the top or bottom of a page, or evenly between the two. This is known as justified vertical alignment. To align the text vertically in Microsoft Word, go to the File menu and choose Page Setup → Layout and use the vertical alignment options.

ALPHABETIZING

After entering data into an application, it's often useful to be able to sort it alphabetically.

To alphabetize data in table form, such as in the Outlook Express Address Book, the most common method is to click on one of the column headers. The table is then sorted by the information in that column. An arrow on the header tells you whether the sort is in ascending or descending order, and clicking on the header again reverses this direction.

More complex, table-based applications have a Sort option in their menu system. You can choose columns to sort, along with the direction (ascending or descending). In Excel you'll find this option on the Data menu. If you want to sort a particular column, click on its header to highlight it and select Sort ascending or Sort descending from the menu bar.

Put the items you use most often first. If you keep accessing the same Favorites in your Web browser, or sending e-mails to the same few people, it makes sense to put the most commonly used items or contacts at the top of your list for quick access. Add a space in front of the name of each item, and they will "float" to the top. All the items with spaces will be sorted alphabetically among themselves.

⇨ See also **Software: Sort.**

HOW TO: ALPHABETIZE A LIST IN MICROSOFT WORD

① Begin by using the mouse to select the text you want to sort. Go to the Table menu and choose Sort. Word will display the Sort dialog box. If your text is formatted in columns, you can choose the sort field here, but for our list the default, Paragraphs, will do.

② Click OK and the list is immediately alphabetized. If the results are not to your liking (sorting free-form text is tricky, and Word sometimes gets it wrong), click on the Edit menu and select Undo to restore your document to how it was before.

ACCESSORIES

Windows is normally installed with a variety of programs in the Accessories menu. They cover everything from scanning your disk for errors to enabling you to create simple graphics. It's worth getting to know all their functions because these programs can save you time and help you optimize your system.

TAKE A CLOSER LOOK

Meet your Accessories.
Go to Start → Programs → Accessories and scroll through all of the items to get an idea of what's available. Most of the program names are fairly obvious. If you want to know more about something, launch it and click Help.

| Accessibility |
| Communications |
| Entertainment |
| Interactive Training |
| Internet Tools |
| System Tools |
| Address Book |
| Calculator |
| Imaging |
| MS-DOS Prompt |
| Notepad |
| Paint |

Need to zoom in on a small area of graphics or tiny fonts on a web page? Select Programs → Accessories → Accessibility and click Magnifier. You'll find the top eighth of your screen now displays a magnified view of the area around your cursor, making it easier to see fine detail. The Windows Accessibility tools are invaluable for visually impaired PC users and those who have problems using a keyboard or mouse.

You've probably taken a cursory glance at your Windows Calculator. The standard view offers basic functions—the most advanced being square-root. If you require a greater choice of functions, look again. Select View → Scientific and suddenly a much more capable utility is presented, including statistical and trigonometric functions and computer-related hexadecimal, octal, and binary figures. This makes it ideal for both advanced math and business applications.

EXPLORE YOUR ARTISTIC SIDE

Make your own images. Paint is a basic program for creating graphics. You can draw and color your own images, but if you only have a mouse to draw with, you may find your images look like the work of a three-year-old! To convert one of your creations into Desktop Wallpaper, select File → Set As Wallpaper.

Recently cut or copied graphics are held in an uncompressed form on the Clipboard. To know what's on the Clipboard at any given time, use the Clipboard Viewer. Go to Start → Programs → Accessories → System Tools → Clipboard. Or select Edit → Delete to clear the Clipboard completely. If it's holding a large picture file, this can free up a lot of memory.

Transfer images from your digital camera. Imaging for Windows is a powerful program that you can use to import your digital images from

---

HOW TO: USE THE CHARACTER MAP

① The Character Map shows all variations of the Western alphabet, such as é or ß. Go to Start → Programs → Accessories → System Tools → Character Map. Choose your font from the Font drop-down menu.

② The Character Map uses such a small font that it can be difficult to distinguish between different symbols such as the Copyright sign or the various mathematical symbols. To view a magnified version, click and hold down the mouse over any one symbol.

③ Double-click on each character to be copied and they will appear in the Characters to copy box. Click on the Copy button to transfer them to the Clipboard. To paste your symbols into a document, open the relevant file and select Edit → Paste.

other hardware such as scanners and digital cameras. You can also use it to view any picture files you might have downloaded from the Internet. It supports a variety of graphics file formats, such as JPEG, GIF, and TIFF.

The Entertainment category of your Accessories is where the multimedia kicks in. In addition to Windows Me's all-singing, all-dancing Media Player—which plays movies and audio CDs, and records tracks to your hard disk—it

features a Sound Recorder. Providing you have a sound card, speakers, and a microphone, you can use it to easily create and edit sound files.

A WAY WITH WORDS
Don't underestimate it—one of the most limited text editors in existence is Notepad, but its sheer simplicity is exactly why it's so useful. Notepad only works with plain text, it doesn't support any text formatting beyond the Tab key, and can't handle files larger than 64Kb. But it's fast to load and, if you

want to view small plain text files or jot down and print out a note or reminder, there's no quicker program to do it.

Try a Notepad trick to create a daily log. Make a text file and type .LOG in the very first line—note it must be in uppercase. Whenever you open this file, Notepad will add the date and time to the end. This is a simple way to keep a set of date-stamped notes, such as a diary.

Wordpad is Notepad's more sophisticated big brother. Although still quite limited in its features, you can style and format text, so it's good for writing straightforward letters. It can also read Rich Text files (*.rtf) and documents in Word 6 format. If your word processor won't read a particular file, try Wordpad. The formatting will probably be lost, but you may well be able to recover the text.

TROUBLESHOOTING
Who's connected to your networked PC right now? Normally, it's surprisingly difficult to tell, but you can run the Net Watcher utility in your System Tools menu to find out.

To study your PC setup, look no further than the System Information program in System Tools. It covers just about all of your hardware and software, including some you probably didn't even know existed. Choose the History option and you'll discover the details of every driver change you've ever made—invaluable if you're trying to restore a device to working order.

Missing an Accessory? Go to Settings → Control Panel. Double-click the Add/Remove Programs icon and select Windows Setup. Select a category in the Components list and then click on Details to see a list of individual programs within that category. Check the box next to the accessory you want to install if it isn't already. You may need your

Windows installation CD-ROM to complete the installation procedure.

▷ See also **Software: Calculators, Clip Art,** and **Dates; Windows: Accessibility, Backing Up, Networks, Optimize Your PC,** and **Windows 95 to Me.**

ACCESSORY SECRETS
Discover some handy little functions tucked away in Windows Me.

- Microsoft Backup is no longer installed with Windows Me, but it's still available on the CD—run \Addons\MSBackup\msbexp .exe to install it.

- For a report on your Internet settings, including your unique IP address, first connect to the Internet and then select Start → Run, and enter WinIPCFG.EXE.

- Computer problems? Dr. Watson (drwatson.exe) in the Windows folder can help you to diagnose them. Select View → Advanced for lots of system information.

- Windows Me comes with a software DVD player. It's called DVDPLAY.EXE, and you'll find it in your Windows folder. Place a disk in your DVD drive, and run the viewer to play your movie.

- If your system takes ages to start up, you can find the culprit by running the System Configuration tool (msconfig.exe) in the Windows System folder. It will tell you which programs are loading.

ARROW KEYS

These keys can help you to navigate a text file, the cells of a spreadsheet, or any other document.

Scroll through a document smoothly, paragraph by paragraph. Hold down the Ctrl key while pressing the up or down arrow for the direction in which you want to scroll.

Highlight text easily by holding down the Shift key while navigating around the document with the arrow keys. If you hold down the Ctrl key too, you can then jump from word to word, or paragraph to paragraph, selecting text even more quickly.

ARROW KEY COMBINATIONS

Navigate windows and documents using Shift and Ctrl with your arrow keys.

TO MOVE CURSOR	PRESS
One character left	Left Arrow
One character right	Right Arrow
One word left	Ctrl+Left Arrow
One word right	Ctrl+Right Arrow
One line up	Up Arrow
One line down	Down Arrow
One paragraph up	Ctrl+Up Arrow
One paragraph down	Ctrl+Down Arrow

TO SELECT TEXT	PRESS
One character left	Shift+Left Arrow
One character right	Shift+Right Arrow
To end of a word	Ctrl+Shift+ Right Arrow
To beginning of a word	Ctrl+Shift+ Left Arrow
One line up	Shift+Up Arrow
One line down	Shift+Down Arrow
To end of a paragraph	Ctrl+Shift+ Down Arrow
To beginning of a paragraph	Ctrl+Shift+ Up Arrow

Mouseless movement between menus! Press the Alt key to take you to the first pull-down menu of an application, for example, the File menu in Word. Then use the left and right arrow keys to move back and forth between the other pull-down menus. For instance, press the right arrow key to move from File to Edit in Word. You can open the desired menu by pressing the down arrow key. Move through the opened menu using the arrow keys again.

Select multiple files, in any window whether in Explorer or on Windows Desktop. First, click on the file icon of your choice to highlight it. Now hold down the Shift key. Keeping it held down, use the arrow keys to move around the window until you've selected all the files you want.

➡ See also **Software: Keyboard Shortcuts.**

ARTISTIC EFFECTS

There's no need to settle for the ordinary with your photographs.

Photo-editing programs provide a variety of effects, allowing you to give your photo the look of an oil painting, a pencil sketch, or even abstract art. Scanners usually come with their own, basic, photo-editing programs. Top-quality software packages, such as Corel Photo-Paint (www.corel.com), can cost hundreds of dollars.

Find your own level. Unless you are a professional who needs the most advanced features, you will probably be perfectly happy with the effects offered by more affordable programs such as MicroGrafx Picture Publisher (www. micrografx.com) or the popular shareware program Paint Shop Pro (www.jasc.com).

Picture Publisher to iGrafx Designer: The Next Step

capabilities of Micrografx Picture Publisher take a leap forward with the advent of iGrafx-packed solution that includes both image editing and high-end vector design and stration. Click below for more information about iGrafx Designer or Micrografx Picture

PicturePublisher iGrafx **DESIGNER**

TURE PUBLISHER SUPPORT
- For Technical Support or Customer Service, click on Support.
- For additional Product Information, view our Online Catalog.
- View our Micrografx Product Evolution Roadmap to help you determine which new iGrafx System Solutions fit your needs.

Problems applying your artistic effects? Check the number of colors used in your image, known as the color depth. Most photo editors will not let you apply effects to 2-, 16-, or 256-

bit color pictures, so you will need to convert the image to 24-bit color. To do this in Paint Shop Pro, select Colors ➔ Increase Color Depth and change the color accordingly.

Less is more. Many bright and gaudy effects are overpowering when applied to an entire image. Instead, use the effect on a selected area of the picture. For example, a "hot neon" effect, looks odd when applied to a whole face, but is more interesting when it's used only on the eyes.

You can add new editing features indefinitely, as long as the photo editor supports plug-ins. A plug-in is a program you can add to the editor, which offers new capabilities and effects to try out. Consult your program manual or go to Graphics UnLeashed (www.unleash.com), the Plugin Site (www.thepluginsite.com), or Planet Photoshop (www.planet photoshop.com/ plugins.html), where you can download lots of free photo-editing plug-ins.

Create your own effects. Some software enables you to make your own effects. In Photoshop, for example, select Filter ➔ Other ➔ Custom, or in Paint Shop Pro select Effects ➔

User → Defined. Just edit a number in a table and see what happens. Bear in mind that you will probably need to experiment a little to achieve results you are satisfied with.

For further advice on applying effects, check the website of your photo editor's maker. Jasc (www.jasc.com/tutorials.asp) provides helpful Paint Shop Pro tutorials, while MicroGrafx

(www.micrografx. com/SUPPORT/ forum.asp) offers forums where you can discuss Picture Publisher issues with other users.

⇨ See also **Software: Color, Photo Editing; Hardware: Digital Cameras, Scanners.**

AUTOCORRECT

Correct basic errors automatically in any of your Office programs.

Correct basic typing errors automatically. If you type "teh" instead of "the," the AutoCorrect feature will automatically spot the problem

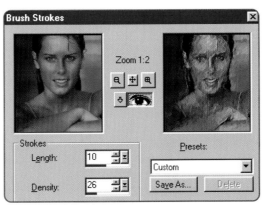

and fix it for you. AutoCorrect has several settings like this one. If one of its rules, such as capitalizing all the days of the week, does not fit in with how you want to work, just turn it off in Tools → AutoCorrect.

If turning off a particular rule seems too drastic, try customizing the AutoCorrect feature instead. For example, two capital letters at the beginning of a word is normally a mistake, but it's not always the case—such as in "PCs." AutoCorrect comes with some built-in exceptions to every rule, but you can always add more to the list by clicking on the Tools menu → AutoCorrect → Exceptions.

Innovation with abbreviation. With a little thought, AutoCorrect can do much more than just fixing mistakes. For instance, you can use it as a time-saving device by inputting an abbreviation for a commonly used phrase, such as "yosi" for "yours sincerely." Go to Tools →

AutoCorrect and enter your chosen abbreviation and phrase. Whenever you type it in, it will be immediately expanded to the full version of the phrase, saving you time and typing. Just make sure you choose an abbreviation that is not an actual word or a commonly used abbreviation, like "etc."

Not just for the Office. AutoCorrect's functionality was originally restricted to the Microsoft Office suite of programs, but Fanix Software has now developed the AutoCorrect Plus program. This tiny utility enables you to use virtually the same automatic error correcting and handy shortcut features for nearly every Windows application on the market. To get this program, download it from the Fanix website (www.fanix.com/ acplus). While you do have to pay for this software, it certainly won't break the bank!

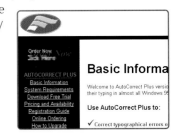

⇨ See also **Software: Access, Autofill, AutoFormat, AutoSum, Excel,** and **Word.**

HOW TO: USE ARTISTIC EFFECTS IN PAINT SHOP PRO

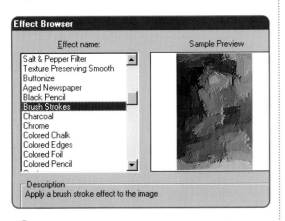

① Select Effects → Effect Browser in Paint Shop Pro to display the list of possible effects. A preview window illustrates how that effect will alter the image.

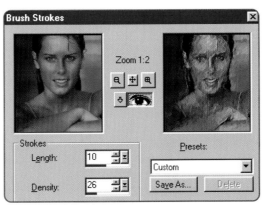

② Here Brush Strokes has been selected. To customize the effect, making it less extreme than it appears in the preview, for example, adjust the settings.

③ Whenever an Effects setting is adjusted, the results are immediately previewed. This makes it easy to tone down the normal Brush Strokes effect and produce the oil painting look that is shown here.

AUTOFILL

Say goodbye to dull, repetitive tasks. Use AutoFill to save time on your Excel spreadsheets.

Fill a range of cells with the same value. Select the cell containing the data you want to copy. Click your mouse at the lower right-hand corner of the cell. The cursor will turn into a black crosshair called the fill handle. Drag the

fill handle over the empty cells to be automatically filled and release the mouse button. The original value is copied into all of the selected cells.

Use AutoFill to create a series of numbers. Select the first cell in the range that you want to fill and enter the starting value for the series—for example, 15. To increment the series by a specified amount, such as 10, select the next cell in the range and enter the next item in the series—in this case, 25. Now select both cells and point the cursor at the lower right corner of the second cell. Drag the fill handle over the

range you want to fill. Drag down or to the right to fill in the ascending order (35, 45, 55, and so on), and up or to the left to complete the descending values.

Make a quick list of days or months. Enter the first day or month in your list into a cell, then drag the fill handle.

	A	B
1	January	
2	February	
3	March	
4	April	
5	May	
6	June	
7	July	

AutoFill will automatically add consecutive days or months. It also recognizes three-letter abbreviations for days and months, like Sun, Mon, Tue, and so on.

Save time with keyboard shortcuts. To quickly fill in the active cell with the contents of the cell above it, press Ctrl+D. To fill it in with the contents of the cell to the left, press Ctrl+R.

Right-click to choose your Autofill. To specify the type of fill series, use the right mouse button to drag the fill handle over the range, then click the appropriate command on the

shortcut menu. For example, if the starting value is the date Jan-2002, click Fill Months for the series Feb-2002, and so on; or click Fill Years for the series Jan-2003, and so on.

Can't find the AutoFill handle? The AutoFill handle can disappear if you have turned off Excel's drag and drop editing feature. To turn it back on, select Options from the Tools menu.

HOW TO: CREATE A CUSTOM FILL SERIES

① You can create your own AutoFill by entering the list of items you want to use as a series on a worksheet and selecting them.

② In the Tools menu, click Options, and then click the Custom Lists tab. To use the selected list, click Import, then click OK.

③ Now enter any item from your new AutoFill list and, holding the left mouse button down, drag the fill handle to complete the series.

Select the Edit tab and make sure the Settings box is checked for Allow cell drag and drop. Try AutoFill again, and the handle should be visible.

AUTOFORMAT

Tired of seeing everything in black and white? Create great-looking tables and charts instantly in Excel.

Make your Excel tables stand out. Select the table you want to format and click Format ➔ AutoFormat. Choose the style that you prefer from the list that appears—such as Colorful, or 3D Effects—and click OK. Excel will now format the selected table in your chosen style.

Pick and choose. You can customize the AutoFormat features to suit you. As before, go to Format ➔ AutoFormat and select your style, but then click Options. Clear the check boxes to remove any of the AutoFormat elements you don't want—such as Font or Patterns or Border. When you're satisfied with your choices, click OK to format the table.

Quickly remove all formatting from a table. You can use AutoFormat to remove borders, colors, and other styles you have applied to a table, even if you didn't use AutoFormat in the first place. Select the range of cells you want to remove all the formatting from, and go to Format ➔ AutoFormat. Select None from the bottom of the list and click OK. The selected cells will now be stripped of all formatting to leave a basic table.

To quickly format charts with Excel 95 and earlier versions, store your favorite chart styles as user-defined AutoFormats. First, open or create a chart with the desired formatting options. Next, choose AutoFormat from the Format menu and click the User-Defined option. Click Customize to activate the User-Defined AutoFormat dialog and click Add. Name and describe your format, and click OK to save it for later use. To apply the AutoFormat to a chart you've just created, go to Format ➔ AutoFormat. In the dialog box that appears, click User-Defined in Formats Used. In the

Formats box choose the style you require and click OK to confirm.

Store your favorite chart styles in Excel 2000 and 97 by creating your own AutoFormats. First, open or create a chart and add any formatting options you wish to include. Click the Chart Type command in the Chart menu. On the Custom Types tab, click User-defined, then Add. Next, in the Add Custom Chart Types dialog box, name and describe your new chart style, and click OK. To apply the AutoFormat to a chart you've just created, go to the Chart Wizard again. Under the Custom Types tab, select User-Defined. Choose your AutoFormat chart style from the list and click OK to confirm.

AUTOSUM

This handy button makes tricky home finance arithmetic easy.

Quickly sum a row or column of figures. Select the cell you want to insert the sum into. Try to

AUTO-ADVICE
Confused by the different Auto functions in Excel? Here's a summary.

● **AutoFill** Creates or completes a series of values in an Excel spreadsheet.

● **AutoFormat** Adds chosen attributes to your spreadsheet, such as Fonts, Borders, and a range of numerical styles.

● **AutoSum** Adds up a column or several columns of figures in a spreadsheet.

choose a cell at the end of a row or column of data, because this will help AutoSum guess which cells you want added together. Click the AutoSum button on the toolbar, marked "Σ," and AutoSum inserts = SUM, and the range address of the cells to the left or above the selected cell. To change this selection, drag over the range you want to use, or click in the Formula bar and type in the cell range formula yourself. Press Enter and Excel will then calculate the total for the selected range.

Make sure AutoSum totals the correct cells. Select the entire range you wish to sum plus the blank cell you want the total to be inserted into. Make sure the blank cell is at the bottom of the column or the end of the row. Click on the AutoSum button and the total will be automatically inserted.

Use AutoSum to calculate grand totals. If your worksheet contains several lists of figures, all in the same row or column, and you have calculated the subtotals using AutoSum or your own formulas, you can create a grand total for the values. Select all the lists together, along with a blank cell to insert the grand total into. Click on the AutoSum button and, instead of totalling the whole list, Excel will add up just the subtotals.

D	E	F
	10	
	15	
	78	
	10	
	50	
	41	
	12	
	=SUM(E1:E7)	

Take a keyboard shortcut. Pressing Alt+= will perform exactly the same function as clicking on the AutoSum button on your toolbar.

Save time creating daily or weekly totals. Use AutoSum to add up several lists of figures simultaneously. For example, if you have a column for each day's expenditure, there's no need to sum each column individually by copying and pasting the formula. Instead, you can select the row of blank cells that the totals are to be inserted into and click on AutoSum. Excel will sum the columns automatically and insert each total in the row you've selected, so you don't have to press Enter each time.

Can't find the AutoSum button? It is normally located on the standard Excel toolbar. However, if you can't see it, click on View ➜ Toolbars and make sure there is a check next to Standard to ensure the normal toolbar is visible. Still can't see the AutoSum button? Try clicking on Tools ➜ Customize. Select the Commands tab and click on the Insert category in the left panel. Scroll down the right panel to find the AutoSum button. Now simply click and drag it to wherever you want it on the Excel toolbar at the top of your screen.

⇨ See also **Software: AutoFill, AutoFormat, Cell, Excel,** and **Formulas.**

BORDERS

Use borders in Word documents to emphasize your text or make a page look more organized and attractive.

Make your paragraphs stand out by adding a border around certain parts of your text. To do this in Word, place the cursor anywhere in the paragraph. Select Format ➜ Borders and Shading. Click the Box setting, then choose a border style you like from the Style option and a color, if desired. Make sure the Apply to: box is set to Paragraph. Click OK. The paragraph border will then enclose the whole width of the page.

Create a stylish look with page borders. Go to Format ➜ Borders and Shading ➜ Page Border. Click on the Box setting and choose a Style setting. If your version of Word has an Art setting, you can choose from a variety of border artwork. In Apply, select the page section, or pages you would like the border applied to, and click OK.

Frame a favorite picture. Select the image in your document that you wish to frame, then go to Borders and Shading ➜ Borders. Choose from the style and color options and click OK.

Use the Outside Border button for fast borders. This tool allows you to create borders with just a click of a button. Highlight a block of text, or click in a paragraph or picture, then click on the Outside Border button. Word automatically decides which type of border to add. To remove, select the text, or picture, and then simply click on the button once more.

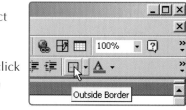

⇨ See also **Software: Word.**

BUDGET PLANNING

Keep your family finances in order with Excel spreadsheets.

Create a budget template. In column A, make two lists: one showing all the different parts of your monthly income and one for your monthly expenditures. These expenses could range from mortgage payments to vacations or doctor's bills. Write the months of the year as headings in columns B to N. Follow your finances by recording each piece of income or outgoing in the relevant spreadsheet cell.

Summarize data with subtotals and totals using Excel's AutoSum feature, which is denoted by the Σ button on the toolbar. Use it to add up the first monthly total for both your income and expenditure sections. Now, at the bottom of the page, subtract your expenditure total from your income total to show how much you have left. Then copy and paste the formulas across the remaining months.

Track your bank balance with a running total. Create a new row below your monthly total row to keep an eye on your account. Enter your bank balance at the start of the year in column A. Create a formula in the same row in column B to add that monthly total to your initial

HOW TO: TRACK YOUR FINANCES

	A	B	C	D
1		Jan	Feb	Mar
2	INCOME	2060	2060	2060
3	John's take home	1000	1000	1000
4	Jane's take home	1000	1000	1000
5	Other	60	60	60
6	EXPENSES	1500	1500	1500
7	Mortgage	600	600	600
8	Food & Utilities	500	500	500
9	Cars	200	200	200
10	Others			200

B2 = =SUM(B3:B5)

= =SUM(B7:B10)

B	C	D
Jan	Feb	Mar

① Key in income and expenditure figures and enter the following formulas for their totals: Income: =SUM(B3:B5); Expenditure: =SUM(B7:B10).

	A	B	C	D
1		Jan	Feb	Mar
2	INCOME	2060	2060	2060
3	John's take home	1000	1000	1000
4	Jane's take home	1000	1000	1000
5	Other	60	60	60
6	EXPENSES	1500	1500	1500
7	Mortgage	600	600	600
8	Food & Utilities	500	500	500
9	Cars	200	200	200
10	Others	200	200	200
11	Monthly Balance	560	560	560

	Others	200
	Monthly Balance	560

=A12+B11

② Enter the monthly total by subtracting expenditure from income. Type in the following formula: =B2-B6. Now enter your opening bank balance in A12 and add a formula for a running total: =A12+B11.

balance. Now you can copy that formula into the cells for all the months of the year.

Use Excel formatting for easy reading. Select the whole budget table and go to Format →

AutoFormat. Use cell formatting to display the figures as currency and use the bottom negative numbers options to show debts in red.

⇨ See also **Software: Money** and **Spreadsheets.**

BUSINESS CARDS

Creating great-looking business cards is easier than you might think.

Make your own business cards in Word. All you need to do is buy pre-cut business-card stationery and use the Envelopes and Labels command on Word's Tools menu to design them to the appropriate dimensions.

Paper's important—use good-quality card stock to make sure you get the best results. Avery Business Card pages are the industry standard—made from thick perforated card stock. The code number, which you'll find in the top right corner of every box, is 5371 for standard business cards that fit ten to a page.

To give your business cards real impact, it's important to keep the main design elements simple. Do not use fancy fonts with lots of swirling lines; this makes the details more difficult to read. Instead, choose a simple font, such as Arial, AvantGarde, or Times, and experiment with bold facing and with type size and positioning. Keep details to the vital minimum, and don't forget your e-mail address.

Use the manual feed setting on your printer so that you can feed the pages through yourself. The thicker paper will now move more easily through the printer from the tray.

Download ready-made business card templates from the Microsoft Office Template Gallery (http://officeupdate.microsoft.com/Template Gallery). In the Stationery, Labels, and Cards section, click on the Business Cards link. Choose a template and click Edit in Microsoft Word.

Spice up your cards with clip art. To make your business cards stand out, you can insert clip art,

---

 HOW TO: CREATE A BUSINESS CARD IN WORD

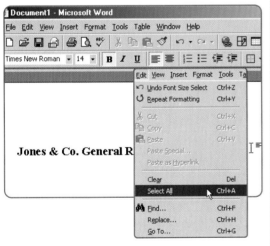

① Enter text in a blank Word document exactly as you would like it to appear on the business card. To highlight it, go to Edit → Select All, or use the keyboard shortcut Ctrl + A.

② Go to Tools → Envelopes and Labels, and click the Labels tab. Your text will now be displayed in the Address box.

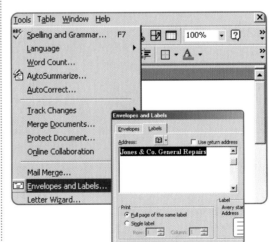

③ Click Options. In the Label Products list, select the type of label you want to use. Choose the same label from the Product Number list and click OK. Insert a sheet of card stock into the printer and click Print to produce a sheet of business cards.

word art, or images into your business card design. You may need to resize the art to stay within the standard card size of 2 x 3.5 inches.

⇨ See also **Software: Clip Art.**

CALCULATORS

Quickly work out those tricky sums without resorting to a spreadsheet.

Windows includes two calculators in one found by clicking on Start ➔ Programs ➔ Accessories ➔ Calculator. The basic calculator is the default, with the usual standard functions. Click on the Scientific option in the View menu and the window changes to add many other functions, such as trigonometry, logarithms, and statistics.

Use your memory. The memory function, indicated by the letter M on the calculator's keypad, lets you perform a series of calculations and keep a running total. Use the M+ key to add displayed

numbers to the memory—an "M" on screen indicates the memory is in use. You can press MR to recall the sum of the memory at any time, and MC will clear the contents of the memory when you've finished.

There are a number of on-line calculators that can help you with specific jobs. For example, The Global Gourmet cooking site (www.globalgourmet.com) has a web-based calculator to help you convert international food measurements. The CNET software library

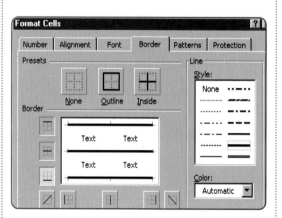

(www.download.com) has a useful collection of calculators for financial matters as well as weights and measures.

Let your PC do most of the work for you. When you've completed your calculations, you don't have to key the sum manually in to your document. Human error can all too easily occur at this stage. It's a much safer bet to use the Copy and Paste function in the Edit menu as an alternative. First, press Ctrl+C to copy the number from your calculator, and then click

where you want the number to go in your document and press Ctrl+V to paste it in.

CELL

The humble cell is the building block of every Excel spreadsheet.

Prepare a rough outline of your spreadsheet using pen and paper before beginning to format your cells. The format options are important for presentation, and organizing them beforehand will help give you a feel for what the completed spreadsheet will look like—particularly if you're trying to fit a large table onto one screen. You can always use the Zoom option on the View menu to adjust the final layout to suit your screen and working preferences.

Make sure you format cells correctly. Any cells intended to hold dates, numbers, or currency must be properly formatted in order to show their values correctly. Highlight all the cells intended for data entry, and then right-click and select the Format Cells option. Under the Number tab, you will be able to identify the type of data that will be entered into the cell and the format in which you want it displayed.

HOW TO: ADD BORDERS TO YOUR CELLS

Direct Savings Account			
Date	Transaction	Amount	Bala
7-Mar-00	Deposit – Joint	$50.00	$
28-Mar-00	Deposit – SD	$1,000.00	$1,0
28-Mar-00	Deposit – Joint	$750.00	$1,8
4-Apr-00	Deposit – Kate	$2,000.00	$3,8
28-Apr-00	Interest	$10.63	$3,8
2-May-00	Deposit – SD	$500.00	$4,3
2-May-00	Deposit – Joint	$700.00	$5,0
15-Jun-00	Kate withdrawal	-$1,000.00	$4,0
15-Jun-00	Deposit – SD	$400.00	$4,4
8-Jul-00	Transfer	$0.00	$4,4
17-Jul-00	Deposit – SD	$200.00	$4,6
24-Jul-00	Kate – Income Tax	-$897.25	$3,7
4-Aug-00	Deposit – SD	$1,000.00	$4,7
22-Aug-00	Deposit – KL	$2,000.00	$6,7
11-Sep-00	Stephen withdrawal	-$1,000.00	$5,7
12-Sep-00	Joint Transfer	-$1,000.00	$4,7

① Highlight the area in your Excel spreadsheet that you want to enhance with a border. Right-click and select Format Cells from the pop-up menu that appears. Click on the Border tab.

② Choose the line style and thickness from the Style window, and then click on the Border preview panel to show where you want your lines to go. In this example, thick horizontal lines separate the entries.

Direct Savings Account			
Date	Transaction	Amount	Balan
7-Mar-00	Deposit – Joint	$50.00	$5
28-Mar-00	Deposit – SD	$1,000.00	$1,05
28-Mar-00	Deposit – Joint	$750.00	$1,80
4-Apr-00	Deposit – Kate	$2,000.00	$3,80
28-Apr-00	Interest	$10.63	$3,81
2-May-00	Deposit – SD	$500.00	$4,31
2-May-00	Deposit – Joint	$700.00	$5,01
15-Jun-00	Kate withdrawal	-$1,000.00	$4,01
15-Jun-00	Deposit – SD	$400.00	$4,41
8-Jul-00	Transfer	$0.00	$4,41
17-Jul-00	Deposit – SD	$200.00	$4,61
24-Jul-00	Kate – Income Tax	-$897.25	$3,71
4-Aug-00	Deposit – SD	$1,000.00	$4,71
22-Aug-00	Deposit – KL	$2,000.00	$6,71
11-Sep-00	Stephen withdrawal	-$1,000.00	$5,71

③ Click on OK to apply the design to your worksheet. If you don't like it, simply press Ctrl+Z to undo the changes and go back and try another combination.

Set Excel 2000 to change the format for a cell for certain values by setting a conditional rule. Go to the Format menu and select Conditional Formatting. In the dialog box that appears, you can define the formula to vary the content of a cell. For instance, if you wanted every value over 2,000 to be displayed in another color, enter the formula "Cell value is" and "Greater than" and "2000" in the dialog boxes. Now you can click the Format button and set your preferred font attributes.

Protect the cells from accidental change. Once you've got your worksheet looking and working the way you want it to, go to Tools → Protection. Before you protect the worksheet, remember to unlock the cells you want to be able to enter data into. To do this, first highlight the cells, right-click, and then select Protection from the Format Cells screen. Uncheck the Locked box to enable data entry.

CELL NAMES

A spreadsheet like Excel 2000 allows you to give proper names to a cell or a range of cells to make navigation and formula calculation easier.

The Name Box is the drop-down box directly under the toolbar that shows the current cell address. On a new worksheet this will always read "A1." If you want to give the cell a label, just click in the Name Box and type the name you want to use. Press Enter and the name will be entered on the drop-down list so you'll be able to jump back to it easily.

A cell name must not include spaces, so if you want to name a cell "Total Cost" you must enter it as "TotalCost." This name will then be used as the reference for the cell on the drop-

down name list. It's worth remembering this process, because it's the standard naming convention for all Microsoft Office products.

Name your ranges. It will greatly simplify the look of your formulas and make the worksheet easier for other people to understand if they have to work on it too. To do this, highlight the cells for your range and type a name into the Name Box. For instance, if you have a column of figures tracking outgoing costs, instead of an unwieldy cell-based formula such as =SUM(B12..B36), you could just name the B12..B36 range

"TotalExpenditure." Your formula would then read: =SUM(TotalExpenditure).

Cell names use absolute cell addresses. This means that if you copy a cell containing a certain name into other cells on your worksheet, the name will always reference the original, named cells. Perhaps most important of all, remember that this will affect the way your formulas work and could completely mess up all your careful calculations!

Avoid confusion—check the exact cells covered by a Cell Name by clicking on the Insert menu → Name → Define. A window will appear on your screen listing all of the named cells in your worksheet. Highlight the name that you want to investigate, then look in the box at the bottom

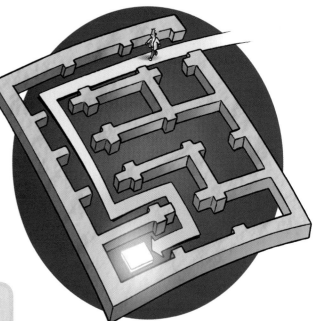

of the window labeled Refers to. The exact cell range covered by the Name will be displayed here. You can now edit or even delete the range, if you want to.

▷ See also **Software: Excel.**

Excel is a very powerful program for analyzing all sorts of data. But when it comes to getting the meaning of the figures across, a spreadsheet full of figures can be hard to comprehend. Fortunately, Excel also has powerful tools that let you turn dull data into colorful and clear charts and graphs.

USING EXCEL'S GRAPH FACILITY

The two types of graphic presentation that most of us are familiar with are charts, where totals are represented as vertical columns or horizontal bars, and pie charts, where they are represented as slices of a pie. You can easily create both of these in Excel, but you can also present your data in a variety of other chart formats. Once you've created your chart or graph you can customize its type, color scheme, and labeling to get precisely the look you want. You can also incorporate it into an Excel spreadsheet or export it to other popular programs like Word and, for presentations, PowerPoint.

CHART YOUR SUCCESS

The Chart toolbar may not be visible on your Excel menu bar. To activate it, go to View → Toolbars and select Chart. The Chart commands will now appear as a floating toolbar.

The quickest way to create a chart is to select the cells containing the data you want to include and then simply press the F11 key. This instantly creates a chart on a new sheet in the default style of a column chart.

If you typically use only one kind of chart or graph—say, a simple pie chart—you can speed up chart creation by changing Excel's default column chart to the one you prefer. Just right-click a chart to call up the Chart menu, then click Chart Type. Select the Custom Types tab,

choose one of the chart types offered, click Set as default chart, and then Yes, followed by OK.

To get your message across with an Excel chart, you have to choose the right one for the job. To see the full range of charts available, activate the Chart Wizard by going to Insert → Chart. Or click the Chart Wizard button on the toolbar. Many of the types available have options that only a specialist would want, such as scatter charts, radar charts, and stock charts. For most users, the most attractive options are column charts, bar charts, pie charts, and line charts.

Use vertical column and horizontal bar charts to emphasize straightforward comparisons

between items or their growth over time, as in a sales presentation, for example. Pie charts are useful where you want to focus on the relation of parts to a whole, as in how much of a telephone bill each member of a family is responsible for, for example.

If you're unsure which type of chart is going to work best, try experimenting with the previews offered by the Chart Wizard. Simply select a sub-type, then click and hold down the button below the preview area. You'll now see your data in the selected chart format. If it doesn't look good, you can continue to try other formats until you find the one that works best for your particular presentation.

THE MOST USEFUL GRAPH STYLES
Make sure you use the right graph for the job.

 Column Ideal for showing comparative totals over specified periods of time.

 Line Good for showing key moments and fluctuations in figures over a period of time.

 Pie Best for showing the division of elements of a whole—for example, allocation of spending.

 Area Can be used to give an overall impression of the extent of change over time.

 Doughnut Useful for drawing comparisons between two relative pie charts but with different totals.

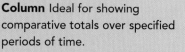

Using copy and paste is an easy way of adding new data to a chart. Select the new cells you want to include and press Ctrl+C to copy them. Click in the chart itself and press Ctrl+V to paste the data. The updated element appears immediately in place in the appropriate style.

You can quickly and easily export charts and graphs created in Excel to other Office applications such as Word and PowerPoint using simple cut-and-paste techniques. Open the Excel document containing the chart and the other Office document that you want to insert it into. Select the chart and copy it using the Ctrl+C. Now select the other Office document, click where you want to place the chart, and use Ctrl+V to paste it.

If an Excel graph pasted into another file is likely to change or be regularly updated, paste the chart in using the Paste Special command in the Edit menu of the other Office program. This will keep the two diagrams constantly linked, so any changes made to the graph in Excel are automatically updated in the graph in the other Office program as well.

The Chart Wizard gives you plenty of options when choosing a chart style. But to get a chart just the way you want, you need to format its various elements, such as type styles and background colors. You can right-click on any element to bring up a format menu. For example, right-click on a column, select Format Data Series, and click on the Patterns tab. Now you can change the colors of the columns by selecting a color in the Area section. You can also alter the color, style, and width of the column borders in the Border section of the window. Click on the graphic background (the "walls") and then right-click to alter its formatting as well.

You can right-click on text elements to format them too, changing fonts and colors from the pop-up menu. In fact, you can do so much in terms of styling your chart that it's easy to do too much, and create something garish and confusing. Remember that the chart should speak for itself; so resist the temptation to add styling just for the sake of it. The simpler the representation of data on your graph or chart, the easier it will be to understand.

See also **Software: Excel, Office, PowerPoint,** and **Spreadsheets.**

HOW TO: CREATE A CHART USING EXCEL'S CHART WIZARD

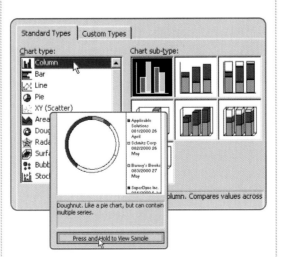

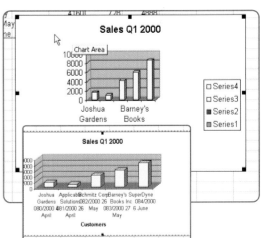

① Open an Excel worksheet and select the cells containing the data to be represented in the chart. Don't forget to include cells containing text if you want the text to appear also. Click the Chart Wizard button. The Chart Wizard appears.

② The default is a column chart. To see others, highlight each name in the list. To preview what your data will look like in a chart, click on a sub-type displayed on the right, then press the Press and Hold to View Sample button to see your data on the graph.

③ Click Next to continue through the Wizard, selecting the data range, title, axes labels, and whether to place the chart in a new sheet or as an object in the existing one. Then click Finish. Alter the size of the graph by dragging the handles at its edges.

CLIP ART

Most clip art is free or very cheap. Use these simple graphics and images to illustrate your documents.

Build up your collection. It's easy to find clip art. There are millions of images waiting to be downloaded from websites (see box, right), or you can buy CD-ROMs of clip art images. Most collections are organized into groups. So, if you're searching the Web for clip art, decide what subjects you want to search for. Set up folders on your hard disk to download the images into, and title them according to topic, such as "people," "technology," or "animals."

Planning to collect a lot of files? Use a clip art manager program, such as Arts & Letters Express (www.arts-letters.com). This will sort your collection into easily navigable groups. It will also provide thumbnail previews of each group to help you track down a particular image and quickly copy it into your document.

Don't collect images you don't need. It's all too easy to clutter up your hard drive with excess clip art. Instead, why not bookmark a few good clip art websites and download images as and when you need them?

Animated clip art only works in web browsers or special animation viewers. If you place a

piece of animated clip art in a Word, Works, or Excel document, only a static image of the animation will be displayed.

Free clip art is meant for noncommercial use in most cases. Make sure you check your rights carefully when you acquire new images. A payment may be required if you intend to use images as part of your business, even if you are not directly reselling the image itself. Even a clip art border added to your business letterhead, for example, technically may be breaching the copyright of the creator.

You can make your own clip art. Clip art dates back to the time when designers and desktop publishers "clipped" and collected small images that might be useful in the future. You can do the same—if you spot an interesting border or illustration, why not scan it into your PC, and add it to your collection. But remember that the copyright issue also applies to images acquired from magazines and other media.

Clip art comes free with Microsoft Word! To see what kind of images you can use, open a Word document and go to Insert → Picture → Clip Art. The Clip Gallery will appear on your screen. To insert clip art into your document, click on the image you want to use. A pop-up bar will appear. Click on the Insert clip icon, and the image will be pulled straight into your document.

Add more images to the Clip Gallery. Open the Clip Gallery as above, and click on the Import Clips button. The Add clip to Clip Gallery dialog box now appears. From the Look in: box, you need to locate the image or "clip" you want to add to your gallery. Click the option labeled Copy into Clip Gallery. You can also download clip art from the Web straight into your Clip Gallery. To do this, just click the Clips Online button on the right of the Import Clips button.

CLIP ART SITES
Grab all sorts of great clip art from these image websites.

All Free Art (www.allfreeart.com)
Visit this site for a feast of free clip art images for your PC.

Clipart Guide (www.clipartguide.com)
A great range, including cartoon characters.

123 Free ClipArt (www.123-free-clipart.com)
Take your pick of the free clip art.

Art Today (http://arttoday.com)
One of the Web's largest graphics resources.

Corel City Clipart Center (www.creativeanywhere.com/clipart)
Ten thousand of the images are free. But if you want to get your hands on the other million, you'll have to pay up!

National Clip Art Gallery of Canada (http://cdnclipart.iwarp.com/)
A useful source of Canadian images.

Clip Art Connection (www.clipartconnection.com)
An award-winning website containing one of the largest collections of free clip art anywhere on the Internet.

COLOR

Try spicing up boring black-and-white documents with colored backgrounds or panels.

The Highlight pen button on the Word toolbar is the quickest way to add a splash of color to text. You can use the tool in the same way as you would a real highlighter pen to draw attention to key parts of a document. In Excel, the Fill Color button performs a similar function.

It's best to use lighter colors, such as yellow or sky blue, to ensure that they don't obscure the accompanying text.

When you want to have a bit more control over the positioning and size of a colored background in Microsoft Word, use the text box feature (see How To below). This powerful tool will make all of your documents really stand out from the crowd.

Use the WordArt feature to add special effects to words or short sentences in Word and Excel documents. Go to Insert ➜ Picture and select WordArt. You can use the tool to color, bend, stretch, and distort your text, to produce all kinds of eye-catching images. The result is treated as a graphic object—not text—so you won't be able to check spelling or include the text in a word count.

Colored paper can enhance your document, with or without additional color effects from the application. Good-quality colored paper can be expensive, but it might add a unique touch or highlight an important page. To see what your document might look like on colored paper, first go to Format ➜ Background and choose a color, and then go to View ➜ Web Layout to view the document. A background color won't print, but it can give you a good idea of the overall effect.

Remember to use color sparingly; otherwise, it will detract from the message contained in your words. Use no more than two or three different colors, and avoid clashing combinations, unless you want to give your readers a headache!

Spruce up your spreadsheets. Highlight column headers or blocks of cells in Excel and color them using the Fill Color button on the toolbar. Color text by using the Font Color button, just to the right of the Fill Color button.

COLUMNS IN SPREADSHEETS

An appreciation of columns is important if your spreadsheet design is going to be effective.

Select a column by clicking its letter heading. For example, click on "A" to select column A, or "C" to select Column C, and so on.

Beware of the AutoSum feature in the toolbar. Clicking the AutoSum button will add up all the numbers in a highlighted column, including any subtotals. This means, for example, that a sum of 2 + 2 = 4 in the column will give an AutoSum of 8 for the whole column. If you don't want subtotals included in your sums, put them into an adjacent column so they're not included in the Autosum.

HOW TO: CREATE A COLOR HEADING IN MICROSOFT WORD

① Go to Insert ➜ Text Box. Position the cursor where you want to create the heading. Click and drag to size the text box. Type in your message, and select it. Click the Center text button on the toolbar to center the text in the box.

② Right-click the highlighted area, and select Font from the pop-up menu.Choose the font style, size, and color. The changes you make will be shown in the Preview window. When you're happy with the results, click OK.

③ Click the border of the Text Box to select it, then right-click it and choose Format Text Box. You can alter the background or border colors, and other features. To create the desired shade, go to the Colors and Lines tab, select Line Color, and click More Colors.

Change the width of a column quickly and easily: just click and drag the borders of the column header. You can also set the width of a column or columns to a specific measurement. Go to Format → Column → Width and type in the figure you require.

If you see a row of "#######" after entering data into a cell, your column setting is not wide enough to display the entry. The quickest way to accommodate wide or narrow data cells is to double-click on the right boundary of that column heading. This process will expand or shrink the column so that it is just wide enough to hold the required information.

Select several columns at once. Click on one column, then hold down the Shift key and click on another column. The new column and any columns in between are highlighted. Or click on one column, then hold down the Ctrl key and click another column anywhere to add just that one to your selection.

You can hide a column by dragging the right border over the left border, effectively reducing the column width to zero. Or you can hide one or more columns by going to Format → Column and selecting the Hide option. Note that hiding a column does not protect it from being viewed in any way. To show the hidden column, simply drag it out again or use the Unhide option.

When sorting columns, always make a copy of the worksheet or save first so you can revert to the previous version if you make a mistake. Highlight all the rows and columns you want to sort, excluding any header titles at the top. Accidentally omitting or including columns and rows can ruin hours of data entry work! Go to Data → Sort. If your table has a headings row, select the Header row option. You can now sort the columns by name rather than letter.

If you make a mistake, press Ctrl+Z to undo it. It's also a good idea to save your new spreadsheet by a different file name.

⇨ See also **Software: Excel, Sort, Spreadsheets.**

Make your Word documents easier to read by formatting your text into columns, newspaper style.

Columns of text work really well on a publication such as a club newsletter or magazine, giving it a professional look. To enter text in columns, click on the Columns button on Word's toolbar, and scroll across to select the number of columns you need. If you can't see the Columns button, click the double arrows on your toolbar to call up more options.

Make your columns bigger or smaller. Check the horizontal ruler at the top of the page and you'll see a marker for each column—click and drag these to adjust the column widths.

HOW TO: ADD COMMENTS IN MICROSOFT WORD

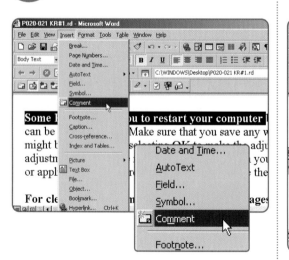

① In your Word document, select the text you would like to comment on, then go to Insert → Comment. You can also click on the Comment icon in the toolbar.

② The Comments window appears at the base of the screen. Type your note into the window, and click in the text area to return to the document. Click Close to hide the Comments.

③ The commented text will remain highlighted in yellow, so you can locate it easily later. Right-click on the highlighted text to edit or delete the comment.

You can reformat an entire text document into columns. Go to Edit → Select All before clicking on the Columns button. To reformat only a part of a document, click and drag to highlight the text you wish to change before clicking on the Columns button.

For the maximum degree of control, select Format → Columns, and enter all the formatting information you require. The dialog box also offers a handy option you won't get elsewhere: you can draw a line between each column.

To remove columns, select the text, click the Columns button, and choose just one column. The text you have selected will now run on across the full page width.

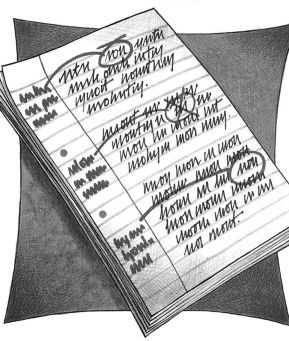

COMMENTS

Use the Comments feature in a Word document to remind you of "things to do".

You're checking a document, or perhaps reviewing one for someone else, when you spot a possible problem. So what do you do? Embedding a note in the document text isn't a good idea, because someone has to take it out later on, and creating a new document for your notes will take more time. The Comments feature, however, enables you to make detailed comments on any word or series of words in a document without changing the text in the original document (See How To opposite).

To make sure you know the comment is there, Word adds a reference mark and shades the commented text in yellow. Leave the mouse cursor hovering over the mark for a few seconds, and the comment will be displayed.

As the document is reviewed and revised, you may probably want to edit comments, or perhaps even delete them. To do this, right-click

on the shaded text and choose either the Edit or Delete options from the drop-down menu.

Word displays the initials of the person who's made the comment next to each note. To change the initials, go to Tools → Options and select the User Information tab. Enter the new details in the Name and Initials boxes.

If you can't see the reference mark when you add a comment, or view the yellow highlighting where the comment has been added, go to Tools → Options, and select the View tab. Make sure you have the ScreenTips and Hidden text options selected.

If your PC has a microphone, you can embed spoken comments rather than just text by clicking on the cassette icon in the Comments window. Keep in mind that recorded speech can take up a lot of disk space. It's probably not a good idea to use this feature on documents you intend to e-mail.

The Comments feature is not restricted to Word. You can use it in Excel, for example, where it works in much the same way. Click on

the cell that you want to remark on, then select Insert → Comment. Just as in Word, once you've entered your notes, the cell is highlighted—this time with a small red triangle. To edit or delete your comments, right-click on the relevant cell.

Don't lose your comments! There's nothing more irritating than accidentally closing a Word document without saving your work. To avoid this happening to you, go to File → Versions, and select the check box next to Automatically save a version on close. After doing this, whenever you close a Word document, with or without comments added in, the latest version will be saved for you!

⇨ See also **Software: Word**.

CONTACT MANAGERS

Keeping track of contact details using a diary can quickly become unworkable as people change address and phone numbers. And, how do you separate your friends, relatives, and business contacts? A contact manager program can do all this, and it has many other features to keep your life more organized.

FIELDS KEEP YOU ORGANIZED

Contact managers store their information in fields like a database record—which gives you an extremely flexible system. A contact record typically consists of a field for your contacts' first names, another for their last names, fields for separate lines of their address, different phone numbers, and so on. If you need to include more information, however, you can easily add your own fields to suit your needs. And, best of all, you can sort and organize your database by fields—such as last name, street name, zip code, or in any order that suits you.

Categorize your contacts. Most popular contact manager programs let you assign categories to contacts, which can be very useful. For example, you could assign a Christmas category to every contact you want to send a Christmas card to, then get the software to automatically print address labels. Or you could categorize every member of your soccer team into one group, so that looking up their details is easy.

Most contact management tools can easily import data from other programs. If you want to upgrade, check the new software's help files for instructions. Importing data is a lot faster than retyping by hand—and more accurate too.

Create a card! Both Organizer and Outlook support vCards—virtual business cards. vCards put contact information into a special format that can be shared between different applications easily. The most common use for vCards is to send them along with an e-mail so that the recipient has all your details. vCards received with an e-mail can be saved in either Outlook or Organizer with all the details entered automatically into your contacts database for you. You can create your own vCard and attach it to e-mails you send.

NOT JUST A CONTACT MANAGER

Lotus Organizer and Microsoft Outlook have many other features related to personal information management.

Outlook components include:
- calendar
- to-do list manager
- phone call log
- email tools
- today view for organizing important tasks for the day
- note pad

Organizer components include:
- calendar
- to-do list manager
- phone call log
- management of information for web pages you frequently visit
- year planner
- note pad
- anniversary viewer

USING OUTLOOK

Add a contact. Switch to Contacts view, then go to the toolbar and click on the New button. A window appears in which you can enter information for a new contact. Use the tabs to organize all the different kinds of information. Click on the Full Name button to enter a complete name and use the address button to enter all the address details correctly. Click Save and Close when you're done.

Lost your way? Outlook has an area on the left of the screen called the Outlook Bar that contains shortcut icons to all its important elements. Single-click the one you want to move directly to.

Manage your Outlook Shortcuts or groups on the Outlook Bar by right-clicking anywhere on the Bar and choosing from the context menu that pops up. If you want to remove an icon that you don't use, right-click on the icon and choose Remove from Outlook Bar.

Save typing time. If you have entered an e-mail address for a contact in Outlook, creating an e-mail to send to the person is easy. Just go to the e-mail view and click New. Then click on the To button, double-click the contact or contacts that you want to send an e-mail to and click OK. Or type the name as displayed in the File as box and press Tab. Outlook will enter the address in the To field for you. This is a lot easier than having to remember and type an e-mail address.

Take a different view. You can view contacts in several different ways in Outlook. Go to View ➔ Current View, then select the view you want from the drop-down menu. If you use lots of different ways to group your contacts, the By Category view may be useful. If you often need phone contacts, then it's quite possible that the phone list may be all you need. You can even create personalized views if the ones provided do not suit your needs.

Take a shortcut. Outlook's pop-up context menus allow you to use the Contacts View as a starting point to initiate many different tasks. To do this, simply right-click on any contact, and then choose from a range of different tasks relating to that contact, from printing personal details or sending an e-mail to automatically contacting the person by phone or even arranging a meeting.

MAKE THE MOST OF ORGANIZER
Add a contact. In the Contacts view, choose the Create menu and click Contact. A Window appears ready for you to add data. Use the tabs to see more information that you can enter. Click OK when you're done.

Organizer is easy to navigate. It takes its design from paper organizers like Filofax and Day Runner, with a column of tabs down the right- and left-hand sides of the main window for moving around. Just click the one you want to open a new view. As with a normal book, the tab moves to the left once opened.

Never forget an important date again. Organizer has a clever built-in feature for reminding you of birthdays and anniversaries. To use it, make sure you enter birthday or anniversary details under the General tab of a new contact. Then you can click the Anniversary tab to see what is upcoming this month. You can also view anniversaries for the whole year or even by Zodiac sign.

To see different views of your contacts in Organizer, first make sure you are in the Contacts area, then click the View menu and choose an option, such as By First Name. You can also change the view simply by clicking on the small icons at the bottom left of the screen. There are lots of views available, and you may find different ones useful at different times.

You can edit your contacts labels by simply clicking on View ➔ Contacts Preferences in Contacts view and then clicking on the Edit Label button.

HOW TO: MAKE A PHONE CALL DIRECTLY FROM OUTLOOK

① First switch to Contacts view using the Outlook Bar on the left. Locate the contact you want to call. Right-click on the name to bring up the pop-up context menu and click on Call Contact.

② A new box appears. If you want to keep notes abouts the call, put a tick next to Create new journal entry when starting new call before you start. You will be able to make notes while the call is in progress. If you don't need a record, just click Start Call.

③ Pick up your handset and, when the call connects, start your conversation as usual. If you have created a journal entry, finish your call by clicking Pause Timer, then Save and Close. If you have not made any notes, just click End Call and hang up the phone.

COPY AND PASTE

Here are some quick ways to copy and move text, graphics, figures, and other items.

To copy and paste between files and programs, click on the item or material that you want to transfer—a graphic, some text, a column of figures—to select it. Then go to Edit → Copy to copy it to a shared area of memory called the Windows Clipboard. Switch to the target file, move the pointer to where you want the data to appear, then select Edit → Paste to complete the transfer.

Sometimes you might want to perform a copy and paste operation in a dialog box, perhaps like the one shown when you select File → Open. Although there is no Edit menu here, you can use the standard keyboard shortcuts instead. To copy an item press Ctrl+C. Go to the destination, place the cursor where you want to transfer the item, and press Ctrl+V to paste.

Keyboard shortcuts can be useful when deciding what to copy, too. The quickest way to copy an entire web page, for example, is to press Ctrl+A (Select All), and then Ctrl+C. Once the whole page is copied, you can then paste it into another file using Ctrl+V and decide what information you want to keep or delete.

Copy and paste keyboard shortcuts haven't always been as now. If you're using an old Windows application and find Ctrl+C and Ctrl+V don't work, try Ctrl+Ins (Copy) and Shift+Ins (Paste) instead.

If a paste option doesn't work, make sure the destination program can accept the type of data you're trying to transfer. For example, only text can be pasted into Notepad. If in doubt, go to Start → Programs → Accessories → System Tools, and select Clipboard Viewer, which will show you what Windows is trying to transfer.

Usually the Windows Clipboard can hold only one object of a particular type. You can copy a picture to the Clipboard, for example, but if you then copy another picture, the first one is lost. If you need to copy several pictures from one

---

HOW TO: DRAW A BEZIER CURVE IN PAINT SHOP PRO

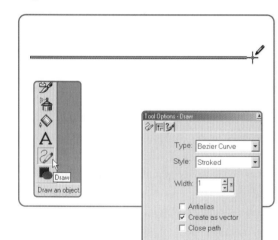

1 Select the Draw tool and then choose Bezier Curve from the Tool Options palette. Click your mouse where you want the curve to begin. Drag the cursor, which has now become a crosshair, to where you want the curve to end, and then release the button.

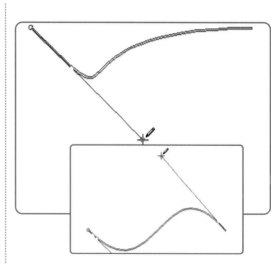

2 The curve appears, but at this stage it is indistinguishable from a straight line. Next, you need to distort the line to produce the curve you need. Click the mouse away from the line, and then drag it to shape the first part of the curve.

3 After you have released the mouse button, repeat the operation to shape the second part of the curve. When you release the mouse button, the finished curve appears! If it is not quite right, use the handles to move, stretch, or rotate the curve.

place to another, you must copy the first, paste it to its destination, and then repeat with each subsequent image.

Microsoft Office applications are more sophisticated. You can copy up to 12 separate

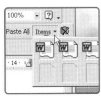

items to the Clipboard. Each item has its own button and can be pasted individually, or you can click on Paste All on the Clipboard toolbar to paste everything.

⇨ See also **Windows: Clipboard.**

Do you have problems using drawing tools on your PC? Try Paint Shop Pro's Bezier curve for perfect semicircles, S-shapes, and more.

Simply knowing that there is a Bezier curve tool won't help you to locate it. Bezier curves are a line type in Paint Shop Pro, but there is no mention of curves in the menus, or on

the toolbar. The secret is to select the Drawing tool. Just select Bezier Curve from the Type drop-down menu in the Tool Options dialog box (if this box is not visible, you can click the Toggle Tool Options Window button).

Bezier curves can seem confusing at first—and even producing a straight line may seem difficult—so start with these simple strategies. To create a symmetrical curve, draw the initial line, then click twice on the same spot. To draw an S-shaped curve, click and drag first on one side of the line, and then the other.

Checking the Create as vector box when you draw a curve is a good idea because you can use the Object Selector tool to select the curve again, and resize, rotate, or distort it as needed.

Do you need more advanced editing options? Click the Vector Object Selection button and then double-click on the curve. In the Vector Properties dialog box can you then change the line width, style, texture, and other parameters.

⇨ See also **Software: Drawing Programs.**

Use this helpful feature to move elements into another file or program.

The copy and paste function is also useful if you want to move text or graphics. To do this, just click on the item to select it, and then go to Edit → Cut; this removes the selected data, and stores it in the Clipboard. Switch to the file where you want to place the data, move the cursor to the required point, and then select Edit → Paste.

You can move files or folders around with ease in the Windows Explorer program. The Cut and Paste options are located in the context menu that appears when you right-click on the item. To use them, right-click on the file or folder to be moved and then select Cut from the pop-up menu. Now right-click on the destination folder, and select Paste.

PAINTSHOP PRO'S LINE DRAWING OPTIONS

There are four basic line drawing tools to choose from.

Single Line
Lets you draw a straight line by dragging from point A to point B and releasing the mouse button.

Bezier Curve
Lets you apply a maximum of two curves to a line and adjust them using movable handles.

Freehand Line
Allows you to draw a line that follows exactly the path of the cursor.

Point to Point Line
Is for drawing a line with multiple smooth curves that can be adjusted seperately using movable handles.

 HOW TO: USE CUT AND PASTE TO MOVE FILES

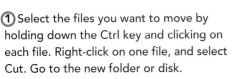

① Select the files you want to move by holding down the Ctrl key and clicking on each file. Right-click on one file, and select Cut. Go to the new folder or disk.

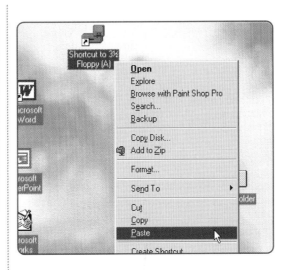

② Right-click on your destination and select Paste. Windows copies the files from the Clipboard to their new home. To undo the change, select Edit → Undo Copy .

DATABASES

Databases are specialized programs that store collections of related information. While you can use a spreadsheet program to create a table—a "flat file" database—dedicated databases such as Microsoft Access are more flexible. You can create multiple tables that let you easily define and extract data.

DESIGNING YOUR DATABASE

So how do you go about creating your own database—for example, if you want to organize an antique auto club? You can use Microsoft Access to store membership details in table form. No matter what information you decide to store later on, details specific to club members will only be held in this table. This way, you'll avoid duplication—and if details change later on, you'll only need to go to one place to modify them.

Create your first table. Start the Access program. Click beside the Blank Access database option and click OK. You'll be asked for a file name—type in "Club," for example, and click on Create. A database window displays all the available options. Double-click on Create table in Design view, and you are ready to get started on your design.

Use the table to store records. You can set up a table with each record giving details of an individual club member. A record is the equivalent of a single card in an index-card box. Each record in the table contains fields used to store facts about each club member. Each field has a data type, too.

Access supports data types such as Text, Number, and Date so that information can be stored efficiently. The data type that you select also affects the kind of operations that can be performed on data—for example, mathematical calculations may be carried out in Number fields but not in Text.

For relational databases, Access needs to identify each data record uniquely. Because of this, you need to designate a "Primary Key." If you decided to make the Primary Key the member's last name, there would be no guarantee that there wouldn't be two members with the same name—Brown, for example. So include a field called Membership Number and select AutoNumber. Access then generates a membership number—starting with 1—for each member added to the database. Right-click on Membership Number and select Primary Key from the pop-up menu to set the field as the one with the unique identification of a membership record.

RELATIONAL DATABASES

When databases are cross-referenced, you get speedy and efficient access to information. Relationships between tables become defined when a record from one table refers to a record from another. Here's an example:

If your auto club teaches classes, it may be useful to create three separate tables which can then be related to each other:

Courses table lists all the courses available.

Members table lists people signed up for the classes.

Attendance table lists people who have attended specific classes, plus dates.

Now define a relationship between them:

If Chuck Layman attends an engine-rebuilding class on August 3, 2001, a record in the Attendance table would show the date. In the Members table there would be a reference to Chuck's record, and in the Courses table a reference to the engine-rebuilding class. Now, when a member is listed on the Attendance table, the Primary Key of a record in the Members table is referenced.

With your fields designed, Access displays your table and field headings, and you can start entering data. Now, the Membership Number field is automatically generated whenever you enter a new record. When you have created all the fields for your database, click Done.

DESIGNING FORMS

Forms are screens that you design to display and enter data from tables. To create a new form, go back to the Club database window, click on the Forms button located on the left, and then double-click Create form by using Wizard in the dialog box. Start by selecting all fields for inclusion in your form, then select a columnar format for the form.

> Create form in Design view
> Create form by using wizard
>
> The wizard asks you questions and creates a form based on your answers.

Experiment with the different options available in the Wizard and view the various results that can be achieved. Once your form is displayed,

use it to enter data and move backward and forward through the records in the table with the video-style control buttons.

EXTRACTING INFORMATION

One of the most powerful database features is the ability to extract information based on specific criteria—for example, you may want to pull out all your members who live in a certain neighborhood or celebrate their birthdays in February. In Access, this is known as a query. Once a query has been created, it can be redisplayed at any time to view the latest results based on current information collected and contained in the tables.

To generate a query, click on Queries in the main database window, then double-click the Wizard option. First, you'll be asked which of those fields from your table you wish to see included in the query results. Click on Modify the query design, then Finish. Now specify criteria for each field in your table—for example, perhaps you want to find all the

members of your auto club who were born during or after 1960. Simply scroll across to the date of birth field and type >1/1/1960 into the

criteria box. To see a set of matching records, click on the "!" button on the toolbar.

⇨ See also **Software: Access, Fields,** and **Records.**

 HOW TO: IMPORT DATA FROM EXCEL

① Go to Access and create a new database. Click on the File menu, select Get External Data and then Import. In the Import window, select Microsoft Excel from the Files of type menu. Select the Excel file and Import Spreadsheet will now start up.

② If your spreadsheet contains column headings, they will be used as the names of the fields in your new table. Decide if you want the new information to be used to create a new table or if you'd like to insert the data into an existing table.

③ You can now change the Field Names if you want. Access also suggests you add a column for primary keys as an identification for each row. Once you've answered all Wizard's questions, click Finish and your data will now form part of your Access database.

DATES

Here are some tips for working with dates in documents and spreadsheets, and keeping dates updated automatically.

A quick way to insert the current date into a document in Microsoft Word is to type the first four letters of the month, such as "Octo" for October. Word will display the full month name and then insert it if you press the Enter key. Press the space bar and the rest of the date will be displayed—once again, just press Enter to insert it.

Word isn't completing dates for you? Go to Insert ➔ AutoText ➔ AutoText, and check the box for Show AutoComplete tip for AutoText and dates.

An alternative approach to adding dates is available by selecting the Insert ➔ Date and Time menu option. Here, you can choose to add the current date, time—or both—in a wide variety of formats.

Another advantage of the Date and Time dialog box is the Update automatically option. Check this and the date is added as a field, and not plain text, which means the date (or time) is automatically updated each time that the document is opened or printed.

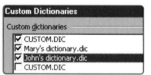

Having learned all the ways of entering dates in Microsoft Word, you will be happy to hear that Microsoft Excel is … completely different. It is just as easy, though. Simply press Ctrl+; to insert the current date, or Ctrl+Shift+: to insert the current time.

The Millennium bug may have failed to cause any significant problems, but the confusion over dates still carries a lesson. When using dates in spreadsheets or databases, use four-digit years instead of two—for example, 2002, rather than 02—and everything will work as expected.

If you come across a system that does use two-digit dates, there are standard Microsoft rules for applying them. The years from 00 to 29 are interpreted as the years 2000 to 2029 (so 4/17/04 represents the 17th of April 2004). Years from 30 to 99 are interpreted as the years 1930 to 1999. So, 11/24/35 is 24th November 1935.

If the normal two-digit date rules don't work for your application, change them. Double-click on the Regional Settings icon in the Control Panel, click on the Date tab, and modify the value in the When a two-digit year is entered box.

When using dates in a spreadsheet or database, you can perform calculations with them, just like any other values. For example, with a simple formula that adds 28 to a date you can discover on which date to expect delivery of an order that will take 28 days.

DICTIONARIES

Need to spell-check a medical, legal, or other specialized document? Buy or create the electronic dictionary you need for the job.

Spell-checking your documents before you send them to someone else makes sure they give a professional impression—but it's not perfect. Microsoft Word, for example, comes with a limited dictionary. If you use names or technical terms, these may mistakenly be flagged as errors. One way to prevent this is to click on the Add button in the Spelling and Grammar dialog box. The word will be added to a custom dictionary and will not be flagged in future.

Make sure you have spelled a word correctly before you add it to the custom dictionary. If you haven't, Word will not detect the error.

Create a custom dictionary for each member of your family or for a special project. Go to Tools ➔ Options, click on the Spelling & Grammar tab, then on the Dictionaries button. In the Custom Dictionaries dialog box click on the New button. Give your new dictionary a name and save it.

To activate a custom dictionary, go to Tools ➔ Options, click on the Spelling & Grammar tab, then on the Dictionaries button. Check the box beside the custom dictionary you would like to apply. Spell-check can refer to several dictionaries, so you can check using more than one.

Editing a custom dictionary to remove incorrect words or add new entries is easy. In the Custom Dictionaries dialog box, select the dictionary you want to edit and click the Edit button to view a list of the words it contains. You may delete or modify words in the same way as in any other Word document. Select File ➔ Save when you're done and close the file.

You don't have to use Word to edit dictionaries. Because dictionaries are plain text files, even Notepad is sufficient to perform the task. Using any text editor, open Custom.dic (usually in the C:\Windows\Application Data\Microsoft\Proof folder), and you should be able to modify it. If you can't, make sure that you have saved the file in plain text format and with a .dic extension.

Need to spell-check documents in languages other than English? The good news is that

Microsoft Office 2000 comes with dictionaries for Spanish and French, too, along with grammar checkers and other proofing utilities. Office automatically detects the language used in a document and loads the correct tools.

For enhanced proofing of documents in 30 different languages—everything from German and Italian, to Japanese or Korean—Microsoft offers the Office 2000 Proofing Tools. Learn more about their capabilities by visiting the Microsoft website (www.microsoft.com).

Online dictionaries can convert one language into another, often free of charge. For free online translation and language software, try

YourDictionary (www.your dictionary.com) and save yourself a fortune in professional translator's fees.

DRAG AND DROP

Want to work more efficiently in Windows, Word, and Excel? Try this neat time-saving feature.

If drag and drop doesn't work, it may be that it hasn't been set to work in Word or another Office program that you are running. Go to Tools ➔ Options and click on the Edit tab. There should be a checkmark next to Drag-and-drop text editing. If there isn't, click once in the box and then click OK.

You can drag and drop a single cell or group of cells in Microsoft Excel, too. Click and drag the mouse to select the cells that you want to move. Then point the mouse cursor at the border of the selected cells. When the cursor changes from a cross into an arrow, you may drag and drop the cells in a new location.

Change the speed of your mouse pointer for more control when dragging and dropping. Go to Start ➔ Settings ➔ Control Panel, and double-

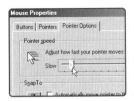

click the Mouse icon. Select the Pointer Options tab. Now adjust the sliding Pointer speed bar to a slower setting. Click OK.

The quickest and easiest way to move files from one folder to another in Windows Explorer is by using the drag and drop facility on your PC. Once you have selected the files that you would like to move, left-click on one of them. Holding down the mouse button, carefully drag the files over to their destination folder, and then release the mouse button to neatly drop them in.

When you drag and drop in Windows Explorer the results might seem a little unpredictable— until you know the rules. Drag and drop a program, and Explorer makes a shortcut, leaving the original program file where it was. Drag and drop files between folders on the same disk, and they move. But, if you drag and drop from one drive to another, files are copied.

The defaults on Explorer's drag and drop facility normally work just fine, but if you want to override them, drag with the right mouse button held down, rather than

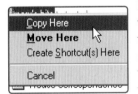

the left. When you drop the objects, a context menu appears showing the different operations that you can perform.

Drag and drop behavior can be modified by using the keyboard. In both Word and Windows Explorer holding down the Ctrl key when you drag and drop copies objects or files rather than moving them.

Drag and drop works in lots of places. If you want to reposition an item on the Start menu, you can drag and drop it to your preferred location.

Drop a file onto a program icon, and the program will launch to display it. Drop a file onto the Recycle bin, and it'll be deleted. Experiment with your applications—they may have other drag and drop shortcuts of their own.

OFFICE DICTIONARY RESOURCES

Whatever your line of business, there's an online dictionary to suit your needs. Prices can vary, so check out a few websites before you commit.

The Hosford Medical Terms Dictionary (www.ptcentral.com/university/ medterms_zip.html)
With around 10,000 terms, this may not be the most comprehensive medical dictionary around, but it's certainly the cheapest.

MedSpel (www.e-medtools.com/medspel.html)
A low-price medical dictionary that makes spell-checking documents easier. Includes over 20,000 words (and 1,500 drug names).

The Science and Technical Dictionary (www.inductel.com)
Although it's not the cheapest one out there

on the market, this Inductel product has dictionaries covering 120,000 definitions in six scientific areas.

The Speller for Microsoft Office (www.spellchecker.com)
Who needs to specialize? The Speller for Microsoft Office includes dictionaries for 12 languages, plus three other dictionaries covering medical, legal, and Internet terms.

Spellex (www.spellex.com)
Whether you're looking for a dictionary covering medical or legal terms—or more specialized areas such as biotechnology— Spellex has something for you.

DESKTOP PUBLISHING

Desktop publishing used to be an expensive, highly skilled affair. Laying out a page involved physically cutting up pieces of printed paper and pasting them into place. But with the advent of PCs and desktop publishing software, anyone with a strong interest can try it out.

GETTING STARTED

Plan your publication before you start. Eventually, you're going to have to copy or print and distribute your newsletter, flyer, business cards, tickets, or whatever—and that's going to be your major cost. If your newsletter is going to thousands of people, consider a black-and-white, easy-to-photocopy design produced on ordinary, white letter-size paper. For party invitations, you might go more overboard—lots of colors, printed using your inkjet printer on good quality card stock.

Setting up a template. If your publication is going to be a regular feature, it's a good idea to set up a template, including column widths, margins, text styles, and standard page elements like page numbers, dates, and mastheads. That way, your publication will have a consistent look and feel.

Make it interesting! Don't get carried away with how your page looks and forget to focus on what you're saying. Everything in your publication should be aimed at making it easy and interesting to read.

SAVING IMAGES

Save photos as TIFFs, using LZW compression (named after its inventors, A. Lempel, J. Ziv, and T. Welch). Because TIFF is a bitmapped, or "raster," image format, if you need to increase the size of the picture in your layout you lose quality, so start with as large an image as possible, using a high resolution like 300 dpi. You can also use a JPEG format, which often reduces file sizes—but with a small loss of image quality because of the compression/decompression method involved; whereas TIFFs use a "lossless" compression method.

What's the best resolution to use? If you're printing your work commercially, use images saved at a minimum of 250–300 dpi to avoid jaggies or blurs. For most home users, images saved at 72 dpi will be good enough quality. Many home printers can be set to around 720 dpi for high quality print results.

LAYING OUT A NEWSLETTER

Put text in columns across the page. Text is more readable in two or three narrow columns than in one wide column—although it becomes unreadable when the column is only two or three words wide. Experiment with your page to find out how wide columns should be to look good while retaining readability. It's traditional to divide the page into equal columns, but sometimes it adds interest to have two wider columns containing the main text, and a narrower side column containing additional material, such as a who's who, a table of contents, or perhaps, a few hints and tips. Set up your columns in your template, so that they'll appear on all pages you add to the document. Don't forget to make facing pages into mirror images. And allow a slightly wider margin on the inner edge for binding.

DESKTOP PUBLISHING

Desktop publishing (DTP) used to be an expensive, highly skilled affair. Laying physically cutting up pieces of printed paper, and pasting them into place. Printing letters into a metal plate by hand, separated by strips of lead. But with the advent publishing software, DTP is available to anyone willing to give it a go.

Use a maximum of three fonts on any page. This helps the page to look less busy and more readable. Use a legible serif font, such as Times, Garamond, Goudy, or Century, for the main text—between 9 and 12 points is a good size, depending on your readers' age and eyesight. Find a complementary san serif font, such as Arial, Franklin Gothic Book, or Gill Sans, for headlines. Then you might like to use a third font for captions, tables, information boxes, or emphasis. Set up text styles for text, headings, captions, boxes, text, and any other features you use regularly—it keeps your pages consistent and also saves you time.

Use upper and lower-case letters in your headlines. All capital letter headlines are difficult to read, and take up more space.

Line spacing can make a big difference to the readability of the main text of a document.

Space between lines of text is called leading. In most desktop programs, it's set automatically to 120 percent of the font size—which would make the leading for 10-point text 12 points. For a special effect, you can vary the rule.

Limit graphics and clip art to two per page, unless you're using a series of images for a purpose. Graphics that compete will distract

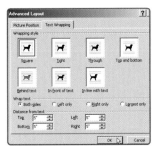

the reader. It's a good idea to line up graphics with columns, and always include a caption if the reader is likely to want to know more about the picture.

DTP PROGRAMS

Check out these programs if you're serious about desktop publishing.

**Adobe PageMaker 6.5
(www.adobe.com)**
Combines templates, stock illustrations, and digital photos with tools for page layout.

**Broderbund Print Shop Pro Publisher 11
(www.mattelinteractive.com)**
Easy-to-use program for the home or office.

**Corel Print Office 2000
(www.corel.com/printoffice)**
Includes photo-editing applications, business images, ready-to-use templates, and support for digital cameras and scanners.

**Microsoft Publisher 2000
(www.microsoft.com/office/publisher)**
Includes templates galore, predefined color schemes, Wizards, and images.

QuarkXPress 4.1 (www.quark.com)
The gold-standard desktop publishing program for design professionals.

Set text that wraps around a picture box so that it is at least 5 points away from the image.

Limit colors to three per page excluding photos to reduce the overall "busyness." At a loss for a color scheme? Then take a look at the main photo on your page. Does it suggest any colors to you? If you select colors from the photo, the whole page will blend together. And don't be afraid to leave plenty of white space around the page. It gives the reader's eye somewhere to rest.

PRINTING

Use a print shop. When you have your publication printed at a print shop, your file must be able to open on the shop's PC. So it's always a good idea to stick to a design using the basic fonts, which the print shop is likely to have available. It's an unfortunate fact of life that while most desktop printers use TrueType fonts, most commercial printers only have PostScript fonts. So you might find it easiest to begin by laying out your publication using TrueType fonts, but be prepared to substitute alternative fonts if you decide to have something professionally printed.

Printing at home? Always print business cards on good quality, even glossy stock—and it's worth looking into the special papers available for inkjet printers. If you're printing flyers, you might want to use sturdy paper, while for a high-volume newsletter, you may reduce the quality of the paper. It depends on what kind of publication you're aiming for.

You can't beat commercial printing—but that involves producing film and plates for the printing press, which is an expensive process and really only viable for large quantities. If you're printing smaller amounts,

digital and high-end color printers will give you the more affordable four-color CMYK printing. In this case, it is usually a good idea to try a copy house such as Kinko's (www.kinkos.com) or Postal Instant Press (www.pip.com).

CMYK? What does that mean? Your monitor uses a mixture of red, green, and blue to create the colors that you can view on your screen. However, a printing process uses a different set of colors—Cyan, Magenta, Yellow, and blacK—to create colors on paper. It's a much more limited range than the millions of colors displayed on your screen. So don't expect your printed colors to appear exactly the way they do on your screen.

Having a publication professionally bound can really give it a competitive, cutting-edge feel. Again, print shops such as Kinkos or Postal Instant Press (PIP) offer a wide variety of binding methods. If you are having your publication professionally bound, make sure you ask your print shop how much extra margin they will need to do this—it's usually an additional half inch.

⇨ See also **Software: Graphics, Grouping,** and **Paint; Internet: Website Creation.**

DRAWING PROGRAMS

Feel like harnessing some of your artistic impulses? Discover a myriad of creative possibilities by using drawing software on your PC. Programs are available in all forms and capabilities to suit your needs, from the simplest of sketching programs to more advanced, professional design packages.

GETTING STARTED

Finding a drawing program to suit your needs is often a case of trial and error, so sample as many as you can before you buy. Some of the best—and most popular—packages are CorelDraw, Freehand, Microsoft PhotoDraw, and Adobe Illustrator. Lots of others are available, some concentrating on special tasks, such as drawing cartoons or drawing for websites. Many demos and time-limited trials can be downloaded from the Internet, too.

At first, the choice and sheer range of tools on a drawing program can be intimidating. Begin by familiarizing yourself with the toolbar. It will be somewhat different to the other toolbars you have used in Windows, and a few of the features—such as Fill and Transparency—may take a little time to get used to. Most programs offer similar tools, such as line and curve drawing, shape drawing, fill options, color palette pickers, and special effects and filters. The best way to learn how to use them is to test them out by working your way through the help files and tutorials supplied with the program.

Once you've mastered the basic tools, you need to either create an image from scratch or import one from ready-made clip-art. If you have an image on your PC already, use the File → Open command to locate the image and double-click to open it.

Drawing programs are easy to use because they work on a point-and-click basis. They offer pop-up windows for various tasks and tool settings, such as pen or brush selection, color picking, or entering text.

Don't underestimate the Undo tool! The key to drawing artwork is to take a methodical approach. Go slowly and save your work when you have reached a point where you are happy with the result.

DRAWING SHAPES

Multiple choice. In some drawing programs—CorelDraw, for example—the freehand and polygon tools have multiple options, often denoted by a small black triangle in the bottom right of the toolbar button. Clicking on this will reveal more available options, such as the Bezier tool, which is used for drawing curves and spiral polygons.

Almost any shape can be created on your PC. Choose from resizable rectangles, circles, polygons, or opt for freehand drawing. The shape options are found on the toolbar under the Freehand, Rectangle, Ellipse, and Polygon tools. You can also draw smooth curves using the Bezier option. Just click on the shape option you want to use, move the cursor to the desired position, and then you're ready to start designing and drawing in CorelDraw!

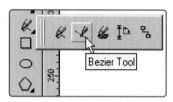

DESIGN PACKAGES

Try these tools and soon you'll be creating dazzling logos and original artwork.

Adobe (www.adobe.com)
The website for the manufacturer of Illustrator includes help files and news.

Corel (www.corel.com)
Home of the popular Corel design package, the site includes tips, hints, and QuickTime tutorial clips on a wide range of topics.

Graphics Software at About.com (www.graphicssoft.about.com)
This is a useful hub for information about drawing and places online to buy software.

SmartDraw (www.tiklsoft.com)
Easy-to-use program for flowcharts, organizational charts, technical drawings, web graphics, and diagrams.

Softseek (www.softseek.com)
This download site has specially crafted drawing and graphics sections, where you can download software demos and plug-ins.

Problem creating that perfect circle or square in CorelDraw? Achieve a perfectly symmetrical shape by holding down the Ctrl key as you draw.

FILLING AND SPECIAL EFFECTS

When you first draw a shape, only the outline is shown. Adding color and texture to shapes is

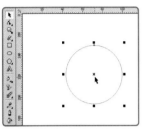

one of the most useful and rewarding elements of a drawing program. Just click on the shape with the pointer or selection tool to highlight it.

To resize a shape in most drawing programs,

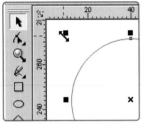

select the Item tool (normally a black arrow) and click on the shape. You can now click and drag on any of the corner or side "handles" to resize the shape.

Options for filling in a drawing for further impact will vary from program to program. In general, you'll be able to use a simple color fill, patterns (which can also be edited), and texture fills. The Fill tool allows you to select from an extensive array of preset or custom colors.

Filters and special effects tools make a big difference to your artwork's originality. To use them effectively, you need to understand the difference between vector graphics and bitmaps. Vector graphics— the mode you're normally working in— are shapes defined by a series of lines and/or curves, which can be edited to alter the outline of the picture. Bitmaps consist of grids of dots and pixels, which can also be edited. Many special effects in drawing programs will only work on bitmap images. To convert an image to bitmap in CorelDraw, go to Bitmap ➔ Convert to Bitmap.

Designing an invitation, letter, or poster? Experiment with the many preset graphics available. In CorelDraw you can view a variety

of clip art for your design by going to Tools ➔ Symbol. Select the one you want to use and drag it onto the page.

MOVING AND ORGANIZING OBJECTS

The easiest way to move objects around is to click on them, and drag them with the mouse to a new position.

Use the Arrange tool to rotate your images. Go to Arrange ➔ Transform in CorelDraw. Enter your chosen angle of rotation in the dialog box. You might need to experiment to get the object in the desired position. Don't forget you can use the handy Undo tool to revert to the object's previous position and try again.

Combine multiple objects simultaneously with the Group command. Hold down the Shift key and click on all the objects you want to keep together. Click Arrange ➔ Group command in CorelDraw to link them. As you move one object, the other selected objects move with it.

DRAWING FOR THE WEB

To create images that work well on web pages, save your artwork as a .gif or .jpg file. In CorelDraw click on the drawing you want to use and go to File ➔ Publish to Internet. Several options on how to save appear. Remember that small is beautiful in terms of web pages.

➔ See also **Software: Clip Art, Graphics, Grouping,** and **Paint; Internet: Website Creation.**

HOW TO: USE THE CORELDRAW INTERACTIVE BLEND TOOL

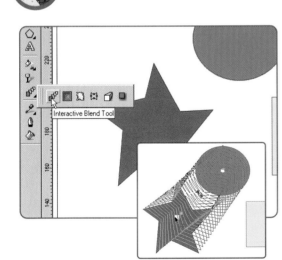

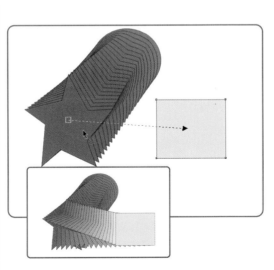

① Open a new document in CorelDraw. Create and color the shapes that you want to blend. Then make sure you have deselected them all. Click on the Interactive Blend Tool in the vertical toolbar.

② Now simply click on the first shape and drag the cursor across the page to the next shape. Release the mouse button and the two shapes will create a smooth and colorful blend. Join the other shapes in the same way.

DROPPED CAPS

Give your Word documents— newsletters, church bulletins, or personal letters—a professional finish by adding large initial letters.

Are your documents dull, with page after page of visually uninspiring text? Fancy formatting might be frowned on in school essays or office reports, but if you are producing something less formal, dropped caps can make your document more approachable and easier to read.

Dropped caps usually fit into the body of the document, so that the text runs around them. However, if you prefer, you can position a dropped cap in the margin to the left of the text.

Your dropped cap will be the same font as the text of your paragraph unless you specify a different font. If your text font is bland, like Arial or Times New Roman, the effect won't be very interesting. Go to Format → Dropped Cap and select a more ornate font, such as Brush Script or Stencil, for more attractive results.

Don't overuse dropped caps. Limit them to the beginning of each major section of a document, once per page, or once per story in a newsletter. Like most formatting options, dropped caps lose their effect if you apply them too often.

You can also create dropped caps in desktop publishing programs, such as Publisher. These often give you greater flexibility than Word.

⇨ See also **Software: Desktop Publishing.**

ERROR MESSAGES

Most error messages relate to problems that are easily resolved, if you follow a few simple rules.

Many errors are one-time-only problems, caused by an unusual set of circumstances that is unlikely to occur again. Shut down your PC, restart it, and try to complete the process you were working on. You might be successful the second time around.

Don't assume you have done something wrong when you see an error message. Every significant program in existence has plenty of bugs and idiosyncrasies, and it's possible that you have encountered one of them. As a result, you should make sure the problem really does lie in your system before taking major action. Reinstalling Windows at the first sign of trouble is likely to cause more problems than it solves.

Look at what the message says. It might appear cryptic, but if you can identify what software or hardware the error relates to, you will be able to consult the appropriate owner's manual for assistance. Refer to the section on error messages or troubleshooting.

The most important thing you can do when you encounter a serious or persistent error message is to write it down. Also, make a note of exactly what you were doing at the time, too, such as saving a file or printing. Technical support people need all the information they can get, so the more details you can provide, the better.

Some errors are caused by file corruption. If a program can't open a document or other type of data file, it's usually because the file itself has become corrupt, and you must recreate that file or restore it from your backup. If the progam files are corrupt, reinstalling the program should fix the problem, because the process will overwrite the faulty program. If it doesn't, uninstall the program using Add/Remove Programs in the Control Panel.

If you have a software problem, the chances are someone else has had it, too. Search for answers online at Deja (www.deja.com/usenet), Google (www.google.com), or Microsoft (http:// search.microsoft.com).

⇨ See also **Windows: Add/Remove Programs** and **Software: Troubleshooting.**

HOW TO: ADD A DROPPED CAP IN WORD

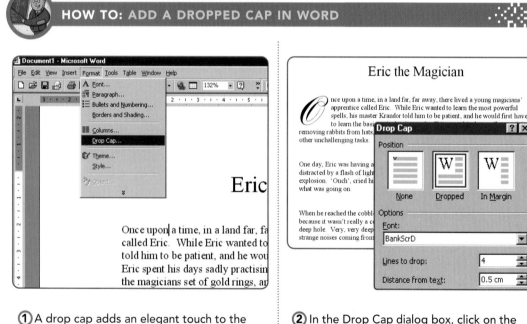

① A drop cap adds an elegant touch to the beginning of your document. Open your Word file and click anywhere in the first paragraph (or in any paragraph where you want the effect to appear). Go to Format → Drop Cap.

② In the Drop Cap dialog box, click on the Dropped option. Choose a font and set the size of the letter by adjusting the Lines to drop number. If the cap overlaps your text increase the Distance from text figure to add space between the first and second letters.

Microsoft Excel is a spreadsheet program designed to manipulate numerical information, but it is also capable of handling text and dates.

Even a beginner can get a lot out of Excel. Type in some figures, then select two or more by highlighting them, and Excel displays the sum on the status line below the worksheet. Right-click on this figure to calculate another value, such as the Average.

Excel's standard spreadsheet templates can help you perform a range of tasks, such as calculating expenses and producing invoices or purchase orders. To find the various templates available, go to File → New, and click on the Spreadsheet Solutions tab.

Learn keyboard shortcuts to reduce the amount of time that you spend switching between your mouse and the keyboard. To select the current row or column, press Shift+Space Bar or Ctrl+Space Bar, respectively. To paste a function into a formula, press Shift+F3. For a complete list, search for "shortcut keys" in Excel's Help.

Make your tables of figures even easier to understand at a glance by turning them into charts. Excel enables you to produce impressive results with the minimum of effort. Choose from a wide range of chart styles, including pie charts and line graphs, in two and three dimensions.

Experienced Excel users can learn about advanced tasks by looking at the file Samples.xls in the folder C:\Program Files\ MicrosoftOffice\Office\Samples. It contains a number of macros that illustrate how to carry out such procedures as communicating directly with a database and copying an Excel chart into a new PowerPoint presentation.

For the latest news on Excel, including articles, support, and upgrades, regularly check the Excel site (www.microsoft.com/office/excel).

⇨ See also **Software: AutoFill, AutoFormat, AutoSum, Cell, Columns in Spreadsheets, Formulas, Number Formats,** and **Spreadsheets.**

HOW TO: CREATE A CHART IN EXCEL

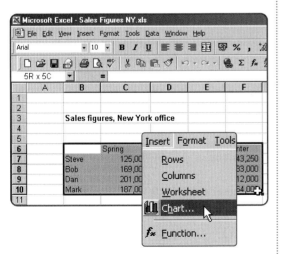

① To produce a chart of your figures, first enter them into a spreadsheet and type explanatory labels along the top (or bottom) and side. Click and drag the mouse from one corner of the figures to the opposite corner to select them all. Go to Insert → Chart.

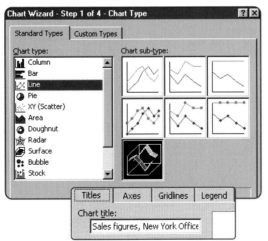

② The Chart Wizard guides you through choosing a type of chart, the precise data range, a heading, and other options. Press Next to proceed through the stages. Don't spend too much time on this because you can edit the settings later.

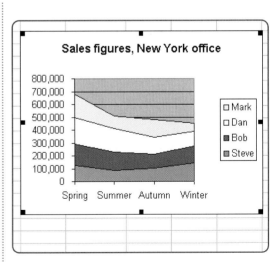

③ The chart will appear when you click on Finish. Right-click on any part of the chart to alter its appearance. The chart is not just a picture—it is a live representation of your data. As soon as you change any of the figures, the chart updates accordingly.

EDUCATIONAL CD-ROMS

Educational CD-ROMs are designed to help you learn. They cover a wide range of subjects and are published to appeal to all possible age groups. CD-ROMs can be a great supplement to classroom-based learning. They are especially good because they let you work at your own pace.

LEARNING FOR THE VERY YOUNG

Preschoolers can benefit from educational CDs as much as school-age kids. There are CD-ROMs for all ages, from the youngest to the oldest. Some are designed for parents to use with their children, and many are largely activity based. They can help children develop hand-eye coordination, basic skills like reading,

CD-ROM PUBLISHERS
The Internet is a good place to go for more information about CD-ROMs.

Dorling Kindersley (www.dk.com)
Offers a wide range of educational software for all age groups.

Encore Software (www.encoresoftware.com)
Includes a selection of educational programs and games on CD-ROM.

Knowledge Adventure (www.knowledgeadventure.com)
Cool CD-ROM games and learning programs for kids of all ages.

Learning Company (www.learningco.com)
A wide choice of games, educational, reference, legal, and biblical CD-ROMs.

Tivola (www.tivola.com)
Provides educational games to help children learn in an adventure or game environment.

and get them used to computers from a very early age. Knowledge Adventure (www.knowledgeadventure.com) produces some excellent early learning software.

It is important to look out for educational CDs that let parents work alongside kids. CDs that tie in with popular movies are often a good idea because familiar characters can help to keep children interested. Disney (www.disneyinteractive.com/learning) has a strong range of interactive CD-ROMs that are very popular with kids. Many parents like to use CDs with activities that can be done away from the computer. For example, some CDs contain audio tracks for you to play and sing along to songs, others have pictures to print and color in, still others offer activities like experiments or games for you to play away

from the computer. When choosing a CD, check on whether it teaches education-based skills or life-skills. Both are valid but a CD should be clear about which it tries to do.

SCHOOL-ORIENTED LEARNING

There are many educational CD-ROMs for school-age children. Some cover specialized school subjects and provide information, exercises, and texts to help supplement classroom learning. Other CD-ROMs take a more roundabout approach, hiding their real subject within a game or other activities. For example, Physicus from Tivola (www.tivola.com) uses a game scenario to test your understanding of physics. It is best suited to users in their early teens.

When looking for educational software don't forget encyclopedias. The Canadian Encyclopedia (www.thecanadianencyclopedia.com) is great for Canadian topics. Britannica (www.britannica.com) and Encarta (www.encarta.com) are fine for students, with Britannica more suited to older users. Both have content on the Web as well as on CD-ROM, so you can keep your encyclopedia up to date with regular downloads from the websites.

NOT JUST FOR CHILDREN

Educational CD-ROMs are not just for children. There is a wide range of CDs that adults can use to help improve their own education, learn new skills, or just brush up on existing ones. CDs can help you learn everything from fancy dance steps to guitar playing, from origami to cooking. Remember, it is never to late to learn!

Some of the best educational CDs are for language learning. They use multimedia to very good effect—for example, showing native speakers to help you improve your accent. You can often record your own voice so that you can listen to yourself and compare your accent with native speakers. Language-teaching CDs may

come with or without exercises and be suitable for school users or for adult tourists. Check the package to find one that meets your needs.

HOW TO CHOOSE SOFTWARE

Choosing educational CD-ROMs is very different than choosing books, in part because it is difficult to browse through them in a store. There are some ways to try and make sure you get good software, though. Talk to your friends for advice, and if you are buying for your kids, ask them what they like. If you are buying to help your kids with schoolwork, remember that kids like to learn in different ways so choose software that suits them best. Look at computer magazines both in print and on the Web. Reviewers see a lot of software and can often help you distinguish good from bad. Try visiting the Children's Software Revue website (www.childrenssoftware.com) for informed critiques of current and recent software titles, videogames, and children's websites. Sometimes you can get a demo CD directly from the

publisher by mail or from its website. Try these before you buy.

In part, categorizing educational CDs as "good" or "bad" is a matter of personal taste—what some people find helpful and fun others might find difficult to get into or dull. But there are some general rules; a well thought-out idea with clear explanation of the aims of the software is a good sign—check the publisher's website and the product box and any review material you can find for this. Also, positive reviews in magazines and on independent websites can be helpful.

You can pay anything for educational software from around ten to hundreds of dollars. Make sure you don't ignore the less expensive software, thinking it is of poor quality. There's some excellent budget software available that is simply part of a back-catalog. Check it out because it may be suitable and have a very appealing price tag.

⇨ See also **Internet: Education**

HOW TO: PLAY TIVOLA'S PHYSICUS

MECHANICS

Force, mass, density | Measuring forces

Forces can have very different causes:
For instance, the mass attraction of the earth causes the force of gravity of a body, the tightening or relaxing of muscles gives muscle power, the force of friction slows down motion, etc. You can measure forces with helical springs (or coil springs), because they will stretch in proportion to the effect of the force (Hooke's law).

Two forces are identical if they have the same effect, e.g. if they both stretch a spring to the same degree.

① Physicus is an adventure game in which Earth has been hit by a meteorite and stopped rotating. Consequently, half the world is covered in ice, while the other half is too hot to inhabit. Can you generate enough electricity to start the Earth turning again?

② As you move around the 3D environment in Physicus, you encounter a variety of different puzzles. You need to solve them, using your knowledge of physics, if you are to complete the rest of the game.

③ Whenever you need a little help, you can use the encyclopedia within the software to do some research. Learn what you need to know, and you can return to the game to apply it.

FAXING

You want to send and receive faxes? No need to buy a fax machine—you may already have a basic fax program on your PC.

Anyone with an old Windows 95 PC can install Microsoft Fax directly. If you are a Windows 98 or a Windows 98SE user, you will find the same software on your Windows CD, in the \Tools\Oldwin95\Message\Us folder.

Unfortunately, Microsoft Fax is no longer provided with Windows Me. You could try installing it from an old Windows 98 CD, but the official Microsoft position is that "using Microsoft Fax in Windows Me may result in errors or data loss, or both," so it's probably not a good idea.

Plenty of other fax programs exist, such as Symantec's WinFax Pro. With Office 2000 you get the Starter edition of this. To launch it, go to File → New → New Fax Message in Outlook 2000. If that option is not available, install the Fax utility from the Office Setup program.

If you have problems sending faxes, check your modem's fax settings. These are buried deep in the Outlook menus. To find them, go to Tools → Options. Select the Fax tab, then click on the Modem button. Choose your modem, click on Properties, and then the Fax tab again (we did say they were buried deep).

There are several modem fax settings that you can change to enable your faxes to get through. Try reducing the maximum transmission speed and turning off some of the various options. You can also disable hardware flow control. However, disabling these options means sending and receiving faxes will take longer, so only do this as a last resort.

To receive faxes as well as send them in Outlook 2000, select Tools → Options, and click on the Fax tab. Check the Automatic receive fax box, and set the other modem

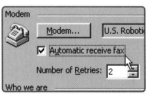

options to suit your needs. You will now be able to receive faxes, but only when Outlook is running.

Microsoft Word also has support for sending faxes, in the form of a range of fax templates and a Fax Wizard, which walks you through the process of sending your document to its destination. For this to work, you must have a fax program loaded on your PC.

Perhaps you don't use Microsoft Word? Not a problem if you have Outlook or an Office suite with Symantec fax software. Create a document in the word processor software of your choice, then select File → Print. Choose Symantec Fax Starter Edition as your default printer, and the document will be faxed to your recipient.

Word 2000 Fax Troubleshooter

Although Symantec's WinFax Pro normally integrates well with Outlook 2000, there are lots of potential problems you might encounter. For information, check the Microsoft support document, Troubleshooting Symantec Fax Starter Edition (http://support.microsoft.com/support/kb/articles/q196/2/72.asp). The Word 2000 Fax Troubleshooter (http://support.microsoft.com/support/word/wordfax) is also helpful.

An alternative approach is to send and receive your faxes via the Internet. Sites such as j2 (www.j2.com), eFax (www.efax.com), and Onebox (www.onebox.com) offer fax and voicemail series (they're free, too).

⇨ See also **Software: Task Wizards.**

HOW TO: SEND FAXES FROM MICROSOFT WORD

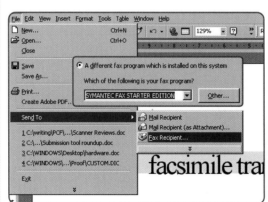

① In Word 2000, select File → New and click on the Letters & Faxes tab. Choose a Fax template from the selection shown (the Preview window on the right will give you an idea of what they look like), and click OK. Type your message into the template.

② Select File → Send To → Fax Recipient, and Word will launch the Fax Wizard. When the Wizard asks you which fax program you're using, for Office 2000, choose Symantec Fax Starter Edition. To send your fax, click Finish when the Wizard has been completed.

FIELDS

Fields are the building blocks of any database, and understanding how they work is the key to using Microsoft Access.

Know the difference between records and fields. At the heart of every Access database is a collection of tables. Each row of the table is called a "record," and contains all the details relating to a particular entry in the database, such as a single person in your Address Book. Every row is made up of a number of boxes, or "fields," each containing one aspect of that record, such as a name or a phone number.

Building your own fields gives you the most control over your database (see How To below), but if you're not confident about setting up a database from scratch, Access offers the Table Wizard to guide you through the process. To open the Wizard, launch Access and select the Access database wizards, pages and projects option in the dialog box that appears.

Give each field a name that describes or identifies its contents. Before creating your fields spend a little time making sure that the

labels you give clearly define the information that the filed will contain. For example, in an order processing system, "Date" would be a poor choice for a field name, since it could refer to the date the order was taken, the scheduled delivery date, or the actual delivery date of the goods. Labeling your fields clearly at the beginning will avoid confusion later.

Don't forget the field properties! To prevent other users from entering inappropriate data, when you set up a field, define a requirement in the Validation Rule box of the General Field Properties at the bottom of the screen. Entering ">0 or <36" would limit numeric values to between 1 and 35, while ">=#1/1/2000#" would not accept dates prior to 2000.

General	Lookup	
Field Size		Long Integer
Format		
Decimal Places		Auto
Input Mask		
Caption		
Default Value		0
Validation Rule		>0 Or <36

Speed up searching, sorting, and grouping operations by setting the Indexed property of a field to "Yes." But be careful! Too many indexes may actually reduce performance in other areas. So, if you're likely to search for, or sort by, a field regularly, such as LastName in an address book, then index it; otherwise, keep the default value of "No."

➔ See also **Software: Access, Databases,** and **Records.**

HOW TO: SET UP FIELDS IN ACCESS

Table1 : Table

Field Name	Data Type	
ContactID	Text	
FirstName	Text	
LastName	Text	
Address1	Text	
Address2	Text	
City	Text	
StateorProvince	Text	
ZipCode	Text	
Country	Text	
CompanyNam		
JobTitle		
WorkPhone		
WorkExtensio		
HomePhone		
MobilePhone		

Microsoft Access
Create a new database using
● Blank Access database
○ Access database wizards, pa

Table1 : Table

Field Name	Data Type	
ContactID	Text ▼	
FirstName	Text	
LastName	Memo	
Address1	Number	
Address2	Date/Time	
City	Currency	
StateorProvince	AutoNumber	
ZipCode	Yes/No	
Country	OLE Object	
CompanyName	Hyperlink	
JobTitle	Lookup Wizard...	
WorkPhone	Number	
WorkExtension	Text	
HomePhone	Number	
MobilePhone	Number	
FaxNumber	Text	
Email	Text	
Birthdate	Date/Time	

Table1 : Table

Field Name	Data Type	
ContactID		Number
FirstName		
LastName		
Address1		
Address2		
City		
StateorProv		
ZipCode		
Country		
CompanyNa		
JobTitle		
WorkPhone		

(right-click menu)
- Primary Key
- Cut
- Copy
- Paste
- Insert Rows
- Delete Rows
- Build...

Contact table : Table

ContactID	FirstName	LastName	Add
1	Edith	Kelton	12 Car
2	John	Smyth	4 Manl
3	Charles	Johnson	
(AutoNumber)			

(1) To create a contacts database, open Access, select Blank Access database, name your file, then select Create table in Design view. In the first cell, type "ContactID." Press the down arrow on your keyboard to move down the column and add the rest of your field names.

(2) In the Data Type column, select the option that most accurately describes the information to be entered in each field from the drop-down menu. A text field allows the greatest flexibility. To give each record a unique number, Choose AutoNumber for the ContactID field.

(3) If the field names are obvious, leave the right-hand field blank. Before saving your table, designate a primary key—the field used to check each record's uniqueness. Right-click on ContactID and select Primary Key. Go to View ➔ Datasheet View to enter your information.

FILE FORMATS

A file's format determines the way in which the information in it is stored on your computer. Here are some hints on choosing formats.

The format of a file is indicated by the three- or four-letter extension following the file name. For example, when you save a spreadsheet

ONLINE FILE FORMAT SUPPORT

Discover the format of unidentified files and convert files to a different format.

Ace Net (www.ace.net.nz/tech/ TechFileFormat.html)
When someone sends you a file with an extension you don't recognize, check the Almost Every File Format in the World list. It should point you in the right direction.

iConv (www.iconv.com)
This site lets you convert a graphics file to another format online. You don't have to download or install any software.

fCoder (www.fcoder.com)
If you frequently convert graphics files from one format to another, you'll appreciate the power and ease of use of ImageConvertor Plus. Download and try out a demo of the program before you buy it.

Gohtm (www.gohtm.com)
As you might guess from the name, this site specializes in converting all kinds of documents (including .pdf, .rtf, .txt, .doc, .xls, and .ppt files) to HTML format.

Wotsit (www.wotsit.org)
Anyone with a more technical interest in file formats will love Wotsit's Format, which contains in-depth information on precisely how file formats work.

in Microsoft Excel, the program always gives it the extension .xls. Files with the extension .doc are Word documents.

If you're sending a Word document to a person whose version of Word is older than yours—or someone who doesn't have Word at all—they will probably not be able to open your file. The solution is to save the file in a different format. Select File ➔ Save As, and choose Word 6.0/95 (*.doc) in the Save as type box. This is a commonly supported file format that virtually every PC is able to view.

When saving graphics for use on a web page, the file format is very important. Always save photographs as .jpeg (also known as .jpg). This keeps the files small and fast to load. The .gif format is generally better for lines, bullet points, buttons, and such. Never include a .bmp (Windows bitmap) file on a web page because they are large, slow to download, and only people using Internet Explorer as their browser will be able to view them.

If someone e-mails you a file simply called "greatpicture," it is virtually impossible to view because there's no extension identifying the file's format. Fortunately, utilities such as Identify

(www.daubnet.com/ english/identify.html) can help you determine the file type by looking at its contents.

FILEMAKER PRO

Need a database? This powerful but easy-to-use program has several advantages over other databases.

FileMaker Pro has simple, intuitive layout tools, logical relational features, and file-lookup procedures. In short, it offers a sophisticated database interface that a beginner will find easy to use. But at the same time, it provides advanced functions for experienced users. You can share files not only with other PC users but also with friends and colleagues who use Macs.

If you already have a database in Excel, Works, or a text file (with tabs or commas separating the data fields), you don't have to start all over again. FileMaker Pro has been designed to make importing existing databases easy.

A number of preset templates can help you to organize your information in a variety of ways. Create and print your own business cards, an inventory of your valuables, or even a set of recipe cards. A database can also help you to keep tabs on your growing book, video, or CD collection. Use the templates as they are or customize them to suit your needs.

The data input panels in FileMaker can be customized by using the Layout Assistant, which guides you through a series of options. You can choose and rename the fields you want to use, but try to keep them as simple as possible and avoid any unnecessary fields.

Want to scan through your records? You don't have scroll through the records one a time, in Form view. Choose View ➔ View as Table to display all your records together in a grid.

There are two ways to access commands in FileMaker Pro 5—pressing buttons on the toolbars, which can be customized, and context menus, which include only options valid for the selected item. To display a context menu, position the mouse pointer over an object or data, and press the right mouse button. The type of object and the mode you are in determines which menu appears.

FileMaker Pro saves your work automatically without prompting, so think twice before making any sweeping changes to your records, especially deleting. When you delete a record, it is completely removed from your database.

⇨ See also **Software: Databases.**

FILE NAMES

Spend a little time working out a file-naming system so that your files are easy to locate and open.

Always give your files names that describe their contents. If you name a series of picture files image1, image2, image3, and so on, chances are you'll never be able to find the picture you want when you try to later.

When you save a file in a Microsoft Office program, it is placed in your My Documents folder, which is generally a good idea. But if you do want to change the default folder, open the program and click on Tools ➜ Options and select the File Locations tab. Select Documents in the File types list on the left, then press the Modify button and select a new default folder.

You can sort your files by name, type, size, or date in Windows Explorer, whether you choose Icon or Display view. To arrange files by name, go to View ➜ Arrange Icons ➜ by Name.

Windows sorts files and folders alphabetically, with numerals at the top of the list. While this might be ideal for someone compiling a dictionary, it is not always the most practical

order. If you want to view the progress of a project over time, for example, consider putting six-digit dates at the beginning of the file names. You can also use numerals or letters to code your files to make certain files sort together.

Sometimes, you can't see all the text in your file names—especially if you select Details from a folder's View menu. However, if you move the mouse to the right of the Name button above the column of file names, you can drag the divider to the right to make more space for the text.

Search out Word files with similar file names, using file properties. In Word, go to File ➜ Open, click on the Tools button on the toolbar and select Find. In the Property box select File name, enter the name or part name in the Value box, and press Add to List. If you enter "letter," for example, all files with "letter" in their name will be listed for you to choose from.

FILEMAKER SITES
Find out about the latest FileMaker developments online.

FileMaker (www.filemaker.com)
This is the official site of the software maker, and features support and news. You can also download a trial version to try out.

FileMaker Magazine (www.filemakermagazine.com)
The latest news and reviews on the software, and a large back-issue library.

FileMaker World (www.filemakerworld.com)
Incorporates news, downloadable files, links to FileMaker websites, and a webring.

FM Pro.org (www.fmpro.org)
A searchable hub site for everything related to FileMaker.

If you can't remember where you put a file, but you know all or part of the file's name, you can use Windows' search facility to look for it. Go to Start ➜ Search ➜ For Files or Folders.

FILL COLOR

Add color to your Word and Excel documents with this graphic tool.

The Fill Color tool allows you to add color and other visual effects to newsletters, reports, or presentations. You'll find it on the Drawing toolbar, where it is represented as a paint bucket, or by going to Format ➜ Background. If your Drawing toolbar isn't visible, click View ➜ Toolbars and check the Drawing option.

The easiest way to use the Fill Color tool is to fill a shape or object with a single color. To do this, click on the shape, then on the arrow next to the Fill Color button on the toolbar, and choose a color from the Colors palette.

For a greater choice of standard colors, click on the More Fill Colors button on the Colors palette. This allows you to mix your own Custom color, if you prefer. Being able to customize a color is especially useful when you're trying to achieve an exact color match, for example, for a logo. If you know the color's composition, enter its RGB (Red, Green, and Blue) values here.

Clicking on the Fill Effects button on the Colors palette gives you access to a wide range of color effects. You can preset or design your own gradients, choose textures and patterns, alter the color schemes, or select a picture to act as a fill. You can combine all the effects, so

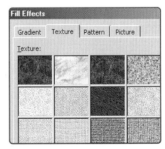

be prepared to experiment. The full scope of the Fill command can be put to good use with a little practice and some imagination.

⇨ See also **Software: Drawing Programs.**

FIND/REPLACE

Use this Word feature to eliminate inconsistencies in a document.

It is easy to lose track of text in a long document. Fortunately, Microsoft Word makes it just as easy to locate it again. Go to Edit → Find, and select the Find tab. Type the text you need in the Find what box, and click on Find Next. Keep clicking on the Find Next button to locate other occurrences of the same string of words.

One reason to find text is because you need to change it. Go to Edit → Replace. Type the word you want to replace in the Find what window

FIND/REPLACE OPTIONS

For these more advanced options, go to Edit → Find and click More in the Find tab.

Find whole words only
This option only locates words that aren't part of a larger word, allowing you to locate a word like "personal," without getting matches like "impersonal" or "personality."

Match case
Check this option to perform a case-sensitive search. For example, perform a search for the word "Fall" and that's precisely what Word will look for; you won't get any hits on "fall" or "FALL."

Search direction
Use All to search the entire document. Up or Down will search in one direction only from the current cursor position and it won't include headers, footers, or comments.

Use wildcards
Use the "?" wildcard to replace one character in a search, or use the "*" wildcard to replace any number of missing letters (for example, "f*t" will match both "fit" and "fingerprint").

and the correct text in the Replace with window and click on Replace All. The changes will occur instantly throughout the document.

Sometimes Replace All can produce unexpected effects. Replace "paint" with "latex" for example, and Word might also replace "painter," with "latexer"—not what you intended. To avoid this, click on Find Next, clicking Replace only when appropriate.

You can use Replace to remove all the occurrences of a particular piece of text throughout the document. Enter the word you want to delete, as normal, in the Find what box and leave the Replace with box blank.

FONTS

Learn how to use, size, change, and find all kinds of type fonts.

The easiest way to change the current font in Word is to select it from the toolbar by clicking

on the arrow next to the name. In the drop-down menu, each font name is displayed in its own typeface, so that you can get an idea of what it will look like.

Windows comes with a reasonable selection of fonts, and other applications install more, but you don't have to stop there. Internet sites have hundreds more. Try the Font Island site (www.fontisland.com) and Font Paradise (www.fontparadise.com)

A drop-down list right next to the font name allows you to select its size. However, you are not restricted to the entries in the list; if you want to choose an odd point size, just type it into the list box. To change the size of the existing text, highlight it first.

For more control, select Format → Font. The dialog box that opens allows you to select such features as font name, style, size, and color.

An interesting range of special effects is available in Word from the Format → Font dialog box in the Effects section. For example, Emboss makes text appear raised from the page; while Engrave produces text that seems to sink into the page; and Outline displays white lettering with an outline around them.

To manage the fonts on your PC go to Start → Settings → Control Panel and click on the Fonts icon. The status bar tells you how many fonts you have, and double-clicking on a particular font displays more information.

Whatever you do in the Fonts control panel, leave the system fonts (the ones with the red A next to their name) alone. Windows uses them and won't work properly until they are restored.

Windows lets you change font size without the letters becoming jagged by applying "font smoothing" to improve the fonts' appearance. But this only works with Microsoft's TrueType fonts. To gain the same features with PostScript or OpenType fonts, install Adobe Type Manager

Light. It's available as a free download from Adobe.com (www. adobe.com/products/ atmlight main.html).

If you have too many fonts—and anything over 1,000 may cause problems—deleting some may speed up your system. Some programs need certain fonts and you will get a warning if a program can't find the one it needs. Store extra fonts on a Zip disk or CD-R to reinstall later.

FOREIGN LANGUAGES

Change some Windows settings and plug in a new spell-check dictionary, and you are ready to go in Spanish, French, or scores of other languages.

All you are likely to see is a few random characters and a mass of square symbols when you view a foreign language document, whether it's a Greek letter in Word or a Chinese website in Internet Explorer. Many languages use different character sets. The reason you will not be able to view them is that they are not supported in your default English language settings. They are displayed instead as little squares or strong characters.

In order to view foreign languages in documents, go to Start → Settings → Control Panel, double-click on the Add/Remove Programs icon, and select the Windows Setup tab. Check Multilanguage Support box in the Components window, click OK, and Windows will install all the languages it supports.

Multilanguage Support doesn't take up much disk space—on our test system, 19 languages took up 5.4Mb—but if space is tight, click on the Details button in Windows Setup and choose only the language you need.

To produce documents in other languages, you will need to remap your keyboard. Go to Start → Settings → Control Panel, and double-click on the Keyboard icon. Select the Language tab and press the Add button. Choose the languages you need, check Enable indicator on taskbar is selected, and click OK. Have your Windows CD ready, if you have one, because your system will need it to install the new keyboard files. Or you can obtain them from www.microsoft.com.

A new input method editor (IME) is installed when you remap your keyboard and reboot. Microsoft may have a more up-to-date version

available, which includes more languages, so check their website (www.microsoft.com/ windows/ie/features/ime.asp) for information.

To change the current language supported by your keyboard, click on the Language icon in the Taskbar, and choose the option you want from the menu. Right-clicking on the Language icon and selecting Properties is a quick way of returning to the Keyboard control panel to add more languages or change your settings.

Your software programs may provide additional language support options. For Office 2000, for example, go to Programs → Microsoft Office Tools → Microsoft Office Language Settings,

choose the languages you need, and Office will let you view and then edit documents in them.

⇨ See also **Internet: Foreign Languages.**

FORMATTING

Don't overlook Word's many formatting features, which help you create attractive documents.

When was the last time you browsed the various examples Word provides? Check the document templates for preformatted letters, faxes, invoices, and much more by going to File → New, and clicking on the various tabs in the dialog box. To preview a template, simply click on the template's icon.

If you can't find a document template to suit your needs, then there's always the option of building your own version instead. Go to File → New, select the Template option shown at the bottom right-hand corner of the box, and click OK. Now you can adjust the document formatting and style as you want; then choose File → Save As to save it as a template when you're done.

 HOW TO: ADD A NEW FONT

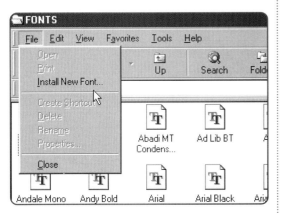

① Insert the floppy disk or CD-ROM containing your new fonts. Go to Start → Settings → Control Panel and double-click on the Fonts icon. From the Fonts window, go to File → Install New Font.

② From the Add Fonts dialog box, select the correct drive in the Drives box, find the font in the Folders box, and then highlight the font in the List of fonts box. Click OK.

An alternative way to format a document, especially suitable for web pages, can be found by selecting Format → Theme. Choose any example you like from the list. Word customizes your background color or graphic, font, and body text and heading styles. Some Themes may not be on your drive, so you will need to insert your Word or Office CD-ROM for them.

If you change your mind and decide you don't want to use a theme after all, click on Format → Theme, and select No Theme from the list.

Get even more themes from the Internet. Select Help → Office on the Web to locate and download the latest examples.

Simple formatting options, such as headings or numbered lists, can be left to Word to handle.

Go to Tools → AutoCorrect and select the AutoFormat As You Type tab to configure precisely what you would like Word to do.

Alternatively, choose Format → AutoFormat, and Word will configure lists, headings, paragraphs, and other document features according to the options you've selected. Click on Options to review or change your options.

Nervous about giving Word too much control over your document? Go to Format → AutoFormat and choose AutoFormat and review each change, and you'll get a chance to reject any modification you don't like. Or just use Edit → Undo to reverse Word's changes.

There is more to document formatting than AutoFormat, Themes, and Styles, so don't rule out the simpler options. Selecting Format → Borders and Shading (see page 64) offers a variety of features, such as putting a box around a paragraph of text, or placing a border around the whole page.

(see page 64)

FORMULAS

Formulas are equations that can automatically perform a wide variety of operations on your Excel spreadsheet data.

Be able to identify your spreadsheet formulas. They begin with an equal sign (=), and might include individual cell references (B7, H4), cell ranges (C3:E3 represents cells C3, D3, and E3), numeric constants (17), or mathematical operators (+, -, *, /). In addition, a wide range of functions is available to help you perform scientific, financial, or statistical calculations.

A cryptic formula, such as (B4/H7) * (C2+C8), may be acceptable if you're building a simple spreadsheet to do one set of calculations, but anything you intend to use regularly needs more clarity. To make formulas easier to understand, name key cells, and then use the names in your formulas, such as =(TotalIncome-TotalTaxes)/12. To give a key cell a name, click on the cell and

---

HOW TO: BUILD A FORMULA WITH THE FORMULA BAR

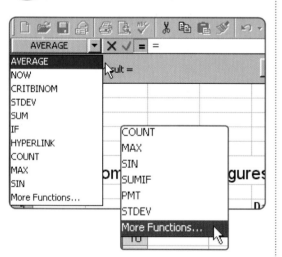

① Select a cell that you want to contain the formula and click on the equal sign on the Formula Bar. If you need to include a function, choose it from the list that appears, or you can select More Functions to explore all the possibilities.

② Use your mouse to select the cells you would like to use in the formula, and Excel will insert the cell references. This avoids the risk of errors made by having to type in cell references.

③ To make the formula active, click OK or hit Enter. To view or edit the formula in the future, click on it, and check the text in the Formula Bar.

press Ctrl+F3. You can name a range of cells, too. Select the cells and press Ctrl+F3, or select Insert ➔ Name ➔ Define.

Use too many names and it's easy to forget which one belongs to which cell. If you get lost, click on the Name list box, choose a cell name, and Excel will take you straight there. If there's no Name list box on your screen, choose View ' Formula Bar to display it. This also allows you to see the formula in any cell by clicking on it.

Using the Formula Bar is a simple way to build formulas. Begin by clicking on the equal sign, then click or select the range of cells you want to use, and Excel will insert the names or cell references for you. Add the operators or functions that you need, and you'll quickly have a working formula.

For an easy way to review any formula, click on the cell containing it, then click in the Formula Bar. Referenced cells are highlighted in different colors, providing a visual indicator of how the formula has been constructed.

If a formula is particularly complicated, click on its cell, select Insert ➔ Comment, and type an explanation of how it is calculated. Any cell containing a comment has a little red triangle in the top-right corner; let your mouse hover over

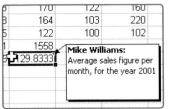

it, and the comment will be displayed. Right-click on the cell to edit or delete the comment.

Spreadsheets are normally very dynamic; change one of the values referred to in a formula, and Excel will recalculate everything to keep the totals up-to-date. This is usually a good thing, but in a really big spreadsheet the constant recalculations might slow you

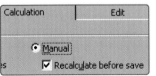

down. If you choose Tools ➔ Options and select the Calculation tab,

and then select the Manual option, Excel will only recalculate when you tell it to do so by pressing F9.

What result would you expect from the formula = 8-2*3? The natural response is to calculate from left to right, producing 8-2 = 6, then 6*3 = 18. Excel, however, performs mathematical operations in a fixed order, and does the multiplication first, giving 2*3 = 6, then 8-6 = 2. To make this formula behave as you expect, surround the part you want to be performed first in parentheses, as in = (8-2)*3.

By default, Excel stores values to a precision of 15 digits, even if it doesn't display them. This can cause problems with financial calculations, where 157.00000025 dollars doesn't make a lot of sense. To turn this off, select Tools ➔ Options, select the Calculation tab, and check the Precision as displayed option.

If you experience a problem with your formula, or the result cannot be displayed for some reason, Excel will show an error value like #DIV/0!, NAME?, #VALUE, or #####. What do they mean? Click on the cell, press F1, and use Excel's Help window to get advice.

➪ See also **Software: Excel** and **Spreadsheets.**

FUNCTIONS

Learn how to use different functions to operate your Excel formulas.

In spreadsheets terms, a function is a predefined formula that performs calculations on a given set of values, or "arguments." For example, the formula = AVERAGE(A1:A10) uses the Average function to produce the arithmetic mean of the first ten values in column A.

Some functions work on text rather than figures, so UPPER (Phoenix, Arizona) returns PHOENIX, ARIZONA. Other functions perform date-related arithmetic. For example, DAYS360 returns the number of days between two dates, so DAYS360 (2001/7/19, 2002/3/21, D) will calculate the number of days (D) between the two provided dates.

Not sure which function to use? Select Insert ➔ Function to get the Paste Function dialog box, where you can browse all the options available to you. For more information on any function that interests you, press F1.

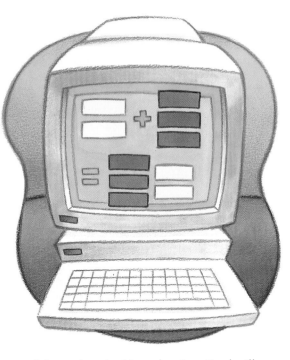

If you're an advanced user explore the User defined category in the Paste Function dialog. Here you can discover, among many other functions, a set of functions for storing and retrieving information in the Registry, the Windows database for how your computer is configured.

For help on functions as you use them, build your formulas in the Formula Bar. If the bar is not displayed, select View ➔ Formula Bar to see it. You can choose from the list of Most Recently Used functions on the left side of the bar. If the function you need isn't listed, however, selecting More Functions will display the Paste Function dialog box. Or you can press the Paste Function button on the toolbar.

GAMES

The PC is an extremely capable game machine, and even the most humble computer is capable of playing engaging games. Whether you prefer games that require razor-sharp intelligence or you would rather switch off and zap aliens, there is a game to cater for your particular brand of fun.

WHAT DO YOU NEED?

The impression many people have is that you must be a teenager to enjoy PC games, but that couldn't be farther from the truth. While it is true that action games are extremely popular, chess, cards, war games, and all types of strategic sports are available for the average PC.

WINDOWS' OWN GAMES

Your PC has several games already in the Games folder on the Accessories menu.

Freecell is a cunning card game. You have to build up the four suits in the slots on the right, in order from ace to king. The cards can be placed on top of each other at the bottom of the screen as long as they are a different color and one rank down (a black 10 on a red jack, for example.) Any of the cards can be moved up to the slots on the left. That's it—seems simple, doesn't it? Try it and you'll find it isn't.

Minesweeper is another seemingly easy game. All you have to do is locate all the mines as quickly as possible without uncovering any of them. The number on each square tells you how many mines are immediately around its edges. If you uncover a mine, you lose the game.

Spider Solitaire is a new spin on an old favorite, which many people find therapeutic to play. If you find Minesweeper too aggressive, or want to take a break from computer work, try this relaxing game.

The kind of add-ons you need to play games depends on the kind of games you play. If, for example, you just want to play an occasional game of cards or chess, then you probably won't have to add anything to your PC. More sophisticated action games, however, do require some special hardware, such as a graphics card, and you may have to upgrade your PC in order to play them.

Generally speaking, the newer the game you want to play, the more up to date your computer should be. Action games, such as Quake 3 and Tomb Raider, place heavy demands on a computer, and you'll need a good graphics card, such as an Nvidia GeForce 2 or later, in addition to a healthy amount of memory (preferably 128Mb) for the best possible textures and smoothest play.

If you plan on playing action games a lot, then invest in a large monitor, at least 17 inches. This not only allows you to get more immersed in the game, since it takes up a greater amount of your visual capacity, but it will also let you view details, such as bonus items and distant enemies, with greater clarity.

For simple real-time strategy games, such as Command and Conquer, a fairly ordinary graphics card, like the ATi Rage Pro, and about 64Mb of RAM will be enough. Before you purchase a game or download a demo version from a website, check the system requirements to make sure that you will be able to play the game on your computer without having to buy additional equipment.

For flight simulations, you need all the processing power you can get. Many of these games, such as Microsoft's FlightSim 2000, require your PC to render vast and ever-changing landscapes with as much realism as possible, so they place heavy demands on a

CPU and graphics card. Choose an Nvidia chip graphics card—either the Ultra or GTS versions—for best performance.

The graphics card market is very competitive, which means it's possible to buy one that suits all budgets and gaming requirements. The chips that drive the best graphics cards are created by Nvidia, and you really can't go wrong if you buy a card equipped with one of their chipsets. But look around carefully before buying because these cards often get heavily discounted.

Getting the right soundcard can make the whole gaming experience a lot better. A standard soundcard will support four speakers, or more, with the very best ones supporting a full six-speaker surround-sound set-up. These multispeaker soundcards can totally immerse you in a game, enabling you to use your ears as much as your eyes.

WHICH OPERATING SYSTEM IS BEST?

Several viable gaming operating systems are available for the PC. Windows is probably the most-used platform for games because it was partly designed with this particular pursuit in mind. New PCs, however, are being supplied with either Windows Me or Windows 2000. Of these two operating systems, Windows Me is the best gaming platform since it was designed for the home-user rather than the business-user.

Microsoft's next operating system is Windows XP, and it offers a number of advantages over Windows 98, Me, or 2000. To start with, it promises to be faster than previous operating

systems. It also has a number of unique features built in, such as voice control, which will add an enjoyable new aspect to future games.

CONTROLLERS

Many simulation games, such as rally, CART or flight simulators, work best with the appropriate controllers. Joysticks, steering wheels, and pedals add that extra bit of realism and controlability to your game play, but at a price. There are many makes available, depending on your budget and the type of game control you want. They include Microsoft (www.microsoft.

com/insider/gaming.htm), Logitech (www.logitech.com), Act Labs (www.act-labs.com), and Thrustmaster (http://thrustmaster.com).

Make sure you buy the right controller for your computer. Generally, most game play controllers are compatible with recent makes of PC. However, if your computer is more than five years old, make sure that the controller you buy

still has a joystick connector and not just the USB connector designed for more recent PCs.

When you buy a new controller, you may need to install software drivers (supplied with it) to allow your PC to understand the controller's movements and translate them into the action you experience on screen. If you don't have the drivers—for whatever reason—you can often download them free from the manufacturer's website. The site's address is often printed on the packaging and the directions that come with the controller.

For added realism, you can buy controllers with force feedback. These contain small motors that create resistance on the joystick or steering wheel to mimic what you would really feel if your tires were fighting to retain grip or if you hit air turbulence in your biplane.

SETTING UP A GAME

So what happens if you discover, after installation, that your game is running really slowly or that it is uncontrollable? Fortunately, developers often include large setup procedures in their games, which enable you to tailor the game's demands to your PC's performance level. Knowing what to change, and when, can make all the difference.

Unless you have an very powerful PC (such as a Pentium 4-based machine), you probably won't be able to run a game (especially a graphics intensive action game) at its maximum resolution. The best way to find out which resolution suits your game—whether it is 640 x 480, 800 x 600, 1024 x 768, 1152 x 864, or even 1600 x 1200—is to start at 1024 x 768 and work your way either up or down until you get acceptable performance.

Many games have options to increase the level of detail in the game world. Although it is always tempting to turn this setting up to full—because you want the game to look its best—the more detail you ask for, the more demands are placed on your graphics card and central processing unit. If you demand too much, the game will slow down considerably. Experiment with the setting until you find a balance between image quality and game speed.

It is not just the graphics settings that can affect your ability to play a game—it is also the way you play the game. For example, you may control the mouse with your left hand and find the default control settings unusable. Just as any

of the control keys from the main setup window in any game can be changed, you can also change the mouse buttons so that the primary button is the right mouse button and secondary one is the left button.

If you find action games too hard to control, try changing the sensitivity setting of the mouse. Again, you'll find this in the game's main setup window, where it is usually depicted by a sliding scale. Move the scale to the far right to have a very sensitive mouse (better for more

advanced players) and to the left for less sensitivity (better for beginners).

GAMES ON A BUDGET

Playing games on your PC doesn't need to cost you lots of money. In fact, if you act shrewdly, it's possible to play games without spending anything at all—thanks to freeware, shareware,

and demo games. Check out the games on offer at GameSpot (www.zdnet.com/gamespot),

Adrenaline Vault (www.avault.com), and the Gamespy Network (www. gamespy.com).

Know the difference between freeware, shareware, and demos. Freeware games are titles released into the public domain by their programmers. They won't cost you a penny to buy, so just download and play. Shareware is "try before you buy." You get a section of the fully functioning game free—usually the first stages—and if you like it, you buy the remaining parts. A demo is a truncated version of a game—often with certain functions disabled. It is designed to give you an idea of whether or not you will like it.

Also check out popular PC magazines, which sometimes come with cover-mounted CDs. It's also worth remembering that all the big publishers have budget games labels. If you wait a year, you can pick up last year's big game for a cut-rate price.

To play the latest games not yet in the stores, you could try being a "beta-tester." These are people who volunteer to try out programs and games in their late development stages to look for glitches and gremlins. You then notify the manufacturer of any problems you've encountered so they can be fixed before the product lands on the shelves of your local store. To find out more, log on to your favorite Internet search engine and type in "beta test." You will see hundreds of companies requesting your help. Simply register with them and read their terms and conditions.

Fancy a mental challenge? Log on to the Internet and try solving the virtual Rubik's cube (www.npac. syr.edu/projects/java/ magic/). Then try solving the 216 cube version— not so easy!

"HELP!" WEBSITES

Where do you turn if you're having trouble proceeding through your game world? The Internet, as always, is crammed full of helpful websites.

What do you do if your game won't work on your PC? Unlike console gaming, it isn't always easy to get a PC game to work. All games come with a manual, so begin there. Look in the back of the manual to find a helpful list of common problems.

Also remember to check the website of the manufacturer. You will find the address in the game manual. The website will invariably have a troubleshooting section for each of its games, and chances are that other people have had the same problem, so the company will very likely have produced a small "patch" that you can download to fix the game.

Find cheat sheets and quick tips to help you. Pay a visit to Gamestat's tips section (www.gamestats.com/tips) and you'll find

everything from cheat codes to entire walk-throughs. Take a look at CheatVault, too (www.cheatvault.com). They even offer an e-mail newsletter with new hints and tips in it. One of the largest and most comprehensive games tips sites is HappyPuppy (www.happypuppy.com). If it can't help you, then no one can.

Visit the forums of some of the bigger games websites, such as Gamespy (www. gamespy.com), GameSpot (www.zdnet. com/gamespot), and Happy Puppy (www.happypuppy.com) to get help on everything from card games to flight simulators. These sites offer users' tips as well as those of games specialists, so you will find some very interesting approaches to a whole variety of games.

visit KidZone (www.gzkidzone.com) for reviews of hundreds of children's games covering all ages, and the opportunity to order games online. Other parents with kids of roughly the same age are, of course, an excellent bet—ask them for their personal, parental endorsement.

In many cases, potentially violent games have in-game settings that allow you to tone down the more violent or frightening aspects of the game for slightly younger children, in exactly the same way as you can change the difficulty setting. You can, for example, often turn off any mature language and/or remove blood and violent, realistic graphics from the game.

Many advanced flight simulation programs are so accurate in their recreations that they can be very difficult for adults to become

ARE ALL GAMES VIOLENT?

If you'd like to buy a game for a child or a teenager, but are worried about the adverse affects it might have on the young person in question, pay careful attention to the age rating on the box before you make your purchase. All computer games are given an age rating in exactly the same way as videos or DVDs. This is generally a good guide to the level of violent content in the game. Alternatively, you could

accustomed to, let alone kids. However, in most of these programs you can also set certain flying options, such as speed, to look after themselves so that you only need to steer and control the altitude of the airplane.

If you'd rather avoid mainstream games with violent themes entirely, several software houses cater to a gentler approach to game play on your PC. Soleau Software (www.soleau.com) make a range of educational, nonviolent, strategy, logic, and arcade games. You'll find other themed games at NiceTime Entertainment (www.nicetime.nu) and Argos Gameware (www.gameware.com). If you would like to get free classic arcade games for your PC,

try visiting Arcade Games Online (www. arcadegames online.com).

See also **Internet: Downloading** and **Shareware.**

 HOW TO: DOWNLOAD AND INSTALL FREE GAMES SOFTWARE

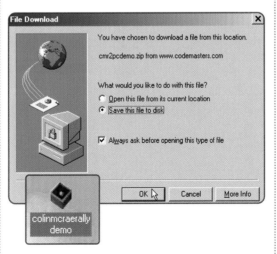

① Log on to the Internet and enter the web address for the games site—here it's www.codemastersusa.com. Most game sites have a Download or Demo section, so click on the appropriate link.

② Locate the demo and click on its link to begin the download to your PC. When the file is downloaded, it may need to be unzipped, so double-click on the Desktop icon. Most programs will unzip and start the installation process automatically.

③ Click Next where necessary and complete any registration information required. Click the Finish button to complete the installation. You should be able to find the game by going to Start → Programs. You can then test your skills before you buy the full version.

GRAMMAR CHECKERS

If you feel that spelling is difficult enough but grammar is even more problematic, the grammar checker in Word can help you.

The best any computer grammar checker can do is offer suggestions. Grammar rules may vary according to sentence structure and the information you are trying to convey, so they require an understanding of language. Unfortunately, this means that you need a basic understanding of grammar to decide whether the suggestions are appropriate.

For the least intrusive method of checking grammar, go to Tools → Options → Spelling & Grammar, and select the Check grammar as you

GRAMMAR-CHECKING OPTIONS IN WORD

Word can check for a host of possible problems in your documents, but what do the grammar rules actually mean?

Capitalization
Checks that you have used capital letters on names and titles, such as "Uncle Buck."

Commonly confused words
Have you used "stationary" when you meant "stationery" (writing paper)?

Contractions
Using contractions, like "don't" for "do not," is not always appropriate in formal writing, and this rule highlights these cases.

Misused words
Checks such confusions as using "who" instead of "whom."

Sentence structure
Checks that your sentences are constructed properly and are not fragments or run-ons.

type box. Word will check your text as you enter it, and any errors will be highlighted with a green wavy underline. Right-click on the underlined text for an explanation of the error, and select Grammar for more information.

If Word keeps flagging text as incorrect, when there are no problems, postpone error-checking until the document is complete. To do this, go to Tools → Options → Spelling & Grammar, and clear the Check grammar as you type box. Instead, select the Check grammar with spelling box. When your document is done, click on Tools → Spelling & Grammar.

If the grammar checker seems too tough (or perhaps too lax, and not detecting every problem in your documents), customize it. Go to Tools → Options → Spelling & Grammar, and choose a new writing style. Casual, for example, enforces only five basic rules, while the slightly scary Formal checks a total of twenty-four.

No matter which writing style you select, the grammar checker will probably still make enough errors to annoy you. Before you give up on it, go to Tools → Options → Spelling & Grammar, and click on the Settings button. Here you can choose exactly which rules you would like it to enforce (see box, left).

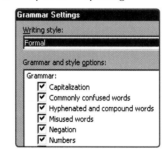

GREETING CARDS

Stop searching for that perfect greeting card, and make your own using Word and your printer.

To help visualize where text and graphics will appear on the page—and which way is up—fold a sheet of paper (in half and in half again, for example) to form the card. Write "Front" and "Back" on the appropriate sides, and "Inside" where the message will appear. Unfold the sheet and you have a layout guide.

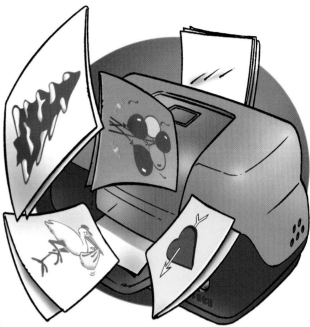

First choose the orientation of your page. Go to File → Page Setup and select Paper Size. Choose Portrait for top-folded cards (short and wide), or Landscape for side-folded cards (tall and thin).

Because you will fold your sheet of paper in half or into quarters, it is helpful to divide up your Word page in a similar way. One method of doing this is to go to Format → Columns, choose two columns, and select the Equal column width option that appears in the pop-up box. Click OK, and the horizontal ruler at the top of the page will show your new page layout; drag each margin pointer towards the edge of the screen if you need more space.

For more complex pages, open a new document, go to Table → Insert → Table. Choose two columns and two rows, set the Fixed column width to Auto, and click OK. Word will now produce two columns that divide the page vertically. To divide it horizontally, select the table, right-click on it, then choose Table Properties → Row. Specify the row height you need (half your page height), and click OK.

If you plan to paste large graphics into your table, lock it into place to avoid accidentally resizing it. Select the table, choose Table → Table Properties → Table → Options, and clear the Automatically resize to fit contents box.

After you prepare your card layout, select File → Save As, and select Document Template from the Save as type box. Give it a name like "Greeting card.doc" and it will be immediately available if you want to make other cards with the same formatting and specifications.

Choose a font that is appropriate for your message. The default Times New Roman is far too official and dull for most cards. Experiment with special effects, using either the Format → Font dialog box or perhaps, the WordArt option on the Drawing toolbar.

Add a graphic for your card. If you're artistic, you can produce a graphic by using a drawing program, such as Paint, to create your own artwork.

 Alternatively, you can use Word's ready-made graphics. Go to Insert → Picture → Clip Art, and choose one of the clip-art images available in Word.

To reposition a clip-art image, click on it, hold down the left mouse button, and drag the picture to its new position. While it is selected, the image will have little boxes displayed on the border, which you can drag to resize it.

Quickly preview your card as you work to check on the design and to avoid wasting paper and ink on trial printouts. Go to File → Print Preview. When you are happy, print it out.

⇨ See also **Software: Drawing Programs; Internet: E-greetings.**

GROUPING

Use Word's Grouping feature to link objects and text together.

Word includes many drawing tools under View → Toolbars → Drawing. They enable you to add lines, clip art, and shapes to a document and to build up designs. But it's useful to group the elements so that if you move one, the others will move, too. To group all the elements in a design, click the Select Objects button on the Drawing toolbar. Click the mouse on the top left

of your design, drag to the bottom right, and release to select all elements. Now, if you click-and-drag a selected item, the others will follow.

To group and move only some of your drawing objects, click on Select Objects, then, while holding down the Shift key, click on each object that you want to move. Select and drag-and-drop one of the elements, and the others will move, too.

To simplify repositioning of objects, the best idea is to select your group using one of the methods above. Click on the Draw button, and select Group. Clicking on any one of these objects selects them all and dragging them

moves them as a group. To make the objects operate individually again, right-click on the group, and choose Grouping → Ungroup.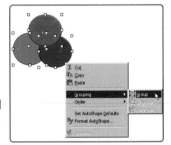

⇨ See also **Software: Drawing Programs.**

 HOW TO: PRODUCE A GREETING CARD IN MICROSOFT WORD

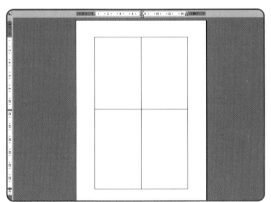

① Open a new Word document. To organize your layout and keep the various elements of the card in the right place, go to Table → Insert → Table to insert a table. Resize the row heights by dragging on the borders so that they take up the full height of the page.

Table Options

Default cell margins

Top: 0 cm   Left: 0.19 cm
Bottom: 0 cm   Right: 0.19 cm

Default cell spacing

☐ Allow spacing between cells   0 cm

Options

☐ Automatically resize to fit contents

② To make sure the table doesn't resize when you add a graphic, right-click on the table, select Table Properties from the menu, and click on Options in the Table tab. Make sure the Automatically resize to fit contents option is clear and not checked.

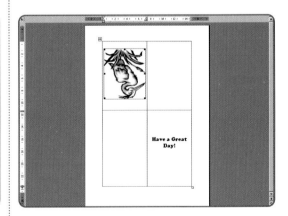

Have a Great Day!

③ Choose a fun font, then type your message in the bottom-right corner. Flip the graphic (see Software: Rotating Items) since the page will be folded, and paste it into the top-left corner. Print out the page, fold it in half, then in half again, with the graphic on the outside.

GRAPHICS

Graphics is often a strange new world for PC newbies. Despite the fact that many image-editing programs seem daunting at first, you don't actually have to be any good at drawing to be able to create your own interesting, fun, colorful, and surprisingly useful graphics.

BEFORE YOU START

What are you going to use your image for? Is it for your website? Or to go in a Word document, or appear in the background of your newsletter? Graphics come in many shapes, sizes, formats, resolutions, and color depths, depending on what they're being used for. So, even before you start creating your design, you need to think about your ultimate goal for your graphic.

Gather your materials. They might be clip art, photos, logos, color swatches, fonts, or various other materials. They need to be in digital format, so scan in anything that's on paper. Use a high resolution, such as 300dpi, and a rich color density, like millions of colors or 24-bit color. Now save all the files you need together in one folder, so that you can locate them easily.

COLORS

Creating your own colors. It's very easy to mix and select your own colors when you're working in a graphics program such as Paint Shop Pro. The Color Palette appears on the right-hand side of the screen. To select a new color, either click anywhere in the Color Palette, or for more accuracy, click on the top-left colored box and either select from the palette of basic colors or click on the color

wheel. Click the Add Custom button to add your selected color to the palette and create your own color scheme.

See a color somewhere that you like? Using Paint Shop Pro, select the Dropper tool, then left-click on the color that you like to select it as your foreground color, or right-click to select it as your background color.

RESIZING IMAGES

Cropping versus resizing images. When you resize an image, you compress the same image into a smaller area, or expand it to fill a larger area, without cutting out any of the image. In Paint Shop Pro, select Image → Resize, then select either a new size or a percentage of the original. It's always a good idea to check Resize all layers and Maintain aspect ratio. When you crop an image, you cut off as much of the outer areas as you want to lose, focusing in on part of the image. The easiest way to crop an image in Paint Shop Pro is to select the Crop tool, draw a box around the

area you'd like to retain, drag the edges to resize it, then double-click within the crop area. You can use both techniques repeatedly.

It's easy to make an image smaller, but not so easy to make an image bigger. When you spread the same amount of image information

IMAGE FILE FORMATS
Images can be saved in a variety of different file formats.

.bmp A Windows format, which all Microsoft Office programs can read.

.gif Use this for images that have large areas of flat color, such as cartoons, logos, maps, and diagrams. Images must be 256 colors or less, and it's suitable for the Web.

.jpg Also suitable for the Web. Use .jpg for images that have lots of colors, subtle shades, and detail, such as photographs. Keep in mind that the compression process results in loss of image quality.

.png A new image format suitable for the Web—but not supported by older browsers— and for images using millions of colors.

.psp Use this format when working on an image in Paint Shop Pro. It stores information about layers, masks, and paths particular to Paint Shop Pro.

.tif A useful image format that most programs can read. It compresses images without losing any information.

over a larger area, you lose detail. So it's always a good idea to start with the image larger than you'll finally need. Before you scale down an image, switch to millions of colors, if you're not already working in that mode. This enables the program to "antialias" the image properly—it uses a blend of different-colored pixels to smooth the edges of the image to avoid jaggies. You can then switch back to 256-color mode, or whatever you were previously working in, and check that the image still looks good.

GRAPHICS IN WORD

Add callouts to draw your readers' attention to hints, tips, or comments. Or maybe pull an enticing idea from the main text and use it to make the reader want to read on. Word offers lots of AutoShapes that make it easy for you to create cool graphics. Select Insert ➔ Picture ➔ AutoShapes to display the AutoShapes toolbar, then click on the Callouts button and select a callout style from the drop-down menu. Click and drag to make the shape the size you want. To insert fully formatable text, just click in the middle of the shape, then type your text. Double-click towards the edge to bring up the options for the shape. On the Colors and Lines tab, you can select a color to fill the shape. Drag the shape to wherever you'd like it to appear on the page, resize it, and you're done!

Are you trying to keep the file size of your document down? You can do this by linking to graphics instead of inserting them. Click at the point where you want to insert your graphic, then select Insert ➔ Picture ➔ From File. Select your picture file, then click the arrow to the right of the Insert button and select Link to File from the drop-down menu. You'll be able to see the picture in your document and print it, but you won't be able to edit it. Your document file size should stay small, but if you want to copy the document onto a floppy disk, you will also need to copy the picture.

Is your document scrolling slowly? Then you need to hide your graphics. To do this select Tools ➔ Options, then the View tab. To hide a picture you've imported, simply select the Picture placeholders check box, and then Word will display an outline of the image instead of the whole picture.

Take care with background graphics. While a picture or AutoShape in the background of your page can look great, you must make sure it doesn't reduce the readability of the foreground text. If you've inserted an AutoShape, double-click on the image, select the Layout tab, and click on Behind text. Now click the Colors and Lines tab and make sure the Semitransparent box is checked. It's a good idea to make sure it has no line around it too—simply click on Line Color and select No Line. Play with the color to make it pale enough to be unobtrusive (or dark enough, if you're running light-colored text over it). If you're inserting a picture, click on it, then, on the Picture toolbar, select Image Control and choose Watermark. Your image should now have faded attractively into the background. For a different effect, try blurring

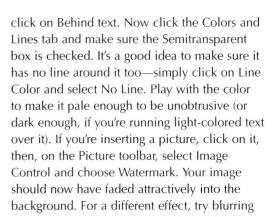

your image in an image-editing program before inserting it in your Word document.

WEB GRAPHICS

The most important rule of web graphics is to keep their file size as small as you possibly can. A web image should never go above 100Kb in size—preferably much less. The average web viewer's modem struggles to download at a speed of anything above 3Kb per second, which means even a 50Kb image can end up taking 20 seconds to download. Reduce your graphics to the smallest file size possible without losing too much image quality.

TECHNICAL TERMS
Understand the terms used for formatting images with these definitions.

Color depth
Color depth tells you how many colors are used in an image. Millions of colors gives the impression of "true color," while 256 or 16 colors are suitable for logos, cartoons, or graphics with large areas of flat color.

File size
The file size of an image is measured in bytes, kilobytes (Kb), or megabytes (Mb). It measures how much hard drive space the image takes up when stored and gives you an idea of how long the image will take to download.

Image height and width
You can measure the height and width of your graphics in many ways: inches, centimeters, and pixels are the most common. For web graphics, it's a good idea to use pixels, but for print, use inches or centimeters.

Resolution
"Raster" images are built up from lots of tiny dots. Resolution measures the number of dots per inch (dpi) used in the image. The higher the resolution, or dpi, the more detailed and the smoother your image will look.

Pick the right format for your web image. If the picture uses lots of different colors—if it's a photo, for example, or if it has large areas of graduated color—then it's best saved as a .jpg. If it uses few colors, and has large areas of flat color—a logo, cartoon, or a line drawing, for example—then save it as a .gif.

Graphics file sizes can easily get out of hand. If you're trying to make the best possible photos for the Web, create two versions—one full-size and one much smaller. Use the smaller one on your pages and make them into a link to the full-size version for those visitors who want to see the photo in the best possible quality

With .gifs, a small color palette means a small image file size. If your image already uses only a few colors, count exactly how many in your image-editing program, then reduce its color depth to exactly that number. To do this in Paint Shop Pro, you first need to flatten the image to one layer by going to Layers ➔ Merge ➔ Merge Visible. Then select Colors ➔ Count Colors Used. In the cartoon of a girl's head, below, the number of colors is only five, which means the palette can be reduced to five colors. To do this, select Colors ➔ Decrease Color Depth ➔ X Colors (4/8 bit). Enter 5 in the Number of

colors box and select Standard/Web-safe and Nearest color for the reduction method. For an image that uses a lot more colors, it's worth experimenting with reducing the color depth to different numbers of colors and seeing how much quality you lose. Often you can reduce an image that uses thousands of colors down to 64 or even 32 colors without losing an enormous amount of detail.

Before you save your image as a .gif or .jpg, save it in its "native" format first. So if you're working in Paint Shop Pro, save it in .psp format. That way you'll preserve the full color depth, layers, effects, vector paths, masks, and other nifty features. This enables you to go back

into your image and make changes to it much more easily at a later date. Once that's done, you can start reducing the color depth, flattening the image, or doing whatever else it takes to get it ready for the Web. Then you can safely save it as a .gif or .jpg, knowing that you've got your original to go back to.

Never resave a .jpg. When you save an image as a .jpg, you compress it, which means the image loses a lot of detail. If you then reopen and resave the image, you compress it further, losing yet more detail. Make sure you always save a copy of your graphic in a noncompressed format such as .psp or .bmp, before saving as a .jpg. That way, if you do need to update the image, you can go to the original file, make your changes to it, and then save it as a .jpg again.

Some people still use 256-color monitors when viewing the Web. If you use a color on your web page that their monitor doesn't support, then their web browser will "dither" your colors in an effort to reproduce a close approximation to your color. Dithering is when the browser mixes two or more colors, using small dots of each. This doesn't sound too bad, but dithering can look terrible on a large area of flat color. So it's generally a good idea to use the "web-safe" palette of colors, which all 256-color monitors can display, no matter which web browser is being used.

Unfortunately, the web-safe palette only offers you 216 colors to work with. A good rule is to make sure that when you design your images, you use a web-safe color for any large areas of flat color, while allowing yourself to use non-web-safe colors for smaller areas like the edges of objects and text.

How do you know if a color is web safe? Just look at the RGB value of the color and divide it by 51. The RGB value will be a number between 0 and 255 for each primary additive color—Red, Green, and Blue. You know your color is safe if each of these numbers is either 0, 51, 102, 153, 204, or 255 (all of which are multiples of 51). Open the color picker by

double-clicking on the color swatches on the Color Palette, and input some of these numbers

into the Red, Green, and Blue boxes. You should find something close to the color you want by typing in different combinations of these "safe" numbers.

➔ See also **Software: Drawing Programs, Photo Editing, Pixel Editing, Vector Graphics; Internet: Website Creation.**

IMAGE-EDITING SOFTWARE

To create your own graphics, check out these popular software programs.

Adobe Photoshop (www.adobe.com)
The professional's choice for image-editing and website graphics creation. It's also available in a less costly Limited Edition.

CorelDRAW (www.corel.com)
This vector-based program makes it easy to create professional artwork from logos to intricate technical illustrations.

Corel Photo Paint (www.corel.com)
Design images for print or the Web and enhance images with lenses, masks, and other editing features.

Paint Shop Pro (www.jasc.com)
Provides you with tools to retouch, repair, and redraw photos with its auto-photo enhancer feature, customize images, and create animations.

Picture It!
(http://pictureitproducts.msn.com)
Discover how to enhance your photos, add templates, and create web page images with Microsoft's Picture It!.

HOW TO: DECORATE A CHRISTMAS LETTER WITH CLIP ART

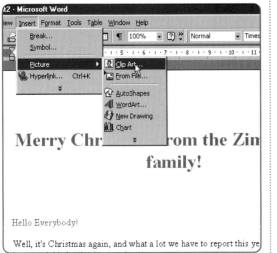

① To create a Christmas letter to send to all your friends, telling them all your news for the year, start by opening a new Word document and typing the letter. Then click at the beginning of the text and select Insert ➔ Picture ➔ Clip Art.

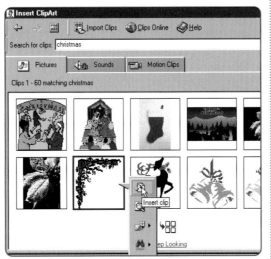

② To search for appropriate images, type "christmas" and press Enter. Select an attractive corner decoration from the variety available. Left-click and select Insert clip. Close the clip art window and return to your letter, and you'll find the corner decoration inserted.

③ Double-click on the image. Select the Size tab and make sure Lock to aspect ratio is checked. Click on the Layout tab and select Tight wrapping style and Other horizontal alignment, then click OK. Now you can move the image to the top-left corner.

④ To flip the image for the other corners, copy and paste it into a graphics program, such as Paint Shop Pro. Then select Image ➔ Mirror to flip it horizontally or Image ➔ Flip to flip it vertically. Save each corner image as a separate file in Windows Meta File (*.wmf) format.

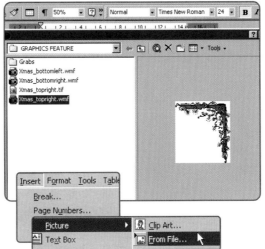

⑤ Back in your Word document, click in the top paragraph to insert the top-right graphic. Go to Insert ➔ Picture ➔ From File, select the image and click Insert. Follow Step 3 to create a floating image, and then move it to the correct position. Repeat for the bottom corners.

⑥ Now all that remains is to edit your text so that it fits perfectly onto the page, then print it on a color printer. For a more personal touch, leave the signature blank and sign your letter by hand. Then send it off to all your friends in their Christmas cards!

HEADERS AND FOOTERS

Use these top and bottom tag lines to make your documents and spreadsheets look more professional.

To display the header and footer areas in Word, go to View → Header and Footer. Click in the Header or Footer box and type the text you want to appear at the top or bottom of every page, such as a title. Style the text as you like within the box. Click Close on the Header and Footer toolbar to return to your document.

Buttons on the Header and Footer toolbar make it easy to format headers and footers. They offer options such as inserting the date, time, page number, filename and author, as well as previewing your document.

Anything you enter in a header or footer will be automatically left-aligned. Use the normal toolbar alignment buttons to center, right-align, or justify the text. To adjust the spacing, go to Format → Paragraph and click the Indents and Spacing tab.

Adjust the area taken up by the header and footer—marked by white bands on the vertical and horizontal rulers. Move your cursor over the top or bottom of the band until you see a double-headed arrow. Click and drag to adjust the size or position of the header or footer.

You can also insert a picture, clip art, or graphic into the header or footer area. Click inside the Header or Footer box, go to Insert → Picture →

From File. Browse to the file where your picture is stored, select it, and click Insert.

Changing headers and footers. To edit your header or footer, double-click on the header or footer and use the toolbar that appears.

You may not want headers or footers to appear on every page. For example, you might want to keep the first page of a report header free. To do this, go to File → Page Setup and select the Layout tab. Here, you will find options to set a different header for the first page, omit headers on certain pages or sections, or to insert different ones on odd and even pages.

Headers and footers in Excel can help you keep track of pages in large spreadsheets. Go to View → Header and Footer and the click the Custom Header or Custom Footer button for a selection of useful automatic options.

HEADINGS

Consistently styled headings in Word make documents easier to read.

The next time you need to create a heading, don't do it manually. Instead, select the text, click on the arrow beside the Style box on the formatting toolbar and browse through the drop-down menu to select a heading you like.

If you don't see a style you want on the Style drop-down menu, go to Format → Style, then select All Styles in the List box to see the full list.

Alternatively, create a new style to fit your exact needs. Go to Format → Style and choose User-defined styles in the List box. Click on the New button. Name your style, then click on Format → Font, and select a typeface, color, style, and point size for your style.

Word can apply headings for you automatically. Although often more annoying than useful, it may work for you. Go to Tools → AutoCorrect and select AutoFormat As You Type. Check the Headings box under Apply as you type.

Text styles can make a heading stand out, but a more eye-catching way is to create a "hanging heading," sticking out to the left of your main text. Click on the line with the heading, and select

Format → Paragraph → Indents and Spacing. Enter a minus figure in the Left indent box.

To review headings in a Word document, go to View → Outline. Each heading has a + symbol beside it. On the Outlining toolbar, click on a number—for example, 3—to display only headings of that number or above.

If you are preparing a glossary, sort your headings alphabetically. In Outline view, go to Table → Sort. Select Paragraphs in the Sort by box, and Text in the Type box. Check Ascending order and click OK.

If a table spans more than one page, you will want the headings to repeat across each page. To do this, select the heading row of the table, then choose Table → Heading Rows Repeat.

⇨ See also **Software: Outlines.**

HELP FILES

Help files make programs easier to understand and assist you with navigation and troubleshooting.

Don't waste time struggling to make a program work. Instead, press the F1 key and browse the program's Help file for advice. For help with Windows, go to Start → Help.

Some Help files have a Favorites tab. Once you've found the information you need, click on Favorites and then the Add button so that you can quickly refer to the information at any time.

When Help doesn't have a Favorites tab, find the Help text you are interested in, then right-click on it, choose Select All, then Copy. Paste it into a new Word document and save the file for quick reference.

Often the text you need will be spread across several pages within a particular Help file. Use the Back and Forward arrows at the top of the Help page to review the pages.

Some programs offer alternative help, indicated by a tiny question mark button on the window's caption bar—the "What's This?" assistance. To use this, simply click on the question mark, then the relevant button or checkbox for an explanation.

Many Microsoft programs, such as Word and Excel, have abandoned the Search tab and now provide an Answer Wizard. Here you can type in a full question, such as "Why don't my files print properly?" and the Wizard will try to help solve the problem. Sadly, the Answer Wizard isn't always quite as helpful as you would like and you may need to resort to the basic keyword searches.

The Office Assistant is another feature of Microsoft Help. To some, the cute animations and helpful comments add a fun element, but to others, the Assistant just gets in the way. If you're in the latter group, right-click on the Assistant and select either Hide or Options. Under the Options tab, you'll find several ways to modify the Assistant's behavior.

Even if you're an experienced user who wouldn't normally bother with Help files, take some time to review the Windows Me Troubleshooter. To access it, go to Start ➜ Help and scroll down to the Troubleshooting link.

Now click on the link any time you need to, and you'll be given step-by-step assistance in

tracking down the solutions to hardware, software, networking, Internet, and many other PC problems.

You can launch a Help file without first running its program. Go to Start ➜ Search ➜ For Files or Folders to locate the program folder. It will also have a .chm or .hlp extension. Double-click on the file to display its contents. Alternatively, go to Programs ➜ Accessories ➜ Windows Explorer and look for the file that way.

Are you short of disk space? Delete Help files you don't need any more. Go to Start ➜ Search ➜ For Files or Folders, and search for "*.chm" or "*.hlp" files. Click on the Size column heading to find the largest files, and delete any Help files of programs you're familiar with.

 HOW TO: USE HEADERS IN WORD 2000

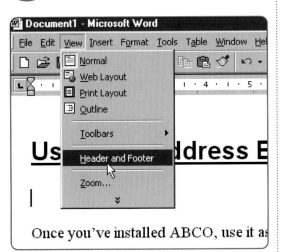

① You can make your name, the page number, and current date appear at the top of every page in your document, without having to type it in each time, by putting the details into a Header. Go to View ➜ Header and Footer.

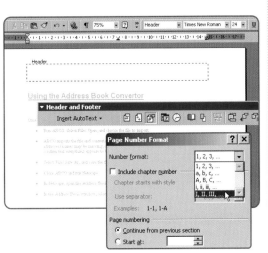

② The document switches to Print Layout view and the Header and Footer toolbar appears. Click on the Format Page Number button to choose a numbering style. Select a number format, such as I, II, III, from the drop-down menu, and click OK.

③ Click on the appropriate toolbar buttons to insert the page number and date, or choose from a range of preset text combinations and other options on the Insert AutoText drop-down menu. Style the text, then click on the Close button to return to your document.

HOME AND GARDEN

Making the most of your home and garden can be a difficult job. Many of us lack the ability to design without any guidance, and it's expensive—and disruptive—to keep trying out new ideas. The ideal solution is computer software that lets you try out ideas quickly and easily without the cost and disturbance.

WHAT CAN YOU DO?

Home design software comes in several forms. Some programs let you work on the interior of your home, adding furniture and general design features to individual rooms. This is useful if you're planning a complete home makeover and want to experiment with several different ideas. Other software actually helps you to build your home, allowing you to configure the size and shape of rooms, add different floors, and even work on the look of the roof. This is useful if you're starting a completely new home or building an extension to an existing one.

Garden design software helps you put plants, water features, and other elements into your plot in the best configuration. These usually include a plant database—so you can easily fill the garden and choose plants that suit your soil and climate and meet your height, color,

fragrance, and other needs. Most databases include information on plant care so that you can maintain your garden once it's in place.

While you can buy software that concentrates on either home or garden design, some software does both—for example, HomeStyles.com (www.store.homestyles.com) or Sierra Complete Home 3D Design (www.sierrahome.com). If you

have a home and a garden design program from the same publisher, you can get integrated tools to work with both, but often the software suites include these extra tools anyway.

Home or garden design software won't produce a perfect plan on its own—it needs some help from you. You need to follow the basic principles of good design, and more often than not, the software includes a design guide to provide these. Keep your budget in mind and don't overspend. Also be realistic about the range of materials and furnishings you can buy locally, and be wary of ultra-fashionable designs that you could grow tired of in six months. Above all, experiment—design software lets you try

as many new ideas as you want without the cost—so make the most of it.

BUYING TIPS

Design software should be versatile and easy to use. You'll want to tinker with your layouts—trying out many different kinds of design features—so it's important to be able to place and move items with just a click and drag.

Make it real. You should be able to import your own scans and drawings in to the software and download images from the Web. Just imagine being able to add your own drapes to a room design with the simple touch of a button! Keep in mind that a feature that creates a shopping list always comes in handy.

Stuck? Your software should offer hints on tricky tasks, provide access to online design guides, and produce 3D views of your designs—invaluable for helping you to visualize the end result.

Garden design software generally comes with a healthy plant database that lets you add to it using scanned pictures of plants. Better still is a program that can mature your design, showing how your garden will look in years to come.

Keep an eye on your software publisher's website. Some publishers provide extras for free download that you can import into your home or garden design software. Typically, they might include new plants for your garden designer, new furniture items, or a range of floor and

wall coverings for interior design tools. These downloadable software extras can help you to keep up with the current fashion trends, and they'll ultimately help you build up a library of objects that you can use in other design projects you might undertake.

Besides garden design software, you can also buy separate garden encyclopedias on CD-ROM or visit a site such as Gardening.com (http://gardening.sierrahome.com/encyc/). The dedicated encyclopedias contain many more plants than your average garden design software. They are also far easier to access than regular printed guides. You can specify certain features you want, such as plant color, height, and fragrance, all in one quick search. Keep a look out for a garden encyclopedia that lets you add your own plants and allows you to annotate existing entries—to help make your entries as useful as possible.

COUNTING THE COST

Design software and garden encyclopedias can be excellent value for the money—some are very moderately priced. Even if you buy the most expensive software, keep in mind that it's still going to be a lot cheaper than an interior designer, and you'll also be able to use the design software over and over again.

⇨ See also **Software: Educational Software; Internet: Downloading; Hardware: CD-ROMs.**

HOW TO: USE THE SIERRA COMPLETE HOME 3D DESIGN COLLECTION

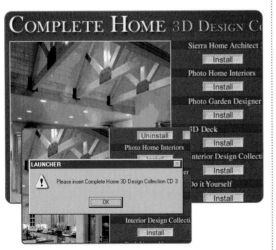

① First install each of the seven program elements that you want. You need to install them individually, so you may need to swap between the installation disks to do this.

② To run any of the different programs, choose it from the Start menu or from the main program screen. The main program screen appears whenever you put one of the program CDs into your CD-ROM drive.

③ Use online assistance to help you access the different applications. Some allow you to import your own scanned photos, which helps you customize your design.

INCOME TAX

Calculate federal and state income taxes with one of the programs available on the market.

The most popular programs for income tax preparation are Kipling TaxCut from H&R Block and Quicken TurboTax from Intuit. They come in standard and deluxe versions. The deluxe version typically contains more detailed tax information, free state-tax software, and sometimes free electronic filing. All versions can import information from your Quicken or Microsoft Money program. If you're affected by some recent change in the tax law, you can get last-minute updates at the software's website.

If you have to file GST/HST returns, check with Canada Customs and Revenue Agency (www. ccra-adrc.gc.ca/tax/business/gsthst/menu-e. html). Here you get all the guides and forms, plus information about filing returns by phone.

Even if you have no financial programs or add-ons, a simple database—even a list of items in a Word document, for example—can often provide a satisfactory means of keeping track of key financial transactions, business expenses, and so on.

Filing your income taxes doesn't need to be a lengthy or difficult experience. Whether you're an individual or a business taxpayer, use Canada Customs and Revenue Agency's NETFILE site (www.netfile.gc.ca).

A range of excellent tools for preparing and filing taxes can be found on the Internet. Sites such as QuickTax (www.quicktaxweb.ca), COOLtax (www.cooltax.com), and Brian Costello's site (www.ufile.ca) are helpful.

Storing tax information on your PC can lead to potentially serious consequences. To avoid losing vital data, make sure that you back up your files regularly and store the copies in another location.

➪ See also **Software: Budget Planning** and **Money; Internet: Income Tax**

INDEXES

Have you created a long report or a family history in Word? Adding an index for quick reference is easier than you think.

Although the Edit → Find function makes it easy to locate topics of interest in a Word file, once a document is printed, readers may need an index. The Index and Tables command will help you create one.

To build an index as you write, select a word or words that you want to include in the index, and press Alt+Shift+X (or go to Insert → Index and Tables, and click on Mark Entry). Now click on Mark to flag the selected word to be indexed, or click on Mark All to index all occurrences of that word in your document.

Wherever you mark an index entry, Word inserts an Index Entry (XE) field, which looks something like: {XE "indexed word or phrase"}. To modify how the entry appears in the index, just change the

text inside the quotation marks. If you want to delete the entry completely, delete the entire XE field, including the braces ({}).

When you've marked all the words you want to index, place the cursor where you'd like the index to appear, usually at the end of the document. Select Insert → Index and Tables, and click OK.

Take a shortcut to creating an index. First, create a "concordance file." Open a new Word document and create a two-column table (Go to Tables → Insert Tables). In the first column, enter the exact word to be indexed as it appears in your document, and in the second column, type the index entry you want for that text. Pressing the Tab key to move between the columns, repeat for all the words you want to be indexed. Make separate entries for plural words. Save the file. Open the document you want to index and go to Insert → Index and Tables. Select the Index tab, click on AutoMark, and choose the concordance file you have just created.

If you add, edit, or delete text after creating an index, click anywhere in the index and press F9. This command will rebuild the index and make sure that all the entries are still correct.

Don't need an index after all? Click anywhere in the index, press Shift+F9, and delete the resulting index field code including the braces.

Want to change the look of your index? Go to Insert → Index and Tables. Before you choose an option, get an idea of each effect by selecting an option and viewing it in the Print Preview panel.

INSERTING

Here's how to insert, link, and embed one type of document into a completely different one.

Need to add a table of sales figures to a report you've produced in Word? One method is to copy your figures from a spreadsheet, then paste them into your Word document. But it's quicker to enter them directly into a spreadsheet linked to your Word document, by using the Insert → Object command (see how to, below).

You can create all sorts of multipurpose documents when you go to Insert → Object in Word. Any application that creates an OLE (Object Linking and Embedding) item registers

on the list of options. In addition to Excel spreadsheets, you can import pictures, video clips, sound files, and presentations.

Make documents richer and more interesting, both in content and visually, with OLE objects. Even in a simple editor, such as WordPad, you can select Insert → Object and add a video clip. View the document and you will see a still of the first video frame; double-click on it to play the whole clip—an instant multimedia presentation.

Whole objects may be "linked" or "embedded" into your documents. To create a link, simply select Insert → Object, and then choose the Create from File tab. Now you can select the file

that you want to link to your document, but before you close, make sure that the Link to File option is checked.

Linking helps keep document files small. When you insert a link to a spreadsheet, for example, all you're adding is a reference to the spreadsheet file, and its location on your hard drive. The data contained in that spreadsheet stays in its original file.

Linked objects are updated automatically whenever the source file changes. For example, if you've created a link to your Personal Finances spreadsheet, then you'll always be able to see the latest financial information when you view the document. Double-click on the linked object, and you can even edit it, without having to start Excel yourself.

A linked object is inappropriate in some cases. Maybe you want to give the document to someone else? Instead of linking the object, embed it in your document instead. To do this, go to Insert → Object, and choose either a new file on the Create New tab or browse to an existing file on the Create from File tab. It is

important not to check the Link to file option. Windows will embed your chosen object in your document when you click OK.

An embedded object is part of the document in which it is created and is not a reference to another file. While this makes it easier for you to send documents to others, remember that there is no guarantee that the recipient will be able to view it. For example, an embedded Excel spreadsheet will be viewable but impossible to edit to someone who doesn't have the Excel program.

Some of your programs may not have an Insert → Object feature, but don't give up. There is another way to achieve the same effect. For example, to insert an Excel table, open Excel, select the table you want to use, and then choose Edit → Copy. Now, open the program receiving the table and click on Edit → Paste Special. In the resulting dialog box, select the object to be transferred to your document and then click on Paste Link.

 HOW TO: INSERT AN EXCEL SPREADSHEET INTO A WORD DOCUMENT

① Open your Word document and position the cursor where you want an existing Excel spreadsheet to be inserted. Go to Insert → Object, and check the Link to file box on the Create from File tab. Click on Browse, then locate and insert your spreadsheet.

② The spreadsheet that appears in the Word document acts like a picture, so if you want to move or resize it, click on the spreadsheet and drag the sizing handles.

③ To edit the spreadsheet, double-click on it. Your original Excel spreadsheet will open, allowing you to make any changes you need. Make your changes then save and close the file. Your Word document will show the modified version.

KEYBOARD SHORTCUTS

Using the same menu command again and again? Often there's a faster method on the keyboard, and if not, you can always create one.

Point and click and drag and drop. In Windows, the mouse is the operational tool. While that makes it easy to use, it's not always the quickest option. Often a keyboard shortcut is the fastest way to perform a particular action. So learning a few basic commands can come in very handy.

Many programs use the same shortcuts. This means that once you've learned them in

KEYBOARD SHORTCUTS YOU MIGHT HAVE MISSED
Save yourself some time with a few simple shortcuts.

DESKTOP

Alt+Enter	Displays the properties of the selected object.
F2	Renames the currently selected object.
F3	Displays the Search for Files and Folders dialog box.
F5	Refreshes the screen.
Shift+F10	Displays the context (right-click) menu of the selected object.

WINDOWS EXPLORER

F4	Opens the Address box.
F6	Moves between the drive, file, and the address panes.
Backspace	Moves to the parent of the currently selected folder.
Keypad *	Expands everything under the currently selected folder.
Keypad +	Expands the currently selected folder to the first level only.
Keypad –	Collapses the currently selected folder.

one program, you can use them almost anywhere. Common examples include Ctrl+O (Open file), Ctrl+S (Save), and Ctrl+P (Print).

Keyboard shortcuts are commonly written with a plus sign (+) separator, as in Ctrl+Alt+Shift+F8, but you don't press the "+" when entering the shortcut. To make shortcuts like this work, you need to hold down the Ctrl, Alt, and Shift keys together, and press the final key, F8 in this case.

Some universally supported shortcuts apply to clipboard operations, such as Copy and Paste. To copy the text on a web page to the clipboard, you can click at the top of the page, hold down the mouse button, drag down to the bottom of the page, and then select Edit → Copy. A quicker way to achieve the same result is to press Ctrl+A to highlight all the text, then Ctrl+C to copy it.

Some programs use their own shortcuts. If a shortcut is available, it's usually shown beside its equivalent drop-down menu command.

Most programs support Windows shortcuts, whether or not they document them. For example, Ctrl+Z will usually undo the last change you made; the Spacebar can be used to toggle the setting of a checkbox; and the down arrow will display all the options in a drop-down menu.

To assign a specific key combination to open a folder shortcut on your Windows Desktop, right-click on it, and select Properties. On the Shortcut tab, click in the Shortcut key box, press

the key combination to be used, and click OK. You can now open your folder by pressing the keys you selected.

You can change existing shortcuts or create new ones to suit your requirements in Microsoft Word. To do this, go to Tools → Customize. In the Customize window, select the Commands tab and click on the Keyboard button. The Customize Keyboard dialog box then allows you to assign or reassign shortcuts to keys—for example, Alt+C to create center-aligned text.

Are your other programs as simple to use as Word? Install a keyboard macro program and you can create keyboard shortcuts to automate the most complex tasks. KeyText 2000 (www.mjmsoft.com/keytext.htm), Keyboard Express (www.keyboardexpress.com), and ShortKeys (www.shortkeys.com) are popular macro programs that you can download from the Internet. You'll find more examples in the big Internet software libraries Softseek (www.softseek.com) and Tucows (www.tucows.com).

➡ See also: **Software: Macros.**

KEYPADS

Using the keypad lets you enter numbers in address books, databases, or spreadsheets quickly and efficiently.

Whenever you need to enter lots of figures in a spreadsheet or another program, the easiest way to do it is to use the numeric keypad (that's the block of keys to the right on most full-sized keyboards). Because all the number keys are grouped closely together on the keypad, this reduces your hand movements, speeding up the data-entry process.

Once you are used to typing figures on a keypad, using any other method can seem slow. So what do you do on a notebook if you find using the "embedded" keypad on the letter keys awkward to use? Buy a separate keypad unit and connect it to your computer through the USB or serial port. Check your favorite computer store to see what's available. Alternatively, search online at Targus (www.targus.com), Beyond (www.beyond.com/computers), or CWOL (www.cwol.com).

You can usually also control your cursor with the keys on your keypad. Keyboards that support this have a Num Lock key and indicator light. With Num Lock on, the keys work as numbers; with it off, they work as arrow keys, moving the cursor left, right, up, and down. The arrows are printed on the relevant keys.

Some people love the flexibility of Num Lock. Others dislike it because they're always toggling the key by mistake, and then discovering that the keypad isn't working as expected. To reduce the chance of this happening, go to Start ➔ Settings ➔ Control Panel and double-click on Accessibility Options. Select the Keyboard tab, and check Use ToggleKeys. In the future, Windows will play a tone to alert you whenever you press Num Lock, Scroll Lock, or Caps Lock.

LABELS

With standard labels and Word or a specialized program, you can print labels for mailing, CDs, or videotapes.

Add an impressive touch to a business letter with a printed address label. Once you've created

your letter, go to Tools ➔ Envelopes and Labels. If the address is at the top of the letter, it will appear in the Address panel on the Labels tab.

The default print option is to print a full page of the same label. It's best to keep this option. You can always save the rest for future letters. Otherwise, go to Tools ➔ Envelopes and Labels, and choose the Single label option on the Labels

tab to print one copy. Or click on the Envelopes tab to print directly to an envelope.

Create your own labels for your CDs and videotapes with specialized programs such as RKS Softwares' Visual Labels (www.rkssoftware.com/vlinfo.htm), Viaprint (www.viablesoftware.com), or one of the Avery packages (www.avery.com/software). A good selection of Word add-ons is available from (www.amfsoftware.com/word.html).

Need to mail a lot of people? Let Word print the address labels, too. Go to Tools ➔ Mail Merge. In the first section of the Mail Merge Helper, select Mailing Labels from the Create drop-down menu, and click New Main Document for your labels. Then use the Get Data option under Data source to tell Word where to find the addresses—for example, they may be in another Word document. Finally, select Merge, then Printer, and your ready-made labels will print out.

➩ See also **Software: Mailings.**

HOW TO: PRINT LABELS IN WORD 2000

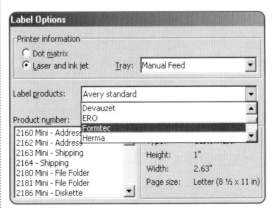

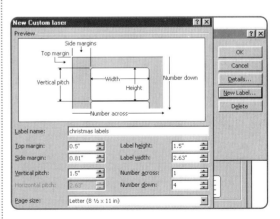

① To print a label on Avery standard labels, go to Tools ➔ Envelopes and Labels, and click on the Labels tab. Type the information for your label in the Address panel. Then, in the section below, choose Full page of the same label or Single label, and click on Print.

② If you're using a different type of label, click the Options button and select the make of label in the Label products drop-down menu. Scroll through the codes in the Product number box, select yours, and click OK. If it isn't listed, click on the New Label button.

③ You can create a label sheet to any specification. Give your label a name, then fill in its details, following the diagram above. Include the page size and click OK. You can now select your custom label in the Product number box in the Label Options dialog box.

LAYERS

Learn how to access and use layers to build up an image in Paint Shop Pro.

A layer is an individual "sheet" of an image that contains part, or all, of the finished artwork. In a layered picture, the "sheets" are stacked one on top of the other. This lets you keep the constituent parts of your image separate, so that you can add and delete layers, alter their order, and edit each one in a variety of ways—without affecting the others. Until you merge the layers, each layer can be treated as a distinct entity. To make changes to a layer, you need first to select it in the Layer Palette.

Layers are ideal for building up an image, since they let you fine tune each component until the overall composition looks just the way you want it to. Layers offer rapid access to each constituent part and give you the opportunity to reposition, overlap, and delete relevant parts of the picture without interfering with the rest.

To show or hide the Layer Palette, open your image in Paint Shop Pro, go to View → Toolbars and select the Layer Palette option. In exactly the same way as an artist's mixing palette, the Layer Palette lets you rearrange and blend the various components of your image.

Create a separate layer for each addition you make instead of putting everything on the single background provided for your picture. Add new layers by selecting Layers → New. Because each additional layer is transparent, your original work is still visible underneath. Paint Shop Pro lets you have up to 64 different layers.

To see a small thumbnail image of each layer, position your pointer over a layer in the Layer

Palette window. This allows you to select an individual component and bring it to the foreground so that you can edit it.

To move individual layers from the foreground to the background, and vice versa, click on your selection in the Layer Palette and drag it up or down the list. The item at the top of the list corresponds to the uppermost layer in the stack.

To delete a layer, select it in the Layer Palette and click the small the Recycle Bin button at the top of the Layer Palette. You can always create a new layer to replace it.

You can temporarily hide layers while you work on others, by clicking on the eyeglasses button beside the layer you wish to hide. Click the button again to reveal the layer once more.

Once you are happy with your layout, merge the layers into a single layer. To do this, select Layers → Merge All from the menu.

⇨ See also **Software: Drawing Programs.**

HOW TO: PASTE AN IMAGE INTO A WINDOW AS A NEW LAYER

① Open the new image, or create an image in a separate image window. Click on the window's title bar. Go to Edit → Copy to copy the picture to the clipboard. Click on the title bar of the window to which you want to copy the image so that it becomes active.

② To insert the image into the selected window, go to Edit → Paste and select the As A New Layer option from the menu. The picture will now appear in your new composition, and its corresponding layer button will be added to the Layer Palette.

LETTERHEAD

Create an impressive letterhead for your business or personal stationery.

Rather than buying costly printed stationery, produce your own using Microsoft Word. Go to View → Header and Footer and type your personalized letterhead in the Header box.

The flashing insert cursor for your text changes to a pointer below the header when you create a letterhead in the header area. To make a deeper header box for your letterhead, press the Return key a few times. The more blank lines you add, the farther down the page the body text will begin. Experiment with the spacing to find one that gives your letterhead and stationery a professional finish.

If you run a small business, include a brief description of the services you provide. The letterhead is an ideal opportunity to remind existing and potential customers of your services, but keep it short.

> **Geoffrey Samuels**
> 624 Greengage Lane
> Springfield OH 45501
>
> *Fine carpentry since 1973*

Add information at the bottom of the page. In the Header and Footer toolbar, click the Switch between Header and Footer button. Type any additional information, such as telephone, fax, and cell phone numbers, in the Footer box.

Create the right impression. Your letterhead could be the first impression a client has of you, so experiment with different fonts—and perhaps add an appropriate graphic that illustrates the service you are offering. Make sure the font is large enough to be easily readable while being recognizable as defining you or your company in a distinct way.

⇨ See also Software: Headers and Footers

LETTER WRITING

Use your PC to produce business letters with a professional touch.

Follow the Wizard. Word's Letter Wizard allows you to enter relevant information, such as the recipient's name, address, the current date, and any special mailing instructions, into text windows, which transfer the information to the letter. In Word, go to Tools ➔ Letter Wizard. The result is an attractive, properly formatted document.

Create a database of regular recipients. Select the Address Book option on the Recipient info tab of the Letter Wizard and click the New option. Type the details for each entry into the relevant text boxes.

Having decided on a style for your letter and on a page design—such as elegant, professional, or contemporary—click on OK to transfer all the information to your document. The letter is now ready to accept the main body of your text.

The Wizard can easily be configured to work in conjunction with preprinted letterhead stationery. For stationery with a heading created using Word's Header and Footer facility, just leave the Pre-printed Letterhead option on the Wizard unchecked.

HOW TO: CREATE A LETTERHEAD IMAGE

① Open your letterhead page. Go to View ➔ Header and Footer. Position your cursor in the Header, where you want the graphic to appear. Go to Insert ➔ Picture and select your graphic in the Clip Art or From File options. The graphic will appear at the insertion point.

② Click on the image that now appears and, using the mouse pointer, drag the corners of the box to resize it. The graphic will remain with the adjoining text. Justifying the image to the left of the screen will also justify the text, so your picture needs to be formatted.

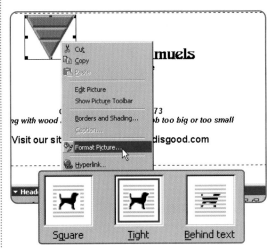

③ Right-click on the graphic to open the Format Picture dialog box. On the Layout tab, choose how to arrange your graphic around the text. Experiment with this, then click OK. The image will be repositioned leaving the text in its original position.

For a one-time-only letter to a client or friend, click the Recipient Info tab. Insert the contact's title and address details. Add a couple of extra blank lines after the address details to create a space between the heading and the body text.

LINES AND BORDERS

Lines and borders are an excellent way to decorate your documents and highlight areas of interest.

To place a border around an existing paragraph in Word, select the relevant section of text by clicking on it three times. Go to Format → Borders and Shading and choose a border.

Select box, drop shadow, or 3D effects and choose a line style under the Borders tab of the Borders and Shading window. Line color and thickness can also be customized. The preview pane displays a small representation of how your border will appear. When you are satisfied with the result, click on OK to apply it.

Activate the Borders and Shading option instantly in Word by pressing Alt+O and then B.

Add decorative lines of separation to your document by clicking on the Horizontal Line button in the Borders and Shading dialog box. This calls up a selection of clip art decorations that you can use to break up passages or simply to enhance your text.

To frame your entire page with a border, go to Format → Borders and Shading and select the Page Border tab. All the same options are available, but the border will now encompass the page. To see the border you must view your document in Print Layout or Print Preview.

Apply full-page borders to the whole document, the first page only, or every page other than the first from the Apply To drop-down menu.

You can set the distance separating your border from your text. Click on the Options button at the bottom right of the dialog box. Then, increase or decrease the numeric point values. The four-way feature allows you to make the border equidistant all around your text or to position it closer or further away at any of the top, bottom, left, or right boundaries. Check the preview of the result at the bottom of the dialog box before clicking OK.

Instead of using straightforward lines to border your page, there are some more artistic alternatives available—these are ideal for a special occasion or party invitation. They can be found in the Art drop-down menu and offer more advanced line alternatives as well as colored symbols and festive motifs. The size of these symbols can be decreased or increased under Width to suit your personal preference.

HOW TO: CREATE AN OUTLINE NUMBERED LIST

① If your list includes subcategories, Word can also number and indent these for you. Go to Format → Bullets and Numbering, click on the Outline Numbered tab, and select a style. If you wish to restyle any of the subcategories in the list, click on the Customize button.

② Each subcategory has its own number style and indent position, which you can adjust. Select a Level in the top left of the dialog box to display its description. Make any style and formatting changes you want. You can define up to nine subcategories in this way.

③ When you've finished customizing your subcategories, return to your document. You can change the level of any paragraph of text by clicking on the Increase Indent or Decrease Indent toolbar button. The numbering adjusts automatically.

LINE SPACING

Change the spacing between lines of text to make reading easier.

Access line spacing options easily from the Format menu in Word. Go to Format ➔ Paragraph to open the Paragraph dialog box. Click the Indents and Spacing tab to give you several line spacing options to choose from.

Save time with a keyboard shortcut. To quickly open the Paragraph dialog box in Word, simply press Alt+O and then P.

Need double spacing for the whole document? You'll find it easier to compose your document using single-spaced text, then change the line spacing on completion. Press Ctrl+A to select all your text and then choose the format option you want from the available alternatives.

No need to highlight a complete paragraph in order to alter the line spacing for it. Simply position your flashing insert cursor anywhere within the paragraph and change the line settings with the Paragraph dialog box. This will adjust the space settings for that paragraph only and will not affect the rest of your document.

LISTS

Microsoft Word can detect when you're creating a list and continues adding list entries.

To begin your list, type the figure 1, i) or an upper or lower case A, followed by a period, dash, or parenthesis. Now hit the Space bar and type the text for your first entry. Press the Return key and Word will create the next sequence in your list for you. Type the text for your second entry, hit Return again, and the sequence continues to form a list. Entries will be automatically indented from the left margin.

Cancel the list process by two methods. After your last entry, hit the Return key twice to create a normal paragraph, returning your insertion point to the original left margin. In indented lists, you can press the Return key once, followed by the Backspace key to go back one indent level.

Convert existing list entries or paragraphs into a numbered list. Highlight the required

passages, then go to Format ➔ Bullets and Numbering and select the Numbered tab to display a choice of seven number and letter styles.

Create a standard numbered list by selecting the required passages, then clicking the Numbering button on the Formatting toolbar. To change the list to a different format, you must go to Format ➔ Bullets and Numbering.

You can choose your own font, size, color, and a range of other numbering formats. Go to Format ➔ Bullets and Numbering, choose a style on the Numbered tab, then click on the Customize button. You can also format the list numbers to left, right, or center justification within the tab stop region and set the alignment and indent distance.

Start a list at any number or letter you choose. Click the Customize button on the Numbered tab (see above) and type your starting number or letter in the Start at box.

For lists that don't need to be numbered, use bullet points. Click the Bullets button on the Formatting toolbar to create your bulleted lists.

Each bullet point can also be customized in various ways. Go to Format ➔ Bullets and Numbering and choose from the bullet options displayed. Alternatively, click the Picture button to reveal a gallery of Clip art images. Or select the Customize button and choose any font symbols, such as Wingdings, instead.

➯ See also **Software: Word**

LINE SPACE LEXICON
Decipher all those space settings to read between the lines.

Single spacing Sets the space from the largest font used in a line. Ideal where there is equal-sized type throughout a document.

1.5 Lines One and a half times that of single spacing. Thus, 12-point font set at 1.5 line space gives a spacing of about 18 points.

Double Twice the spacing of single, so a 10-point font gets a line spacing of approximately 20 points.

At Least Displays the minimum line spacing that Word can adjust, so as to handle larger font sizes.

Multiple Increases or decreases the line spacing by a percentage amount set by you.

Exactly Fixes the line spacing at a preset distance throughout the paragraph.

MACROS

To some people, macros—a series of actions or keystrokes saved as a sequence and run automatically—may sound intimidating, but macros can be useful to anyone, even computer beginners. While macros are usually set up to do very complex jobs, they can also perform straightforward, but repetitive, tasks.

COMMON USES FOR MACROS

When do you need to make a macro? Keep a mental note of any tasks you perform regularly, and consider whether a macro might help you be more productive. Even a simple job that only requires a few keystrokes, like formatting the text in a paragraph in Word or formatting a column of a spreadsheet as a currency column, can be made quicker and easier with a macro.

In a spreadsheet, macros can be used for formatting cells or performing complex operations across different workbooks.

If you use relatively complex spreadsheet formulas a lot, but use them on different groups of cells every time, you can create a macro that has empty spaces in the formula, ready for you to insert cell ranges manually.

In a word processing program, it is possible to set up a macro to automatically type a phrase you use frequently; for example, the closing sentences of a letter, or the spelled-out name of your organization.

WHAT PROGRAMS SUPPORT MACROS?

It is not just the big office suites that support macros. Many other programs can run them, too. If you are unsure whether a favorite program runs macros, check its help files for this information.

When searching for macros in your software's help file, be aware that the software may not actually refer to "macros" as such. Some other terms you can try looking for information on are "scripts" or even "automated procedures" to see if macros are supported.

You can also get specialized macro programs that run macros under Windows, rather than working directly in individual programs.

Under Windows, take a look at the Task Scheduler—a Windows program that runs maintenance macros. To do this, go to Programs → Accessories → System Tools and select Scheduled Tasks. You can use the Scheduler to run programs automatically—for example, to perform regular backups or check for e-mail.

CREATING AND RUNNING MACROS

When you create a macro in a Microsoft program, every mouse and keyboard action you perform is recorded. This information is then stored in a special form known as Visual Basic. In order to view Visual Basic in Word, go to Tools → Macro → Macros. Then select the macro and press Edit.

Test a macro first on a copy of a document before you apply it to your real document. This way, you avoid altering vital data if the macro does not perform correctly. To duplicate a document, select the file name and go to Edit → Copy, then to Edit → Paste.

Add a macro to a toolbar to make the macro easy to run. In Word 2000, click on the down arrow at the far right of the toolbar and select Add or Remove Buttons. Click on Customize and select the Commands tab. Scroll through the Categories and click on Macros. Choose the macro you want from the list and drag it to the toolbar.

FINDING READY-MADE MACROS

You can share macros with friends and other people on the Internet. Look at popular shareware websites, such as Jumbo (www.jumbo.com), ZDNet (www.zdnet.com/downloads), and CNET (www.cnet.com), and search for "macros" to find out more about doing this.

Microsoft publishes a free collection of macros for Word 2000. You can download them from their website (www.microsoft.com) or from CNET (www.cnet.com).

Both Corel (www.corel.com) and Lotus (www.lotus.com) provide online help about using macros with their office suites. Search for macros at their sites for more information.

MACRO SECURITY

Many computer viruses are actually macros that are attached to Word or Excel documents. They run automatically on your computer, without you knowing it, when you open an infected document or disk. If you send a document with a macro virus to another user over the Internet or pass it on to them on a disk, they will become infected, too.

Although most macro viruses won't cause too much mayhem, a few are highly damaging. Protect yourself with good antivirus software.

Make sure you update the software frequently and check the manufacturer's website for news on the latest viruses and alerts.

Besides running virus-protection software, you can avoid passing a macro virus on to someone else by sending document files as .rtf or .txt files—this way, a macro virus can't be attached.

You can set different security levels in Microsoft applications to help protect against a macro virus. In Word, Excel, and PowerPoint 2000, go to Tools → Macro → Security, then select a security level. If you choose High security, the macros must have a digital identification stamp, indicating they have not been altered. Microsoft Office can then check and disable macros automatically. Medium security setting prompts you to enable or disable macros each time you open a document that contains them. Low security does not check macros at all.

If you want set virus protection in Word 97 or Excel 97, go to Tools → Options. Click on the General tab and make sure Macro Virus Protection is checked.

Security software patches for macro-supporting applications can also be downloaded from the Internet. Check your software supplier's website regularly for updates.

Take precautions! Macros are now the most popular form for virus transmission, designed with programs, such as Microsoft Word and Excel in mind. But you can protect your programs by not opening documents from unknown sources. Keep your browser current—Netscape (www.netscape. com) and Microsoft, (www.microsoft.com) publish free updates regularly.

→ See also **Windows: Viruses; Software: Menus and Toolbars.**

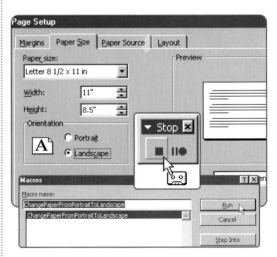

 HOW TO: RECORD AND RUN A MACRO IN WORD

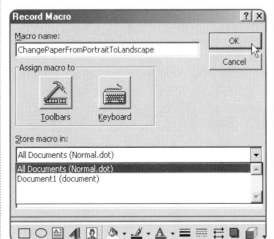

(1) In Word, position the cursor at the top of the document, and go to Tools → Macro → Record New Macro. Give the macro a name. The name can contain up to 80 characters, but spaces and nonalphanumeric symbols are not allowed.

(2) Decide where to store the macro. Select Normal.dot to make the macro accessible to all documents. Choose the current template if you are using a template. Or select your current document if the macro is document-specific. Click OK.

(3) To record the macro, run through the series of actions you want performed. When you have finished, click the square button on the Stop Recording toolbar. To run the macro, go to Tools → Macro → Macros, select your macro, and click Run.

MAILINGS

Using Word's Mail Merge and an address database can speed up mailing for newsletters, business letters, or even Christmas cards.

If you already have an address database, use it for a Word mail merge. There is no need to retype the information into a Word table. You can use an existing Microsoft Word document, Excel spreadsheet, Access database, or other list.

To merge your main document directly with an electronic address book, created with Microsoft Outlook or another program, go to Data source in Mail Merge Helper. Click Get Data and select Use Address Book. Select the address book and click OK.

Customize your mailing so that, for example, only people in a particular city will see news about a special event. First click on the location in the main document where you want the special text to appear. Click the Insert Word Field button on the Merge toolbar and select If… Then…Else. Select City under Field name and Equal to under Comparison. Type the city name into the Compare to box. Now type the special text you want to appear into the Insert this text box, including a Return if you want the text to appear as a separate paragraph. Then type the text to be seen by people not in your chosen city into the Otherwise insert this text

box. Leave that box blank if you don't want them to see any extra text at that point in the letter. Click OK.

To preview merged documents, click anywhere in the main document and click View Merged Data (the ABC button) on the Mail Merge toolbar. Word displays information from the first data record in place of the merge fields. To see information from other data records, click the arrow buttons on the Mail Merge toolbar, or type a record number in the Go to Record box and press Enter.

You do not need to send your mailing directly to the printer after merging. After clicking Merge in the Mail Merge Helper, select New Document in the Merge to box, then click Merge. The information will be transferred to a new Word document, with each letter on a separate page. Name and save the new document. You can then edit the pages on-screen or print some pages out. Click Edit in the Mail Merge Helper to return to the main document or data source to edit them. When you are happy with the results, print the mailing.

Look out for spacing errors when checking merged documents. These errors are easy to make when two fields, such as First name and Last name, are next to each other. Print out a page or two, since mistakes are often easier to spot on the printed page than they are on-screen. To edit the pages, click Edit under Main document in the Mail Merge Helper.

You can restore your mail-merge document to a normal Word document. After you have finished your mailing, go to Tools → Mail Merge and select Document Type. Click Restore to Normal Word Document. The Merge toolbar will disappear

CREATING A DATABASE IN MAIL MERGE
Mail-merged documents can be sent by e-mail or fax. Here's how.

1. In Mail Merge Helper, click Create Data Source to start a new address database.

2. Look through the field names and remove any you don't want to use by selecting them and clicking Remove Field Name.

3. If desired, create your own data fields by typing a name into the Field name box and pressing the Add Field Name button.

4. Click OK. A Save As dialog box will open. Name and save your data file.

5. You'll now be prompted to fill in the fields on your data file. Click Edit Data Source.

6. Fill in the fields for each record, clicking the Add New button icon along the bottom to add each new entry.

7. Click OK when you have finished.

and the document will no longer be connected to the data source that you originally selected.

⇨ See also **Software: Databases** and **Fields**.

MARGINS

How to adjust margins in your Word document for a variety of effects.

To adjust margins in a Word document, go to View → Print Layout. Rest the mouse pointer on a margin boundary on the horizontal or vertical rulers. When the pointer changes to a double-headed arrow, drag the boundary to where you want it to go.

To specify exact margin measurements, hold down the Alt key while dragging the margin boundary. The ruler displays the measurements while you drag. Alternatively, you can type in the measurements. To do this, go to File ➜ Page Setup and select Margins. Tab through the boxes, typing in the margin sizes you want, or click the arrows by each box to increase or decrease the margin widths by increments of 0.1 inch.

To change the margins for part of a document, first select the text you want to set off, then go to File ➜ Page Setup, click Margins, and set your desired margin widths. Choose Selected text in the Apply to box. Click OK. The new margin settings are applied to your selection.

Word inserts a section break before and after text that has been set-off by new margins. If you switch back to Normal view, you will see this as a double dotted line containing the words Section break. To make further changes to the margins, click anywhere in the section. If you have several sections in a document, you can highlight them by clicking and dragging and make changes to all of them at one time.

When the margins in a section have been changed, the section may stand alone on a separate page. To change it back to normal continuous text, click in the section, go to File ➜ Page Setup and click the Layout tab. Select Continuous in the Section start box. rather than New Page.

To change the margin settings permanently, go to File ➜ Page Setup, click the Margins tab, and enter the settings you want. Click Default. From then on, each new document you create will automatically use these new margin settings unless you change them for that document.

MEMORY

Here are some tips to help you decide how much RAM you need to run all your programs properly.

You can tell you need more memory when your programs run slowly. Often this happens when you have several programs open. When your PC has run out of RAM, it uses virtual memory, which means it uses some of the free space on your hard drive to simulate extra RAM.

You can increase or decrease the amount of space Windows uses for virtual memory, but the simplest approach is to let Windows decide. Right-click the My Computer icon and select Properties. Select the Performance tab and click the Virtual Memory button. Make sure the Let Windows manage my virtual memory settings entry is selected. Windows then adjusts the amount of disk space used for virtual memory based on the amount of RAM you are using at the time. To set the values yourself (although this is not recommended), click Let me specify my own virtual memory settings and enter them (in Kb) under Minimum and Maximum.

 HOW TO: MAIL MERGE IN WORD

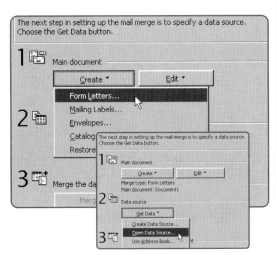

① To send a form letter to multiple recipients, go to Tools ➜ Mail Merge. Under Main document, click Create, select Form Letters, and click Active Window. Click Get Data in the Mail Merge Helper, click Open Data Source, and locate your data file.

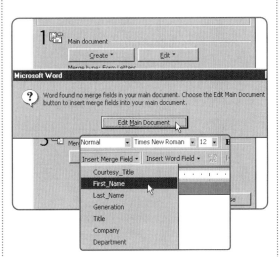

② Now you must insert merge fields into the main document. Click on Edit Main Document. Position the cursor where you want a field to be inserted, then choose the appropriate entry under the Insert Merge Field button.

③ Continue until all the merge fields are entered. Name and save the document. Click the Mail Merge Helper button and then click on Merge. Make sure New Document is selected under Merge to and click Merge.

Having a hard drive that is almost full can cause problems, so periodically have a house cleaning. Empty your Recycle Bin and delete unnecessary programs and files. Delete any unwanted temporary files and activate Disk Cleanup (see page 30).

When your memory resources are limited, make sure you close programs that are not in use. Open programs take up memory even if you are not using them. Occasionally, closing a program doesn't free the RAM it was using. If your PC is still slow, save any open documents and restart it to free the space.

To find out how much RAM is installed in your PC, right-click the My Computer icon on your Desktop and select Properties. Click the General tab. Information about your PC appears in a dialog box, including the amount of RAM.

Every PC has a maximum amount of RAM that it can contain. Older models can be upgraded and continue their active lives for years, but at some point you may reach the maximum amount of RAM that can be installed. There is nothing you can do then, except buy a new PC. Newer models have the capacity for huge RAM upgrades, so you will only be limited by your budget. Memory can be expensive, but it is a false economy to buy a tiny RAM upgrade, because you may soon find you need more.

Whenever you upgrade a program or buy a new one, the program will inevitably require more RAM to operate than previous versions. Check on the box or ask your PC dealer for the recommended minimum amount of RAM needed to run the program. Many games, graphics, movie, and 3D programs require huge amounts of RAM. If such a program recommends, for example, a minimum of 32Mb of RAM, you will find that it runs faster and smoother with even more—perhaps as much as 64Mb or even 128Mb.

⇨ See also **Windows: Hard Disk Space** and **Hard Drive.**

Menus provide easy access to all of the the features of a software package, such as Word or Excel.

Menus are usually organized using a standardized system, which makes it easy for you to learn new applications quickly. For example, the far left menu in most applications is called File, and under it you find options to open new files, to save your work, and to print. The next menu is called Edit, and provides cut and paste options. Help is usually found as the far right menu item.

Although you can use the mouse to make menu selections, many menus also have keyboard shortcuts. One letter of each menu option is underlined. Press the Alt key and that letter to access that menu item. Or you can use the keyboard arrow keys to move through the options, pressing Enter when the one you want is highlighted.

HOW TO: INSTALL MORE RAM

① Unplug your PC and disconnect your monitor and peripherals. Open up your PC by unscrewing the holding screws (usually at the back) and sliding off the outer case.

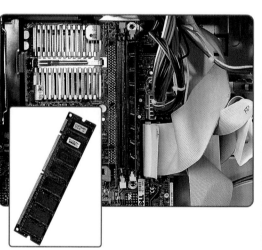

② Locate the spare RAM socket inside your PC, near the white PCI and green AGP slots. One RAM socket will already be occupied with the PC's existing RAM card, looking similar to the one you're installing. The spare RAM slot should be located next to that.

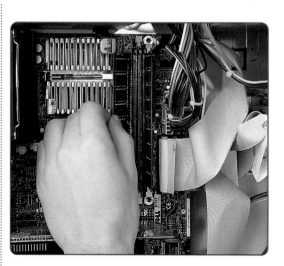

③ Holding the new RAM module by the edges, carefully insert it into the slot. The module will only go in one way, indicated by a notch at one end, which corresponds with a bump in the slot. Don't force it in—it should slot in gently.

By default, all Office 2000 programs show only the menu items that you use most frequently. Pass the pointer over the downward arrow at the bottom of a menu and more commands appear. If you would rather see all the options all the time, go to Tools → Customize and select Options. Now uncheck Menus show recently used commands first and click Close.

A lot of software also offers a shortcut menu with fast access to frequently used features that you can access by clicking the right mouse button. Its options vary, depending on context, and it is sometimes called a Context menu.

MERGE

Merging is a system used to combine the contents of one file and another to create a completely new file.

Use Mail Merge in Word to create identical copies of a single letter for multiple recipients. Mail Merge can be a great time-saver, and if you are involved in a club or charity, you can easily create individually addressed letters to all the members without having to type each letter over again or entering each address every time you want to do a mailing.

When you run Mail Merge, the software looks at your data source and, one record at a time, grabs the information it needs and inserts it into a copy of the main document. The process is automatic, so you can set the production of letters or other documents to run while you work on another job.

To get help for setting up a data source, open Word Help and type Merge into the search box. Choose Create a new Word data source from the list of topics.

See also Software: Databases and Mailings; Internet: Outlook Express.

MONEY

Using software, such as Microsoft Money, is a convenient way to organize financial information.

Every time you run Money, you will start at the Money home page. This is an information center displaying vital information about the state of your finances. Set it up to show your main accounts, upcoming bills, provide shortcut links to your most frequent tasks, and even show a graph of the day.

To get the most out of Money, you need to tell the program everything about your financial situation. That means gathering information about your finances and entering it into the software. This can take time, but once it's done, you will have a single centralized record.

Money can help you with short- or long-term budgeting. If you want to keep track of day-to-day spending, Microsoft Money can be used to balance your checkbook on a daily basis. If you prefer to keep control of the bigger picture, use it to manage investments, loans, savings, and retirement plans.

In the black, or the red? Money can analyze how you spend and produce reports based on this information, enabling you to identify areas where savings could be made or where investment opportunities may lie.

 HOW TO: CUSTOMIZE MENUS IN WORD

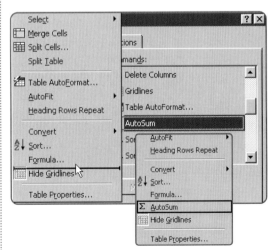

① Adding menu commands in Word 2000 is easy. Simply go to Tools → Customize and choose the Commands tab in the Customize dialog box. Now select a category, and scroll through the Commands list that appears until you find the item you want to add.

② Drag the command to the menu that you want it to go onto. The menu should drop down. Move the cursor to the command's new position, and then release the mouse button. Close the Customize window.

MP3 PLAYERS

Find out how to use these popular multimedia programs.

Windows Me includes an MP3 player called the Windows Media Player. Double-click on its Desktop icon and use the File menu's Open command to select and play your MP3 files. It comes with some great 3D visual effects that move in time with the music.

To "test-drive" an MP3 player, download one for free from Download.com (www.download .com). Click the MP3 & Audio link, then click Players. There are hundreds of MP3 and CD players to choose from, and the page displays the player's name, a brief summary, and the file size. Browse through the list, and click on one to go to its download page. There you'll find a full description and technical specifications. For more information, read the reviews and user comments. Check the links under Related Resources on the right side of the page, and then click Download Now.

Go to the CNET Music Center (http://music. cnet.com) and click Play Music to get all the facts on MP3 players, including reviews and user comments. You can also learn about streaming audio, MiniDiscs, and even how to connect your PC to your home stereo!

"Skins" are add-on software that change the look of an MP3 player. To view and download some great-looking skins for your Winamp player, go to the Winamp site (www.winamp .com) and click Skins & Plug-ins, or check out the other sites listed in the box at right.

Like most MP3 players, Winamp uses the standard buttons, such as Play, Pause, and so on found on all CD players. But in addition, it has features like Shuffle, Playlist, and a graphic equalizer. For an interactive visual guide to Winamp's control panel, go to the Winamp site (www.winamp.com). Click Get Winamp Now and select the walk-through. For a graphic that shows the controls, click the Winamp main window; then select any button to see a description of what it does in the window below.

➪ See also **Internet: MP3; Hardware: MP3 Players.**

NEWSLETTERS

Create interesting and attractive bulletins for your community, club, or church group using just Word.

To lay out a story in columns in Word, go to View ➔ Print Layout. Then select all the text to be formatted. Click the Columns button on the Standard toolbar, then click on the number of columns you want.

To adjust column widths and spacing, drag the column markers on the horizontal ruler. Exact column widths and spacing can be specified by going to Format ➔ Columns and entering your measurements in the Widths and Spacing boxes.

To create a heading that spans the columns like a newspaper, go to View ➔ Print Layout. Then type your heading at the beginning of the first column and press the Enter key. Highlight the heading text, click the Columns button, and select 1 column.

To add visible lines between columns, switch to Print Layout view and click in the section you want to change. Go to Format ➔ Columns and check Line between. Or draw lines by using the Line button on the Drawing toolbar. To change the appearance, thickness, or color of the line, right-click it, and select Format AutoShape from the pop-up menu. Choose from the options available under the Colors and Lines tab.

"Balancing" is spreading text in linked columns evenly between them so that the text in all the columns ends at the same point on the page. If you are planning to insert a headline, story, or picture directly below the text columns, it is important to get the columns to balance. Make sure you are in Print Layout view, then click at the end of the columns to be balanced. Go to Insert ➔ Break and select Continuous to insert a

WINAMP SKINS ON THE WEB

Customize your Desktop MP3 player with some fantastic downloadable skins.

AAASkins (www.aaaskins.com)
This site carries skins for different programs. Look under the extensive Winamp Skins list for a category that interests you.

mp3.com (www.mp3.com)
Wood effect or DJ turntable? Click MP3 Software ➔ Windows ➔ Skins to browse through some creative visitor-submitted skins, each with a small screen grab.

Winamp (www.winamp.com)
There are tens of thousands of skins to choose from at Winamp. Check out the Top Ten Skins, or browse under Futuristic, Retro, Stylish, Cars, Sport, Music, or Movies!

Winamp Skins (www.winamp-skins.com)
Hundreds of skins arranged by category: themes include music, TV, movies, cartoons, celebrities, and games.

section break at that point. Text will now be balanced equally among the columns.

Download newsletter templates from the Web. Open Word, click Help, and click on Office on the Web. Your browser opens and connects to Microsoft's Office Update web page. Click USA or Canada, scroll down to Word Help Favorites, and click Template Gallery. Find Marketing and click Newsletters to see a templates list. Click the Word icon next to each template to preview. Click Edit in Word to download a template and edit it in Word.

The Newsletter Templates page has a Newsletter Wizard to help you create a template in minutes.

To get information about any new updates and additions, click Sign up to hear about new templates and enter your e-mail address.

Save a created or downloaded template file in the Templates folder so that it appears under the General tab when you click File → New. The Templates folder is usually in C:\Windows\ApplicationData\Microsoft. Create a new folder in the Templates folder, then save your template into it. Your folder name shows up as a new tab.

⇨ See also **Software: Columns of Text, Desktop Publishing, Publisher, Templates,** and **Text Boxes.**

NORTON UTILITIES

Use Norton Utilites to increase your PC's performance, solve, and prevent problems, and rescue your computer in case of meltdown.

Norton Utilities 2001 is three programs in one. It's a continual-monitoring system that finds problems. It then corrects them automatically to help prevent your PC from crashing. And it's a tool for optimizing your system's performance.

Don't install Norton Utilities if you are already having problems with your PC. Make sure your PC is healthy first. If your PC can be booted up from a CD-ROM, insert the Norton disk into your PC and start—or restart—it. Run Norton Utilities from the CD. When Norton has given your PC a clean bill of health, you can then install Norton onto the hard drive.

If your PC can't be booted from a CD, make a set of emergency startup floppy disks. Ask a friend if you can use their PC for a few minutes. Take your Norton Utilities CD-ROM and some blank floppies to the guest computer, insert your Norton CD-ROM, and click Browse the CD. Double-click the Support folder, then the Edisk folder, and double-click on Ned.exe. Follow the instructions, then go home and fix your PC.

To find and fix Windows problems, go to Start → Programs and select Norton Utilities → Norton WinDoctor. WinDoctor identifies and fixes problems with Windows' file-tracking registry, system files, and programs, checking for

---

HOW TO: USE WORD'S NEWSLETTER WIZARD

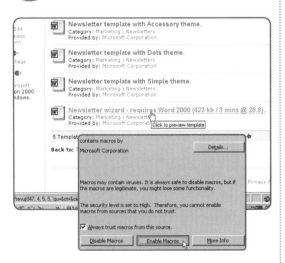

① With the Newsletter Wizard downloaded, a security warning appears about macros. Check the Always trust macros from this source box, and click Enable Macros. The Newsletter Wizard window appears. Click the Next button to begin.

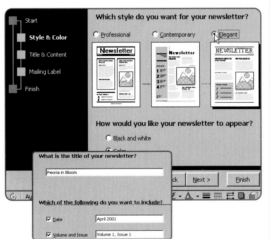

② Choose a style for your newsletter by clicking, for example, Elegant. Select Black and white or Color. Click Next. Enter a title, the date, and the volume and issue number. Click Next. Choose the mailing label option you want and click Next again.

③ Click Finish to close the Wizard and view the newsletter. You can overwrite all of the text, but read each section first for pointers on using the template correctly. You also have the Office Assistant to answer some of your queries, if necessary.

problems such as lost shortcuts, invalid registry entries, or faulty programs. Click through the WinDoctor Wizard to check your system. A list of any problems will be displayed. Click Repair All to automatically fix them. Or you can select a specific problem and click Repair; However, having to sift through all the computer-speak really isn't worth the effort, so let WinDoctor sort it instead.

Norton System Doctor is installed by default and works in the background, checking your system for problems while allowing you to continue working on your computer.

If you haven't installed Norton utilties yet and want to recover an erased file with Norton Unerase, don't install Norton— if you do, it will write it to your hard drive and run the risk of overwriting the file you want to recover. Instead, insert the Norton Utilities CD-ROM and click Launch Utilities. At the next screen click Norton Unerase. When the Norton Unerase Wizard starts, select Find any recoverable files matching

your criteria, and click Next. The Wizard will display a list of possibilities.

Speed up your system performance by running Norton Speed Disk. The disk defragments your hard drive so that all the files of one type are stored close together. Run it periodically, or whenever your system slows down. In Speed Disk, select C: drive, click Start, then Full Optimization. As the disk works through checks, it displays a colorful map of your hard drive, with colored squares for different files. Watch the squares line up as your hard drive is being defragmented. Click Legend to see what all the squares mean.

Run Disk Doctor to test your system files and

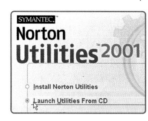

check for hard drive surface errors. To start it, select your C: drive in Norton Utilities and click Diagnose. You can configure Disk

Doctor to repair any problems automatically in the background, so you can continue using your PC. System Doctor works in conjunction with Disk Doctor to monitor your drive for problems.

⇨ See also **Software: Help Files** and **Troubleshooting.**

HOW TO: CHECK USING NORTON SYSTEM DOCTOR

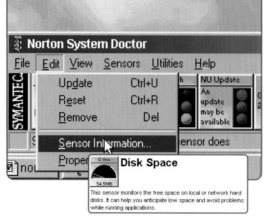

① If you see a red light on the Systems Doctor icon on the Windows Taskbar, click the icon to open the System Doctor. Check the Disk health sensor. If you see a green light, there are no serious errors with your hard drive (C:).

② To discover the problem, go to Edit → Sensor Information. The Disk Space window shows the Disk Space sensor registering an alarm. Click Show Current Alarm. A Caution box appears saying Disk space on drive C: is low. Click on Click here for details.

③ The next window explains the problem and how you can fix it. The trigger setting—the point at which System Doctor activates the low disk space alarm—can also be changed. The default setting is 10 percent of disk space free.

NOTEPAD

Use this accessory program to jot down notes or copy pieces of text.

Notepad is a simple text editor that opens and saves files in text-only format. You can't change fonts or apply any formats. To run Notepad, go to Start → Programs → Accessories → Notepad.

Notepad does have some limited tools for text editing. To find specific characters or words, click at the beginning of the text, then click Search and Find. Type the text you want to find in Find what, then click Find Next. You can also use the F3 key as a shortcut for Find Next.

Some keyboard shortcuts can be used in Notepad. You can use the standard keyboard shortcuts of Ctrl+X, Ctrl+C, and Ctrl+V for Cut, Copy, and Paste respectively. However, the Ctrl+A keyboard shortcut, used to select all text, can't be used. Instead, go to Edit → Select All.

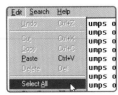

To wrap text in Notepad, go to Edit → Word Wrap. All text will become visible, but it won't affect how the text appears when you print it.

Notepad only works with files smaller than 64Kb. To work with larger files, try using WordPad instead. It is also a text editor, but documents can be formatted with font and paragraph styles.

⇨ See also **Software: WordPad.**

NUMBER FORMATS

Learn to adjust decimal places, currency, dates, and other number formats in Excel.

When you are entering figures into an Excel spreadsheet, amounts such as 3.45 display correctly, but a figure such as 3.40 will display as 3.4, which can cause confusion if it refers to a currency.

To format cells to display two decimal places, select the spreadsheet cells, go to Format → Cells, and click the Number tab. Select Number in the Category list and make sure that a 2 appears in the Decimal places box. If you want to use a comma as a marker for thousands ($1,000), check the Use 1000 separator box; otherwise, leave it unchecked.

To display the dollar sign, select the cells to format, go to Format → Cells, and select the Number tab. Click Currency. In the Symbol window, select English (United States).

Special formatting can be applied to a single cell. For example, you might only want the total—out of a list—to have a dollar sign. To do this, just select the cell containing the total figure, then right-click on it. From the pop-up menu, select Format Cells → Currency. Click the arrow next to the Symbol box and select $ English (United States).

To arrange a column of figures so the decimal points all line up, first select the column by

clicking on the letter at the column head. Then go to Format → Cells, click on the Number tab, and select Accounting in the list of categories. You can add dollar signs (which will also be lined up) by selecting them in the Symbol window.

Include phone numbers and zip codes in your cells. To format a column for phone numbers, select the column and go to Format → Cells. Click on Special and Phone Number. Now you can enter a 10-digit number with area code as a continuous stream of numbers. When you click away from the cell, you'll see it change into a correctly formatted phone number.

Apply customized number formats by typing in a formula. To display "Surplus" next to positive values and "Deficit" next to negative values, for example, select the cells to be formatted, go to Format → Cells, and click Custom. In the Type window, carefully type in $0.00 "Surplus"; $-0.00 "Deficit". Include a space after $0.00. Spaces typed in the formula will show up as spaces on the spreadsheet, as will such characters as $, +, -, =, /, !, and &. In the Type box, several common formats for custom numbers are shown. Experiment with some of them to see what they do.

Need to hide some confidential figures? There may be times when you want to hide your formatted figures away from prying eyes Highlight the formatted cells that you wish to hide, then go to Format → Cells and click on the Number tab. When the Category list appears, click Custom. Select the existing numbers and press Backspace. Finally, type three semicolons (;;;) in the Type box. The values in your cells will now be hidden.To unhide your figures again, highlight them and simply click on Number in the Category list instead of Custom. The figures will reappear.

⇨ See also **Software: Cell, Columns in Spreadsheets, Excel,** and **Formatting.**

OFFICE

Microsoft Office is a complete software suite, designed to fulfill all your needs right out of the box.

An office suite is a collection of programs that, together, meets a wide range of general needs. Besides Microsoft Office, other popular office suites include Lotus SmartSuite (www.lotus.com) and Corel WordPerfect Office (www.corel.com). One great advantage of an office suite is that

it is designed so that its components integrate with each other.

The most important part of any software suite is its word processor, because it is used so frequently by so many. In the case of Office, this is Word. The next most used program is likely to be either Outlook, which organizes contacts, manages your diary, and sends e-mail, or Excel, the spreadsheet.

Microsoft Office comes in several different versions, but they all contain three core applications: Word, Outlook, and Excel. Each version caters for a specific type of user.

Working on a document and need to e-mail or fax it immediately? Microsoft Office will allow you to e-mail or fax from within any application, provided you have the correct software installed. To do this in Word or Excel, just click Send To under the File Menu and choose whether you want to send the document as an e-mail or as a fax.

Need help with a program? Or want to learn how to work faster and more efficiently? Microsoft supports Office users by providing information at its website, including detailed troubleshooting, upgrades, and new software. It also offers downloads that add new features or fix past problems. Some templates (preformatted documents) and wizards (step-by-step instructions) for use with Office programs can also be downloaded.

If even the stripped-down Standard version of Office provides more software than you need, Microsoft Works might be a more suitable alternative for you. It is a suite designed with home users in mind, and, like Office, it comes in several versions. Many PCs come with Works already installed.

⇨ See also **Software: Access, Excel, PowerPoint, Publisher, Word,** and **Works 6.0; Internet: Outlook Express.**

VERSIONS OF OFFICE 2000
Choose the best suite for your needs from the following packages.

Office 2000 Standard
Geared for the home-based computer user, this basic version contains Word, Excel, Outlook, and PowerPoint.

Office 2000 Small Business
The Small Business Edition adds Publisher for desktop publishing and a set of business tools to the suite, but removes PowerPoint. It contains Word, Excel, Outlook, Publisher, and Small Business Tools.

Office 2000 Professional
This version adds Access and brings PowerPoint back into the business tools. If you need to organize lots of information, or work regularly with outside clients, this is the best choice. This suite includes Word, Excel, Outlook, Publisher, Small Business Tools, Access, and PowerPoint.

Office 2000 Premium
Premium adds graphics and web design software to the Professional suite. If you need to produce high-quality printed matter, in addition to good websites, then this version is the one to choose. It includes Word, Excel, Outlook, Publisher, Small Business Tools, Access, PowerPoint, FrontPage, and PhotoDraw.

ORDER

This Word function enables you to change the way objects—photos, text, and shapes—are stacked.

Microsoft Word, like other desktop publishing tools, such as CorelDRAW and Microsoft Publisher, allows you to use graphics and text on the same page. Although Word is not a sophisticated desktop publishing tool, its Order options enable you to layer text, shapes, and graphics to produce basic leaflets, banners, and bulletins, create shadow effects, position text inside a graphics box, and layer multiple images.

Setting the order in which different graphics appear on the page allows you to achieve interesting effects. For example, part of one graphic can be hidden behind another.

To access Order, go to Draw on the Drawing toolbar and select Order. If the Drawing toolbar is not open, go to View → Toolbars and select it from the toolbar options. The pop-up menu gives you possible options for layering images.

Use Send to Back to place a selected item behind all other items and Send to Front to bring an item to the top. The Send Forward and Send Backward buttons allow you to place items in different layers within a complex multilayered design. Use Send Behind Text to place graphic images behind words.

⇨ See also **Software: Desktop Publishing, Drawing Programs,** and **Layers.**

OUTLINE

Use Outline in Word to organize the information in your documents and draw up first drafts.

To access Outline in a Word document, go to View → Outline. A new toolbar will appear, offering various outline features. These include

Do you have lots of headings and subheadings in your document? You can use Word's Outline feature to automatically display the different levels of heading in different fonts. Indents help make these clear on screen.

To change the default settings for your headings, go to Format → Style. Here you can click on the different headings and assign new font styles to each one. For example, choose Heading 1 in the Styles panel of the Styles dialog box. Click on the Modify button. In the pop-up menu, click on Format. From the drop-down Format menu, select Font. Change the font style, then click OK. Check the Add to template box in the Modify Style window to apply the changes to the default setting; otherwise, the changes will only apply to the open document.

Customize how headings appear by configuring a paragraph style for each level. You can even set up different styles of headings for different kinds of documents, such as for reports, business

letters, or job reviews, making creating documents for a range of purposes quick and easy.

If you are writing a meeting agenda, or want to impose a structure on a long document, number the headings to make it easier to refer backward and forward through the document. To assign numbers to an existing document, go

to Edit → Select All. Then go to Format → Bullets and Numbering. Click the Outline Numbered tab, choose the style of outline you want, and click OK.

In Outline view, a plus symbol beside a heading tells you that there is subtext—body text or lower level headings—below the heading. Double-click on the plus symbol to hide or reveal the subtext. A line appears under the heading when text has been hidden. Headings with a minus symbol have no subtext.

being able to format different headings according to their position in the outline hierarchy. You can also use such outline features to hide or display text under particular heading levels. This allows you to show some headings but not others in different document views.

HOW TO: CREATE A HEADING USING WORD'S ORDER FEATURE

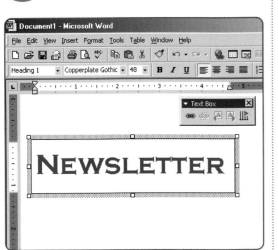

① Open a Word document, then go to Insert → Text box. Click and drag on the document to create a text box. Type in the text you want to appear as the heading. Style your heading with the font, size, alignment, and color options on the Formatting toolbar.

② With the Rectangle tool on the Drawing toolbar, create a box slightly larger than the heading box, elsewhere on the page. Color it using the Fill Color tool. Set the rectangle to appear behind your text box by right-clicking on it, then going to Order → Send to Back.

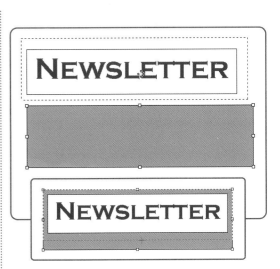

③ Click on the border of the colored box and drag and drop it in position over the text box. To enlarge or reduce the size of the box, click and drag on any of the corner or side "handles" of the box. You can adjust your text box in the same way.

If outlined headings are distracting, change the view by going to View → Normal. The heading fonts will remain in place, but the indents and the heading markers (indicated by plus signs) will no longer appear, making it easier to read the document text on screen.

⇨ See also **Software: Headings** and **Style.**

PAGE BREAKS

Learn how to specify exactly where you want a page break in Word.

When typed text exceeds the amount that fits onto a page, Microsoft Word creates an automatic page break and a new page. When viewed with View → Normal, this break appears as a single dotted line across the page.

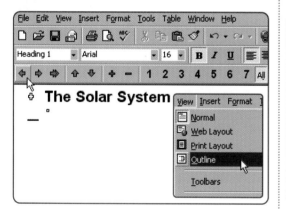

Force a new page at any designated position by manually inserting a page break. Place the cursor on the line above the text that you want to appear on a new page, then go to

Insert → Break. Select Page break and click OK. In Normal view, these breaks appear as a more solid dotted line with the words "Page Break" in the center.

If you can't see the page breaks in your document, and are in either Print Layout view or Outline view, click on the Show/Hide button (¶) on the toolbar. This will reveal all hidden text, tab characters, spacing, and paragraph marks within the document, allowing you to locate any page breaks.

To delete a manual page break, click anywhere on the line then press the Delete key on your keyboard. Be aware, however, that automatic page breaks cannot be deleted in this way. One way to remove unfortunate automatic page breaks is by adjusting your margin settings.

You do have control over where Microsoft Word creates automatic page breaks. Go to Format → Paragraph, and select the Line and Page Breaks tab. Use the options under Pagination to specify formatting for your document. To prevent the first or last line of a paragraph appearing by

itself at the top or bottom of a page, check Widow/Orphan control. To make sure that a page break is not created within a paragraph, first select the text, and then check the Keep lines together box. To lock a paragraph or chapter heading with the text that it refers to, select the text, and then check the Keep with next box.

HOW TO: ORGANIZE A WORD DOCUMENT IN OUTLINE VIEW

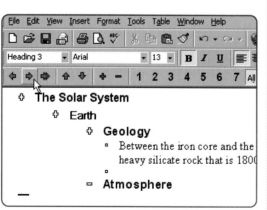

① To display the structure of your document and the Outlining toolbar, go to View → Outline. Type in your main heading, then set it in Heading 1 style by clicking the green arrow at the far left on the Outlining toolbar.

② Continue typing your headings and subheadings. Use the Demote button (right arrow) to style subheadings and the Promote button (left arrow) to make higher-level headings. Click the double-pointing right arrow to create Normal-style body text.

③ Use the Show Heading buttons on the Outline toolbar to hide everything except the headings in your document. Click on Show Heading 3 to display only headings of style 3 and above. You can reorder whole sections with the Move Up and Move Down arrows.

PAGE NUMBERS

Add page numbers to identify the sequence of multipage documents.

To number pages in Excel, go to View → Header and Footer and click on the Header/Footer tab. Select your numbering choices for the document from the header or footer boxes.

Several formatting options for page numbering are available in Word. In each case, the numbers are included within the header and footer areas.

To number each page individually in Word, go to View → Header and Footer, and click the Insert Page Number button on the pop-up toolbar. The number will appear in the header. To insert the number in the footer, first change views by clicking the Switch Between button.

To number pages automatically in Word, go to View → Header and Footer, and click the Insert Auto Text button. From the drop-down menu, select Page. Options also appear for automatically adding other details, such as names and dates.

Reposition page numbers to the left, right, or center while the header and footer areas are displayed by using the normal alignment buttons on the standard toolbar.

Make the page numbering more visible. Instead of using only numbers to identify your pages, add the words "Page #"or "Page Number" to your header or footer before inserting the numbering option.

To make a clean-looking cover page, hide the first page number. Some documents, such as ones that have a contents page, may not require a page number on the first page. If you hide the page number, it will still be counted as page 1 but the numbers will only show from page 2 on. To do this, go to Insert → Page Numbers and uncheck Show number on first page.

To display both the page number and the total number of pages in a document, as in "Page 4 of 20," go to View → Header and Footer, click the Insert Auto Text button, and choose Page X of Y.

Customize the wording of a page number and total number sequence. Type the required text into the header or footer area, click the Insert Page Number button on the Header and Footer toolbar, and then click the Insert Number of Pages button. Each numbering option appears where the cursor is positioned. You can reposition them anywhere within the header or footer.

⇨ See also **Software: Headers and Footers.**

PAINT

Here are some tips to help you use this fun accessory program included with Windows.

Microsoft Paint may seem a little basic, but it does contain several features often only found in more comprehensive paint packages. The lack of confusing icons and features make it a fun accessory that is very easy to use and, in addition, has useful applications for graphics work. To open the program, go to Start → Programs → Accessories → Paint.

The pencil is the default tool and will produce a freehand line that is 1 pixel wide. To create a differently shaped line, choose one of the other drawing tools, such as the Brush tool. A selection of brush tips you can choose from are available from a "pick box" below the main drawing toolbar.

The Line and Curve tools offer a selection of line weights, from 1 to 5 pixels in width, but only a limited number of shapes can be created using the tools. The Line tool draws a straight line between your starting and finishing point; the Curve tool allows you to create a line that

---

HOW TO: ADD PAGE NUMBERS IN WORD

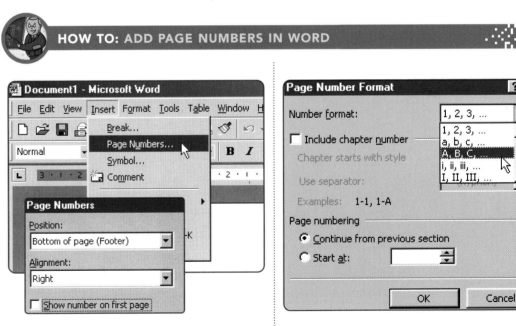

① Open your Word document and click Insert → Page Numbers. In the Position box, select Top of page (Header) or Bottom of page (Footer). In the Alignment box, choose to place the numbers on the left, right, center, inside, or outside of your pages.

② Click on the Format button on the right of the dialog box to choose a style of numbering. The option allows you to select a standard number format, alphabetical increments, or Roman numerals. After selecting, click OK twice to return to your document.

can be bent in any direction by left-clicking away from the line and then dragging.

The Rectangle, Ellipse, and Rounded Rectangle tools enable you to quickly produce images. Simply select one of the tools and click-and-drag until the desired size is reached. To use the Polygon tool, left-click at various points to create an irregular-shaped polygon connected by straight lines. Each of these tools has three available options, found in the pick box below the toolbar; they allow you to create outline shapes, overlays, or filled shapes.

Other drawing tools include: an Airbrush with three nozzle sizes; a Fill With Color tool, which

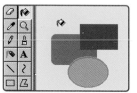

fills shapes or background with color; an Eraser to delete little mistakes; and a Color Picker to match colors exactly.

Use the colors at the bottom of the Paint window or create your own custom-made shades to fill in your design. To mix your own colors, go to Colors ➜ Edit Colors. Click Define Custom Colors. In the color palette that appears, mix the exact shade you want, and then click the Add to Custom Colors button.

You can assign a different color to your left and right mouse buttons, which is particularly useful when filling in a large design. To do this, just left-click on one color, and then right-click on another. Now both colors are available to you at a click of the mouse. This can save time when editing your image, and it works with all the shapes, lines, brushes, and fill tools.

The images that you create using Microsoft Paint can be used as Windows wallpaper for your Desktop. Create your picture, save it as you would normally, and then go to File ➜ Set As Wallpaper (Tiled) to repeat the image to fill your screen or Set As Wallpaper (Centered) for a single image on your screen.

Interesting effects can be achieved by mirror-imaging your picture. The Image ➜ Flip/Rotate

feature offers you the opportunity to flip an image vertically or horizontally, or to rotate it through 90, 180, and 270 degrees.

An image can also be stretched or skewed using the Image ➜ Stretch/Skew option. Stretching allows you to dictate the height and width of an image by adjusting either dimension in increments as small as 1 percent. By adjusting both height and width options by the same degree, you can resize the picture. Skewing, on the other hand, twists an image through either the vertical or horizontal plane in increments of 1 degree at a time.

The top two buttons on the Paint toolbar let you cut or copy a particular section of an image, either a free-form area or a rectangular portion. With these tools, you can remove or reposition a complete area or a detailed section around an irregular object.

Paint can also be used to view and edit other artwork files. Use the paste feature to import .jpg, .gif, or .bmp files into your picture, or scan in images or photographs and alter them.

➪ See also **Software: Drawing Programs.**

PASSWORD PROTECT

Here are some tips for keeping Word and Excel documents out of the sight of prying eyes.

You can password-protect a Microsoft Excel worksheet. After you have saved the file, go to Tools ➜ Protection ➜ Protect Sheet. Enter a password of your choice and click OK. You will then be prompted to re-enter the password, to make sure that you spell it correctly both times. Anyone who then tries to modify the sheet will be prompted to enter the password.

Protect specific elements of an Excel document by selecting any of the three options in the

Protect Sheet dialog box. To prevent any changes to cells in worksheets or to data in charts, check Contents. Check the Objects box to prevent changes to graphic objects and to prevent adding or editing comments. To prevent changes to the definitions of "what-if" scenarios on a worksheet, check Scenarios.

To protect an entire workbook in Excel, go to Tools ➜ Protection ➜ Protect Workbook. In the dialog box that appears, check the Structure option to prevent users from moving, deleting, hiding, or renaming worksheets, inserting new worksheets, or moving or copying worksheets to another workbook. Users will also not be able to run a macro that includes a protected operation. Check the Windows option to prevent users from moving, resizing, or closing the windows.

To prevent users viewing a worksheet at all, hide it before password-protecting it. Select the sheet by clicking the relevant Sheet tab at the bottom left of the Excel window. Go to Format ➜ Sheet ➜ Hide. The sheet then disappears. Now password-protect the sheet and save the file. When a user opens the file, they will not be able to see the hidden sheet unless they enter the correct password and then select Format ➜ Sheet ➜ Unhide.

Hide and protect certain rows or columns of a sheet. Highlight the rows or columns, go to Format ➜ Row (or Column) ➜ Hide. Password-protect the sheet and save the file. To hide and protect an entire workbook, go to Window ➜ Hide and password-protect it.

Hide and password-protect formulas to prevent them from displaying in the Formula bar. To do this, first select the range of cells containing the formulas you want to hide. Go to Format ➜ Cells and select the Protection tab. Select the Hidden option and click OK. Now go to Tools ➜ Protection ➜ Protect Sheet and make sure that the Contents box is checked.

number. If you think you might forget a password, write it down and store it in a safe place.

If you want to protect your work so that you can't accidentally change it, but you are not worried about security, then do not enter a password. Users will be able to unprotect the sheet or workbook without entering a password.

Protect a Word or Excel document with a password when you save it. With your document open, go to Tools ➜ Options and click on the Save tab. In the File sharing options section of the dialog box, type a password in the Password to open box, and click OK. Type your password again in the Confirm Password dialog box, click OK, and then click Save. If you type a password into the Password to modify box, users will be able to open the document but won't be able to modify it without typing the password. Go to File ➜ Save As and save your document.

➡ See also **Internet: Passwords** and **Security on the Net.**

You can protect some cells but leave others unprotected. This is useful if you are using the worksheet as a form and you want to protect cells containing labels, but leave other cells unprotected so users can fill them in. To do this, select all the cells and lock them by going to Format ➜ Cells, selecting the Protection tab, checking Locked, and clicking OK. Now unlock your chosen cells by selecting them, going to Format ➜ Cells, unchecking Locked, and clicking OK. Finally, password-protect the sheet.

To remove password protection, go to Tools ➜ Protection ➜ Unprotect Sheet (or Unprotect Workbook). You will then be prompted to enter your password. If desired, opt to unprotect a workbook but leave the current sheet protected.

For extra security, mix up a word with a number to create a unique but memorable password. This method makes it especially difficult for someone to guess the password. Your password might be "D1a2v3i4d5," which mixes up "David" and "12345." Passwords are case-sensitive, meaning that if you use a lower-case "d," the password will not be recognized. Don't use any words or numbers that might be guessable, such as your name or telephone

PHONE DIALER

Use this Windows miniprogram to dial your phone for you, wherever you are in the world.

Your phone and modem must be on the same line for the program to work. To dial a number, go to Start ➜ Program ➜ Accessories ➜ Communications ➜ Phone Dialer. Type in the number you want to call and click Dial. Add the Phone Dialer as a shortcut to your Desktop if you use it frequently. Just right-click on the Phone Dialer icon and select Send to ➜ Desktop (create shortcut).

Use the speed-dial facility to store your eight most frequently used numbers. In Phone Dialer, click one of the empty speed-dial buttons on the right. In the Program Speed Dial dialog box, type in the

name and phone number and click Save (or Save and Dial to dial the number immediately). The name will appear on the speed-dial button you selected. To dial that number at any time in future, simply click on the button. To edit or delete any of your stored speed-dial numbers, go to Edit ➜ Speed Dial and change the details.

Tired of dialing long access and PIN numbers? Program the Phone Dialer to use a calling card. Go to Tools ➜ Dialing Properties. Check the box beside For long distance calls, use this calling

card. Select your card from the drop-down menu. To enter or change your chosen card, click the Calling Card button, select New, and enter the card information.

If you need to dial a number to reach an outside line, you can program the number into Phone Dialer. This way you don't have to enter it every time you make a call. Go to Tools ➜ Dialing Properties and fill in the access numbers for local and long distance calls under the When dialing from here section. Click OK.

To select a phone line when you have multiple lines, go to Tools ➜ Connect Using. In Address, insert the phone number to use when dialing out. For more options, select Line Properties.

To simplify phone-calling when using a laptop and making calls from a number of different locations, enter all the relevant information in the Dialing Properties dialog box. Set up a new location for the each place you use your laptop by going to Tools ➜ Dialing Properties, and clicking on the New button. If you are abroad, scroll through the country/region list to select the country. Fill in the necessary information relating to the way calls are dialed there, and then click OK. Locations are given the names "New Location 1," "New Location 2," and so on. These names can be replaced with more meaningful names of your choice by typing into the I am dialing from box.

PHOTO EDITING

Photographers are losing their monopoly over the world of beautifully retouched photos and special effects. With only a PC and some photo-editing software, you can now achieve effects that used to be limited to professionals working in darkrooms with specialized tools.

PHOTO REVOLUTION

The development of scanners, digital cameras, and photo CDs from film processors means you can now easily transfer all your photos to your PC. It's impossible to take a perfect picture every time, but with photo-editing software not only can you retouch and improve your photos—you can create collages and montages, convert color photos to black and white, add unusual color casts, and convert photos into watercolor prints. You can turn your favorites into calendars, postcards, greetings cards, or jigsaw puzzles. Microsoft Picture It! Photo is used here—but you can try any of the software listed in the box below, left.

GETTING STARTED

Want to display your photos at their best? Go to Start → Settings → Control Panel → Display, and click the Settings tab. Select True Color, if it's available, or High Color and click OK. Now your images will display in as many colors as your monitor is capable of displaying.

Scanning your photos? Wipe any dust off your photo before you start, then put it onto your scanner. If possible, make sure that it's lined up with one of the edges of the platen (the full scanning area on which your photo sits). Using your scanning software, click Preview and the scanner will perform a quick scan, just so that you can see exactly where the image sits on the screen. It doesn't matter if you scan your image upside-down or sideways—you can always rotate it later. Good settings for scanning photos are around 300dpi and scaled to 100 percent. Now simply click Scan, and the image will be scanned into whichever image-editing program you're using.

Keep a copy of your original scan. That way you have an original to go back to when your clever effects make grandma look a little more frightening than you'd anticipated. All you need to do is rotate the image so that it's square on the screen, and crop any extraneous areas, then save your image, and call it something like "grandma_original." Once you start making major changes to the image, save the changed image under a new name, so that you've always got the original to revert to.

Fix dust, scratches, and blemishes. Most photo-editing software comes with photo repair tools. Some will even offer to automatically fix all scratches for you, but this can have unpredictable results, so it's better to fix each one manually yourself. Zoom in on the blemish before you start working on it, then zoom back out to check the overall effect. You'll be amazed what you can achieve.

Crop in on the interesting parts of your photo and don't feel bad about throwing away large areas of the background. Try to crop your image so that the focus of attention is in the center.

Zap red-eye. One of the most instantly effective improvements you can make to a photo using your software is to remove red-eye from your pictures. Just focus in on the eyes, click on the red bits of the pupils, and tell your software to remove the red-eye. Suddenly little Emily doesn't look quite the demon she used to.

Get rid of date stamps on photos by using the Cloning tool to carefully copy nearby parts of the photo and clone them over the date stamp. Zoom in so that you're working close in on the date stamp area. Keep changing the area of the image that you're cloning from to make sure it will look correct when reproduced in the area you're cloning to. You can get rid of unsightly telephone wires or even an out-of-place tumbler the same way.

Adjust brightness and contrast to lighten dark pictures, add depth to flat pictures, and darken washed-out pictures. If your image-editing software has an automatic contrast/brightness setting, give it a try to see if it improves your image. If it doesn't, adjust the settings manually. In our photo of Carol and Dan by the sea, their faces are in shadow. We used Picture It's Touchup Painting tool to increase the brightness

and contrast of their faces slightly. Then we reduced the brightness of the white chair, to make it less distracting.

Fix old black-and-white photos. You've got a lovely old photo of your grandparents' wedding, but it's not aged well. Convert the image to grayscale to remove any unsightly color cast. If your software has an option to remove fading, select that—otherwise adjust the brightness and

contrast to improve the image. Your software should have a tool for sharpening photos—sometimes misleadingly called Unsharp mask. See how much you can sharpen the image without making it look too grainy. You should end up with a much-improved photo.

What resolution and format should you save your photo in? If you're e-mailing it or posting it onto the Web, you need to get the file down to a reasonable size—preferably below 100K—without losing too much quality. Reduce its resolution to 72dpi, and save it as a JPEG. Many photo-editing programs offer a Save as Web image option, so make the most of it.

If you're planning to print your image, then file size is not a problem—but picture quality is. Save the picture at a resolution of at least 300dpi. A good file format is the TIFF format, which uses LZW compression to reduce file size without losing quality. Image files saved for printing can take up a lot of disk space, so consider storing them using a removable storage medium like a Zip disk or writable CD-R.

Use your images on postcards, greetings cards, calendars, invitations, or business cards. Picture It! offers a wide range of predesigned templates

for your photos. On these pages, for example, a collection of photos of family and friends were

given a variety of uses. The photo of a girl on a beach became a calendar, the shot of a couple by the sea was made into a postcard, and the composite photo of the girl and the canoeists turned into a magazine cover.

⇨ See also **Internet: Website Creation; Hardware: Digital Cameras** and **Scanners.**

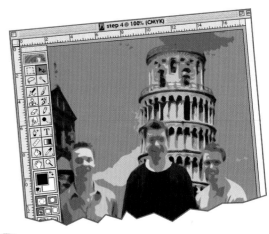

MERGE TWO PHOTOS TO MAKE A COOL MAGAZINE COVER
We're going to take an image of a girl in a pool and add to it two tiny guys in canoes—all using Microsoft Picture It! Photo. The result is above.

1. Scan both pictures and make them approximately the same size.
2. Cut out the two canoeists and their canoes. We cut them out manually with the help of the Picture It! Edgefinder tool.
3. Merge the canoeists onto the image of the girl in the pool. Make sure they're layered above the image of the girl, so that they can be seen clearly. Get the positions roughly correct and resize them.
4. Add a drop shadow to the canoeists—only a very slight one, because the sun is

directly in front. Make it reasonably transparent, so you can see the water through the shadow. This gives the canoeists some relief against the water.
5. Add ripples. To do this, copy the image, make it 80 percent transparent, then paint 100 percent transparency over the parts that you don't want to appear.
6. Open up Picture It's preformatted designs, and under Fun Stuff, you'll find magazine covers. We opened up a cover, then dragged our composite image onto it.

PIXEL EDITING

Make micro-adjustments in Microsoft Paint to leave all your images as sharp as possible.

A pixel is a single point in a graphic image—its name comes from a meld of the words Picture and Element. Every computer image is made up of millions of pixels arranged in rows and columns.

Most graphics programs on the PC can zoom in on an image, allowing you to edit small and delicate parts of a picture that other painting tools—such as the airbrush and fill tools—are too big to handle.

Microsoft Paint is usually found in the Start → Programs → Accessories menu. It has a simple toolbar that lets you open, navigate around, and alter an image in a few simple steps.

For pixel editing, the main tools are the Pencil and Magnifier on the toolbar. The Magnifier tool gives you a choice of zoom levels in a drop-down box below the toolbar itself. You can also customize the zoom in the View → Zoom menu to suit your needs.

Clean cut. Pixel editing is particularly useful when cleaning up the rough edges of an image part that has been cut out and moved. In Paint, you can use the Free-Form Select tool to outline and move an image element.

POWERPOINT

PowerPoint is a versatile program allowing you to incorporate words, sounds, images, and animations into dynamic slide shows.

Need to make a presentation? Microsoft's PowerPoint program offers you a range of

professional features and flexibility that goes far beyond the traditional slide show and overhead projector sequence.

When you first start up PowerPoint you will be given the option of how you want to create your presentation or slide show. Choosing the Design Template option will open the New Presentation window. From here, you can choose the template that is best for your purposes—these include combinations of colors, layouts, and images.

When the template appears, click on the area you want to work in, and type in the text or place the images you want to include on the slide.

When you finish one slide and want to move on to a new one, use the Insert → New Slide command. You can create as many slides as you wish, but remember, if you print them, they use a lot of color ink, which can prove expensive.

You can apply ready-made backgrounds to jazz up your slide shows and even use your own photographs or designs as a background. The quickest way to modify the design of all of your slides is by using View → Master → Slide Master. When the master slide appears, add your image or clip art, and it will appear on all the slides in your presentation.

Add special effects to your presentation by choosing Preset or Custom Animations in the Slide Show Menu. Once you have highlighted a piece of text or clicked on an image, you can choose from a range of animation effects to add movement and sound.

If you have a sound card in your PC, you can record a short voice-over narration for each slide using the Slide Show → Record Narration command. You will need a microphone (either external or internal) and speakers to be able to use this option.

HOW TO: EDIT PIXELS IN PAINT

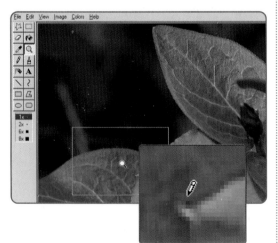

① Once you have opened the image you want to re-touch, use the Zoom tool to magnify it. The Zoom tool brings up a rectangle that you place over the area you want to enlarge. Click to see a closeup of the image and the pixels.

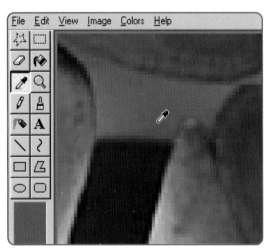

② To get a perfect color match, use the Pick Color tool. When you click on the image, the Picker will copy the tone it is placed over and switch to the Pencil tool. Then fill in the areas you want to change pixel by pixel.

Showtime! Run a slide show by going to Slide Show → View Show. This steps through your slides in the sequence you have ordered them—you can choose whether or not to automate events in your slide instead of manually clicking through them. Don't be afraid to experiment to find what suits your presentation best. Finally, when you're ready to return to editing the slides, simply press Esc.

PREFERENCES

Customize the look and functions of your Office programs to suit your working style.

In most Office programs, including Word, using the Tools → Customize command allows you to add or remove buttons and menu items. There is a huge variety of actions you can include on your toolbars, giving you one-click access to almost any Office function.

Don't go overboard—it's easy to get carried away and add too many options to your toolbars. Be careful to choose the functions you use most and need ready access to. Cluttering up your toolbars with unnecessary buttons could slow you down—you don't want to be fumbling through an overcrowded toolbar in the middle of an important presentation.

The Tools → Options command in Word lets you set the way the program reacts in certain situations. You can set up a customized dictionary to include specialized words or phrases that repeatedly show up in your

Spelling and Grammar checks. Using the View tab, you can choose which screen elements are visible—for example, highlights and hidden text.

In the Excel spreadsheet program, use Tools → Options to set preferences such as the color of chart fills and chart lines. You can also choose whether to edit data directly on your worksheet or whether pressing the Return key activates the next cell for editing.

In Outlook Express, the Tools → Option command lets you choose how your e-mail is managed. Under the General tab you can choose to be notified when new mail is received, how often the program checks for messages, and whether to connect automatically when it's checking.

Customize your Internet Explorer. You can alter how the Internet Explorer browser operates with the Tools → Internet Options command. Go to the Temporary Internet files section under the General tab to control how Windows stores temporary Internet files. Click the Colors and Fonts buttons to set different display options. Under the Connections tab choose which

HOW TO: ADD IMAGES TO A PRESENTATION

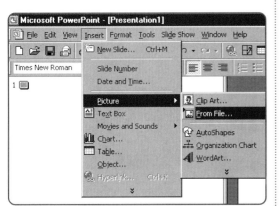

① Choose a picture you have already downloaded from the Internet or scanned in to be placed into your presentation. Go to PowerPoint's Insert menu → Picture → From File. You will then be asked to locate the picture you want.

② When you have found the image you are going to use, double-click on it. To re-size an image, click on it to select it, and then move the handles or boxes on the corners and edges in the desired direction. You can also apply animations to images.

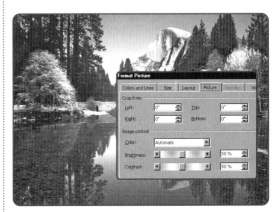

③ You can alter the contrast and brightness of the image by first selecting it and then going to Format → Picture and using the sliders on the Picture tab of the Format Picture dialog box. Click on the Preview button after each change to see the results.

Dial-Up connection Internet Explorer will dial when the program is launched.

Content Advisor → Enable. This Internet Explorer option lets you specify which websites users can visit according to content. You can also use the Security tab to set the level of safeguards your browser uses when downloading sites. This is particularly useful if you are concerned about viruses, although you should note that a high security settings can slow down your browsing.

The Advanced tab in Internet Explorer's Options is better left to the experts. Unless you really know what you're doing, tinkering with these settings can adversely affect your PC's

PRINTING
SOFTWARE SITES
Advice and software to help
improve your printer's output.

Avery
(www.avery.com/software/index.jsp)
Explore Avery's titles and download the free wizard to personalize printouts.

Fine Print
(www.fineprint.com)
The program brings increased versatility to all your requirements and is downloadable.

ScrapbookScrapbook (www.scrapbook scrapbook.com/printtips.html)
This site gives updated advice on the best papers to use and offers articles on printing.

SierraHome
(www.sierrahome.com/software/)
Visit the Publishing section for a wide range of printing software for every need.

Smart Computing
(www.smartcomputing.com)
Detailed easy-to-follow guides, including how to print envelopes and select a printer.

performance. If you stumble into a problem, don't worry—you can hit the Restore Defaults button and everything should return to normal.

The General tab in Internet Options gives you the option of setting your default home page. This is the page which is automatically loaded when you open Internet Explorer. Type the web address in the box. Or select Internet Options when you get to the page you want, then hit the Use Current button.

PRINTING
Get great results when printing your Word and Excel documents.

The speediest way to print out any Office document is to click the Print button on the Standard toolbar. The document will then print immediately, based on the settings you last specified in the Print box.

To print specific pages or ranges of pages in a Word document, go to File → Print and select the button next to Pages. Then enter the numbers of the page or pages you want to print, separated by commas.

In an Excel spreadsheet, go to File → Print Preview and select the Page Break Preview to see where the page breaks are. After that, you can simply click and drag the blue lines to set new page breaks.

Sometimes you may only want to print a small area of a spreadsheet. To do this, select the area by clicking and dragging over it. Go to File → Print and choose Selection under Print what. Now click on OK, and only the selected area appears on the page.

Print several Word documents at the same time, without even opening them. Click the Open button on the Standard toolbar, and use

the Open dialog box to navigate to and open the folder containing the documents you want to print. Highlight the documents. Select Print from the dialog box's Tools menu and all the documents will print out.

Printing a draft copy in Word. Go to Tools → Options and select the Print tab. Check the Draft output box and then print the document.

Select the best page orientation—landscape or portrait. Go to File → Page Setup, click the Paper Size tab, and choose the appropriate option under Orientation.

Gridlines can help guide the eye through columns of figures in a complicated spreadsheet. To print them in Excel, go to File → Page Setup, click the Sheet tab, and select the Gridlines box. All the data in your sheet will now print along with the fine gridlines as displayed on screen. Alternatively, apply borders from the toolbar, using the Border button and the drop-down menu from the arrow next to it.

When there is too much Excel data to fit on a single sheet, try shrinking the printed image. Go to File → Page Setup and select the Page tab. Now you can shrink the page manually by selecting the Adjust button under Scaling and entering a percentage. Or select the Fit to button, and specify how many pages wide and tall you want the sheet to print on.

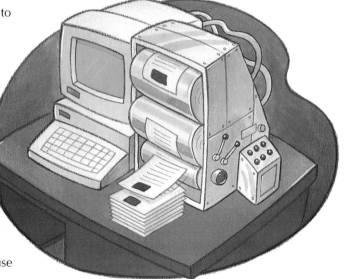

Dividing long Word documents into sections makes reviewing and printing easier. To create a new section, go to Insert → Break and highlight the kind of section break you want. To print the section, go to File → Print and, in the Page range dialog box, enter s followed by the section number, for example, s5.

Missing Headers and Footers? Get them back on your printed page by checking that your page margins are wide enough. Then go to File → Page Setup, click the Margins tab, and in the From edge section, enter a figure larger than the printer's minimum margin setting.

Row numbers and column letters can be a handy reference on a spreadsheet printout. Go to File → Page Setup and click the Sheet tab. Now select the Row and column headings box.

⇨ See also **Hardware: Printers**

PRINT PREVIEW

Use Print Preview to get perfect printouts every time.

Get an instant Print Preview in Word by clicking the Print Preview button on the toolbar.
 Or go to File → Print Preview. You can visually click and drag the margins rather than setting them in Page Setup.

Headers and Footers are invisible in Normal View, but will appear when you print the document. Switch to Print Layout view or use Print Preview to check they are there.

Use Multiple Pages in Word's Print Preview mode to see several pages at once. Click on the Multiple Pages icon on the toolbar and select the number of pages you want to see. Click the One Page icon to go back to a single page.

Netscape Navigator and Internet Explorer have Print Preview features available from the File menu. Use them to check that web pages will output correctly before hitting the Print button.

Use the Magnifier tool to zoom in on areas where graphics and text run up against each other to make adjustments before printing.

To really enlarge a page element, use the drop-down Zoom menu in Word's Print Preview. You can choose from as high as 500 percent magnification.

Page breaks. Use Print Preview to make sure they are in the right place.

Avoid printing out blank pages in Word. Click
 the Show/Hide button on the Standard toolbar. Then delete any blank lines at the end of your document.

Editing text in Word's Print Preview. Click on the text and Word will zoom in. Click the Magnifier button to change the cursor to an I-beam and then make your changes.

HOW TO: CREATE PRINTED ENVELOPES

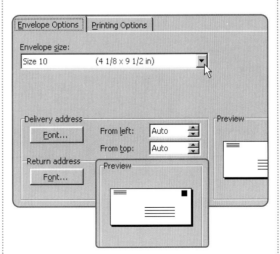

① In Word, go to Tools → Envelopes and Labels. Type the delivery address in the top box. Check the Omit box and click the Options button. Select the envelope size you want from the drop-down menu. The Preview will change as you select the options.

② To change the address's position, use the up and down arrows to alter the From left and From top settings; the address will move on the Preview as you enter new values. Now select the Printing Options tab.

③ You may have to try various options until your envelopes print properly. Make sure that Manual feed is selected in the Feed from box and click OK. Then insert an envelope in the manual feed tray of your printer and click on the Print button.

PUBLISHER

Publisher 2000 is part of the Office 2000 suite. It is a desktop publishing program that uses templates and wizards to automate the process of creating professional, colorful documents for print or posting on the Web. Many of the templates are specially designed for small businesses, community groups, and families.

Click on an option to select the type of information required. The first time you use this function, a form will pop up for you to fill in with your details. If you decide your document doesn't need any personal information at all, just click Finish. This will end the wizard.

Once you have a basic document, you can customize it to suit your needs. Click the Hide Wizard button in the bottom-left corner to see your document more clearly. To preview it as it will print, go to View ➔ Hide Boundaries and Guides. When the wizard is through, highlight the sample text and start typing your own text.

You can return to the wizard at any time to make changes. For example, to select a different scheme, click Color Scheme in the top panel and the name of the scheme below. When you select text and click the Font Color button, the pop-up dialog box displays all the colors used in your color scheme. If you want to choose a color that is not part of the scheme, click More Colors.

USING A PUBLISHER WIZARD

When you launch Publisher, the Catalog opens up, displaying the templates and wizards available. The first tab, Publications by Wizard, shows you the documents that have a wizard. The second tab, Publications by Design, groups together similar styles of documents. While the last tab, Blank Publications, is for starting a document from scratch.

To start using a wizard, click on the Publications by Wizard tab in the Publisher Catalog. Select a category, and view the previews on the right. Browse the options and double-click on the one you want. When you select options in the left window, you can preview the effect on your document on the right.

You will be prompted to enter personal information relating to your home or business.

CREATE A DOCUMENT FROM SCRATCH

To get started, go to the Publisher Catalog, click the Blank Publications tab, and select the type of document you want—a blank full page, or perhaps a postcard, web page, poster, or banner.

To structure your document and position text and images, use the Layout Guides. Go to Arrange ➔ Layout Guides, and select the number of columns and rows you want. To change the margins, enter a figure in the boxes at the top of the dialog box. To move margins or layout guides, go to View ➔ Go to Background. Hold down the Shift key, click on a guide, and drag it to its new location.

For extra help positioning your page elements, use a ruler guide—a nonprinting horizontal or vertical line. To create a guide, hold down the Shift key, click on the horizontal or vertical ruler, and drag it to the required position.

Every object in a Publisher document must be in a frame. Create a text frame by clicking the

HANDY KEYBOARD SHORTCUTS
Some hints to help you navigate your way around Publisher.

Ctrl+Shift+N	Inserts a new page.
Ctrl+Shift+Y	Shows and hides special characters.
Ctrl+Shift+O	Shows and hides boundaries and guides.
Ctrl+Shift+L	Displays the whole page.
Ctrl+M	Moves between the background and foreground of a document.
Ctrl+W	Snaps text to the guides.
Ctrl+K	Inserts a hyperlink into a web page.

Text Frame Tool button on the Objects toolbar. You can edit text in a text frame just as you would in Word. Other tools allow you to insert pictures, Clip Art, WordArt elements, lines, and shapes, including oval, rectangles, and more.

To add a picture, you need to create a picture frame. Select the Picture Frame Tool button, click where you want one corner of the picture frame to go, and drag diagonally until the frame is the right size. Now double-click in the frame, browse your hard drive for the graphic file you want to use, and click Insert. Double-click on any existing picture to replace it with another.

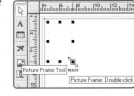

To browse through a library of design "building blocks" for your page, click Insert → Object → Design Gallery. You can add a masthead, table of contents, sidebar, or choose from boxes, borders, and other decorative elements.

ABOUT TOOLBARS

When you select a text box, the Word-style text-formatting toolbar appears below the Standard toolbar. First select the text to be modified, then click the appropriate arrows or buttons. You can opt to change the font, style, size, or color of the text, to align the text, or fill the text box with a color.

When you select a picture box, the picture-formatting toolbar appears. Click the buttons to wrap text to the frame or the picture, to select a fill color or line color, to open the Picture Frame Properties dialog box, or to rotate left and right.

CREATING A WEB PAGE

Use a web-page wizard in the Publisher Catalog as the starting point. Choose your basic layout and color scheme, replace the headline and sample text with text of your own, and then add hyperlinks, forms, or clip art.

To change a Design Gallery element you've included, click the "magic wand" icon below the frame. Use the wizard to preview and select a different design from the list.

To preview a web page as you work, go to File → Web Page Preview, then select Current page. To preview a whole site, select Website. Your page will appear in your default browser. If you've opted to view an entire site, you can check all your hyperlinks by clicking on them.

Publish your web page using the Microsoft Web Publishing Wizard. Go to Start → Programs → Internet Explorer, and select the Web Publishing Wizard. If the Wizard was installed with a previous version of Publisher, look under Start → Programs → Microsoft Web Publishing → Web Publishing Wizard. If you don't have the wizard, you can install it by reinstalling Internet Explorer 5 and choosing Custom Install.

FUNCTIONS AND FEATURES

What is it? Sometimes it's hard to tell by sight exactly what an element in your document is—whether an image is an imported graphic or a composition of objects created in Publisher, for instance. Float your mouse pointer over an object and a pop-up label tells you what the object is—a picture frame, line, rectangle, custom shape, or text frame, for example.

To zoom in on a particular element, you need to select it, click the Zoom percentage window arrow, and scroll down to Selected Objects.

You can jump pages to navigate through a multipage document, such as a newsletter. To jump to a particular page, simply click on the numbered icon of the page you want to view in the bottom left of the screen.

To wrap text around objects, right-click on a text frame and select Change Frame → Text Frame Properties. In the dialog box that appears, make sure that the Wrap text around objects box is selected, then click OK. To select

a paragraph when editing text, click three times anywhere in the paragraph concerned.

To resize an object, simply float your mouse pointer over one of the "handles" located at the corners and middle of each side of the selected object. When the pointer turns into a Resize icon, click and drag this icon to enlarge or shrink the object.

⇨ See also **Software: Desktop Publishing; Internet: Website Creation.**

THE STANDARD TOOLBAR
A few clues to help you understand the buttons on the Standard toolbar.

Bring to Front/Send to Back
Place a selected element on the top or bottom layer of your document if elements are stacked on top of each other.

Show Special Characters
Display or hide nonprinting characters, such as paragraph marks and spaces.

Zoom box
Click the arrow to select the zoom percentage you require, up to 400 per cent.

Zoom Out/Zoom In
Click the – button to view more of a document and the + button to zoom in.

QUICKEN

Take control of your finances with the complete money management program from Intuit.

Seven Up. Quicken 2001 Deluxe from Intuit (www.intuit.com) is a powerful program with features that help you organize the seven key areas of your home finances: banking, taxes, investments, planning, loans, insurance, and finally, your spending and saving.

Use the Accounts feature to keep track of all your expenses. Quicken's Accounts are great for helping you manage your bank accounts and credit cards, but they're also handy for any area where you regularly exchange funds. If you've lent a friend a lot of money, why not set up an account to help you track the repayments? You could also set up accounts for your children to keep a record of their allowances and gifts.

Get your Categories right for your needs. Quicken includes a number of preset Categories for producing reports and tracking types of expenditure and income, such as viewing and paying bills online and watching your

investments accrue. You can add and delete items from the Category & Transfer List so that the options always reflect your spending habits.

Not sure how you want to use Categories? Start by using just two or three for expenditure, such as "bills," "leisure," and "household." Over time, you'll see how the information entered against each transaction builds up a picture of where your money goes. If you find this function useful, you can easily add Categories at a later date.

Quicken lets you automate regular transactions. If you have any regular incomings and outgoings of a fixed amount—such as your monthly paycheck, loan repayments, or annual insurance policies—you can configure Quicken to enter these sums automatically. You can also set up Quicken to prompt you to confirm whether a payment has been made or received, and to remind you that payments need to be made or policies renewed.

Quicken's Reports provide statements, graphs, and tables to help you see where your money has gone. If you customize a report that you might want to use regularly, you can get

Quicken to memorize it and add it to the toolbar for instant access in the future.

Keep your receipts! Quicken is only useful if the data you enter is accurate and complete. Going on vacation? Keep your credit and bank card receipts in a safe place so you can update Quicken on your return. Shop online? Make sure you print out your order information so that you don't forget to add the transaction to Quicken next time you have an account session.

LEARN THE LINGO
Familiarize yourself with these terms first to get the most out of your Quicken program.

- **Account:** A set of common financial transactions—such as a credit card—that you want to track.
- **Category:** The group label or name you attach to a Transaction. This helps with reporting.
- **File:** A group of Quicken accounts kept together for easy management.
- **Memorize:** Quicken can remember your transactions and reports, which is handy if you need to re-enter text and parameters.
- **Online banking:** Quicken includes a powerful suite of tools to enable you to

pay bills and transfer funds over the Internet by directly linking with your bank.
- **Reconcile:** The act of comparing your bank statement with your Quicken record to confirm there are no irregularities.
- **Reports:** Quicken's own statements and analysis graphs and tables so you can see exactly where your money has gone.
- **Quicken:** A timetable that you can set up to automatically track regular outgoings, such as mortgage payments.
- **Transaction:** A movement of money into—or from—an account recorded by Quicken.

RANGES

Creating a range beforehand allows you to perform an action on a group of cells in an Excel spreadsheet quickly and easily.

Create a range by selecting an area of cells in your spreadsheet. Simply click and drag the mouse over the area you wish to select. Release the mouse and the cells remain highlighted—this is your range.

Once a range has been set, any action that you decide to select from the Format menu—and some options from the Tools and Data menu—can be carried out on all the cells in the range. This is a very quick method for standardizing all the fonts, colors, and borders for a worksheet.

A range is denoted by the two cells marking the upper left-hand and lower right-hand corners of the selected area. For example, a range covering those cells in columns B, C, and D and rows 3, 4, and 5 is identified as B3:D5 in a formula, or as 3R x 3C in the address window, denoting a range that is three rows deep by three columns wide.

To define an area of a worksheet for printing, create a range covering the area to be printed. Go to the File menu, and choose Print Area → Set Print Area. Once you've printed, you can delete the print range if you don't need it again. Go to File → Print Area → Clear Print Area.

Sort the items in a range by selecting Sort from the Data menu. The Sort dialog box lets you choose which columns to sort by and whether your list is in ascending or descending order. It also warns you if you try sorting only part of a collection of data.

Think you'll need to repeat the same range? Why not save and name it? Your named ranges

can be quickly identified and used in formulas and macros to simplify your worksheet design. See the How To box below for a step-by-step guide to naming a range.

Ranges don't have to be rectangular! If you have a number of separate blocks of cells to integrate into a single range, hold down the Ctrl key and click on the cells you want to select. This allows you to define a range with as many cells as you need, no matter where they are on the worksheet.

READ-ME FILES

"Read-me" files contain useful information about installation, version changes, and compatibility problems for software.

"Read-me" files are generally found along with any files you download from the Web or on the installation discs for programs you buy. They're normally text files containing the latest

information about the product, which needs to be brought to your attention before you install it.

Save heartache. Before you install any software, read the "read-me" file. Use Windows Explorer to browse the program folder for a "read-me" file. The file may contain important information regarding the program's compatibility with your existing hardware and software, and you may choose not to proceed with installation.

Most CD-ROM software will auto-install and offer you the option to read the "read-me" file after the installation is complete. These files often include sections on problems and system requirements that may differ slightly from the information published with the package.

If you want to check the "read-me" file before installing new software, turn off the auto insert notification feature to stop the software from auto-installing when you insert the CD. Right-click on My Computer and select Properties. Click on the Device Manager tab, click on the

HOW TO: NAME A RANGE IN EXCEL

① Highlight the data cells you want to include in the range. First place the cursor in the top left-hand cell (B2). Hold down the left mouse button and drag the mouse to the far right-hand cell (G3), then release the button.

② Click in the Name Box below the main toolbar and type the name you want to use for your range. Do not include any spaces between characters. Press Enter to assign the name to the range. Name as many ranges as you wish for quick reference.

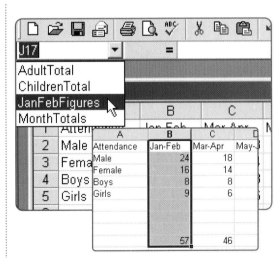

③ The named ranges can now be accessed by clicking on the down arrow at the side of the Name Box. To view a named range on your worksheet, select it from the list and the cells will be highlighted automatically.

"+" sign beside the CD-ROM icon, and then double-click on the CD-ROM drive that appears. Select the Settings tab and uncheck the Auto insert notification box in the Options section. Click OK to close the dialog boxes. Or you can override the auto insert notification by holding down the Shift key while inserting the CD-ROM.

If your new software is compressed into a Zip file, read the "read-me" file before you unzip the contents. Browse the contents of the Zip file using an unzipping program, such as WinZip. When you double-click the "read-me" file its contents will be displayed. This avoids unzipping files unnecessarily, should the "read-me" file decide you against installing the product.

Not all "read-me" files are called "ReadMe.txt." Look out for variations such as "Readme1st.txt" or "ReadThisNow.txt." Any files with a .doc suffix ("ReadMe.doc"), need Microsoft Word or WordPad to open them. Files named "file_id.diz" contain short text descriptions of the shareware or freeware products to which they're linked, to help you decide if a certain program is for you.

RECORDS

Records are the basic building blocks of a database program such as Microsoft Access.

What exactly is a record? It can be compared to a Rolodex card with an address on it, or a recipe card in a kitchen recipes file. It's a collection of data items—called fields or cells—that have structured content. The type of entry that goes into each field or cell is clearly defined, like a date, name, or zip code. When the required information is entered into the fields, the record can be saved into a database file.

Use record validation to protect the integrity of the database. Validation checks that a record meets specific requirements before it is saved to the database file. This is why some data entry screens only let you enter certain data in specific ways. For example, validation will check that you've typed a date of birth in the correct format and that the date is consistent with other fields

on the record; that is, a date of birth cannot be listed as being later than a date of marriage.

Make sure you protect your records by only allowing authorized people to edit and delete information. If you share your database, allow others to look at the information ("read-only access"), but make sure you control their access by ensuring that their log-on password doesn't authorize them to make changes. Anyone wanting to make a change will need to request a special password to grant them permission, or they will need to get someone with the appropriate password to make the changes for them. To set these options in Access, go to Tools → Security and select User and Group Permissions.

Normally, records are listed in the order in which you entered them. Often you want to change the order; for example, you might want to see all of your contacts or customers listed together according to their last name. To do this, click on the surname field and click the Sort Ascending button on the Toolbar.

Want to work with a subset of your records? Perhaps all those people in Idaho? Set a filter. To do this in Access, locate one of the records where the State is Idaho, select the "Idaho" text and then click on the Records menu, Filter then Filter by Selection. Access hides all other records so you can concentrate on these. To

view all the records, select remove Filter/Sort from the Records menu.

Microsoft Excel also uses database records. A series of worksheet rows in a table containing structured data—such as an address and phone number list—constitute a record set, in which Excel rows are the records, and the columns are the fields. The first row (or record) will generally be used for headings or labels to identify the field names.

B	C	D	
First Name	Last Name	House No	Str
Allan	Fredericks	552	Cas
Julia	Miller	14	Der
Tom	Barwell	2887	Car
Carolyn	Wilmot	136	Ple
Barbara	Graham	16	Fou
Miranda	Fraser	555	Jers

⇨ See also **Software: Access, Databases, Excel,** and **Spreadsheets.**

RESIZING

Resize your embedded clip art and bitmap images in Microsoft Word and Excel to produce the perfect image for your page.

Resizing an image is straightforward. Click on your image to select it and you'll see sizing "handles" appear at each corner and on the edges of the selection area. To resize the image,

RECORDS KEYBOARD SHORTCUTS
Speed your progress when working with Access 2000 databases.

Ctrl+ "+"	Adds a new record.
Ctrl+ "–"	Deletes a record.
Ctrl+ ";"	Inserts today's date.
Shift+Enter	Saves the current record.
Ctrl+ "'"	Inserts the data contained in the same field in the previous record.

you just click and drag a sizing handle towards—or away from—the center of the image. Release the mouse button to set the new size. You can then click and drag the image if you need to reposition it.

To resize an image by a specific percentage, select the image by clicking on it. Go to Format → Picture. When the dialog box opens, click on the Size tab. Enter the percentages you want in the Height and Width boxes. Click OK.

If your image won't stay in proportion, press the Shift key while dragging one of the corner resizing handles. This forces any changes to be made to both axes of the image. To keep the image's current central point, press Ctrl while resizing; the image will then resize from the center outward. Remember, if you're not happy with the result, you can always use Ctrl+Z—the Undo feature—to reset the image and try again.

Force an image to be resized consistently in proportion. Just check the Lock aspect ratio box on the Size tab of the Format Picture dialog box. While you won't need to press the Shift key when resizing, you will need to uncheck the box if you want to distort the scale in the future.

There are two image types in Microsoft Office: drawing objects and pictures. Both can be resized in the standard way, but there are some differences. Pictures formats, such as GIF and JPEG, can also be cropped. Drawing objects, such as geometric shapes, can be grouped and ungrouped (selected or deselected) for resizing and editing separately or together.

Not sure whether your image is a picture or an object? Select it and then click on Format. The option "Picture" or "AutoShape" appear in the menu, depending on which one your image is. Both choices take you to the Format dialog box.

An alternative to resizing for picture images is cropping. This allows you to fit an image in a space without reducing its size—by cutting away any part of the edges that you don't need. Right-click on the image and select Show Picture Toolbar. Click on the Crop tool on the

toolbar and drag the handles to reduce the image size. When you release the mouse button, the area outside the crop mark will be deleted from the image.

⇨ See also **Software: Clip Art, Drawing Programs, Graphics,** and **Photo-Editing.**

RESUMES

Treat your resumé as an important sales document to help you sell yourself to a prospective employer.

Use Word's Resume Wizard to get started. Go to File → New and click the Other Documents tab. Double-click on the Resume Wizard and follow the steps onscreen to create a contemporary, professional, or elegant resume. The Wizard tailors the document for entry-level or other positions, and helps you write a covering letter.

Keep resumés simple! For best results, resist overly elaborate fonts and borders, and don't use too much color. Don't use clip art or other graphics illustrations unless they demonstrate a skill or achievement. Avoid mixing different bullet or numbering styles, and minimize the use of bold, underline, and large fonts.

Don't forget that the covering letter you send out with your resumé is just as important as the resumé itself. It's probably the first impression the company will have of you. Don't make your letter too long—keep to the point. You can support the content of your letter by designing a simple but effective letterhead for yourself. too.

If you want to send your resumé directly to a potential employer as an e-mail attachment, it's always best to check with them beforehand that this is OK. If so, also ask what format you should use——for example, a Word document. Make sure you virus-check any files first, as you're unlikely to endear yourself to a future boss if you infect his or her computer!

⇨ See also **Internet: Job Hunting.**

HOW TO: RESIZE AN IMAGE IN WORD 2000

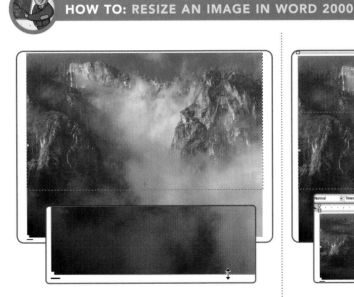

① Click on a picture or drawing object to see a frame around its edge. Place the mouse over one of the handles, and then click and drag the frame until it reaches your required size. Release the mouse button and the image will distort slightly to fit the new dimensions.

② To anchor the image to its current central point, press Ctrl while you are dragging the handle. Again, the image will appear to be squashed to fit the new frame.

ROTATING ITEMS

Spin around your text and images with Microsoft Word.

All the tools you need to rotate text and images in Word can be accessed through the Drawing toolbar. To display it, go to View ➔ Toolbars and click on Drawing. It will appear at the bottom of the screen, but you can drag it to the top or have it as a free-floating palette.

You can only rotate text that is in tables, text boxes, and AutoShapes. You can't rotate standard document text.

To quickly change the direction of text, put the text in a text box. To do this, click on the Text Box button on the Drawing toolbar. Click on your document and drag to create a box, then cut and paste or type your text into the box. Go to Format ➔ Text Direction and choose the new alignment from Orientation. Once rotated, you may need to resize your text box.

Use WordArt to create "free rotating" text. Although you can't rotate standard text in Word, you can create a graphic that looks like text and rotate that instead! WordArt, normally used for fancy headings, can be used to rotate standard-looking text (see How To, below).

Normally, imported pictures and graphics cannot be rotated in Word. The only images you can rotate are drawing objects, or Clip Art that has been converted to the drawing format. However, you can import pictures and graphics into a graphics application, such as Paint Shop Pro, then rotate and save the image there, before reimporting it into the Word document.

To rotate an AutoShape or drawing object, select the object by clicking on it. Click on the

Free Rotate button on the Drawing toolbar. Four small green circles will replace the

image handles, one at each corner of the shape. Click and drag on one of these handles to rotate the object in the direction you want.

To control the amount of rotation, use the Rotate or Flip options. Rotate turns an image through a set angle; Flip turns the whole image back to front, as in a mirror. Go to Draw ➔ Rotate or Flip and use the drop-down options.

➪ See also **Software: Drawing Programs.**

SAVE AS

Use the Save As option to change file names and formats.

Clicking the Save icon on the toolbar is a fast way to save your work, but doing this overwrites any previous version of the document. Instead, create "incremental backups"—older drafts of your document, which you can retrieve—using the File ➔ Save As option. Add a number or date to each draft so you can tell the versions apart.

 HOW TO: ROTATE TEXT USING WORDART

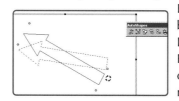

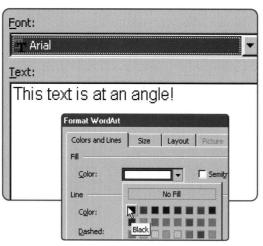

① Open a Word document and click the WordArt button on the Drawing toolbar (or go to Insert ➔ Picture ➔ WordArt). Select the first WordArt style option in the top left corner and click OK.

② In the WordArt text editor, type in your chosen words and then set the font and font size to the required settings. Now click OK. On the WordArt toolbar, click the Format WordArt button, set the Fill Color to black, and click OK.

③ Click the Free Rotate button on the Drawing toolbar. Now rotate the text in the same way as a drawing object; that is, by clicking and dragging one of the round, green "handles" on the corners of the text.

Some programs—like Word and Excel—let you add a Save As button to your Standard toolbar, so it's just as accessible as the Save button. Go to View ➜ Toolbars and select Customize. On the Commands tab, find Save As in the Commands panel and drag it to your toolbar. Click the Modify Selection button on the Commands tab, then select Change Button Image to assign an icon to the new button.

Remember to use Save As if your source document is read-only. All files originating from CD-ROMS will be read-only by default, as will files from a floppy disk if the write-protection tab is set. Using Save As lets you give your document a new name, or change the directory to which it is saved, without changing the protected original.

Use Save As to change the format of your file. This is useful if you want to convert Word or Excel files to text only files, or to HTML files for the Internet. In the Save As dialog box, click on the Save as type arrow to see the different formats in which your document can be saved.

| File name: | video capture.doc |
| Save as type: | Word Document (*.doc) |

Word Document (*.doc)
Web Page (*.htm; *.html)
Document Template (*.dot)
Rich Text Format (*.rtf)
Text Only (*.txt)
Text Only with Line Breaks (*.txt)

which allow the defaults on the previous and next buttons to be changed for another object, such as a graphic. The Next page and Previous page buttons now jump to the next or previous graphic, instead of the next or previous page.

The size of the scroll bars can be enlarged in all Windows programs by editing the scroll bar properties. Right-click on an empty area of the Desktop, select Properties, and click on the Appearance tab. Select Scrollbar from the Item menu and increase the pixel width in the Size box. Finally, click OK.

Avoid horizontal scrolling—it's too difficult to read. If necessary, you can reduce the text size or margin widths. If the document is a Notepad text file, go to Edit and check the Word Wrap option to fit text to the Notepad window width.

If you navigate a lot of large web pages or electronic documents, consider switching to a scrolling mouse, such as Microsoft's IntelliMouse. This mouse has an additional wheel built in between the mouse buttons that controls scrolling. It can even auto-scroll a document so that it moves up the screen at a constant slow speed while you read.

⇨ See also **Software: Keyboard Shortcuts.**

SCROLL BARS

Here are some shortcuts to help you use the scroll bar sliders.

Controlling the scrolling speed is sometimes difficult when you're trying to navigate a large document. Often you can whizz past the point you were looking for. To keep track, look at the small yellow box that appears when you click and drag the scroll box along the scroll bar in Microsoft Office programs. The current page number and heading will appear in the box.

Microsoft Word's scroll bar also has viewing buttons at the bottom of the right vertical scroll bar. The top one scrolls down one line at a time, The next goes back to the previous page, and the bottom jumps to the next page. When you click the third, round button a menu appears,

KEY TO SUCCESSFUL SCROLLING

With the right keyboard and mouse combinations, you can move through a document, or a web page with ease and speed.

STANDARD MOUSE
Scroll up one line Click the up scroll arrow (at top of scroll bar).
Scroll down one line Click the down scroll arrow (at bottom of scroll bar).
Scroll up one screen Click in the scroll bar above the scroll box.
Scroll down one screen Click in the scroll bar below the scroll box.
Scroll to a specific page Click and drag the scroll box and watch the page number in the small box that opens.
Scroll beyond the left margin Press Shift and click the left scroll arrow.
Scroll right To move across to the right in your document, click the right scroll arrow.

MICROSOFT INTELLIMOUSE
Scroll up three lines Rotate the wheel in the middle of the Intellimouse one click forward.
Scroll down three lines Rotate the mouse wheel one click back.
AutoScroll Click and hold the wheel button. Move the pointer up or down to control speed and direction.
Cancel AutoScroll Click either the mouse button or press any key on your keyboard.
Pan Hold the wheel button, drag the pointer left or right to move through the page.
Zoom Hold down the Ctrl key on your keyboard and rotate wheel forward or backward to zoom in or out.

SORT

Organize your lists and tables using the Sort tools in Word and Excel.

Both Word tables and Excel spreadsheets sort in similar ways. First select the entire area of information to be sorted. Then go to Table → Sort in Word, or Data → Sort in Excel. Both applications will then provide a similar dialog box, where you can set the ascending or descending order and the columns to sort by.

Save your work first and select the correct information before you sort. Information can get jumbled if you don't select all the information associated with each item, and any unsorted columns will end up out of sync. You should get a warning about this, but it's best to be safe.

Any text in Word can be sorted; it doesn't need to be in a table. When sorting ordinary text Word uses the hard-return paragraph marks (¶) to separate the items to be sorted. To check that all items are properly separated, click on the Show/Hide toolbar button to display the marks.

To sort a list of text other than by first-word, insert a comma or tab before the text you want to sort by. This identifies the next item as a new "field," and it appears as an option in the Sort dialog box. To sort cities by country, place a comma after each one: Paris, France¶ London, England¶, and so on. Select a column from the "Sort by" dialog box in the drop-down menu.

When sorting by number, Word ignores all characters except numbers. This is useful because it allows you to place numbers in any location in a paragraph or table cell. However, Excel sorts don't have this ability, so in some circumstances, it might be quicker to copy an Excel table into Word for sorting. For instance, the fields Harry 5, Anne 9, and George 2 could not be quickly sorted in number order in Excel, but in Word you just need to select Number from the Type box in the Sort Text dialog.

If your table or list has headings describing the contents of each column, include these in your selected area for sorting and select the Header row option in the Sort Text dialog box. This prevents the first row of your sort area from being included in the sort. Instead, the heading of each column is shown in the Sort by list as substitutes for column names or field numbers.

If a sort operation in an Excel worksheet does not work properly, check that the values are all correctly formatted; re-enter them, if necessary. Excel will sort number fields before text fields, so try not to mix formats in the same column.

 HOW TO: SORT A WORD LIST

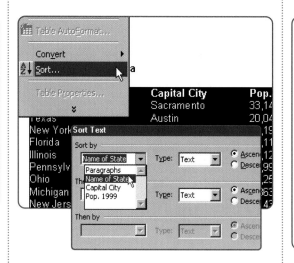

① Create your list, making sure that a single tab is placed between items on each row. Highlight the entire table, including the category headings, to select it.

② Click on Table, then choose Sort to access the Sort Text dialog box. Select the Header Row option, and then choose the column to sort by in the Sort by drop-down list.

③ Now click OK and watch as the data reorganizes itself according to the criteria you have set.

SOUND RECORDER

Windows' Sound Recorder is a great utility for capturing audio from CDs, microphones, and other sources.

Want to play and record from CDs or copy audio from Internet broadcasts? Sound Recorder will do this, and more, but you need a PC with a sound card. Make sure the card has a "line in" socket that lets you capture sound from an external source, like your stereo, a microphone, or a tape recorder, as well as from the Net or a CD drive. To open Sound Recorder, go to Start → Programs → Accessories → Entertainment.

If you have problems getting Sound Recorder to capture your audio, check that the recording settings are correctly configured for the device you want to record from. Go to Edit → Audio Properties, and then click on the Volume button in the Sound Recording settings section. The Recording Control panel will open up, where you can set the balances and inputs that Sound Recorder uses. Make sure that your input device is checked and its volume control is not set to zero. If your device is not displayed, go to the Options menu, click on Properties, and review the checklist of audio sources.

When capturing sound, close other applications that might be working in the background and affect the quality of the recording. Do a dry run of your sound source first to check that it's working before finally clicking the Record button. You won't be able to check the green modulation line (which monitors the sound levels) in your dry run; it will not start until you have clicked on the Record button.

Edit the sound file by moving the slider to the point in the sound clip where you want sound to stop. Save the file, go to Edit, and select either Delete Before Current Position or Delete After Current Position, depending where the section you want to remove is. Play back the edited file to check that the cut has been made in the right place. To undo any edit, select File → Revert. If you haven't saved the file, the Revert command cannot work.

Sound Recorder provides three adjustable settings that define the quality of the recording. The better the quality, the larger the file. CD quality is the best sound quality, at 44.100kHz 16-bit stereo. Radio quality offers good quality sound at 22.050kHz 8-bit mono. Telephone quality is the poorest at 11.025kHz 8-bit mono. To set the quality, see the How To below.

⇨ See also **Hardware: Microphones, MP3 Players,** and **Speakers; Software: MP3 Players.**

SPELL CHECKER

There's no excuse for poor spelling with Word's spell-checking tools.

The Spell Checker feature checks your spelling as you type, placing a wavy red underline on words it thinks may be misspelled. A wavy green underline indicates possible grammatical errors. Right-click on the word and either select an alternative suggestion from the list offered or choose Ignore All to leave the spelling as it is.

If you don't like the Spell Checker feature querying your work while you are typing, turn it off. Go to Tools → Options and select the Spelling & Grammar tab. Uncheck the Check spelling as you type box. Or hide wavy lines temporarily by checking Hide spelling errors in this document.

When you add a word to the spell-checker database, it places it into the current custom dictionary. You can specify other dictionaries to use in different circumstances. This is useful if you work in several languages or frequently prepare documents relating to a special field, like medicine. To create a new dictionary, access the Spelling & Grammar tab on the Options dialog, click on Dictionaries, then click the New button.

⇨ See also **Software: Dictionaries** and **Grammar Checker.**

HOW TO: SET SOUND RECORDER QUALITY

1 Go to File → Properties. In the Properties dialog box, click on Convert Now. Under Name, select the setting you want, such as CD, Radio, or Telephone quality. A description of the setting will appear in the Format and Attributes windows below.

2 If desired, adjust the settings and save the new format by clicking Save As. Click OK. The file will be saved in .wav format, which is best for shorter clips, such as to add audio to documents and PowerPoint presentations. By default, recording is limited to 60 seconds.

SPREADSHEETS

Many people think spreadsheets are just for number-crunching. While it is true that spreadsheets have many complex mathematical formulas built in, and can whiz through jobs that might take hours to do with a calculator and paper, they have potential far beyond simply manipulating figures.

SPREADSHEET BASICS

Spreadsheets arrange their information in rows and columns. These can be sorted in any way you choose, making it easy to see the same information from different perspectives. You can employ different fonts and colors in a spreadsheet, and even import graphics. These kinds of features make spreadsheets ideal for

WHICH SPREADSHEET?

Several spreadsheets come as part of full office suites, and it's likely one of these came with your PC.

Excel (www.microsoft.com/office)
Part of Office, this is by far the most popular spreadsheet for business.

Quattro Pro (www.corel.com)
Comes as part of WordPerfect Office.

Lotus 1-2-3 (www.lotus.com)
Lotus is part of the SmartSuite office suite.

Microsoft Works (http://works.msn.com)
Comes as part of the Works suite of applications and is designed with home users in mind. Works contains plenty of template spreadsheets ready for your data.

Shareware
You can also find shareware spreadsheets and calculating programs that meet your needs, for example, for tax calculations. Search shareware sites like www.tucows.com and www.jumbo.com to see what is available.

jobs like keeping a family calendar, planning a garden maintenance schedule, or even organizing information for a vacation trip. Think expansively about your spreadsheet and it could become a vital companion.

Most spreadsheets share a set of basic conventions when it comes to moving around and entering data. In most cases you can move between cells using the Tab key. You will be able to align the contents of a cell or group of cells so that, for example, decimal points are centered or text is flush to the left or right of a cell. Don't forget your right mouse button either. It usually provides access to cut, copy, print, and other frequently used features.

Working with groups of cells. Often you need to move a group of cells, or apply formatting, such as a color, alignment, or font change to a group. Most spreadsheets allow you to select a group by dragging the mouse cursor across your selection. Then you can make changes to all the cells at once.

Use data types. Spreadsheets have different types of cells and can automatically format information in them for you as you are entering. Two of the most useful formats are Number, which allows you to make calculations to a set decimal place, and Date, which makes sure the look of date and time information is consistent across the whole of your spreadsheet.

Recalculate in a second. One of the neatest things about spreadsheets is that once you've set them up, you can try lots of "what if" scenarios. As soon as you change a number in one cell, the spreadsheet recalculates every formula that uses the cell in an instant. With a calculator you'd have to go through the whole calculation again.

MATH MATTERS

Spreadsheets can do very complex math on your behalf. You do need to learn how to enter formulas but this is generally clearly explained in the software's help menu. The basics of how formulas work are fairly straightforward.

To add the numbers in a column in Microsoft Excel, the formula is =SUM(C2:C7). The = sign tells the software you are using a formula. SUM indicates it is a simple adding job. The letters and numbers inside the brackets indicate the range of cells to be added up. Excel highlights

these on screen when you double-click on the formula cell so that you can check the formula. The : symbol indicates that you want to add up all the cells between—and including—the two you name.

SMART AND EASY TO READ

Spreadsheets are excellent for making calculations based on different scenarios. A spreadsheet will rapidly calculate repayments of loans at different interest rates or how your savings will grow if you save different amounts over a set period. You can design a simple spreadsheet on which you enter one value in a cell and the calculation is completed automatically. Note that cutting and pasting formulas is often quicker than retyping.

Sometimes a spreadsheet can become so packed with information that it is difficult to read. If this happens, consider using color in the cells to highlight particular sections or try

changing font size to emphasize important sections of a spreadsheet.

Many spreadsheets include the ability to draw graphs automatically. This can be a really useful way to create a visual representation of how numbers "stack up" because it is often a lot easier to grasp the meaning of a graph than of rows and columns of numbers.

Why limit your use of spreadsheets to math? Because they are so good at structuring information and let you use color, and sort and resort information in different ways, spreadsheets are great for a host of other tasks. Some people use them to hold booklists, record collections, fitness schedules, household valuables lists, and much more.

Sometimes spreadsheets are a nuisance to print when just one or two rows or columns spill over to a separate sheet of paper, making the table difficult to read. To solve the problem, try changing the paper orientation from portrait to landscape in Page Setup. In most cases, this should fix it. Alternatively, many spreadsheets have a Fit to page option in their printing controls, which automatically reduces a spreadsheet so that it prints on a single page.

➔ See also **Software: AutoSum, Budget Planning, Cells, Columns in Spreadsheets, Copy and Paste, Excel,** and **Ranges.**

 HOW TO: SET UP AN EXCEL SPREADSHEET

① To create a new spreadsheet in Excel, click on Start ➔ Programs ➔ Microsoft Excel. Go to File ➔ Save As and name your file. To draw up a rudimentary three-year savings plan, click in cell A1 and type a main heading, then enter a row of headings for your columns.

② In the Percent column, type in your base interest rates. In the Over 1 Year column enter the formula to calculate the interest earned: =SUM([savings amount]*[percent cell]/100). In the Over 2 Years column enter the same formula with *2 on the end. For 3 years, add *3.

③ To choose a currency symbol for your figures, highlight the cells and go to Format ➔ Cells. On the Number tab, click on Currency and choose a symbol from the drop-down menu. To round the figures to the nearest dollar, set Decimal places to 0, and click OK.

STYLE

Standardize your Word documents by using the Style feature to format your text.

Word's styles are often overlooked, but they are a powerful way of quickly and consistently applying a set of formatting characteristics to text throughout your document. Word allows you to set a range of different styles for titles, headings, subheadings, lists, body text, and other standard features.

You might think that you're not using styles, but whenever you open a blank Word document, you are. This is the Normal style that defines the starting font, size, line spacing, and other text characteristics before you start typing. You can see which style you're currently using in the Style box on the Formatting toolbar. To see the other default headings styles, click the arrow next to the Styles box.

Turn on the View Styles feature if you're working with styles for the first time. This identifies the style applied to each paragraph on-screen. Go to View ➔ Normal. Then, go to Tools ➔ Options and select the View tab. Under Outline and Normal Options, set the Style area width box to 0.7. Click OK to return to your document, and you will see a column going down the left side of your document listing the styles used.

To quickly apply a style, click anywhere within the paragraph and then select the style you want to apply from the drop-down Style list on the Formatting toolbar. To save time, you can use a keyboard shortcut to this menu by pressing Ctrl+Shift+S to open the Style box, then use the up and down arrows on your keyboard to work through the list.

The Style box only includes the default and previously loaded styles. To access the full list, go to Format ➔ Style. Make sure the List option is set to All Styles.

Word templates have preconfigured styles that you can apply to your document. To see how the options might change your document, go to Format ➔ Theme and press the Style Gallery button in the dialog box. Click Document on Preview, and then click on the templates to see how the styles work in the Preview window. To apply one of the templates to your work, click OK. Or click Cancel to quit.

If a particular style isn't to your liking, you can modify it in the Format ➔ Style dialog box. In the style description window, the styles described as Normal + means that it takes the settings from the Normal style as the default and just adds the changes defined to the document.

This means you do not have to enter in all the basic characteristics for every style.

Use Automatic update to apply style changes throughout a document. If you want to change

HOW TO: MODIFY A WORD STYLE BY ADDING COLOR

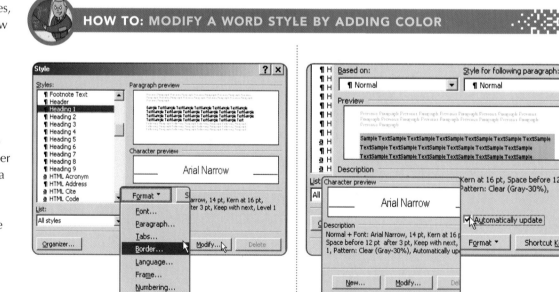

① In Word, go to Format ➔ Style. Highlight the Heading 1 under the Styles window. Click on the Modify button. In the Modify Style dialog box, click on the Format button, and select Border. Under the Shading tab, select a gray fill shade. Click OK.

② Check Automatically update on the Modify Style box, and then click OK. Click Apply to close the Style window. Look at your Heading 1 text to see the changes.

the font size of a heading in Heading 1, for example, and to then have that change applied to all other headings in the document, just go to Format ➜ Styles and click the Modify button. On the Modify Style window, check the Automatically update box. Word will watch for and automatically apply the changes throughout the whole document to maintain its consistency. Do not enable Automatically update for the Normal style, because any changes to it will affect the template.

If paragraphs with the same style seem to look different, it may be because some manual formatting has been applied to text within a paragraph. To remove any manual formatting, select the whole paragraph affected by triple-clicking within the affected text , then press Ctrl+Spacebar. This will reset the text to your chosen style.

➪ See also **Software: Fonts** and **Outlines**.

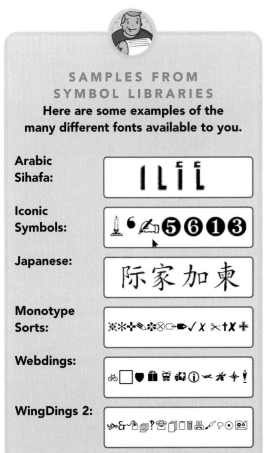

SAMPLES FROM SYMBOL LIBRARIES

Here are some examples of the many different fonts available to you.

Arabic Sihafa:

Iconic Symbols:

Japanese:

Monotype Sorts:

Webdings:

WingDings 2:

SYMBOLS

Fonts don't need to be restricted to just A to Z and 0 to 9. Symbols can add useful and fun graphics to text.

Symbols come in font family sets used specifically for graphics and special characters. Other font families, such as "san serif" or "decorative" are made up of alternative designs of the alphabet (upper and lower case) and numbers. Symbols, though, can be of anything. To try it out, select the Webdings font in your word processing application, and type "hello." It will come out as five preselected symbols.

Graphic symbols are also called "dingbats," and there are plenty available on the Internet from commercial, shareware, and freeware suppliers. Enter the words "font," "symbol," and "dingbat" into your search engine to get a list of websites with these symbols. If you need a specific subject symbol, include that word, too. "Symbol" is a wide-ranging term, but "dingbat" is a useful keyword that refers specifically to graphic fonts.

Unless you can remember exactly which key a symbol is mapped to, your keyboard will be of no help to you when you are trying to add a symbol to a Word document. Go to Insert ➜ Symbol to access the character screens for all the symbol fonts that you have installed on your computer. Select the appropriate font, locate the symbol you want to use, and click on Insert.

To enlarge or reduce a symbol, simply increase or decrease its font size. First, highlight the symbol to select it, and then choose the new point size from the Font Size drop-down list on the toolbar. Or you can type in your own point size. The symbol can be enlarged up to 10 or 20 times its normal size and still retain good image quality.

The font and the background color of symbols can also be changed in Word, in the same way

as you would change a normal character. If you use a 3D text package—like Simply 3D (www.micrografx.com)—you can also turn your symbols into animated, textured 3D images.

Foreign language characters can be entered using the Symbols dialog box. Non-Western alphabets and scripts—including Arabic, Hebrew, Hieroglyphic, and Japanese—can all be installed as symbol font sets and inserted into a document. Although this is a good way to include an occasional word or expression in a foreign language, if you want to write or edit extensively in another character set, then you should install Word's Multilanguage Support (see Software: Foreign Languages for more information on this program).

A symbol, like any other font, can normally be seen or used only if it is installed in the Windows font directory. This can cause problems if you want to send an electronic document to someone who doesn't have the same fonts installed in their machine. However, you can get around this by embedding TrueType symbol fonts into your document. Go to Tools ➜ Options, and then select the Save tab. Check

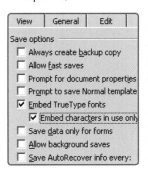

Embed TrueType fonts and Embed characters in use only boxes. The document can now be saved normally. Note that some TrueType fonts can't be embedded in the text because of licensing restrictions.

Any symbol that you want to use regularly—a heart or a star, for example—can be assigned its own AutoCorrect combination or Shortcut key in Word. To do this, just go to Insert ➜ Symbol and click on the symbol or character you want to assign. Now click on the Shortcut key button to assign the character to a keyboard combination, or click on AutoCorrect to use the AutoSpell check function of Word to substitute a symbol for a text code. For instance, pressing the Ctrl+Alt and C shortcut inserts the copyright symbol (©) into your document.

Typing (c) initiates an AutoCorrect to replace it with the copyright symbol.

⇨ See also **Software: Autocorrect, Fonts,** and **Keyboard Shortcuts.**

TABLES

Use Word's Table feature to produce attractive and useful tables.

Do you frequently use the same format for tables? If so, then you can set it as your default table. To do this, simply go to Table → Insert → Table. In the dialog box that opens, enter the specifications for the table in the Table size and AutoFit boxes, then check Set as default for new tables. In the future, whenever you want to create a new table, it will be in this specified format. To change the default setting later on, simply alter the specifications following the same method as you did before and then check the default option again.

To select a row in a table, place your mouse pointer to the left of the row until it turns into an arrow, then click. To select a column in your table, hover your pointer above the column until it turns into a downward-pointing arrow, then click. Select multiple rows or columns by holding down the Shift key as you select them one at a time.

To move a row or column, simply cut and paste it in exactly the same way as you would treat any other piece of text. First, select the row—or column—and then press Ctrl+X. Now select the new location, right-click, and choose Paste Columns from the pop-up menu.

To move the entire table, switch to Print Layout view, and then float your mouse pointer over the table until a four-sided arrow symbol appears at the top-left corner of the table. Now click on the arrow symbol and drag the table to the desired position.

If you are working with figures that are not in

Table AutoFormat...	
AutoFit	
Heading Rows Repeat	
Conver	
Sort...	

a table but in a list separated by tabs, you can quickly convert the document to a table. Select the whole list and then go to Table → Convert and scroll across

Text to Table. Enter in the specifications and click OK. You now have an instant table with which to work.

When you convert text to a table, using AutoFit, the table is arranged to fit the width of the page. If you don't have many columns or don't have much information in each cell, the cells will look too wide. To cut the extra space, right-click anywhere in the table and then select AutoFit → AutoFit to Contents from the pop-up menu.

To resize columns manually, carefully place the mouse pointer over the border between two columns until the pointer changes into two arrows separated by two short parallel lines. Click-and-drag to make the column wider or narrower. You can resize the outer boundaries of the table the same way.

To see an options menu for formatting a table, right-click anywhere on the table and scroll down to Table Properties. The Table tab allows you to align the table on the page or wrap text around it. The other tabs allow you to format rows, columns, or cells. You can add borders or shading, align text within a cell, or perform many other operations.

HOW TO: USE THE AUTOFORMAT GALLERY FOR A TABLE

Table	Window	Help
✏ Draw Table		¶ ② » Normal
Insert ▸		⊞ Table...
Delete ▸		Columns to the Left
Select ▸		Columns to the Right
Merge Cells		Rows Above
Table AutoFormat...		Rows Below
Sort...		Cells...
Table Properties...		
⌄		

① AutoFormat is a simple way to create tables. In Word, go to Table → Insert → Table and click the AutoFormat button. Select a format from the list to see a sample of each one. Choose from different styles, such as colorful, classic, contemporary, web, or 3-D effects.

Formats:
(none)
Simple 1
Simple 2
Simple 3
Classic 1
Classic 2
Classic 3
Classic 4
Colorful 1
Colorful 2

Preview

	Jan	Feb	Mar	Total
East	7	7	5	19
West	6	4	7	17
South	8	7	9	24
Total	21	18	21	60

Formats to apply
☑ Borders ☑ Font ☑ AutoFit
☑ Shading ☑ Color

Apply special formats to
☑ Heading rows ☐ Last row
☑ First column ☐ Last column

② Each design can also be modified by checking or unchecking the boxes at the bottom of the dialog box. Here, items like color, borders, and shading can be changed to create your own design. The Preview panel will show each change you make.

TABS

These word and number aligners in Word are not as tricky to use as they sometimes seem.

To change the spacing between default tab stops, select the paragraphs you want to apply the changes to. Go to Format → Tabs. In the Default tab stops box, enter the spacing—in inches—that you want between tab stops. Or click the arrows to move up and down in increments of 0.1 inch. Finally, click OK.

When you are using a table or spreadsheet, clicking on the Tab button allows you to move from one cell to the next. It's also possible for you to insert a tab into a cell. All you need to do is hold down the Ctrl key when you click the Tab button.

Tab stops can be set with a leader—a dotted line that draws the reader's eye from one item to another. Leaders are often used in lists, like a table of contents. To create a leader, select the paragraph where you want to insert the leader, go to Format ➜ Tabs. In the Tab stop position box, enter the second tab location in inches. Under Leader, select a dotted line style. Click Set and OK.

If you find that the second tab with a leader is in the wrong place on your page, repeat the step above, changing the inches figure for the tab position. If you have several lines that need leaders with identical tab positions, you can format one line, and then copy and paste it as many times as you need. Change the wording for each line as necessary.

Use Word's click-and-type facility to insert a tab stop anywhere on a blank line. Switch to View ➜ Print Layout, or View ➜ Web Layout. Move the I-beam mouse pointer until you see either an Align Left, Align Center, or Align Right symbol, then double-click.

TASK WIZARDS

These miniprograms take you step-by-step through common computer tasks, and they can be customized.

Create and send a fax with Microsoft Word's Fax Wizard. Click on File; then New. Select the Letters and Faxes tab, and double-click on the Fax Wizard icon. Follow the steps in the Fax Wizard. Look under the other tabs and you'll find Wizards for resumés, memos, calendars, reports, legal pleadings, and other documents.

Word's Web Page Wizard has a number of "themes" that you can choose from. Each one is a distinctive design using complementary backgrounds, colors, and fonts. Not all the themes are available when you install Microsoft Word—the Office 2000 CD-ROM has extra ones. Click on the theme "Nature," for example, and Word prompts you to install it. Click Install to start the process. You'll be

prompted to insert your Office 2000 CD-ROM, and Word will extract the theme from it. Once it has been copied, you'll see a sample of the new theme in the right window.

Use Outlook's Import and Export Wizard to import a list of contacts created in another program, like Word. Open Word and create your contact list or open your existing contact file. Information (like name, address, and phone number) in each individual record should be separated by tabs or commas. Make sure the file is saved as a .txt file, and close the document. Open Outlook and go to File ➜ Import and Export, and follow the instructions. Outlook Express uses a slightly different procedure with a dialog box instead of a Wizard.

Use Word's Letter Wizard to write a letter. Go to File ➜ New and select the Letters and Faxes tab. Choose a layout for your letter, and a style—Formal, Informal, or Business. Enter the

recipient's name and address, and the greeting. At the key points, you select what you want to write from a list of common letter elements.

Microsoft Excel makes number-crunching easier. Use the Chart Wizard button on the toolbar to create bar, line, and pie charts of data. Some Wizards help you use two Office programs together—the Access Import Spreadsheet Wizard makes it easy to transfer data from Excel to Access, for example.

If you ever get stuck while writing a letter the old-fashioned way, use the Letter Wizard to modify or complete it. Go to Tools ➜ Letter Wizard to start it up.

While running Letter Wizard, the Office Assistant provides hints along the way. But there may be times when it's help is not welcome. To hide the Assistant, click the Office Assistant and click Options from the pop-up menu. Under the Options tab, uncheck Help with Wizards. If the Office Assistant is hidden, go to Help ➜ Show the Office Assistant.

You can include extra Wizards not incorporated in a regular Word installation. Some Wizards are installed on your hard drive in compressed form. Windows extracts them the first time you double-click on their icons. There are also other Wizards on the Office 2000 CD-ROM that are not copied to your hard drive when you install Word. To install them when you first install Word, choose Customize, instead of Install Now, while running Setup. Already installed Word? Run Setup again. Go to Start ➜ Settings ➜ Control Panel ➜ Add/Remove Programs, and highlight Office 2000 (or Word 2000). Click Add/Remove and select the Add or Remove Features option.

Even more Wizards can be downloaded from the Net. In Word, go to Help ➜ Office on the Web. This takes you to the Microsoft Office Update site, where you can download any additional Wizards and templates you want.

➾ See also **Internet: Downloading.**

TEMPLATES

Templates are documents set up with a particular set of specifications. You use a template as the pattern or model for many documents, without having to reconfigure the basic settings every time. Many popular office program suites support templates and provide ready-made ones.

SPECIFIC TYPES OF TEMPLATES

If you work from home or just need a few specific kinds of documents for personal business, templates can be especially useful. If a program supports them, you can create templates for any kind of document it produces. Within Word, for example, you can design templates for short documents like letters, faxes, memos, and meeting agendas. You can also produce templates for more complex documents, such as reports or newsletters, complete with column settings and headings.

If you use Word to design a simple web page for your club or society, you can set up templates to help. In fact, if you produce any kind of newsletter or document regularly that involves reusing the same basic settings, a template is ideal.

Microsoft Word 2000 uses two types of templates: Global and Document. Global templates are the most simple and have settings that are used by all documents. Word opens a Global template, which is a blank Normal document, every time you start the software.

Document templates, though, are templates that produce a specific type of document, such as a fax or letter. These have to be opened manually every time you want to use them.

Keep your options open. When using templates three choices are available to you. You can open and use an existing template as it is, open and modify a template, saving it with a different name, or create your own template from scratch.

CREATE AND MODIFY TEMPLATES

To produce a document based on an existing template in either Excel or Word, first go to File ➔ New. Click on the tabs in the New dialog box and choose the template that you want by double-clicking on it. If it is not loaded, you may need to install the template from your Office installation CD—just follow the instructions that appear onscreen. The document window will open, ready for you to insert data. Make sure that you remember to use File ➔ Save As to save the document.

You can open a new document as a template. Go to File ➔ New. Click the General tab, then select the type of document you wish to use— Blank, Web Page, or E-mail message. Click the Create New Template button, and click OK.

Don't like the existing template font? Change it by opening a new document as the template (see above) Then go to Format ➔ Font. Choose your font type, size, and style settings, then click the Default button. Now click Yes to change the default font for the next new document created with that template.

If you modify a template in Word 2000, documents you created using the template before it was modified will not be affected by the new changes. If you want the changes to reflect the new template, then go to Tools → Templates and Add-ins. Make sure that the Automatically update document styles option is selected, then click OK.

Create a template from an existing document. If you've designed a really good document, with special formatting and other features, save it as a template to use next time you're faced with the same situation. To do this, first make a copy of it, giving the copy a name, like "Special Cover Letter." Make sure the copy only has the elements in it you want to use again—delete any text that is specific to the current use, for example. When you have finished, go to File → Save As. In the Save As type box, choose Document Template. Word 2000 will automatically find the template's folder. You can navigate to a subfolder or simply save it in the templates folder that Word has found.

COLLECT AND ORGANIZE TEMPLATES

You can download more templates from the Internet using any Office 2000 program. Make sure you are online, then go to Help → Office on the Web, and click on the Template Gallery icon at the top right. Any of the templates found

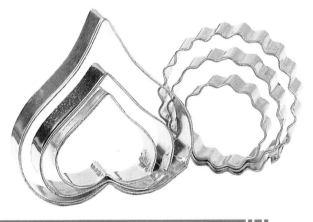

here can be downloaded for use with your software (see also box, opposite, for other sites).

Keep your Word templates in folders. When you create new templates in Word, they are stored in a special folder, which Word locates automatically. To create more folders with different names, use Windows Explorer to go to C:\Windows\Application Data\Microsoft\Templates. Then click New and add the new folders you want. You can now save document templates to these folders, which will be available as new tabs in the New dialog box.

Use your new or downloaded templates to build a comprehensive library. Among the templates that come with Excel are invoices, purchase orders, and expense statements. Word 2000 has a strong range of templates, including fax cover sheets, letterheads, resumé formats, and some web page designs. Many of these have instructions in them on how and where to add your own data. Follow the instructions, usually by clicking and typing as directed, and you can easily create personalized documents from them.

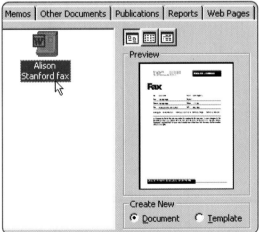

HOW TO: CREATE AND SAVE A FAX TEMPLATE IN WORD

① The easiest way to create a template is to edit an existing one. Go to File → New and click the Letters & Faxes tab. Select the Template option under Create New, then select one of the Fax templates to open—use the previews to help you choose. Click OK.

② Now edit the template, adding your own information where required and changing any of the data types. Insert your phone number or any other information that never changes. A macro is included to automatically insert the current date, so don't change this.

③ When you have completed your new fax template, save it with a meaningful name, so that you will remember to use it. The next time you need it, go to File → New, and select your personalized fax template.

TEXT BOXES

Want to insert some extra text material in a framed box on a letter or a report? Here's how.

To create a text box in a Word document, go to Insert → Text Box. Alternatively, go to View → Toolbars, select Drawing, and click the Text Box button. The mouse pointer turns into a cross shape. Click at the point where you want the top left corner of your text box to go, and Word will create a 1-inch square box. You can also click and drag in any direction to specify the approximate size and position of your text box.

To reposition a text box, place the mouse pointer on the side of the box, between the little boxes. The pointer turns into a four-sided arrow. Click and drag the box to its new position.

You can resize text boxes easily by clicking on one of the little boxes, or handles, on the edge of the box and dragging outward or inward. If you down hold the Shift key while you drag a corner handle the box resizes proportionately. To resize a text box vertically, horizontally, or diagonally from the center outward, hold down the Ctrl key as you drag.

Want to add a color background to your box? You can use the buttons on the Drawing toolbar to modify a text box just as you would any other object. Click the arrow next to the Fill Color paintbucket button to select a background color for your text box.

If the Text Box toolbar has disappeared, click on any text box in your document, or go to View → Toolbars → Text Box. If you haven't yet created a text box in a document, you won't be able to see the Text Box toolbar.

When you count words in a document by going to Tools → Word Count, Word does not include text in text boxes. However, you can count the words in individual text boxes. To select a text box, place your mouse pointer over the border

until it turns into a four-headed arrow, then click. Don't click inside a text box—that's what to do when you want to edit the text. Now, select Tools → Word Count

To rotate the text in a text box—to arrange text vertically on a poster, for instance—select the text, then click the Change Text Direction button on the Text Box toolbar. Don't use the Rotate and Flip commands on the Draw menu on the Drawing toolbar—those commands rotate the box, but not the text inside it.

Link text boxes in a document so that copy flows from one to the next. This is how to make text in a newsletter, for example, flow from a panel on the left page to one on the right page. Select the first box, then click the Create Text

TEXT BOX TOOLBAR
The center of text operations.

This toolbar appears when you create a text box with the Text Box tool on the Drawing toolbar or by going to Insert → Text Box.

Use the Create Text Box Link tool (left) to make text flow from one text box to the next like newpaper columns. To stop text flowing beyond a selected box, click the Break Forward Link button (right). The links before and after will then remain intact.

Click the Previous and Next Text Box buttons, in Page Layout view, to move between and select the linked text boxes in a your document ready for editing.

Each time you press the Change Text Direction button, the rows of text turn 90° clockwise inside the text box you have selected.

Box Link button on the Text Box toolbar. The mouse pointer—now a pitcher—turns into a pouring pitcher when it's over an empty text box. Click inside the next box that you want the copy to flow into. Repeat the procedure to link additional boxes. When you paste text into the first box, it will flow through all the linked boxes.

To copy linked text boxes, including their text, to another document, go to View → Print Layout. Select the first text box in the document, then hold down the Shift key and select more text boxes. Then copy and paste to your new document as you would with text.

To change the size, position, and layout of a text box, as well as the colors, right-click on the box's border and select Format Text Box from the pop-up menu. Click on the Colors and Lines tab to give your box a black or colored border.

Just because it's a box, a text box doesn't have to be square. You can use any of Word's AutoShapes as a text box, including geometric shapes, scrolls, and stars. Select the text box that you want to reshape. On the Drawing toolbar, go to

Draw ➜ Change AutoShape, choose a category, and click on the shape you want.

➪ See also **Software: Desktop Publishing, Drawing Programs,** and **Newsletters.**

TEXT WRAPPING

Here are some tips to make text run neatly around pictures in Word.

To wrap text around a drawing or text box in Word, place your mouse pointer over the border. When the pointer turns into a four-sided arrow, right-click and select either Format AutoShape or Format Text Box. Select the Layout tab and click on the Tight option, then OK. The text will now wrap around the shape of your object.

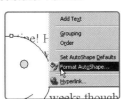

Under the Layout tab, you can specify other ways to position text and pictures. For example, if you want a square blank border around all four sides of your object, select Square.

For greater control over how the text wraps, click the Advanced button on the Layout tab. Select the Text Wrapping tab and choose to wrap text on the left, right, or both sides. You can also specify the distance between the text and image on any side by adjusting the figures in the Distance from text boxes.

When you insert a picture into a newspaper-style column, click the Top and bottom option on the Text Wrapping tab to produce complete lines of text above and below the picture. This is most important if the picture is narrower than the column of text. If you select Tight text wrapping, short words will trickle unevenly around the left and right sides of the picture.

Text may not wrap evenly around a drawing created with the Line tool (under AutoShapes ➜ Lines), because the tool often produces jagged edges. For smooth curves, use the Curves tool instead. Another approach is to create a background shape with smoother edges; make it

slightly larger than your drawing and the same color as the background. Wrap the text around this background shape for a neater look.

➪ See also **Software: Desktop Publishing.**

TEXTURES

Find, choose, and add textures in Word to make backgrounds for web pages and text boxes.

To add a textured background to a web page you're editing with Word, go to Format ➜ Background ➜ Fill Effects, and select the Textures tab. Click on one of the texture squares to select it as a background and click OK.

Create a textured background for a text box or an AutoShape, and it will show up when you

SITES FOR DOWNLOADING TEXTURES
Spice up your backgrounds.

Absolute Background Textures Archive (www.grsites.com/textures)
A huge site with over 3,000 different textures, arranged by color and subject, such as wood, marble, nature, or animals. It has a very useful preview feature where you can see which text colors show up best against a selected background.

Nik Palmer's Aquatic Tilable Textures (www.3dcafe.com/textures/nik/niktext.htm)
Offers colorful, splashy, and psychedelic patterns, plus cloud and marble effects.

Julianne's Background Textures (www.sfsu.edu/~jtolson/textures/textures.htm)
The patterned backgrounds offered are sorted by color and/or pattern. Click on a tile to preview it.

print your document. Select the text box or AutoShape, click the arrow next to the Fill Color button on the Drawing toolbar, and click Fill Effects. Select the Texture tab, choose a texture square, and click OK.

You are not limited to the textures that come with Word; you can use any image you like as a background texture. On the Texture tab, click Other Texture to bring up the Select Texture dialog box. Here you can browse the hard drive to locate your texture files. When you click on a file name, you will see a preview of the image on the right of the dialog box. When you've selected your choice, click on Insert.

Lots of free textured backgrounds can be downloaded from the Web. Sites usually show a range of different "tiles," which make up a seamless background. Save the file to your PC. Then, from your Word document, source the background as described in the previous hint.

Any scanned-in photograph or graphic downloaded from the Web can be used as a background for a web page created in Word. Go to Format ➜ Background and select Fill Effects. Click the Picture tab, and then Select Picture. Browse your PC for the desired image, select it, and click Insert, then OK. The picture will be displayed as a tiled, or repeated, background. You may have to lighten your image or change the color of your text to make it readable.

If you add a fancy background to a flier or other document, you may find that the background doesn't print, even though it displays on screen. You can get around this problem. Open a new document, create a text box that is the same size as your page, and copy and paste all the text back into it. Now it will print. Remember to select Print Preview to find out what your page looks like before printing.

➪ See also **Windows: Desktop; Internet: Free Graphics** and **Website Creation.**

THESAURUS

Lost for words? Let these word-finding programs jog your memory.

Sometimes the word you are looking for is on the tip of your tongue, but trying to remember it can be frustrating. Websites and software packages (see box) can help you retrieve the "lost" word, as well as help you increase your vocabulary—on-screen or off.

Whether you are working in a document or want to type in a single word and find its meanings, you have a wealth of words at your disposal with a couple of clicks of the mouse. Just use Word's built-in thesaurus.

Make sure the word you want to replace is spelled correctly using the Tools ➔ Spelling and Grammar menu. This saves both time and anxiety by cutting out long fruitless searches.

THESAURUS SITES
Many online pages are dedicated to word searching.

Wordsmyth (www.wordsmyth.net)
A dictionary and thesaurus in one. Free registration, 50,000 headwords, flexible searches, and words of the week.

Merriam-Webster (www.m-w.com)
This online dictionary and thesaurus includes www.wordcentral.com, an educational resource for building your own dictionary.

thesaurus.com (www.thesaurus.com)
Includes a variety of options to help you search this online version of Roget's Thesaurus, plus free tools and games.

Bartleby.com (www.bartleby.com/110)
Roget's Thesaurus of English Words and Phrases is just one of the hundreds of reference books you can search at this site.

A thesaurus can help pep up a document filled with repetitive words. For example, if you use the word "ridiculous" a lot in a Word letter or report, using the thesaurus will provide you with at least ten alternatives.

Be selective. Overusing fancy words from a thesaurus can make your documents sound long-winded and pompous. Keep your language simple and use alternative words only when you really need to avoid excessive repetition or to find the right nuance.

Make sure you check that the meaning of the alternative words offered by the thesaurus makes sense in the context of your text. Be aware that the thesaurus doesn't distinguish between nouns and verbs when answering queries.

⇨ See also **Software: Dictionaries.**

TOOLBARS

Customize any useful shortcut tools on your toolbars and save time and effort with your documents.

Toolbars are the rows of buttons that appear along the top of your screen with your program window when it is open. They are perhaps the most used parts of any program because they offer speedy ways to get things done. Simply clicking on a button will take you where you need to go.

Each program's toolbar comes with default settings. However, once you have used a program for a while, you may want to customize the options available. With many programs, in a few easy steps, you can get the toolbars to suit the way you work.

To find the full range of toolbars available for the program you are working in—for example Word, Excel, or other Office programs—go to View ➔ Toolbars. Alternatively, you can position the mouse pointer over an empty part of the toolbar and right-click. The pop-up menu gives you the option to show or hide any of the toolbars listed.

The Standard and Formatting toolbars in Word contain all the buttons you need to work with text, draw tables, scale, and print. But there are lots of other toolbars to choose from, such as Database, Drawing, and Web. However, they are not all applicable to all programs. To view a full list of toolbars, go to Tools ➔ Customize. On the Toolbars tab you can select the toolbars you want to display. Take the time to open a document and try all the toolbars to see which of them are useful to you.

To personalize your toolbars, you can simply go to Tools ➔ Customize. The Commands tab gives you total freedom to create and customize your own toolbars. When you click on it, the dialog box shows you different categories of commands, so that you can then focus on certain types of functions—for example creation and maintenance of a databases, formatting Word documents, or manipulating graphics.

The Options tab in the Customize window can be a very useful feature, allowing you to set large icons on the buttons, adjust the animation for drop-down menus, and customize and display keyboard shortcuts.

To add buttons to your toolbar, begin by scrolling through the categories on the Commands tab and looking through the lists of commands on the right. Click on a command you want to create a button for, and drag and drop it anywhere on your toolbar. Repeat to add as many buttons as you like and build a set of shortcuts for the commands you use most.

There is no limit to the number of buttons you can place on your toolbars, but try to keep it simple. Too many toolbar buttons can lead to tired eyes and even delay your progress because you have to search out the relevant functions from all the surrounding ones time after time.

Too many toolbar buttons? Streamline your toolbars by deleting the buttons you can live without. Select Tools → Customize. Click on the toolbar button you want to remove and drag it away from the toolbar. When a small box with a

cross in it appears, release the mouse button and the button will disappear from the toolbar.

TROUBLESHOOTING

When things go wrong, don't panic. Help may already be at hand.

PCs are likely to go wrong at some point, often for small, easily rectified reasons, and sometimes because of major faults. Windows software contains a number of troubleshooters to guide you through problem-solving tactics. Trying these first can often save you a lengthy and frustrating call to a customer service line.

To find troubleshooters in the program you are working in, look in the program's Help file. You'll find it on the Help menu. Click on the Index tab and type in "Troubleshooter" or "Troubleshooting" to display a list of options. Select the subject that suits your problem. Keep the dialog box open while you work, so you can carry out any instructions then and there.

For help with Windows, go to Start → Help and select the Contents tab. Click on Troubleshooting

and choose an option from the list. Windows offers suggestions on how to rectify problems or, if it's unable to offer a solution, suggest you contact a specialist. It also offers tutorials to guide you through procedures on your PC, and a list of the topics you've recently asked about—in case you need another look.

Troubleshooters work in two ways: by simply giving you a hint or tip or by working through a gradual process of elimination. In the last case, you will be prompted to give information about your particular problem by selecting boxes that are relevant to your situation.

Having trouble with your troubleshooting? If you can't find what your looking for in Microsoft Help, try searching with just the key words. If you need help with formulas in Excel, for example, type "Excel" and "Formula" rather than "How do I create formulas in Excel?

⇨ See also **Software: Help Files.**

 HOW TO: USE WORD'S BUILT-IN THESAURUS

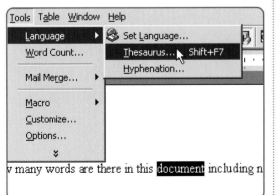

① Select the word in your document you want to replace, and go to Tools → Language → Thesaurus. If you open the thesaurus without selecting a word, you must type a word to look up in the Insert box on the right, then click on the Look Up button.

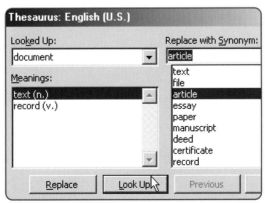

② Definitions of the original word appear in the Meanings section, and alternative words are listed on the right. To see more alternatives for each synonym, select a word and click on Look Up. Click on Previous to go back and work your way through the list of definitions.

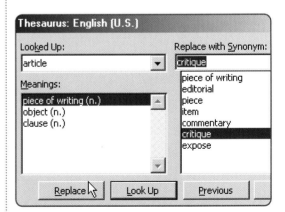

③ When you find a word you want to use, click on it, then on the Replace (or Insert) button. Word will replace the word you selected in your document with your choice. If you didn't highlight a word at the beginning, Word will add the word where your cursor is.

UNDO

This important command allows you to reverse, or "undo," an action.

We all make mistakes! Undo them by going to Edit and selecting to Undo. Alternatively, use the keyboard shortcut Ctrl+Z. This function will undo the last thing you did on the PC. In Word, Excel, and many other programs, a curved arrow button can be found on the toolbar, which is the equivalent of the Undo command.

Most actions normally performed on a PC—such as typing, cutting, pasting, formatting, changing the font size, and even accidentally deleting a paragraph or the entire contents of a file—can be reversed by using the Undo command or clicking this button.

If you click the arrow next to the toolbar's Undo button in Word, you will see a list of all the recent actions you can reverse. Scroll down the list until you find the one you want, and click on it to select it. Word will then cancel, or undo, that action and all the actions above it in the list. Alternatively, you can press Ctrl+Z several times to undo your most recent actions in the reverse order they were performed. Remember to stop pressing Ctrl+Z when you reach the last action you want to undo.

If you decide you didn't want to undo an action after all, go to Edit and select Redo. Alternatively, use the keyboard shortcut Ctrl+Y.

Only some programs allow you to undo multiple actions, and they may differ in the number of steps you can undo. Other programs allow you to undo only your most recent action.

The Undo command can be used while you are in My Computer or Windows Explorer, as well as when using a program.

UPGRADING SOFTWARE

If you are happy with your tried-and-tested version of a software program, when should you switch to a new version?

Software is constantly being improved and upgraded, but that doesn't mean you should rush out to buy newer versions of all your programs. Look at the features being offered. Do you really need them? Is it worth the money, considering what you will be using it for? The latest graphics software may be useful to professional designers, but if you're just scanning and retouching family photographs, an earlier version will probably do the job just as well.

Newer versions are invariably bigger and require more memory. Check the demands to see if you have enough disk space to install a new version, and enough RAM to run it. You'll find this information on the product's box or at the manufacturer's website.

Provided your system can handle it, upgrading your web browser is always worth it because it's free! Later versions of Internet Explorer, for example, include RealPlayer and plug-ins for displaying movies and Flash animation. Complex graphics are more

common on websites, and you simply won't be able to view some sites unless you have version 5 or above of Internet Explorer.

When you're using RealPlayer, for example to listen to Internet radio, you will be automatically prompted to download a newer version if the one you are using isn't recent enough. To go about this just click Download now in the dialog box to go directly to a download site and get the new program. Some recently recorded files won't even run on older versions of RealPlayer.

Always check the free CDs on some PC magazines. Many contain recent versions of software like Internet Explorer and Netscape Navigator. For a few dollars or nothing at all, you can avoid long connect times while downloading from the Net.

When installed, Netscape places a Smart Update shortcut on the Start menu. Click Start and then Netscape Smart Update. You will be automatically connected to the update page on Netscape's website, where you can browse through the most recent updates and additions and download any software you want.

Go to Start and scroll up to Windows Update to connect to the Microsoft website, where you can find and install product enhancements and files applicable to your own computer, including device drivers and Windows Me system files. The site scans your computer and displays a list of applicable components along with the approximate download times. It also informs you of any components that you may have already updated. You can choose to download one item or several. After an item is downloaded, Windows automatically installs it for you.

Make sure you have your original software disk handy when you are about to install a software upgrade. You may well be prompted to insert it during installation to prove that you are a registered user, because an upgrade is usually cheaper than buying a completely new version.

Shareware relies on the honor system. When you download shareware, there is nothing to stop you from not paying. But if you don't pay, not only will you be cheating the manufacturer, but you won't be able to upgrade the software. Registered users are kept informed of changes, improvements, and updates to shareware, so it is worth paying the small fee for this information.

➡ See also **Internet: Downloading** and **Shareware.**

UTILITIES

Use utility software to keep your PC running smoothly and to troubleshoot problems.

Your utilities are listed under System Tools. To find them, go to Start ➔ Programs ➔ Accessories ➔ System Tools.

Using extra utilities. The utilities in Windows' System Tools folder cover the most basic needs, but it's worth checking out add-on utilities from other companies, such as McAfee Office and Norton Utilities. These help check your PC and keep it in peak condition.

If you need to free up space on your hard drive, run Disk Cleanup. This utility scans your hard drive and lists temporary files, Internet cache files, and unnecessary program files that you can safely delete. It can be accessed through System Tools or by double-clicking My Computer, right-clicking the C: drive icon and clicking Properties. Click Disk Cleanup under the General tab. Highlight each entry in the Files to delete box to see a description of each item—for example, it may offer you the option of emptying the Recycle Bin. Click View Files to see the files contained in each folder. Check the box next to the folders that you want to remove, then click OK.

For other options with Disk Cleanup, click the More Options tab and then Clean up to search for any unwanted Windows components or installed programs or to reduce the amount of storage space used by System Restore. Click the Settings tab to run Disk Cleanup automatically if your hard drive space is running low.

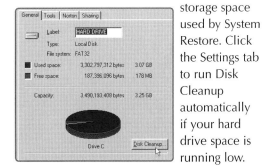

ScanDisk checks your files and folders for errors and automatically repairs them. It also checks your hard drive for physical damage. To activate ScanDisk go to Start ➔ Programs ➔ Accessories ➔ System Tools ➔ ScanDisk and click on your hard drive. Under Type of test, you need to select Standard and click Start. To scan the surface of the drive for physical errors, click Thorough instead of Standard. Right-click an item in the dialog box and click What's This? for more information.

When you save a file, especially a large one, your PC uses whatever available space on your hard drive it can find. This means that files may be split up and located in several places. This slows your PC because it has to search for file fragments all over the drive. Disk Defragmenter groups files together, which helps speed up the PC's performance. To start this utility, select Disk Defragmenter under System Tools. Make sure Drive C is highlighted in the Select Drive dialog box and then click OK. Select Show Details to see a graphic representation of the types of files on the hard drive and the progress of the defragmentation. Select Legend to see what types of files the colored squares represent.

➡ See also **Windows: Hard Drive; Software: Task Wizards; Hardware: Hard Drive.**

NORTON UTILITIES
When your PC is unwell, this software package will come to its aid.

This brand is the world leader—the best-known commercial diagnostic and repair software for PCs. Available as a software package separate from the Utilities options on your PC, it can run similar checks and organize your space, as well as repair files and recover information that has been accidentally erased.

VECTOR GRAPHICS

Vector graphics could be the key to the future of fast Internet graphics.

A vector graphic is a digital image that has been created by using geometric formulas to draw lines and fill in colors. Vector graphics are used mainly by drawing and Computer Aided Design (CAD) programs, such as Adobe Illustrator, CorelDraw, and AutoDesk, to create images that can quickly change their scale and also easily be edited. The instructions for creating a vector graphic are stored in an eps (Encapsulated PostScript) file.

Vector graphics have a number of advantages over bitmap formats, which have to hold information about every pixel in the image. This information makes the file sizes of bitmaps much larger and also means that any changes to the picture could result in a loss of information and quality. Bitmap files (such as .bmp, .jpg, and .gif) are best used for working with photographs and scanned images in programs like Adobe PhotoShop or Jasc Paint Shop Pro. Many applications (like Paint Shop Pro) now allow you to work on both vector and bitmap formats.

If you've ever tried to zoom in on a photograph using a graphics application, you'll have noticed that the image soon becomes blocky and distorted. Do the same with a vector graphic in a drawing application and the image will remain clear. This is because the drawing recalculates itself for each resolution. An image can be scaled as large or as small as you want with no loss of quality.

Printers and monitors are generally "raster" devices—that is, they rely on a grid (called a raster) to tell them what color to display where.

This is fine for bitmap images, but it means that vector graphics need to be rasterized before they can be displayed or printed. The software will normally handle this for you, but if you ever need to convert a vector graphic to a bitmap for printing or editing in another application, make sure you export your image at the required size. Once it is in a raster bitmap format any further resizing will probably result in loss of quality.

The success of vector graphic animation over the Internet has prompted the launch of a new standard, Scalable Vector Graphics (SVG), based on the new Extensible Markup Language (XML), which looks to be the future standard for creating documents that can be shared across many computers, mainly over the Internet. In addition to having a small file size, SVG files support high resolution printing and, because the code is text-based, as opposed to binary, additional information can be included (such as author copyright and search engine details).

VIDEO CLIPS

Get the most out of your PC's multimedia capabilities by watching video clips online.

"Streaming" is the name given to the process by which your PC is able to download digitized video from the Internet and to start playing

PC FREE PLAYERS
Tune in to music videos or online radio programs with these video players.

RealPlayer
RealNetworks (www.real.com)

Windows Media Player
Microsoft (www.windowsmedia.com)

Quicktime
Apple (www.apple.com/quicktime)

back that video without waiting for the whole file to download. The data "streams" almost directly from the Internet onto your computer screen. This means that the waiting time before you see the video is reduced and that you don't need to store large video files unnecessarily on your hard drive.

To be able to watch video on your PC, you need to download the appropriate free player from one of the main video format software companies. In fact, you should install all three of the main players—RealPlayer, Microsoft Windows Media Player, and Apple Quicktime—because video content on the Web generally needs a specific player to play.

Install the players and you'll be ready to start watching online video. The free video players "plug-in" to your standard web browser and they will automatically activate themselves whenever you click on a compatible video clip. They'll manage the process of streaming the data file into your computer and showing it on your monitor.

Thanks to the market competition between the three main suppliers of streaming video, there is a host of free material available for you to watch online. The most popular of these are music videos, movie trailers, and TV news channels. The website of each video software company provides lots of links to video content. You can also use your players to listen to online radio stations. RealPlayer has 2,500 online radio stations around the world that you can tune into.

To work effectively, streaming audio and video requires a consistently good quality connection to the Internet. If the servers are busy or if there are problems with your line quality, the content may occasionally pause or get blocky. These blocks are called "artifacts" because they are the remains of previous images that haven't been updated because of the data delay. Turn off any background browsing or downloading that might be stealing the available bandwidth from the streaming content.

VOICE RECOGNITION

Look—no hands! Voice recognition has come a long way in a short time.

Voice recognition software isn't just for dictation. Most packages allow you to control Windows as well, so that you can launch programs and open and close documents with just a quick word.

All voice recognition packages are supplied with headset microphones, but if you're uncomfortable with them, you can substitute your own headphones and a high-quality desktop microphone.

Online chat can become more like real chat with voice recognition software. There's no more tiresome typing-in your side of the conversation. Just say it instead.

Don't even think about using voice recognition in a noisy open-plan office or anywhere with

lots of background noise—whether it is kids playing or audible traffic. The microphone will pick up surrounding noise, which will make recognition difficult and decrease accuracy.

Take training seriously if you want to get the most out of your voice recognition program. The more time you give the program to learn the peculiarities of your voice, the more accurately it will carry out your commands or reproduce spoken words as text.

Check the specifications on the box before you buy a voice recognition package. The program will work more effectively if you have a fast processor, plenty of memory, and lots of available hard drive space.

Speak naturally and steadily when dictating text. Any undue emphasis will lead to mistakes. You can make dictation even more effective by buying specialized add-on vocabulary packages, such as those tailored for medicine and law. They will vastly increase the range of words the software recognizes without having to be taught.

 HOW TO: DOWNLOAD REALPLAYER AND PLAY A VIDEO CLIP

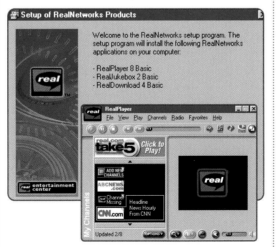

1 Open your browser, go to www.real.com, and scroll down to the Top Free Downloads box. Double-click on the RealPlayer Basic Free Download link, complete the questionnaire, and download the software.

2 Double-click on the downloaded file to start the installation procedure. This will set up the viewer software. Once installed, try out the program. Log onto the Internet and go to Start → Programs → Real → RealPlayer.

3 RealPlayer includes a list of Channels that you can access for the latest video news, music and entertainment channels. Click on a link and enjoy the show!

WATERMARKS

Adding a subdued background to your Word document is actually a way of highlighting key information.

Watermarks can be text or images positioned behind the main text on printed documents. The main use of a watermark is to provide you with certain information about the status of a  document with text, such as "Draft," "Confidential," or "Overdue." Alternatively, a watermark can establish the source of the document, for example, by watermarking it with a corporate logo.

To create a watermark that will be printed on every page of your document, insert it into a header or footer. To do this, go to View ➔ Header and Footer. Items can be positioned anywhere on the page, not just within the Header and Footer areas. Click the Show/Hide Document Text button on the Header and Footer toolbar to hide the main document content. Create your watermark with the tools on the Drawing toolbar, such as AutoShapes, Text Box, WordArt, Clip Art, and drawing objects, or insert a picture. Resize and position the watermark wherever you want it to appear on the page, then click Close. If you want your watermark displayed only on the current page, insert it directly into your text instead.

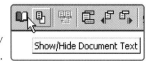

To format your watermark so that the main text of the document flows over it instead of wrapping around it, right-click on the object and select Format for the object type. Click on the Layout tab and select Behind text. Your main document text will ignore the watermark and run above it independently.

If the watermark is too dark, it will distract from—and even prevent you from reading—the main text on the page. To lighten text watermarks, select the text, click on the Font Color button, and choose another color, preferably a light gray. To

lighten an AutoShape or drawing object, double-click on it and change its line color to a light gray and select the lightest shade of any fill color.

If you've chosen a picture file for your watermark, you can adjust the properties to levels that won't interfere with your main text. To do this, right-click on your picture and select Format Picture. Click on the Picture tab and, in the Image control section, select Watermark from the Color drop-down menu. If you need to adjust the image further, use the brightness and contrast slider controls.

If you want to see your watermark on a page while you type, work in Print Layout View. You can also see your watermark in Print Preview. Remember, it's a good idea to print a page containing only your watermark so that you can verify its quality and position before using it with actual documents.

WORD

Microsoft Word can be daunting for new users. Here are some general tips to make it less scary.

If you're new to Word, adjust the Save Document settings to give yourself extra security while you're getting up to speed. Go to Tools ➔ Options and select the Save tab. Click in the Always create backup copy checkbox to have Word save a copy of any file you're currently working on with a .bak extension. This means you'll be able to go back to the previous saved version of your document if you run into difficulty. (Keep in mind that only one backup copy is kept on file, and it is progressively replaced as you resave your work.)

Creating a backup. Go to Tools ➔ Options, select the Save tab, and check the Save AutoRecover info every box. Set it to save every five or ten minutes. This forces Word to take another backup of your work at the

interval specified by you. This backup will only be available to you if Word or your PC crashes. When you exit Word in the normal manner, the AutoRecover file is deleted.

To make sure that your documents are saved in the correct folder, check the save location settings. Go to Tools ➔ Options and click on the File Locations tab. Documents are normally saved in your My Documents folder—C:\My Documents. To choose a different default folder, click on the Modify button, browse to and select your preferred folder, and then click OK.

Typing text into a Word document is straightforward, but when it comes to applying formatting and making changes it can be a bit confusing at first. Word provides three or four different ways to achieve most of its simple functions. Learning just one of them can be tricky.

The drop-down menu at the top of the window is the traditional way to get to the option you want. Word 2000 hides the options it thinks you won't need and lists just those you've used recently. This makes the menus less overwhelming, but if you're not sure where to look for these options, it can make finding an option even more difficult. If you'd rather turn this feature off until you know your way around, go to Tools → Customize, select the Options tab, and clear the Menus show recently used commands first box.

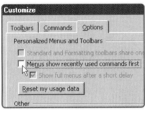

WORD TOOLBARS, MENUS, AND KEYBOARD SHORTCUTS

Pick the best ways for you to achieve common functions in Word.

Toolbar button	Menu	Keyboard shortcut
New Blank Document	File → New	Ctrl+N
Open	File → Open	Ctrl+O
Save	File → Save	Ctrl+S
Print	File → Print	Ctrl+P
Cut	Edit → Cut	Ctrl+X
Copy	Edit → Copy	Ctrl+C
Paste	Edit → Paste	Ctrl+V
Undo	Edit → Undo Typing	Ctrl+Z

There are 16 different toolbars available in Word 2000, each providing graphical access to various functions. Once you're familiar with Word, you can edit these toolbars to remove the buttons you don't use and add ones you do. To do this, go to View → Toolbars → Customize. Click on the Commands tab and drag and drop buttons for the commands you use onto the toolbars to build your own interface. To remove a button, simply drag it away from the toolbar.

Make accessing commands less of a drag. To save moving the mouse pointer to the top of your screen, many of the most common formatting commands are available to you by right-clicking the mouse button. The pop-up menu that appears shows a shortened version of the Format menu. If you want to apply a formatting instruction to an area of text, remember to highlight it before accessing the menu.

If you want to move text from one place on your document to another, you don't need to access a menu at all. Simply highlight the required text, then click on it again and, keeping the mouse button depressed, drag it to the new location and release the mouse button.

Taking shortcuts. Many keyboard users prefer not to use the mouse unnecessarily and learn keyboard shortcuts instead. Most people find it quicker and easier, for instance, to press the Ctrl and Z keys together (Ctrl+Z) to undo a mistake than to select Undo Typing from the Edit menu. Most commands have a keyboard shortcut already defined, but you can create your own commands for those that don't.

To quickly open an existing Word document for editing, locate the document in Windows and double-click on its icon. This will automatically launch Word, if necessary, and open the file. Make sure all your files have a Word icon or a .doc extension to support this facility.

Need assistance? There's plenty more help available with Word Assistant—the animated guide to the Word Help system. If you need help, go to Help → Show the Office Assistant, and type in questions or keywords relevant to your problem. You can also get additional support by going to Help → Office on the Web. This connects you to resources on the Internet.

WORD COUNT

If you need to know how much you've just written or got left to read, then the Word Count feature is just what you need.

Finding out the number of words in your document is straightforward. Just go to Tools → Word Count to get an onscreen summary of your document. The number of characters, lines, paragraphs, and pages is also shown. Word Count includes special characters and numbers, and considers anything a word that is followed by a space, so 1 + 1 = 2 will be counted as five words, while 1+1=2 will be counted as one word. Words not separated by spaces, such as http://www.twindata.com, will also be counted as single words.

To count the words in a part of a document, highlight the area to be counted and then go to

Tools → Word Count. You can't exclude selected text from a word count, so you have to count any words to be excluded separately and then deduct them from the total.

Another way to get a word count is to go to File → Properties and click on the Statistics tab. This gives you a report on count information as well as the date and length of time the document has been worked on. If you divide the number of words written by the number of minutes the document has been edited for, you can get a quick estimate of your words per minute.

If you use Word Count regularly, add a button to your toolbar or define a shortcut key so that you can quickly access this information when you need it. Go to Tools → Customize and click on the Commands tab. Select the Tools category on the left and scroll through the list on the right to Word Count. Click on the command and drag and drop it on your toolbar or you can click on the Keyboard button to create a keyboard shortcut for it.

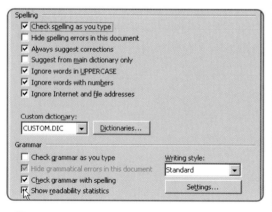

Want to check how many words you write, on average, in a sentence, how long your words are, or how many sentences you write in a paragraph? Word can tell you all these statistics and many more. You'll need to change your Spelling and Grammar options to enable this feature, which provides an additional report at the end of a spell check (see how to, below). In addition to your word counts, this report includes an assessment of the readability of your document based on a number of language rules incorporated into the grammar checker. You'll have more statistics at your fingertips than you'll ever need.

WORDART

Create fancy graphic text for your documents using Microsoft Word's WordArt feature.

In Word 2000, WordArt text is inserted by clicking on the WordArt button that appears on the Drawing and WordArt toolbars. If neither of these toolbars is displayed on your screen, go to View → Toolbars and click on the WordArt option. While you can apply WordArt to long sentences, it is generally more effective with shorter pieces of text, such as headings and notices with a maximum length of 200 characters.

Remember that any text included in your WordArt will not be included in your spelling or grammar checks. Either check WordArt text carefully yourself or prepare your text in Word and run the spell check before cutting and pasting it into your WordArt object.

WordArt is a feature available on most Microsoft Office programs. Once you know how to insert a WordArt image into Word, you'll be able to add WordArt text images to Excel

worksheets and PowerPoint presentations. To find the WordArt command in these programs, look on the Drawing toolbar or under Insert → Picture.

If you've upgraded to Word 2000 from Word 95 or earlier, you may find that you now have two versions of WordArt. The independent applet that came with earlier versions of the program and the new integrated WordArt that Word 2000 installs. You can use either version to create objects. The main difference between them is that Word 2000 WordArt creates actual drawing objects and provides additional 3D and texture tools.

To give your text a 3D effect, increase the line weight. You can increase the contrast further by changing the Line Color. After creating your WordArt (see how to, opposite), click on the Format WordArt button on the WordArt toolbar. Select the Colors and Lines tab and increase the line weight to about 4pt and view your change.

HOW TO: SET UP WORD COUNT WITH AVERAGES AND READABILITY SCORES

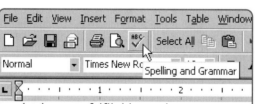

① In Word, go to Tools → Options and click on the Spelling & Grammar tab. In the Grammar section of the dialog box, select both the Check grammar with spelling and Show readability statistics options by clicking in the checkboxes, then click OK.

② When you're ready for a word count, word and sentence averages, or information about the reading level of your document, click on the Spelling and Grammar button on the toolbar. Work your way through the spelling and grammar check of the document.

③ When the spell check is complete, your document's statistics are displayed. The higher the Flesch Reading Ease score, the easier the document is to understand. The Flesch-Kincaid Grade Level rates text on a U.S. school-grade level. When you're ready, click OK.

safely answer yes and go ahead and read the file in the WordPad program. Nonetheless, if you make any changes to the file while you're working, make sure you have saved the file as a Text Document to retain the original format.

Notepad

Many Word keyboard shortcuts also work in WordPad. The Home and End keys take you to the beginning or end of the current line. Ctrl+Home takes you to the start of your document and Ctrl+End takes you to the end.

WordPad also supports the Document Scraps feature that lets you select any area of a document and drag it to your Desktop or to a folder. The text will then be copied and saved as a Document Scrap that you can use whenever you want.

WordPad normally saves files with the .doc extension, which is also the recognized

Microsoft Word default. You can specify any other Windows extension (for instance, .txt or .ini) when saving, but if you specify an unrecognized extension—say, file.zzz— WordPad renames the document file.zzz.doc.

If you want to save a WordPad file without the .doc ending, all you need to do is enclose the filename in quotes—for example, "file.zzz". If you save your file as a Text Document, you can then make WordPad the default application for editing files with the .zzz extension. Simply right-click on the icon for the file, select Properties, and click on the Change button. Now, just select WordPad as the program you want to use, and click OK to confirm your decision.

⇨ See also **Software: Keyboard Shortcuts.**

You can set any image file so it can be used as a texture for your text. Click on the Format WordArt button and select Fill Effects from the drop-down Color menu that appears. On the Texture tab, click Other Texture, select your image and click Insert. Select your image texture and click OK to apply it.

WORDPAD

Don't overlook this handy word-processing program included with your Windows accessories.

WordPad might not pack in all the features of a program such as Word, but it can format text and include graphics perfectly adequately. You can also use the WordPad program to read and edit any Microsoft Word files that you might have received—even if you don't have Word available on your own PC.

Windows Notepad is your normal viewer for text files with a .txt extension. However, if you were to click on a large text file the error message "This file is too large for NotePad to open. Would you like to use WordPad to read this file?" will appear on your screen. You can

HOW TO: INSERT A WORDART HEADING IN YOUR DOCUMENT

1 Go to View → Toolbars → WordArt to open the WordArt toolbar. Click on the Insert WordArt button, select your preferred text style, and click OK. Choose a font and type size, type in your text, then click OK.

2 Resize, reshape, and change the colors of your image using the options on the WordArt toolbar and the "handles" on the object. You can also change and amend the chosen style here if you need to. To return to normal editing, click outside the WordArt area.

WORKS 6.0

Microsoft Works is a suite of programs providing an all-in-one solution for the home PC user. It contains all the essential tools for day-to-day tasks, from word processing to spreadsheets, databases, and a calendar. There's also a special area to store your favorite photos and Internet pages.

GETTING STARTED

There are two ways to launch Works. You can go to Start → Programs → Microsoft Works to display the Task Launcher and open your desired program. Alternatively, you can click the Works icon that appears on your Desktop automatically when you install Works, which will bring up the Task Launcher.

WORDS OF WISDOM
Learning the main terms used in the programs will help you understand Works better.

Task: Any activity you carry out in Works, from adding appointments to the calendar to creating a spreadsheet.

Template: A ready-made document that helps you get started and can be customized to your individual needs.

Wizard: A step-by-step guide that helps you create a document, such as a letter or fax.

Task Launcher: The home page of Works—the area from which you can launch all your tasks—just like a home page on a website allows you to access the rest of the site.

History: Click on the History link on the Task Launcher to find any previous documents you have created in Works.

Task Search box: Use the box to ask Works which program to use for a particular task.

If you know which program you want to use, save time by accessing it directly from the Programs menu. Go to Start → Programs → Microsoft Works, then simply click on the program you want to open and work on.

What is the Task Launcher? Think of it as the control center of Works. When you launch Works from Start → Programs, the Task Launcher Welcome Page appears. Any of the Works tasks can be started with the Launcher. You can open a document you're working on, check your calendar, or access one of Works' wide range of programs or wizards—including ones for the Web, databases, and spreadsheets.

Feeling a bit lost? Take a tour. If you're not sure where to start with Works, go to the Task

Launcher welcome page and click Take A Tour. Works will give you an illustrated tour of some of the main features it offers.

BASIC PROGRAMS

Use the spreadsheet program for calculations. If you need to plan your vacation budget, figure out your loan repayments, or evaluate your physical fitness, this is the program you need. While it's not as powerful as Excel, it's handy for domestic planning, and the templates can get you number crunching a lot quicker than starting from scratch in Excel.

The database program is for making lists and keeping records. All items you want to keep track of can be recorded under convenient categories, and you can retrieve all or just part of them whenever you want. You could record

the service history of your car, with mileage, oil changes and repairs, so that you will be able to provide a comprehensive history when you want to sell it. You can also cross-reference categories so that you can check details of your car insurance against your house insurance.

Works provides a variety of templates for spreadsheets and databases, which can be customized for your requirements.

Use word processing for writing letters and other text-based documents, such as resumés and personalized stationery. You can create typed envelopes and address labels to make mailing them quicker, too. The program has all the features you need to create the perfect document, and even allows you to insert information from your Works spreadsheets, databases, or calendar.

Works Word Processor
Create great-looking letters, reports, form letters, flyers, and resumes. The Word Processor is your home base for all your tasks. Or, learn more about Works Word Processor on the Web.

Start a blank Word Processor document

Bibliography
Brochures
Caregiver instructions
Certificates
Cover letters

Letters
Create letters for all occasions. Choose from a variety of letter styles/templates. Create mass mailings to family and friends.

Start this Task

Check out the letter wizards to see ready-made formats. Go to the Works Task Launcher ➔ Works Word Processor ➔ Letters, then click Start this task to display the letter wizard. Now follow the wizard's onscreen instructions.

STAY IN TOUCH

Never forget another appointment with Works' invaluable Calendar. You can organize all your events, set reminders to make sure you don't miss appointments, and even e-mail other

people your schedule straight from the Calendar. You can access Calendar by clicking Programs on Works' Task Launcher.

Set Works' Calendar as the default calendar for your PC. Your computer may have various calendars available already, such as the one that comes with Outlook. Making Works your default calendar means that any appointments you make on your PC are in one calendar, so appointments never get overlooked. To do this, start the Works Calendar from the Task Launcher and a message appears to ask if you'd like to make Works your default calendar. Click OK.

As with Outlook, you can create your own address book in Works. Use it to store all your names, addresses, anniversaries, and e-mail contacts. You can even e-mail people directly from the Address Book.

To add a new contact, open the Address Book and go to File ➔ New Contact. Now click Name. Type in the contact information of the person that you're adding to the Address Book. You'll probably find that you don't always want to fill in every section, but it's wise to include a first and last name and an e-mail address.

Can't find a contact in the Address Book? Your Address Book may soon add up to hundreds of entries, so rather than searching for a needle in a haystack, you need to be able to find the contact you want quickly. Go to the List area of the Address Book, then simply type in the first

few letters of the person's name in the search box and click through the list to find them.

Sort your list of contacts by last name, first name, e-mail address or any other criteria. For example, in the Address Book home page, go to View ➔ Sort By and click the method of your choice—Last Name will list contacts alphabetically by last names.

WORKS PORTFOLIO

Works 6.0 offers something completely new —the Portfolio. This feature provides a way to store data from a number of sources—from articles and images downloaded from the Web to simple written documents—in their own neat portfolios. Think of it as a giant scrapbook (only rather more organized!) where you store the computerized equivalent of newspaper clippings, magazine pictures, and such.

How do I access the Portfolio? The Portfolio runs whenever you start your computer, and its icon appears on the Desktop. However, if you

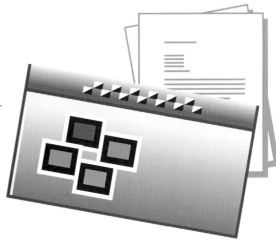

don't want the Portfolio icon to appear every time you start your PC, you can easily turn it off. Open the Portfolio, go to Tasks ➔ Options and uncheck the Start the Works Portfolio every time I start Windows preference. Now you can open the Portfolio only when you need it, by going to Start ➔ Programs ➔ Task Launcher ➔ Works Portfolio.

HOW TO: ADD A PICTURE FROM A WEBSITE TO A PORTFOLIO

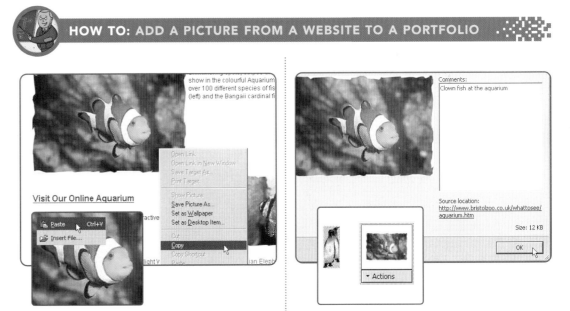

① Click on the website image to select it, then right-click it. Select Copy from the pop-up menu that appears. Open the Portfolio, right-click on a blank area and select Paste from the pop-up menu.

② The Item Details dialog box should now appear. If it doesn't, go to Tasks ➔ Options and check the box that says Add comments to items when copying them into a collection. Add any comments you want, to label your picture, and click OK.

WRAPPING TEXT

If you want your documents to turn out just as you've visualized them, it's essential that you understand word wrapping.

A word "wraps" when it places itself on a new line without an end-of-line or paragraph code to force it on to a new line. Word processing programs wrap text according to document page and margin settings. Text processors, like Notepad, don't tend to wrap text because they're often used for programming and other situations where each line is numbered. Any wrapping would cause problems.

To turn wrapping on in Notepad, check the Word Wrap option in the Edit menu. This automatically wraps text to the window dimensions and won't wrap the text if you print the document.

Text wrapping is dealt with automatically in Microsoft Word until you want to insert a graphic or other object on a page. You'll then need to decide how you want your text to wrap around it. Various options allow you to force text to flow around, under, or over your object.

Make sure you have the Print Layout option selected from the View menu or you won't be able to see your graphic—or the effect that the

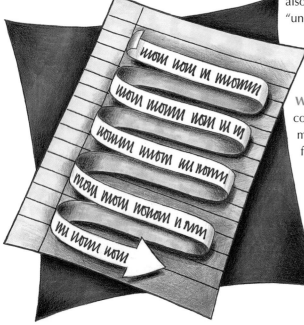

wrapping options have on your page design. Print Layout lets you see the page as it would print out.

To set a text wrapping style for a graphic, right-click on it to access the Format menu, and choose Format. Click on the Layout tab and choose the wrapping style.

Don't be square. Usually, Word will wrap text around the box, which creates a square, or newspaper-style, wrap. However, for many images, following the shape of the image inside the box, instead of using the normal square wrap, can help you create a great-looking design. Use the Tight option to get this effect.

ZIP FILES

For archiving and quick downloading, the .zip file format is the standard method for compressing files on your computer.

Zip is a file compression utility—an essential piece of software to help you manage your files. It lets you condense a large group of files into one smaller file. If you download or receive a compressed file from a friend or colleague, you'll also need to have the utility to decompress or "unzip" the files. The most popular Zip utility is WinZip 8.0 (www.winzip.com). A trial version can also be downloaded for free from many shareware sites.

While many files achieve a very high compression rate, others won't compress much at all. Some files—especially graphic formats, such as the .gif or .jpg—are already highly compressed. Zip files need to be able to reconstruct the original files exactly, so they are not able to reduce much more the size of files that have already been reduced themselves.

WinZip integrates itself with Windows Explorer so you can easily create a Zip

TEXT WRAPPING OPTIONS IN WORD

Learn how to work with text, and you'll soon have text wrapping all wrapped up.

Behind text: Allows text to flow over the object, removing any wrapping restrictions.

In front of text: Removes text wrapping, placing the object in front on the document.

In line with text: Slots your object into position on a text line in the document.

Square: Wraps the text around all sides of the object's rectangular box.

Tight: Moves text on each line as close to the image as possible. Adjust the closeness by clicking the Advanced button and then the Text Wrapping tab.

Through: Click the Advanced button on the Layout tab to wrap text into any open areas.

Top and Bottom: Simply wraps text around the top and bottom of an object.

file. Highlight the directory or files you want to compress, and then right-click the selection. Select Add to Zip from the pop-up menu and WinZip generates the file and asks you to name it.

You can also unzip a file within Windows Explorer. Right-click on it and select Extract To from the menu, and choose the folder you want WinZip to decompress the files to. Make sure the Use folder names box is checked so any specified folders are recreated. If the box is left blank, all the different files will be unzipped into the single selected folder.

Before you unzip a compressed file, make sure you run a virus scan first. Locate the file that you want to virus check in the virus scanner section of WinZip's program location screen.

Go to Options → Configuration. Now Scan the Zip file, by selecting the Virus Scan option under the Actions menu.

Need to send zipped files to someone without a Zip program? To do this, create your Zip file as normal, click the Actions menu, and choose the Make .Exe File option. This creates an "executable" file that can be decompressed and opened on the other person's PC without WinZip.

Free up more space on your hard drive. WinZip is ideal for archiving files that you may not need to see for a while. Create a new folder on your Desktop and name it. Drag your files into the folder and right-click on it. From the pop-up menu, select Add to [folder name].zip. WinZip will start and automatically create a zipped file containing all the files in the folder.

ZOOMING

Don't strain your eyes—use your program's Zoom facility to enlarge graphics and text.

Enlarge or reduce an area of your screen by zooming. Enlarging a section of the screen lets you focus more clearly on a detail of text or graphics, while zooming out—perhaps prior to printing—allows you to see how your work looks as a whole.

Under the View menu, Office applications include Zoom tools for scaling your document. Microsoft Word contains preset percentages for enlarging or reducing your document. The useful Percent box on the toolbar allows you to specify any zoom setting for your document.

One way to zoom in on an Excel table is to highlight the first row, and select Fit Selection from zoom options. This expands the row across the visible screen for maximum visibility.

A more efficient way to view your page layout is to click the Print Preview button. Print Preview puts one or more fully formatted pages onto the screen so you can see how they'll look.

Zoom in and out with a Microsoft IntelliMouse or similar scrolling mouse. Use your mouse without accessing the zoom menu by pressing the Control key as you rotate the scroll wheel.

Graphics packages—such as Paint Shop Pro and CorelDraw—provide zoom tools so the user can edit even the smallest pixel on a large image. Programs like Paint Shop Pro and Adobe Photoshop provide flexible and fast zooming. To access these zoom tools, press Ctrl and the "+" sign to zoom in or Ctrl and "-" to zoom out.

⇨ See also **Software: Scroll Bars.**

 HOW TO: USE ZOOM WITH A WORD DOCUMENT

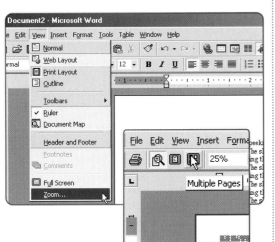

① To adjust the viewing area on your document, click on View → Zoom, or click on the Print Preview button to get a view of the whole page. To view several pages, click on the Multiple Pages button and drag the mouse across the pages you want displayed.

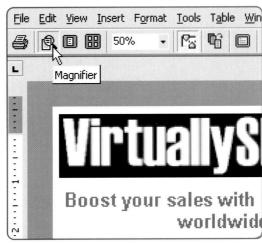

② To find minor errors that will show up on a printout, click on the Magnifier button in Print Preview and click on the document. You can now move around the page to check that it's ready to print. To make any adjustments, click Close to return to Print Layout view.

③ Check your changes in Print Preview again, and print your document. Click on Close to return to Print Layout view. Return your file to a comfortable zoom setting before saving it—only save it with a specific zoom setting if that's how you want to see it next time.

The Internet

Join the information revolution and learn to surf with confidence. Speed up your Internet access, brush up on your online etiquette, and come to grips with the biggest data bank on the planet.

ADDRESS BOOK

Outlook Express comes with an Address Book to store your e-mail addresses, but it can do much more.

Use a keyboard shortcut to open the Address Book quickly by pressing Ctrl+Shift+B while Outlook Express is open. Alternatively, click on the Address Book button on the toolbar.

Sharing a PC with others? Make sure each user sets up a separate identity, so each member of your family or work group has their own Address Book. In Outlook Express, go to File → Switch Identity and click on Manage Identities. In the pop-up dialog box, click New and enter the name and password for a new identity.

To add a new friend to the Address Book manually, open the Address Book and click on New → New contact. In the Properties box, enter in the details under each of the tabs, clicking OK when you complete all the details.

Remember that the Address Book can store much more than just e-mail addresses. Use it to record home and business telephone numbers and addresses, as well as personal information about family members and business colleagues.

Add contacts to your Address Book instantly when you receive an e-mail. Open the message, right-click on the person's name, then click Add to Address Book. To add from your Inbox or another folder, right-click on a message in the message list, then click Add Sender to Address Book.

Automatically add e-mail addresses to your Address Book whenever you reply to a message. Go to Tools → Options. On the Send tab, check the box that reads Automatically put people I reply to in my Address Book.

Address Book can also be used on its own without running Outlook Express. This allows you to update contact details independently. To access the Address Book from the Windows desktop, go to Start → Programs → Accessories and select Address Book.

Transfer contacts from another program, such as Netscape Messenger or Eudora to Outlook Express. To import the data directly into your new Address Book, go to File → Import → Other Address Book. Choose the program you've been using and click on the Import button.

Need a hard copy of your Address Book contact details? You can print them out easily in any one of three formats, depending on whether you want all the information (Memo), business information only (Business Card), or simply phone numbers (Phone List). Go to File → Print and select the appropriate button in Print Style.

Your Outlook Express Address Book is a kind of database—and it gives you powerful database-

---

HOW TO: SET UP A MAILING GROUP IN OUTLOOK EXPRESS

1 In the Address Book, highlight the folder from which you want to create your mailing group. Select New Group from the File menu. The Properties dialog box appears. Enter a name for your group in the Group Name box and click on Select Members.

2 Your main contacts list appears on the left. Highlight a name and click Select to add that person to the list of group members in the box on the right. Continue until you have selected all the members of your group, then click the OK button.

3 To add a person who isn't in your Address Book to your group, enter a name and e-mail address in the boxes at the bottom of the Properties dialog box and click Add. To send a group message, type the group name in the To box, write your message, and click Send.

style methods for organizing and viewing your contact details. You can sort the contacts alphabetically by first name, last name, or by e-mail address. In the Address Book, go to View → Sort By, and select the desired option from the drop-down menu.

Often you may want to send messages, such as an invitation, to a large group of people. With the Address Book, you can organize your contacts into mailing groups for different purposes so that you can send e-mail to all in the group (see How To opposite). You can have any number of different groups, and contacts can belong to as many of these groups as you wish.

⇨ See also **Internet: Outlook Express.**

AIRLINES

The Internet makes it easy to book flights, shop around for the best deals, or grab that last-minute, bargain vacation of your dreams.

Airline ticket websites all plug in to one of the four global computerized airline reservation systems for their information. So when you're looking for the best flight deal, always check out at least two—and preferably three or four—agencies to make sure you cover all the bases and get the best possible deal.

Try specialized airline ticket and travel sites for spur-of-the-moment getaways. The Last Minute Club (www.lastminuteclub.com) offers all sorts of travel deals. You'll find this website provides daily updates on cruises, package holidays, and many other travel possibilities. Travelprice.ca (www.com/CA_EN/Index.htm) has its last-minute packages right on the home page.

There's more to air travel than just buying a ticket; a little extra information on airplanes and airports can make the whole experience much more enjoyable. Try etravel (www.etravel.org), which offers useful hints and tips from other travelers, as well as information on all aspects of travel.

Lost baggage, delayed flights, rude staff? They can all happen. When you want to let the world know about it—and have your complaint forwarded to the offending airline—go to the Air Travel Complaints Commissioner (www.cta-otc.gc.ca/cta-otc2000/menu_e.html). Here you will find out how to file a complaint and where to send it. There are links to airlines, airports, tour operators, and Transport Canada. The site lists FAQs, and explains the meaning of arcane phrases, such as "terms of carriage," that appear in small type on air tickets.

For the young—or the young at heart—one of the cheapest ways of hopping on a long-distance flight is to offer your services as a courier. In exchange for carrying a small pouch of documents, you can get massive discounts on fares around the world. Visit the Air Courier Travel website (www.courier.org) for all the details.

AIR TRAVEL SITES
Want to make a quick getaway? Check out the following sites.

Air Canada (www.aircanada.com)
This is an easy-to-navigate site for booking tickets online, using credit cards or frequent flyer points.

Airline Guide (http://the-travel-guide.com/airlines.htm)
A listing of all the world's best and most reliable airlines with links to their websites.

Expedia.com (www.expedia.com)
This site is a giant of the online travel world. There's an easy search for the cheapest air ticket, plus lots of travel-related content.

Travel Links (www.ipclangley.com/IPC-Client-webs/Links/Travel.htm)
This portal offers guides to various Canadian and international reservation websites and links to Canadian tourism sites.

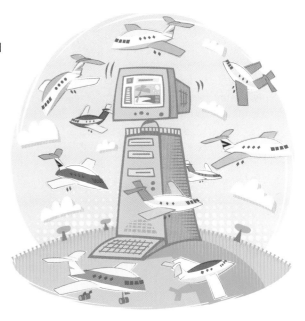

Are your travel plans flexible? Flight Network (www.flightnetwork.com) offers discount airfares from Canadian consolidators, who deal in international business and first-class tickets. Cancellation can be expensive. Even if it is permitted, there is a $300 fee. Once your trip is underway, no refunds are allowed.

⇨ See also **Internet: Credit Cards** and **Travel Planning.**

ALTERNATIVE HEALTH

Get healthy, and stay healthy with alternative advice from online sites. But always consult your doctor first about any serious conditions.

Check out online newsletters for the latest in alternative health developments. Alternative Health News Online (http://altmedicine.com) aims to separate the hogwash from the effective. Updated daily, it offers a free, weekly e-mail newsletter, plus bulletins and alerts on health matters. VitalCast.com (www.vitalcast.com) offers health news and updates, reference, shopping, discussion groups, and chat.

Learn how to give a massage and buy massage gear from online sources. Bodyworkmall.com (www.bodyworkmall.com) is a source for massage lotions, oils, specialist chairs, and tables, plus information on professional massage. The Massage & Bodywork Resource Center (www.massageresource.com) has a wealth of information on techniques, finding professional practitioners, books and supplies, associations, and includes a message board.

Learn how to use herbs and plants to keep you healthy. The Medicinal HerbFAQ (www.ibiblio. org/herbmed/mediher1.html) offers a useful resource list of herbs and FAQ. Algy's Herb Page (www.algy.com/herb) will teach you how to grow your own medicinal plants and create decoctions and other herbal remedies.

An annotated, extensive directory of alternative health sites is provided by McMaster University (www-hsl.mcmaster.ca/tomflem/altmed.html). The Canadian Health Network, in partnership with Health Canada, also includes alternative medicine websites (www.canadian-health-network.ca/1alternative_health.html).

Homeopathy is a widely accepted alternative therapy, gaining in popularity and often used with traditional medicine. Canada Homeopathy (http://canadahomeopathy.com) offers descriptions of the therapy, FAQs, and links to homeopathic practitioners across the country.

In China, alternative medicine is mainstream. NewCenturyNutrition (www.newcentury nutrition.com) has a Chinese herbal database, a search service for Chinese herbs, and more. Chinese Medicine and Acupuncture in Canada (www. medicinechinese.com) provides details about practitioners, schools, and government regulations in Canada. Chinese Herb Garden (http://healther.

stormloader.com) has articles on scientific principles, recipes, products, and the pharmaceutical factors of Chinese medicine.

➾ See also **Internet: Health.**

ALT NEWSGROUPS

Accessed in the same way as regular newsgroups, alt newsgroups can turn up some fascinating news and views.

You can find alt newsgroups by using the list of archived groups available at Deja.com (www.deja.com/usenet), where there is also

a search engine to help you dig out some of the more obscure topics.

Make sure you read the newsgroup's FAQ before you dive in; it will give you a good idea of whether it's the kind of place you want to be. Check out FAQs by Newsgroup (www.landfield.com/faqs/by-newsgroup).

Don't be baited into an argument that could make you look foolish. Some people—on alt newsgroups, in particular—post "trolls" (outrageous messages) to provoke arguments.

Not everyone wants to reveal his or her true identity in an alt newsgroup. To remain anonymous, open another account with your ISP using a nickname, or use an alternative screen name if you're an AOL user. Alternatively, open a new account with another ISP, maybe even a free one, or use a web-based e-mail service, such as Hotmail (www.hotmail.com).

Exercise extreme caution if your children want to participate in alt newsgroups. While most are perfectly safe—if sometimes a little eccentric—there are many others that are extremely objectionable. Try using software that blocks any material that you may disapprove of (see Internet: Security on the Net).

Want to start up your own newsgroup? It's much easier to do so under the alt hierarchy than under the traditional hierarchies. Check out Landfield's guide (www.landfield.com/faqs/alt-creation-guide) for further details.

SITES SPECIALIZING IN ALTERNATIVE HEALTH MATTERS
Use natural remedies to ease your aches and pains.

The Alternative Health Channel Index (http://onhealth.webmd.com/alternative/home)
A complete list of alternative health sites, from the reliable people who brought you WebMD.

Biorhythm Generator (http://the.sitefoundry.com/biorhythms)
Prepare for your ups and downs in advance with this Biorhythm Generator. Fill in the onscreen form and check out your best days.

The Official Deepak Chopra Website (www.deepakchopra.com)
Deepak Chopra's site. Meditation and mindfulness tips from the master.

Quackwatch (www.quackwatch.com)
Before you buy that potion or follow the latest offbeat health fad, check it out first.

Yahoo!Health (http://ca.yahoo.com/Health/Alternative_Medicine) Links to myriad sites, from aromatherapy to yoga.

Conspiracies—from Area 51 to the assassination of JFK—are one of the liveliest and most intriguing topics on alt newsgroups. Scan them all at Liszt (www.liszt.com/news/alt/conspiracy).

⇨See also **Internet: Newsgroups.**

AMAZON

The world's largest online bookstore, with no long checkout lines.

Amazon (www.amazon.com) is so big that it has spawned other sites that exist just to make your Amazon shopping easier. If you want to compare Amazon's prices with those at

other online stores, try Amazon's zBubbles, a software application that pops up as you shop, and tells you how much an item costs from Amazon.

Got your own website? You can earn revenue through the Amazon Associates Program. This program lets you refer customers to Amazon's site in exchange for a commission. Get more information from the Amazon website.

While you can't purchase anything from Amazon until an account is set up, you can still add items to your shopping basket. Buying from Amazon for the first time? Shop first, then click Proceed to checkout. The sign-in page will appear. If you don't have an account with Amazon, select I am a new customer and follow the prompts.

Entered the checkout and account pages? The address should change to https:// and a closed lock should appear on the bottom bar. If this doesn't happen, don't buy anything—it means your browser doesn't support secure shopping.

Buying several items? Pay close attention to the shipping instructions. Remember, there is a minimum shipping cost. If the items are not all

in stock, Amazon may ship them one at a time, thus increasing your shipping fees. If you can stand to wait, it will be much cheaper to have everything shipped at once.

Buying something for delivery in Europe? Amazon has online stores in the U.K. (www.amazon.co.uk) and in Germany (www.amazon.de), too. More to the point, their U.K. and German sites ship from warehouses in the U.K. and Germany, which could mean a lower shipping cost for items going to Europe or locations other than North America.

See also **Internet: Shopping Online.**

AMERICA ON LINE (AOL)

Here are the ins and outs of the world's largest Internet Service Provider.

With over 23 million subscribers, AOL is regarded as the newbie's on-ramp to the Net. But the sheer number of subscribers has led to problems, especially when they try to sign on at peak times (for AOL, that's anytime between 9 a.m. and 6 p.m.) While AOL makes your life

easier at first, when you're more experienced, you may want to consider switching your ISP.

Accidentally delete an important e-mail? All is not lost. With AOL 5.0 and later, you have 24 hours to retrieve deleted e-mail. Click on the Mail Room and select Recently Deleted Email. Choose Keep As New or Permanently Delete.

AOL members can create a 10Mb website for free. AOL also has a place to publish business websites, called Business Park. For more in-depth coverage, check out AOL's Prime Host. For a monthly fee, you can set up an easy-to-create, 50Mb, professional-looking website and get online technical support.

Don't want to tie up your phone line? Want to read and answer e-mails on the move, or cut

online time if you have AOL at limited-hours? Do your e-mail offline. Go to the Mail Room menu and choose Set Up Automatic AOL. Check the dialog boxes of the options you want.

To compose an offline message, launch AOL, but don't sign on. Compose your mail, but click Send Later instead of Send Now. When you are ready to send offline mail, choose Run Automatic AOL from the Mail Room pull-down menu. AOL will automatically log you on, send and receive your mail, log you off, and confirm delivery.

Read mail and newsgroups offline. There's no need to stay online to read your mail. To read mail in date order offline, choose Read Offline Mail from the Mail Room menu. Alternatively, you can read copies of mail you've sent by

ENJOY THE AOL EXPERIENCE
These hints can help you get the best from your AOL software.

- Customize the AOL controls. E-mails, ads, and access to sites can all be controlled or restricted if you look through the options.

- Routinely empty AOL's cache folder. It doesn't automatically empty itself, and when the number of temporary files gets too large, your AOL software may stall.

- From Display, increase the screen resolution to make AOL's screenscape more readable.

- Upgrade to the most recent version of the software from time to time.

- Get AOL add-ons. ZDNet's software library (www.zdnet.com/products) has many such products, including pingware that keeps AOL from kicking you out if you're reading or writing—activities that AOL counts as inactive.

choosing this option from the Mail Room menu. Find and read newsgroups offline by going to Files → Newsgroups offline.

Keywords let you navigate the AOL service. Press Ctrl+K and type in a keyword, such as "entertainment." Or type the keyword in the Find field of the toolbar. Then click the Keyword button to view a list of related channels.

The bookmark feature on AOL is called Favorite Places. Here you can list both AOL areas and websites. To add a web page, click on the Favorites icon on the toolbar and choose Favorite Places. Click New and type in (or cut and paste) the name of the site and its web address.

AOL has a lot of fun extra features. You've Got Photos delivers your photographs online. You can keep track of appointments, key dates, and other events with My Calendar. Mail Extras lets you create your own stationery, change the color and style of e-mails, or add photos or hyperlinks. Create personalized signatures, too.

⇨ See also **Internet: E-mail** and **Internet Service Provider.**

ANIMATION

From commercial banners to cute animated links on personal home pages, the Net is full of animations.

Spotted a particularly good animation on somebody's web page? You might be able to save it to your hard disk by right-clicking on the picture and selecting Save image as. This only works with animations in the GIF graphics format though, and you will probably only be able to view the animation later by opening it in your browser.

Why create your own animations for your web page when it's so easy to save other people's animations to your own hard drive? Because it's a breach of copyright unless the website owners have specifically given permission for you to use their work. A better solution is to

visit a library of animated GIFs, such as AnimatedGif.net (www.animatedgif.net), which contains a vast selection of images that are free for anyone to use, grouped in dozens of categories.

Animations from a free library won't make your site look particularly original, so why not build some of your own? Visit the Animated Banner Maker (www.3dtextmaker.com). Here you can create simple but effective animation online by entering some text and choosing the special effects you'd like to apply.

More complex animations require you to install a special animated GIF editor to produce them. But don't rush to buy one just yet—you may already have the tools you need. Some design software, such as Paint Shop Pro 6, comes with its own animation program, and

 HOW TO: USE AOL ANYWHERE

① The main advantage of AOL Anywhere is that you can use it on any PC with any ISP. You don't need AOL software. Connect to the Internet and go to www.aol.com. If you are not an AOL member, click on the AOL Online button beside the Members Sign In.

② Follow the simple download and registration instructions to become an AOL member. When you are registered, return to the AOL Anywhere website at www.aol.com. Enter your screen name and password and click on the Go button.

③ You then have a range of choices of personalized services, including being able to collect your e-mail and send new messages. You also get to use the AOL Instant Messenger program to chat with friends around the world in real time.

HOW TO INSTALL MACROMEDIA SHOCKWAVE

Advanced web animations use Macromedia Flash or Shockwave. To enjoy them, get a copy of the latest player—it's free and easy to install.

1. Visit the Shockwave download page (www.macromedia.com/shockwave/download), read the instructions, then click on Auto-install now.

2. After a short delay, you will be asked if you want the installation to go ahead. Just click on Yes.

3. Your browser now downloads the Shockwave players and installs them automatically. After a few minutes the animated Shockwave logo will appear on your Desktop, which indicates the installation is complete.

these can be as powerful and easy-to-use as many stand-alone animation programs.

So you need an animated GIF editor? You'll find a selection at any of the big Internet shareware libraries. Start at the WinFiles page (http://winfiles.cnet.com/apps/98/graph-gifanim.html), where you'll find a detailed list of 20 GIF animation editors and a download link.

Animations, by definition, contain several different pictures, so they can potentially take a while to download—bad news if you have a slow dial-up Internet connection. So anything that reduces animation size is welcome. For advice on helpful tools, check out WebRef (www.webreference.com/dev/gifanim).

While animations are fun—and look great on a personal home page—be careful if you plan to use them for a business site. Many people consider animations to be overly cute and annoying, so business sites tend to use them sparingly, if at all.

You could liven up an e-mail by embedding an animation in it, but this only works when the recipient is using a mail program that can display HTML messages. If your recipient has old software, or checks mail on a Net-connected cellphone or handheld computer, the animation won't be visible, but it will still download, taking a long time. So send animations only to those whom you're certain can access them.

If you find animations distracting or if they are slowing down your surfing, Internet Explorer lets you turn them off. Click on the Tools → Internet Options, and choose Advanced. Scroll down to the Multimedia section and uncheck the Play animations option.

Even if you think you've disabled animated effects on web pages, there's a chance some advertisements won't be affected because there are several ways of producing them. Turning off Java will disable just about everything. Click on Tools → Internet Options. Click on the Security tab, then Custom Level. Finally select Disable Java. Remember that once Java is disabled, you won't be able to run any Java applets.

APPLETS

An applet is a small application in Java programming, usually embedded in a web page to add features or page transition effects.

To speed up browsing, turn off the applets on your PC by disabling Java. In Internet Explorer, click on Tools → Internet Options. Select the Security tab, click on Custom Level, and check Disable Java. But remember: if the applet is needed for something like a chatroom on one of your favorite sites, it will no longer work.

Want to try creating your own applets? Internet sites such as Java (http://java.sun.com) and Java Programming Resources (www.apl.jhu.edu/~hall/java) offer resources and information that

help you. However, creating applets is not a job for the faint-hearted. Java can seem complex, even for people who have programming experience. But be patient, do a little at a time, and don't be discouraged.

To add advanced capabilities to your own web page, you can download free Java applets from libraries such as The Java Boutique (http://javaboutique.internet.com/applets) and Javapplets (http://javapplets.com). Remember though, that visitors to your website may have disabled Java—or their browser might not support it—so don't assume that everyone will be able to use all your new features.

Diagnosing problems with Java applets is often tricky, but if you're using Internet Explorer, there is a way to make it easier. Just go to Tools → Internet Options. Select the Advanced tab, and under Microsoft VM, check Java console enabled. Click OK and restart the program. Now choose the Java Console option under the View menu, where you will find a window that provides status information on any applets that you might have running.

Cruising eBay or any of the other Internet auction sites can be addictive; you suddenly realize that you can't live without that string-art kit, like the one you had in the 1970s. Whether you're bidding once in a while, or serious about buying and selling, there's no denying that Net auctions are just plain fun.

GETTING STARTED

Take advantage of interactive auction sites that generate automatic bid alerts, send auction schedules to your Inbox, and deliver a running commentary during the action. Or eliminate days of hassle and nail-biting by waiting to the last minute to bid. Esnipe (www.esnipe.com) will help you get a better price at eBay (www.ebay.ca) by bidding for you at the last minute.

Tired of having to check site after site to see if anyone is auctioning that lava lamp you want? Use a search site such as Auction Watch (www.auctionwatch.com) or Bidder's Edge (www.bidx.com) to search hundreds of auctions simultaneously.

There are two types of online auction sites: commercial and person-to-person. At a commercial site, such as WebAuction (www2.warehouse.com) or First Auction (www.firstauction.com), buyers compete with one another to buy goods owned and stored by a company. A person-to-person auction site, such as eBay or Auctionweiser (www.Auctionweiser.com), acts as a go-between for buyer and seller. After the bidding, the site notifies the winning bidder and the seller, who then make their own arrangements to complete the transaction privately.

BEFORE YOU BID

One way that person-to-person sites try to prevent fraud is by posting buyer and seller feedback. On eBay, for example, other buyers and sellers can attach their positive, negative, or neutral comments to your account. If your feedback rating falls to minus four, your account is terminated. Always check a seller's feedback rating before you make a bid.

All bidding is not the same. Some auction sites will allow you to state just how much you want to pay and will let you know if anyone accepts your bid. In reverse auctions, such as the ones held at Pricemate (www.pricemate.com), the prices go down until someone buys. Other auction sites work by searching merchants for the price that you specify. Collaborative sites, such as Mercata (www.mercata.com), pool buyers and search out the best deal from merchants. But if you'd rather barter than bid, check out NexTag (www.nextag.com).

COMMERCIAL SITES
All of these sites require a no-cost membership, including credit card information, to bid.

Bargoon (www.bargoon.com)
This Canadian commercial site deals in everything from antiques and automobiles to real estate.

Bidder Network (www.bidder-network.com)
Collectibles, antiques, hardware, software, and more for sale or up for auction. Registration is confidential.

DealDeal (www.dealdeal.com)
Sale items at DealDeal include computer gear, small office or home office goods, auto electronics, sports equipment, and more.

First Auction (www.firstauction.com)
Part of the consumer network that also sponsors the Internet Shopping Network and the Home Shopping Network, it offers lots of name-brand equipment and appliances.

UBid (www.ubid.com)
Refurbished computers, software, home equipment, plus home electronics devices.

Some commercial auction sites, such as Egghead (www.onsale.com) and First Auction (www.firstauction.com), have live bidding forms. With these you can make bids in real time, so you don't have to sit there waiting for your e-mail to eventually show up. However, you'll find that you really get addicted to auctions much faster this way.

Want to know the value of a family heirloom or just to find out more about its history? Visit the auction house Sotheby's (www.sothebys.com) for

BIDDING DOS AND DON'TS
Enjoy the thrill of bidding but keep it safe, armed with these tips.

- Do use credit cards to make purchases. They protect you against fraud.

- Don't ever send cash. If someone demands cash, it's a sure sign of fraud.

- Don't deal with people who won't provide their name, street address, and telephone number. Several auction sites supply information about how long a seller has been a member and whether they have had previous sales. Others require a valid credit card number from anyone who wants to buy or sell via their site.

- Don't be afraid to ask the seller lots of questions. If a seller is not able to answer a question, perhaps they don't want to.

- Do check out what similar items have sold for in previous auctions. EBay and several other auction sites let you look at the history of items sold in the past 30 days.

- Do get help if you are a victim of mail fraud. The use of the mail to defraud someone is an offence under Section 381 of Canada's Criminal Code. Call the police fraud squad if you have a complaint.

possibly the most extensive database of antiques, collectibles, and memorabilia on the Internet. Alternatively, Christies (www.christies.com), which has salesrooms in New York and Los Angeles, lets you see upcoming auctions and locate specific lots for sale.

Auctions usually run for three to seven days. The last hour of a multiday auction is a consumer-psychology wonder. It often features such players as the Gotta-Make-A-Deal Rookie, who indiscriminately fires bids into the upper price range; the Stealth Bidder, who sneaks in under the bell to grab your gear; and the Shopping-Is-Hell Grunt, who has invested too much time over the last five days to walk away now. The final few minutes can be brutal—and expensive if you don't watch out.

SECRETS OF SUCCESS
If you crave quick action, jump into short-term auctions, such as FirstAuction's 30-minute Flash Auctions (www.firstauction.com) or Edeal's nonstop one-hour Express Auctions (www.edeal.com). These lightning rounds always start at crazy low prices, but the bids don't stay there long.

Before you make your first bid, check out the shipping costs at the auction house's FAQ page. Shipping fees vary widely from site to site, even though all auction houses use standard courier services. These costs can easily run up the price of your fabulous find if you're not careful.

Investigate a product and its retail price first. Check out the item you are interested in with a consumer product site, such as mySimon (www.mysimon.com), ConsumerREVIEW (www.consumerreview.com), or Product ReviewNet (www.productreviewnet.com).

Done your research? Set your top price and don't falter. Put in a low bid first, and if you receive notice that your bid was trumped, you can always move higher. If you might weaken, submit your price and don't get updates.

Are you going to be buying high-priced items? Consider an escrow service, such as Tradenable (www.tradenable.com) or Fort Knox (www.fortknoxescrow.com). These companies charge a percentage of the price to act as go-between. You mail payment to the escrow service, they verify it, alert the seller when everything checks out, and the goods are shipped. After an examination period, you notify the service, which cuts a check and mails it to the seller. Escrow services often accept credit cards, so buyers get extra protection.

Buying and selling online for profit? You may have to report any of your profits on your tax returns. If you've auctioned off your Star Wars collection for more than the 1976 purchase price, Canada Customs and Revenue Agency may consider your profit a capital gain that must be reported. To find out your tax situation, check the CCRA's website (www.ccra-adrc.gc. ca/tax/individuals/topics/capital_gains/menu-e.html).

Buying from abroad over the Net? In this case, you may have to worry about duties. Check with the Canada Customs and Revenue Agency (www.ccra-adrc.gc.ca/customs).

⇨ See also **Internet: Ebay** and **Shopping Online.**

AUTOMOBILES

Research, compare, and purchase the car of your dreams.

OK, so you can't test-drive a car online, but it's the perfect place to kickstart your initial research. Visit the sites of all the main manufacturers, such as Ford (www.ford.ca), Chevrolet (www.chevrolet.ca), and Toyota (www.toyota.ca). There you will find information and specifications on the latest

models of cars, special offers, brochures, upcoming models, plus dealers in your area, and online shopping.

Search for local dealers. When you feel it's the right time to start looking for a new

CAR SITES

Put yourself firmly in the driver's seat by browsing online before you buy.

Canadian Driver (www.canadiandriver.com)
Features test-drive reports, a price guide, and links to clubs and other car enthusiasts.

CarClick (http://carclick.canada.com)
Links to car makers, dealers, financing and insurance groups. Offers road test reports, and a database of new and used cars.

Car Stuff (www.car-stuff.com)
Whatever car you own, there's probably an owner's club for like-minded enthusiasts.

Sympatico Automotive (www1. sympatico.ca/Contents/Automotive)
Buying guide to new and used cars. Here you can compare the prices, safety features, and specifications of two cars.

automobile, visit the websites of local dealers. Use Autonet.ca (www.autonet.ca/Dealers) where you can search by make, province, and even by postal code. Even if you'd prefer to complete the deal in person, browsing online can get you in the right direction quickly.

Get quotes from several different sites before you buy. Information is power, especially when negotiating the best price for your new car. Obtain quotes from Autobytel.ca (www.autobytel.ca), CarsbyNet (www.carsbynet.com), and Auto123 (www.auto123.com). You can also access wholesale and retail market guides for vehicles from The Canadian Black Book (www.canadianblackbook.com).

Don't fancy haggling for your car?
Take a look at the service offered by Dealfinder (www.dealfinder.com). Select the model you're looking for, the area in which you want the service to search, and let Dealfinder do the rest for you (see How to box opposite).

You can find bargains on auction sites like eBay (www.ebaymotors.com) or Bargoon (www.bargoon.com), but there are lots of overvalued cars, too. Take note of eBay's warning: "The seller assumes all the responsibility for listing this item. You should contact the seller to resolve any questions before bidding." Buying at auction is a gamble. Dare you take the risk?

Need financing for your car? Remember, there's no need to take out a loan with the same dealer who is selling you your car—unless they can offer you a competitive rate of interest. Visit different dealers and online banks to compare repayment rates.

Want some extra reassurance? Even if you've found the car you want all on your own, some websites can help before you make your final decision to buy. For example, Carfax (www.

carfax.com) provides detailed information on the history of a used car and whether it's been damaged or the odometer rolled back. Transport Canada (http://apps.tc.gc.ca/roadsafety/Recalls/recintro_e.htm) lets you check for all recall notices for cars by make, model, and year. The site also offers general information about road safety.

After buying a car, search for the history of that make using a search engine like Google (www.google.com). Unless your choice of car is very rarel, you will probably find one or more examples. Discover owners clubs, too. These are sites where people who own the same car keep in touch and share information such as news, recommendations, and servicing advice.

Own a classic car? There's a vast online community out there, where you can swap everything from advice to car parts and news. To hook up with other classic car owners, or browse the classified ads for your dream motor, try Canadian Classics magazine (www.canadianclassics.mag.com), which has links to classic car clubs. Also check out the classifieds at Excite's website (www.excite.ca/autos/vintage_and_classic/buying_and_selling/).

⇨ See also **Internet: Auction Sites, Banking,** and **Shopping Online.**

BACK BUTTON

This essential button reconnects you to web pages you've already visited.

If you've gone one link too far, click the Back button on your browser toolbar to take you to the previous page. Finding what you need on the Internet often involves a lot of exploration, clicking on every link in an effort to locate something useful. Often you'll want to retrace your steps, and this is the easiest way to do so.

Jump back several pages to your starting point. The golden rule for website design is that you're never more than two clicks away from the page you want. Unfortunately, not everyone sticks to this principle, and some sites bury their information very deeply. To skip back several pages, click on the down arrow to the right of the Back button, and you'll be able to choose

from a menu of recently visited pages. It's a much quicker process than pressing the Back button over and over again.

If the Back button is grayed out, then the last link followed may have opened a new browser window. Minimize your current browser window to find out where you are. Is there another window behind it? If so, you should be able to use its Back button to retrace your steps.

Occasionally you'll get yourself in a loop. If you visit a site that has changed its address, the page will probably redirect you to the right location. That's fine until you click on the Back button. Your browser returns to the redirect page, which then sends you to the page you've just left. Just click the arrow next to the Back button and select a page farther down the list.

⇨ See also **Internet: Browsing, Forward Button, Maximize/Minimize,** and **Refresh/Reload.**

BANDWIDTH

Discover how bandwidth affects the speed of your Net access.

Bandwidth means the amount of data that's transmitted within a fixed amount of time. For digital devices, it's usually expressed in

terms of "bits" per second (bps) or "bytes." Thus, a modem that works at 56,000bps has twice the bandwidth of a 28,000bps modem.

Bandwidth is directly proportional to the amount and complexity of data that is transmitted or received per unit of time. For example, more bandwidth is required to download a single photographic image in one second than it takes to download a whole page of text in the same amount of time. Large sound files and animation require a much higher bandwidth for fast downloading. Virtual reality (VR) and full-length, three-dimensional, audio-visual presentations require the most bandwidth of all.

The more bandwidth you have available on your modem, the faster you'll be able to surf. But even if you have a high bandwidth connection to the Internet, you can still get stuck in a data bottleneck. At peak times of day, when lots of people are online, your speed of access may slow down dramatically, as the big servers and those servers with low bandwidth reach their full capacity.

⇨ See also **Internet: Baud Rate/BPS** and **DSL.**

HOW TO: GET A GREAT DEAL ON A CAR FROM DEALFINDER

1 If you think negotiating the best car price seems too much like hard work, log onto Dealfinder, Inc. (www.dealfinder.ca). The firm will search for the car of your choice in any geographic area you indicate.

2 Enter your personal details and select the car you want. Specify the color, additional accessories, car payment methods, and the area that you wish searched. The process starts with the payment of Dealfinder's fee.

3 Within three days, Dealfinder will let you know what it has found for you. You can always decide you're not going to buy the car, but you will still have to pay the fee.

BANKING

Why spend your lunch hour standing in long bank lines, or manually updating your checkbook, when you can track your finances online? Paying bills, transferring money, and viewing transactions electronically is what online banking is all about, and it's never been easier.

GETTING STARTED

First, visit your current bank's website and find out whether it offers online banking. The chances are that a variety of features are already provided. Think about the type of banking you do most frequently—business, personal, loan management, or investments—and select a service that suits you best. While some banks offer free services online, others, like Bank of Montreal's BMO mbanx Direct (www.bmo.com/banking/ways/online.html) charge a monthly fee. Some also require that you install their software.

Can't find your bank's site? Consult Canadian Bankers Association site (www.cba.ca/eng/links_index.cfm), which has links to banks, financial institutions, and government sites.

In addition to your PC, all you need to get started is a modem and web access. In a few cases, you'll need bank-specific software, too.

Millions of people already bank online. Make sure your bank offers all the services you need. The best bank websites go beyond bill-paying and balance updates to let you check your credit card accounts, link banking and brokerage accounts, make trades, and get free stock quotes. Some update account information in real time, and not overnight.

SAFETY AND SERVICE

Is web banking safe? The general consensus is "Yes." All banks use the industry standard Secure Socket Layer (SSL) encryption in the interactive sections of their sites. For even tighter security, use either Navigator 4.0 or Explorer 4.0 or later versions, which are capable of 128-bit encryption. Check the padlock symbol on your Taskbar. If you get a message saying the browser can't communicate with the site, don't do business there. Be sure to grill banks on customer service: How quickly do they respond to e-mail? How do you reach a live person? If you find that your bills have not been paid, how will the bank respond to your query?

The biggest security breaches come after setting up super-secure encrypted and password-protected banking accounts, when people then enter their security information into the computer and walk away from the desk to have lunch or run an errand. To keep your banking details safe, make sure you always log off whenever you are away from your PC.

Make sure your bank has enough live support. Accidentally sent someone the wrong amount, or discovered that checks have not been going out when they should? Make sure your bank has enough live phone support to fix it fast.

Backup, backup, backup! While this should be obvious, make sure that you keep backups of all your banking information. Filing paper copies away doesn't hurt either.

BILL-PAYING

Many banks will let you check your account and pay bills using your own copy of Quicken or Microsoft Money. Sympatico Finance (www1.sympatico.ca/Contents/Finance/banking.html) has links to online banks and other financial sites that let you check balances, transfer money, or pay bills online. You can also bank online using Sympatico's Amicus Financial (www1.sympatico.ca/amicusfinancial/).

ONLINE BANKING
Want to set a budget, keep data for more than three months, or track your portfolio? Consider banking online.

CNET (www.cnet.com)
PC Magazine (www.zdnet.com/pcmag)
Both these sites offer detailed software reviews, which may help you make a choice.

Money (www.microsoft.com/money)
Quicken (www.intuit.com/canada/quicken)
These straight-to-the-source sites are where you will find the rundown on the two most popular banking software programs.

MoneySense.ca (www.moneysense.ca)
An online magazine with banking guides, news, investing tips, and more.

Bill-paying online is much more efficient than using written checks and Canada Post. The first time you make a regular payment, you enter in the name and address of the recipient. After that, all you have to do is choose a payee, enter in the amount, and select the date you want the payment sent. The bank then sends money to the payee by wire, or prints and mails an old-fashioned check if the payee can't accept electronic payments.

Most bill-paying programs allow you to schedule recurring payments by the month, week, or quarter, which may be a useful system for your cable or mortgage bills. If you make a mistake in an electronic check, you can usually stop it, provided you catch the error at least five business days before the check was scheduled to be issued.

Electronic Bill Presentation and Payment (EBPP), the banking system many banks use, renders the banking process more convenient—the entire bill system becomes faster and more secure, and you can access it all through one archive, as opposed to rooting around in a messy pile of papers that can get lost.

BANKING SOFTWARE

Want to turn your computer into a checkbook? Your best option may be to visit your bank's own website. But to integrate bill-payment information with your software, use the full versions of Quicken (www.intuit.com/canada/quicken) or Microsoft Money (www.microsoft.com/money). Both come with budget-, and financial-planning information, along with

electronic bill-paying, banking, and online brokerage access; and convenient links to the Web for investment tools and research.

Quicken and Microsoft Money add an array of alerts, which let you know—for example—when an account balance slips below a specified amount, as well as more advanced online banking and bill-payment functions. Money 2001 tends to have better help sections and account-setup guides, and appears to be designed specially for newcomers. Quicken 2001—on the other hand—has several extras that have been created for the more experienced computer user. It also pays greater attention to year-round tax planning, as well as free tax filing via TurboTax Online.

SMALL-BUSINESS CONCERNS

Setting up your own business? Look at the Business Development Bank of Canada site (www.bdc.ca/bdc/home/Default.asp), which offers advice and financing. Industry Canada (strategis.ic.gc.ca) has guides to business start-ups, market research, employee management,

www.cbsc.org

Canada

financing, and more. Canada Business Services Centres (www.cbsc.org/english) is the gateway to government information about employment issues, exporting, taxation, and other matters. It also offers a step-by-step guide on how to create a business plan, as well as an online small-business workshop.

Some online companies—EZ-e-Accounting (www.ez-e-account.com), for example—will help budding entrepreneurs to manage their money better; to set up, organize, and maintain bookkeeping; to give advice on controlling cash flow; to prepare remittances for PST, GST, and payroll; to reconcile statements; and to prepare business plans. Another company, AssetFindCanada.com (www.AssetFindCanada.com), will check the credit of customers and corporations. Dun & Bradstreet Canada (www.dnb.ca/creditexpress/index.html) offers a credit check of over a million Canadian companies.

⇒ See also **Internet: Bill Paying.**

ONLINE BANKING SERVICES AND INFORMATION

Most of the major banks now offer banking and bill-payment services. Find out which ones do what from the sites listed below.

Banks of the World (www.gwdg.de/~ifbg/bank_2.html)
Links to U.S., international, and offshore banking businesses.

Consumer Connection (http://consumerconnection.ic.gc.ca)
Industry Canada (strategis.ic.gc.ca/SSG/ca00669e.html)
Consult these sites when you want to check and make comparisons of banks' service charges.

Ing Direct (www.ingdirect.ca)
Citizens Bank of Canada (www.citizensbank.ca)
These branchless banks provide the same services as old-fashioned banks, including checking accounts, credit cards, and loans.

MoneySense.ca (www.moneysense.ca)
Provides guides to financial management, as well as general financial information and articles.

BAUD RATE/BPS

Understand how the speed of your Internet connection affects your ability to surf the Web.

Is it baud rate or bps? Baud rate represents the number of frequency changes made per second on a phone line. Bps stands for bits per second, and bits are the data that make up web pages. So bps measures the number of bits that pass through the phone line in a single second. Today, a modem's speed is usually quoted in bps rather than baud rate, but people still use the terms interchangeably. Previously, the two terms were effectively the same, but modern modems can transmit, for example 1,200bps at 600 baud, which can lead to confusion.

When 56 is really 53. The standard modem usually fitted in new PCs is capable of downloading information at 56Kbps. But, in reality, quirks on the phone lines caused by electrical interference and bottlenecks in the Internet mean the connection speed changes continually. That's why the same web page might appear almost instantly one day but take an age to download the next. Moreover, the standard maximum speed for data transfer over the Internet has been set at 53 Kbps.

Don't open too many windows in your web browser if you are suffering from slow connection speeds. Every extra web page will put more demand on the capacity of your modem. Often, you can open a couple of new windows without too much slow down, but go beyond that and the pages will take forever to load. Once a page has fully loaded, however, it can be left in a window without impeding access in your other windows.

Downloads are quicker than uploads. This is because the Net can download files to your PC much faster than your PC can upload files to the Web. If you are e-mailing digital photographs to a friend, it can take almost twice as long to send them as it would take you to retrieve them from your e-mail account. With really big files, these times can add up to hours. So, where possible,

point friends to websites where they can retrieve the relevant graphics or music files themselves.

⇨ See also **Internet: DSL, Internet Service Provider; Hardware: Modems.**

BILL PAYING

Take control of your finances—pay your bills online.

Does your bank support Internet bill paying? Most do. Find out your bank's web address at Sympatico Finance (www1.sympatico.ca/Contents/Finance/banking.html), which lists online banks.

Get Yahoo! to pay your bills. The popular Internet search engine offers its very own bill payment system (http://finance.yahoo.com/bp). Yahoo! Bill Pay enables you to pay your bills online and provides handy financial planners such as payment schedulers. Similar services are available at Sympatico's Amicus Financial (www1.sympatico.ca/amicusfinancial/).

Set up an automated online payment system for your fixed bills. These could include

mortgage, rent, personal loan repayments, and even some utility bills. Even if you forget to pay the bill before you head off on vacation, the system will remember and pay it for you.

Protect your personal details. If you're considering becoming a customer of a bill payment site or even of your bank's bill payment site, check that it has a decent privacy policy. It's vital that your personal information is sufficiently protected, especially from your

WHERE TO PAY YOUR BILLS
Planning to handle your finances online? Try these sites.

TelPay (www.telpay.ca)
A full-service bill-payment service, allowing billing and payment of bills through one site.

**eroute inc.
(www.eroute.com/Default2.asp)**
This service consolidates and presents bills to customers who can pay online or at their financial institution.

Canada Post's Electronic Post Office (www.epost.ca)
At this site, you can receive mail, pay bills, and transfer funds electronically.

**Royal Bank (www.royalbank.ca)
Bank of Montreal BMO mbanx Direct (www.bmo.ca)**
These and other Canadian banks let you download your account history into various financial and accounting software packages.

Canadian Bankers Association (www.cba.ca/eng/Consumer_Kiosk/kiosk_contips.cfm)
This site has information about consumer protection and codes of practice. You can also locate the Canadian Banking Ombudsman here.

payees. It's also worth making sure your financial status won't be passed on to other companies for marketing purposes—or you may find yourself deluged with advertising.

Faster payment means faster debits. Bear in mind that online bill payments are received faster than when you send a check in the mail, and your payment may be debited sooner than you expect. Count this into your calculations, or you might suddenly go into the red!

If you have more than one bank account, consider an online bill-paying service that offers multiple bank account features, such as TelPay (www.telpay.ca). This setup would suit you if, for example, you run a business from home, and use one account for personal finances, and another to settle your business affairs.

Some payees refuse electronic payments. If you want to handle all your finances online, make sure the system that you choose can mail them a paper check. Because of the extra time it will take to mail the check, schedule the payment several days ahead of the due date.

Make sure your bill payment system uses a Secure Sockets Layer (SSL) to stop anyone reading the data transferred between its website and your computer. For better protection, get the most up-to-date version of your web browser, which will support 128-bit encryption. This makes the code used to scramble your data virtually uncrackable.

⇨ See also **Internet: Security On The Net.**

BOOKMARKS

Access your favorite websites easily with Netscape Navigator's handy Bookmark feature.

To keep the addresses of your favorite web pages handy in Netscape Navigator, use the Bookmark feature. When you find a web page you like, click on the Bookmark icon on Navigator's toolbar and choose Add Bookmark.

When you want to visit that site again, click on the Bookmark icon and select your site from the drop-down menu.

Remove tired or incorrect bookmarks to keep your Bookmark list up to date. Click on the Bookmarks menu and select Edit Bookmarks. In the window that appears, highlight the bookmark you want to remove. Then choose Edit and Delete.

You can view your Bookmark list as a web page with hyperlinks—you may find it easier to organize and navigate. To do this, click on File → Open Page → Choose File. Open the bookmark.html file in the Netscape directory. If you have trouble tracking this file down, you can use the Search utility in the Start menu. When you locate the file and open it, your

Bookmark list will appear as a web page containing clickable links to each site.

You can set Navigator to check for and purge web addresses that no longer exist. Go to Bookmarks → Edit Bookmarks, and select Update Bookmarks from the View menu of the window that appears. Your browser will hunt down any "dead" links and remove them.

Transfer your Bookmarks or a list of bookmarks between Internet Explorer and Netscape Navigator. You'll need to download the program Favtool from Microsoft (www.microsoft.com/ msdownload/ieplatform/favtool/favtool.asp).

Make your Bookmarks list easier to read by inserting breaks. Go to Bookmarks → Edit Bookmarks. Highlight the Bookmark you want to add a visual separator before, click on the File menu, and choose New Separator.

⇨ See also **Internet: Netscape Communicator** and **Favorites.**

HOW TO: ORGANIZE YOUR BOOKMARKS INTO FOLDERS

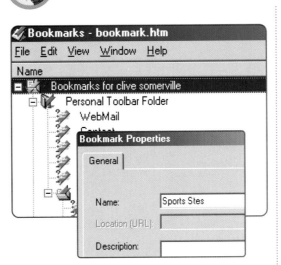

1 Click the Bookmarks icon, choose Edit Bookmarks. This opens up the Bookmarks window, displaying all your Bookmarks. To create a new folder, go to File → New Folder, enter an appropriate name, such as "Sports Sites," and click OK.

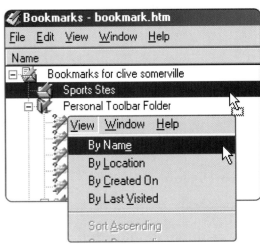

2 To move a bookmark into the new folder, highlight it in the Bookmarks window and drag it over to the folder icon. Open the View menu from the Bookmarks window to see your bookmarks by name, location, date created, or the last time you visited them.

BROWSING

Make your Web browsing as pleasant and speedy as possible!

Keep your browser up to date if you want to visit web pages using all the latest multimedia features. Updates are freely available for Internet Explorer (www.microsoft.com/windows/ie) and Netscape Navigator (www.netscape.com).

Older PC? If your computer is less than 350Mhz, it may work better with an older browser, such as Internet Explorer 4. Or you could try a less well-known browser such as Opera (www.operasoftware.com), which is more compact than Navigator and Explorer.

The surf's up in the mornings and the evenings. This is when the Net is least busy and browsing times are fastest. Your access will be slower if lots of people are using your ISP at once, or if the websites you use are very popular.

Choose your look—you can customize the way web pages appear in your browser. In Netscape Navigator, click on Edit → Preferences. From the dialog box, you can go to the Appearances category to change your fonts or colors, or to the Navigator category to change the language. In Internet Explorer, click on Tools → Internet Options. At the bottom of the General

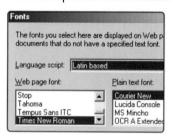

tab, there are four buttons: Colors, Fonts, Languages, and Accessibility. Use these buttons to customize your web page view.

Download several web pages all in one shot. Click on File → New Window and enter a web address. Do this for as many sites as you wish to visit. Leave the windows open and click on the page you want to see. Remember that opening extra windows slows down your connection.

Increase your browsing speed by regularly clearing your cache (see Internet: Bookmarks).

Your cache saves any web pages recently visited. This also protects your privacy, since other users can't see the sites you've been browsing.

All those fancy graphics and pop-up ads can really slow your download speed. Disable graphics and Java applications to make pages

load faster. In Explorer, go to Tools → Internet Options → Multimedia. Deselect Show Pictures, Video and Animations. Under the Java listing, uncheck the Java Enabled Box. In Navigator, go to Edit → Preferences → Advanced. Deselect the box for Automatically Load Images.

Fingers tired from too much clicking? To skip back and forth through pages without using the mouse, press the Alt+Left Arrow keys to go to previously displayed pages, and Alt+Right Arrow to move forward.

⇨ See also **Internet: Cache, Cookies, Internet, Internet Explorer** and **Netscape Communicator.**

BULLETIN BOARDS

Swap information and gossip at the wired world's oldest meeting posts.

A Bulletin Board Service (BBS) is a self-contained online community, a bit like a miniature Internet. People use Bulletin Boards

---

HOW TO: CHANGE YOUR HOME PAGE

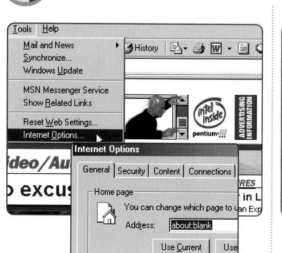

In Internet Explorer change your homepage by going to Tools → Internet Options. Click on the General tab to see your current home page URL. You can choose to type in a new web address, or use the current page, the default page, or a blank page.

If you use Netscape Navigator, click on the Edit menu and select Preferences → Navigator. Click on the Home page radio button in the Navigator starts with section. Type the URL of your choice into the Home page Location section.

both to post messages and to exchange files. Like newsgroups, they cover a myriad of subjects, from stamp collecting to bodybuilding. Depending on your interests, you can choose to access a local Bulletin Board, or one hosted in another country.

No, not everyone uses the Internet! Over 20,000 Bulletin Boards are inaccessible from the Net. Instead, you have to connect directly to the computer that hosts the BBS service using special dial-up software.

You can download shareware dial-up software from The Directory's BBS Corner (www.thedirectory.org/diamond/usoft.htm). BananaCom's software is one of the free ones. Once you've installed it, select the BananaCom icon from the Start menu. Enter a BBS telephone number and dial up to connect.

Hundreds of Bulletin Boards can also be accessed from your web browser. All you need is Telnet software, which comes free with Windows. Double-clicking on an Internet BBS link in your web browser will bring up a Telnet window, which displays the text-based home page of the BBS. If this doesn't happen, you will need to manually show your browser the telnet.exe file, which you'll find in the Windows folder. Refer to your browser's Help file for details on how to do this.

Be warned—when dialing a BBS directly, you're charged as if you were making a normal voice call. If the BBS is on the other side of the globe, it could cost you a small fortune! To help keep it cheap, choose a BBS that's local to your area. You'll also be talking to your neighbors, enhancing the community feel.

Read your BBS messages offline with an offline mail reader program. If you do want to use a foreign BBS this will help to keep your costs down. The mail reader software downloads

messages to a virtual mailbag on your computer, where you can read and reply to them at your leisure. When you're ready to send your replies, the application creates a new mailbag, which you can upload by redialing the BBS. This system means that fewer users are connected at the same time, keeping the service speedy and easily accessible for everyone who wishes to use it. You can download an offline mail reader from BBS Archives (http://archives.thebbs.org/).

BUSINESS

The Internet can be a cheap and easy way to make your business a truly global affair.

The Internet is a real boon to small businesses. It can help them to compete in the free market, providing access to a potentially worldwide customer base, yet keeping running costs relatively low.

Keep all your business accounts up to date and stored at secure online site with software like NetLedger (www.netledger.com) or BS/1 Small Business from Davis Business Systems (www.dbsonline.com). Both programs can help you manage all aspects of invoicing, receipts, bills, bank accounts, checks, time billing, and inventory.

Behind the times? Don't panic! The Canadian Business Services Centres can provide advice and help. The main website (www.cbsc.org/english) has links to guides about e-commerce and other business matters. The section on how to start up a business covers topics such as market research, development plans, and financing. The main site has links to provincial centers, where you can get online or in-person assistance through seminars, training programs, and access to legal and accounting advice.

Smarten up your professional image by printing custom stationery and business cards from your

SITES FOR SMALL CANADIAN BUSINESSES
Keep your business affairs in order and your stress levels down.

Business Gateway (www.businessgateway.ca)
An official federal government site that provides information on business start-ups.

Canada Customs and Revenue Agency (www.ccra-adrc.gc.ca/tax/smallbusiness/index-e.html)
This site has details about GST/HST, small business seminars, and info-fairs.

CanadaOne (www.canadaone.com)
Site features include a free online magazine, business directory, and offers pertaining to human resources, e-hiring, and more.

Canadian Federation of Independent Business (www.cfib.ca)
This lobby group deals with the laws that

relate to small businesses. The site has research reports and valuable links. Once you become a CFIB member, you can use the site for business hints and tips.

Legal Line (www.legalline.ca)
Look here for FAQs pertaining to business law. You can find a lawyer who specializes in legal problems that may concern you.

Strategis (strategis.ic.gc.ca)
An Industry Canada site offering information on all aspects of business.

Workopolis (www.workopolis.com/content/recruiter)
A Canadian recruitment resource where jobseekers can post their résumés and employers can search for potential hires.

PC. Sites like Printomat (www.printomat.com) and Color It (www.coloritprinting.com/canada/index_cdn.htm) offer letter and card templates, and an affordable one-stop printstore.

⇨ See also **Internet: Banking.**

CACHE

Manage your browser's cache settings to speed up your surfing.

When you connect to the Web, the server stores temporary files in a folder called the "cache" (pronounced "cash") in Netscape Navigator, or "Temporary Internet Files" in Internet Explorer. Visit the same sites regularly? You'll find pages download onto your screen much faster, since your computer pulls up files it recognizes from your cache instead of waiting to download them.

Speed up your surfing by increasing the amount of hard disk space allocated to cached files. As a rule of thumb, you should set aside around

five percent of your hard disk space for the cache. However, if you have a very large hard disk, you might want to use more space—up to a maximum of ten percent.

To increase your cache size in Netscape, go to Edit → Preferences and double-click on Advanced. Now highlight Cache, highlight the figure in the box next to Disk Cache, type in your new, larger figure and click OK. In Internet Explorer, go to Tools → Internet Options and click Settings in the Temporary Internet Files area. Drag the slider to the right to increase the amount of disk space allocated and click OK.

Keep your online shopping for family presents a secret. Open your web browser's cache folder and locate the pages for the site you visited. Select each page and press Delete to erase it.

Remember that ISPs also cache frequently used websites and, even if you clear your cache or refresh your page, you may just be getting the ISP's cached page. To avoid this problem, regularly click the Refresh or Reload button on your browser's toolbar.

⇨ See also **Internet: Refresh/Reload.**

CALCULATORS

There's a free online calculator for every job, from working out loan repayments to solving equations.

Work out whether you can afford that new house, and how long it will take you to repay the loan, using an online mortgage repayment calculator. These are available at many different sites, including Canada Mortgage and Housing Corporation's site (www.cmhc-schl.gc.ca/en/bureho/fiop/index.cfm), and at Canoe's Money site (www.canoe.ca/MoneyBankingTools/generalMortgage.html).

HOW TO: CLEAR YOUR CACHE IN NAVIGATOR AND EXPLORER

① In Netscape Navigator, go to the Edit menu and click on Preferences. This opens up the Preferences dialog box. In Internet Explorer click on the Tools menu and then select Internet Options.

② In Navigator, click the plus sign (+) next to Advanced option. Click on Cache and select Clear Disc Cache. Click OK when warned that this will remove all files in the disk cache. Now click Clear Memory Cache, then OK. Click OK once more to finish.

③ Instead of "cache," Internet Explorer uses the term "Temporary Internet Files." Go to the Temporary Internet Files section and select Delete Files. Click OK when warned that you're removing all temporary Internet files. Click OK to finish.

Plan for your own or your children's college education. The Education Savings Calculator at Human Resources Development Canada (www.hrdc-drhc.gc.ca/cgi-bin/english_calc_page1_cesg.cgi) enables you to calculate the amount required for college, taking into account the Canada Education Savings Grant. The Dundee RESP Calculator (www.dundeefunds.com/Dynamic/Education/RESPCal/RESPCal.cfm) lets you adjust all the various RESPs with or without the Canada Education Savings Grant. Mohawk College's Cost of College Calculator (calculator.mohawkc.on.ca/) looks at all the costs of schooling. The resulting figures will be applicable to any Canadian community college.

Solve that tricky math or statistical problem with a little bit of help from the Calculators On-Line Center (www-sci.lib.uci.edu/HSG/RefCalculators.html). There are over 11,000 specialist calculators online here, covering everything from basic math to linear equations and fluid mechanics.

Planning a big trip to several countries? Get to grips with foreign money by using a currency conversion calculator, such as those at the Bank of Canada site (www.bankofcanada.ca/en/exchform.htm) or Yahoo! Canada Finance (ca.finance.yahoo.com/m3). With minimal mental gymnastics, you will soon be confident at

converting dollars into a foreign currency, or vice versa perhaps.

Fine-tune your fitness program. Use a daily activity calculator to figure out how many calories you burn in a typical day (www.thriveonline.com). Tick off your daily activities and the calculator works out how many calories you burn. Are you in a panic because summer is just around the corner? Now may be the best time to increase your exercise program. Health Canada's Physical Activity Guide (www.paguide.com) tells you how to start an exercise program and how to do it safely. Dietitians of Canada (www.dietitians.ca/english/healthy/bod_info.html) helps you calculate your body mass index. This site tells you your BMI score and offers tips on controlling fat intake and achieving your ideal weight.

CELEBRITIES

Keep up with all the latest news on your favorite stars.

Try typing your favorite star's name as a web address, sandwiched between www and .com—for example, you could try Shania Twain (www.shania-twain.com). There's a good chance that you will go straight to the official website of that celebrity.

You can expand your collection of celebrity memorabilia by buying photographs, books, and other associated items online. To get you started, try visiting special websites such as Celebrity Bookstore (www.celebritybooks.com) or CelebrityCD (www.celebritycd.com).

Get up to speed on the latest news and rumors about the rich and famous. Sites such as E!Online (www.eonline.com), Showbizwire (www.showbizwire.com), and that bastion of colorful gossip, The National Enquirer (www.nationalenquirer.com), will help you to keep track of all the stars.

Ask Mark McGwire how you hit a home run or consult Tom Cruise for advice on acting. Popular stars make regular appearances in special live chatroom events set up at websites such as Yahoo! Chat (http://chat.yahoo.com), CBS Sportsline (http://cbs.sportsline.com), and ESPN Network (http://espn.go.com).

⇨ See also **Internet: Television.**

CELEBRITY SITES
Star struck? Feed your obsession the easy way.

Celebrity Site of the Day (www.csotd.com)
Exactly what it says on the package—a new celebrity site every single day of the year.

Entertainment Tonight Online (www.etonline.com)
The latest gossip on Hollywood, TV, and music industry stars, updated daily.

Stage Names (www.usfanclub.com/realnames.html)
The true identity of dozens of stars revealed. For example, Marvin Lee Adair is Meatloaf!

Biographical Dictionary (www.s9.com/biography)
The Biographical Dictionary contains a searchable database of 28,000 celebrities through the ages.

People Magazine (www.people.aol.com)
News, features, and interviews on the inevitable celebrity theme in this online version of the popular magazine.

Celebrity EMail (www.celebrityemail.com)
Send e-mails or view messages to celebrities.

CHATROOMS

One of the most popular uses of the Internet is as a forum for people all over the world to communicate in real time. This is done using IRC (Internet Relay Chat), which consists of various separate networks of servers that allow you to "chat" online with anyone, anytime.

WHAT IS A CHATROOM?

A chatroom is an online discussion group where you can converse with your friends and e-colleagues in real time. This means that, instead of having to wait for a reply, as happens with ordinary e-mails, your message is sent simultaneously to all the other people in the chatroom and appears on their screens at the same time, too. Similarly, any reply or new message that they type will appear on your screen and those of the rest of the group.

What about my children? As with the rest of the Internet, children should be supervised at all times when using chatrooms. While most rooms follow a code of conduct that means they are likey to be polite and friendly, some are certainly not suitable for children. Your Internet Service Provider should be able to block access to chatrooms if you want.

GET CONNECTED

The IRC networks vary in size. The largest nets are Undernet, IRCnet, DALnet, NewNet, and EFnet.

EFNET was the original IRC net and often has more than 32,000 people on it at once.

To connect to an IRC server, you need to run a program known as a "client." Head for mIRC (www.mirc.com) to download a free client. This site will walk you through the download

process, which takes just a few minutes. Once connected to a server, you can join one or more "channels," devoted to topics ranging from baseball to Beruit to small talk.

You don't have to connect to IRC to have a chat. Thousands of Internet sites, such as Yahoo! (http://ca.chat.yahoo.com) and MSN (http://communities.msn.ca/home/) have their own chatrooms. And there are also web-based chat sites with hundreds of "rooms," such as Talk City (www.talkcity.com) and Web City (http://chat.webcity.ca/). None of these alternative chat facilities require special software. For a list of popular web chat channels, check the 100 Hot Web Rankings (www. 100hot.com/chat).

Conversations may be public (where everyone in a channel can see what you type) or private (messages between just two people, who may or may not be on the same channel). There are hundreds of IRC servers worldwide. To find a list of

servers around the globe, go to the IRC Help site (www.irchelp.org/irchelp/networks/).

Once you have downloaded your IRC client software and logged onto one of the servers, you'll be able to see what channels are available on that server by typing /list. You can then view literally thousands of listed channels. If you find that you need to narrow the list down still further, simply type /list-min 10, for

example, to view all channels that currently have a minimum of 10 users.

FAVORITE SMILEYS AND ABBREVIATIONS

Chatrooms use a variety of abbreviations and symbols called "smileys." Here are a few of the most common.

:-)	A smiley face (on its side).
:-(	A frown.
;-)	A wink.
:-P	Someone sticking their tongue out.
X=	Fingers crossed.
{}	Hugging.
$-)	Greedy.
OJ	Angel.
}:>]	Devil.
brb	Be right back.
bbiaf	Be back in a flash.
bbl	Be back later.
ttfn	Ta ta for now.
np	No problem.
imho	In my humble opinion.
lol	Laughing out loud.
j/k	Just kidding.
wb	Welcome back.
rotfl	Rolling on the floor laughing.

To navigate the IRC, you need to use commands. All commands start with /. If you omit the /, anything you type will be transmitted to the channel as a message. Although there are hundreds of commands, you can get by adequately with 20 or 30 basic ones (see box for shortcuts). For a complete list of commands, check either the help file of the server or Connected Media (www.newircusers. com/ircmds.html).

CREATING A CHANNEL

A channel is a chat forum. Begin by picking a name that is not already in use. For example, to start a channel called "film real," type /join #film real. A window pop ups showing you as the only person on film reaL. Promote yourself to channel operator by typing /op, followed by your nickname. Your nickname will now appear with an @ in front of it. Now you are the operator, you can change the topic at will by typing /topic, followed by the channel name and the new topic. Type /quit when you want to leave the IRC.

Every user on the IRC is known by a nickname, such as "Thunder Thighs" or "Smart Chick." To avoid conflicts with other users, it's best to use a nickname that is not too common. The nickname for nickname is "nick." For a full list of the e-mail addresses and nicknames of everyone on a channel, type /who *.

Channels are run by channel operators, or "ops," who control the channel by choosing who may join, banning mischievous users, and moderating the channel (in other words, choosing who may speak). Channel ops are like baseball referees. They have complete control over their channel, and their decisions are final. If you are banned from a channel, type /msg to the channel op and ask nicely to be allowed back in. If that doesn't work, go to another channel and try not to get banned this time!

NET SPLITS AND OTHER PROBLEMS

You may occasionally be disconnected from a channel by a net split. Net splits occur when networks become divided, thus separating you from other participants with whom you were speaking. Splits are often relatively short, but quite common on very busy days. When one occurs, wait a while, then try to connect again.

One frequent IRC problem is lag—the noticeable delay between the time you type something and the time when someone else gets to read it. One way to reduce lag is to choose a nearby server. You can measure how bad the lag is by using the /ping command, which tells you the length of delay you are experiencing. On most clients, typing /links shows a list of servers on your current net. Use this command sparingly, or you may be mistaken for a "link-looking" troublemaker. To avoid lag, use the /dcc chat command to establish one-on-one connections, which won't be broken by a net split.

In most clients, you can set up a DCC chat connection by typing /dcc chat "nickname of other person." To talk through that connection, just type /msg =nick (note the = sign). In mIRC, you can also start a DCC chat session by selecting DCC and then Chat from the Menu. Now enter the nickname of the user with whom you wish to chat. A new window will open for that DCC chat session.

Whenever you leave a chatroom, remember your Internet netiquette and say goodbye, especially if you've been involved, as opposed to just lurking. To quit IRC completely, and so the others on the channel see that you're leaving, type "/quit good night."

It's easy to change IRC servers. If you want to leave one server and try out another, it couldn't be easier. Simply type /server followed by the server name. It's always worthwhile trying a few different IRC servers to see what the service is like and which one will best suit your particular chatting needs.

⇨ See also **Internet: Netiquette.**

Dialog box

Connect to IRC Server | Sort

Full Name: lisa magloff
E-Mail Address: lmagloff@planet3.com
Nickname: scribbler
Alternative:

☐ Invisible mode

OK | Cancel | Help

While the Web provides vast learning opportunities for kids, it's also a worry for many parents. How much time online is too much? Are your kids viewing harmful information? Who are they talking to on chat lines? However, there are a host of child-friendly resources and ways to keep kids' surfing safe.

SAFE SURFING

Consider filtering tools. Concerned your kid may be reading or viewing material online that is inappropriate or harmful? There are lots of different filtering tools but they don't all work along the same lines. Some companies decide what is filtered, some let parents pick among preset categories, while others provide a "starter list," which parents can add to or remove sites from. Also, some tools allow a parent to override the filter if they consider a site appropriate for their child to view. For reviews of the filtering tools available—many of which have downloadable free demos—go to ZDNet (www.zdnet.com) or CNET (www.cnet.com) and search for "filtering."

Avoid blocking good information. Use a filter, such as CYBERsitter (www.cybersitter.com), to analyze language around key words. For example, if you have set a filtering tool to limit access to sites containing potentially inappropriate words such as "sex" or "breast," you may be better off using a filter. That way, you'll avoid blocking entries such as "breast cancer" or "chicken breast recipes."

CYBERsitter™
For a Family Friendly Internet

"CYBERsitter is the most advanced and effective product available for restricting access to objectionable Internet material."

<u>Download Now!</u>

No filtering or blocking system is foolproof. The only way you can be positive that your child is surfing safely is to become—and stay—involved in your child's online exploration. Set clear rules for using the Internet and make sure your kids know what the rules are. That way they will stay safe.

GET INVOLVED

Surf as a family. Before you start shopping for the kids, explore fashion trends together with them, thus avoiding arguments and cries of "Oh, Mom, that looks awful." Visit DailyFashion.com's Real Fashion for Real Girls (www.dailyfashion.com), GapKids.com (www.gapkids.com), and Teenmag.com's styling section (www.teenmag.com).

Teach your child financial management, and "money sense" with The Allowance Room and Money Machine (www.cibc.com/ smartstart/general/AllowanceRoom.html) and Kids' Money Q&A (www.kidsmoney.org/ advice.htm). There's Something About Money (www.yourmoney.cba.ca/eng/index.htm) is a Canadian Bankers Association site that helps young people learn about money.

Is your child an Internet zombie? Concerned they may be spending too much time online? Perhaps you don't want them to use the Net when you're asleep or away from home?

SAFE SURFING GUIDELINES FOR KIDS
Handy hints to ensure happy times online.

1. Take the trip together. Make time to see what your kids are doing online and discover their interests.

2. Teach your children never to give personal details to people they meet online, especially in public places such as chatrooms and bulletin boards.

3. Instruct your child never to plan a face-to-face meeting alone with an online acquaintance regardless of how old they say they are.

4. Tell your child not to respond to offensive or dangerous e-mail, chat, or other communications. Have them tell you so that you can report it to the site operator.

5. Establish clear rules for Internet use for your kids and make sure they follow them.

6. When you are home, limit your kids' noneducational surfing time by placing your computer in the family room or another open area.

Special software, such as NetNanny (www. netnanny.com), allows you to set limits on how much time your child spends online, and what time of day they can go online. (You might also try shooing them outdoors to get some exercise, or signing them up for an after-school activity!)

INTERNET FUN FOR KIDS

Plan a kids party online. There are plenty of ideas for the cutest crafts, games, refreshments, and more at ZDNet Family PC (www.familypc. com). You can also make a website to invite everyone to your birthday party. Find out how at thePlunge. com (www. theplunge.com).

thePlunge.com

Event Planning Made FUN!

Holidays	Just For Fun	Mil
• Valentine's Day	• Cocktail Party	
• Hanukkah	• Movie Night	
• Christmas	• Dinner Party	

Many browsers are created just for kids' use. While they work in the same way as adult browsers, such as Internet Explorer or Netscape Navigator, they are easier to use and also filter out inappropriate words or images. Kids can search from over 10,000 safe sites using ChiBrow (www.childrenbrowser.com), a free browser that lets parents decide what is appropriate first. TermiNet (www.danu.ie) is a browser that acts as a firewall, while also restricting and blocking access to sites and protocols. Or set KidDesk at Edmark.com (www.

FAMILY EDITION KiD DESK

Hard Drive Security for Parents and Computing Fun for Kids!

edmark.com/prod/kdfe) to start automatically when your computer starts so that your child only has access to what you want them to. It comes with a kid-friendly browser based on Internet Explorer 4.

Child-oriented search engines work just like regular search engines, but special features protect kids from inappropriate material while helping them to locate information easily. Some of these search engines will only look within a certain group of preapproved sites and others will search the whole Web but withhold inappropriate results. Try AOL NetFind Kids

Only (www.aol.com/netfind/kids/channel) for links to kid-safe sites only. Or visit Ask Jeeves for Kids (www.ajkids.com), which allows children to ask a question in plain English, presents a list of matching questions for selection, and takes them to a kid-safe website for the answer.

Kids love to chat with other kids in chatrooms. But how do you know when your child is chatting about a topic that you approve of—and with another child as opposed to an adult masquerading as a child? You can breathe easy and know that your children are chatting safely when they use a monitored chatroom, where adults keep tabs on what's being said—and by whom. FreeZone (www.freezone.com) offers five monitored chatrooms of fun while Graffiti Wall (www. graffitiwall.com) has separate chatrooms for

under- and over-12s. Kids can also share writing ideas at Creative Writing For Kids (http:// kidswriting.about.com/mpchat.htm).

⇨ See also **Internet: Chatrooms, Education,** and **Passwords.**

HIP AND HAPPENING SITES FOR KIDS
Encourage the next generation of PC users to get online and learn more about the world around them.

CBC4Kids (www.cbc4kids.ca)
This site offers news, music, science, history, and much more on this easy-to-navigate and colorful site.

Canadian Kids Page (www.canadiankidspage.net)
Hundreds of fun, funky, and educational links to safe sites, all annotated and organized in age ranges from preschool to college.

The Cartoon Network (www.cartoonnetwork.com)
Home to favorites such as Fred Flintstone, Scooby-Doo, and Space Ghost.

FreeZone (www.freezone.com)
A unique online community where kids come to interact with other kids. Includes

an online tutorial program so that children can teach adults how to use computer and Internet technology.

Kids' Castle (www.kidscastle.si.edu)
An interactive site looks at the treasures and the educational program at the Smithsonian Institution in Washington, D.C.

Yuckiest Site on the Internet (www.yucky.com)
Science site with a definite lean toward the yucky, the sticky, and the creepy crawly.

Zoom Dinosaurs (www.zoomdinosaurs.com)
An interactive online hypertextbook about dinosaurs. It's great for younger children, their parents, and their teachers.

COLLECTIBLES

The world's largest marketplace, the Internet, puts you just a few clicks away from millions of individual buyers, sellers, and merchants.

Come together. "Wanted" or "For Sale" notices on collectible sites put buyers and sellers together, and posting a request for a particular item on a site's message board is likely to bring you quite a few offers. The more message boards you try, the more chance you have of finding what you want.

Try using an "upside down" auction site such as eWanted (www.ewanted.com). You post a "Wanted" message for items that you wish to buy and the sellers do the bidding.

More than a garage sale. Collectibles sites are a great resource for learning as well as trading.

They often allow you to swap information with other collectors, or get the benefit of expert advice and background material on a particular item.

If you're a beginner to the world of collectibles, start with a community guide, such as About.com's (http://collectibles.about.com). You'll find plenty of sensible advice from the more experienced enthusiasts on how to start building collections. You can also use the message boards to ask for advice, check on the availability of items, and compare prices. Collectors love to share their enthusiasm and knowledge, making this an excellent way to get up to speed.

Hang out in a virtual mall to get a feel for the collectibles market, and maybe discover your very own passion. A virtual mall, like its bricks and mortar counterpart, is a collection of individual stores under one roof—the roof in this case being a single website.

Narrow down your choice of sites when using a search engine. Instead of typing in a request for "collectibles," which will bring up hundreds of websites, try, for example, "baseball collectibles." To make sure you find precisely what you're looking for, you can define the search even further, by typing, say, "Babe Ruth baseball collectibles."

Attend sales at online auction sites, such as eBay (www.ebay.ca) and iCollector (www.icollector.com). Vendors post their goods with a "reserve" price—the absolute minimum price they're prepared to accept. The item remains on the site for a fixed period, typically 10–14 days, and the highest bidder wins. With some persistence and a bit of luck you can snap up a real bargain.

Broaden you horizons. Visit a website where collectors from all over the world meet to trade and chat. Sites such as World Collectors Net (www.worldcollectorsnet.com) can open up different sources, especially in Europe, or may inspire a new area of interest.

Find out what your collectibles are worth. Use an online price guide, such as Kovels (www.kovels.com). Registration is free and you will find current price guidelines for thousands of antiques and collectibles. Alternatively, get an online appraisal for items you suspect may be valuable. Some major auction houses, such as Sotheby's (www.sothebys.com), provide online valuation forms.

A picture's worth a thousand words when it comes to selling a collectible. It's a lot easier for buyers to make a decision if they can see what the object looks like. Use a digital camera, or scan in a conventional photograph, then upload the image from your computer to the website where you wish to sell the item.

⇨ See also **Internet: Auction Sites, eBay,** and **Shopping Online; Hardware: Digital Cameras.**

COLLECTIBLE SITES
Whether you're buying or selling, soak up the atmosphere here...

Antique Antics (www.antiqueantics.com)
A Canadian collectibles site. View the item here, and negotiate by e-mail.

Collector Online (www.collectorsonline.com)
A virtual mall with dozens of stores to browse—or you can rent vendor's space.

eBay Collectibles (http://pages.ca.ebay.com/collectibles-index.html)
With more than one million items up for grabs, there's something for everyone.

Gerry's Sports Cards (www.gerryssportscards.com)
This site specializes in vintage hockey cards and memorabilia.

Best Antiques and Collectibles Sites! (http://computrends.com/antiquering)
Dozens of dealers are linked in this web ring. View one site, then click the Next button to visit the next dealer, and so on.

COOKIES

These tiny files are sent to your PC by websites to help personalize your surfing experience, but some people view them as snooping.

On the record. Ever wondered how a website knows who you are before you even log in? When you first visited and registered your name, e-mail address, and other details, the website dropped a cookie onto your hard drive to record your details. So, the next time you visit, you don't even need to log in—the site recognizes your PC and already knows you.

Personalizing pages. Shopping sites such as Amazon (www.amazon.com) use cookies to track your browsing on their sites and work out your preferences. Next time you visit, they can recommend products you might like to buy.

A cookie is only a simple text file. It isn't a program, so it can't alter or do any harm to your

PC. Only the website that sent the cookie can retrieve it, so no other sites have direct access to the information it contains. However, the company owning the website can pass on the information to other companies, if it wants to.

Some cookies are called "persistent cookies". While most cookies are deleted as soon as you finish surfing, others stay on your PC until their expiration date is reached. Rather like your browser's History file, persistent cookies leave a record of the sites you have previously visited.

Don't like the idea of cookies? Your browser can block or delete them. Or you can opt to be prompted whenever a site tries to put one on your hard drive—so you can choose whether or not to accept it. However, many shopping sites send and receive cookies every few seconds. If your browser prompts you each time, it could make things excruciatingly slow!

⇨ See also **Internet: Privacy** and **Security On The Net.**

COPYRIGHT

Copyright laws apply to the Internet just as they do to other media. If you have your own website, they can protect your content.

Why does copyright exist? To protect the rights of the creator. This means that the text, images, animations, video, and overall design of a website belong to the copyright owner. You can still download copyrighted text, images, or music for personal use, just as you might tape a song or photocopy a news article. But you can't take somebody else's material and republish it on your website without permission.

Don't copy—link. If there is an article or picture you particularly wish to draw to the attention of your audience, why not provide a link to that site? That way you avoid any legal problems, since a website address, like a telephone number, is not subject to copyright. And you'll give the site publicity too.

 HOW TO: BLOCK COOKIES

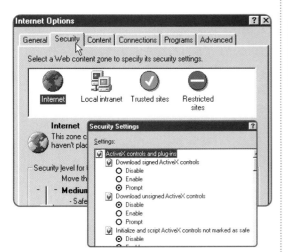

1 Run the Internet Explorer program if this is your main web browser. Go to Tools → Internet Options. Click the Security tab, then the Custom Level button to access the Internet Explorer security settings.

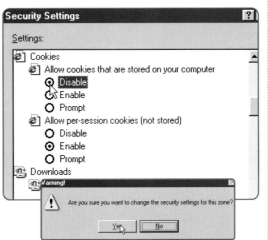

2 Scroll down to the Cookies section. Highlight the appropriate radio buttons to disable only cookies that are stored on your computer ("persistent" cookies), or only cookies that are retrieved at the end of a session, or both. Click OK.

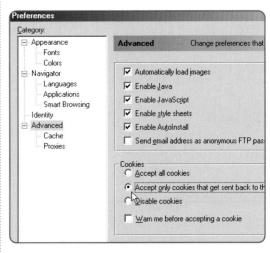

3 If you use Netscape Navigator, to disable cookies or persistent cookies go to Edit → Preferences and select Advanced in the Category box on the left. Choose one of the three options under Cookies and click OK.

If in doubt, ask the originator of the material for permission to use it. Be clear about the exact use and any revenue that might be generated. Consider the options and have a fallback plan ready if the answer is "no."

While a copyright notice is not strictly necessary, it reminds visitors to your site that this is your content and they should respect it! For example, you could include a note at the foot of your website's homepage, such as "© Copyright 2000 John Smith."

Want to protect your copyright? You can register your content with Industry Canada's Canadian Intellectual Property Office (CIPO). You get copyright automatically under the Copyright Act. But registration provides a certificate that you can use to sue anyone who infringes your rights. Registration is inexpensive and can be done online. For details about copyright, fees, and registration, go to CIPO's site (strategis.ic.gc.ca/sc_mrksv/cipo/cp/cp_main-e.html).

CREDIT CARDS

Concerned about credit card fraud? Exercise a little caution, and online shopping can be safe and fun.

Keep your standards. Apply the same rules to purchasing online as you do when buying from a store or over the telephone. Before reaching for your credit card, make sure you are satisfied that the company you're dealing with is trustworthy. Are they a reputable established business or are you responding to an unsolicited

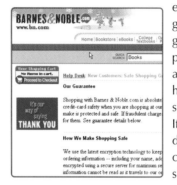

e-mail promising goods at "too good to be true" prices? Is there a telephone helpline and a street address? If the website does not inspire confidence, then shop elsewhere.

Can your browser use Secure Sockets Layer? SSL is a data encryption system used by websites to ensure that your personal details are transmitted in a secure format. Version 2 and later of Netscape Navigator and Microsoft Internet Explorer support SSL. To see whether a website is operating the Secure Sockets Layer before submitting your details, look out for a small locked padlock symbol or key at the bottom of your web browser window.

 HOW TO: DOWNLOAD A FILE USING DOWNLOAD ACCELERATOR PLUS

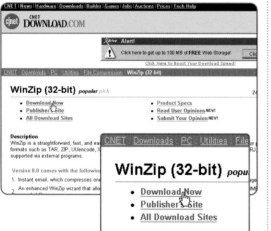

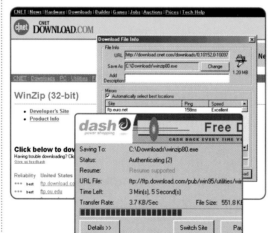

1 Find an Internet site that has the file you want. The site should provide information on the size of the file and whether it is .zip, .exe, or another type of archive, as well as confirming that the program is compatible with your operating system and hardware.

2 Download Accelerator will load automatically. The tracking bar shows you how long the process is taking, where the file is being stored on your hard drive and whether the download can resume if the connection is lost.

3 When Download Accelerator has completed its work, you can quickly find your file by using Windows Explorer. Don't forget to scan for viruses before opening any file downloaded from the Internet.

Look for a Digital Authenticate Certificate.
This certificate guarantees that the site you're looking at is what it purports to be, and not a

front set up to deceive you into releasing your financial details. Click the key or padlock icon to view the certificate.

You have limited liability for fraud. MasterCard limits your personal liability for fraudulent use of your credit card by someone else to $50. Visa has waived this with its Zero Cardholder Liability Policy. With both, you have to notify the card issuer as soon as you become aware of the fraud. This enables the issuer to block the card's use and issue you with a new one. To make sure your credit rating isn't sullied, you should also notify the credit-tracking agencies.

Never use a debit card (an ATM or bank card) to pay for a purchase on the Internet. It does not have the limited liability protection that a regular credit card does.

⇨ See also **Internet: Banking**, **Security On The Net**, and **Shopping Online.**

DOWNLOADING

By following a few simple guidelines, you can avoid the common problems of downloading data to your computer.

Be organized. If you don't already have one, set up a dedicated download folder on your hard drive to help you find your files after downloading—for instance, C:\Downloads. It also makes sense to keep an archive directory to store your downloads in, such as C:\Downloads\Archive. Then, should you need the original file, you won't have to download it all over again.

Checking for viruses is a sensible precaution, even with the most reputable of sites. Make

sure your resident virus scan program is operational while you're downloading. Also check the downloaded file with your anti-virus software before you open it.

For speed, use a download accelerator. Programs such as Download Accelerator Plus (www.downloadaccelerator.com) can speed up your downloading by up to 300 percent for certain file types.

Use an archive program such as WinZip. Most websites prepare their files for downloading by compressing them with a "zip" utility. This packages up multiple files into a single file and reduces its size to make it quicker to download. WinZip will "unzip" this

package once you have downloaded it. WinZip is available as shareware (www. winzip.com). You can download it for free and pay later if you like it.

Download files from FTP sites. FTP stands for File Transfer Protocol—it's an old but fast method of sending files over the Internet. Sites that use this format tend to send files more quickly than straightforward web pages do. If you have the program Download Accelerator Plus, it will automatically look for faster sites, including FTP ones. Large software libraries will also usually offer an FTP site.

Try using a download scheduler program. Software like Gozilla (www.gozilla.com) can manage your downloads for you, scheduling them for less busy times on the Web, when

the files will copy across more quickly. Like Download Accelerator, Gozilla can also resume a broken download later on.

Missing files? If you can't find a file on your computer that you're confident you've already downloaded, there's a simple procedure you can follow to locate it if you use Netscape Navigator. If Navigator is still running, click File → Save As. When the Save As dialog box appears, it will automatically open to the same folder you selected for the previous download. Make a note of the folder listed in the Save In field at the top of the dialog box. Click the arrow to the right of the Save In field to identify the path to this folder. Make a note of the file path and click Cancel to track down your file.

⇨ See also **Windows: Folders** and **Viruses; Software: Upgrading Software; Internet: FTP.**

RESUMING INTERRUPTED DOWNLOADS
File download gone amiss?
Find out what to do next.

1. The Resume function of Download Accelerator can save you lots of time if you suffer a lost connection or have to halt a file transfer. To resume an interrupted download, just run the Download Accelerator program and double-click on the file in the entry list. The status column will indicate how much of the file has already been successfully downloaded.

2. Some older Internet servers and some connections channeled through another networked computer may not support this function, so watch for the confirmation message on the Download Accelerator panel when you begin a transfer.

3. Download Accelerator 4 includes an AlwaysResume feature that, for files less than 10Mb, will support resume even on those connections where the standard resume is not available. This should not be used as part of your standard configuration, because it slows down the transfer speed.

DSL

A Digital Subscriber Line (DSL) provides you with a fast, permanent connection to the Internet.

DSL is a way of transmitting digital data on regular copper phone lines and is great if you need use the Net a lot, because you get a fast, 24-hour connection. It's available in various standards, but the best for home or small business use is ADSL (Asymmetric Digital Subscriber Line). This is usually the cheapest option and your current telephone line can probably be converted with the minimum of

DSL INFORMATION SITES
Thinking of joining the DSL bandwagon? Do your research first!

AT&T Canada (www.attcanada.ca)
This provider is geared up to serve business customers with high-speed access, but it does not yet have home service.

NBTel
(www.nbtel.nb.ca/English/AtHome/Vibe)
Vibe Service is NBTel's DSL service. The site has FAQs and a list of local providers.

Sprint Canada (www.sprintcanada.ca)
DSL is offered here, but it serves only small-business customers, with pricing geared to business needs.

Sympatico (www1.sympatico.ca)
Bell Canada's Internet provider offers high speed access and advice to potential DSL customers. It provides answers for FAQs about availability, compatibility with other phone features, and technical matters.

PC Magazine (www.zdnet.com/pcmag/)
This and other computer magazines offer advice about DSL, comparing it to cable-service high-speed link and dial-up service.

hassle. One advantage of ADSL is that you can use your phone on its existing number at the same time as using the Net,

Check with your phone company to make sure that you can receive DSL. Lines can only be installed within certain distances of the phone substation. Speed of the connection deteriorates with distance, so phone companies impose limits on how far they will roll out a line.

A special DSL card or modem will connect your PC to the data line. A DSL supplier may provide these as part of the contract for the service. The cards are generally PCI cards for PCs. If you have a Windows 98/Me PC, use a USB DSL modem. There are varying standards of DSL modems, so, if you need to buy one, get a recommendation from your supplier first.

Choosing the right provider is always tricky! When comparing contracts, look for guarantees for committed information rates and minimum service levels. What happens when your provider fails to meet its promises? Are there hidden charges, and do you need to pay extra for installation or equipment rental? If, at sometime in the future, you are not satisfied with the service, how much will it cost to terminate the contract?

Protect against virtual intruders. An "always on" DSL connection increases the risk of unwelcome visitors, so use firewall software to protect your system. A free application, such as Zone Alarm from Zone Labs (www.zonelabs.

ZoneAlarm

Easy, Always-On Internet Secu

ZoneAlarm™ is essential solid protection against them dead in their track More than **6 million** PC **ZoneAlarm is compati**

com), monitors and protects your ports from attack by rendering the system invisible to roving hackers and preventing unauthorized access to your PC.

New standards of DSL include VDSL—the "V" stands for "video." VDSL uses new technology to transmit interactive video streams. It integrates your phone line with your TV set so

that caller information can be displayed on the TV screen. The data rate is over ten times that of ADSL and includes the ability to stream high-definition television signals. It might well be the next big thing in data transmission.

⇨ See also **Hardware: Modems.**

EBAY

The auction website at eBay (www.ebay.ca) is a great way to buy and sell just about anything, from CDs to cars.

Don't dive in and start bidding immediately. Take time to research the item and the seller—eBay provides plenty of help. Most pages include lists of frequently asked questions (FAQs). Online tutorials and community forums also mean you can learn from the experiences of others.

Check the feedback and add your own. Sellers will often ask buyers to comment on the service being provided. Regular sellers quickly build up a profile, which should reassure you about their honesty and ability to honor a sale. Whenever you complete a buying or selling transaction on eBay, it's always a good idea to contribute your feedback, whether it's positive or negative. This will help future bidders to make a valued judgment when dealing with the same seller.

ebY	ID card	adirondackd
Member since Sunday, Aug 13, 2000		☆

Summary of Most Recent Comments

	Past 7 days	Past month	
Positive	1	5	
Neutral	2	2	
Negative	1	2	
Total	4	9	
Bid Retractions	0	0	

Only deal with sellers who are ID verified. All sellers have to start somewhere, so not everyone is going to have dozens of positive feedback reports. If a new seller has an ID Verify logo in their Feedback Profile, it means they have satisfied an independent agency, acting for eBay, that they are who they say they are and that they currently reside at the address supplied. So at least with this method you know whom you are dealing with!

Check where in the world the item you want is located. Since eBay is now a global service, items listed in eBay's search engine may be drawn from the United States, Canada, Europe, Japan, Australia, or New Zealand and you may incur additional shipping fees and import duties when you buy. If you're considering an international purchase, make sure before you bid that the seller will send the item abroad. Otherwise you'll be wasting everyone's time.

Bids move up in even, incremental amounts, but these are just a minimum and you can sometimes get an edge by increasing your bid slightly above the minimum amount. For example, in a $5.00 increment auction, you can increase each of your bids by $5.01.

Planing to sell an item? Consider the situation from the buyer's position. Would you bid for the item you've presented? Reassure your potential customers by giving as much information about yourself and your items as you can without compromising your personal safety. Set up an "About Me" page of relevant information, and get ID Verified in the rules and safety section if you don't have positive feedback in place yet.

Think visually—scan in a photo of your item. People like to see what they're buying. A picture reassures buyers that the item exists and gives them an idea of its condition. Keep the image file size small enough so potential buyers don't lose interest waiting for it to load onto their screens, but large enough to show it's condition. Instructions on uploading a picture to the eBay server are given on the eBay site.

Set a reserve price. Unless you want to risk selling for less than you expected, set a minimum acceptable final bid. So if the auction fails to reach the reserve, you don't have to sell. The reserve is not the same as your starting price, which can be low to start the bidding.

Post a link to your auction in relevant newsgroups and forums to draw potential buyers. If you plan to be a regular seller, create a web page to advertise your upcoming sales.

If your item doesn't sell, you can try again for free, but it's a good idea to change the formula. You could swap the image, change the lot title, and lower the minimum and reserve prices.

⇨ See also **Internet: Auction Sites** and **Collectibles.**

HOW TO: BID FOR AN ITEM IN AN EBAY AUCTION

All Items	All items including Galler
Status	**Featured Items - Curren**

📷	NO reserve! Kodak DC290 2.1 Megapixel! Dutch!
🖼️	KODAK DC240 DC 240 DIGITAL CAMERA *1 YR.
📷	KODAK DC200 DIGITAL CAMERA+EXTRAS! DC 2
🖼️	KODAK DC280 DIGITAL CAMERA 20MEG MEM
🖼️	*** NEW *** Kodak DC240i Digital Camera ***

(1) When you see an item you're interested in, click on the description to find out more about it. The item line tells you the current highest bid, how many bids have been made, and how long the auction has to run.

KODAK_DC280_DIGITAL_CAMERA_2

Item #448871979

Photo & Electronics:Photo Equipment:Dig

Currently	$355.50 (reserve not yet met)
Quantity	1
Time left	**8 days, 4 hours +**
Started	Sep-24-00 18:27:59 PDT
Ends	Oct-04-00 18:27:59 PDT
Seller (Rating)	jziggy (508) ☆ me
	view comments in seller's Feedback Profile | view seller's
High bid	aac_jk@yahoo.com (0) 👓
Payment	Money Order/Cashiers Checks, Personal Checks, Other
Shipping	Buyer pays fixed shipping charges, Will ship to United charges

(2) The next screen gives you access to information about the item and the seller. The icons next to the seller name indicate how many previous auctions the seller has run and whether the seller has a personal information page. To place a bid, click on the bid icon.

AK_DC280_DIGITAL_CAMERA_20MEG_MEM

Item #448871979

Current bid:	$355.50 (reser
Bid increment:	$5.00
Your maximum bid:	420

(Minimum bid: $360.50)

[Review bid]

crementally on your behalf **up to your maximum bid** y users. The eBay term for this is proxy bidding.

(3) At the bidding screen, enter your maximum bid. eBay acts as a proxy bidder on your behalf, bidding in the stated increment until your maximum bid is reached. If you are successful, the seller should contact you within three days to make arrangements.

EDUCATION

In the Internet age, education has become not just a case of how many facts you know, but whether you understand where to look for them in the first place. The Net contains sites to help you learn, sites where you can find schools and colleges, and sites to teach you fun or more serious subjects.

ONLINE LEARNING OPTIONS

Begin your search for knowledge with an education-oriented metasearch. Education World (www.education-world.com) is simply a database of 110,000-plus educational sites available on the Net. Search by keyword, using advanced search options such as Boolean (see page 271), or you can search by region, event calendar, K12, and other categories. You can

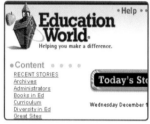

also search with Yahoo! (http:// ca.yahoo.com/), which will come up with thousands of sites in over 100 categories dealing with education.

Going to college is one of life's major steps and finding the right one for you can be a tough job. But you can actively speed up your search by going on the Internet. The Association of Universities and Colleges of Canada (www.aucc.ca/en/index.html) has details about programs, facilities, enrolments, fees, and housing. The Canlearn Interactive site (www.canlearn.ca/English/eng.cfm) can help you plan your education taking into account your goals and your financial situation. This Human Resources Development Canada site has links to provincial and federal loans programs, including the Canada Student Loans Program. School Finder (www.schoolfinder. com) lists over 600 colleges, universities, graduate schools, and online training centers.

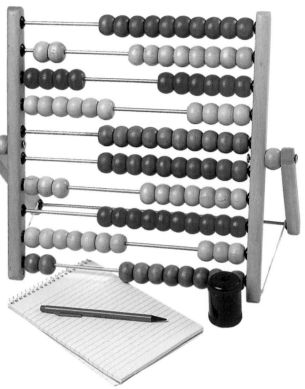

Internet Age demands require that you know more than ever before. With so many options for online learning, you needn't go back to college to acquire new skills. World Wide Learn (www.worldwidelearn.com) lists online courses and learning resources available from around the world on almost every topic, from classical animation and cartoon development to an accelerated online MBA program. Canadian Education on the Web (www.oise.utoronto. ca/~mpress/eduweb/eduweb.html) provides an extensive directory of distance education

courses available across Canada at university, college, and secondary school levels.

More and more schools are now offering online learning. Are you interested in an institution or a program, but don't know if the courses you'd like to study are offered online? Check with the

KIDS' EDUCATION
Covering preschool through high school, here are some websites where your child can have fun and learn.

**Colorful Mathematics
(www.math.ucalgary.ca/~laf/
colorful/colorful.html)**
A lively, exciting site using games to teach math concepts to students. The games are about the discovery of patterns at the very heart of mathematics.

FunBrain.com (www.funbrain.com)
Great fun! The Internet's advanced alternative to old-fashioned flash cards, these learning games are divided into specific age categories and provide a fun, easy way for your child to learn.

Science Brainium (www.brainium.com)
This interactive site has educational games and self-paced learning activities designed for the grade 4 to 8 crowd. The BugZone presents an animated adventure series that illustrates scientific concepts.

**TeenOutReach.com
(www.teenoutreach.com/index.shtml)**
Search here for great sites featuring music, movies, games, and many other topics. Parents, too, have their own corner here with links to sites about adoption, single parenting, and more.

institution. If you or your child intends to take a course online, pay close attention to whether the school is accredited or not. While this may not matter for some courses, if you need to have a written certificate at the end of the course, the school needs to be accredited through a national accreditation agency.

Most colleges and universities now maintain websites with up-to-date details about their programs, faculties, and facilities. Online sites where this information is listed include The Association of Universities and Colleges of Canada (www.aucc.ca/en/acuindex.html), Canadian Education on the Web (www.oise. utoronto.ca/~mpress/eduweb/eduweb.html), and School Finder (www.schoolfinder.com).

LEARNING CAN BE FUN
When your learning needs are less academic and more growth or hobby oriented, visit Elspeth Sladden at The Learning Studio (www. thelearningstudio.com). For a small fee per course, the site offers online instruction, often using webcasts in courses such as "Ten Steps to Great Relationships," "Speak and Grow Rich," and "Champagnes and Sparkling Wines." FreeSkills (www.freeskills.com) specializes in free online computer tutorials to help you bone up on Windows, Unix, Novell, graphics, and many of the other technical subjects, while Inner Learning Online (www.innerbody.com) offers online courses such as automotive repair. The websites and Usenet groups covered above have

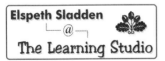 message boards that could provide answers to any queries you have.

Didn't get your high school diploma? With online study options, it is never too late to start. The Independent Learning Centre (ILC) (http:// ilc.edu.gov.on.ca/01/home.htm) of the Ontario Ministry of Education provides a distance education program with an extensive series of

high school correspondence courses. Manitoba Education and Training, Distance Learning and Information Technologies Unit (www.edu.gov. mb.ca/metks4/instruct/ddu/handbook/index. html) offers correspondence courses for elementary and secondary school. Alberta Online Consortium (www.albertaonline. ab.ca/) has an online school for grades 1 to 12, as well as regular distance education.

There's more to education than the three R's! These days, kids use the Internet to discover all kinds of different subjects. Learn2 (www.learn2. com) covers such practical subjects as how to fix a zipper or raise goldfish. But if you want to mix fun and education, Starchild (http://

starchild.gsfc.nasa.gov) is NASA's site for young aspiring astronomers. Find out what you need to know for homework assignments. Educator's Choice Search (http://www3.ns.sympatico.ca/ educate/home.htm) has thousands of links, all organized by topics such as "Places," "People," and "Canadian Information."

INTRODUCE THE NET EARLY
Internet education starts once a child learns how to use a computer. Speed up the process by introducing your child to the educational aspects of the computer. Funschool (www. funschool.com) has educational games for preschoolers. Teach them to enjoy music by singing along to songs for preschoolers at the U.S. National Institute of Environmental Health Sciences site (www.niehs. nih.gov/kids/ musicchild.htm).

Home schooling is increasingly popular. The Internet allows house-bound kids, or those in rural areas, to attend classes virtually. Canadian Home Based Learning (http://www.flora.org/ homeschool-ca/) is an educational resource for home-school parents. Kids' Town (http://www. kidstownglobal.com/) is an online magazine for home-schooled kids.

⇨ See also **Software: Educational CD-ROMs.**

E-GREETINGS

Snail-mail cards may go the way of the horse and buggy now that e-cards come with full-color illustrations, sound, and animation.

The easiest way to send an e-greeting is to log-on to one of the many sites offering thematically sorted images (see box at right). Just select the image, type in a message, and the address of the recipient, and off it goes.

Before you send an e-greeting, use the site's Preview facility to see the card. You can also alter the delivery time and date if appropriate.

The same e-card can be sent to many different people, as a party invitation for example, by simply clicking the site's Add Recipient, or similarly named, button.

If a simple photograph or cartoon doesn't seem exciting enough, use animation instead. Remember that you will need the Flash plug-in to view it, as will your recipient. You can download Flash free from the Macromedia site (www.macromedia.com).

Want to make sure a greeting card got there? Ask for e-mail confirmation to be sent to your

own mailbox. Assuming your recipients check their mail, you'll know they've seen your cards.

Many sites allow you to add a voice message to your e-greetings, normally recorded via a toll-free number. To hear the message, your recipient needs the RealPlayer plug-in (downloadable from www.real.com).

Use your favorite e-greetings website's address book to store e-mail addresses and important dates so all the information you need is in one place.

⇨ See also **Internet: E-mail**.

E-MAIL ADDRESSES

Get an e-mail address that you can take with you wherever you go.

Keep up with your e-mail while you're on the road or on vacation. Subscribe to a web-based provider, such as Hotmail (www.hotmail.com) or Yahoo! Mail (http://mail.yahoo.com). These services let you check mail from any computer connected to the Net. You can set them up to retrieve mail from your other e-mail accounts.

Don't forget to delete mail you've read from an account mailbox. If you exceed the fixed amount of space such services allocate to you, the provider may delete messages for you.

If you are an AOL user, you can retrieve your e-mail from a computer without the AOL browser. Just go to the AOL site (www.aol.com/aolmail) and enter in your screen name and password when prompted.

When your first-choice name is already taken on one web-based e-mail provider—and you don't want to be "janedoe98"—try another site. There are many providers, and one of them will have your name available. For an extensive list of web-mail providers, check out the Free E-mail Directory (www.e-mailaddress.com).

Get a free e-mail address for life. Sign up with a mail-forwarding organization such

as Bigfoot (www.bigfoot.com) or Mail-X-Change (www.mail-x-change.com). You get one e-mail address to give out, and the mail will be forwarded to any account you want.

Check web-mail accounts regularly. Some services terminate your account if it is not used for a given period—typically, 90 days.

About to change your ISP, job, or city? Fear you'll lose touch by having a new e-mail address? To avoid this, you can register your details with an online service such as ContactDetails (www.contactdetails.com). All you do is list the site ID on e-mails, business cards, and so on, so that others have access to the site. If you change your e-mail address, the

E-GREETING SITES
Delight friends and family with an original online greeting.

Blue Mountain (www.bluemountain.com)
One of the biggest selections of e-greetings images on the Web, organized in categories. There's also a Card of the Day.

Comedy Central (www.comedycentral.com/greetings)
Humor dominates, with a good range of cards for most occasions.

Expressit (www.expressit.com)
This site specializes in 3D and animated cards, although there are plenty of more conventional images, too.

Hallmark (www.hallmark.com)
A cleverly designed site from a "real world" card manufacturer. Especially strong in photographic images.

Yahoo! Canada Greetings (http://ca.greetings.yahoo.com)
An extensive range of greeting cards organized in categories.

updated details will always be available at the ContactDetails site.

⇨ See also **Internet: E-mail.**

ENCYCLOPEDIAS

Online or CD-ROM encyclopedias are ideal for quick information access.

Get free access online to one of the world's best information sources: Encyclopedia Britannica (www.britannica.com). Check out the Canadian Encyclopedia (www.thecanadianencyclopedia. com) for details about all things Canadian.

Got a DVD-ROM drive in your PC? DVD editions of *Britannica 2001* and *Encarta 2001* have more photos than their CD counterparts, and hours of extra video and audio material.

Need a specialized encyclopedia for focused research? Just add the topic to your Internet search term; for example, use "encyclopedia

physics" or "encyclopedia wine." The hits will cover sites relevant to the latter word as well.

Stumped by that trivia quiz question? Try the encyclopedic Fun Trivia site (www.funtrivia. com/trivia.html). Its searchable database has thousands of categorized trivia entries.

Beef up your homework and get extra tips from the Microsoft Encarta site (http://encarta.msn. com/homework). There is also a selected collection of links to related websites.

⇨ See also **Internet: Education.**

ENVIRONMENT

The Internet has ideas to help you save energy and money, and make the world a better place.

If you want to drive a clean machine, visit the U.S. Environment Protection Agency's Vehicle Emissions Guide (www.epa.gov/autoemissions).

They've rated every new passenger vehicle for tailpipe emissions. Also, visit to Office of Energy Efficiency (http://energy-publications.nrcan.gc. ca/index_e.cfm) to calculate fuel consumption for your current or future car.

Do the environment a favor and save money on home heating and power bills by switching to solar energy. The Solar Energy Society of Canada (www.solarenergysociety.ca/discover1. htm) provides details of what's involved. For an overview of alternative power, visit the website of Natural Resources Canada's Renewable and Electrical Energy Division (www.nrcan.gc.ca/es/ erb/reed/public_e.htm).

Environmental programs can extend across communities. To get the lowdown on programs countrywide, visit the Sustainable Development Information System site (www.sdinfo.gc.ca/ ENG/Default.cfm). The International Institute for Sustainable Development (http://iisd1.iisd. ca/comm/) has a listing of publications about community initiatives and "how to" guides.

 HOW TO: CREATE AN E-GREETING IN OUTLOOK EXPRESS

① Open a new message in Outlook Express. Type in your greeting and format it the way you want. Centering short phrases can add impact. Go to Insert → Picture. Click Browse in the dialog box and navigate to where the picture is stored. Select it and click Open.

② Then click OK in the Picture dialog box. The picture appears beneath your message. To add some space between the two, right-click on the picture and select Properties. In the dialog box under Spacing, change the figure beneath Vertical to 10, and click OK.

③ If the picture is too large or too small, you can resize it by grabbing the handles at the edges and corner and dragging to the required dimensions. Now you can save the message and e-mail it to your friend.

E-MAIL

Before there were e-companies, e-business, eBay, and e-commerce, there was e-mail. Even people who don't use their PC for much else find e-mail invaluable. E-mail makes communication easier. Letters and files can be sent and arrive almost immediately, and there's no need to coordinate phone calls.

KEEPING TABS

What can you do if you want to send someone an e-mail, but you don't know what the e-mail address is? Normally, you would go to the "From" field of the last e-mail the person sent you to obtain the return address. But what if the person has never e-mailed you? Well, the first solution—and the simplest one—is to phone the person and ask for the address. Alternatively, you could try accessing an online directory of e-mail addresses (you can find a directory of directories at www.emailaddresses.com).

But what if the name you need isn't in an e-mail directory, or you can't decide which "John Smith" is the one you want to get hold of? Many people give their e-mail address out when they contribute to online discussion groups or place information on the Internet. You can also use a search engine to look for a name and a keyword, and you just may turn up a page featuring the person's e-mail address, too. For example, if your friend Beth Jones is

an avid gardener, you can try typing "Beth Jones" and "garden," into a search engine.

FAXING VIA E-MAIL

It was only a matter of time before someone worked out how to turn a fax into an e-mail. In fact, there are numerous services that enable you to use your e-mail account as a fax machine. Some supply you with a personal fax number and when anyone faxes that number, the fax is converted into an e-mail attachment and sent to the e-mail address you specified. eFax Plus (www.efax.com) requires you to sign up for a toll-free U.S. number and charges a monthly fee, as does Protus IP solutions (www.protus.com/index.cfm).

If fax to e-mail works, then e-mail to fax must also be possible. And it is—you can send a message or document via e-mail to the fax service's site and then have it forwarded via fax to the number you specify. eFax Plus (www.efax.com) and Protus IP solutions (www.protus.com/index.cfm) again offer this service, as does j2 Global Communications (www.j2.com). Most of these Web companies have a set-up fee and charge on a per-fax and per-minute basis.

KEEPING IN TOUCH

Want to send a phone message to someone who doesn't have computer access, but you don't want to speak to them directly? Or maybe you'd like to send yourself an automatic wake-up call? Then try the Nortel Networks website (www.nortelnetworks.com). The site takes your e-mail message, converts it into a voice message through a

speech synthesis process, then delivers it to your chosen phone number at a time you choose. It's ideal for communicating across different time zones.

Traveling lightly with just your cellphone? Try UnifiedMessaging (www.unifiedmessaging. com)—a service for business—which lets you use your phone or Internet connection to check your voice messages, faxes, and e-mails.

WEB-BASED E-MAIL SERVICES
Check out these special sites for help with your e-mailing needs.

Anonymizer (www.anonymizer.com)
Mask your ISP address by sending mail through this third party re-mailer.

Canada.com (www.canada.com)
Canoe.ca (www.canoemail.com)
These two Canadian sites offer free e-mail. With a Canada.com account, you can have "your name@canada.com" as your address.

Email.com (www.email.com)
The site offers free e-mail accounts.

Hotmail (www.hotmail.com)
This is Microsoft's very popular, free e-mail service.

Mail.com (http://corp.mail.com)
A good—free—e-mail service with lots of different domain names.

SpamFree (www.spamfree.org)
Learn how to deal with (and ditch) any junk e-mail that comes your way.

Do you want to keep using your regular e-mail address with your ISP while you're on a business trip or vacation? Use an e-mail gateway site to access your account and read and send your messages. All you need when you're traveling is access to any PC with a web browser, so you'll be able to send messages from any cybercafe or other Internet-connected PC. One such gateway is Mail2Web (www.mail2web.com). You will need to give the name of your e-mail server (this is usually the part after "@" in your e-mail address), your user name (usually the part before "@"), and your e-mail password. When you send your answer to mail, your reply will look as though it has come from your usual e-mail account even though you've accessed it elsewhere. The service is free, but the one price that you'll have to pay is that your e-mail will have a short advertising message for Mail2Web.

E-MAILING WITH FLAIR

Ever wonder how some people manage to get such funky e-mail addresses as joecool@ wrigleyfield.com? They use a forwarding service. These services let you choose almost any kind of groovy address. Anything mailed to that address is re-routed to your "real" e-mail service provider. Forwarding services also let you keep one e-mail address, no matter how many times you switch ISPs. Both ForeverMail (www.forevermail.com/) and V3 (www.v3.com) offer an e-mail forwarding service where you can choose your own address.

Few people realize that it's sometimes possible to recall and delete an e-mail message before it reaches its destination. To carry out these tasks from Outlook 2000, you open the message from your Sent Folder and click on Actions. Now select Recall this message. If the message still resides on your company's or ISP's mail server, it will be deleted and you'll be informed that the process of deletion has taken place. But remember you will need to react almost immediately to recall the message in sufficient time.

Concerned about hacking and e-mail privacy? In fact, the person most likely—and most interested—in reading your e-mail is probably your boss. Don't assume that anything you send from your office e-mail is private. When you want to criticize the management via e-mail, do it from a third party account, such as HushMail (www.hushmail.com), which offers secure and

encrypted mail, or Hotmail (www.hotmail.com).

SORT YOURSELF OUT!

Do you receive a lot of regular mail from the same people all of the time? Set up an e-mail filter. E-mail filters look for names, words, or phrases within the letters, and transfer them straight to a designated mailbox as soon as you receive them. Automatic sorting makes your mail easier to keep track of (or to ignore)—indispensable if you are on a number of mailing lists or receive a lot of junk mail. In Outlook Express, filters are stored under Message Rules in the Tools menu. To activate the filters, check the boxes that apply to you. In Netscape Messenger, you will find Message Filters in the Edit menu.

> 1. Select the Conditions for your rule:
> ☐ Where the From line contains people
> ☐ Where the Subject line contains specific wor
> ☐ Where the message body contains specific v
> ☐ Where the To line contains people

Setting up an e-mail to exchange files? There's no guarantee that the attachments will arrive intact. Your best bet is for both parties to enable the MIME (Multipurpose Internet Mail Extensions) standard in their e-mail software. Eudora, Outlook, Outlook Express, and Messenger all support MIME. Even with MIME engaged, expect some quirks. For example, the only way to reliably transmit from Eudora to Lotus Notes is by stuffing files inside Zip archives before sending them. To engage MIME, refer to your Help file.

ADDRESSES EXPLAINED

Internet e-mail addresses typically have two main parts, separated by an "at" sign (@). Take joebusiness@businessdude.com, for example. The user name (joebusiness) refers to the recipient's mailbox. The host name

(businessdude), which is also called the domain name, refers to the mail server—the computer where the recipient has an electronic mailbox. The host name is generally the name of a company or organization. Finally, there's a dot (.), followed by three letters (com), which indicates the type of domain.

An address ending with .com typically means that the host is a business or commercial enterprise, or an online service, such as Canada.Com. Most companies use this extension. A host name ending with .edu indicates a university or educational facility; .org shows the host is a non-commercial organization; and .gov is used by government agencies and officials. Other extensions include .mil for military and .net for network. There are also plans to add additional domains, such as .web and .store. Foreign e-mail addresses often contain a dot (.), followed by two letters that represent the country. For instance, .uk stands for United Kingdom. Sometimes the address is not obvious. For example, .es stands for Spain (Espagne), and .de for Germany (Deutschland).

Want to find someone's address? If you know where they work, you can guess the domain name part of their address. But what about the user name? The recipient's name may be just their last name, their first initial and last name, or their first and last name separated by a dot, dash, or underscore. Take a little bit of time to work your way through these variations, and you'll probably get the right address.

ETHNIC INTERESTS

The Internet gives people with minority interests a place to communicate and share information. Whatever your ethnic interests are, you can find others who share them. Brush up on the language of your forebears, correspond with pen pals, buy rugs from Pakistan and baskets from Mali, or simply research a topic.

ETHNIC RIGHTS

Find out about civil rights and civil liberties from the Canadian Civil Liberties Association (www.ccla.org)—our country's civil liberties watchdog. The Canadian Human Rights Commission (www.chrc-ccdp.ca/), created by the Canadian Human Rights Act, works to resolve individual complaints, promote knowledge of human rights, and reduce barriers to equality in employment and services. The Canadian Human Rights Foundation (www. chrf.ca/english/general/files/master_eng.htm) is a private body dedicated to promoting human rights through education, both here and abroad.

Are you a victim of racism or is it an issue that concerns you? The Canadian Race Relations Foundation (www.crr.ca/EN/default.htm) was founded to foster racial harmony and cross-cultural understanding, and to eliminate racism.

Celebrating our diversity. Heritage Canada's Multiculturalism website (www.pch.gc.ca/multi/main_e.shtml) aims at increasing cross-cultural understanding and discouraging discrimination. The Canadian Council for Multicultural and Intercultural Education (www.ccmie.com/) encourages public participation and respect for cultural diversity.

CAREERS

A large number of Internet sites exist to help with the career-related needs of minorities. One is the Human Resources Development Canada's Workplace Equity site (info.load-otea. hrdc-drhc.gc.ca/~weeweb/homeen.shtml). Alliance for Employment Equity (www.web. net/~allforee/) is a national lobby group that is working toward mandatory employment equity.

Do you own or start your own business? The Aboriginal Banking Unit of the Business Development Bank (www.bdc.ca/bdc/home/Default.asp) is a site aimed specifically at assisting Aboriginal entrepreneurs get their businesses up and running.

Find a role model of your own ethnicity for inspiration. Windspeaker (www.ammsa.com/windspeaker/index.htm), a national Aboriginal news source, profiles outstanding Aboriginal people. Artists Against Racism (www. artistsagainstracism.org) features a wide range of artists—actors, musicians, dancers, painters, writers—who, in speaking out against racism, provide role models to youth.

CULTURE

Are you a member of the Cree First Nation? Learn more about your culture by studying Cree Language Lessons (www.nisto. com/cree/). Reconnect with your ancestry and culture at the Native Trail (www.nativetrail com/en/index.html) or the Aboriginal Youth Network (www.ayn.ca) where you can chat with friends, read about lifestyles, and follow links to education, health, entertainment, and employment sites.

Anyone interested in learning about Canada's Native peoples can begin at Windspeaker (www.ammsa.com/windspeaker/index.htm). This national news source features profiles of prominent figures, news, editorials, links to provincial papers and radio, and information about jobs, community events, health, government, and politics. The Assembly of First Nations (www.afn.ca) is the place to see the progress of leaders' efforts in the areas of treaty and land rights, environment, employment initiatives, health, housing.

For African-Canadian cultural links, click on the African-Canadian On-line (www.yorku.ca/research/aconline/) site. Here you can find out about the newest documentaries, latest publications, dance events. AfriCanada.com (http://africanada.com/default.cfm) has features, news, music, chat, and forums to keep up to date with what's happening in the Black community not only in Canada but around the world.

Asians from all countries have a wide variety of Internet sites and resources geared toward their interests. AZNLink.com (www.aznlink.com) is a fast-growing directory that lists Asian sites. ChinaDotCom (www.china.com) presents news and information from China, Hong Kong, and Taiwan. NewsAsia (www.newsasia.com) contains current news and financial information from Asian publications across the Internet, while aForums (www.aforums.com) provides the opportunity for online discussions of Asian news events, culture, and history.

If you are going to do business in Asia, Asiaville (www.asiaville.com) is an invaluable site, listing online resources for information on business in Asia. To complement this, Asia Source (www.asiasource.org) gathers information regarding the cultural, economic, historical, and political dimensions of Asia.

Keep up with current events around the world through Ethnic NewsWatch (www.ethnicnewswatch.com), a full-text collection of newspapers, magazines, and journals created by and for minorities.

Learn the language of your ancestors online or go to International Language Development (www.ild.com), which provides shareware language lessons in German, Japanese, Korean, and Russian using RealAudio. Study foreign languages online, with Language Lessons on the Web (http://languagelab.bh.indiana.edu/lessons/wlessons.html).

If you speak a language, such as Chinese or Arabic, that doesn't use Roman-style letters, you may need to download special software in order to read websites written in that script. Go to a shareware site, such as ZDnet (www.zdnet.com) or CNET (www.cnet.com), and look for the language reader you need.

ETHNIC GOODS ONLINE

The Internet lets you shop globally, often buying directly from the craftsperson. Crafts Fair Online (www.craftsfaironline.com), everywhere store (www.everywherestore.com/artisan groups.htm), Native Arts Trading (www.nativeartstrading.com), and Tribal Planet (www.tribalplanet.com) are among the thousands of sites that carry native crafts from many different places around the world.

Do you live in a small town that doesn't have any local ethnic grocery stores? Then order ingredients from the CMC Company (www.thecmccompany.com) or Far Away Foods (www.farawayfoods.com). Such companies will ship you food from many countries, including Bangladesh, Greece, Egypt, and Malawi.

Thinking of opening a Mexican restaurant but aren't sure where to get your supplies? Visit Pacific Island Market (www.asiamex.com/tayabas), where you'll find a vast range of Asian and Mexican cooking ingredients that can all be delivered to your door.

Want to learn to cook ethnic ingredients? Culinary World Tour (http://gumbopages.com/world-food.html) contains recipes from around the world. International Recipes Online (www.simpleinternet.com/recipes) is a culinary exchange group. And The Recipes Folder (http://eserver.org/recipes) contains thousands of vegetarian recipes from such places as India, the Middle East, the Mediterranean, and Asia.

⇨ See also: **Software: Foreign Languages; Internet: Foreign Languages.**

MINORITY-ORIENTED SITES
Check out these sites pertaining to ethnic interests.

HEALTH
Canadian Health Network, Ethnic Groups (www.canadian-health-network.ca/1ethnic_groups.html)
Links to sites and articles dealing with health issues in a multicultural society.

First Nation and Inuit Health Programs, Health Canada (www.hc-sc.gc.ca/msb/fnihp/index_e.htm)
Covers national projects including telehealth, substance abuse programs, care programs.

GENERAL
Canadian Council for Multicultural and Intercultural Education (www.ccmie.com)
Find out more about news, youth projects, education, and exchange opportunities.

Canadian Ethnocultural Council (www.ethnocultural.ca)
A coalition of ethnocultural organizations with links to their members.

Asian Canada (www.asian.ca)
Wide range of links for Asian communities.

Black Cultural Centre for Nova Scotia (www.bccns.com)
Ontario Black History Society Online (collections.ic.gc.ca/obho/)
Two sites looking at the history of black settlement in their areas.

NativeTrail (www.nativetrail.com/en/index.html)
An online portal for First Nations and Inuit people of Quebec and Labrador.

FAQs

Almost every website has a FAQ page —a file of Frequently Asked Questions. Make it your first stop for info.

You can pronounce it "F-A-Q," but you might lose credibility with the techies if you do. It's more commonly pronounced "fak."

It's only polite to read the FAQs before you join a newsgroup, whatever the topic. That way, you run less risk of cluttering up the information exchange by asking questions to which the answers already exist.

Most FAQs are relatively brief and load into your browser instantly. So if you're new to a site, program, or a topic, it's worth taking extra time to browse the whole document. Not only might you find the precise information you need, you'll also discover lots of other things that will enhance your experience.

Does your website need FAQs? Frequently asked questions (FAQs) can be very useful if you are running a business or an educational site, but if it's a personal or family site you shouldn't really need them. For detailed advice on how to prepare and publicize FAQs, go to Infinite Ink's Writing Periodic Postings site (www.ii.com/ internet/faqs/ writing).

ii WRITING PERIODIC POSTINGS ('FAQs' & 'PIPs')

Print out the FAQs as a handy hard-copy reference. You'll avoid the need to keep an extra window open on your Desktop.

FAQs can be a great way to find solutions to computer problems when you've exhausted other possibilities. ZDNet (www.zdnet.com/ zdhelp) has an extensive collection of links to FAQs relating to hardware problems.

Searching an archive of FAQs can be a good way to find out whether a newsgroup is the one for you, especially if you're interested in an obscure topic. Try the searchable archive from the Internet FAQ Consortium (www.faqs.org).

⇨ See also **Internet: Newsgroups.**

FAVORITES

Save frequently accessed sites in your Favorites folder in Internet Explorer—to make surfing the Net faster and more effective.

Keep Favorites in themed folders, like Travel or Health. This makes them easier to access and gives you a tidier list. The same applies to using Bookmarks in Netscape Navigator.

If you're not using a Favorite, delete it. It's just taking up valuable space. Right-click on the name and select Delete from the menu.

Set aside regular time to organize your Favorites or Bookmarks. Move the ones that aren't in a folder to the appropriate one—create a new folder, if necessary.

Don't annoy the rest of your family by hogging the phone line. Organize your Favorites offline. That way, you can take your time and consider carefully what you want to keep and where you want to store it.

Name a Favorites folder "Temporary," or something similar. Use it when you're online to store sites that don't fit easily into your categories, or any you're not sure that you want to keep. Once a week or so, decide which Favorites to keep and where to put them, and delete those you no longer need.

A site may assign a Favorite a name that won't remind you of what it is when you look at it later. "User FAQ," for example, could be just about anything. In Internet Explorer, use the Rename command to give your Favorite a more meaningful title. Right-click on the Favorite (or Folder) and select Rename from the drop-down menu. Type a new name then press the Enter key.

Many websites have a page of links to related sites. Make that page a Favorite and you'll have a ready source of reference for whatever your choice of subject.

Need to work on another computer? Take your Favorites or Bookmarks with you. Both Internet Explorer and Netscape let you save them as a portable HTML file, which either program can open. In Internet Explorer, go to File ➔ Import and Export, and follow the Wizard's instructions. In Netscape Navigator, go to Bookmarks ➔ Edit Bookmarks, then go to File ➔ Save As.

⇨ See also **Internet: Bookmarks, Internet Explorer** and **Netscape Communicator.**

FILTERS

When the sheer volume of incoming e-mail gets overwhelming, filtering functions let you file and store messages in a manageable way.

Set up folders and filters for each of the main categories of e-mail you receive, such as Work, Finance, Family, and so on. As mail is received, it is automatically stored in the relevant folder.

Filters are a great way to organize newsgroup messages, which can often be overwhelming in number. You can create newsgroup filters in the same way as e-mail filters.

Are you being bombarded by junk e-mail—or spam, as it's known—from one or more specific addresses? Use Outlook Express's filters to keep unwanted messages out of your Inbox in the future. Go to Tools ➔ Message Rules ➔ Blocked Senders List, and add the address or addresses. Now all e-mails from that source will go immediately to the Deleted Items folder.

Reorganize that bulging Inbox in Outlook Express by applying a newly created filter (or filters) to messages that have already been downloaded. Go to Tools ➔ Message Rules ➔ Mail. In the Message Rules dialog box, click on the Apply Now button. Select a rule or rules; press the Browse button and choose the folder to which you wish to apply the rules. Click on Apply Now and the rules will take effect.

➪ See also **Internet: E-mail** and **Outlook Express.**

FOREIGN LANGUAGES

Discover how to display foreign language characters, use translation services online, and decipher foreign sites with a built-in browser.

The main challenge in reading most foreign-language websites is getting the browser to display them accurately in the first place. To start with, you might need to install fonts

containing the foreign characters you require (see Software: Fonts). Internet Explorer users will find such fonts available for download by clicking Products Update at the Microsoft site (http://windowsupdate.microsoft.com). Help for Netscape browsers may also be found online (http://home.netscape.com/menu/intl).

It's not enough to install fonts to support a particular language—you have to tell the browser about it, too. To do this in Internet Explorer, choose Tools ➔ Internet Options and click on the Fonts button on the General tab. Select the language script you wish to configure and the fonts you would like to use with it.

Enabling multilanguage support in a browser isn't too complicated, but there are simpler ways of viewing foreign language web pages. Shodouka (www.lfw.org/shodouka), for example, is a website that accepts the URL (web address) of any Japanese-language page and displays it as an image. Although this can slow things down, it will work in any browser.

For complex languages, including Chinese and Korean, which contain more unusual characters, try using a completely new tool. NJStar (www.njstar.com.au) offers a free browser, called Asian Explorer, specially designed to work with Asian languages. TwinBridge (www.twinbridge.com) also has some useful language add-ons.

HOW TO: SET UP FILTERS·IN OUTLOOK EXPRESS

① Go to Tools ➔ Message Rules ➔ Mail. Click New and in the top section of the dialog box set the conditions for the rule (Outlook Express's name for a filter). Scroll through the options and check the conditions you want the program to examine incoming e-mail for.

② In section 2 select the action your rule is to carry out. You may select more than one. You can place messages in a particular folder, for example, or choose not to download a message from the server. Click on all the underlined text in section 3 in turn to define the rule further.

③ Follow the instructions in the dialog box that appears. In the top line of the Select People dialog box, type the text you want the rule to search for, click Add, and then OK. Finally, give the rule a name and click OK. The new rule is now listed in the Message Rules window.

Are websites you need in a foreign language? While there's nothing wrong with that, it's not very helpful when you don't speak the language. Before you give up, try a free online translation service, such as Babel Fish (http://babelfish.altavista.com/translate.dyn) or Free Translation (www.freetranslation.com). To receive a translation, choose the language and enter the page address. Don't expect perfection, but the translation should be close enough for you to figure out its meaning.

Even if you have a good understanding of a foreign language, you may still discover one or two words on the page that stump you. In situations like this, you need a good online dictionary. Sites such as Your Dictionary (www.yourdictionary.com) and Foreign Word (www.foreignword.com) contain comprehensive collections of hundreds of glossary listings, including four separate links to the Prussian language.

Some browsers come with built-in translation facilities. Some of the best examples of these are Neoplanet (www.neoplanet.com), Mozilla (www.mozilla.org), and later versions of Netscape—Netscape 6 and higher (http://home.netscape.com/download). They are all much smaller downloads than Internet Explorer, so why don't you give them a try?

While free translation sites on the Internet might give you a general idea of what a particular document means, they are often full of errors. For greater accuracy, try a professional service such as Plus Translation (www.plustranslation.com). Or look for a real

live translator near you. Check out the Canadian Translators and Interpreters Council site (www.synapse.net/~ctic/cticlink.htm).

If you want to read foreign language material, a more satisfying solution might be to learn the language. Eloquence (www.elok.com) offers free courses in Spanish and French for

complete beginners, while CyberItalian (www.cyberitalian.com) is a website that takes an unusually interactive approach to learning. Travlang (www.travlang.com/languages) has lots of links to other helpful sites.

Once equipped with a deep knowledge of your chosen language, or a translation tool, you will be able to understand many more pages on the Internet. The challenge will be finding them, since foreign language sites are not highlighted at Yahoo! or Google. For a list of foreign search engines, visit www.bizforms.com/search.htm.

FORWARD BUTTON

Use the Forward button on your Web toolbar to navigate easily through website pages.

Your Internet browser keeps a list of all the pages you are currently viewing on the Internet. Click on the Back button, and the browser will take you to the preceding page in the list. Changed your mind? Click Forward to move one site down the list. If the Forward button is grayed out, you've reached the end of the list.

HOW TO: GET FREE ONLINE TRANSLATIONS

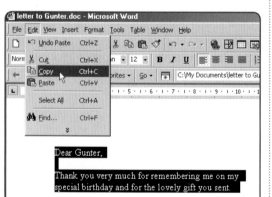

① Use the mouse to highlight the text you want to translate (you can only translate a few sentences at a time). Choose Edit → Copy to copy it to the clipboard, then in your web browser, go to http://babelfish.altavista.com/translate.dyn.

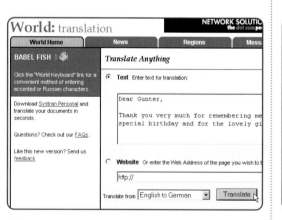

② Click in the Text box, then select Edit → Paste to paste your text for translation. Now choose the kind of translation you want (English to German, in this case), then click on the Translate button.

③ The translation you requested will appear after a few seconds. You can copy and paste this text into your Word document or e-mail. If the result is not accurate enough for your needs, try an alternative service.

It's easy to lose track of where you are, especially after a lengthy Internet session, and you may not always know where the Forward button will take you. Internet Explorer users can regain their bearings by allowing the mouse cursor to hover over the Forward button for just a few seconds; the title of the next page will then be displayed.

When you've pressed Back several times, clicking Forward once may not be enough. But don't click on the Forward button over and over again—waiting for each page to display is a waste of time. Instead, click on the down arrow to the right of the Forward button, and choose the page you want from the list that appears.

⇨ See also **Internet: Back Button**

Whether you are interested in photographs, clip art, or graphics, you can get them on the Internet.

Found an image you like? Just right-click on it, select Save Image As, and it's on your hard disk for you to access whenever you wish. Bear in

mind, however, that although copying for personal use—for wallpaper, for example—is not a crime, reusing material in a newsletter or on a website without the owner's permission means you are in breach of the creator's copyright. So, why not choose from the vast array of free online images for your website?

Want some special graphics for Halloween, or Christmas? Claire Amundsen Schaeffer's Free Graphics site (www.freegraphics.com) has links to 130 sites in her holiday section alone. The site provides an excellent directory of other graphics sites, too.

A larger directory, covering everything on the Internet that's free, is the FreeSite (www.thefree site.com). Its biggest sections cover such topics as web space and software, but it also has a useful list of free graphics resources. To get a regular e-mail with details of its latest discoveries, register for its weekly newsletter.

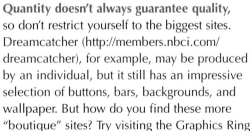

Quantity doesn't always guarantee quality, so don't restrict yourself to the biggest sites. Dreamcatcher (http://members.nbci.com/ dreamcatcher), for example, may be produced by an individual, but it still has an impressive selection of buttons, bars, backgrounds, and wallpaper. But how do you find these more "boutique" sites? Try visiting the Graphics Ring

(www.graphics ring.com), where you can find hundreds of them.

Still haven't found a site that provides what you need? Visit your favorite search engine. For example, you could enter the phrase "free graphics" at Google (www.google.com), and you would get over 103,000 hits.

You can get photographs from the Web, too. It's not just graphics that are available free of charge on the Internet. Although they're harder to find, there are some great websites, such as Free Images (www.freeimages.co.uk), that provide a host of stunning downloadable photographs at no cost.

⇨ See also **Internet: Copyright; Software: Graphics.**

FREE GRAPHICS SITES
Get yourself some groovy graphics without spending a penny.

Brown Bag Graphics (http://members. aol.com/dogscratch/graphics)
A collection of animated images and textured web page backgrounds.

Canada eh? (www3.sympatico.ca/taniah/Canada/)
A source of Canadian-related images, both original and in the public domain.

Free Graphics (www.free-graphics.com)
This Clip art site has more than 20,000 graphics, including buttons, backgrounds, unusual fonts, banners, and 3D animations.

Free Images (www.freeimages.co.uk)
Free photographs are harder to find on the Internet than buttons and backgrounds, but you can discover some excellent downloadable examples at this site.

Kodak (www.kodak.com/go/play)
Once you've found all the free graphics you need, try out some of the special effects at Kodak's free online image processing site.

Rozie's Alpha-Bytes (www.geocities.com/rozie/alphabet.html)
If you want to liven up your website's headings, check out Rozie's colorful letter GIFs on different-colored backgrounds.

FREEWARE

Who said there is no such thing as a free lunch? A mass of freeware is available from Internet libraries— quality software, entirely free, nothing to pay, no catches at all.

Different people define "freeware" in different ways. It is quite common for applications to be free only for home use, while business users have to pay. Other freeware libraries may contain restricted demo versions of a software package or programs that are only free because they force you to watch advertisements. Make sure you read all the details before you download a program—it is time well spent, and you'll appreciate it later on.

Do be wary of free software. Make sure you consider the consequences when you download files from an unknown source, such as someone's home page. Also, some hackers create apparently useful freeware programs, which have a hidden, malicious function, such as installing a virus on your computer (these are called Trojans). Wherever your freeware comes from, make sure you check it over with an updated antivirus program before using it.

Where can you find freeware? All the best libraries on the Internet have a few freeware programs at least, and a wide selection of sites specialize in freeware and nothing else. There are plenty out there. Just enter "freeware" in your favorite search engine to find them, or try some of the freeware sites listed in the box at right.

Searching the Internet for freeware can be a time-consuming exercise, so why not have someone else do all the work for you? The oddly named Lockergnome (www.lockergnome. com) produces a free daily newsletter, sent to you by e-mail, with lots of pointers to useful freeware, good websites, fonts, drivers, and more.

⇨ See also **Internet: Downloading.**

FTP

Get to know the ins and outs of this extremely useful Internet file transfer system.

Before web pages and browsers became popular, File Transfer Protocol (FTP) was the standard way of transferring files on the Internet. Browsing an FTP server isn't exactly user friendly—all you see is a text-based list of file names and directories, not all of which are clear as to their content—but FTP's speed and efficiency keeps it in common use today.

All the major browsers provide some level of support for transferring FTP files. With Internet Explorer, just type ftp://ftp.microsoft.com into the address box. Once the browser has connected to the FTP site, you'll see a list of files and folders, just as in Windows Explorer. Navigation works in a similar way too; click on a folder to open it and click on a file to display or download it.

There are lots of files available on FTP servers all over the Net, but you won't find them by using a regular search engine like Yahoo! or Google. The best place to look is on the Lycos

Fast FTP Search page (http://ftpsearch.lycos. com), where you will find all categories of software, MP3, and graphics FTP files among the 100 million files indexed.

One of the most common applications for FTP is providing a means for people to upload files to their own website. While your browser may allow you to perform some of the functions you need, a special FTP program, or "FTP client," offers the most features. Sites such as Strouds CWSApps (http://cws.internet.com/ftp.html) and WebAttack (www.webattack .com/shareware/ ftp/swftp.shtml) offer a wide and varied selection.

One program specifically for FTP downloads is WS FTP Pro (www.ipswitch.com). For various technical reasons, this type of program downloads files of more than 1Mb in size quicker than normal web servers.

FREEWARE SITES
Work your way through this list to build up your collection of software.

**Freeware Files
(www.freewarefiles.com)
Freeware Arena
(www.freewarearena.com)**
These sites have extensive searchable databases of both popular and specialized freeware packages.

**Tucows (www.tucows.com)
Soft Seek (www.softseek.com)**
Two good Internet libraries from which to start a search for freeware.

WebAttack (www.webattack.com)
WebAttack has a big library of freeware utilities. Try browsing the different categories for interesting programs.

POPULAR FTP PROGRAMS
Visit these sites to help you choose your file transfer client.

CuteFTP (www.cuteftp.com)
GlobalSCAPE Inc.'s FTP client is one of the most powerful and easy to use.

FTP Voyager (www.ftpvoyager.com)
FTP Voyager from Rhino Software is easy enough for beginners, but with enough depth for expert user.

Terrapin FTP (www.us.terra-net.com)
Terrapin's helpful features include Site Maps, which let you browse previously visited FTP servers for useful files without connecting again to the Net.

WS_FTP Pro (www.ipswitch.com)
Ipswitch is constantly developing this program, which now features SSL encryption to make sure your data is secure during Internet transfer.

Some download programs also help with FTP file downloads. Go!Zilla (www.gozilla.com) is ideal for all Internet downloads, but it also has a "Leech" feature that detects when you are trying to link to an FTP site. It automatically locates any files for download from that site. Once you've chosen a file, Go!Zilla makes sure that the download is successful—it's even able to resume a download if the connection is either deliberately or accidentally cancelled.

Sometimes you might be prompted to enter a user name and password before you can log on to an FTP server. Most servers will accept "anonymous FTP," which means that you can type in "anonymous" as the user name and enter your e-mail address as the password. If the server doesn't allow you to do this, then e-mail "webmaster@[The FTP site name]" to request a real user name and password.

Windows comes with its own FTP client (FTP.EXE), which can be found in the Windows folder. Unfortunately it is DOS-based, so for beginners it is not at all user friendly. However, a knowledgeable user may find it handy to perform a simple FTP task or two on a computer

that doesn't have a full FTP client. Sites such as Tucows (http://html.tucows.com/webmaster/tut/dosftp.html) or http://home.att.net/~knoblock/dosftp.html offer helpful instructions on using the Windows FTP.EXE.

When transferring files using an FTP client, you need to be aware of a potential snag. Files may be transferred in either Ascii (text) or binary (program) mode. If you get this wrong (in particular, transferring a ZIP, EXE, or other binary file in Ascii mode), then the file will be corrupted. Most FTP clients can figure out which mode to use—most of the time—but it is not guaranteed, so check your FTP programs preferences for guidance.

FTP can seem quite a complex process, but there is a tutorial called "Zen and the Art of FTP" (www.eurekais.com/brock/ftp_tutorial/) that can help you, and lots of others are available, too. For a list, just enter "ftp tutorial" into your favorite search engine.

Zen and the Art of FTP:

HOW TO: DOWNLOAD AND INSTALL AN FTP CLIENT

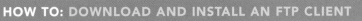

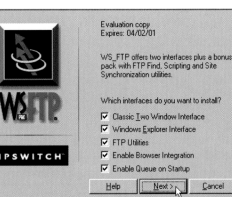

① Connect to the Internet and go to www.ipswitch.com. Click on the Try Now hyperlink in the WS_FTP Pro section. Fill in the registration information on the next page. Click Next and select the version and the download site on your PC you want to use.

② Once the program is downloaded to your PC, double-click on the WS_FTP Pro file to open it. Click Next through all the windows and click OK at the Program Manager Group dialog box. Then restart your computer to activate the installation settings.

③ Now, when you connect to an FTP site, WS_FTP automatically takes over and finds all possible downloadable files. Click on Continue Evaluation, locate the file you want, and click on the left-facing arrow. Your FTP file download will then begin.

GAMES

Join in the fun by playing interactive games with thousands of others.

You will need a fast connection to play 3D games online, as well as a fast processor, lots of RAM, and 3D video acceleration. Also check that your computer has a videocard before you start downloading.

There are two types of online games: those on private networks and those on commercial networks. If you are just starting out, you may want to begin with a private network. The best games on the commercial networks—called premium games—are either pay-to-play or require a subscription to connect to the network. For available private network games,

GAMES SITES
Here are some sites for traditional and not-so-traditional gaming.

Canada Gaming (www.gamedownloadsonline.com)
News and reviews of all types of games available to download.

Chess Federation of Canada (www.chess.ca/page1eng.html)
News, details about learning chess, chess software, clubs, tournaments, and so on.

Free Games Online (www.freegamesonline.com)
Hundreds of freeware, shareware, and online games.

Free Gaming (www.free-gaming.com)
Puzzles, card games, single player games, crosswords, trivia, and more.

Game Pod (www.purplelion.com/games)
At the Game Pod, you'll find many of your favorite casino, arcade, and trivia games.

download either GameSpy (www.gamespy.com) or Kali (www.kali.net). These programs will

enable you to connect to available games, a few of which are text-based play-by-e-mail (PbeM) games.

Commercial networks provide Internet-accessible game servers. Mplayer (www.mplayer.com), Heat (www.heat.net), and MSN Gaming Zone (www.zone.com) are some networks that give priority to games. The speed of the networks is usually fast, but they do charge a premium to play. This is also where you will find many of the team games, called MMORPGs (Massively Multiplayer Online Role-Playing Games), which allow hundreds or thousands of players to play in the same interactive world.

Never played a role-playing game before? Get experience by "lurking" in a play-by-e-mail (PbeM) game. The PbeM and private network games are all about creating a fantasy character and immersing yourself in that character during the game. This can take some practice. Many e-mail games allow lurkers—people who follow the game but don't participate—to read the same game e-mail messages as the players do. Alternatively, check out the newsgroups, alt.mud ("mud" stands for multiuser dungeon), and rec.games.mud, or the site www.godlike .com/muds/, for tips on how you can join and take part in a role-playing game.

Chat with your teammates or opponents while you play a MMORPG, using Roger Wilco (www.resounding.com). Roger Wilco is a free voice chat application that allows players in an online game to talk to each other, thus eliminating text messaging—a slower means of communication. The program allows hundreds of players to chat by mixing their voices with the game's audio in real time. So why not buy yourself a cheap microphone and start chatting while you play?

If you are looking for a new game, try buying specialist gaming magazines, such as Computer Gaming World and PC Gamer, rather than download demos from the Web. Since most decent games are at least 20Mb, and the magazines feature free CD-ROMs full of games, the magazines can save you time and money.

Before playing a PbeM game, make sure you are familiar with your e-mail program. Many players are overwhelmed by the amount of e-mail they receive once they start playing. Setting up aliases and filters will make sending e-mail easier. Also make sure you know how to organize your e-mail using folders.

Looking for professional chess or poker players to match your skills against? Then you may well be better off in a pay-to-play or fee-based gaming site. These sites attract the more serious-minded and tournament-quality players.

Play premium online role-playing games for free by participating in the beta-testing stage. Many game designers let people play for free in order to establish characters before the game is released to the public. Online magazines such as Zdnet and manufacturers' game sites will sometimes carry ads for beta-testers.

Play your favorite Shockwave games without a web connection. Once you've initially played a

Shockwave game on the Internet, you will find it stored in your browser's cache directory. Look for a file with *.dcr in the name. Move this file to a different folder, so it doesn't get deleted when your browser empties its cache. Now, whenever you want to play the game, fire up your browser (there is no need to actually connect to the Internet), select File ➔ Open File, and open the .dcr file. Because Shockwave games are cross-platform, you can take this file to any computer with the Shockwave plug-in installed in its web browser and play the game.

You don't have to be an adolescent to find interesting games on the Internet. If you are a crossword puzzle fan, head to your favorite newspaper site and print out the puzzle. Even better, try Yahoo! (http://ca.yahoo.com /recreation/games/ puzzles) or 4Anything (www.4crosswords. 4anything.com) for a large selection of crosswords.

⇨ See also **Software: Games; Hardware: Joysticks** and **Plug-and-Play**.

GARDENING

Use the Net to design landscaping, order plants, and help you look after your garden.

Don't leave your plants out in the cold. Make sure your local climate is right for the plants in your garden by checking the plant hardiness zone map at Agriculture Canada (http://sis.agr. gc.ca/cansis/nsdb/climate/hardiness/webmap. html). It will help you to determine what kind of plants will grow best in your region. To make sure that you set out your bulbs and shoots at the right time, keep up-to-date on the weather forecasts and frost predictions at Environment Canada (http://weather.ec.gc.ca/current_e.html).

Choose the best plants for home or garden by checking out a plant finder. Plant finders ask questions about your region, such as soil type,

climate, and exposure, and then recommend suitable plants. Many gardening sites, like Canadian Garden (www.canadiangarden.com), Canadian Gardening's GARDENet (www. canadiangardening.com/GARDENet/gardenet. html), and Canadian Wildlife Federation's gardening site (www.wildaboutgardening.org) have plant finders. Dial-a-Garden (www.dial-a-garden.com) sells disks that offer advice

about the right plants for specific areas, growing conditions, etc.

A land designer program will help you plan large gardens, letting you try different layouts, suggesting plants, and allowing you to model your garden in three dimensions. Land designers work best when you have a large area and a lot of plants to organize, and it may not pay to invest money in a land designer if you only need a few plants. Land design software can be purchased on CD-ROM from Sierra (www.sierra.com) and Yahoo! (http://store.yahoo.com). Sierra also features regional guides, design guides, a plant finder, and articles about all types of gardening.

Information on city gardening topics—such as home composting, worms, rooftop gardening, and sprouting on your kitchen countertop—can be found on the Internet. One good source of information is the City Farmers Urban Agriculture (www.cityfarmer.org), a Vancouver-based nonprofit organic gardening collective that encourages the growth of greenery within our concrete canyons.

GARDENING SITES
Everything comes up roses when you visit these sites.

Canadian Garden (www.canadiangarden.com)
This site includes tips on all types of plants, a resource list leading to information about gardening in different seasons and settings.

Cyndi's Catalog of Catalogs (www.qnet.com/~johnsonj)
Searching for that perfect plant or a specific tool? Check out this site, which features over 1,850 gardening catalogs.

Gardening.com (www.gardening.com)
This site offers a large database of plant types to search and purchase.

The Garden Gate (http://garden-gate. prairienet.org/homepage.htm)
Track down newsgroups, mailing lists, software, online books, databases, and discussion groups on plants—or tour a virtual garden. Plus hundreds of other links.

GardenNet.com (www.gardennet.com)
A useful starting place for up-to-date horticultural information, as well as news on events and travel, a jaunt through selected online catalogs, and an exhaustive list of gardening associations. The Garden GuideBook is a database of gardens, open to the public around the world, that is searchable by garden type or location.

Garden Web (www.gardenweb.com)
This megasite specializes in seed, plant, and equipment exchanges, and online forums with gardeners all over the world. Has frequent contests with garden-related prizes.

Wild About Gardening (www.wildaboutgardening.org)
Visit this site to learn how to map a garden, grow native plants, attract wildlife. Here you'll find a growing calendar, as well as an extensive plant encyclopedia.

GENEALOGY

The Web makes researching your family tree fast and easy. A lot of information is available online, from ships' passenger lists to church records and census data. There are also online genealogical societies and libraries offering all sorts of data and tips. So here is some advice to help your family tree research bear fruit.

GETTING STARTED

Begin with yourself. Write down your name, birth date, place of birth, and parents' names. If you're married, record your husband's or wife's name, and the date and place of your wedding. Note any children's names and their dates of birth. Do the same for any other relatives you know. Before you know it, you'll have the makings of a family tree.

Quiz any living relatives for first-hand accounts and recollections. All those stories your grandparents told you when you were a child could come in handy now! When you've found out as much as you can about your family history, it's time to follow up your leads online.

Your genealogical information can be broken down into family groups—your family, your mother's family, your father's family, and so on. To help you organize all this information, keep a group sheet and a pedigree chart for each family in your line.

You can download family group sheets and pedigree charts for free at Ancestry.com (www.ancestry.com), but you will need Adobe Acrobat reader (free at www.adobe.com) to use them. If you don't have Adobe Acrobat, try the group and pedigree sheets at American Genealogy Mall (www.genealogy-mall.com/fgr.htm and www.genealogy-mall.com/pedchart.htm). Cyndi's List (www.cyndislist.com/supplies.htm) provides links to sites offering similar charts.

Keep printouts of your family group and pedigree sheets for offline research—the more involved you get in your hobby, the more you'll find yourself traveling in the pursuit of knowledge! Even if you keep your records on a handheld PC or laptop, it's worth having printouts available for quick and easy reference.

ONLINE DETECTIVE WORK

Find out if anyone else has already researched your surname or family history. The Canadian Genealogical Projects Registry (www.afhs.ab.ca/registry/) lists research projects completed or being planned. For links to Usenet groups to help with a specific name, visit Canada-Roots-L (www.rootsweb.com/~jfuller/gen_mail_country-can.html#CANADIAN-ROOTS). Also helpful is RootsWeb's GenConnect (http://genconnect.rootsweb.com/index/ Canada.html). Many of the groups covered at this site have message boards that could provide vital clues.

Cut down on search engine time—many genealogical websites have done the donkey work for you. One such site is Canadian Genealogy and History Links (www.islandnet.com/~jveinot/cghl/cghl.html). It links a wide range of sites, giving access to everything, including the First Census of New France in 1666 and materials relating to the Loyalists. The Alberta Family Histories Society (www.afhs.ab.ca/aids/index.html) offers links to a wide range of genealogical sources. Cyndi's List (www.cyndislist.com) provides links to tutorials and guides, organizing your research, and all kinds of data, archives, and records. Bob's Your

POPULAR GENEALOGY PROGRAMS

Give your research a kickstart with this handy software.

Ancestral Quest (www.ancestralquest.com)
Family tree software designed for Windows.

Brother's Keeper (www.bkwin.net)
Shareware for the novice genealogist.

Clooz (www.clooz.com)
An electronic filing cabinet to help organize your genealogical records.

Family Reunion (www.famware.com)
A free download from the Web that collates all your family data efficiently for you.

Family Tree Maker (www.familytreemaker.com)
America's best-selling family tree program.

The Master Genealogist (www.whollygenes.com)
Comprehensive genealogy software.

cngenwebe.html) links up with provincial and county sites where you can locate a particular community. This lists volunteers who will do genealogical research tasks for you.

GATHER OFFICIAL DATA
Looking for official documents? Visit The National Archives of Canada (www.archives.ca/02/020202_e.html) can tell you where to look for specific records—birth, death, marriage, divorce, adoption, land, wills, and more. Here, you can access a free publication, *Tracing Your Ancestors in Canada.*

For census records, go to Statistics Canada (www.statcan.ca/english/census96/list.htm). Census Links (http://censuslinks.com/Canada/) connects to the census records of nine provinces. A lot of U.S. census data is located online at the U.S. Census Bureau (www.census.gov) and through sites such as the Mormon Church's Family History Centers (www.familysearch.com).

MAKE THE MOST OF YOUR PC
Your computer could be your most valuable tool! As well as using it for group and pedigree sheets, you can also download shareware programs to create your own family tree or

Uncle, eh! (http://indexes.tpl.toronto.on.ca/genealogy/index.asp) looks for specific records (baptisms, for example), people (by religion, ethnicity, and race), and geographic location.

Sooner or later, you'll meet a "brickwall"— an ancestor who evades your most zealous research. If you're drawing a blank, head for Genealogy's Most Wanted (www.citynet.net/mostwanted). It includes links to a staggering number of surnames and posts messages from people all over the world who are trying to hunt down elusive ancestors. The site reports an excellent success rate at helping amateur genealogists get past their brickwalls.

Knowing where your ancestor once lived may help you find a record. The Canadian County Atlas Digital Project (http://imago.library.mcgill.ca/countyatlas/default.asp) has a searchable database of property owners' names that appear on country altas maps. The Canada GenWeb Project (www.rootsweb.com/~canwgw/

ancestral and descendancy charts dating back centuries. Legacy (www.legacyfamilytree.com) has a range of comprehensive and easy-to-use family history software free to download (see the box opposite for other useful sites). Alternatively, you could use Ancestry.com's online family tree organizer (www.ancestry.lycos.com/main.htm) which incorporates several specialist search engines and historic document retrieval facilities.

Scan in any first-hand data you can, such as photographs, birth, marriage, and death certificates, and even correspondence. It's a handy way to keep a record of what you have, without constantly having to shuffle through shoeboxes and files. After all, what better and more accessible filing cabinet do you have than Windows Explorer?

You could even create your own unique genealogy website of results and queries—who knows what contacts you could make through an online presence. Maybe some unknown third cousin twice removed will suddenly drop you an e-mail out of the blue.

⇨ See also **Internet: Web Rings, Website Creation** and **Software: Databases.**

TOP TEN RESEARCH TIPS
Handy hints to help you trace your roots.

1. Contact living relatives for assistance.
2. Get to know the history of the area in which you are conducting research.
3. Use period-appropriate maps of the area where your ancestors were living.
4. Use family group sheets and pedigree charts or group sheet software to help organize your data.
5. Don't gather information on everyone with the surname you are researching, unless it is an uncommon name.
6. Never assume that a surname was always spelled the same way.
7. Use common sense when reading family histories. If a source for information is not listed, be cautious about accepting it—it could be hearsay.
8. Use primary sources, such as land, probate, church, and county records, and rely on printed histories.
9. Keep a master copy of your data somewhere safe in case you lose anything. When you're traveling for research purposes, take a duplicate copy of your information.
10. Persevere—it's worth it!

GOVERNMENT

Governments generate vast amounts of information. Knowing where to find exactly what you need will help you cut through the red tape.

Start your search with a site that organizes government files, such as the Government of Canada site (http://canada.gc.ca/menu_e.html). It has links to all departments, agencies, and crown corporations, as well as gateways for consumers, business people, and non-Canadians who are visiting or working here. Departmental sites offer data files accessible by the public. The site's popular features include links to jobs and career training (www.jobsetc.

TAP INTO GOVERNMENT FILES

Want to know the official line? Time to go surfing.

Canada Information Office (www.infocan.gc.ca/index_e.html)
This site informs you about the availability of government programs and services.

Government Electronic Directory Services Direct500 (http://canada.gc.ca/search/direct500/geds_e.html)
Want to contact a department or an official? Search here by name, title, phone number, or organization/department.

Governor General of Canada (www.gg.ca/menu_e.html)
Explore Rideau Hall on a virtual tour. Read about various honors such as the Order of Canada and Decorations for Bravery.

Parliament of Canada (www.parl.gc.ca)
Here you can track the progress of bills, read Hansard, and find out about tours and other activities.

ca/cgi-bin/loader.pl?lang=e), job openings in the public service (http://jobs.gc.ca/home_e.htm), and the tax department (www.ccra-adrc.gc.ca/tax/individuals/menu-e.html).

Need government statistics for your business? Statistics Canada (www.statcan.gc.ca/start.html) offers all kinds of economic, business, and trade information. An online publication, *The Daily,* contains newly released data, as well as schedules of major upcoming releases and announcements of new products and services. The Community Profiles section looks at 6,000 towns and cities across the country. To access a provincial government online, type "www.gov. [the two-letter provincial postal abbreviation]. ca" or use Yahoo! (http://ca.yahoo.com) and search under the appropriate category.

All official Canadian sites contain .ca in the address or URL. Government organizations and political parties will usually have .org in their address. If you absentmindedly add the wrong ending to an address, you may find yourself visiting at a very different site. For example, www.parl.gc.ca is the official site for Parliament of Canada. But, www.parl.org takes you to the Providence Animal Rescue League site in Rhode Island, U.S.A.

To find out about international government and legislation, visit the United Nations Development Program website (www.undp.org), which features a wide range of information on all global issues concerning the UN. Read the views of world leaders, view explanations of new initiatives, and locate UN offices worldwide.

Can't resist a bit of real-life gossip? For fascinating facts on the famous, access FBI documents that have been released as part of the Federal Freedom of Information Act. The FBI has a freedom of information reading-room site (http://foia.fbi.gov), which includes intriguing, declassified information on Marilyn Monroe, Elvis Presley, and the British royal family, as well as other, less famous, people. To use the reading room, you'll need the Adobe Acrobat program, which you can download for free (www.adobe.com).

GREETING CARDS

Design and make your own card, download an e-mail postcard, or order and send a snail mail card courtesy of the Internet.

Afraid an e-mail card is not personal enough, but there's no time to hunt down a paper version and send it? Some U.S. sites such as Amazing Mail (www.amazingmail.com), Sparks (www.sparks.com), and Snailgram (www.snailgram.com) now send real postcards. All you have to do is to log on, select from a variety of pictures and card styles, type your message, and click Send. The postcard is automatically printed, mailed, and delivered to

the recipient's mailbox. Easy! Not only do you save a friendship, but it doesn't cost much more than buying and mailing a card in the usual way.

Is a relative about to celebrate a milestone birthday or anniversary? Would you like the Queen to send a congratulatory greeting? Go to the Canadian government site (http://canada.

gc.ca/comments/faq_e.html#ann), where you will find forms and information about obtaining best wishes from the Queen, the Governor-General, or the Prime Minister.

In love, but don't know how to say it? To step up the pace of your romance, get a little help from PassionUp (www.passionup.com). This site contains a large selection of fill-in-the-blank e-mail love letters, poems, songs, and other greeting cards. Your loved one will never know you didn't write it yourself!

Roses For You...

Because you're a beautiful person, I wanted to send something beautiful to you.

Some free greeting card services exist purely to collect lists of e-mail addresses. Beware of using any services affiliated with groups or organizations that you don't approve of—once they have your e-mail address, you may be bombarded with junk mail.

If you are familiar with HTML code (the code that's used to create websites), look for greeting card sites that allow you to use the HTML format to write your own cards. This feature is a great way to personalize your cards to family members and close friends, because you can provide links to other sites.

Pushed for time? To show you still care, order both e-cards and paper cards, along with flowers and other goodies, through Hallmark (www.hallmark.com). Other great sites for free e-greeting cards include Blue Mountain (www.bluemountain.com) and NetGreeting (www.netgreeting.com).

⇨ See also **Software: ClipArt** and **Desktop Publishing**; **Internet: E-greetings**.

HISTORY

Use the web browser's History button to view websites offline, or engage in some covert spying on your kids!

As you surf the Web, your browser lists any pages you visit in what's known as your "History." This is particularly handy if you want to download web pages and read them later on your laptop or palmtop, or free up the phone line for other members of the family to use. When you're online, just make sure you fully load each page you want to read. Then go to the File menu and select Work Offline. You can now call up the sites you've already visited by clicking on them in your History file.

If you have Internet Explorer 5 or a later version, the History button allows you to sort the files according to date, order of visit, number of visits, or name, and then search their contents. Keep in mind that pages stored in this way will be overwritten the next time you visit that address online. If there are any pages you want to store permanently, click on your browser's File menu and select Save As.

Worried your kids have been visiting unsuitable sites? To keep their browsing in check, hit the History button on the toolbar. Now right-click on any site you're curious about and left-click on Properties. You'll then be able to tell when the site was last visited.

To keep your surfing secret, delete the History button from your toolbar. Right-click on any of the toolbar buttons and, in the pop-up menu that appears, left-click on Customize. You will now be able to remove the History button. While this won't fool everyone, it should be enough to keep the Net novice at bay. In turn, if you want to snoop and find that someone else has deleted the History button, you can restore it in the same way, using the Customize feature.

Cover your tracks! If you want to clear all current History entries, go to Tools ➔ Internet Options and hit the Clear History button.

Make your History as long or as short as you want. You can set it to record just a day of browsing or to save a week's worth of surfing. Go to Tools ➔ Internet Options, select the number of days desired, and hit OK. Be careful though, if you set it to 30 days and do a lot of surfing, you'll end up with an enormous list!

⇨ See also **Internet: Saving Web Pages.**

HOW TO: FIND FOREIGN GOVERNMENT INFORMATION

Department of Foreign Affairs and International Trade — Ministère des Affaires étrangères et du Commerce international

Embassies and Missions

Contact Lists

- Canadian Representatives Abroad
- Offices of the Trade Commissioner Service Abroad
- Canadian Diplomatic and Consular Missions Abroad

Canadian Mission Web Sites

* = Embassy or High Commission

• **Argentina**	• **Costa Rica**	• **Japan**	• **Spain**
• **Buenos Aires** *	• San Jose *	• Tokyo *	• Madrid *
	• Côte D'Ivoire	• **Korea**	• **Sweden**
• **Australia**	• Abidjan *	• Seoul *	• Stockholm *
• Canberra *	• **Czech Republic**	• **Kuwait**	• **Switzerland**
• Sydney *	• Prague *	• Kuwait City *	• Berne *
• **Austria**			

① As a jumping-off point, use diplomatic links, which offer up-to-date information for a general audience. Try the Department of Foreign Affairs and International Trade's listing of Canadian embassies (http://www.dfait-maeci.gc.ca/dfait/missions/menu-e.asp).

The WWW Virtual Library

- **Agriculture**
  Agriculture, Gardening, Forestry, Irrigation...
- **Business and Economics**
  Economics, Finance, Marketing, Transportation...
- **Computing**
  Computing, E-Commerce, Languages, Web...
- **Communications and Media**
  Communications, Telecommunications, Journalism...
- **Education**
  Education, Applied Linguistics, Linguistics...
- **Engineering**
  Civil, Chemical, Electrical, Mechanical, Software...

- **Information & Libraries**
  General Reference, Information Quality, L...
- **International Affairs**
  International Security, Sustainable Develo...
- **Law**
  Arbitration, Law, Legal History...
- **Recreation**
  Recreation and Games, Gardening, Sport...
- **Regional Studies**
  African, Asian, Latin American, West Eu...
- **Science**
  Biosciences, Health, Earth Science, Physi...

② Use a website which offers links to government information, such as The WWW Virtual Library (www.vlib.org). Alternatively, for geographically arranged sites, visit The Worldwide Governments (www.gksoft.com/govt/en/world.html).

We all want to stay healthy and have access to the latest information on trends, medicine, and treatments. The Net allows you to do all this, and more. When surfing for information, select sites and products backed by accredited organizations—but remember, nothing can replace a real live doctor!

FEELING A BIT BELOW PAR?

Give yourself an online checkup at the Mayo Clinic site (www.mayoclinic.com). Here, you can fill in a personal health scorecard, read the lifestyle planners, and review health options. Medbroadcast.com (www.medbroadcast.com) lets you find out more about illnesses and how to keep well. It provides an online place for your health records, and features multimedia presentations on preventive health techniques, coping strategies, and more.

Check out your medication's compatibility with over-the-counter drugs at Medbroadcast.com (http://drugs.medbroadcast.com/drugpages/). You'll find out other details. Type in the name of your medication (either brand or generic) for a description of its purposes, ingredients, side effects, and contraindications for use. Sympatico's HealthCentral (http://healthcentralsympatico.com/mhc/index/drugidxa.cfm) also has lists of drugs, their uses, possible side effects, and other details.

Do some serious research. Peruse the medical journals to learn more about your condition. Access the U.S. National Library of Medicine's database (www.nlm.nih.gov) with over 3,500 medical journals and archives dating back to 1966. Or join Medscape (www.medscape.com). Here, you can search MEDLINE, and read its newsletter and web-enhanced full-text articles. McGill University's Health Sciences Library (www.health.library.mcgill.ca/) also offers a full range of online journals.

Need advice on workplace health and safety? Go straight to the source—Health Canada's Occupational Health and Safety Agency (www.hc-sc.gc.ca/ohsa/nehsi.htm).

Organize your medical records and manage health information with a health information manager. Medbroadcast.com (www.medbroadcast.com/main.shtml) offers a free health record service. GlobalMedic (www.globalmedic.com/home.htm), part of the Canadian Medical Association, offers a secure and interactive secure health record. Or, you can buy Health-Minder Software from www.health-minder.com.

LINK UP WITH OTHERS

If you or a loved one is afflicted with a medical condition or disease—or in need of an operation—you'll know that keeping well informed and talking to others who have had similar experiences is vital. You can do this via the Net. Many sites, including those listed in the box to the right, have chatrooms. Or try typing the name of the condition into a search engine like Yahoo! and see what comes up. There's a website and an associated chatroom for almost every ailment.

To find a doctor, check the site of the licensing body in your province. If you live in Toronto, for example, go to the College of Physicians and Surgeons of Ontario site (www.cpso.on.ca/) and click on the "Find a Doctor"

YOUR VERY GOOD HEALTH!
Enhance your well-being—log on to thousands of topics, Q&As, and more.

Achoo (www.achoo.com)
Links to thousands of health-related sites, e-zines, headlines, and a unique Human Health and Disease directory.

Canadian Health Network (www.canadian-health-network.ca)
This site is organized by topic and has an extensive FAQs list. If you can't find what you're looking for, e-mail it for answers.

Internet Mental-Health (www.mentalhealth.com)
This Canadian site's goal is to improve understanding, diagnosis, and treatment of mental illness.

MayoClinic.com (www.mayoclinic.com/home)
Take charge of your health: check out the personal scorecard, lifestyle planners, and health decision guides here.

link. Away from home and feeling ill? Head for World Clinic (www.worldclinic.com). This site offers medical advice and will help you find a doctor virtually anywhere. Responses are given by phone or fax, in addition to e-mail.

GET THE SCOOP ON GOOD HEALTH

Can't get to a drugstore for your prescription? Use an online service, such as Pharmacy.ca (www.pharmacy.ca/home.html) to obtain prescription and non-prescription products. Once you're registered, you can submit an order, check the cost, and fill in your name,

address, and the method of payment. Delivery of purchases occurs within two or three business days, depending on where you live.

Beware of any site selling medication that's usually only available on prescription. Many of these sites specialize in offering Viagra online. As much as you might want to try Viagra—or any other miracle treatments they offer— remember, most of these sites are scams offering—at best—sugar pills.

Avoiding quackery. While there are many websites offering reputable advice and treatment, others only want your money.

Check these sites out first at Quackwatch (www.quackwatch.com) or Healthwatcher (www.healthwatcher.net). If you have complaints of inappropriate healthcare practices, get in touch with your provincial licensing body. For example, if you live in Alberta and wish to complain about a doctor, contact the College of Physicians and Surgeons (www.cpsa.ab.ca/) and click on "Complaints" to find out what to do.

How are you doing, healthwise? Get an online assessment. Body Break Online (www. bodybreak.com) lets you evaluate your fitness level, get real information about health, diets, and dieting. The site also features nutritional and exercise tips, videos, and advice. HealthStatus (www.healthstatus. com) offers personalized calculations for body mass, body fat, target heart rate, and more. How Is Your Health? (www.howisyourhealth. com) has various assessments to work out your individual risk and suggests ways to

improve your health. But take any results not based on an actual physical exam with a grain of salt.

Planning a trip overseas? For health advisories, go to the World Health Organization's site (www.who.int) and Health Canada's Travel Medicine site (www.hc-sc.gc.ca/hpb/lcdc/ osh/pub_e.html). Or, visit the Department of

Foreign Affairs and International Trade's travel information site (http://voyage. dfait-maeci.gc.ca/ destinations/ menu_e.htm).

Ever wondered about the inside of your body? Satisfy your curiosity (or get the information for school projects) by visiting The Visible Human Project website (www.nlm.nih.gov/research/ visible/visible_human.html).

⇨ See also **Internet: Alternative Health.**

FLEX YOUR FINGERTIPS
Tap in to the latest health trends, find out more about nutrition, and improve your overall fitness levels with the help of the Web.

Canada's Food Guide (www.hc-sc.gc.ca/hppb/nutrition/pube/ foodguid/foodguide.html)
This sets the standards for eating wisely.

Dietitians of Canada (www.dietitians.ca)
An "Eat Well, Live Well" section lets you compare your nutritional profile to others, test how much you know about food, and calculate your body mass index.

Health Canada's Physical Activity Guide (www.hc-sc.gc.ca/hppb/paguide/)
An introduction to getting and staying fit that even includes exercises that you can do while at work.

Luckymag.com (www.phys.com)
The Condé Nast fashion doyens will help you assess and improve your health and fitness.

Real Age (www.realage.com)
Find out how old your body feels—as opposed to how old it really is. Use this information to create your own age-reduction plan. This health assessment program also evaluates how genetics, nutrition, fitness, and stress affect your well-being.

Women's College Online (www.womenscollege.com/home.html)
Get reliable information about women's health issues from Toronto's Sunnybrook and Women's College Health Sciences Centre.

HOME BUYING

It is now possible to locate a home, apply for a loan, and even complete the deal all on the Internet.

Find your ideal home, without resorting to weekend open houses. Go to the site with the most listings—MLS Online (www.mls.ca)—and search by province, area or city, and then by price, type of house, and more. Because the site gets its listings from brokers, not individuals, expect to negotiate with a real estate agent.

Other information sources. Canadian Real Estate Pages (www.realestate-canada.com/) is a site for home buyers, real estate agents, and those selling their own homes. It has information about real estate, finances, and contractors, as well as links to appraisers, mortgage sources, and legal information. The Canadian Real Estate Association (http://crea.ca/english/public/about/index.htm) represents real estate agents, but it has information about home buying and selling, types of mortgages, offers, conditions, and the services offered by realtors.

Skip the middleman and think selling your home directly on the Net. Sites such as For Sale By Owner (www.forsalebyowner.ca) and Can-Estate For Sale By Owner (www.mortonweb.com/canestate/canestate.htm) let you list your home yourself, for free, on their site, and you can also supply a photograph. Selling privately means no real estate agent or no broker's commission, although you do have to spend more time filtering out undesirable offers.

Make a Net gain. Use Realty Referral Network (www.rebate20.com) to find the agent that best suits your needs. You then deal with that agent for the transaction, be it buying or selling. Once the real estate transaction has been closed, you get a rebate for 20 percent of your real estate agent's commission.

Apply for a mortgage online. Shopping on the Web may work for buying gifts and airline tickets, but what about a mortgage? Most banks now offer mortgage services online. The Web also enables you to find and compare thousands of different options, then apply online for the one most suited to your needs. The best sites

will ask detailed questions and then recommend the most appropriate loan product, such as fixed rate, adjustable rate, and so on. Look for sites such as The Mortgage Group (www.mortgagegroup.ab.ca/). This is a mortgage broker that offers a fast response time, a wide choice of mortgage lenders, a variety of rates and terms, as well as prequalifying for a mortgage.

Buy from the government. Legally, mortgages have to be insured if the down payment for the home is less than 25 percent and Canada Mortgage and Housing Corporation (CMHC) is one of the insuring bodies. So, if someone with a CMHC-insured mortgage can't meet the payments, the lender forecloses on the home. CMHC pays the lender what is owed and takes ownership of the home. Then, CMHC sells it at market value (usually an MLS-listing) as quickly as possible, sometimes giving buyers access to an easy purchase. You can check on listings of CMHC homes at their regional offices (www.cmhc-schl.gc.ca/en/index.cfm) or on the MLS website (www.mls.ca).

Not sure of your asking price? A search of sites such as MLS Online (www.mls.ca), Century 21 (www.century21canada.com/home_index.html), or RE/MAX (www.remax.ca) will give you a reasonable idea of what other homes in your neighborhood have sold for. Basic listings for these properties appear in the Owners' database for three months. If you want a "premium" placement—meaning your property is given priority in the search results—you'll have to pay.

HOME-BUYING HELP
Seek some useful online advice for buying or selling your property.

Canada Mortgage and House Corporation (www.cmhc-schl.gc.ca/en/index.cfm)
This all-inclusive site authoritatively answers questions about buying, building, renovating, and maintaining a home. It covers mortgage information, public and private financial assistance, and housing markets.

Canada's Most Referred Real Estate Agents (www.cmrr.com/index.html)
Here you'll find top agents in the location of your choice. Just type in the city and province, and you'll get a list of agents, recommended by their peers for expertise and professionalism.

HomeFinderCa (www.homefinder.ca)
Canada-wide listings, some with virtual tours.

Moving in Canada (www.movingincanada.com)
Compare population figures, employment opportunities, household incomes, climate, schools, and a host of other statistics for cities across the country.

The International Real Estate Directory (www.ired.com)
Over 25,000 links to real estate sites throughout the world. IRED reviews hundreds of sites each week, to eliminate the purely advertisement-oriented.

Islands in the stream. If you're looking for a gift for the person who has everything, how about buying them an island? For listings of islands for sale, take a trip to Private Islands (www.vladi-private-islands.de). Some islands, notably those along the coast of Canada's Maritime provinces, sell extremely cheaply. Before you make up your mind to buy that lovely offshore getaway, remember to make sure it has a sustainable source of fresh water.

Looking for something a bit larger? Purchase a castle, chateau, or vineyard through French Castles (www.french-castles.com), Best Properties (www.best-properties.com), or Castles-for-Sale (www.castles-for-sale.com).

⇨ See also **Internet: Legal Advice.**

HOME IMPROVEMENT

Do it yourself or find someone else to do it for you on the Web.

The Internet is an enormous how-to manual. Access a huge range of tips and instructions for just about any home improvement project, from unclogging a drain to roofing a house. Good sites include Do It Yourself (www.doityourself.com), Natural Handyman (www.naturalhandyman.com), Hometips (www.hometips.com), and DIYonline (www.diyonline.com). Print out the information and create your own

manual for a project. DIYonline also offers free design software, so you can plan the job before you start knocking down walls.

Be sure of finding the best contractor for your home improvement job and screen out potential cheats and rip-offs. Check Handyman Connection (www.handymanconnection.com/). This site recommends craftsmen with at least 10 years' experience who will handle small to medium-sized home repairs and renovations. Moreover, their work is guaranteed for one year.

Visit the who's who of glue. People have a need to glue things to other things, and as long as they do, they'll find Thistothat (www.thistothat.com) indispensable. This site tells you exactly what glue to use to attach just about any two things together. Manufacturer's specifications on hundreds of glue products are given, as is helpful advice on gluing.

Be a materialist. Get a good estimate of material costs before you start buying for a project. Working out how much you need will help you avoid overspending. Many sites, such as Interior Decorating (http://interiordec.about.com), have a variety of calculators to help you estimate costs for everything from paint to decking. There are also sites such as Construction.com (www.construction.com), which offer online estimators for your project, so you can see if you're being overcharged by a contractor.

Never be stuck for a decorating idea again. You can look up decorating ideas from your favorite magazines online. Try Martha Stewart (www.marthastewart.com), Better Homes and Gardens (www.bhg.com), or Canadian House and Home (www.canadianhouseandhome.com) to get you started.

See others do it for themselves. If all that home repair is wearing you out, why not watch someone else doing the hard work for a change? Drop in on a home improvement project on the This Old House webcam (www.pbs.org/wgbh/thisoldhouse/works). You can check on the progress 24 hours a day and maybe get some inspiration while you're there. Or, go to Debbie Travis's Painted House (www.painted-house.com/) to get instructions for painting walls, furniture, and all other household items.

Do-it-yourself feng shui. Feng shui is the Chinese art of designing living and working spaces to allow for the most harmonious flow of energy, and it has become tremendously

popular. To find out more, visit The Ultimate Feng Shui Resource (www.qi-whiz.com) and World of Feng Shui Online (www.wofs.com).

Search for a super sofa. Once you've finished refurbishing your home, why not fill it with new furniture? Have that new sofa delivered to your door with shops like Concordian Chesterfield (www.concordian.com). Alternatively, order it direct from your favorite store's website.

Make your own furniture. Are you handy with the chisel and plane? You can do it yourself with furniture too—just browse through the publications at Lee Valley (www.leevalley.com)

HOME IMPROVEMENT INFORMATION SITES
How to keep up with the Jones's.

BH&G How-To Encyclopedia (www.bhg.com/homeimp)
A comprehensive site covering topics such as plumbing, wiring, and carpentry, with handy calculators to estimate materials.

Canada Mortgage and Housing Corporation (www.cmhc-schl.gc.ca)
Lots of advice on how to plan a renovation, solve home improvement problems, save energy, and do all these things safely.

Home Ideas (www.homeideas.com)
Research that project before you start tearing the house down.

The Home Improvement Fan Club (www.morepower.com)
Information for fans of the TV sitcom *Home Improvement.*

Homestore (www.homestore.com)
Tips, how-tos, and all the gear you need.

Rona (www.rona.ca)
Covers all aspects of home improvement.

under "Books, Woodworking" for information on furniture design and construction.

⇨ See also **Software: Home and Garden.**

HOMEWORK

Stumped by your studies? There's online help for students of all ages.

Don't waste time surfing. If you need help with your homework, the last thing you want to do is spend hours searching the Web. Head straight for the homework metasites such as the Discovery channel's school pages (www.school.discovery.com). The site contains over 600 links

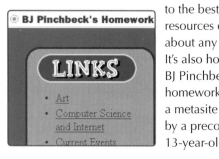

to the best resources on just about any topic. It's also home to BJ Pinchbeck's homework helper, a metasite created by a precocious 13-year-old!

Ask an expert. Stuck on a tough question? Sometimes it helps to seek expert advice. Several sites provide real people who will answer almost any question you can think of. Ask an Expert (www.askanexpert.com) is a directory of links to people who volunteer their time to answer questions, and to web pages that provide information. Alternatively, try asking What Is? (www.whatis.com) for help. Sites like these are especially useful for questions that are complex or that require in-depth knowledge to answer. Bear in mind, though, that the experts usually take a few days to respond. So, for more basic information, look elsewhere.

For a complete listing on homework subjects visit the About.com Homework Help website. It

has an extensive list of topics divided into subject areas such as art, history, languages, and sciences. Click on

a suitable link, for example, Creative Writing for Teens, to see advice and titles of articles written by teachers and education specialists. The homepage also has links to advice on homework and study tips and help for beginners on using the Web.

No time to read the whole book? Read the notes instead. Several websites like SparkNotes (www.sparknotes.com) and EssayEdge (www.essayedge.com) provide free notes and test preparation aids on a wide range of scholarly and literary works. Even if you've read the book, they can help you bone up before the big test.

⇨ See also **Software: Educational CD-ROMs; Internet: Bookmarks, Education** and **Encyclopedias.**

HYPERLINKS

Use the hyperlink feature to make documents faster and easier to move around and access.

Hyperlinks, or just links, are clickable text or icons on a web page, that take you to another place on that page or to a different web page. They contain hypertext mark-up language (HTML)—the coding used for web pages.

Find a hyperlink easily. Your mouse pointer changes from an arrow to a hand when you pass it over a hyperlink. The link itself may also change color as you do this.

Create hyperlinks in Word. First, highlight the text that you would like to make into a hyperlink. Then go to your toolbar and click on the Insert Hyperlink button. A dialog window will appear on your screen, allowing you to easily designate a location on the Web, your company's network, or somewhere else in a document or on your hard drive.

Keep activating links accidentally? You can often find yourself wanting to edit the text of a link in Word, but activating the link instead. Right-click the link and choose Hyperlink → Edit Hyperlink from the pop-up menu. The Edit

Hyperlink box now appears. Edit your hyperlink text in the Text to display section.

Create a hyperlink quickly in FrontPage Editor. Highlight the section heading and then right-click it, drag it to the appropriate point on the

page, and choose Link Here from the shortcut menu. FrontPage Editor will create a text link that duplicates the subheading's text.

Divide your web pages into smaller segments to make it easier to read and navigate. Use

subheadings to create themed sections within a page. Then, at the top of the page, you can create individual hyperlinks to each subheading. By clicking one of the hyperlinks, it allows visitors to your website to go straight to the relevant section in the web page without having to scroll down through the document.

Remember to check edited hyperlinks on your website before you upload it to the Internet. If you have edited any hyperlinks in a web document, check that they read correctly, and that the web addresses in the links are correct by clicking on each to make sure that they take you to the intended websites.

⇨ See also **Software: Word; Internet: HTML** and **Website Creation.**

INCOME TAX

Reduce the stress of paying your taxes by filing your return online.

If you decide to file your own return online, go straight to the source and visit the Canada Customs and Revenue Agency website (www.ccra-adrc.gc.ca/menu-e.html) first. The CCRA provides help and links to authorized e-file providers—all without the two- to three-hour wait you may sometimes get when you phone in. If you decide to file online, you must file through an authorized e-file provider, which will charge for the service. The authorized provider's software is tested early in the year, and a list of approved providers appears on the CCRA site.

Have a home-based office? Be sure you know the deductions you are entitled to and the rules that govern business and personal expenses. The CCRA site provides a wealth of information. For example, it can show you how to calculate the percentage of home use for business, and how to account for the business and personal use of your car. Download the *Guide for Canadian Small Businesses* (www.ccra-adrc.gc.ca/E/pub/tg/rc4070ed/rc40702-e.html) and check out the "Business-use-of-home expenses" in the Business and Professional Income guide (www.ccra-adrc.gc.ca/E/pub/tg/t4002eq/README.html). You can also use this official site to get sound information and tips about possible deductions related to support for family members with disabilities, education deductions, and moving expenses.

Crunch the numbers with a calculator. Ernst & Young (www.tax.ca) offer a tax calculator on their site, so you can do a quick estimate to find out what you will be getting back from—or what you might owe—the government.

Hold on to your tax return. When you file your return electronically, you don't have mail in your supporting documentation, but you do have to keep it available just in case the CCRA wants to examine it.

E-filing is not for everyone. In some cases, it is not possible to file your tax return electronically. You have to go the regular filing route if you want to submit an amended return for a year other than the one for which taxes are due. This applies if you are bankrupt or a nonresident, or if you owe tax to more than one province.

⇨ See also **Internet: Business.**

TAX SURVIVAL SITES
Explore the sites below to help find your way through the tax jungle.

CCRA
(www.ccra-adrc.gc.ca/menu-e.html)
Here is all the information you need to file your return electronically. Links to authorized tax-filing software, access to forms, publications, and tax advice.

COOLTax (www.cooltax.com)
This site allows you to prepare up 20 tax returns. The user, guided step by step through the process, can log on as often as may be required to compete the return.

Ernst & Young
(www.tax.ca)
Provides a calculator for personal tax and for the savings produced by RRSP contributions. Features links to other tax-related sites.

Quicken
(www.quicken.ca/eng/taxes/index.jsp)
The site includes all the tax forms. There are tax tips and sections on home business tax deductions, and lets you calculate the GST.

QuickTax
(www.quicktaxweb.ca)
Takes you step by step through the tax completion process and allows multiple log ons. There are tax tips and page-by-page clarifications of the tax form.

Taxbyte T1 (www.taxbyte.com)
This software, designed for the professional tax preparer, offers a variety of choices for different tax situations.

HTML

You can create a web page in a few minutes using the formatting code called HyperText Mark-up Language, or HTML. All websites use HTML "tags" (commands) to tell the browser what to display and how to display it. There are programs to create HTML code for you, but learning the basics is good experience.

VIEW SOME HTML

To see what HTML code looks like, launch your browser, and visit any web page. Right-click on the main part of the web page, and select View Source from the pop-up menu. A page of plain HTML code will open up on your PC.

Meet the tags. All web pages have an <HTML> tag at the top and an </HTML> tag at the bottom (in either upper or lower case). The <HEAD></HEAD> tags enclose information about the page, including the title. The <BODY> </BODY> tags enclose all the words and pictures that you see on a web page.

Working in pairs. Most HTML tags come in pairs, surrounding the information they format. For example, <B>**This text is bold**</B>. The opening tag switches the formatting on; the closing tag with the backslash switches it off.

To create a web page, you will need a web browser, such as Internet Explorer or Netscape Navigator; a folder on your hard drive in which to store your web pages; and a text editor, such as Notepad, to write and save your code. Avoid using Microsoft Word for writing straight code, because its clever formatting tools will wreak havoc with your HTML. If you want to put pictures on your web page, you'll also need an image-editing program, like Paint Shop Pro (www.jasc.com).

A GOOD STUDENT

Begin with a lesson. A beginners' tutorial will help you to decide what you want to do with your page. Try Pageresource.com (www.pageresource.com/html/index2.htm) or The Easiest HTML Guide For Beginners (www.tips-tricks.com/begin.shtml). Dreamink (www.dreamink.com) also has an HTML Guide For Total Beginners.

Always nest your HTML tags correctly. Think of the system as "first in, last out." For example,

 HOW TO: CREATE A BASIC WEB PAGE USING HTML

```
index.htm - Notepad
File  Edit  Search  Help
<html>
<head>
<title>Test page</title>
</head>
<body>
This is my web page.
</body>
</html>
```

① Type the following in Notepad:
<html> <head>
<title>Test page</title>
</head>
<body> This is my web page. </body>
</html>

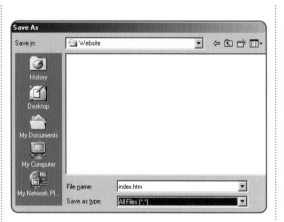

② Click on File and then Save. Name the document "index.htm" and in the Save as type: panel select All Files (*.*). Save it in your website folder on your hard drive.

③ Now view the page in your web browser. Open Internet Explorer and go to File → Open → Browse. Go to the location of the file, select index.htm and click Open. You'll see a web page with the words, "This is my web page."

MORE HANDY TAGS
Basic commands to get you started.

- **<HTML></HTML>**
  Tells web browsers that your page is written in HTML.
- **<HEAD></HEAD>**
  Sits below the HTML tag. Contains information about the document.
- **<TITLE></TITLE>**
  Specifies the page's title, which appears in the web browser's title bar.
- **<BODY></BODY>**
  Contains all the text and pictures that appear on the web page, plus all the HTML that formats the page.
- **<H1></H1> to <H6></H6>**
  These set your heading font sizes. **<H1>** is the largest; **<H6>** is the smallest.
- **<CENTER></CENTER>**
  Centers text, images, tables, and other elements on your web page.
- **
**
  Breaks text onto a new line (leaves no space between the lines). There's no closing tag needed for this command.
- **<P></P>**
  Breaks text into a new paragraph (leaves a blank line in between).
- **<I></I>**
  Italicizes text.
- **<B></B>**
  Boldfaces text.
- **<IMG SRC="file name">**
  Inserts an image.

this is correct: <B><I><U> **_bold, underlined, italic text_**</U></I></B>.
This is NOT correct: <B><I><U> bold, underlined, italic text</B> </I></U>.

Don't type special characters, such as & or ©, straight into your HTML code because they won't appear correctly in all browsers. Always use special ASCII codes. A good ASCII character conversion chart is available from ZDNet (www.zdnet.com/devhead/resources/ref/ascii.html).

Organize your code neatly so that you can easily read it. Write code on separate lines, and use organizational comments to remind yourself what is where, and why. An ! with dashes inside chevrons (<>) signals a comment that stays in the source code and won't appear on your web page. For example:
<!-- Navigation bar starts -->
<!-- Navigation bar ends -->.

Link to other sites. A good web page can be made even better if you provide hyperlinks to other relevant websites. This is the code you need to create a link:
<A HREF="http://www.thewebsiteaddress">website name or any other text you want to appear as the link</A>.

Choose fonts that most people have installed on their computers. If you use a fancy font, they might not have it, and their browser will use a font that they do have instead. Safe ones to go with are sans serif fonts, which include Verdana, Arial, and Helvetica. A good idea is to specify more than one font, just in case—and don't forget those Mac users. In the example <FONT FACE="Arial,Helvetica,sans-serif">, Arial is a Windows font, and therefore almost all PCs have it installed, and Helvetica is the Mac equivalent. If the viewer has neither, the browser will look for another sans serif font.

TIPS ON COLOR
You can specify colors in two ways: by name or by a special code known as hex values. For example, <FONT COLOR= "#FF0000"> and <FONT COLOR="Red"> both give exactly the same instruction. Although it is easier to use color names than hex values, color names are not recognized by all web browsers.

If you want to choose your own range of colors for the elements of your website but don't know the hex

values for them, most HTML editors and image-editing programs have built-in color mixers that will work out the hex value for you.

Define your colors. The <BODY> tag is where you define the page's background color, the color of the text, and the link colors. This means your page won't appear against a dull gray background in old browsers. Also, it saves you having to define your font colors throughout the page. <BODY BGCOLOR="White" TEXT="Purple" LINK="Red" VLINK="Green" ALINK="Aqua"> sets the background color of the page to white, the text to purple, the link color to red, the visited link color to green, and the active link color to aqua. The active link is the color of the text while you are clicking on it.

A FINAL ONCE-OVER
Check your code works before you go live. Consider investing in an HTML validator to check your code for you, such as CSE's Validator (www.htmlvalidator.com). Or check it online with ZDNet's Online Code Validator (www. netmechanic.com/cobrands/zdnet/htmlcheck/).

⇨ See also **Software: Clip Art, Graphics,** and **Photo Editing; Internet: Hyperlinks** and **Website Creation.**

INSTANT MESSAGING

Instant messaging lets you know when friends are online so that you can chat with them privately.

Instant messaging is a communications system that allows you to create a private online chat room with another person. There are various competing systems, but the other person involved must use the same system as you.

The major instant messaging systems include AOL Instant Messenger (www.aol.com/aim), which comes with Netscape Communicator, ICQ (www.icq.com) and Microsoft's MSN

Messenger (http:// messenger. yahoo.com).

If you are using Netscape Communicator with Windows and the America Online Instant Messenger keeps popping when you don't want it to, there is a fix. Go to the Setup button on the Instant Messenger sign-on screen, select the Misc tab, and uncheck Start Instant Messenger when Windows starts. Now the program will only load if you request it to do so.

ICQ ("I-seek-you") is the most popular online instant messaging system. It is similar to AOL's Instant Messenger program. Once you have downloaded and installed

ICQ on your PC, you can create a list of friends, family, business associates, and others who also have ICQ on their PCs. ICQ uses this list to find your friends for you, and notifies you once they have signed onto the Net.

Don't forget to apply the usual security precautions when using instant messaging. Never run files sent to you by strangers, and for extra protection operate behind a firewall such as Zone Alarm (www.zonealarm.com).

INTERNET

A global network of millions of computers providing the largest information and communications system in the world.

What do you need to get on the Net? You need a PC with a modem (a device that can send digital data over a phone line). Then you need to sign up with an Internet Service Provider (ISP)—a company that provides Internet access.

Anarchy by design. The Internet is decentralized by design. Each Internet computer, called a host, is independent of any others. Its operators can choose which Internet services to use and which local services to make available to the global Internet community.

There are a variety of ways to access the Internet. Complete online services—such as AOL or Sympatico.ca—offer Internet access along with their menu of special features. It is also possible to gain more direct access through a more bare-bones Internet service provider (ISP).

An amazing information resource. You can find information on every possible subject from the Web's global network. The amount of information is so

vast that it's usually best to use a search engine—a powerful website that will scan the Net for relevant sites for you. The most popular search engines are Go2Net (www.go2net.com), Yahoo! (www.yahoo.com), Excite (www.excite.com), and Lycos (www.lycos.com).

Worldwide communication. The Internet also enables you to send e-mail (electronic mail) to other Internet users anywhere in the world, contacting them in a matter of minutes rather than days by postal or "snail" mail.

Interactive opportunities. The Web also allows you to interact with others. Apart from sending and receiving e-mails, you can buy goods and services, chat online with friends, or join a discussion group to meet others with similar interests to yourself.

INTERNET ERRORS

Whenever there is a problem with connecting to a site, an error message will appear.

Received the "400 Bad Request" error message? This message means there is something wrong with the web address you typed in. Either the server you're contacting doesn't recognize the document you're asking for, or the document doesn't exist, or you're not authorized to access it. Check that you have typed in the address correctly. Pay special attention to uppercase and lowercase letters, colons, and slashes. Many sites put initial capital letters on directory names but not file names. If you get this message repeatedly, it's possible that the source you copied the website address from uses an incorrect mixture of uppercase and lowercase letters.

"401 Unauthorized" signals that you are probably accessing a protected site and you're not on the host's preferred guest list. Or you may have typed your password incorrectly. Some sites also put a block on domain types. If you're not from a .gov or .edu domain, for example, you may not be able to gain access. If you're sure you are permitted in, try again, but make sure you type correctly. Passwords are often case sensitive, so check that your Caps Lock is off.

"404 Not Found" pops up when the server that hosts the site can't find the HTML document specified at the end of the web address. It may be a simple case of mistyping, but it may also mean that the document doesn't exist anymore. To see if the website is still live, try deleting the last part of the web address to the nearest slash. If it is live, check if there are links to the document you're looking for. Failing that,

> **HTTP Error 404**
>
> **404 Not Found**

delete the last slash and try typing .html instead, to see what that gives you.

"503 Service Unavailable" has several possible causes. Your access provider's server may be down or your own system might not be working. Wait a minute and try again.

"Bad File Request" means that your browser is unable to work with some of the form you're trying to access. Perhaps there's an error or unsupported feature. Contact the Webmaster—the site's administrator—by e-mail (key in webmaster@[site's name]), or try accessing the form again some other day.

When the "Host Unknown" message appears, it usually means that either the server is down for maintenance, or you have lost the connection. It could be that your modem was disconnected from the server for some reason. First check the website address for errors. Then click on Reload, which will reestablish the connection in many cases.

 HOW TO: SET UP AOL'S INSTANT MESSENGER

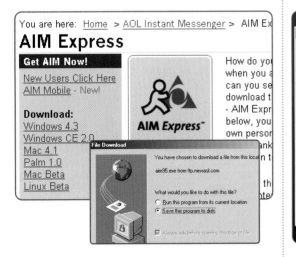

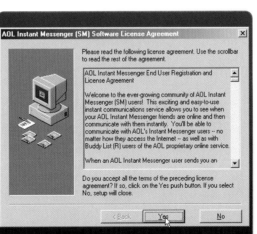

(1) Go to the AIM download page (www.aol.com/aim) and select your operating system—in most cases, Windows 98 or Windows Me—to begin downloading the installation program to your PC. If you don't have one, create a folder called Downloads in which to store it.

(2) When the download is complete, double-click on the aim95 file in your Downloads folder and follow the instructions to install the software on your hard drive. The New User window appears when the installation has been completed.

(3) To run AIM, establish your Internet connection and double-click the AIM icon. Enter your screen name and password into the dialog window and click the SignOn button to connect to the AIM network.

"Connection refused by host." You may not be allowed to access this document, because it's blocked to your domain or it's password-protected. If you know the password, try again. If you don't know the password, but think you might be eligible for one, e-mail the site's webmaster and ask for it.

"Failed DNS lookup" means the Domain Name System can't translate the web address you used into a valid Internet address. It's either a harmless blip or the result of a mistyped host name. Blips in DNS lookup are common, and often you can rectify this by clicking the Refresh or Reload button. If the problem persists, try again later.

"File contains no data" indicates the site you've accessed is the right one, but the web page HTML has errors in it. You may have stumbled upon this site just as updated versions are being uploaded. Try again in an hour.

INTERNET EXPLORER

Get to know the ins and outs of using this popular Web browser.

Customize Internet Explorer's toolbar to make the functions easier to access. To see the names of the toolbar buttons, go to View → Toolbars → Customize, and select Show text labels. To add and remove buttons on the toolbar, right-click the toolbar and click Customize. Scroll through the buttons and highlight the one you want.

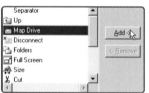

Click Add and it will move to the current toolbar buttons menu. To remove a button, reverse the process.

For basic browsing and specific information about Internet Explorer and its features, go to the Help menu and click Contents and Index. To find out about, and install more components of, Internet Explorer, go to Tools → Windows Update. You will then be connected to the Internet, where you can download components such as Internet Explorer Error Reporting for overcoming browser errors.

Already familiar with Netscape? Learn about differences between Internet Explorer and Netscape Navigator by going to Help and clicking For Netscape Users. To learn more about how to use the Internet, you can go to Help and click Tour.

Searching is easy with Internet Explorer. To search from the Address bar, type "go," "find," or "?," followed by a word or phrase, then press Enter. To search for a word or phrase within a web page, press Ctrl+F to open the Find dialog box, type in the word or phrase, and click Find Next.

Learn to move quickly around the Address bar. You can move the cursor into the Address bar by pressing Alt+D. To move the cursor back and forth between parts of the address, press Ctrl+Left Arrow or Ctrl+Right Arrow. To go to a new website, press Ctrl+O.

Save time typing in addresses. Type the URL words in the Address bar and press Ctrl+Enter to add http://www. and .com on either side of the word. So when searching for the Microsoft site, enter "microsoft," press Ctrl+Enter, then Enter again, and http://www. microsoft.com will appear.

Learn to move quickly around a web page. To move to the end of a document, press the End key on the right-hand side of your keyboard. To move to the beginning, press the Home key directly above it.

Move between pages faster. Rather than clicking the Back and Forward buttons on the browser toolbar repeatedly, use keyboard shortcuts instead. To move back a page, press either Backspace or Alt+Left Arrow. To move forward a page, press Alt+Right Arrow. To stop a page from loading, hit the Esc key.

Get the latest version of a website. A good website is updated on a regular basis, but you might not necessarily be looking at the latest version. Your PC caches (stores) web pages on

the hard disk to speed up access times. Press F5 to download the latest version.

⇨ See also **Internet: Back Button, Browsing, Cache, Downloading, Favorites, Forward Button, History,** and **Saving Web Pages.**

INTERNET OPTIONS

Adjust the settings in Internet Explorer to speed up and smooth out your surfing sessions.

Alter the amount of disk space assigned to temporary files by going to Tools → Internet Options → Temporary Internet Files. Click Settings and change the amount of disk space used. If you have lots of hard disk space, leave the figure higher because it will speed up your Internet access. To quickly delete all temporary Internet files, click Delete Files.

Protect your kids by screening the websites they view. Go to Tools → Internet Options → Content and click Enable. Here you can configure the browser to block websites that contain varying levels of bad language, nudity, sex, and violence.

Does the sound of the modem dialing and connecting drive you nuts? Set your modem to dial silently to the ISP by selecting Tools ➔ Internet Options ➔ Connections. Select your ISP from the list and click Settings ➔ Properties ➔ Configure. Move the Speaker Volume slider to Off. Now click OK back through the screens, and enjoy the sound of silence.

Turn off sounds and pictures for speedy surfing. Go to Tools ➔ Internet Options ➔ Advanced. Under Multimedia turn off the Play sounds and Show pictures options. Websites will load much faster. The downside is that many sites use graphics extensively, and you might find it difficult to make sense of sites without them.

To remove underlines from hyperlinks, go to Tools ➔ Internet Options and click the Advanced tab. In the Underline links section click Never.

Tired of the same old web page every time you open a new browser window? You can change your home page to any page you like. Go to Tools ➔ Internet Options, click on the General tab and type a new web address into the Home page section. Or, to use the page currently on

view, click Use Current, or for speed, select Use Blank. If you change your mind, you can click Use Default to restore your original home page.

➪ See also **Internet: Cookies** and **Security On The Net.**

INTERNET SERVICE PROVIDER

Wondering where to start? These tips will help you find the best ISP.

What is an Internet service provider? An ISP is a company that provides you with dial-up access to the Internet. You need to sign up with an ISP in order to browse the Web.

Ask a friend. The best place to get information about an ISP is from someone you know. If their experience sounds good, visit the ISP websites on your friend's computer, if they'll let you.

Try before you buy. Pick an ISP that offers a free trial without a start-up fee, and try it out. You

could even evaluate several providers at once. Access them at the times when you plan to be online—peak hours are usually between 3 pm and 9 pm. Try several times, especially during weekdays. If you regularly hear the busy signal, try another ISP.

E-mail an ISP and ask them a question, such as how much they charge for technical support or if they support your Internet software. Send it to sales@[name of ISP] or info@[name of ISP], or both. You can learn a lot about an ISP from their response, and how long before it arrives.

Is it local? Make sure the ISP you choose has a phone number that is a local call for you, not a long-distance call. Otherwise, you will get a shock when your next phone bill arrives.

Make sure technical support is an 800 number, and that there are no fees associated with it. Ask what hours it is available. Phone the number and see how long it takes for the call to be

ARE YOU BEING SERVED?
Evaluate your ISP or shop around for others with these websites.

Daily eDeals Free ISP Comparison (www.dailyedeals.com/free_internet)
Click the Free ISP comparison link to view a regularly updated table of ISP companies, or click the Best Free Internet Provider link.

ispnut.com (www.ispnut.com)
A weekly list of regional popular free ISPs.

Freedomlist (www.freedomlist.com)
A website providing lists of free ISPs throughtout the world, with appropriate reviews of each one.

The List (http://thelist.internet.com)
Search for local and national ISPs.

About.com's Family Internet pages (http://familyinternet.about.com/library/ weekly/aa020200a.htm)
What to consider when you're looking for an ISP. This site includes a list of ISP types, and regularly updated reviews.

Internet Access Provider List for Canada (http://herbison.com/iap_meta_list/ iap_meta_list_ca.html)
Search for regional and national ISPs.

Longmont.com (www.longmont.com/mnc/classes/ chamber/on101/15ques.htm)
This site provides the kinds of questions to ask before you sign up an ISP.

CNET Web Services Dial-up Access at CNET (http://webservices.cnet.com/html/aisles/ Dialup_Access.asp)
Click on User Opinions for a list of popular ISPs and what Net users say about them.

Search at CNET (http://webservices.cnet.com/html/aisles/ Internet_Access.asp)
Search for an ISP by area code, filter your results, and develop comparison charts.

Download at CNET (http://download.cnet.com/downloads)
Click on Internet and then ISPs for a wide choice of rated ISP software to download.

answered and how helpful the customer service people are. For example, do they support your version of Windows and your software? Are they willing to help you get set up?

Read the ISP's terms of service. You should be able to find the terms on the ISP website, but if you can't, or you can't understand them, take your business elsewhere. Will they sell on your name and personal information? Are there penalties if you leave before the end of your contract? Do they mention additional, unusual charges? Are you limited by the number of hours you are allowed online?

Want to create your own website? Make sure your account includes web space. They should offer at least a free 5–10Mb of space, and some offer an unlimited amount. And ask about web bandwidth: how much the ISP will let people download from the site each month. About 300Mb per month is a reasonable amount. Make sure you won't get hit with enormous charges if you go over that limit.

Are free ISPs worth it? Watch out for reliability and customer service. Some free ISPs may cut you off (with notification) if you haven't clicked on any of the ads in the last 20 minutes or so. However, for the home user, most offer an acceptable level of service and can save you several dollars a month in subscription fees. Since they're free, subscribe to several and go with the one that suits you best.

INTERNET STORAGE

Free up space on your hard drive by storing files on the Internet.

Most Internet service providers supply you with some web storage space of your own, but

you don't have to use it just to house web pages. Check with your ISP for site specifics. If the information you want to store is sensitive, use a utility such as

WinZip (www.winzip.com) to compress the file and give it a password. Be sure to keep track of how much space you are using because extra charges may be incurred for using more space than your ISP has allocated you.

If your ISP doesn't supply web space, or if you need more, other companies can provide you with up to 100Mb of your own storage space. Most do not charge for the first 25Mb, which is enough to store the equivalent of 17 high-density floppy disks, 200 word processing documents or spreadsheets, 10 PowerPoint presentations, or thousands of images or MP3 files. For online storage options try Xdrive (www.xdrive.com) and FreeDrive (www.freedrive.com).

Access your files from anywhere in the world with Internet storage space. Do you have an important business meeting in France but you want to travel light? If you store your files on the Internet, you can retrieve them from any computer with an Internet connection, or from a WAP (wireless access protocol) phone. An entire presentation can be sent to a business contact without you having to be there yourself—just store it online and send your contact the web address and password.

Want to send some very large files? Don't e-mail them—store them on the Internet

instead. Large e-mails can take a long time to download, and attachments do not always open. Create a collaborative workspace with web-based storage. Some services, such as FreeDrive.com, will allow you to create a folder and type in the e-mail address of people you want to share it with. It will then send an e-mail on your behalf granting people access to the folder.

Use Internet storage to create a photo album. Upload your digital photos to your web storage space and send far-flung friends and family the web address. They can then visit the site for themselves, eliminating the need to e-mail them the photos.

If you're a teacher, create online storage space for your class. Students who are sick or unable to attend class can pick up their assignments or hand them in online.

Students can also access documents at school or home without the need to carry easily lost or damaged Zip disks and floppies.

Don't wait for files to download while surfing the Net. Save them directly to your Net storage. When you type in the URL of a file or web page address with FreeDrive, the file is automatically sent to a special Surf-N-Save folder.

JOB HUNTING

Use the Internet to speed up the search for a new career.

The **"extreme resumé drop" technique** is the e-mail equivalent of blindly sending your resumé to every company with a pulse. While mass-mailing is ineffective nine times out of ten, there is always that tenth time. Also, the technique is so quick and easy that your details can reach large numbers of companies inexpensively and efficiently. The concept is simple. Companies who are hiring have e-mail addresses. Collect them all together and send your resumé to everyone on the list. Resumé Path (www.resumepath.com) can help you organize a speedy extreme resumé drop to over 200 different companies.

Are you a student looking for work? Want to sound more experienced? Be aware that your campus e-mail address—with an ".edu" extension on the end—advertises both your student- and entry-level status. Consider hooking up with a local ISP for the duration of your job search. Serious searching online is best done with a .com or .net account.

Internet resumés need to be computer searchable. Most employers search for nouns, not verbs, so your resumé needs to emphasize these. Nouns act as buzzwords that employers look for in potential candidates. If the keywords describing your strengths—team player, Excel, Word, schedules—are not already in your

resumé, redesign it so that it includes them in a separate keyword section.

There are active and passive Net resumé postings. Passive posting includes posting to primary job sites, such as Canada.com Careers (www.canada.com/careers/), Jobshark.com (www.jobshark.ca/caeng/index.cfm), and Monster.ca (http://english.monster.ca/). The key to getting responses is simply to force as many keywords into the subject line as possible.

Active posting involves surfing individual employer postings or job postings and responding directly with an e-mail resumé. This can be a very productive method, since it is more direct and personal. It also gives you the opportunity to add comments about yourself that are relevant to a specific employer, as well as your contact details.

LEGAL ADVICE

The Internet can't argue for you in court, but it can help you to find the right lawyer or advice.

Want to talk to a lawyer but can't afford it? To access legal aid, go to your provincial government site to find information about this service in your province.

For every possible legal link, visit Duhaime's Canadian Legal Information Centre (wwlia.org/ca-home.htm). This site also provides a "plain language" legal dictionary that will tell you exactly what legal terms such as *res ipsa loquitur* mean. Canadian Legal FAQs (www.law-faqs.org/) covers a multitude of topics at both federal and provincial levels.

Find a qualified lawyer specializing in the area of law you need. CanadaLegal.com (www.canadalegal.com) allows you to search for a lawyer or firm that can handle your problem. This site also has information and articles in more than a hundred different areas of law.

Search for lawyers and law firms by name, by practice area or geographic location at

Canadian Lawyer Index (www.canlaw.com/). Most of the lawyers on the site will give you a free half-hour consultation to make sure your styles mesh. Another useful site is the Canadian Legal Lexpert Directory (www.lexpert.ca/), which allows you to search by practice area and find the most highly recommended firms or individuals.

ONLINE LEGAL TIPS AND TACTICS
These hints can help guide you safely through the legal jungle.

- Evaluate your legal needs carefully before you try to solve them online. As a general rule, the more specialized your needs are, the harder you will have to search to find web information relevant to your situation.

- Make sure you know the source before you begin to act on it, especially if it's from a questionable source such as a newsgroup or chatline.

- Check the authenticity. If a site is billing itself as offering legal advice, especially if it is charging you, with the American Bar Association (www.abanet.org).

- What is the date of the information? Last year's rulings may not be relevant today. Advice that may be accurate in one state may be inapplicable in another.

- Don't be too quick to use legal forms downloaded from the Web or copied from a CD-ROM. Your local legal system may require more specific or different forms than those you have downloaded.

- Find out if you need a professional lawyer. Some cases legally require that a member of the Bar represent you whether you actually need them or not.

INVESTING ONLINE

Trade shares on the Internet and get a taste of how it feels to be a professional stock trader. Net-based stock brokerage firms let you look at financial portfolios, obtain quotes on stocks, get financial data on public companies, and execute securities trades—but first make sure you are aware of the pitfalls.

STOCKMARKET SERVICES

Many services make it simple for you to obtain current stockmarket quotes on your computer. At StockHouse Canada (www.stockhouse.ca), you can get up-to-the-minute quotes and information, news, and track your own portfolio. Both Yahoo! Finance (http://quote. yahoo.com) and Wired News (www.wired.com) allow you not only to get quotes and generate charts of stock performance, but also to save a profile

of your portfolio and gauge your overall performance as well. If you're on AOL (www. aol.com), the keyword "quotes" allows you to do all of the above.

With Netscape Navigator you can gain access to stock or mutual fund quotes from anywhere on the Web, simply by typing the word "quote," followed by a ticker symbol, such as IBM in the Navigator location bar. You can also set up a personal financial portfolio either in the Personal Finance channel or via My Netscape. To see your portfolio, you only need to type "my stocks" in the location bar. If you have not set this up and you type "my portfolio," you will get a default portfolio that you can then customize.

Most sites offering stock quotes over the Internet delay their quotes by 15 to 20 minutes because of restrictions and fees imposed by the stock exchanges. If you need your quotes faster, you'll have to pay. Standard & Poor (www. standardandpoor.com) and Quote.com (www. quote.com) offer this service for a fee, while Freerealtime.com (www.freerealtime.com) provides limited quotes for free. Canada Stockwatch (www.canada-stockwatch.com) charges for realtime quotes, statistics, charts, as well as "market depth" service, but offers a month's trial subscription to entice you. To have automatic quotes and news headlines flowing across your Desktop throughout the day, download Yahoo! News Ticker (http://my.yahoo.com/ ticker.html).

TRADING STANDARDS

Online brokerages must meet the same requirements as traditional firms. They have to be registered with the provincial and territorial

securities commissions. Check the provincial governments' websites for the addresses. You can also check a brokerage's reputation at the Investment Dealers Association of Canada (www.ida.ca/index.html), a national self-regulatory body that regulates the activities of investment dealers. The Canadian Investor Protection Fund (CIPF) (www.cipf.ca/) safeguards customers' securities up to $1,000,000. But the securities commissions advise you to steer clear of unlicensed individuals and brokerage firms, to consider all offers with scepticism, and to avoid any online investments that are offered anonymously.

GETTING STARTED

While you won't need special software to trade online, you must open a trading account. Look for a broker who will let you transfer money into the account on a regular basis. If you intend to trade online regularly, it might be easiest to transfer a set amount each month direct from your checking account into a money market fund until you invest it. In order to trade, be aware that you will have to keep a minimum balance in your trading account and, as with traditional brokerages, you are required to pay for the securities within three days.

Although buying online won't do away with the commission normally paid to a broker, it is considerably reduced. Online commission charges vary from broker to broker, so make sure you know what a broker's prices are before you start buying shares. And don't forget that a commission is charged any time you buy or sell—online brokerage firms may also impose a number of other fees and charges.

Before you go wild and start buying and selling stocks or mutual funds online on a large scale, think about what the tax bite would be as a result of such trading. Profits made on your investments when you sell them are considered capital gains, but only a portion of the gains are taxable. Also, if you are not quite so successful in your investing, capital losses can be used to reduce the capital gains. However, be warned about daytrading. If you trade frequently, hold your stocks for a short period of time, spend quite a bit of time studying the markets, Canada Customs and Revenue Agency might view your activities as your prime occupation and tax your income as business income.

WHISPERS AND GLITCHES

A stock price may fall because the company concerned did not meet its "whisper number." This term refers to rumors relating to a firm's possible quarterly earnings and the number usually differs from Wall Street thinking. Many investors use whisper numbers to make investing decisions. To find out what it's all about, look over the analyst estimate and whisper number listings at Whisper Number (www.whispernumber.com) and Earnings Whispers (www.earningswhisper.com).

Trading online isn't foolproof. At times you won't be able to access your account, you could be away from your computer when the market makes a major move, or your Internet connection could be down. Heavy trading, software glitches, or a natural calamity could cause an online brokerage's system to crash.

POTENTIAL PITFALLS

Online investors often turn to stock chatrooms for information, but be wary—a lot of incorrect information is passed on here. Chatroom contributors talk about stock as if they were the world's greatest experts, and some of them even make up fake press releases. These people have two goals: to drive the stock price up so they can sell before you have a chance to realize the stock's true lower value; or to drive the price down so they can "buy to cover" their "short" position for a profit. Some firms have begun to take legal action against this on the Internet.

Because of the time lag in processing both buy and sell orders, you'll want to make sure you protect yourself from paying more than you can possibly afford by using stop orders, and limit orders. A lot can happen in 20 minutes on Wall Street. An order for a fast-moving stock may not reach the market until the price has doubled. Limit orders guarantee that you do not pay over a certain amount for a stock. The buy order will only go through if the market price has not moved beyond your price limit. A stop-loss order sets the sell price and when the security's price drops below this level, it is automatically sold.

Don't get caught up in the dot.com hype. There are a handful of websites designed to inform consumers about the increasingly frequent demise of various Internet companies. Dotcom Flop (www.dotcomfailure.com) is one such site that features verified information as well as company rumors. Also try the Webmergers (www.webmergers.com) website for similar information on many different companies.

ONLINE INVESTMENT BASICS
Here's what you need to know to make your pile.

1. Choose your broker carefully—search filings for brokers through the provincial securities commissions or the Investment Dealers Association of Canada.

2. To avoid losing large sums—should the market suddenly shift—always use limit and stop-loss orders for trading online.

3. Use the free services offered by online brokers that allow you to receive automatic e-mail messages whenever there is news about your stock.

4. Professional traders don't buy and sell on whim, nor should you—do research.

5. Keep a careful watch on where you get your information. Take advice from reliable sources, not anonymous "experts" you come across in chatrooms.

6. As with betting or buying, decide first how much money you can afford to spend and do not exceed that limit. As a beginner, you may want to stick to lower-risk investments such as mutual funds.

MAILING LISTS

A mailing list brings together people with a common interest and lets them communicate by e-mail. Subscribe to a list and you're given an e-mail address that you can send your comments and questions to. Your e-mails are posted to all the other subscribers. It's a great way to swap ideas and info.

CHOOSING A LIST

There are thousands of mailing lists, covering diverse, wide-ranging, and often bizarre topics, from flower arranging to wildlife conservation. So if you're a huge Rolling Stones fan, you might like to find out about Rolling Stones mailing lists, where you can talk by e-mail to your heart's content with other fans.

LISTS OF LISTS
Want to know more about mailing lists? Visit these sites of directories.

Liszt (www.liszt.com)
This directory, of over 63,000 mailing lists, is not only organized into subject categories, but it's also searchable. It covers the major Listserv, Majordomo, and Listproc lists as well as independently managed ones.

Topica (www.topica.com)
Another searchable list that sorts your results by category.

Tile.net (www.tile.net/lists)
Search or view by name, description, or host country. Only includes Listserv mailing lists.

PAML (http://paml.net)
Publicly Accessible Mailing Lists is one of the original directories of lists.

Prodigy (www.goodstuff.prodigy.com/ Mailing_Lists/index.html)
An index of this ISP's own up-to-date mailing lists, searchable by name or subject.

How do you find a mailing list? There are several directories of mailing lists on the Web (see box). Or use a search engine, such as Alta Vista (www.altavista.com) or Google (www.google.com). For example, entering "Rolling Stones" and "mailing list" into a search engine should bring up a few Rolling Stones mailing lists. Remember that behind every list is a list manager, the real person who runs the list.

Check your favorite websites. Another way to find mailing lists is to scour websites about the topic you're interested in. The sites might include links to relevant mailing lists.

If you can't find a list you like on a specific subject, host your own. You can set up a list for free at websites like Yahoo!Groups (http:// groups.yahoo.com) ListBot (www.listbot .com), or CoolList (www.coollist.com).

JOINING A LIST

So, you've found out about a mailing list that interests you. But how do you subscribe? Wherever the mailing list is shown—such as on a website—you should also find clear instructions on how to subscribe. This will generally involve sending an e-mail to the mailing list administration address provided, along with a special command, such as "subscribe" followed by your e-mail address.

When you send your subscription e-mail, open up a new, blank e-mail, type the address into the "To" field, leave the "Subject" field blank, and type any subscription commands in the

body of the e-mail, right at the top. Usually you don't need to type anything else. If you have a signature file with your name and address, disable it.

Keep the welcome note! Once you have subscribed to a mailing list, you'll receive a welcome e-mail, giving you more information about rules for the list, how to post to the list, and how to unsubscribe from the list. Save this e-mail somewhere safe. It's a good idea to create a folder in your e-mail program for keeping all these registration details.

Having problems subscribing? Even if you've used slightly incorrect terminology for the mailing list software, it can usually recognize that you're trying to subscribe and will send you a Help file containing a detailed explanation. If you still can't figure it out, you can take a look at the Mailing List Gurus' advice (www.gurus. com/lists/subbing.html).

Mailing List Gurus	Subscribi List Optic
	How to subscribe to l receive individual mes
Intro to Mailing Lists	To subscribe to the li the mailing list manag server containing one list server manages th the command. Read o mail, and receiving m ListProc, MajorDomc
Participating in Lists:	
Finding Lists	

Lurk for a while. Don't fire off your opinions, questions, and comments right away. Spend some time just reading through the e-mails that come through, to get a feel for the list. If the list has an FAQ document, read that.

SENDING MAIL

Turn off any request for a confirmation of delivery that your e-mail program provides. These confirmations—known as "receipts" or "confirm delivery options"—are a big annoyance to list administrators. If you fail to disable them, every time you receive a message from your mailing list you'll automatically send a confirmation reply, which will go to the administrator and everyone on the list. Not the best way to make yourself popular!

Don't use Rich Text Formatting (RTF) or HTML formatting in the e-mails you post to the list. A mailing list will have people using all kinds of e-mail programs, some of which have problems dealing with RTF or HTML e-mails. Check through your e-mail software to see if there's an option to turn either of them off. Rootsweb (http://helpdesk.rootsweb.com/help/html-off.html) has instructions for various e-mail programs. In Outlook Express, for example, go to Tools ➔ Options, click the Send tab, and select Plain Text, not HTML, for both settings.

MAIL ETIQUETTE

Stick to the topic. If you've joined a list about the Rolling Stones, the other list members would love to read snippets of news, stories about when you met the drummer, song lyrics, opinions, or anything else about the band. They probably don't want to read the George Dubya joke your friend just sent you, no matter how hilarious it is, or receive virus warnings—most of which are hoaxes anyway.

Make your e-mails easy for others to read. Remember, your e-mails could be reaching hundreds or thousands of people. Use short, informative subject lines. Don't type in capitals. Don't use acronyms, unless you are sure that everyone else on the list will instantly know what you are talking about. Leave lines between paragraphs, use punctuation, and re-read and spell-check your e-mails.

When replying, include enough of the original e-mail to give context. Not everyone will have read the original e-mail. On the other hand, don't quote absolutely everything in your reply. Feel free to delete earlier, irrelevant threads of replies in the e-mail you receive. If you're replying to someone who wrote at great length before actually posing their question, delete everything but the question you're replying to.

Don't send file attachments. If you have a file you'd like to share with the list, post a note asking if anyone wants it. They can then e-mail you separately to request the file.

Consider replying privately instead of to the whole list. Think about whether everyone is really interested in an endless discussion you and one other person are having. The same goes for arguments. If you want to get heated, take it offline for a while. Most people don't want to read other's "flame" wars.

Be considerate. A mailing list is a community and its tone is set by the e-mails you and other users send. Always try to be polite and friendly. The other people on the list could come from anywhere in the world and may have very different beliefs and humor than yours. Think carefully about how you'd present yourself in person and try to do the same online.

MOVING ON

Aaargh! How do I unsubscribe? Remember that e-mail you received on subscribing? Now's the time to dig it out and scan it for instructions on unsubscribing. Alternatively, next time you receive an e-mail from the list, look carefully at the beginning and the end. There may be instructions on how to unsubscribe. If you still can't work out how or if the information isn't clear, then visit the Publicly Accessible Mailing Lists website (http://paml.net/gettingoff.html), where you will find a detailed guide on the best way to unsubscribe.

Changing e-mail address? When changing your e-mail address, make sure you unsubscribe from all mailing lists first. Otherwise, any e-mails sent to your old address are eventually going to bounce back to each mailing list. The unfortunate list owners will be avalanched with lost e-mail and will have to delete you from their lists manually.

Off on vacation? If you're planning to set up a "Bill's on vacation" autoreply message, unsubscribe from all mailing lists to avoid bouncing messages and autoreplies. Mailing list administrators hate it when mail bounces back to them—and since they're usually volunteers, it seems unfair to make them unhappy.

➪ See also **Internet: E-mail, Filters, Netiquette, Outlook Express,** and **Signature Files.**

MAPS

Need to find the fastest route to Kalamazoo? Get a map for every adventure on the Internet.

Navigate anywhere in Canada without leaving your PC using sites such as Yahoo! Canada Maps (http://ca.maps.yahoo.com/), Mapquest (www.mapquest.com), or Canada.com Travel (www.canada.com/travel/resources/maps.html). These sites feature online address finders, route maps, driving directions, and city information. Canada.com Travel has convenient links to special attractions such as golf sites, festivals, and wine tours. Mapquest features live traffic reports and up-to-the-minute travel information.

The National Atlas of Canada Online (http://atlas.gc.ca/english/index.html) is an interactive atlas with information about Canada as a whole. The Geography and Map Division of the Library of Congress (http://lcweb2.loc.gov/ammem/gmdhtml) holds over 4.5 million items. The Map Collection is a catalog of maps from around the world dating back to 1544. It is organized according to seven categories, including towns

and cities, and military campaigns. The indexes for all categories are searched simultaneously, and maps can be downloaded.

For maps of the world, no publication is more trusted than National Geographic. Their website (www.nationalgeographic.com) includes a detailed map section, providing maps from all over the world, a name finder for locating hard-to-find places, constellation maps, photos of Earth from space, information on cartography, and more.

If you are going backpacking, you will need a heavy-duty topographical map. Luckily, the Centre for Topographic Information of Natural Resources Canada has mapped much of the country for you. Many large outdoor-sports gear stores can provide maps of the wilderness in

your area. However, if you are going farther afield, you can find the map you're looking for on the Canadian Topographic Maps website (http://maps.nrcan.gc.ca/main.html). You can buy any of these maps online.

If you need specialized maps, here are some resources. The Canadian Hydrographic Service (www.chs-shc.dfo-mpo.gc.ca/chs/) has up-to-date charts for recreational boaters. Nautical Data International (www.ndi.nf.ca/) is their offical distributor of electronic marine charts. Aeronautical and Technical Services (aero.nrcan.gc.ca/english/ATS_e.html) publishes Canada's official aeronautical charts. Fugawi World Maps and Charts (www.fugawi.com/docs/mapframe.html) lets you create digital maps from any scanned map or existing map database, marine, topographical, or street.

What does your house looks like from space? GeoGratis (http://geogratis.cgdi.gc.ca), created by the Canada Centre for Remote Sensing, lets you search Landsat imagery, watershed maps,

BEHIND THE SCENES
There are hundreds of sites offering all sorts of film-related information.

Abbycon (www.abbycon.com/entertainment/MovieStarsandActors.htm)
At Abbycon, you get biographies, pictures, and links to lots of sites about lots of stars.

Movie Stars (www.fortunecity.com/lavendar/tombstone/95/)
Grab some pictures of movie stars old and new with from the Movie Stars site.

Film100 (www.film100.com)
This is a comprehensive list of the hundred most influential people in the history of movie making, including biographies and timelimes. You can customize the list to view actors, critics, or even special effects people.

Great Lakes mosaics, cities, land inventory, and much more. You can view and/or download aerial charts for free.

For links to more map sites than you can shake a stick at, check out The University of Iowa Center for Global & Regional Environmental Research (www.cgrer.uiowa.edu/servers/servers_references). This random—but thorough—selection of links to map sites includes EarthRise: Map Index to Space Shuttle Imagery; Xerox PARC Interactive World Map Viewer, the BigBook Yellow Pages and Map Locator, and hundreds more map sites.

Create interactive maps for free with MapBlast Interactive Maps (www.aquarius.geomar.de/omc/). Fill out the online form—giving the map boundaries as latitudes and longitudes, if possible, and the type of projection you would like—and a page with the desired map will be returned to your browser. You can pan around, zoom in on a map, then download it straight onto your hard drive.

MICROSOFT NETWORK

The Microsoft Network (MSN) is an online service that connects to, and forms part of, the Internet.

In common with AOL and CompuServe, MSN offers a wide variety of services, such as news, chat, and travel sites. MSN.com (www.msn.com) features a home page with easily accessible links to other areas, such as autos, games, and news, as well as Search, Hotmail, Shopping, Money, and People and Chat. MSN.com's shopping area, the eShop, includes links to preferred stores, daily specials, gift centers, third-party shopping content, and a shopping search engine.

MSN's most popular feature is probably Hotmail—a web mail account (available to all, whether or not MSN is your ISP), which allows you to send and receive e-mail to and from any computer hooked up to the Internet. While Hotmail is highly useful when you are traveling without a computer and want to check your e-mail at Internet cafés or via a friend's PC, it is not the kind of upscale address you might want for a business account. Also, because the Hotmail service is web-based, it can be slow with a low bandwidth Internet connection.

One unique feature of MSN.com is the Message Center, which lists new e-mail messages currently in the user's Hotmail Inbox, along with the names of any friends who are currently online. This is a free service, but in order to get the most use out of Message Center, it makes

MOVIE MAGIC
Check out the latest movie news, reviews, and celebrity gossip.

Filmbug (www.webfind.net/people)
A large database of movie stars, writers, directors, and others involved in films.

Hollywood (www.hollywood.com)
Get the scoop on the celebrities and their latest films at the Hollywood site.

Hometurf (www.hometurf.com)
Can't remember what that long-forgotten star looked like? Head to Sandy's Faces for the Faceless at Hometurf for hundreds of photos of the stars and not-so-stars.

**Joblo's Movie Trailers
(www.joblo.com/movietrailers2Mi.htm)**
At Joblo's Movie Trailers you get a huge collection of—you guessed it— downloadable trailers and movie scripts from all your favorite films.

Moviefone (www.moviefone.com)
Dial up Moviefone to check show times and book tickets for theaters around the country. You can also catch up on the latest movie news and reviews.

sense to have both a Hotmail account and MSN.com Messenger.

⇨ See also **Internet: America On Line, E-mail,** and **Internet Service Providers.**

MOVIES

Movie reviews, show times in your area, information on your favorite film celeb, and even made-for-PC movies—it's all at your fingertips.

Coming soon from a studio near you. The major film studios have their own websites giving news of upcoming movie releases. Visit Paramount (www.paramount.com), Universal Studios (www.universalstudios.com), or MGM (www.mgm.com) to see what's due for release.

Use the yellow pages at Yahoo! (www.yp. yahoo.com) or Movies.com (www.movies. go.com) to search for a movie theater or video rental store near you.

Get the scoop on the latest releases at Reel.com (http://reel.com). Download trailers for current flicks, but be prepared to wait several minutes for the clip to download.

Stay on top of what's coming out by getting the ReleaseDates program, which sends upcoming film, movie, music, and software releases dates straight to a datebook on your PC or Palm. ReleaseDates is available as shareware through the Zdnet website (www.zdnet.com)—just search for "releasedates" and look in the Downloads section. Once it is installed, choose the film category you want and the database is automatically sent to your e-mail address.

Ever wish for your own private movie critic? Someone familiar with your personal taste, to tell you what's good and what's bad? Well, with a little help from a website called Movie Critic (www.moviecritic.com), you may never waste the price of a ticket on a bad movie again. First, you rate 12 movies from "loved it" to "hated it." The site uses the information to group you with other users who have similar

tastes; then the site extrapolates what other movies you might enjoy.

The Internet Movie Database (www.us.imdb. com) is "the" online movie reference site. Started way back in 1990 on the rec.arts.movies newsgroup, the site catalogs information on over 200,000 different movie and TV shows, as well as more than 400,000 actors and actresses, nearly 40,000 directors, and hundreds of thousands of production people. Use it to settle a family argument about a movie, or find that half-forgotten film—that you now want to watch—instantly, even if you can only remember one of the actors who appeared in it.

Many small studios are making short films with original and innovative content just for the Web. Download a short film to take a break during a stressful day or just broaden your horizons. Atomfilms (www.atomfilms.com), ifilm (www. ifilm.com), imovies (www.imovies.com), and Mediatrip (www.mediatrip.com) are just some of the sites that allow you to download original movies to your PC for free. You may also need to download a movie player from one of the film sites.

MP3 is a digital music format that compresses large audio files into much smaller, near CD quality, files. The files are shrunk by a process in which all the inaudible and superfluous information is stripped from the file by an encoder. The music industry hates it, but Web surfers can't get enough of it.

SMALL IS BEAUTIFUL

With minimal effort, you can track down your favorite songs on MP3 sites and download them to your computer or portable MP3 player. MP3s also make it extremely easy to transport music around. For example, the classic Beach Boys song *God Only Knows* would fill up 29Mb of hard drive space as a standard CD file and take almost two hours to download with a 56Kbps modem. When converted to MP3 format, this same file is just over 3Mb, one-tenth the size. Although most people find the quality of MP3

sound perfectly fine, some people say they find it inferior to CD discs because an MP3 file is created by the compression of sound.

We usually associate MP3 with music, but there are also popular spoken-word selections, such as Audible.com (www.audible.com). Audio books, newspapers, and jokes are easily available—the comedian and actor Robin Williams even has his own show on the Web (RobinWilliams@audible.com).

ALL ABOVE BOARD

While MP3s are surrounded by controversy, they are in no way illegal. In the same way that you can make a tape of a music CD, you can make an MP3 copy of any CD you own, so long as it's for your own use. Distributing MP3s, though, is illegal, unless you own the copyright or the songs are in the public domain. But, there are numerous file-sharing sites, such as Napster (www. napster.com) and Gnutella (http:// gnutella.wego.com). Less popular titles are free on such sites, but you'll have to pay for any popular tunes.

To play MP3 files, you'll need at least a 75MHz Pentium processor computer with 16Mb of RAM, a 16-byte sound card, a CD-ROM drive and speakers or headphones. Creating MP3 files requires a 133Mhz Pentium processor, or better,

with 32Mb of RAM. You'll also need a lot of hard drive space to store MP3 files—they may be small, but even at 3Mb to 5Mb per file, you can fill up a hard disk very quickly. It is reasonable to budget a couple of gigabytes of hard disk space for your MP3s or plan to store them on Zip disks or CD-Rs.

DOWNLOAD AN MP3 PLAYER

Windows Me has its own MP3 software, called Media Player. You can launch Media Player by clicking on its button in the Quick Launch area of your Desktop, next to the Start button. If you are using Windows 98, you can download the player from Microsoft's website (www.microsoft. com/windowsmedia). Alternatively, there are other MP3 players such as Winamp (www.winamp. com) or MusicMatch Jukebox (www. musicmatch.com) available as free downloads.

MP3s ON THE INTERNET
Music used to be hard to find on the Web. Now, MP3s are everywhere.

Audiofind (www.audiofind.com)

Findsongs (www.findsongs.com)

Free-MP3s (www.free-mp3s.net)

HitSquad (www.hitsquad.com)

Liquid Audio (www.liquidaudio.com)

Look4MP3 (www.look4mp3.com)

MP3 (www.mp3.com)

Music4Free (www.mp3-music-4-free.com)

SoundClick (www.soundclick.com)

2000 MP3 (www.2000mp3.com)

Once you start to accumulate a collection of MP3s, you'll need more than just a player; in fact, you'll need a whole jukebox. Luckily, jukeboxes are easy to download and some are available for free (although, you may find that it's worthwhile paying extra to get more features). MP3 jukeboxes will organize your collection and playlist, look up track listings, search your hard drive for media files, and more. Download RealJukebox from Real (www.real.com), WinAmp jukebox from WinAmp (www.winamp.com), or the Shareware Music Machine from HitSquad (www.hitsquad.com).

ONLINE RADIO STATIONS
Perhaps even more popular than downloading the actual files is listening to streaming MP3 online radio stations. Windows Media Player has a Radio Tuner built-in. Or RadioSpy (www.radiospy.com) is a downloadable program that makes it easy. Select the category of music you want to hear, and the program automatically seeks out the stations playing that type of music. You can search for specific songs that are being played and even chat with other people listening to the same station as you.

PLUG-INS
If you're planning a Karaoke night, there are shareware plug-ins available that try to remove the vocals from your MP3 files. Vocal Recorder (www.analogx.com) is available in WinAmp format—you need WinAmp 2.0 or higher, a

stereo system, and high byte rate. You can also use it to remove some of the instrumentals from your files. Or try Soritong (www.sorinara.com/soritong/), an MP3 player that comes with a vocal reducer.

EDITING MP3s
You may find that you want to edit your MP3s. Most songs that you download have a few seconds (or more) of silence on either end. These sounds of silence can not only spoil a party for an aspiring DJ, but they also take up

valuable hard drive space. Although MP3s have a small file size, multiply that by a hundred and the amount of wasted space is quite noticeable. Trim the fat with MP3Trim—available from websites like MP3.com (www.mp3.com) and Logiccell.com (www.logiccell.com/~mp3trim/). This is a free program that lets you remove unwanted sound and silence from the start and end of MP3 files. It has features such as auto detect silence and preview so you can hear your new edited version before saving. A

similar program called PCDJ is available from the same sites. It has a more elaborate interface and a built-in player, which makes things a little easier.

ENCODING
When encoding MP3 files, be sure to use a high enough byte rate to produce good quality music. For most people, this means using a byte rate of 128Kbps or higher. Anything below that and the treble tends to sound "thin." Byte rates above 128Kbps give higher quality, but of

course, the file sizes are correspondingly larger. If you're not getting decent music at 160Kbps, you need a better encoder. It's worth considering the version of MusicMatch Jukebox 5 that you pay for, which uses Fraunhofer's FastEnc encoder. This encoding program and others, such as RealJukebox and iCast, are widely available on the Net. They're either free or low cost at websites such as MP3 (www.mp3.com).

⇨ See also **Software: MP3 Players; Internet: Music and Radio Online; Hardware: MP3 Players.**

MP3 RECORDING RIGHTS AND ROYALTIES
What the heck is file-sharing and why are the record companies so fired up over it?

At the eye of the storm is the file-sharing program that lets you convert your Desktop into a Web-based trading room, where millions of music fans can swap MP3 digital music files. When you can get the music for free, why would you want to pay, argue the record companies? And this, they say, robs them and their artists of their rightful royalties to copyrighted material.

File-sharing sites like Napster turn your PC into a mini-Web server from which you can upload and download music files. Everyone with the same file-sharing software can then rummage through your music collection, and you can pick through theirs, for free.

The design and application is very simple. You download the file-sharing program as you would any application, walk through the nearly automatic installation, and start.

Recently, many record companies have been adopting an "if you can't beat 'em, join 'em" philosophy, and they have been combining with file-sharing sites like Napster (www.napster.com) and Gnutella (http://gnutella.wego.com) to form a legally approved way to share tunes. Is this the end of free music? Probably not, but the new deals will doubtless improve the quality of the music while at the same time guaranteeing royalties to the recording artists.

MUSEUMS

Tour the world's most interesting exhibits, research collections, and shop from a museum store—all from your living room.

Take a virtual tour of the world's museums. Even if you don't have the time or money to travel, you can still visit thousands of museums without leaving your home. Virtual museums allow you to research and experience art, artifacts, collections, and exhibits from all over the world. For the most comprehensive lists of virtual and online museums, visit MuseumStuff.com (www.museumstuff.com) or ICOM (www.icom.org). MuseumStuff also has one of the most complete listings of museum links, all organized by subject.

If you're after pictures of celebrated art, Museums Online (www.museums-online.org) has hundreds of famous works of art that are available for downloading. You can beautify your desktop, illustrate a report or document, or browse by artist, movement, country, or period, and buy posters and prints at Artcyclopedia Online (www.artcyclopedia.com).

Take a real tour of a museum. Find out what shows and exhibits are on view all around the world. Traveling to Paris, Singapore, or Atlanta

and want to take in some art? You can look at what's on offer and when at the Virtual Library museums pages (www.icom.org/vlmp/).

Shopping for unusual gifts and educational items? There's nothing as special as a museum store. With the Internet, you can shop at hundreds of museum stores, specializing in everything from dinosaur memorabilia to replicas of ancient Egyptian art, to collector Pez dispensers. You will find a comprehensive list of online museum stores and catalogs at MuseumStuff.com (www.museumstuff.com).

⇨ See also **Internet: Education.**

MUSIC

Find a score of the music that's been going around in your head, create an original soundtrack, or simply listen to the latest single.

Sample CDs before you buy from online stores, listen to online concerts, and tune in to live and archived radio broadcasts from around the world with an audio player. You will need to download RealPlayer (www.real.com) or MediaPlayer (www.microsoft.com/windows/

windowsmedia). To run an auxiliary MP3 player, download Winamp (www.winamp.com). For music shareware, head straight to HitSquad (www.hitsquad.com/smm).

Need some funky music for your next '70s theme party? Order your own custom-made CD. Online compilation shops will let you preview and order tracks from their catalog, then they burn them onto a disc and send it to you. Try Custom Disc (www.customdisc.com), Music à la Carte (www.musicalacarte.com), or MixFactory.com (www.mixfactory.com).

To purchase ready-recorded CDs, try HMV Canada (www.hmv.com), MyMusic.ca (www.mymusic.ca), A&B Sound (www.absound.ca/index.html), Columbia House Canada (www.columbiahousecanada.com), or CD Plus.com (www.cdplus.com).

Use a search engine to answer your musical questions. MusicSearch (www.musicsearch.com) is one of the most comprehensive guides on the Web. Along with a full search engine dedicated to music, there are lists categorized by artist, kind, instrument, and events. A regional section allows you to focus on a your chosen continent, country, or artist.

MUSEUM SITES
Grab a piece of the cultural action when you take a virtual museum tour.

ArchNet (http://archnet.uconn.edu/museums/museums.html)
Get a glimpse of archaeological and cultural history museums worldwide.

Canadian Museum of Civilization (www.civilization.ca/cmc/cmceng/welcmeng.html)
A gateway to the story of Canada and its peoples. Take a virtual tour through the exhibits. Visit the Canadian Children's Museum (called The Great Adventure), an intriguing and absorbing place to be.

Musée (www.musee-online.org)
An interactive directory of collections from around the world.

Virtual Museum Canada (www.virtualmuseum.ca/English/index_flash.html)
Find out what's on at Canada's museums.

World Wide Arts Resources (www.wwar.com)
Here you can search for thousands of museums, artists, and art resources.

MUSIC SITES
Hit the right note with these sites.

Global Electronic Music Market (http://gemm.com)
GEMM lists over 2 million new and used recordings from around the world.

NME (http://nme.com)
NME—the influential indie tabloid—offers reviews, chats, archives, and online gig and chart information.

RecordFinders (www.recordfinders.com)
This site stocks hundreds of thousands of vinyl (remember those?) records.

Rollingstone (www.rollingstone.com) and MTV (www.mtv.com)
For more mainstream music news and information, try one of these sites.

The Virtual Gramophone (www2.nlc-bnc.ca/gramophone/src/home.htm)
A National Library of Canada project devoted to cataloging and preserving recordings from 1900 to 1950. The site features digital audio reproductions of selected 78s, artists' bios, and details about music styles and recording technology.

Having trouble remembering the lyrics to the third verse of "Louie Louie"? Never fear. Several lyric websites are available to remind you of them—and many other lyrics that are better off forgotten. Start with Songfile (www.songfile. com) or Lyrics (www.lyrics.ch).

Rock fans are not the only music-lovers on the Internet. There are many sites and zines exclusively devoted to classical music. Recording company BMG runs GetMusic—a magazine-style site (www.getmusic.com/ classical) or you can go to strictly Net-oriented sites such as Musdoc (www.musdoc.com/ classical). If your computer has a sound card, PM Classical (www.pmclassical.iicinternet.com)

has an extensive range of classical masterpieces in MP3 file format to transform your Desktop into a concert hall. And for fans of Gilbert and Sullivan, there's the G&S index (http://diamond. boisestate.edu/GaS/l).

View your favorite diva in the buff plus plenty of other light-hearted info on opera at the Virtual Opera House (http://users.lia.net/dlever). More serious-minded fans can plan their vacations around the performance of *La Traviata* by using the Opera Schedule Server (www.fsz.bme.hu/opera), which lets you choose concerts by date, city, artist, composer, and title. The librettos for hundreds of operas— in original languages and translation—can be found at Bob's Opera site (www.castle.

net/~rfrone /operas /operas.htm) and at E-libretti (www. geocities.com/ voyerju/libretti.html).

⇨ See also **Software: MP3 Players; Internet: MP3** and **Shareware.**

NETIQUETTE

Learn the basics of good Internet behavior and how to use the Net politely and responsibly.

The first rule of netiquette is always try to give people you meet—and converse with—online the same respect that you would give someone in person. Get the full scoop on netiquette hints and tips from the online book *Netiquette* by Virginia Shea (www.albion.com/netiquette).

Flame on/flame off. "Flame" is personal abuse or strident language. When Internet conversation degenerates into name-calling, it's known as a flame war. Although avoiding all troublemakers may be difficult, if things do start to deteriorate, break off and move on. Every newsgroup has its own FAQ, describing the

rules of the group—reading it first may save you from a flame war and may make new friends.

Watch those capitals! Be extremely careful about the excessive use of capital letters. The chatroom version of yelling is to write in capitals. If you do it too much, others will quickly scold you for it.

Don't get suckered into e-hoaxes. If it sounds too strange to be true, then it probably is. To learn the truth about an e-hoax, urban myth, chain e-mail, or any of the pervasive flotsam and jetsam floating around on the Internet, check it out at ZDNet's E-Hoax Central (www.zdnet.com/zdhelp/filters/ehoax/).

Be nice to newbies. Everybody has to begin their chatroom life at some point, so if someone stumbles into your chatroom who is obviously new to the medium, show them some patience and help them get the hang of it. Similarly, if someone has a problem and you can help, then do so. They may repay the favor some day.

Mailing out cute jokes and video clips? Make sure the people who receive them actually want them. When you spend 15 minutes downloading your e-mail only to find huge video joke files, it's not so funny.

When attaching files to an e-mail, make sure you send virus-free files and inform the recipient of the size and type of file.

Don't spam. Spam is that dreaded unsolicited commercial e-mail spouting subject lines such as REDUCE YOUR MORTGAGE PAYMENTS NOW! It's irritating and congests the Net.

Flooding is bad chatroom behavior. This is when messages are repeated over and over, or when you fill the screen with gibberish.

Give your friends a break and let them know how much time to spend on your e-mail by using meaningful subject lines.

⇨ See also **Internet: Chatrooms, Cookies, Security On The Net,** and **Spam.**

NETSCAPE COMMUNICATOR

Tips and tricks for using this popular web browser.

Communicator is an omnibus program that includes the Navigator browser, the Messenger e-mail program, the Composer home page-editor, AOL Instant Messenger, and Multimedia support. It can be set to block access to objectionable web content with NetWatch (search for netwatch at www.softseek.com). To set it up, you'll need to go online.

If you are researching a topic, Communicator's Smart Browsing feature will give you a link of sites related to the one you are on. For example, if you are at Digimedia (www.digimedia.com),

SHORTCUTS TO USE WITH COMMUNICATOR
Tricks to make browsing easier.

Ctrl+Home Goes to the top of a page.

Ctrl+End Goes to the base of a page.

Ctrl+A Selects all the text on a page.

Ctrl+B Automaically opens your Edit Bookmarks page.

Ctrl+C Copies selected text to the Clipboard.

Ctrl+D Adds a new bookmark to your Bookmarks file.

Ctrl+F Opens the Find On Page dialog box.

Ctrl+P Prints the current page.

Ctrl+N Automatically opens a new browser window.

simply click on the site name, then select What's Related, under the Netscape "N" in the top right-hand corner, for a list of related sites.

If you have an old version of Communicator, but would still like to try Smart Browsing, just type "go" followed by the word or phrase in the website Location box—for example, "go oil rigs."

To head directly to a search engine, type "search" and the word or phrase in the website location box. For example, type "search oil rigs" in the URL Location box to look for oil rigs.

Check the freshness of your bookmarks. Let Communicator flag any that have changed or that it can't verify. To do this, go to Bookmarks ➔ Edit Bookmarks and click to highlight the bookmarks you'd like to check, holding down Control as you select. Go to View ➔ Update Bookmarks, choose Selected Bookmarks (or All Bookmarks), then Start Checking. Changed pages will be marked, while the ones that can't be verified by Communicator can't verify will have a question mark next to them.

Speed up your research when looking through long documents by using the Find Dialog box. Just press Ctrl+F and your browser will display a Find Dialog box. Enter your most promising keyword, then click the Find Next button. The dialog box searches the web page until it locates the keyword. Then use either Ctrl+G or the Find Next button.

Increase browsing speed with Communicator by turning off graphics. Go to Edit ➔ Preferences ➔ Advanced and unclick Load Images automatically. The whole page will now appear almost instantly. If you want to see a particular graphic, simply right-click on the placeholder (usually a square with an "x" in it).

Bypass search engines completely with Communicator's Internet

Keywords feature. Just type the term in your browser's Location box. There are three types of keywords. The first group includes the names of places, products, or institutions, such as Dumbo University or Miami, Florida. The second are commands that must be followed by an object, such as "shop CDs" or "search History." The third combines the names of cities with specific activities and local information—for example, "Dallas movies" or "Los Angeles dining." Keep in mind that these keywords are Netscape's— that is, what you may regard as a keyword may differ from what Netscape regards as one.

Becoming a no-lifer and spending too much time in cyberspace? To find out what's going on tonight in your hometown, just type the word "zip" plus your zip code in the Location box. This will take you to Netscape's Digital City page, where you'll find what bands are in town, what exhibits are at the local galleries, and what restaurants and bars are worth going to. While the service doesn't work everywhere, it's active in most major cities and towns.

Take aim. When you download Netscape Communicator, you get AOL's Instant Messenger (AIM) as part of the deal. AIM's random pop-ups and memory gobbling can be annoying. To remove it, go to the Start menu ➔ Search ➔ For Files or Folders. Search for the word "aim." The Find tool should turn up an AIM folder and a file, LAUNCH.AIM. Delete both and AIM will not bother you again. Want it back? Go to AOL's website (www.aol.com) and download it.

To maximize the amount of space used to display actual web pages, you can switch to a version of the Navigation toolbar that uses smaller icons or plain text. It's easy. Just go to Edit ➔ Preferences in the main menu, and select the Appearance category. In the Show Toolbar As area, choose either Pictures Only or Text Only to make the toolbar smaller.

NEWS REPORTS

Have regularly updated news reports sent to your e-mail or Desktop.

Searching through online newspapers for stories on particular topics can be a time-consuming exercise. Instead, have news headlines and reports on subjects of interest to you sent directly to your e-mail inbox every day. News services like CNN (www.cnn.com) MSNBC (www.msnbc.com), and Canadian Press (www.cp.org) will send you news reports by e-mail. Sign up for categories like All Politics, E(ntertainment), Sports, Law Watch, Space Update, and more. European Internet Network (www.einmedia.com) delivers breaking European news to your e-mail address.

Get up-to-the-minute news reports by installing a news ticker tape on your desktop. News Index (www.newsindex.com), DeskTopNews (www.desktopnews.com), ABC News (www.abc.com), and Yahoo! (www.yahoo.com) all offer personalized news tickers. Stay in the know with a daily delivery of a stream of news and information on your favorite subjects. The sites all have their own downloadable software.

Many news sites put up headlines and offer links to the stories. This way, you can rapidly search the content of hundreds of newspapers for the most interesting stories. Try the following news sites: NewScan (www.newscan.com), Moreover (www.moreover.com), CanadaDaily.com (www.canadadaily.com), or eNewswires.com (www.enewswires.com).

Create a custom news page online, featuring stories on only the topic you want, culled from many different news sources. Both Crayon (www.crayon.net) and Infobeat (www.infobeat.com) offer this service. You can also select news and weather conditions for your locality by entering your zip code. Crayon will also deliver your news by e-mail.

Watch and listen to the news over the Net. Let streaming technology bring up-to-the-minute news clips to your computer. You will need the RealPlayer media player program (www.realplayer.com). For videos on demand, try CNN Videoselect (www.cnn.com).

Want to know what's happening in the House of Commons? Read all about the Commons' committees' deliberations—where the main work is done before bills become law. Go to Committee Reports on the Parliamentary website (www.parl.gc.ca/common/committee.asp?Language=E&Parl=37&Ses=1).

WorldNewsTV (www.foreigntv.com) is an international Internet daily news channel that provides English-language broadcasts from media outlets around the world. It also offers videos of the latest headlines from Reuters and inside coverage of the United Nations.

Broadcast.com (www.broadcast.com) and Worldwide Broadcast Network News (http://wwnews.net) offer television news broadcasts over the Internet, plus regular entertainment, arts and sports updates. Or browse current and past news stories with video and audio news from the BBC (www.bbc.co.uk) and CBC News (www.cbcnews.ca).

More specialized news reports online include the Obscure Store and Reading Room (www.obscurestore.com), offering offbeat stories. Opinion Pages (www.opinion-pages.org) lets you to search editorials and commentaries from English-language papers and magazines. Straight Goods (www.straightgoods.com) is Canada's independent online source of news.

➾ See also **Internet: Plug-ins.**

NEWSPAPERS

Save a tree by perusing your favorite paper on the Internet.

Newspapers rarely put entire editions online. But online editions let you search for related and past published stories, as well as find in-depth background information on current events that you want to follow.

Are you searching for a particular story? Try looking in a news directory such as AJR Newslink (http://ajr.newslink.org), Editor and Publisher (www.mediainfo.com), News Directory (www.newsdirectory.com), or Metagrid (www.metagrid.com). Or, you can look in a multiple news archive (although these often charge a fee) such as Electric Library (www.elibrary.com) or NewsLibrary (www.newslibrary.com). For a particular paper, try Newspapers Online (www.newspapers.com). The Paper Boy (www.thepaperboy.com) offers links to thousands of newspapers worldwide.

NEWSPAPERS ONLINE
Check out your favorite dailies online.

Associated Press (http://wire.ap.org)

Globe and Mail (www.globeandmail.com)

Los Angeles Times (www.latimes.com)

Le Monde (http://tout.lemonde.fr)

National Post (www.nationalpost.com)

New York Times (www.nytimes.com)

Reuters (www.reuters.com)

Toronto Star (www.thestar.com)

USA Today (www.usatoday.com)

NEWSGROUPS

Despite the name, newsgroups are not essentially concerned with the latest events happening around the globe. Newsgroups are the Internet's primary discussion areas where you can talk openly with experts in almost every field. Also, newsgroups are not a part of the World Wide Web, but part of Usenet.

ACCESSING USENET

To access Usenet, you will need an Internet connection, a newsreader program, access to a news server, and an e-mail account that supports the protocol POP3. This means web-based accounts like Hotmail, Juno, or Excite won't work unless you've upgraded them to allow POP3 access. Netscape and Internet Explorer come with newsreaders already installed, and most ISPs (Internet Service Providers) maintain a news server as part of their access package. Call your ISP's support line or check their home page to find your news server address.

If you are using Outlook for your e-mail, then you will have to download a newsreader. Try Agent (www.forteinc.com). You can also access

Usenet through one of many Web interfaces such as Deja.com (www.deja.com/usenet/) or Supernews (www.supernews.com).

deja.com	eBay's Half.com acquires Deja.com's Precision Buying Service
Thursday, Jan. 18	Search Discussions Power Search	Search Tips
	[Search]
	Search recent ▾ discussions in the standard ▾ archive
Welcome to Deja.com's Usenet	**BROWSE DISCUSSIONS**
	alt. (alternative)
	news. (news)

Newsgroups are divided into topics according to a naming system known as a "hierarchy." Hierarchies include alt., for alternative topics; biz., for business topics; soc., for social, cultural, and religious topics, and many more. Newsgroup names are structured with the main topic first, down to the specific subject area. For example, the group rec.sport.baseball.info takes you to information all about baseball.

When you get a list of newsgroups from your news server, some of the names may contain a wildcard character (*). You might, for example, see alt.football.*. All this means is that there are several groups under the alt.football discussion hierarchy. Just double-click the name (or click the plus sign to the left) to expand the list of groups.

Finding newsgroups is no problem at all, but finding the ones that contain the information that you really want is not an easy task. If you want to access a particular discussion, there are search services that target newsgroups. One of the best known of these is Deja News (www.dejanews.com). Tile.net (www.tile.net) also offers excellent newsgroup search engines to help you.

If you use Outlook Express to subscribe to and use newsgroups, by default it only downloads the header—or subject line—of the new messages. It does this to save time, so that you can browse through the headers. To see the message itself, you must click on the message header and press the spacebar. Within a few moments the message will be downloaded to your PC and displayed in the bottom panel of the Outlook Express window.

NEWSGROUP MESSAGING

Most newsgroups receive hundreds of new messages every day. When you are downloading them automatically that can quickly add up to thousands of messages. For this reason, Netscape Communicator allows

THE BIG EIGHT
Here are the eight main categories of newsgroups, known as "the Big Eight."

Comp. Lists computer science, technology, and development newsgroups.

Humanities. Discusses fine arts, literature, music, philosophy, and the classics.

News. Network news and Usenet itself.

Rec. Shows a list of recreational pastimes, hobbies, and arts newsgroups.

Sci. Records and discusses scientific research and applied computer science.

Soc. Pertains to social issues, such as history, culture, religion, and lifestyle.

Talk. Online live group conversation.

Misc. Carries topics that don't fit into any of the above categories.

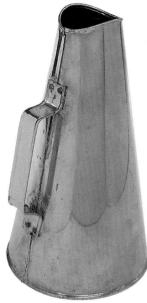

you to limit the number of messages it downloads automatically. To set this option, select Edit ➜ Preferences from the Communicator menu, which opens the Preferences dialog box. From the Category menu, select Mail & Groups ➜ Groups Server, which opens the Groups Server window. Now check the Ask Me Before Downloading More Than option, then enter a number for the message limit. Before downloading any messages, Communicator will inform you when the amount of messages on the server exceeds the limit you've set and that way you can override your limit if you're feeling a little reckless. To save your settings and close the Preferences box, click OK.

You can also download messages to read offline at a later time. To do this in Outlook Express, click on the File menu and choose Work Offline before you connect to the Internet. Select the newsgroup you want, then go to File ➜ Properties ➜ Synchronize. Check the When synchronizing this newsgroup, download box and then select the New messages (headers and bodies) option. Now click OK and then select Synchronize Newsgroup from the Tools menu. Outlook Express will then connect to the Internet and collect all of the new messages for the newsgroup. You can then disconnect and read the messages at your leisure.

Switch Identity...	
Identities	
Properties	Alt+Enter
✓ Work Offline	
Exit and Log Off Identity	
Exit	

In a newsgroup, raising a new topic is known as "starting a thread." Any replies to the initial message are then added to that thread. Your newsreader program can sort messages by thread, sender, subject, size, and date.

CREATING A USENET NEWSGROUP

Setting up a newsgroup is a little complicated because each Internet service provider decides for itself whether to carry any new newsgroup. Starting a "big eight" newsgroup (in the comp., humanities., misc., news., rec., sci., soc., or talk. hierarchy), as opposed to an alternate (alt.) group, requires that you adhere to very specific rules. Here's the basic procedure:

The discussion
1. Submit your initial outline to group-mentors @acpub.duke.edu for advice.
2. Post a Request for Discussion to news. announce.newsgroups, news.groups, and any other newsgroups hosted by your server other than those related to the topic.
3. Put your proposal in the proper format. You can find this format on "How to Format and Submit a New Group Proposal," which is posted regularly to the news.announce .newgroups and news.groups hierarchies.

The vote
1. Usenet Volunteer Votetakers (U.V.V.) take the request and post a call for votes in newsgroups related to the subject or type of group that you want to set up.
2. Voting occurs over a 21- to 31-day period, and only votes sent directly to the vote taker are counted. These include mass acknowledgments (a list of all names who are opposed to or in favor of the group) and are strictly nontransferable.

The result
1. There is a 5-day waiting period after the voting ends. To be approved, there must be no serious objections from voters to your newsgroup. There should be at least 100 more "yes" votes than "no" votes, and at least two-thirds of voters need to favor the new group.
2. If all the above requirements are met, news.announce.newsgroup will send out a new newsgroup message to announce the establishment of your newsgroup.

For detailed instructions on creating a newsgroup, you can go to Geocities (www.geocities.com/nnqweb/ncreate.html) and Homepages (http://homepages.go.com/ ~eacalame/create.html).

NEWSGROUP SITES
A useful selection of newsgroup resources and advisory services to point you in the right direction.

GO.com (www.go.com)
Usenet newsgroup articles and FAQs (frequently asked questions).

HotBot (http://hotbot.lycos.com)
Hotbot lets you search newsgroup postings.

Media Awareness Network (www.media-awareness.ca/forum/mnetnews.htm)
Introduction to newsgroups, netiquette, etc.

Netizens: An Anthology (www.columbia.edu/~rh120)
The history of Usenet, a description of what Usenet is, and speculations about its future.

Sympatico (www1.sympatico.ca/help)
This site offers an Internet tutorial for beginners, with a description of the three types of dicussion groups.

Tile.Net/News (http://tile.net/news)
The place to view the latest newsgroups.

Usenet Help (http://ibiblio.org/usenet-i/usenet-help.html)
An extensive collection of helpful Usenet guides, including Netiquette, Usenet writing tips, and creating your own newsgroup.

OUTLOOK EXPRESS

Outlook Express is the ideal e-mail and newsgroup program for home users with a dial-up connection. You can store your friends' and colleagues' e-mail addresses and other details, set up folders in which to store messages, and work offline or online. Follow our guide to setting up your first e-mail account.

SENDING AND RECEIVING E-MAILS

Outlook Express checks for new messages every 30 minutes by default, but if you are waiting for an important message you can get it to check more often. Go to Tools ➔ Options, select the General tab, and add the new time interval in the Send/Receive Messages section.

Send a file as an e-mail attachment. You can transmit almost any type of file—a photo of your new baby, for example—but avoid attachments larger than 1Mb. Write your e-mail, click Attach on the toolbar, select the file, and send as usual.

Accessing attachments you've received. E-mails with files attached have a small paperclip icon beside them in the message list. When viewing the message in the preview pane, click on the large paperclip on the far right to open the attachment or save it to your hard drive.

Received more than one attachment? Save them all at once by going to File ➔ Save Attachments.

Forgotten your friend's birthday? E-mail them a greetings card. Click on the arrow next to New Mail and select a design, such as Running Birthday, from the drop-down menu. Or, click Select Stationery to see more designs. Choose one, type your message, and click Send.

Deleted an e-mail containing vital instructions? Take a peek in the Deleted Items folder. It might still be there—if you haven't emptied the folder since you deleted it. To empty the Deleted Items folder select Edit ➔ Empty "Deleted Items" Folder. If you're confident you won't want to look at deleted e-mails again, set Outlook Express to empty the folder each time you exit the program. Go to Tools ➔ Options, select the Maintenance tab, and check the top box.

MULTIPLE USERS AND ACCOUNTS

Separate personal mail from hobby newsletters. You can easily set up two different mail accounts (see How To opposite), each one with a different e-mail address. You can monitor them both at once by clicking the Send/Recv button, or check just one of your accounts by clicking the arrow beside the Send/Recv button and selecting that account.

OUTLOOK EXPRESS TOOLBAR BUTTONS
Here are the tools of the trade for an Express ride with e-mail.

 Addresses: Opens your address book, where you can store and retrieve e-mail addresses, phone numbers, home addresses, and much more.

 Find: Lets you search e-mails by word, topic, or name. Click the arrow next to the button for more options, such as online directory searches.

 New Mail: Opens a new message. Click on the arrow to the right of the button for stationery options, or type the address of a web page to send.

 Forward: Opens the selected e-mail so you can send it on to another person. Any attachments received in the original e-mail remain attached and are sent to the new addressee.

 Reply: Opens a new message window in which to type a reply to the sender of the selected e-mail.

 Reply All: Opens an e-mail for replying to everyone to whom the selected e-mail was first sent. Use with great care, particularly if your reply is at all sensitive to some of those concerned!

 Send/Recv: Tells Outlook Express to connect to the server, download incoming e-mails, and send any outgoing e-mails waiting in your Outbox.

 Print: Allows you to print out the e-mail you have selected, to keep a hard copy of it for your records or perhaps to read later at your leisure when you're away from your computer.

Set up separate Inboxes and address books for each member of your family. Go to File ➔ Identities ➔ Add New Identity. Type in a name and password, if required. To switch identities, go to File ➔ Switch Identity, and select a new name. There's no need to close Outlook Express or your Internet connection.

THE ADDRESS BOOK

Add your new neighbors' e-mail address. Click the Addresses button on the toolbar. Click New ➔ New Contact. Select the Name tab and type the name. Add the e-mail address or addresses below, and any other information on the other tabs, as desired. Click OK to create the contact.

Do you regularly e-mail your softball team? Create a Contact Group so that you can send the same e-mail to several people at once. Open the address book, select New ➔ New Group and name your group. Click on Select Members and choose all the people in your address book you want to include by highlighting them and clicking the Select button. Next time you e-mail

your softball team, click the small Addresses button next to To: at the top of your message, and select your group from the pop-up menu.

NEWSGROUPS

Use Outlook Express as a newsgroup reader. A newsgroup is a discussion forum on the Web, where users air their views on a particular topic. In order to join one, you need to set up a news account. Contact your Internet service provider (ISP) and ask them for their News server (NNTP) address. Go to Tools ➔ Accounts, and select the News tab. Go to Add ➔ News, and enter your ISP's NNTP server information.

There are millions of newsgroups worldwide, covering everything from local news to knitting. But how do you find them? Go to Tools ➔ Newsgroups and type in a word or topic. All the newsgroups on that topic will appear. Click the most likely looking group, press Subscribe, then OK. To unsubscribe, right-click the group and click Unsubscribe. You can't view newsgroup listings until you've set up a news account.

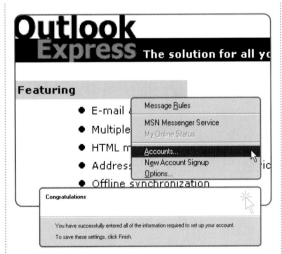

WORKING MORE EFFICIENTLY

Inbox out of control? Make separate folders for storing different types of messages. Click on the Local folders icon. Go to File ➔ Folder ➔ New and type in a name. Click OK. Now simply drag and drop messages into the appropriate folder.

To locate a message quickly, click on the Find icon on the toolbar. Type in a keyword, such as a name in "From" or specify a file received before or after a certain date. Click Find Now.

➔ See also **Internet Service Provider.**

HOW TO: SET UP AN E-MAIL ACCOUNT

1 Sign up with an Internet service provider, such as AOL (www.aol.com), that includes e-mail addresses and newsgroup access. Your ISP will give you all the details you need to set up an e-mail account: your account name, password, e-mail address, and their SMTP server address.

2 Open Outlook Express and go to Tools ➔ Accounts and click on the Mail tab. Click on Add ➔ Mail. Type the details as prompted, clicking on Next to proceed. When you have entered all the information, you are ready to start receiving and sending e-mails.

3 Click the New Mail button in the toolbar. In the To: field, type your friend's e-mail address. Outlook Express automatically enters your e-mail address in a From: field. Fill in the subject line, type your message in the main body area, and finally, click Send.

PASSWORDS

Protect your files by giving them a password that's known only to you.

A password is a secret series of characters that enables an authorized user to access a website, private files, computers, and programs. On multiuser systems each user must enter his or her own password before the computer will respond to commands. A password ensures that unauthorized users can't access your computer or private files.

The password that you choose should be a word that n one else could possibly guess. In practice, most people select something that's fairly easy to remember, such as their name or initials. But this is one reason why breaking into most computer systems is surprisingly simple. For secrecy, select a word that means something to you personally, a word you haven't already shared with co-workers—and not the name of your child or the family pet.

One common cause of security breaches is putting passwords down on paper, especially when they're stickered to computer screens. It's always best to choose a password that you won't need to write down. Use a character substitution scheme to create one that's easy to remember, but hard to crack. For example, take your date of birth and substitute the equivalent letter in the alphabet for the numbers. For example 11/26/1959 could become AABFAIEI.

You can also devise a code to replace the letters of your name or a phrase with letters that are a certain number of keys away on the keyboard. So if your name is Freddie, you could count two keys to the right of each letter to make the code HYtGGpe (uppercase for vowels and lowercase for consonants). If you do write your password down, keep it in a safe place known only to you.

For extra protection, have a different password for every application. Within each password, combine upper and lowercase, and a digit or two. Passwords should be at least six characters

long, but the most secure are 13 or more. You could create words that stand for the date and place of a big event—for example, 90wa66 could be a June 6, 1990 wedding anniversary.

The most unique devices won't make it any easier to memorize lists of lengthy character passwords, but you can always get a little extra help. Software is available to generate passwords for you and then encrypt them so that no one else will ever figure them out. One such program—Norton's For Your Eyes Only —is available wherever Norton is sold, or through Symantec, the Norton website (www.symantec.com). Or search shareware sites such as Jumbo! (www.jumbo.com) or

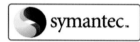 CNET Shareware .com (www.shareware.com).

The most common way for others to gain access to password-protected documents and accounts is when you don't log out once you've finished with your computer. If you're using a site from a public terminal, be sure to close the browser to end the session once you're done.

HOW TO: PASSWORD-PROTECT YOUR PC

① Use your screensaver to lock out access by anyone else. Right-click on the Desktop, click on Properties and then click on the Screen Saver tab. Check the box beside Password protected and click Change. Type your chosen password in both boxes and click OK again.

② Set the time lapse before the screensaver is activated—for best security choose one minute. Make sure a screensaver is selected in the drop-down menu, click Apply and OK. With the screensaver on, your password will have to be entered to return to the Desktop.

PEOPLE FINDER

Wherever they're hiding, you can always find people with the help of the Internet.

There are many sites to help you track down individuals and businesses, and some of these sites are free. Try YellowPages.ca (www.yellowpages.ca) or InfoSpace Canada (www.infospace.com/canada/). Trace phone numbers and addresses with Canada411 (http://canada411.sympatico.ca/), Reverse Directory (www.reversedirectory.net/), and 555-1212.com (www.555-1212.com).

For a fee, information look-up services and online investigators will dig out personal details on almost anyone. Falcon Collection and Investigations Inc. (www.falconcanada.com/) does individual and business background investigations and locates people, among other services. AssetFindCanada.com

related searching, plus links to legal, social and other issues, search tools, registries, etc., all organized by province/territory. Adoptee Searcher's Handbook (www.ouareau.com/adoptee/) gets you started with free online advice and links. Canadian Adoptees Registry Inc. (www.canadianadopteesregistry.org/index.html) has a free searchable database for adoptees, birth parents, foster parents, and adoptive parents. Or, enlist the assistance of Adoption Searches and Investigations (www3.sympatico.ca/searches/), which searches for members of the "adoption circle."

You can track down your long-lost classmates from college or high school via ClassMates.com (www.classmates.com) or by clicking on Alumni.net (www.alumni.net)).

Looking for a cellphone number? Try Cellow pages.com (www.cellowpages.com). Or log onto the Contacts Directory (www.555-1212.com/index.jsp) for a reverse directory, where you can find cellphone and fax numbers or e-mail and website addresses when you've just got a number without a name.

Learn all the tricks of the investigation trade and make your search more professional at Backgrounds Online (www.backgroundsonline.com), Robert Niles.com (www.robertniles.com/data), How To Investigate (www.howtoinvestigate.com), and Navy Spies (http://members.aol.com/navyspies/tips.htm).

Bring an end to world poverty and warfare by pestering politicians to take action! Their addresses and phone numbers can often be found at Politicians (http://www.trytel.com/~aberdeen) and The Environmental Forum (http://cyberbuzz.gatech.edu/tef/links).

You can search for war veterans, through the Canadian Virtual War Memorial of the Veterans

Affairs Canada website (www.vac-acc.gc.ca/general/). Another useful site for obtaining information is the Royal Canadian Legion (www.legion.ca/). To locate military services records, check the National Archives of Canada (www.archives.ca/02/02020201_e.html#6).

Have you lost a friend and are your worried about their whereabouts? Get people worldwide looking for them by registering their name, details, and a photograph at Mispers.com (www.mispers.com).

START YOUR OWN SEARCH
Use online resources to get your investigation off the ground—fast! You'll soon be able to find almost anyone.

Canada411
(http://canada411.sympatico.ca/)
Click on the Reserve Search by Phone hyperlink to locate people in Canada.

internet@address.finder (www.iaf.net)
Online white pages of Internet addresses, including a search engine for rapid results.

Net Detective 2001
(http://powerpromotion.net/go/091504)
Better than hiring a private investigator!

People Finder (www.peoplesite.com)
Alert thousands of pairs of eyes to help you look for your first love or lost relative.

Reverse Phone Directory
(www.reversephonedirectory.com)
This directory has three search capabilities in one. It also has links to other types of searches.

Who Where?
(www.whowhere.lycos.com)
Trace people and businesses, worldwide by e-mail, telephone, or Web presence.

(www.assetfindcanada.com) will tell you about a person's assets, income sources, and credit history. It also will investigate the marital and employment status among other things. The company profiles businesses and will give you a complete corporate picture—full history of the business, its officers, equipment, its inventory, supplier payment record. Net Detective (www.researchingtools.com/) is not free but is downloadable and is a way of checking criminal records, adoption records, backgrounds, credit reports.

Searching for phone numbers abroad? Try the WorldPages International Directories (www.worldpages.com/global). White Pages OnLine (www.whitepages.com.au/wp) and

Yellow Pages OnLine (www.yellowpages.com.au) will find Australian phone numbers and addresses. For the UK, use 192.com (www.192.com) and BT (www.bt.com/phonenetuk/).

If you're an adopted child searching for your birth parents or if you want to find a child you gave up for adoption, then CANADopt (www.canadopt.ca/) is a good place to start, and it is free. Here you will find details about adoption-

PETS

People love their pets! Many of the most popular online sites are about keeping pets happy and healthy.

Looking for a pet? The most humane option is to adopt one from a shelter. Almost a million pets are euthanized every year in Canada. Start with your local Society for the Prevention of Cruelty to Animals; a list of the provincial associations is found at the Canadian Federation of Humane Societies (www.cfhs.ca).

There's nothing quite as heartbreaking as losing a pet. After you have called the local shelters and put up signs around your neighborhood, try Missing Treasures Lost and Found (www. missingtreasures.com)—a nationwide lost and found service to help reunite pets and other

ONLINE PHOTO-SHARING SITES
Create your own screensavers, greeting cards, and online photo albums.

- **Club Photo** (www.clubphoto.com)
- **FotoTime** (www.fototime.com)
- **Microsoft Photo Album** (http://communities.msn.com/content/features/photoalbum.asp)
- **Ofoto** (www.ofoto.com)
- **Photofun** (www.photofun.com)

PHOTO-SHARING AND DEVELOPING SITES
Learn how to use your camera creatively when you log on here!

- **Black's Photography** (http://blacksphotocentre.com)
- **Future Shop.ca** (www.futureshop.ca/photo)
- **Kodak** (http://photonet.kodak.ca)
- **Photoloft** (www.photoloft.com)
- **PhotoPoint** (www.photopoint.com)

treasures with their families. If a beloved bird has flown the coop, contact Bird HotLine (www.birdhotline.com), a worldwide bird lost and found service.

When your pet is sick, you want help fast. Find a veterinary hospital or clinic near you through VetQuest (www.vetquest.com), which lists 25,000 veterinary facilities in Canada, the United States, and Europe. Or, search your province's veterinary association. For example,

the College of Veterinarians website has a list of veterinary clinics throughout Ontario.

There's no need to leave your pet behind when you go on vacation! Travel Pets (www. travelpets.com) list over 20,000 pet-friendly bed and breakfasts, inns, hotels, motels, and resorts in Canada, the United States, and abroad. If you're going to be traveling in the United States, check out Takeyourpet (www.takeyourpet. com) and DogFriendly's Travel Guide (www. dogfriendly.com) that list pet-friendly hotels and attractions.

PHOTO SHARING

Put your photo gallery on the Net, share photos with friends and relatives, and send prints without going through a photo developer.

Sending photos by e-mail can be slow and e-mails with large attachments can take forever to download. The alternative is an Internet photo gallery that lets you share your photos with anyone you want, quickly and easily.

Before you can share your photos via the Web, you must have a digital photograph. Don't have a digital camera? You can still put your photos on the Internet. Many retail photo developers will scan and upload your images to a website, or transfer your paper images onto a CD-ROM.

The fastest way to upload images from a PC to the website is by client application. This is a

program that runs on the PC and manages the uploading process for you (once you have selected the photos to be uploaded). Many Web photo-sharing and photofinishing sites provide free client application software.

Don't be tempted to speed up your upload time by reducing the resolution or applying more compression to the pictures. To get photographic-quality prints from the images you display on the Web, upload the largest image file size you have. A large .jpg file (the type that comes from the camera) only takes a few minutes to upload over a 56Kb modem.

Another advantage of Web photo-sharing is access to top-quality prints without a trip to the developer. At most photo-sharing sites, you can have prints made on the same kind of photographic paper used for 35mm film developing. Sites will send a print to any address you choose. You can also buy items such as calendars, mouse pads, and T-shirts with your photo printed on them.

Web photo-sharing is free on most sites. There are limitations on how much storage space you can occupy on the servers, but you can fit more than 100 images in 50Mb. Select which album or photos you want to share, choose whom you want to share it with—check that they will want to receive all those pictures

beforehand!— and the site will send them an e-mail message with the link. The sites also let you set up mailing lists.

⇨ See also **Software: Photo Editing; Hardware: Digital Cameras.**

PLUG-INS

Pump up your browser to enjoy new capabilities and improve your Web experience by adding plug-ins.

A plug-in is an auxiliary program that works alongside your Internet browser. Download the free program, install it, and your browser calls on it automatically whenever it needs to. Without plug-ins, the Web would have no sound, moving pictures, sophisticated animation, or 3D virtual reality.

Every browser comes with some plug-ins already installed. Netscape Navigator includes an older version of Apple's QuickTime as well as several Netscape-made plug-ins, such as LiveAudio and Live3D. Microsoft's Internet Explorer comes with Progressive Networks' RealAudio 2.1.

The most popular plug-ins are RealAudio from www.real.com, which plays sound within seconds of an audio file being downloaded; QuickTime (www.apple.com/quicktime/download), which plays video within the browser window; and Macromedia's Shockwave (www.shockwave.com), a plug-in for playing interactive animation.

Download plug-ins before you start surfing to save time. Check out the Netscape plug-in page (http://home.netscape.com/plugins/) for a complete list of what's available.

Download a plug-in as you would any file from the Internet. If you are using Internet Explorer, make sure you click the button marked Save It when the dialog box appears. After the download is complete, exit the browser, locate the file you just downloaded, and double-click on it to install it on your hard drive.

Before downloading a plug-in, check the installation notes to make sure that your browser can use it. Many plug-ins, such as Apple's QuickTime, offer several installation files for download. Read the descriptions because choosing the appropriate file may save some download time.

Installing too many plug-ins may slow down your system. To remove an unwanted plug-in, look for the plug-in in the Plug-ins subfolder in your browser's folder. Delete or move the file, and your browser will not load the plug-in.

If you use Internet Explorer, you'll come across ActiveX controls. These are small pieces of software that run within Internet Explorer and enhance Web pages. They are automatically downloaded for you (unlike plug-ins).

⇨ See also **Internet: Downloading.**

 HOW TO: DOWNLOAD AND INSTALL A PLUG-IN

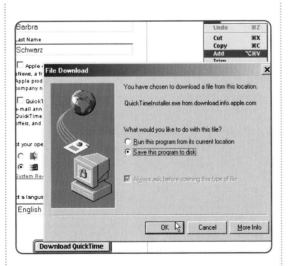

① Use these steps to install any plug-in. (Apple QuickTime is used here.) From the Apple website (www.apple.com/quicktime/download), enter your e-mail address and name and then select the Download QuickTime button.

② The File Download window will now appear on your screen, choose Save this program to disk, and click OK. Next you need to save QuickTime to your Desktop and the Download will begin.

③ A shortcut to QuickTime will appear on your Desktop. To access the QuickTime player click on the QuickTime icon and open the file menu to load the player. When downloading files from the Internet, your computer will automatically default to your QuickTime player.

POLITICS

Stay informed, get active, and keep up with politics around the world.

Get the lowdown on who got how much, from whom, and to do what. Politics Watch (http://politicswatch.com/index2.html) has the latest from Ottawa and around the country, press releases, and links to all political parties (as well as spoof sites). Or, try Mapleleafweb (www.mapleleafweb.com/main.shtml) for news, polls, and forums on social and political issues. Tired of tax-cut promises, cheerful jaw-boning, and transparent baby-kissing? Look at Outrageous Canadian Political Facts (www.islandnet.com/~luree/politics.html) where you will get lots of information, what your M.P.'s pension will be, and lists of broken political promises.

Far-flung activists can now work together. Canada Protest Page! (http://www.tpg1.com/protest/canprot.html) lets you protest various laws, events, and decisions in Canadian life. Here are links to politicians and citizen groups that are taking action. The Council of Canadians (www.canadians.org) is a non partisan citizens' group working on important Canadian issues. The Citizens' Handbook (http://www.vcn.bc.ca/citizens-handbook/) tells you how to organize at the grassroots level. Play a part in helping to save the environment and go to Greenpeace Canada (www.greenpeacecanada.org) or Sierra Club of Canada (www.sierraclub.ca).

No more writing letters to elected officials by hand. Contact them by phone, fax, and e-mail. Get the information about your federal, provincial, and local politicians at About.com's Canadian politicians site (http://canadaonline.about.com/aboutcanada/canadaonline/msub304.htm). Or, go to the Canadian political parties site (http://home.ican.net/~alexng/can.html) where there are links to every conceivable political Canadian site.

There are elections happening all the time, all around the world. With outcomes that affect business and politics in many regions. So follow election news worldwide. Klipsan Press (www.

klipsan.com/elecnews.htm) provides concise coverage. Elections Around The World (www.agora.stm.it/elections) is an international database with the latest results of elections worldwide, plus vital statistics for many nations.

While you can't vote via the Net yet, you can use it to keep track of federal elections. Start with Elections Canada (www.elections.ca), which has reports and statistics about the most recent election. If you would like to know who was the victor of the 1896 federal election, go to PoliticX (http://www.politicx.com/elections/federal/history.shtml) where there are results of elections from 1867 onward. Elections (www.sfu.ca/~aheard/elections/) gives election results broken down by ridings, parties and candidates, and analyses of past elections.

Stay informed on political news. Find out who's in and who's out, and what they're getting up to in between with Politics Watch (http://politicswatch.com/index2.html), a site on top of all the government news with hundreds of links. Frank (www.frankmag.net/), the satirical publication, gives you the scoop on everything that moves on the Hill. Canoe's CNews (www.canoe.ca/CNEWSPolitics/home.html) offers the latest headlines, forums, and CapitalWatch. Sympatico's NewsExpress (www1.sympatico.ca/news/) updates its news hourly.

PORTAL

A website that specializes in directing you to other sites.

A portal is a site designed to be your all-in-one entree to the Internet. Not just a search engine, it's also a site that provides Internet services such as e-mail, chatrooms, free personal web pages, shopping, directory, plus original content. Yahoo! (www.yahoo.ca) and Excite (www.excite.ca) are popular portals. AOL Canada (www.aol.ca) is another favorite portal designed to make it easy to access information.

Portals are good for helping new users to get acquainted with what's out there and what can be done. Their downside is that they filter the sites they offer you. Portals tend to point you to sites that have the same kind of commercial link as themselves, rather than to the most relevant or informative site on a given topic.

MORE POLITICAL SITES
For the full range of news and views about political activity across Canada.

Canadian Politics on the Web (http://politics.nelson.com/canpol.html) Portal to find out all about government, politics, activists, and more.

FindPolitics.com (www.FindPolitics.com) Index to Canadian and provincial websites.

Parliament of Canada (www.parl.gc.ca) Commons and Senate debates on the Net.

Rabble.ca (www.rabble.ca) Bills itself as a place to get involved, express your opinion, and connect with others.

Straight Goods (www.straightgoods.com) Independent news and commentary on the Canadian government.

Different portals will suit your needs better than others. If you can't find what you're looking for at Yahoo! or Excite, then try Canada.com (www.canada.com), Canoe (www.canoe.ca), Sympatico-Lycos (www1.sympatico.ca), or others until you find the site that suits you.

Navigating the Web can be complicated. To make things easier, make one of the major portals your home page, so that every time you launch your browser you'll start at their site.

PRIVACY

Explore the Internet without leaving any tracks behind.

Your browser is probably giving personal information to marketers, who will bombard you with product offers and ads. Once the marketers have your e-mail address, there's nothing to stop them from selling it to still more marketers. To keep from being bombarded with adds and solicitations to BUY NOW!! LAST CHANCE!!, you need to stay anonymous.

You can maintain a low profile while browsing the Web by using a proxy server, which forms a kind of wall between your PC and the sites you visit. Instead of capturing your information, web servers see only the proxy's identity. If you surf the Web via a T1 line at your office (as many companies do), then you're probably already protected by a proxy server or a firewall. And if you connect at home, you can use one of the free public proxy servers such as

Anonymizer (www.anonymizer. com), which protects your identity by keeping your e-mail address and your surfing a secret.

Take a do-it-yourself approach to anonymizing. One way is to temporarily remove your personal information from your browser. After you remove details such as your name and e-mail address from your browser, the only information

a website can sniff out is your ISP's address and geographical location.

While it's tempting to use the same password for all of the online services you join, resist this urge. You don't necessarily have to use a different password for each service, but you should definitely make sure that your e-mail passwords are unique. If you were to use the same password, getting access to your private e-mail messages is easy for an unscrupulous website owner.

Forewarned is to be forearmed. You can configure your browser to notify you if any sites that you visit could put your personal security at risk. With Internet Explorer running, click on Tools → Internet Options, and select the Advanced tab. Scroll to the Security section and check the boxes beside Check for publisher's certificate revocation, Warn about invalid site certificates, and Warn if changing between secure and not secure mode. Click OK, and in the future you'll be warned of potentially risky sites where security might be compromised.

If you share a computer, or use a PC at work, others will probably have access to your e-mail. Protect your e-mail privacy by collecting and sending your e-mail from a web-based service such as Mail2Web (www.mail2web.com) or

MSN Hotmail (www.hotmail.com). Hushmail (www. hushmail.com) also offers secure storage and encrypted messaging.

Digital signing is a method of protecting the privacy of your e-mail correspondence by letting e-mail recipients confirm the identity of the sender through a third party certificate of authenticity. Download the software from VeriSign (www.verisign.com).

Protect your private correspondence and surfing from online snoopers with shareware privacy software. Pretty Good Privacy, Inc.'s Personal Privacy v6.0 (www.mcafee.com)

FREE ADVICE AND SERVICES FOR YOUR SITE
Find out how you can promote and market your website— often without spending a penny—when you log on to these sites.

The Art of Business Web Site Promotion (www.deadlock.com/promote)
A step-by-step guide to promoting your own commercial website.

FreePage Web Site Hosting (www.ncf. carleton.ca/ncf/freeplace/freepages)
An offering of National Capital Freenet, this site not only hosts your site but also offers advice for creating and designing pages, a newsgroup for Q&As, and an IP newsletter.

100% Free Web Page Hosting (www.magma.ca/~mvpinct/fhec.htm)
A list of free website hosting services, some available only in Canada.

PR2 (www.pr2.com)
This site provides a very useful free biweekly e-mail newsletter packed with tips on various ways to market and promote your website.

WebStep Top 100 (www.mmgco.com/top100.html)
Here's how to get your address listed as one of the top websites with 100 of the best search engines and databases.

Yahoo! Canada GeoCities (http://ca.geocities.yahoo.com)
Here you can have your website hosted for free. And, if you are new to this, there are Wizards to help you construct your page.

encrypts personal items like e-mail attachments and files, allowing only those recipients with the proper key to open them. BlackBoard Software's Blackboard Internet Privacy v5.0 available from ZDNet (www.zdnet.com) removes your cache, history, downloads, and trash with one click of a button, allowing you to surf without the fear that anyone can find out what sites you have visited. Most of this shareware is relatively inexpensive.

PROMOTE YOUR WEBSITE

Once your website is up and running, you need to let people know where to find it.

It's not enough to just build a website and hope people will come—you have to actively promote your site to draw users. One simple way to do this is by using web spiders, such as Submit It! (www.submitit.com), that will submit your website to hundreds of other sites, directories, and search engines.

If you submit your site to search engines manually, then you should focus on the major— or deep—search engines. These use programs known as web crawlers to roam the Web, searching for new or updated pages. But if your site isn't linked from anywhere else and you haven't registered it at all, it will be invisible to the web crawlers. Normally, to register your site you'll need to supply your web address, name, and e-mail address, and sometimes give a description of the website and contact details. Deep search engines include Google (www.google.com), AltaVista Canada (www.altavistacanada.com), Go.com (www.go.com), Excite Canada (www.excite.ca), HotBot (www.hotbot.lycos.com), Lycos (www.

lycos.com), Northern Light (www.nlsearch.com), Raging Search (www.raging.com), and, finally, Yahoo! Canada (ca.yahoo.com).

Before you register with a search engine, you should check their advice on how to use key words in your web pages. For example, if your site is about teddy bear collecting, type "teddy," "bears," "furry," "stuffed," and "toys" as keywords. Avoid using words like "web," "internet" or "services," since they won't help to target searches specifically at your site.

If you have a large list of keywords, your pages will be found with a broad spectrum of search strings, but they're less likely to be at the top of the results lists (this is a "blanket strategy"). If you use a limited number, it increases the density of those few keywords and therefore puts them high up the list (a "targeted strategy").

If any of your keywords are routinely misspelled, include the incorrect version in your list so your site can still be found. Selling satellite TV dishes? Include "sattelite" on your list.

To help you choose the right keywords for you website, try the free Wordtracker trail (www.wordtracker.com). You enter keywords and the site suggests how useful these would be in the targeting of your website by search engines.

The URL-minder NetMind (www.netmind.com) can help you to let people know when your web page has been updated. By signing up for the service at their site, and then adding a little bit of HTML code to your own site, your visitors can automatically be sent e-mail whenever you update your pages. Saves you a lot of work!

Another key to promoting your website is to build a large group of core viewers. There are many ways to do this. You can keep the information on your site as up to date as possible. Or you can try to make it so complete that it effectively becomes the "bible" for whatever subject your site deals with. This way people will come back to your site again and again to keep on checking the information.

One way to build community around your site is to start a mailing list to keep people enthused

HOW TO: SUBMIT YOUR SITE TO A SEARCH ENGINE

1 Connect to the Internet and go to one of the main search engines, such as Altavista (www.altavista.com) or Yahoo! (www.yahoo.com). Click on the Submit a site link in Altavista, or click on a category for your site in Yahoo! and then click on Suggest a Site.

2 Simply follow the step-by-step instructions for entering your website URL and personal details. Unless yours is a business site, you should select the free submission option. Then once you've completed the details, your site should be included in all future searches.

about your subject. Design a subscription form (www.pr2.com/feature10.htm) and include relevant news, helpful tips, and discussions. Make sure you only mail people who have asked to be put on the mailing list, and don't forget to make it easy for people to unsubscribe.

RADIO

Listen to hundreds of radio stations on your computer. Author Tom Wolfe was wrong when he said radio was just "something people listen to while they're doing something else."

In order to listen to radio online, all you need is a computer with a soundcard (in other words, any recent PC), a free streaming media program such as RealAudio (www.real.com) or WindowsMedia (www.windowsmedia.com), and a station to listen to. Once you're set, you'll find it easy to turn your dial to CBC nationwide, Studio 1 in Chelyabinsk, Russia, or Grooveradio.com in Miami.

Online radio stations can only transfer data (music) as fast as your connection will allow. But don't rush out and upgrade your connection speed yet. A fast connection doesn't necessarily translate into better sound. Sound files are usually encoded at a low enough rate for the average connection speed. While you can't expect perfect fidelity over the Net, sound quality should be between AM and FM.

There are two types of online radio—live broadcasts and prerecordings. The live broadcasts are just like radio, except that you can listen to thousands of stations across the world, broadcasting everything from speeches to concerts (and, of course, recorded music). With on-demand audio, the material is prerecorded, so no matter when you decide to log on to a broadcast, you will always start at the beginning.

Overwhelmed by all the radio content online? In fact, there is so much choice available these days that your main concern will be to narrow

down what you want to listen to. To get started, you may want to use an Internet radio directory to find a site playing something that appeals to you. Tune in to these directories: Internet Radio List (www.internetradiolist.com) and Virtual Tuner (www.virtualtuner.com). Radio Station Listings and Histories (www.rcc.ryerson.ca/schools/rta/ccf/ccf_radiolistingsandhistories.html) has a comprehensive listing of radio stations, arranged by province and region.

Start up your own pirate online radio station. You can always set up your own online radio station. Unlike traditional radio, no special licenses are required. For more information on do-it-yourself broadcasting, or to listen to the attempts of others, visit the following sites: Icecast.org (www.icecast.org), About (http://pirateradio.about.com), SHOUTcast (www.shoutcast.com), or Live365 (www.live365.com).

And once you've set up your own radio station you can market and promote it for free online through RadioSpy (www.radiospy.com).

Want to find your favorite jock in Vancouver? Simply type his station's call letters into your browser's address window (after www.) and you'll stand a better chance of finding him.

Missing your favorite old-time radio shows? Now you can tune in to shows such as The Shadow, Jack Benny, Fibber Magee and Molly, Bob Hope, Burns and Allen, and the Lone Ranger. Head for Boston Pete's Old Time Radio Place (http://bostonpete.safeshopper.com).

Want music that's not mainstream? Tune into 1groove.com (www.1groove.com) for music of the clubs and rave culture. Bonzaroo.com (www.bonzaroo.com) has every type of music, from jazz, dance/hip-hop, R&B/soul, to nostalgia, and Grooverince (www.grooverince.com) features underground dance music.

MORE GREAT RADIO SITES
Live concerts, broadcasts, and interviews with your favorite artists are all online.

CBC (www.cbc.ca/onair)
National radio featuring popular, classic, and alternative music plus interviews and commentaries.

ChickClick Radio (www.chickclick.com)
The first nationally syndicated radio show to be spawned by a website and quite possibly one of the first radio shows to specifically target young women.

LiveConcerts.com (www.liveconcerts.com)
A huge online archive of live concerts as well as press conferences and interviews with popular musical artists, including audio files from the KCRW radio program Morning Becomes Eclectic.

Radio-locator (www.radio-locator.com/cgi-bin/page?page=provs)
Search by city, station name, call sign, and also internationally.

The Score (www.headlinesports.com)
For 24-hour sports news.

RECIPES

Use the Internet to look up new recipes, put together a personal cookbook, or collate your own recipe collection.

There's no need to clutter up your kitchen with collections of heavy cookbooks. The Internet gives you access to tens of thousands of recipes from all around the world. You can even create your own customized cookbook by putting together a unique database of delicious downloaded recipes.

Cooking Thanksgiving dinner, but can't remember mom's sweet potato recipe? Just look it up in your own online recipe book. Sites such as Cookbook Wizard (see box below) contain thousands of recipes that you can access anywhere, any time you wish.

Read your favorite cooking magazines online. Epicurious' cooking megasite (www.epicurious. com) offers *Bon Appétit* and *Gourmet* magazines online, including recipes, cooking tips, techniques, guides, and glossaries. Other gourmet magazines include *Fine Cooking Online* (www.taunton.com/fc/), which focuses on the science of fine cooking, and *American Connoisseur* (www.americanconnoisseur.com), which features gourmet recipes and cooking tips. It's also well worth looking at *Chatelaine* (http://recipes. chatelaine.com) has triple-tested recipes, ranging from snacks through meals in a hurry, to desserts.

Take a cooking course over the Internet. Today's video streaming technology enables you to view audio and video clips of cooking techniques in your own home. You'll have to pay for some of the courses on offer, but there are plenty of free ones too. Learn basic techniques, such as how to sauté vegetables or roast a turkey for Thanksgiving, or try your hand at sushi-making and gourmet cuisine. You'll find a whole catalog of online cooking courses at World Wide Learn (www.worldwidelearn.com).

Ever wondered what the Vikings ate when they set off to explore the New World? Or who invented the potato chip, and why? Taking an historical approach, the Food Timeline (www.gti.net/mocolib1/kid/food) tracks the development of food from 17000 BC to the present day, and offers an assortment of recipes from the various eras. The Boston Cooking School Cook Book (www.bartleby.com/87/) is a 1918 cookbook of 1,849 recipes. Its no-nonsense approach means you don't have to be an expert chef to understand the old-fashioned ingredients and instructions.

Want to duplicate a Babe Ruth bar or a McDonalds Quarter Pounder in your own home? The Cook's Thesaurus (www.foodsubs. com) is an encyclopedia covering thousands of

ingredients and kitchen tools. The entries include pictures, descriptions, synonyms, suggested ingredient substitutions, plus correct pronunciations.

RECREATION

Bored? Watching too much TV? You need a hobby, and the Internet is there to help you find one...

The first place to look is in a directory. DMOZ (www.dmoz.com) and About.com (www.about. com) are two of the best for listing hobby resources, newsgroups, and information about almost every recreation imaginable.

Don't be alone: join a sports club. Head to the sports pages of Canada.com (www.canada.com) to discover listings of thousands of clubs across Canada, on every kind of activity, from baseball to rock climbing. Or join the Sierra Club of Canada (www.sierraclub.ca) and peruse their listing of walks, hikes, and outdoor activities near you—including singles walks, nature hikes, and full-blown mountain expeditions.

RECIPE WEBSITES
Catch the word on the culinary scene, and cook up something special for dinner!

Cookbook Wizard (www.cookbookwizard.com)
Tens of thousands of recipe listings. Whatever you want to cook, it's here!

Foodgeeks (www.foodgeeks.com)
Thousands of online recipes and culinary suggestions.

Food Network (www.foodtv.com)
A vast site for food-related matters, with online menus, recipe searches, cookbooks, and info on TV programs and celebrities.

Foodweb (www.foodweb.com)
In addition to reader's recipes and recipe cards, this site offers lots of links to food and drink, restaurants, and much more.

The Kitchen Link (www.kitchenlink.com)
Comprehensive cookbook site with message boards, recipes, offers, and daily menus.

Martha Stewart (www.marthastewart.com)
Lifestyle guru Martha Stewart offers recipe favorites plus interactive search facility.

entries, proposals and papers, fellowships, festivals, funding... you'll find it all here.

Are you an aspiring coin collector? Check out Numismatic Network Canada (www.nunetcan. net/), where you can subscribe to a newsgroup and find a valuable set of links to coin dealers and other experts. Canadian Coin Reference site (www.canadiancoin.com) is a wealth of information re coins, also with good links.

Seek and you shell find. Discover what sea creature lived in the shell you found on the beach. Go to Conchologists of America, Inc. (http:// coa.acnatsci.org/conchnet) or Conchology (www. conchology.uunethost.be).

Simply out of this world! You can collect lumps of outer space from the Meteorite Shop (www. meteoriteshop.com) and Meteorite Central (www.meteoritecentral.com). Want to know more? Find out what planet you've bought a piece of at Meteor Lab (www.meteorlab.com). Also, check out the Canadian Meteorite Catalogue site (http://tabla.geo.ucalgary.ca/ cdnmeteorites/) for information about meteorites in Canada.

Pieces of eight... You won't find pirate maps with X marking the spot, but there are lots of treasure hunting tips to be gleaned from the Web. Try On-Line Treasure Hunter (http:// onlinether.com) for the lowdown on coin and relic hunting, prospecting, and treasure diving. For newsgroups, go to Treasure Net (www. treasurenet.com).

Go out with a bang! If your hobby involves countdowns and complex discussions on the merits of various flammable propellants, look up Rocketry.Org (www.rocketry.org) for information on amateur and experimental rocketry. To get

technical, try Rocket Equations (www.execpc. com/~culp/rockets/rckt_eqn.html), and learn how to predict your rocket's speed and altitude from weight, motor thrust, and impulse.

Need expert advice? Get an online copy of the book *How to Design, Build and Test Small Liquid-Fuel Rocket Engines* (www.im.lcs.mit. edu/rocket). Alternatively, Model Rocketry for Educators (http://home.earthlink.net/~voraze/ toc.html) provides teachers and students with information and lessons in the use of model

ARTS AND CRAFTS
Get in touch with your creative side.

The Crafts Fair OnLine (www.craftsfaironline.com)
Links a go-go.

The Crafts Report Online (www.craftsreport.com)
A comprehensive online resource.

DLTK's Crafts for Kids (www.dltk-kids.com)
Holiday blues? Lots of printable activity templates suitable for ages two and up.

The Kit Connection (www.kitconnection.com)
Fun and challenging craft kits for sale.

KnitNet (www.amagickgarden.com)
An online knitting magazine, featuring patterns you can print, knitting news, how-to videos, and catalogs.

The Secret Crafters Club (www. geocities.com/secretcraftersclub/ index.html)
Women exchange craft ideas and chat.

Stitchers Web (www.stitchersweb.com)
Order online or with a toll-free number to purchase needlework supplies.

Get outside and in action even faster—search the metasites. GORP (www.gorp.com) offers over 100,000 pages on everything outdoors, from exotic international destinations to more accessible outdoor environments, such as a local state park. Planet Free Time's (www.planetfreetime. com) motto is "Get off the couch." There are links to hundreds of how-to associations, message boards, and places of interest for every recreational activity, from auto touring to watersports.

Feeling arty? There are thousands of sites worldwide devoted to just about every form of creative art known, from the International Guild of Glass Artists (www.igga.org) to Ceramic Art (http://karaart.com/ceramic/index.html).

Make the most of your talent. Sign yourself up for the Arts Deadlines List (http://artdeadlines list.com), a monthly e-mail newsletter listing every opportunity going for artists, art educators, and art students. Contests and competitions, scholarships and grants, juried exhibitions, jobs and internships, calls for

rocketry as a learning tool. Also, visit the Canadian Association of Rocketry sites (www. promotek.com/car/), which promotes model and high-power rocketry in Canada.

Are you a rail buff, who can't get enough of chugging steam locomotive and quaint cabooses? Railfan Network (www.railfan.net) offers a variety of information and services for rail fans, as does Railroading in the North East (www.northeast.railfan.net) and Rick's Train Server (www.trainpage.com), where you can chat with other train lovers.

Hot to try firewalking? John Shango (http:// shangofire.com) takes you through the steps required. Or consult Tolly Burkan, the father of firewalking (www.firewalking.com). Learn all about preparing to take your first steps. You can even order instructional videos to help you build your will power.

⇨ See also **Internet: Sports** and **Travel Planning.**

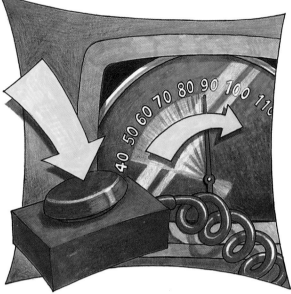

REFRESH/RELOAD

Called Refresh in Internet Explorer, or Reload in Netscape Navigator, this button can speed up download time and increases browser performance.

If a web page is loading very slowly compared to normal load times for your computer, or you get an error of some kind, try reloading the page by first clicking the Stop button, and then the Reload or Refresh button on your web browser's toolbar.

Still elements to download into a page? To check, look at the animation in the top right corner of your browser. If it's moving, the page is still loading. You may also see progress indicators in the status bar in the bottom left corner of the browser window. If there are lots of graphics, Java applets, or elements that need plug-ins, the page will load more slowly.

If you think the contents of a browser's window may have changed since the last time you

viewed it, then simply click the Reload or Refresh button to update the page.

Sometimes, a web page just won't fully download, however long you wait. Perhaps you can't scroll all the way to the bottom of the page, or the pictures and graphics aren't fully displayed. Clicking on the Refresh/Reload button instructs a new page transmission to your computer, which usually solves the problem.

⇨ See also **Internet: Downloading.**

RELIGION

Gather information about the world's religions, study scripture, or find a place to worship near you.

Search classic scripture texts online. Scholars and students of religion will find the Internet a useful source for comparing and researching texts. Whether you're a student or just want to know more about a particular religion, try Academic Info (www.academicinfo.net). It offers a comprehensive guide to religious studies.

When using a search engine to find religious links, it makes sense to enter the name of the religion you're interested in. If you're unsure about the religious base of an inquiry, or are looking for something more general, some of

the best metasites are sponsored by academic institutions. Try Mount Royal College's Internet guide on Religious Studies (www.mtroyal.ab. ca/) or the University of Calgary's Religious Studies Web Guide (www.acs.ucalgary.ca/).

Check the date of major religious holidays so you can wish your friends a happy Diwali or Rosh Hoshanah on the right day each year. Whatever your friends' religion, the Calendar Zone (www.calendarzone.com/Religious/) can provide you with an online list of holidays. Alternatively, the Worldwide Holiday and Festival Site (www.holidayfestival.com) lets you search by country, religion, and month.

Find a retreat geared to your interest, location, sense of adventure, or spiritual path. All About Retreats (www.allaboutretreats.com) and Retreats Online (www.retreatsonline.com) should have soemthing to suit your needs. But if you'd rather not leave your computer, you could always visit An Online Retreat (www.creighton.edu/ Collaborative Ministry/cmo-retreat. html) instead.

Need to know the answer to questions like "What percentage of the world is Zoroastrian?" If so, visit Adherents.com (www.adherents.com), a research organization containing over 50,000 different statistics and geography citations for references to published membership/adherent statistics and also the congregation statistics for over 4,200 religions, churches, denominations, religious bodies, faith groups, tribes, cultures, and movements. For Canadian figures, check Statistics Canada's website (www.statcan.ca/ english/Pgdb/People/Population/demo32.htm).

Pray online. Get a live view of the Western Wall in Jerusalem at Aish Ha Torah's Window on the Wall (http://aish.com/wallcam). You can even have your prayers sent directly to the wall with Virtual Jerusalem (www.kotelkam.com). Just send an e-mail and someone at the other end will write it out and place it in the wall for you.

Find Mecca. If you aren't quite sure which way to face for Mecca, or exactly what time to pray, log onto Salam Iran (www.salamiran.org/ Religion/ Praytime). All you have to do is enter your location and the website will point you in the direction of Mecca and give you the times for daily prayers.

REMINDERS

Arrange an e-mail to remind you of special anniversaries, birthdays, or those mundane chores that always slip your mind.

There are hundreds of reminder services on the Internet that will help you keep track of minor events, such as when to change the oil in your car, or major events, such as anniversaries or business meetings.

Need help getting your day organized? uRemember.com (www.uremember.com) is both versatile and free. Enter any important dates and the service will send you reminders via e-mail or voicemail, to your computer, phone, PDA (Personal Digital Assistant), or pager. Alternatively, you can use a scheduling service that lets you perform a wide range of helpful tasks. ScheduleOnline (www.scheduleonline .com/login.php3) helps you to schedule meetings and tasks, create to-do lists, broadcast e-mail invitations, and send e-mail reminders.

Use an online personal organizer. A free virtual notepad that stores phone numbers, addresses, e-mail addresses, Web bookmarks, and notes is available from Web Address Book (www.web addressbook.com). Or organize your daily activities with shareware such as RedBox

Organizer, which you can download from Pass the Shareware's website (www.passthe shareware.com.

Get your life organized with a free calendar service. SuperCalendar (www.supercalendar. com) displays all group and personal events on an integrated, color-coded calendar, with graphics stickers to highlight events. Alternatively, try Virtual Perpetual Calendars (http://www.vpcalendar.net).

Set different reminder applets to appear on your screen at different times of day. Reminder (www.geocities.com/SiliconValley/Lakes/5365/ reminder.html) provides a free applet that acts as a reminder note. Once launched, it runs in the background as a small and unobtrusive window on your PC's Desktop.

Create colored notes to display on your Desktop. There are lots of shareware sticky note programs available on the Internet. You can use your virtual notes to write messages to yourself on your computer Desktop. Choose different color notes. Some even come with alarms, too. Try Tenebril StickyNote 7 (www.tenebril.com/products/stickynote/) or Stickynotes 1.0.2 (www.cs.utexas.edu/ users/tbone/stickynotes.html).

Get an e-mail alert any time a topic or keyword is mentioned on TV. TV Eyes

(www.tveyes.com) is a free service that sends you such e-mails according to any key words that you specify. Be careful to keep the topics narrow, though, or you'll be inundated with mail. You can also follow the latest news or keep up with your investments. TVEyes monitors broadcasts in real time and "watches TV for you when you're not able to."

Problems keeping those New Year's resolutions? Resolution Reminders (www.hiaspire.com/ newyear) is an award-winning site that offers a free e-mail reminder service. It includes goal-tracking tools, and lots of information on making and keeping resolutions of all kinds, from

losing weight to quitting smoking. As if you didn't feel guilty enough already…

Play the lottery regularly? If you're too busy to check your tickets, get a reminder site to do it for you. LottoBot (www.lottobot.net) checks your tickets against the latest draw and sends an e-mail notification of your results. It covers all the national (6/49, Super 7) and provincial lotteries, such as Lottario and Western 6/49.

SCRIPTURE WEBSITES
Worship your chosen faith from wherever you are in the world.

Bible Gospel Net (http://bible.gospelcom.net)
Features nine different versions of the Bible.

Find A Church—The Church Locator (www.findachurch.com)
Traveling across the country? Use these listings to find your local church.

Humanities Text Initiative (www.hti.umich.edu)
Peruse the Book of Mormon at the University of Michigan's website.

ISKON (www.iskcon.org)
A chapter-by-chapter translation of the Baghagvad Gita at ISKON, the Krishna site.

Islami City (www.islamicity.com)
Search the Koran in Arabic or English or hear any sura (passage) recited on audiofile.

Jewish Torah Radio (www.613.org)
At this site, you can study the Torah online in Hebrew or English, or view the largest collection of Torah audio and video files on the Net.

SAVING GRAPHICS

You can save pictures and graphic images found on the Net onto your hard disk.

To save a graphic image from the Web for later use, just right-click on it. A list of options will appear. Choose the Save Image As or Save Picture As option, and save the file to your hard disk. Use the default name—the name used by the web page for the file—or type in your own.

When copying images for text from web pages don't forget to note where they came from and whether or not they were copyright-free. That way, if you want to publish the text or images in your own report or website, you will know where to seek permission. Always respect the terms of any copyrighted material.

SAVING WEB PAGES

You can save a complete web page, including all the images, for later viewing online.

If you are saving just the web page text, one simple way to do this is to open a new Word or Notepad document on your Desktop, then transfer the text into it using copy and paste.

Just click on the page and use Ctrl+A to select all of the text, Ctrl+C to copy it, and Ctrl+V to paste it into your document. Of course, the text you paste into your document will look just like any other text document and not like the original text on the web page. Before doing this, always check to see if the web page has a print as text or download as text option.

You can also save a web page simply by clicking on Save As in the File Menu on your browser's menu. On some older web browsers, however, this may save only the HTML text of the page, and when you come to open it later, the graphics will be missing. You may even find that the page is hard to follow because often the headings are in graphics form on a web page. If this happens, consider upgrading to the latest version of your browser.

If you use Internet Explorer 5+, you can save a complete web page for later browsing. When you save, choose Web Page, complete (*.htm, *.html) from the Save as type box. This lets you save a web page or a web archive to your hard drive and then look at it later on.

There are many shareware programs that allow you to save complete web pages onto your hard drive with the click of a button. CatchTheWeb (www.catchtheweb.com) is one such program. Search for more offline web page shareware at ZDNet (www.zdnet.com) and SuperFiles.com (http://superfiles.com/downloads/offweb.shtml).

SCIENCE

There's a wealth of scientific information on the Internet to help you understand the world better.

Interested in space? The Web is the place to be. Head over to the Canadian Space Agency (www.space.gc.ca) for information about Canadian astronauts, the International Space Station and the Canadarm2, how to become an astronaut, and even a site for kids. NASA's site (www.nasa.gov) provides updates and details about all their programs. Get shuttle assembly statistics, crew information, and flight schedules

from ShuttlePressKit (www.shuttlepresskit.com) and the NASA Human Spaceflight site (http://spaceflight.nasa.gov).

Find out where ET went! Help the search for extraterrestrial life by having your PC analyze data downloaded from the Arecibo Radio Telescope as part of the SETI (Search for Extra-Terrestrial Intelligence) project. The program works as a screen saver, analyzing data when you're not using your computer, and sending it back to SETI whenever you connect to the Internet. One of the largest combined computing efforts ever attempted, SETI at Home now involves hundreds of thousands of PCs. Join at http://setiathome.ssl.berkeley.edu.

HIP AND HAPPENING SCIENTIFIC SITES

Get browsing, learn lots, and have some fun with these innovative websites.

Access Excellence: About Biotech (www.accessexcellence.org/AB/index.html)
This site explores applied biotechnology, plus issues and ethics in this field.

Canada-France-Hawaii Telescope (www.cfht.hawaii.edu)
Study spectacular stellar images taken by this joint project atop Hawaii's Mauna Kea.

The Interactive Frog Dissection (http://curry.edschool.virginia.edu/go/frog)
Now you don't have to sacrifice a real frog to learn about its anatomy!

Robohoo! (www.robohoo.com)
Discover all there is to know about robots.

ScienceCanada (www.mts.net/~dforbes/ScienceCanada.html)
A wealth of information and annotated link, organized into categories, plus a "Just for Kids" section.

Ever come across a science word you've never seen before? Wondering what it is? Head for the Net, where you'll find hundreds of scientific dictionaries. For gardeners, there's Garden Web (www.gardenweb.com). Budding genetic researchers can turn to the dictionary at (www.gdb.org), while biologists can use The Dictionary of Cell and Molecular Biology (www.mblab.gla.ac.uk/dictionary). And you

can find definitions for space terms at the NASA Jet Propulsion Laboratory (www.jpl. nasa.gov).

Thousands of science journals and magazines exist online to help you research and keep up to date with the latest breakthroughs and experiments in your area of interest. Find out what antiquities have been uncovered lately at Archaeology (www.archaeology.org); keep

up with new medical research at The Lancet (www.thelancet.com); explore the wonders of the world with National Geographic (www.nationalgeographic.com); and delve

deep into hard science with Scientific American (www. sciam.com) and Technology Review (www. techreview.com).

Catch scientific news every day with Scitech Daily Review (www.scitechdaily.com), where stories from different sources are collected. Or subscribe to Netsurfer Science (www.netsurf. com/nss) and receive weekly bulletins on subjects that interest you. If you're interested in popular science, Discover (www.discover.com), the Discovery Channel Canada's EXN.ca (http:// exn.ca), Popular Science (www.popsci.com), and Canadian Nature Federation (www.cnf.ca) offer science news, updates, and articles.

Have your questions answered on the Internet. Ever wondered how a refrigerator keeps food cold, or why a bridge stays up? Get the answers at HowStuffWorks (www.howstuffworks.com). Or select a site where scientists will personally answer all your questions. Try Mad Sci Network (www.madsci.org) when you absolutely must know why the sky is blue at 4 a.m. Ask Dr. Science (www.ducksbreath.com), Ask Dr. Universe (www.wsu.edu/druniverse), and Pitsco's Ask an Expert (www.askanexpert.com) are also available to answer your questions about science online.

Build your own Tesla coil, fly a small rocket, try cold fusion at home, or do other weird and wonderful science projects with information from Rocketry Online (www. rocketryonline. com) or Eskimo (www.eskimo. com/~billb/ weird.html).

HOW TO: SAVE WEB PAGES TO USE AS BACKGROUND WALLPAPER

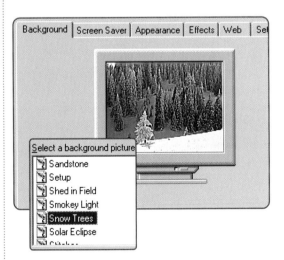
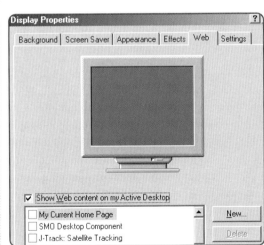

① Web images can be made into Wallpaper with just a few clicks of your mouse. Open the web page you want to use in Internet Explorer, choose File → Save As, and locate a suitable folder on your hard disk. Then store the file there as an HTML document.

② Right-click on any empty space on your Desktop and select Properties from the pop-up menu that appears. Select the Web tab, then check the Show Web content on my Active Desktop box.

③ Finally, select the Background tab, click the Browse button, and locate the file you stored. Select it and click OK. The image will now appear as the Desktop Wallpaper design on your PC.

SEARCH ENGINES

The Web is home to over a billion pages of text with about a million more being added every day. So how on earth do you find anything in all that electronic noise? By using a search engine. But there is more to it than just typing a word into Yahoo! and seeing what pops up.

TYPES OF SEARCH ENGINES

If you want to find something specific, you need to know how to use the correct search tool for the job and how to tell it exactly what to look for. Most people just fumble around the Internet, missing out on the best stuff. The real art of Internet searching is knowing how to find exactly what you are looking for. Luckily, it is an easy art to master.

When you use a search engine, what you are really doing is searching the engine's database of web pages. When someone submits a web page to a search engine they give each page "metatags"—keywords which help to describe the content. The database is compiled by a web crawler, or web spider, which is a program that explores the Internet looking for both new sites and changes to sites it already has in its database.

The thoroughness of a search engine depends on how much text its crawler collects and how often. While there are many different search engines, some of them use the same crawler technology, so they produce virtually identical results. GoTo, MSN, and HotBot all use the same crawler, while Raging Search and AltaVista share the same database.

To keep up with what's happening on your favorite search engine, check out Search Engine Watch (www.searchenginewatch.com) and Search Engine Showdown (www.searchengine showdown.com). These sites will come up with the latest scoop on how different search engines work, which one currently offers the most pages, and more.

Search agents are a type of search engine that gathers information, but only from a limited number of sites. The best are programs that you download. They are very useful if you want to query several different search engines at once. Copernic (www.copernic.com), Search.com (www.search.com), and Metacrawler (www.metacrawler.com) will all query hundreds of search engines, directories, e-mail archives, and Usenet archives at your command.

Subject directories are search engines that will allow you to browse a range of sites under a specific topic. In a directory, the sites are arranged by subject or by another criteria, such as entry date or rating. Also, directories are not compiled by web crawlers, but by

real live people. Popular ones include Yahoo! (www.yahoo.ca), Open Directory (www.dmoz.com), and About.com (home.about.com/aboutCanada/).

To find really specific stuff, use a specialized directory. These directories will find sites on the Internet for almost any subject or interest. They will collect pages that the major directories might miss. Start by searching a directory that lists such directories, such as Directory Guide (www.directoryguide.com), Earthcam (www.earthcam.com), Go Gettem (www.gogettem.com), and Search Bug (www.searchbug.com).

2,600 Specialty Directories : General Directories | Advertising | Veterinary | Art Artists | Automotive | Aviation | Books Publications | Bus Internet | Culture Peoples | Education | Employment Jobs | Entertainmen Food Drink | Government Politics | Health Medical | Law Legal | Local R Shipping Parcels | Media News Weather | Meta-Search | Miscellaneous Email | Real Estate | Recreation Sports | Reference | Religion | Science Shopping | Social Science Humanities | Software | Travel Lodging Maps

POPULAR SEARCH ENGINES
Surf the Net easily and efficiently using a search engine.

AltaVista Canada (www.altavistacanada.com)
Canada.com (www.canada.com)
Excite Canada (www.excite.ca)
FAST (www.alltheweb.com)
Google (www.google.com)
GoTo (www.goto.com)
HotBot (www.hotbot.com)
Infospace Canada (http://home.infospace.com/canada/)
Looksmart (www.looksmart.com)
Lycos (www.lycos.com)
MSN (www.msn.com)
Northern Light (www.northernlight.com)
Open Directory Project (http://dmoz.org)
WebCity.ca (www.webcity.ca)
Yahoo! (www.yahoo.ca)

BOOLEAN OPERATORS

To limit the number of hits you get from your searches, use Boolean logic, which helps you search for a subject by narrowing down the options. Go to a search engine and type in "dog" and you will get about ten million hits. Boolean logic uses words called operators (AND, OR, NOT, NEAR) to create relationships among words and concepts. In most search engines, you can use the plus sign (+) instead of AND, a blank space instead of OR, and the minus sign (-) instead of NOT.

Type the Boolean operators (AND, OR, NOT, NEAR) in uppercase letters so the search engine can recognize them. Using lowercase letters makes the operators "stop words"—words that a search engine ignores because they are too common and will create false hits.

Most search engines use Boolean operators. For example, if you enter the query "ben jerry," most search engines will interpret the keywords as if they contained an OR operator, as in "ben OR jerry." The search will contain all results for "ben" and all results for "jerry."

The OR operator can be useful when searching for alternative spellings, such as "color OR colour," or in order to broaden a query when searching for synonyms, such as "city OR urban."

The NOT operator excludes part of the search entry. It can also be used to help restrict the search, as in: "ghosts OR apparitions OR spirits NOT moonshine NOT alcohol."

NEAR and AND operators work in a similar way to retrieve documents that contain two keywords from a search. The only difference between the two is that NEAR operators limit the results of your search by requiring the keywords to be within 10 words of each other—this is useful when searching for names. For example, "John NEAR Doe" retrieves documents containing Doe, John or John A. Doe.

Nesting is a method of combining operators in a logical order. Most search engines evaluate Boolean operators in the order NEAR, NOT, AND, and OR. So, if you enter the search "hardware software+Internet," the results would include all documents that contain the words software and Internet, and then look for documents containing the word hardware. To avoid this problem, use parentheses. The query for retrieving documents about Internet hardware and software would then be "(hardware OR software) AND Internet."

NAVIGATING AROUND THE BROWSER

Speed up your site checking by opening the sites that look most promising in new browser windows. You can do this by holding down the Shift key as you click on the site address that appeals to you.

If you are interrupted while going through your Internet search results and have to close your browser, you can bring up your search results again later on. To do this in Internet Explorer, simply open the History panel. Under the date that you made the last search, click on the entry for the appropriate search engine. This will reveal a complete list of the searches you have made using that particular engine. Allow your pointer to hover over the entry. Once you have located the interrupted search, click on it to return.

⇨ See also **Internet: Browsing** and **Yahoo!**

HOW TO: SEARCH ALTAVISTA USING BOOLEAN OPERATORS

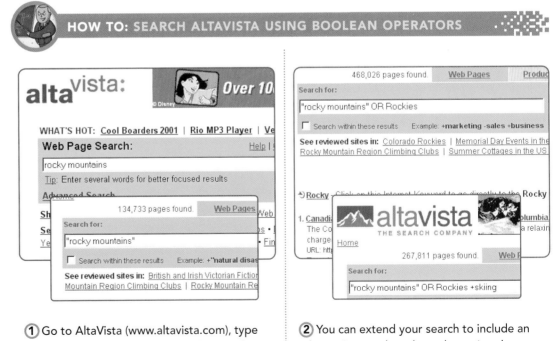

1 Go to AltaVista (www.altavista.com), type in two words, and click Search. The search returns a list of web pages containing one or both words in small or capital letters. To search for a phrase, rather than single words, place quotation marks around the words.

2 You can extend your search to include an alternative word or phrase by typing the word OR before it. And limit your search to sites that include a key word or phrase by typing a plus sign immediately before the word. Scroll through the resulting list of links.

SECURITY ON THE NET

Every day there seem to be new reports of million-dollar Internet frauds or of hackers breaching the networks of Microsoft or the CIA. So it's no wonder that home shoppers are concerned about the safety of making online purchases by credit card. But there are ways to safeguard yourself on the Net.

HOW TO TELL IF A SITE IS SAFE

Most retailers that offer value for money and treat their customers fairly at their bricks-and-mortar stores do the same online. In many cases these companies make an effort to reassure nervous online shoppers by creating secure locations online for their customers to carry out transactions in confidence.

HACKER SITES
Give your research a kickstart by visiting these informative sites.

CSIS (www.csis-scrs.gc.ca/eng/opert/ io2_e-html)
Find out about how the Canadian Security Intelligence Service deals with cyber threats.

FBI (www.nipc.gov)
Visit the FBI's anti-Internet crime work at the National Infrastructure Protection Center.

Hackers Hall of Fame (www.discovery.com/area/technology/ hackers/hackers.html)
At this Discovery Channel site, you can learn about infamous hackers of recent years.

Happy Hacker (www.happyhacker.org)
Read about the state of hacking and have a free vulnerability scan of your computer.

RCMP (www.rcmp-grc.gc.ca/html/ ecweb2.htm)
Learn about the RCMP's Economic Crime Program, which investigates computer crime.

If you're dealing with a company for the first time, be sure to look through the site for a real address and phone number, plus at least one contact name. If you don't see these, you should think twice about shopping there.

Safeguard yourself against third parties fraudulently using your credit card. Before you type in your credit card details at an online store, make sure you're at an encrypted site to prevent unauthorized access. In Internet Explorer, a padlock symbol appears on the status bar; in Netscape, the normally open padlock in the bottom left-hand corner turns into a closed one. Most secure sites use a URL that begins "https://"; note the "s."

Each site you visit using Internet Explorer can be assigned to one of the four following zones: Internet zone, Local intranet, Trusted sites, or Restricted sites. All websites are placed by default in the Internet zone, with a medium security level. Local intranet covers all addresses on an internal server, like an office network. Trusted sites are on another server, and are websites whose content you trust. Restricted sites are ones where you believe there is risk in their content. You can adjust the security settings for all sites under the Security tab in Internet Options (see how to, opposite.)

WHAT DOES BIG BROTHER KNOW?

When you shop online, many companies you deal with collect two kinds of information: personal, and data about the pages that you have visited, as well as purchases that you have already made.

Personal information is collected so that the site has a record of your name and address for shipping products. It's also used to customize the site so that, for example, it greets you by name when you log on, or displays your favorite products on the first page. All of this information is kept strictly between you and the online store. It is not revealed to third parties.

The other information is on your purchasing preferences and favorite pages on the site. This information may be given to third parties, such as advertisers or marketing agencies, who want to know what kind of people visit the site. The information given out won't personally identify you and will generally be used as part of the site's usage statistics.

Many sites have security statements giving details of their policies. You can often find a link to the legal and privacy policies on the company's home page if you want to find out more about your consumer rights.

What are hackers? A hacker is anyone who gains access to the data within a computer system without authorization. Their reasons vary. Sometimes it's to play a prank, sometimes the motivation is political, and occasionally the intent is criminal—to obtain classified or private information, steal money, or cause damage.

COOKIES

Sometimes when you go back to a site, you'll find it has remembered your name or what you bought the last time. The site can do this because of a "cookie." When you give your details online or when you make a purchase, the site you are visiting packages this information into a tiny text message called a cookie. The site then sends you the cookie and it is stored on your hard drive. The next time you visit, the site retrieves the information on the cookie and is able to personalize your visit.

You can locate and delete unwanted cookies with Internet Explorer by finding the Temporary Internet Files folder within the Windows folder on your hard drive. Simply right-click on the cookie with the appropriate web address in the Name column and click on Delete.

You can set your browser to reject cookies. In Internet Explorer, go to Tools → Internet Options and select the Security tab. With Internet selected, click on Custom Level and scroll down to the Cookies heading. Under the first option, click Disable—or Prompt, which lets you decide each time whether to accept a cookie or not.

Are cookies dangerous? No. Cookies are simply text files. They are not programs, so it is impossible for them to contain viruses, to access your hard drive or to read personal information.

Cookies contain personal information that you've provided. The open nature of the Net means that people could access this information with time and effort. And some Internet presences are unprincipled about passing on personal details they receive. In other words, cookies aren't dangerous, but they are an aid to gathering information about you. To learn more, visit Cookie Central (www.cookiecentral.com).

E-MAIL ENCRYPTION: PRETTY GOOD PRIVACY (PGP)

E-mails are not secure. In theory, anyone who really wants to could intercept and read your e-mails, and more alarmingly, send out e-mails in your name. There are millions of e-mails zapping around the world daily, so the risk of being intercepted is slim. But if you're sending sensitive information and want it to be secure, download the free e-mail encryption software Pretty Good Privacy (www.pgpi.org).

> **The International PGP Home Page**
> Download the latest version
> Here you may download the latest freeware PGP version for your platform, whether you

PGP is a "public key" cryptography program. Each PGP user has a private key, or digital signature—a unique number known only to themselves, which is never given out to e-mail recipients—and a public key that you give out freely. Each time you send an e-mail, PGP uses your private key to create an encrypted message. With PGP, the recipient uses your public key not only to decrypt your message but also to confirm your identity and verify that the message has not been altered en route. And your private key has remained private.

AM I LIABLE IN CASES OF FRAUD?

You have limited liability for fraud. MasterCard limits your personal liability for fraudulent use of your credit card by another person to $50. Visa has waived this with its Zero Cardholder Liability Policy. With both, you have to notify the card issuer as soon as you become aware of the fraud. This enables the issuer to block the card's use and issue you with a new one. To make sure your credit rating isn't sullied, be sure to notify the credit-tracking agencies.

⇨ See also **Internet: Credit Cards, Privacy,** and **Shopping Online.**

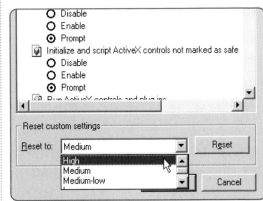

HOW TO: SET SECURITY LEVELS IN INTERNET EXPLORER

**① To specify the security settings for each zone, go to Tools → Internet Options. Select the Security tab, then click on the zone you want to change: Internet, Local intranet, Trusted sites, or Restricted sites. Click on the Custom Level button.

**② Choose a security level from the Reset to drop-down menu. All the settings in the main section of the dialog box can be customized within your chosen security level. Return a level to its default settings by clicking on the Reset button. Click OK when you've finished.

SENIORS

It's never too late to enter the electronic age, and there are many sites geared for seniors.

There's no need to travel alone. Use the Net to find like-minded travelers and tours geared to seniors. Try the following travel information sites: Senior Tours Canada (www.seniortours.ca), Canadian Senior Citizens Information and Services Center (www.infoseniors.com/ travel), and Seniors Vacation and Home Exchange (www.seniorshomeexchange.com).

There are many tours geared just for seniors. For worldwide exotic travel, try ElderTrek (www.eldertreks.com) or Golden Escapes (www.goldenescapes.com). Elderhostel (www. elderhostel.org) runs educational adventure programs for seniors. GORP Travel has programs for energetic seniors, European Walking Tours (www.gorp.com/ewt) and Senior World Tours (www.gorp.com/seniorwo/). The Canadian Association of Retired Persons travel section (www.fifty-plus.net/travel/) caters to groups.

Don't be upset if a travel website asks your age. Some sites, like OneTravel (www.onetravel.com), ask your age when you are searching for flights to make sure that you get the best possible discount. However, hotel and airline websites do not always clearly list the senior discounts currently available. So, to locate special deals,

try doing a search for "seniors" on these sites, or consider e-mailing the sites to ask.

While many chatrooms focus on 20-somethings, there are plenty of sites for seniors looking for companionship. Check out Sassy Seniors (www. sassyseniors.com), a personals and dating site for seniors and baby boomers. Senior Friend Finder (www.seniorfriendfinder.com) offers a chat site. Single Seniors in Canada (www.singlescanada. com/Seniors.htm) and SeniorsCircle (www. SeniorsCircle.com) carry personals and pen pal links for 50-plus Net users.

To make web pages easier to read, increase the size of the type. In Internet Explorer, go to View → Text Size and select Largest. In Netscape, go to Edit → Preferences, select Appearance → Fonts, and choose a larger point size.

For even better legibility, change the typeface that a website displays. Sometimes typefaces are ornate, but it's easier to read a plain typeface, such as Arial, Helvetica, or Verdana. To change the typeface in Internet Explorer, go to Tools → Internet Options, and from the General tab, select Fonts. In Netscape, go to Edit → Preferences, and select Appearance → Fonts. Do not check the "Use my default fonts" box because using your choice all the time may cause some web pages to look odd.

Many government and nonprofit sites have information useful to seniors. The government portal for seniors is Seniors Canada Online (www.seniors.gc.ca). For Old Age Security or Canada Pension Plan information, go to Human Resources Development Canada (www.hrdc-drhc.gc.ca/isp/common/home.shtml). For health news, visit Health Canada's Aging and Seniors site (www.hc-sc.gc.ca/seniors-aines/ index.htm). Click on Duhaime's Canadian Legal Information Centre (wwlia.org/ca-home.htm) where you can search by topic and province. When in doubt, contact Canada's Association for the Fifty Plus (www.fifty-plus.net/).

CaregiverNetwork (www.caregiver.on.ca)
Online information for caregivers. Topics include day care, home support, and care for the caregiver.

ElderWeb (www.elderweb.org)
ElderWeb is a virtual community of computer-using older adults.

Hells Geriatrics (www.hellsgeriatrics.com)
Interactive forum for over-50s on health, humor, chat, and serious issues.

Senior.com (www.senior.com)
Chatrooms, discussion groups, and information on financial, travel, and housing services for seniors.

Wired Seniors (www.wiredseniors.com)
This site offers seniors a web of their own, with a whole network of senior-oriented sites, including SeniorsSearch.com.

SHAREWARE

Inexpensive software programs, distributed on the honor system, can be downloaded and purchased over the Internet.

Is it the program for you? Before buying expensive software, check to see whether there's a shareware program that performs exactly the same task. You can sample shareware for free before deciding to buy. Excellent shareware is often available at very low prices.

Shareware is often offered free to nonprofit or educational institutions. If you are a student, teacher, or work for a nonprofit institution, you may be able to get a program for free.

Although most shareware is free of charge, the author usually requests that you pay a small fee if you like the program and use it regularly. By sending the fee, you become registered with the producer so that you can receive service assistance and updates. You can copy shareware and pass it along to friends and colleagues, but they too are expected to pay a fee if they decide to use the product.

Shareware differs from public domain software in that shareware is copyright protected. This means that you cannot sell a shareware product by passing it off as your own.

Trying to choose between different software programs that do the same thing? Many shareware sites list how many other people have downloaded the program. If it is very popular, the chances are that the program is the one you want. Alternatively, use a site that rates shareware, such as ZDNet (www.zdnet.com).

To avoid viruses, download shareware from one of the more dependable sites on the

Internet, such as Tucows (www. tucows.com) or CNET (www. download.com).

Remember, shareware is a method of distribution, not a statement of quality. There are a lot of great shareware products out there, and a few duds. That's why it's best to try out the program first before you pay for it, which is the beauty of shareware. But if you do keep the program, don't forget to pay. Using a shareware program beyond the trial period without registering it is—quite simply—stealing.

If you have problems downloading or using a shareware program, you can always contact the author directly. Most problems can be easily cleared up this way. If the author is a member of the Association of Shareware Professionals, and you are unable to resolve a dispute, then try contacting the ASP ombudsman directly for help by sending an e-mail to the following address: omb@asp-shareware.org.

Shareware organizations can also help with PC problems and questions. The Association of Shareware Professionals (www.asp-shareware.org) is an organization made up of Shareware authors and distributors; the Educational Software Cooperative (www. edu-soft.org) is a professional association of shareware authors and distributors, who produce various educational software. One of the most useful online, Cnet's Shareware.com (http://shareware.cnet.com), has an extensive range of problem-solving guides in its support

section— there's a hyperlink to it at the base of each page.

SHAREWARE AND SHAREWARE INFO SITES
Your guide to free Internet downloads.

CNET Shareware.com (http://shareware.cnet.com)
This service lets users browse and download freeware, shareware, demos, and upgrades.

FileFarm (www.filefarm.com)
FileFarm is best for standard downloadable software for all Windows computers.

Shareware FAQ (www.faqs.org/faqs/shareware-faq)
A two-part frequently asked questions site regarding shareware, from the alt.comp. shareware newsgroup.

Slaughter House (www.slaughterhouse.com)
A library of shareware specializing in game, Internet, and media-related programs.

Tucows (www.tucows.com)
Tucows offers a large selection of top shareware, from fun screen savers to high-tech design software.

If you have written a program and would like to distribute it on the Internet as shareware, upload your program to one of the top Shareware sites by FTP. Uploading instructions can be obtained from Coast-to-Coast (send an e-mail to cctarch@mail.coast.net), DotNet (www.dotnet.com/wsftp.html), and SimTel.net (www.simtel.net/simtel.net/upload.html). You may also want to use a shareware file distribution service. An excellent list of shareware author resources can be found at www.ramsisle.com/othrsite.htm.

⇨ See also **Internet: Downloading.**

SIGNATURE FILES

End your e-mails with a signature, joke, or your contact information.

All e-mail programs let you end your e-mail with a personal "signature," which appears automatically at the end of the e-mail.

To create a signature file in Outlook Express, go to Tools ➔ Options. Outlook Express will display a dialog box. Click the signatures tab to create a simple text signature or configure the program to use a specific file for your signature. You can configure Outlook Express to include the signature in every message, too. To add a signature on a message-by-message basis, open a New Message window, then go to Insert and select Signature.

In Netscape Messenger, first create a separate text file that includes your signature information. You can use any text editor—for example, NotePad, WordPad, or Word (so long as the file is saved as Text Only). Save the text file to your hard drive in your e-mail program folder. After you create the text file, use Edit ➔ Preferences ➔ Identity ➔ Choose, to tell your e-mail program where to find the file so that it can attach copies to your e-mail messages.

SHOPPING ONLINE

There are thousands of online shopping sites, selling everything imaginable, giving you access to a wider range of goods and services than ever before—often at lower prices. You can shop for bargains, find unusual or rare items, or just buy your groceries. With such a variety, here are a few points to consider.

IS THE PRICE RIGHT?

Many websites claim to offer huge discounts, but to know if they're accurate, you need to know what the standard retail price is in the first place. Before making a purchase online, compare the price with those in local brick-and-mortar stores or newspapers.

Get the scoop on the best products. Productopia (www.productopia.com) tells you what to look for before you buy. Read reviews, look at popularity ratings, and learn, for example, whether a 19-micron video head in a VCR is something you need. Epinions.com

(www.epinions.com) rates all sorts of products from minivans to pots and pans. Or search for a product at Sympatico Shopping (www.shopping.sympatico.ca) by keyword or by store categories, choosing either Canadian or U.S. sites. At this site, you can create a "virtual model" of yourself to make clothes buying easier.

Find the best prices fast—comparison shop at price clearing houses. Sites such as BizRate (www.bizrate.com) and My Simon (www.mysimon.com) list prices from hundreds of different vendors on thousands of different products. Others, like CNET Shopper (www.cnet.com),

specialize in one kind of item—in this case, computer equipment and gadgets—but from dozens of vendors.

Check the Internet for sales in your favorite bricks-and-mortar stores. CanadaSale.com (www.canadasale.com) tracks advertised deals across the country. Before you buy online, however, check that the same item isn't on sale for less elsewhere. Also, check the safe shopping tips from Sympatico (http://shopping.sympatico.ca) if you are new to online buying.

Don't forget the hidden shipping and handling costs of any items you purchase. Additional costs can sometimes be added off-screen, and the true total purchase price is only sent to you at a later date in the e-mail order confirmation. If you cannot get specific charges in writing or

printed from the website, shop elsewhere. It may not be that the company is hiding costs, but it is best to be cautious. Many e-retailers also charge you when you return unsatisfactory merchandise. Be sure the e-tailer states this "restocking" fee before you buy.

Sometimes the shipping and handling fees cancel out the discount of shopping online. To avoid this, buy in bulk whenever possible. Consider mentioning to colleagues and family about the opportunities offered by bulk-buying, especially around Christmas time. The savings can be spent on more treats for the family.

TIME TO HIT THE SHOPS

Shopping with a conscience. Want to be sure overseas workers get a fair wage for their labors? Try Global Exchange (www.globalexchange.org/stores), or Level Ground Trading (www.levelground.com) for "coffee with a conscience." Bridgehead (www.bridgehead.ca) has gift baskets, coffee, tea, chocolates, cards, and CDs—all purchased from the grower or artisan at a fair price.

Would you like to shop for groceries online and get them delivered right to your door? Food Fare (www.foodfare.com) and TeleGrocer (www.telegrocer.com) partner with grocery stores. Some of these online grocery operations focus on specific urban areas. For example, OnlineGrocer.ca (www.onlinegrocer.ca/shop/homeasp) delivers only in the Ottawa area.

Save time: always make a list before you place your online grocery order. There might be as many as 196 cereals at an online grocer. Ordering more than one kind may mean waiting for the whole list to disappear while the first item is tallied, then waiting for 196 items to download onto your screen again. You'll find it a lot quicker to search for products by brand name.

So many shopping sites, so little time. How do you find what you want? Some stores are bundled together into virtual malls, but nowadays many have their own domain name. To find your favorite chain store, try typing in the name, sandwiched between www and .com. If that doesn't work, or if you're looking for a smaller store, check one of the huge shopping directories. Visit All Internet Shopping Directory (www.all-internet.com), Canada Shopping Links (www.canadashopper.com), Shopping Search (www.shoppingsearch.com), and Yahoo Canada Shopping (http://ca.shopping.yahoo.com).

FOREARMED IS FOREWARNED

To prevent fraud, shop by credit card. Most card companies will cover your entire loss if you do get caught out. Consider a separate card for e-commerce to keep track of spending.

To avoid schemes and scams, always look for a physical mailing address and phone number—a P.O. box number is not enough. If the company refuses to hand out this

information, be suspicious. Legitimate retailers will always have these details clearly stated. Never trust a vendor who asks for highly personal information such as your Social Insurance Number, bank account number, or your mother's maiden name.

Do your research first. Fraud-alert websites, such as Internet ScamBusters (www.scambusters.org), list reports of unscrupulous characters and scams. Or post a message in a relevant newsgroup or chatroom to see if anybody knows of a particular e-tailer. You can also call the Better Business Bureau in the city where the seller is located to check for negative reports. Still concerned? Try another site!

You can get arrested for seemingly innocent transactions. For instance, beware of buying a "new credit identity," which often uses fake Social Insurance numbers. The Employment Insurance Act makes it an offence to knowingly apply for more than one SIN.

You may be shopping electronically, but you still need to keep paper records. If the company site has any guarantee regarding the item you are buying, print it out. Also print out a copy of the order confirmation and save any paperwork

shipped to you. Most Internet fraud centers around "small print" that was never there. A paper trail may help you fight this type of fraud. In Canada, online purchases are considered "distance contracts," and provincial laws apply. But if the retailer is in another country, you will have only limited options to get your money back because of the different legal jurisdictions.

To avoid floods of junk mail, unwanted phone calls and spam, make sure you shop only at sites that post a privacy policy. Otherwise, the owners of the site can sell your name and personal information on to other sources.

➪ See also **Internet: Amazon, Auction Sites, Automobiles, Credit Cards, eBay, Games, Home Buying, Music,** and **Security On The Net.**

MAJOR SHOPPING SITES
Millions of sites are devoted to online shopping, so pull up a credit card and dig in!

Arts and crafts
Unique gifts made by skilled craftspeople:
FolkArt Gallery (www.thefolkartgallery.com)
The Arts & Crafts Society (www.arts-crafts.com)

Books
There are oodles of online bookstores:
Amazon.com (www.amazon.com)
Barnes and Noble.com (www.bn.com)
Indigo.ca (www.indigo.ca)
The World Scientific Bookshop
(www.wspc.com/books/)

Home electronics
Where better to buy home electronics?
AVdeals.ca (www.avdeals.ca)
FutureShop.ca (www.futureshop.ca)
Panasonic Canada (www.panasonic.ca)
Toshiba Canada (www.toshiba.ca)

Toys
Find a gift for the child who has everything?
Elements of Nature
(www.elementsofnature.com)
EuroToyShop (www.eurotoyshop.com)
FAO Schwarz (www.fao.com)

SPAM

Spam is the Internet version of junk mail—unwanted and unsolicited e-mail that clogs up ISPs and slows down the Net.

Think twice before you allow your name to appear in member directories or other locations where e-mail addresses gather. Spammers (people who send spam) use programs called web crawlers, which trawl the Internet looking for web addresses.

Use an internet service provider that gets tough with spammers. Since there is currently no law targeting spam, it's up to ISPs to stem the junk mail tide. Sympatico, Information Gateway Services, and Yahoo! Canada Mail will take action against spammers. These ISPs are strict about their members using the service to send spam and will suspend or discontinue service for those who abuse their e-mail accounts.

Do not respond to spam. Don't buy anything from spammers and don't ask to be removed

from their list—if you do, you're just letting them know you exist. The best solution is to delete any spam you receive.

Retaliation almost never hurts spammers, but you could end up hurting yourself. One of their favorite tactics is to forge the e-mail address of the last ISP administrator to boot them off. When people retaliate—by sending the spammers back 50 copies of what they sent, for example—the forged ISP administrator receives your retaliation instead of the spammer. The ISP then complains to your ISP, and you risk being the one to lose service for harassment.

You can try to throw web crawler programs off their track by placing a set of invalid characters in your e-mail address. For example, if your address is "john@aol.com," you can put "john@NOSPAMaol.com" in your return address field. Include a note in any e-mails you send explaining that, to respond to you, they'll need to remove the "NOSPAM" from your address.

If you can't beat it, file it. One of the most effective ways to deal with incoming spam is to

filter it. Most e-mail providers offer filtering features. You can get all of your incoming messages screened, as they download, for specific words and known spammer e-mail addresses. Your e-mail account will automatically reroute the suspect spam to a designated folder. Then you can delete the spam without even reading it.

 HOW TO: SUBSCRIBE TO A SITE USING INTERNET EXPLORER

① Visit your chosen site and click Favorites → Add to Favorites. In the dialog box, check Make Available Offline and click Customize. The Offline Favorite Wizard will appear.

② Read and click through the instructions. Select I would like to create a New Schedule and click Next. Now choose how often you want Explorer to update the page.

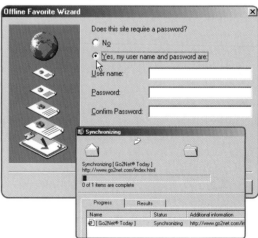

③ If you need to log in to enter the site, type in your user name and password in the next screen. Click Finish. Your browser will now copy the site to your hard drive.

Microsoft Outlook (www.microsoft.com/office/outlook) lets you easily add spammers to a special "dispose of" file. To turn on these e-mail features in Outlook, go to Inbox ➔ Organize and click Junk E-mail. Then highlight a message and select Junk E-mail from the Actions menu. Choose Add To Junk Senders List or Add To Adult Content Senders List.

For even more protection, try a third-party solution such as Novasoft's program SpamKiller (www.spamkiller.com) or Contact Plus's SpamBuster (www.contactplus.com/spam/spam.htm). These programs offer more options to deal with and report spam.

One unique solution to spam comes from Junkbusters (www.junkbusters.com). This site offers information on spam, junk mail, and telemarketing calls. It also has a Notification and Offer section, containing a text passage that you can cut and paste into replies to spammers, offering to "purchase" spam messages for $10 a shot. In other words, if they send you spam, they must pay for the right to do it!

SUBSCRIBING

By subscribing to a site, you can get the browser to automatically check for new content. Receive regular updates on anything you like.

When you subscribe to a site, your web browser copies that website to your hard drive so that you can view it offline. During the setup procedure for your subscription, you tell your browser how often you want it to update the site, so that it will do it automatically for you. This means that you don't have to worry about viewing out-of-date content, even though you are reading the site offline. (To find out how to subscribe, see the box opposite.)

Want to unsubscribe from a site? In Internet Explorer, go to Favorites ➔ Organize Favorites. Right-click on your chosen site and select

Properties. Click the Schedule tab and tick Only when I choose Synchronize from the Tools menu. Click OK. Now Explorer will only update your website subscription when you instruct it to.

Keep track of the headlines! Use the Windows Active Desktop feature to put web pages directly on your Desktop, and they will automatically refresh their content. But don't set up too many; they will slow down your PC.

➪ See also **Windows: Active Desktop; Internet: Favorites** and **Saving Web Pages.**

SUPPORT GROUPS

When you need to seek advice or just talk to someone, get online and receive support from others in similar situations.

Online support groups exist for just about every ailment, disease, condition, or state of mind you can think of. For disability-related resources, Family Village (www.familyvillage.wisc.edu) is a good place to start. Otherwise, try typing the name of your concern into your favorite search engine. You'll find plenty of links.

The most private type of support group is a mailing list (a discussion conducted via e-mail). Write to the list and everyone else sees your message as an e-mail in their Inbox. To find a mailing list on any topic, go to Publically Accessible Mailing Lists (www.neosoft.com/internet/paml/).

To set up a mailing list support group of your own, contact someone in charge at your ISP's company, such as a system administrator or customer service representative. They will assist you in setting up and running it.

Discussion groups are another type of online support group. They work similarly to

chatrooms. For lists of web-based discussion groups, visit Sympatico-Lycos forums (www1.sympatico.ca/forums/).

Get 12-step help online. Online meetings, lists of meetings around the world, and lists of newsgroup and bulletin board 12-step support groups are all available on the Internet. Take a quick trip to the 12 Step Cyber Café (www.12steps.org), 12 Step IRC Information (www.users.cts.com/crash/e/elmo/ircinfo.htm), or Emotional Health Anonymous (http://home.flash.net/~sgveha/).

➪ See also **Internet: Chatrooms, Mailing Lists,** and **Newsgroups.**

SUPPORT GROUP SITES
Connect with others via the Net to share information and experiences.

Beseen (www.beseen.com)
Free message boards on any issue.

Drkoop.com (www.drkoop.com)
Every condition covered, from acne to vision problems. There are health forums where you can start your own chatrooms too.

Grohol.com (www.grohol.com)
More online support groups.

Internet Mental Health Web Communities (www.mentalhealth.com/fr16.html)
Community discussion groups and counseling in mental health.

Mental Help Net (http://mentalhelp.net)
Web-based discussion groups and chats.

Neurology WebForums (http://neuromancer.mgh.harvard.edu/cgi-bin/ultimate.cgi)
Discuss neurological conditions on message boards and in chat areas.

SPORTS

The Internet has enough live coverage, information, and trivia to keep all sports fans happy. In addition to baseball, football, and basketball stats, the Internet can tell you where to go skydiving and how to hit a better backhand. So get your sporting apparel on and get ready for a wild Web workout.

WATCH THE WEB

If you love to watch sports coverage on TV, why not watch it on the Net? You can find sports not usually broadcast on TV, as well as more complete coverage of sports that are. Japanese baseball, golf competitions, tennis matches—watch it all online.

Most websites offer video streaming using the plug-ins QuickTime or RealPlayer. As long as you have an up-to-date web browser, you won't need to download any extra software to view the video. Quokka (www.quokka.com) provides excellent live coverage of a wide variety of sports, as well as graphics, scores, and updates on everything from golf to sailing. For highlight videos and live games, try NBA Canada

(www.nba.com/canada/), Canadian Football League (www.cfl.ca), Baseball Canada (www.baseball.ca), and Hockey Night in Canada (cbc.ca/sports/hockey). For news, interviews, and general information on sports events and personalities, go to CBC Sports (http://cbc.ca/sports/), SLAM! Sports (www.canoe.ca/slam/), Fan.ca (www.fan.ca), or TSN Canada (www.tsn.ca).

Buy a ticket to a baseball, football, basketball, or hockey game online. Ticketmaster (www.ticketmaster.ca) and Tickets.com (www.tickets.com) get you to the game.

Is golf your passion? Great Canadian Golf (www.greatcanadiangolf.com) has listings and reviews of courses country-wide, tips, and online golf instruction. Score Golf (www.scoregolf.com) has instruction articles, news, profiles of Canadian golfers, equipment reviews and links, lists and reviews of courses in Canada, the United States, Europe and other international locations. Or go to Tiger Woods' official site (www.tigerwoods.com) to read about this golfing superstar.

ONLINE LESSONS AND OTHER INFO

If you're dying to take lessons in softball or surfing, but can't spare the time, take an online lesson instead. Learn how to throw, hit, or swing like a pro with My Sports Guru (www.

COMMUNITY SPORTS
Link up with sporting people and events in your area.

Eteamz (www.eteamz.com)
Players, coaches, families, and fans are brought together.

International Olympic Committee (www.olympic.org)
Go to this official site for news on future Olympics, and more.

Commonwealth Games Association (www.commonwealthgames.ca)
Get news of preparation for the next Games, look at the athletes and coaches, and read about the history of these events.

SIRC Sports (www.sportquest.com.sports/index.html)
Long lists of sports, with links to events, biographies, history, rules, clubs, and more.

Canada's Sports Hall of Fame (http://home.inforamp.net/~cshof)
Check out this site for information about Canada's most famous athletes.

Canada: Our Century in Sport (www.ourcenturyinsport.com)
Relive exciting moments in the history of Canadian sport.

EXTREME SPORTS

If extreme is your scene, or you just love vicarious thrills, start here.

**Adrenalin e-zine
(www.adrenalin-magazine.com)**
Interviews with sporting legends, equipment reviews, and other top-notch info.

**Adventure Directory.com
(www.adventuredirectory.com)**
Choose adventures from over 75 activities.

**ESPN Extreme Sports
(http://expn.go.com)**
Headline news from the adventure sports scene. Chat with sporting legends and read features on exotic destinations.

**Extreme Mountain Biking
(http://extreme.nas.net/)**
Bike reviews, technical tips, news, crashes, and preparation for the ride.

**Extreme Sports
(www.extreme-sports.com)**
Links to water sports, skateboard, and motocross sites, among others. Plus X-sport TV show listings.

Xtri.com (www.xtri.com)
The magazine for iron men and women competing in triathalons.

mysportsguru.com), which features advice and video lessons from professionals in a variety of sports. ThrottleBox (www.throttlebox.com) has a free instructional video that you can download—although you'll need to download the free Throttlebox player too. Among others, the site offers lessons on golf, snowboarding, and skiing. Fancy something more tranquil? Discover how to tie flies, pick up a few fly fishing techniques, and learn how to tell a tall fishing tale at Flyfish (www.flyshop.com).

Place your bets! Sites such as EZ Sports Betting (www.ezsportsbettingonline.com) offer real-time Las Vegas lines, and odds for all games and events. To get reviews of betting sites and lots of links, head to Vegas Casino (www.vegasino.addr.com), or try the Gamblers Edge (www.gamblers-edge.com). First, however, you

should make sure that online betting is legal in your state. Most sites require you to make an initial deposit into an online account, from which you can make bets.

Skiing is unpredictable—you can plan your trip months in advance, but the snow still falls when it wants to. So get the scoop on where to find the "fluffiest pow pow" and keep track of the latest conditions with on-mountain snow cams. For up-to-the-minute reports, try Ski Central (www.skicentral.com), or GoSki Canada (www.goski.com/canada.htm), or On the Snow (www.onthesnow.com). You can even buy new skis or a snowboard, and book your vacation.

GET IN ON THE ACTION

Follow your favorite game while you're on the move—arrange for the scores to be sent to your pager or cell phone. Try Yahoo's messenger service (http://alerts.yahoo.com). You can be notified when the game starts, get instant updates on score changes, or find out the score once the game has ended.

Learn from the experiences of others. Read about the adventures of adrenalin junkies and explorers at Global Online Adventure Learning (www.goals.com). Mick Bird, for instance, is

rowing from Australia to Christmas Island. Bill and Helen Thayer have been to the Arctic, the Amazon, and the Sahara. While Chris Duff has paddled round Ireland and New Zealand's South Island in a kayak.

New in town? Use the Internet to find a reaction sports team or event near your new home. One of the best sites is the webcrawler DMOZ (www.dmoz.org). Type in the sport you're interested in and the search engine will come up with hundreds of teams around the world. For example, for lacrosse teams, try www.dmoz.org/Sports/Lacrosse/Clubs.

Calling all armchair jocks! Indulge your imagination—buy and trade players in huge online fantasy leagues. For the television connection, try Fox Sports (www.foxsports.com/fantasy). Stats Inc. (www.stats.com) specializes in real-time statistics, which are essential for the best fantasy league play. And keep up to date on all the hoop news on the Fantasy 2000 Report at Fantasy Sports (www.fantasysports.com).

⇨ See also **Internet: Recreation.**

TELECOMMUTING

Don't spend hours driving—telecommute instead! Use your PC to stay connected to the office.

Depending on your job, telecommuting may require specialized technology. But the basic equipment you will need is a computer, printer, phone and data lines, Zip drive, and fax machine. Some telecommuters may also need access to their corporate LAN (Local Area Network). Try to get your company's IT (Information Technology) staff to visit your home so that you're hooked up correctly from the start, and get a dedicated DSL

SOFTWARE FOR INTERNET TELEPHONING

Check out these sites for the latest telephony software.

e-button (www.e-button.com)
Website to telephone, so visitors to your website can talk to you directly!

**FreeWebCall.com
(www.freewebcall.com/index.cfm)**
PC-to-PC and PC-to-phone services.

**iConnectHere.com
(www.deltathree.com)**
Text and voice e-mail, voicemail, faxing, PC-to-phone long-distance calling.

**Microsoft NetMeeting
(www.microsoft.com)**
Check out this service, which is free to thousands of users.

Net2Phone (www.net2phone.com)
Place a call anywhere through the Internet.

Netscape CoolTalk (www.netscape.com)
Provides audio conferencing, whiteboard, and text-based communications.

(Digital Subscriber Line) that allows you to stay connected to the Net 24 hours a day for a set fee.

If you work from home, you can deduct a portion of your mortgage or rent from your taxes. You may also be eligible for other deductions such as heating and electricity costs, insurance, and so forth. Check the detailed rules on home-based offices in Interpretation Bulletin 514 (it514e.txt) at Canada Customs and Excise Agency's site (www.ccra-adrc.gc.ca/tax/technical/menu-e.html).

Establish clear working hours. This will keep you on track and prevent people from calling you at odd hours. It is a good idea to get a separate phone line for work and put it on an answering machine or service after hours.

Keep your working routine as businesslike as possible. At first you may enjoy the novelty of being able to watch *The Jerry Springer Show* as you work but, in the end, you'll be less productive.

Telecommuting is a great way to add more flexibility to your life and increase family time, but it can also create feelings of isolation. Don't forget to build socializing into your schedule. Find a way to stay in touch with co-workers and other people. Some telecommuters form informal networks by taking coffee breaks together in local cafes or meeting each other for lunch.

Let your family know not to bother you with nonwork-related matters when you're at work. Many people telecommute for reasons of child-care. Keep in mind that it is very difficult to work full time and simultaneously tend to children. Set definite family and work hours—and keep them separate.

Link up with other telecommuters! The Canadian Telework Association website (www.ivc.ca/part3.html) is a great place to learn about the advantages (and disadvantages) of teleworking. It surveys the Canadian and U.S. telework scenes, looks at taxes, and offers

advice for both teleworkers and managers. Telecommuting Jobs (www.tjobs.com) has job postings in several telecommuting categories. You can also visit Canadian Home & Micro Business Federation (www.homebiz.ca) dedicated to serving home-based and small business professionals.

TELEPHONE

Now you can make phone calls over the Net for a fraction of the cost of using a land line.

Have you got free—or fixed-price—Internet access? Internet "telephony" software essentially provides free computer-to-telephone calls anywhere in the world.

Windows users may already have the software to make computer-to-telephone calls. Check to see if you have Microsoft's NetMeeting installed by clicking on Start → Programs → Accessories → Communications. If so, NetMeeting will appear in the drop-down menu.

Phoning via the Internet does not yet offer the same quality of phone service as direct connections. When you use this service, your voice is digitally encoded, then broken up into packages, and sent out across the Net. You may end up talking over each other, when you and the person you're talking to aren't in sync.

To make calls over the Net, you'll need some basic equipment, the first being a computer. Most of the latest Internet telephony products are PC-only, but iVisit (www.ivisit.com) and CUseeMe (www.cuseeme.com) are good for people who need to set up communication between Macs and PCs. You'll also need a 100-MHz or faster processor, a soundcard (preferably a full-duplex, SoundBlaster-compatible model), plus a microphone and speakers. A headset is highly recommended since it'll give cleaner audio input and prevent feedback or echo. You also need a modem or network connection to the Net.

Want to make video calls? You'll need a Webcam or video capture card and camera, like the 3Com's WebCams (http://ca.3com.com) or Winnov Videum (www.winnov.com).

For the fastest connection and fewer delays, turn off all the other programs on your computer before making a Net phone call. Most computers come with a built-in recorder to allow you to record your Internet phone conversation. To find your recorder, check your computer's help guide.

ICQ ("I seek you") is a buddy list to help you find your friends online and connect up with them. The NetMeeting Zone (www.netmeet.net)

explains how to use ICQ with Internet telephony software like Microsoft's NetMeeting.

Want to use e-mail, but don't want a computer? Cidco's iPhone is a telephone with a small screen, built-in Net connection, and a keypad for writing e-mails.

TELEVISION

Enjoy TV? Sure you do, and you can also discover all kinds of useful information about it on that other electronic medium—the Net.

Want to know when your favorite TV show is on air? Don't have a TV guide? There are lots of listings site. Try TV Guide Canada (www.tvguidelive.com), Canada.com TV listings (www.canada.com/tvlistings/), Jam! Showbiz (www.canoe.ca/Television/home.html). Search by specific programs, time slot, or day of the week.

Find out when your favorite Seinfeld episodes are on! These sites offer episode guides to the most popular shows: Epguides.com (http://epguides.com), Hu's Episode Guides (www.episodeguides.com), and Mighty Big TV (www.mightybigtv.com).

Faster than an online guide, independent TV listing utility Electronic TV Host (www.microserve.net/tvhost/etv) lets you browse TV programming offline. Alternatively, you can have Spyonit (www.spyonit.com) notify you by e-mail when your favorite show is on.

Play along with game shows. Most TV stations and networks maintain their own sites, complete with listings, live sports coverage, documentary follow-ups, news, and more. Visit TV Show (www.tvshow.com) for links to all the TV stations and network home pages.

Watch live TV on your computer with Live TV (www.comfm.fr/live/tv) and WorldWide Internet TV (http://wwitv.com). Live TV lets you watch live video feeds from hundreds of different TV stations, while WorldWide Internet TV connects you with sites from around the world.

Know someone who wants to get online but is wary of PCs? Sony's WebTV is designed to access e-mail and the Web without a computer. WebTV uses your TV as a monitor and is similar to setting up a VCR. It includes a remote control that's used to compose e-mail and offers Picture in Picture display so you can watch TV in a small window while browsing online. To get more information, check out the Sony WebTV site (www.sel.sony.com/sel/consumer/webtv).

NEWS OF THE TV WORLD
Enjoy soaps, celeb news, and gossip? Want a TV career? Then visit these sites.

E! Online (www.eonline.com)
Check out the popular TV gossip show on a computer near you.

The Friends Place (www.friendsplace.com)
This website allows you to read every script of every episode of the extremely popular TV series.

Screen Trade Canada (www.screentradecanada.com)
The latest news about the people, the films, the TV and radio shows.

Showbizwire (www.showbizwire.com)
Showbizwire provides TV, film, and celebrity buzz collected from many different entertainment news services.

Soap City (www.soapcity.com) and Soap Digest (www.soapdigest.com)
There's plenty of soap stuff for fans at these two sites!

TVEyes (www.tveyes.com)
Enter your search term—Middle East peace, for example—and TVEyes will let you know when and where it is mentioned on TV.

TRAVEL PLANNING

The Internet has become a popular destination for people planning their family vacations, business trips, or romantic weekends away. You can book airline tickets and hotel reservations, and find currency conversion rates and first-hand accounts of remote places. So log on and make that dream holiday a reality.

PLAN AHEAD

Go paperless by buying e-tickets for flights online—it's one less thing to leave behind on the dresser! Most airlines now offer this facility with e-mail booking confirmation. Many even give you a discount for booking online. All you need for check-in is proof of ID, such as your driver's license or, if you're traveling abroad, your passport.

Research your destination before you go. There are thousands of online travel guides and magazines. The award-winning Rough Guides website (www.roughguides.com) contains a vast resource of detailed information on more than 14,000 destinations around the world, and it has a weekly Spotlight feature focusing on one specific location. Lonely Planet (www.lonely planet.com) is less comprehensive, but it's a great place for first-hand advice and inspiration, where you can check out the opinions and experiences of novice and seasoned travelers.

SNAP UP A BARGAIN

Ticket prices can determine whether you set off on that big great adventure or decide it's out of your reach. Keep the following resources in mind when hunting down a good deal.

Current Sales

Depending on the number of tickets sold up to the point of sale, ticket prices are often adjusted up or down. To get the best deals, plan your trip as far in advance as possible. Many websites have an e-mail support service, which will let you know when the price to a particular destination reaches the amount you're willing to pay.

Internet Specials

Look out for special deals that are only available through the Internet. Often major airlines offer bonus frequent flyer miles when you purchase tickets in this way. Other sites, such as Clickrewards (http://ca.clickrewards. com), offer incentives for using their service.

Last-minute Bargains

Internet-exclusive deals are usually offered through airline, hotel, and travel operator sites. Try Yahoo! Canada Travel (http://ca. travel.yahoo.com), the Last Minute Club (www.lastminuteclub.com), or Travelprice.ca (www.travelprice.com/CA_EN/index.htm).

Travel Auctions

Several auction sites specialize in airline tickets. Get the thrill of an auction and the chance for a bargain holiday in one fell swoop! To place your bid, try GoingGoingGone (www.goinggoinggone. com), SkyAuction (www.skyauction.com), Amazon (www.amazon.com), or BidTripper (www.bidtripper.com).

Name Your Price

Some websites allow you to bid on a destination, then wait for a matching price. Because you must commit to buying the ticket if your price is reached, these sites work best when you're certain of your destination, travel dates, and how much you want to pay. So do your research first and make a realistic bid. Airfare reverse-auction sites include Priceline (www.priceline.com) and Expedia.com (www.expedia.com).

Consolidators

Consolidators buy tickets in bulk when they're cheaper, and sell them at a discount. An online source of consolidator fares is Flight Network (www.flightnetwork.com).

TRAVEL SITES

You know where you want to go, it's just a matter of buying the plane ticket, booking the hotel, printing out a map...

Expedia (www.expedia.ca)
Travelocity (www.travelocity.ca)
Exit.ca (www.exit.ca)
The "big players" of online airfares, listing tens of thousands of flights and prices.

Airline Tickets Direct
(www.airlineticketsdirect.com)
The Last Minute Club
(www.lastminuteclub.com)
Travel CUTS (www.travelcuts.com)
Check out this discount air travel sites.

All Hotels (www.all-hotels.com)
Book online from an amazing array of 40,000 hotels, some at reduced rates.

Abercrombie and Kent
(www.abercrombieandkent.com)
If you're saving for that dream holiday, look no further for the ultimate in luxury adventure travel and safaris.

Hotel Discount (www.hoteldiscount.com)
Allows travelers to compare and make reservations at 2,000 hotels in 40 cities in the U.S.A., Europe, and Canada. It specializes in finding accommodation during peak times.

Places to Stay (www.placestostay.com)
More than 10,000 hotels, bed-and-breakfasts, inns, and resorts online. Receive instant confirmation when you book, modify, or cancel reservations.

Mapquest (www.mapquest.com)
National Geographic
(www.nationalgeographic.com)
Afraid you'll lose your way? Look up maps for almost every imaginable destination.

Many travel magazines have online editions. For tales of daring do, visit Outside magazine (www.outsidemag.com). If you prefer safer sounding travel options, visit Epicurious Travel (travel.epicurious.com) or take a look at Travel and Leisure magazine (www.travelandleisure.com).

For an in-depth profile of foreign lands, head for individual government websites. Alternatively, the CIA World Factbook (www.odci.gov/cia/publications/pubs.html) is unbeatable for global facts and statistics. Or, consult the Department of Foreign Affairs and International Trade site (http://voyage.dfait-maeci.gc.ca/menu-e.asp), which also has information and advice for travelers.

GO NATIVE!

Look up an online city guide to discover the hippest happenings and exciting cultural events taking place in the destination of your choice.

TimeOut (www.timeout.com) has weekly listings of attractions and events for 25 major cities around the world, as does WCities (www.cities.com.city_info.html). You can also investigate what's happening at major Canadian cities with Travel Canada (www.travelcanada.ca).

Picture this—you need to plan a conference call with Beijing, but you're in Belgrade and your boss is in Bogota. If you have Netscape 4 or Internet Explorer 3 or later, you can use the International Java Clock at the BioTactics Clock page (www.biotactics.com/clockjava.htm) where "times are simultaneously posted for a dozen cities around the world." The page also lists other time references, including the CIA's World Time Zone map, and hyperlinks to sites that can help you calculate time differences.

Before traveling to a foreign country, it's best to brush up on a few basic phrases. Travlang (www.travlang.com/languages) offers tutorials to over 74 languages. Combined with some vigorous hand waving, you'll be able to make just about anyone understand you!

BE PREPARED

Avoid "Montezuma's revenge" and other illnesses. Before you go, look up a medical site. Health Canada (www.hc-sc.gc.ca/hpb/lcdc/osh/travel/clinic_e.html) offers a list of clinics and guidelines for health problems. For the truly paranoid, the U.S. Center for Disease Control (www.cdc.gov/travel) carries the latest news about diseases around the world.

Medicine Planet (www.medicineplanet.com) provides a travel health service for Web-enabled phones and palm computers.

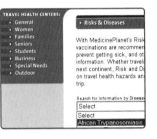

Going on a big trip to several countries? Don't spend your time struggling to convert local currencies. Use the Bank of Canada's currency converter (www.bankofcanada.ca/en/exchform.htm) to figure out values in over 60 currencies. Just select the date and the currency or currencies.

⇨ See also **Internet: Airlines** and **Weather.**

TRIVIA

Useless knowledge fascinates us all, and on the Internet you'll find a treasure trove of trivia questions and answers.

Think you know everything about Canada? Test your knowledge at the Canadian Trivia Game (www.simutech.on.ca/trivia/). This site has questions covering everything from history and sports to genius-level facts. For slightly less exhaustive coverage of cities in Canada and elsewhere in the world, try FunTrivia (www.funtrivia.com).

Muscle up on your movie knowledge with the inexhaustible reference source that is the Internet Movie Database (www.imdb.com). If you want to know who was in what movie and when, or just about any fact related to the movies, this is the best place to start your search. If you don't find what you're looking for, try the more light-hearted Mr. Showbiz (www. mrshowbiz.com).

Try looking for the answer to your trivia question at a searchable archive such as Useless Knowledge (www.uselessknowledge.com). There are more than 20,000 trivia items to discover here with a reasonably efficient search engine to ferret them out. The site also offers changing daily doses of trivia in the form of facts and quotations.

UPLOADING

You've designed your web pages— now it's time to put them online.

What does it mean? Uploading is the process of copying files from your computer onto another computer, via the Internet. For instance, if you have designed a website on your computer at home, you need to upload it to an Internet server before the rest of the world can visit it. The same goes for e-mails and attachments—

when you click Send, the e-mail is uploaded to the recipient's mail server until they request their e-mail program to retrieve it.

It's a basic point, but you can't upload anything to the web unless you have some web space to upload it to. If you have an account with a conventional ISP (Internet Service Provider), you almost certainly have a generous amount of web space you can use for your own site. Check your registration information or your ISP's site for details; most free ISPs don't offer web space.

Test, test, and test again before you upload your new site to your web space. To check your web pages in Internet Explorer or Netscape Navigator, go to the File menu and select Open, then browse your hard

TRIVIA SITES
Become a mine of useless information!

FunTrivia.com (www.funtrivia.com)
130,000 questions and answers, games to play, and a very large archive of trivia that you are free to use for your own games.

Oldies Music (www.oldiesmusic.com)
A treasure trove of info on music of the 50s, 60s, and 70s.

Simpsons (www.geocities.com/ Hollywood/Hills/7637/main.html)
At this site, you'll find everything you ever wanted to know about television's favorite dysfunctional cartoon family.

Ted on TV (www.tedontv.com)
Ask Ted anything about the TV past or present on this astonishing one-man site.

Triviastic (www.triviastic.com)
A growing archive of trivia built by its visitors. You can check out a top trivia 25 and the latest 25 contributions.

drive for the pages. If you can, give a friend a copy on a disk to check that links work and that the navigation is logical.

Get some help. It's worth checking the Help section of your ISP's website before you upload your site to make sure the details you last used, such as the server name, are still valid.

The most common way of getting your site onto your web space at your ISP's web server is to use an FTP (File Transfer Protocol) program. Most FTP programs look and feel similar to Windows Explorer, so they are relatively easy to use. And most are freeware or shareware, so you can at least try them out free for 30 days before you need to buy. Some popular ones include FTPExplorer (www.ftpx.com), CuteFTP(www. cuteftp.com), and WS_FTP (www. ipswitch.com).

Before you begin to upload your website files, check that you have on hand all the relevant information from your Internet Service Provider. You will need an FTP log-in name and password; these are probably the same as your normal account log-in details, but check the server name to which you connect.

Use all lowercase letters for your file names and extensions when you upload, since some web servers are case-sensitive.

If you use FrontPage 2000 to create your website, you can upload pages to your site without using an FTP program. Go to File ➜ Publish Web and type in the location of your web space after the http:// prefix. Click the Options button to choose to publish only changed pages. The "all pages" option will overwrite any pages already on your site that have the same file name. Click Publish.

First time nerves? Try uploading a test web page if you're worried about getting things right. Just create a basic HTML document in your web editor with a few lines of text and use that to try out the procedure. When you upload your real page, you can simply overwrite the test page.

Test your site thoroughly as soon as you've uploaded it. You don't want to "go live" and tell people about your site if it has problems.

Keep a copy of your site on your PC's own hard drive. This is particularly important if you're going to update the site frequently, because you can alter any given pages and upload only those specific ones to refresh the site.

➪ See also **Internet: FTP** and **Website Creation**.

UPGRADING SOFTWARE

Keeping your operating system and software up to date is increasingly a matter of downloading upgrades and bug fixes from the Internet.

Check the Microsoft Update website (http://windowsupdate.microsoft.com/) if you haven't already set your PC to automatically check for updates. If you don't check for updates, you may miss out on useful or essential software.

Set up your system to check automatically for Windows updates so that it's always running with the latest system software. From the Start menu, select Settings ➜ Control Panel and double-click Automatic Updates. In the dialog box there are two options: for Windows to be automatically updated without notifying you; or to be notified before updates are downloaded. Select the one you prefer. Now Windows will periodically search for updates when you are online.

Don't download beta-test software unless you are something of a PC expert and feel confident that you can fix any problems the software might cause. Beta-test versions of programs have not completed testing, so they may contain potentially annoying or damaging bugs.

Set a regular time. If you have any shareware software, it's worth checking the websites you got the programs from originally—for example, every three to six months on average—to see if any updates are available.

HOW TO: UPLOAD A FILE WITH CUTEFTP

① Download CuteFTP from www.cuteftp.com and install it on your PC. Make sure you're online and have details of your ISP's settings on hand. Open CuteFTP. The Site Manager window should appear—if not, go to File ➜ Site Manager. Select File ➜ New Site.

② Name the site and then enter the ISP settings. In the FTP Host Address box, enter the upload address. Enter your password. Make sure the Normal Login type option is set, unless your ISP has told you otherwise. Click Connect, then OK.

③ The panel on the left shows the contents of your hard drive and the one on the right shows any files already in your webspace. Navigate the hard drive to find the files you want to upload. Select the file or folder, right-click on it, and select Upload from the menu.

Don't get caught in the rain. Use the Internet to get the latest weather information.

Wondering what to wear? Have the daily weather report sent to you by e-mail by Weather By E-mail (www.weatherbyemail.com). Or, go to the Meteorological Service of Canada (www.msc-smc.ec.gc.ca/index_e.cfm), which offers not only weather news, but is also a source of weather facts. Another site is the Weather Office (www.weatheroffice.com), which lets you check

current weather and forecasts. It has marine forecasts, wind chill and humidex calculators, UV forecasts, and even radar imagery for pilots!

Going on a trip and want to know what the weather will be like? Try CBC Weather (http://cbc.ca/weather/), which has in-depth weather and forecasts for cities in Canada and the rest of the world. The Weather Network (www.theweathernetwork.com) has forecasts for Canadian, American, and international cities, maps, radar, marine forecasts, pollen and bug reports.

Get the same forecasts from Environment Canada Weather (http://weather.ec.gc.ca/index_e.shtml). It has reports on all the regular weather conditions, plus marine forecasts and warnings, scientific analysis, and satellite shots.

Be prepared for severe weather by getting up-to-date storm warnings. The Weather Office (www.weatheroffice.com) and the Weather Network (www.theweathernetwork.com) cover floods, blizzards, and hurricanes. The Canadian Weather Almanac (http://members.tripod.com/~MitchellBrown/almanac/index.html) explains various weather phenomena around the world.

Learn more about meteorology. In Canada, the Meteorological Service (www.msc-smc.ec.gc.ca/index_e.cfm) conducts research into climate

and climate change, and provides information about these issues and concerns. The Canadian Hurricane Service (www.ns.ec.gc.ca/weather/hurricane/index_e.html) offers details about this phenomenon, as well as animated satellite shots, and a section for kids. The National Earthquake Hazards Program (www.seismo.nrcan.gc.ca/english/) has details about recent earthquakes, how earthquake data is collected, and how to prepare for such an event.

If you are a storm chaser, then you know that up-to-the-minute notice of weather is crucial to catching that storm. If you are not a storm chaser, but want to be, find out how from the NOAA site (www.nssl.noaa.gov/~doswell/Chasing2) or StormChase (www.stormchase.com). View and download storm chasing information and logs from Severewx.com (www.severewx.com) and the Storm Prediction Center (www.spc.noaa.gov).

WEB ADDRESSES

Understanding how those names you type into your browser work will help explain why they don't always work.

Web addresses are also called URLs (Uniform Resource Locator). Every web page has its own URL, which is made up of three parts. The first part is the protocol, such as http://. Next comes the host, or domain, name, which is everything before the first forward slash. After the slash comes the file name.

The full domain name identifies and locates a host computer on the Internet. It breaks down into the subdomain, domain name type, and country code. For example, in www.prowriter.com.fr, www stands for worldwide web, the subdomain is prowriter, the domain type is .com (suggesting a commercial site), and the country code fr locates it in France. Most sites in Canada do not include the country code. You can often guess an organization's web address by learning the domain types (see box opposite).

For more details on how domains work, visit InterNIC FAQ (www.internic.net/faq.html).

The http:// prefix is not the only protocol. The FTP (File Transfer Protocol) lets you download a file quickly. To use it, just type ftp:// before the domain name. If you are trying to reach ftp.bogus.com, for example, type ftp://ftp.bogus.com into your browser. To access newsgroups, use a news: opening and omit the //; for example, to reach the newsgroup alt.bogus, type in news:alt.bogus.

It is often enough to enter just a company name into your browser. Netscape, AOL, and Internet Explorer will all add the http://. and www. for you. For example, to reach Yahoo!, simply enter "yahoo" into the Address bar of the browser, and it will complete the http://www.yahoo.com

for you. AOL, Explorer, and Netscape also let you enter a keyword or phrase instead of a URL and will direct the query to a search engine (see Internet: Search Engines).

Every so often, you will type in an address and get an error message. This happens because either the site has gone offline or moved—or you may have typed the address incorrectly. First try retyping the address. Then try eliminating everything after the first forward slash of the address. For example, if www.notworking.com/computer /hassle/html did not work, try www.not working.com. Otherwise, wait until later; the site may be down for repairs or uploading. If you still have no luck, use a search engine, such as Google (www. google.com) or Fast Search (www.fastsearch.com).

If you don't want to set up your own site, you can still watch the action. Many sites are educational, although adult sites are the most popular. All you need is RealPlayer from either Real.com (www.real.com) or ZDNet (www.zdnet.com).

Your webcam's frame rate (how many new images are generated every second) is influenced by many factors, including the hardware connection, your computer processor's speed, the webcam itself, the software's video compression and decompression settings, and your Internet connection. If your images are slow or freezing up, then one or more of these is probably too slow, and it is time to upgrade.

A web camera is like any other camcorder or camera. To get the best picture, you need to position the camera (and yourself) correctly. Try pointing the camera at an angle so that there is a wall or screen behind you. Or place a light nearby to illuminate your face and shoulders.

⇨ See also **Internet: FTP** and **Website Creation.**

WEBCAM

Create your own Big Brother show with a camera and a computer. Or keep an eye on the babysitter.

Set up a webcam to send live pictures over the Internet. You will need a webcam connected to

DOMAIN TYPES
Domain name suffixes all have meanings related to the owner's business.

.ac	Academic (mostly outside the U.S.)
.com	Commercial or company
.co	Commercial or company (usually non-U.S.A. and usually followed by a country abbreviation)
.edu	Educational institution
.gov	Government
.mil	Military
.net	Internet gateway or administrative host (some commercial sites now use .net, too)
.org	Nonprofit organization

your PC, a video card, and a website (the free website that comes with most ISP accounts is fine). You will also need a software program, such as RealPlayers Spycam or Webcam, to take the pictures automatically and send them by FTP to your website. All in all, the total cost is not as high as you might expect. The shareware for RealPlayer or Webcam can be downloaded for free from the ZDNet Software Library (www.zdnet.com).

Once you have downloaded the required software, it will walk you through how to configure your website and how often you want pictures taken. Then simply leave the software running. The live updating only works while your computer is online. Programs like SpyCam will dial out, get an Internet connection, upload the image, and then hang up. If you want to run a live, continuous webcam broadcast, make sure you have a fast Internet connection or set SpyCam to upload at longer increments.

There are many versatile uses for webcams. You could broadcast your wedding ceremony, a christening, or a graduation to friends and relatives who couldn't make the event. Set up a connection with your children when they go off to college and you can see if they are really eating right and cleaning up their rooms.

WEBCAM SITES
Find out how to set up a webcam, or watch the action on other webcams.

EarthCam (www.earthcam.com)
EarthCam is a collection of all kinds of spycams from all over the place.

WebCam Central (www.camcentral.com)
This site cross-indexes a listing of thousands of live webcams on the Internet.

WebCam World (http://developers. webcamworld.com)
Learn how to set up a webcam by using the site's tutorial. The main site also offers technical support, an online store, and a top 100 webcam list.

WEBSITE CREATION

Whether it's to keep distant relatives up-to-date with family news or family history, a hobby, a special area of interest, a community or church group, or even a business enterprise, creating your own website is a great way of communicating with people, and it has never been easier.

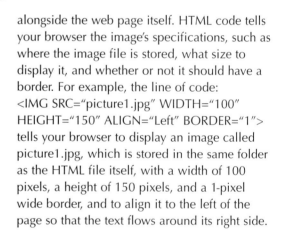

BEFORE YOU START

Pick up a basic understanding of how a web page works. A web page is actually just a simple text file that contains the information to be displayed in the page. It's "marked up" using a special computer language called HTML (HyperText Markup Language). Instead of a .txt extension, it's saved with a .htm or .html extension, which is how your browser knows that your document is a web page, and not just a regular text file.

HTML code is a simple programing language that is based on the formatting "tags," or commands, that word-processing programs used to use. In its most basic format, it's merely a series of tags that you can use to format the structure and layout of a web document (see also HTML tag box, page 233). To display a sentence in bold, for example, simply include the sentence in your HTML code, and put a <B> tag before it and a </B> tag after it. Other HTML tags give your browser extra information about the web page—such as its title, a description, and any keywords—which are particularly useful when your page is listed in a search engine.

Aside from formatting text, HTML can be used to create tables, which help you to control the layout of your page more easily and powerfully. You can also use HTML code to tell your browser to display images on your page. Images are separate files that are stored alongside the web page itself. HTML code tells your browser the image's specifications, such as where the image file is stored, what size to display it, and whether or not it should have a border. For example, the line of code:
<IMG SRC="picture1.jpg" WIDTH="100" HEIGHT="150" ALIGN="Left" BORDER="1">
tells your browser to display an image called picture1.jpg, which is stored in the same folder as the HTML file itself, with a width of 100 pixels, a height of 150 pixels, and a 1-pixel wide border, and to align it to the left of the page so that the text flows around its right side.

HTML code can create links to other pages on the World Wide Web. This is especially useful if you want to give your viewers more in-depth information or show them a cool site. To make a piece of text into a hyperlink, you only have to put simple HTML tags before and after the text, including the address of the web page you want it to link to. For example, the line of code reading <AHREF="http://www.microsoft.com"> Take a look at the Microsoft site for more information!</A> turns the line of text saying "Take a look at the Microsoft site for more information!" into a hyperlink connecting directly to the Microsoft site.

CREATING YOUR SITE ONLINE
Create your own website online without HTML.

Moonfruit
(www.moonfruit.com)
A Web community site that can also help you create an interactive, animated website. If you don't have Flash technology installed on your computer, you must download it first.

MSN.ca
(http://communities.msn.ca/home)
Lets you get together with people who share your interests and set up your own website. Create and post a page to web communities, family sites, personal pages, or make your own online photo album.

Sympatico-Lycos
(www.tripod.ca/index.html/)
This website builder from Lycos Network provides you with the facilities, including Tripod Site Builder and Lycos Photo Center, and information to create your own website.

Yahoo! Canada GeoCities
(http://ca.geocities.yahoo.com/home)
A publishing community that allows you to set up your own website for free, using File Manager, HTML Editor, and Page Builder. Choose a preformatted template, fill in the blanks, add pictures, and then publish it.

Before you even switch on your PC, think a little about the factors that affect the design of your site. What do you want it to achieve? What type of people will visit your website? What will they be looking for? How Internet-savvy will they be? Will they be using the latest version of Internet Explorer or an old broken-down version of Netscape Navigator? Will they have a super-fast connection or a 28.8K modem? Will they have a huge monitor, or a small 640x480 monitor? All of these factors will influence your site design. Try to cater as much as possible for your target "viewership." Think about them now and it'll save you work later.

WEB CREATION PACKAGES
Create your own site with these advanced website creation packages.

Adobe GoLive (www.adobe.com)
This package has been compared to Macromedia's highly rated Dreamweaver in its approach to website creation. Based on HTML code, Adobe GoLive lets you create and manage professional database-driven websites.

FrontPage
(www.microsoft.com/frontpage/)
A web-authoring package produced by Microsoft. One of the leading website creation and management tools, FrontPage uses HTML, Dynamic HTML, script ASP, and cascading style sheets to format your website.

Macromedia
(www.macromedia.com)
Presents the web-authoring packages Director, Shockwave, Dreamweaver, Fireworks, and Flash. Considered to produce the best web-creation packages available. The Dreamweaver 4 Fireworks 4 Studio allows you to design and produce your own site by combining graphics design with website development.

Gather your material. Pull together all the information that you want to put in your site—text, photographs, and existing graphics. These elements should give you an idea about how to organize your site, and they might even inspire a look and feel or certain theme. You might want your site to reflect the style of your own marketing brochures or flyers, for example.

Sketch out the structure of your site. Put pencil to paper and divide your site into sections. Note what your section headings will be, what information will appear under each section, and how your users will navigate through the site. Mock up your front page and a few subpages.

SOFTWARE AND HARDWARE
You can create HTML using something as basic as Notepad, or try out a fully featured HTML editor. If you use Notepad, you'll have to code all your HTML by hand (see Internet: HTML). The next step up is an HTML editor, like HomeSite, in which you still code by hand, but which offers toolbars and buttons to make coding quicker and easier.

There are also WYSIWYG (what you see is what you get) editors, like FrontPage and Dreamweaver, which hide the HTML code from you. The editor creates all the HTML for you in the background. Microsoft Word offers a similar feature to the WYSIWYG editors—you can convert any Word document to a web page simply by selecting Save as Web Page. This creates all the HTML for you (see How To, page 232). Try a few versions of editors and see which one suits you best. Most HTML editors are available to download and try free for a limited time.

If you're planning to include images of any kind on your site—photos, logos, menu bar graphics, animations, and so on—you'll need an image-editing program such as Paint Shop Pro or CorelDraw.

If you want to use a lot of photos on your site, consider buying a digital camera. Your photos will be saved in JPEG format, which you can

then easily open in Paint Shop Pro and manipulate to the size you require. Not sure you want to invest in a digital camera? When you have your photos developed, ask for them in digital format on CD. The CD will also include software for touching up your images.

Take a look at the Kodak site (www.kodak.com) or Snapfish (www.snapfish.com) for more information.

If your images are already printed on paper or as slides, you can have them scanned at an office services store like Kinko's (www.kinkos or Le Print Express (www.leprint.com)—although if you have a lot of images, it'll be cheaper in the long run to buy a scanner.

CREATING YOUR SITE
An inconsistent site is confusing for a viewer. Try to reuse the same elements on each page. It's a good idea to have a consistent navigation bar or menu that appears in the same place on every page to give viewers an idea of where they are. A logo or heading at the same place on every page reassures them that they are still on the same site. And a consistent color scheme—background, text, and links, particularly—helps tie the pages together visually. Word's Web Page Wizard can help you achieve this.

Put the most important information at the top of your web page. People will only scroll down the full page if there is something of value in the information they first receive—so take care to avoid hiding the most important details at the bottom of the page.

Some people still have monitors that are only 640 pixels wide. Try not to create web pages any wider than this—tables and frames are usually the culprits. Viewers don't mind scrolling down through pages, but they hate to scroll across.

Keep your images small in terms of file size. One simple way to check an image's file size is to list it in Windows Explorer, then go to View → Details, and take a look at the figure under the Size column. For a user with a 28.8K modem, each 1Kb in file size takes about a second to download, so that fancy 120Kb image you just created might not be such a good idea. Ways to cut an image's size include reducing the number of colors it uses, reducing its physical height and width, and saving it in the most suitable format—GIF or JPEG.

Use tables to reduce the width of text columns. The default in HTML is for lines of text to stretch all the way to the right side of the browser window before starting a new line. On a typical monitor, optimum line length for ease of reading is actually around 10 words, so consider putting the text for your web page into a table, and setting the table width to 400

pixels at the most. A table is easy to create with any web-authoring software, including Word.

Always give every page a title. The title of a web page appears at the very top of the browser when it's being viewed, and also in the button in the status bar at the bottom of your screen. An informative title is useful to the viewer who stumbles across your web page in a search engine's results.

Remember that not everyone who enters your site will come in through the front door, so try to make their first impression as appealing as possible—every page should be well designed.

PUBLISHING YOUR SITE
It's possible to turn your PC into a web server —capable of storing web pages that anyone else in the world can access—but it's not a task for beginners, and it requires a permanent, expensive connection to the Internet.

If you already have an account with an ISP (Internet Service Provider), find out if the deal includes web space—most ISPs offer you around 5 to 12Mb of web space. Ask your ISP how much it will allow other people to download from your website—around 300Mb a month is reasonable. Some Internet companies also offer free web space. A good place to start is The Free Site (www.thefreesite.com) or Dreamwater (www.dreamwater.com), which list free web hosting services. The downside is that you usually have to display an advertising banner of some kind on your pages, but shop around to see what you can find.

Transfer your site to your web space using FTP (File Transfer Protocol). Most Internet service providers still insist that you use the FTP system for uploading websites. It sounds scarier than it is. You'll need an FTP program like CuteFTP (www.cuteftp.com) or Terrapin

FTP (www.softwareblast.com). Both are available to download and test for free.

Before you start uploading with FTP, you need to go through the folder in which you've created your site, and remove the files that are not part of the site. You will also need to find out from your ISP the address of their FTP server, your user name, and your password. Open up your FTP program, and create a new connection (see also Internet: FTP). Drag and drop your web folder onto the server and watch it copy over.

When you've finished FTPing your site, open up a web browser, and plug in the URL of your site (your ISP can give you this information). Check that all your pages work, your links point to the right places, and that your images are displayed.

➪ See also **Internet: FTP** and **HTML.**

USEFUL SITES FOR WEB AUTHORS
These sites can help you develop your website.

CNet (www.cnet.com)
The Web Building section of this site provides tutorials, useful downloads, and reference guides.

Reallybig.com (www.reallybig.com/reallybig.shtml)
Links to free web resources, including Clip art, sounds, and other add-ons, such as guest books and hit counters.

Webmonkey (http://hotwired.lycos.com/webmonkey)
A huge range of practical tips, tutorials, and information, covering all the skills you need for every aspect of site-building.

HOW TO: CREATE A WEBSITE IN WORD

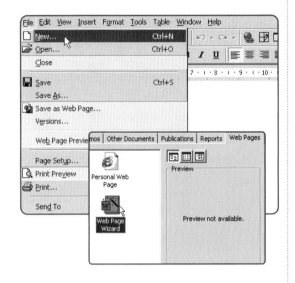

1 Sketch out the pages you'll be creating on paper first. Plan to give each section of your website its own page. The pages will be linked automatically. Open Word and select File → New. Click the Web Pages tab, then double-click the Web Page Wizard icon.

2 The Web Page Wizard guides you through naming your site, choosing a page layout, adding different types of template pages, reordering pages, and choosing a color theme. Your page names appear as links to help navigate your site, so name pages appropriately.

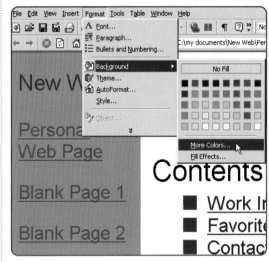

3 You're not stuck with the design you've selected. To change the background, click in a frame, go to Format → Background, and choose a new color. Click More Colors to mix your own, or Fill Effects to add a texture or pattern. Changes are applied to the whole site.

4 Overtype the sample text on the template pages with your own text. If your website contains a blank page, type your text directly onto the page, or copy and paste text from a Word document. For consistency, use Word's Style options to style your text.

5 Before inserting a scanned image or digital photo, tidy, crop and resize it in Paint Shop Pro. Graphics must be transparent GIFs: select the CompuServe Graphics Interchange (*.gif) in the Save as type box. To insert an image, click Insert → Picture → From File, and select it.

6 Upload your website to your web space on your ISP's server. Microsoft Word saves all the files you need for your site in one folder, so all you need to do is copy that folder over to the ISP's FTP server. Make sure the Upload Subdirectories option is checked.

WEB RINGS

Web rings are a collection of linked sites on the same topic that allow web users to share interests and hobbies and to pool information.

Web rings are one of the hottest new ways to organize websites on the Internet. People like them because they often have noncommercial information and don't rely too much on intrusive banner ads.

Use a web ring as a refined search engine. Once you've found a web ring that interests you, track down more information within it. Search within a ring on a selected topic and save trawling through hundreds of irrelevant sites on

a search engine. Yahoo! (www. yahoo.com) lets you search by individual rings or via its entire, gigantic network of web rings.

Use navigation buttons at the end of a web ring page to work through web ring sites. After you visit one site, a mouse click takes you to the next site, another click takes you to the next, and so on until you complete the ring back at the first site. You can also view sites at random or in lists of five.

Look out for structures similar to web rings, such as The Rail (http://therail.com), which takes you straight through the sites without looping you back to the beginning.

Can't find a web ring that suits your interest? Start one of your own. Some rings have just a handful of sites; others have hundreds. By logging onto and joining Yahoo! WebRing (http://dir.webring.yahoo.com/rw), you can create your own ring in simple steps. When you have finished, your new web ring appears on the side of your Yahoo! home page. Click on this link to bring up details of your ring.

Web rings make great promotional tools—if only for your own site or home page. In fact, the web ring was created because of the explosion

in personal home pages. You could start off a web ring to celebrate all birthdays on a certain day, perhaps, or to sell memorabilia.

WEDDING PLANNING

Weddings can cause stress. But don't fret if you're about to walk up the aisle–help is at hand.

The best day of your life means getting hitched, not hitting a hitch! With online services (see opposite), you can plan it all in advance. My Wedding Organizer (www.weddingsoft.com), lets you try before you buy. Have a look, too, at Smart Wedding Wedding Planner Software for Windows (www.smartwedding.com) with its guest list manager and expense tracker. The idoido site (www.idoido.com) has planning tools, and lets you create your own "wed-site."

Send e-mail invitations. Cheaper than snail mail, this high-tech method is also much more fun. Look for free e-mail software that allows you to send cartoons or graphics. Or simply attach a photo file of the happy couple.

HOW TO: FIND A WEB RING IN YAHOO!

1 Log onto the Internet and type the Yahoo! WebRing website address (http://dir.webring.yahoo.com/rw) in your browser's Address box.

2 Search for a web ring on your desired topic by typing a subject into the box and clicking on the Search button. Alternatively, select a category in the Yahoo! directory.

3 A list of web rings will now appear, with the number of sites in each ring. Simply click on one you like to begin navigating your way through the web rings.

Design your own wedding album in Word. Style your pages using words and fonts of your choice, then go to File ➔ Picture ➔ Insert and pull in the photos. Use scanned pictures or download shots from a digital camera.

Find your perfect wedding music on the Web with Windows Me's Media Player. Click on the Media Player icon, then the Media Guide button. Click the Music tab and you'll be taken to the Music related Web sites. You can search the sites for Albums to buy or even download

MP3 files to play on your PC. You could even download several MP3 tracks and create your own personalized playlists of music.

If friends and family are scattered far and wide, beam the ceremony live across the Net. Using a webcam and a laptop running Windows 98 or higher, send the video to a website that will host it (some offer the service free, but without sound). The Lycos VideoCenter (http://video. lycos.com) lets you store up to 10Mb free.

Your wedding video is only a mouse-click away with Windows Media Player. Windows Me has its own video-editing application, called Windows Movie Maker. It is a very basic editor that captures video (as well as still images and audio), slices footage into segments based on scene changes so you can rearrange it, and

converts it to a highly compressed format so you can e-mail it or post it on the Web.

➩ See also **Software: Video Clips; Internet: E-mail, Webcam; Hardware: Digital Cameras** and **Scanners.**

WINDOWS EXTRAS

It's the little extras and add-ons that you discover that make Windows such fun to use.

You can download sounds, such as favorite lines from films, and assign them to events, such as starting Windows or closing programs. Sounds need to be in .wav format. Check out SoundAmerica (www.soundamerica.com), which has almost 30,000 sounds to download. Remember: when you assign a new sound to an event (which you do via the Sounds and Multimedia icon in the Control Panel), you'll need to find it using the Browse button.

Want to change Windows icons or cursors? If you don't like the Desktop options, download new ones from the Net. Look at the Freeware Home site (www.freewarehome.com/desktop/ icons_ag.html) or Cool Fun Clicks (www. coolfunclicks.com). To change icons, simply right-click on your Desktop and select Properties. Go to the Effects tab, select the icon to be changed, then click Change Icon. Use the Browse button to find and select the new icon from your hard drive.

Jazz up Media Player with help from the Web. If you're bored of the standard Media Player interface, click on Skin Chooser in the Player's menu and choose from a range of fun alternatives. Simply click Apply Skin to see how each one looks on your Player. If you click on the More Skins menu, you'll be taken to the Skin gallery on the Media Player website, (www.windowsmedia.com) where you can download even more great designs.

Find new wallpaper on the Web to brighten up your Desktop. Find an image that you'd like to use on a website, right-click on it, and choose Set as Wallpaper from the pop-up menu. The image will now be displayed as your Desktop's background pattern or "wallpaper." To change the wallpaper back, right-click on the Desktop, select Properties, and click the Background tab. Now reset the pattern from the list provided.

Use the Net to enhance on-screen features. CNET shareware site (http://shareware.cnet.com) has terrific free or trial packages for Windows.

➩ See also **Windows: Icons; Internet: Free Graphics.**

WEDDING SITES
Make it a day to remember when you organize your wedding on the Web.

BridalPlanner (www.bridalplanner.com)
Advice column, planners and checklists, tips, wedding shows in your region—all this is available at this site.

Bridal Showers (http://allaboutshowers.com/bridal)
Find out how to organize a great shower.

FrugalBride (www.frugalbride.com)
The name explains the focus, and the site is well worth a visit. Lots of information about how to plan a wedding on budget.

Wedding Bells (www.weddingbells.com)
The Internet equivalent of a glossy bridal magazine with lots of excellent pictures. Don't miss the showroom of designer wedding gowns.

Wedding Canada (www.weddingcenter.on.ca)
A good starting point for planning the big event, with links for choosing your gown, organizing the reception, and more.

WOMEN'S INTERESTS

Women may be from Venus and men from Mars, but the Internet has done a lot to bring women's interests and concerns down to Earth. There are a profusion of sites seeking to empower women. Explore online and you will find a plethora of woman-oriented information and possibly some new friends, too.

ALL-ROUND SITES

Search for sites with relevance to women's issues with Women.com (www.women.com). The site screens every link submission for its appropriateness to women's interests. Or, try the Canadian Women's Business Network (www.cdnbizwomen.com) for a directory of women's organizations and businesses.

SITES FOR AND ABOUT WOMEN

Here are a few of the many women's interest sites worth visiting on the Web.

For Women Only (www.cyberparent.com/women)
Delves deeply into the topics of work, relationships, health, and sex.

Herspace.com (www.amazoncity.com)
An online community for creative women, centered around music, art, and writing.

Moxie (www.moxie.ca)
A network of sites on subjects such as music, health, sex, technology, sports, and fashion.

Oxygen (www.oxygen.com)
Oxygen aims to create a new kind of relationship between women and the media.

Today's Parent (www.todaysparent.com/index.jsp)
This online version of the print magazine offers advice on parenting, child health and behavior, safety, and a Q&A section.

Many general interest and gateway sites are geared just for women, acting as a kind of women's MSN. The sites contain chat and content focused on parenting, health, fitness and beauty, relationships, sex, jobs, cooking, money, and other topics of special interest to women. For the biggest variety of women-centered topics, try iVillage (www.ivillage.com), Cybergrrl (www.cybergrrl.com), or Women.com (www.women.com).

WOMEN AND POLITICS

Get politically active on women's issues. WomensWeb (http://community.web.ca/womensweb/) concentrates on issues, resources, and tools for women's social activism. The Status of Women Canada (www.swc-cfc.gc.ca/direct.html) is a government agency that works for women's equality. The National Council of Women of Canada (www.ncwc.ca) is the Canadian branch of the International Council of Women. This organization is involved with international issues of interest to women, such as landmines, social assistance standards, and workplace childcare.

Find out about women's rights around the world. Learn what Amnesty International (www.amnestyusa.org/women) is doing to increase the human rights of women around the world. Or investigate WomensNet (www.igc.apc.org/womensnet), a global community of women activists and organizations who use computer networks to promote women's rights. WomenWatch (www.un.org/womenwatch) is a gateway for UN research and information on women's issues worldwide.

HEALTH CONCERNS

When it comes to health, it's good to talk. Luckily, there are a growing number of places on the Web where women can get health information and discuss issues with specialists and those who know what they are going through. Online women's health forums on a variety of topics can be found at OBGYN.net (www.obgyn.net) and Women's Health Interactive (http://women's-health.com/about).

Learn about government health resources and your rights. Canadian Health Network Women (www.canadian-health-network.ca/1women.html) is sponsored by Health Canada. It is a gateway to information on health issues specific to women.

HOME HELP

Whether you employ a nanny, gardener, or cleaning lady, you can use the Internet to get information on taxes and deductions. Canada Customs and Revenue Agency's Employers' Guide: Payroll Deductions (http://www.ccra-adrc.gc.ca/E/pub/tg/t4001eq/t4001eq-01.html) deals with payroll tax, CPP, and Employment Insurance deductions. Employers Online (http://employers.gc.ca/pager.cfm?sid_lang=e) covers health and safety, labor laws, training and skills development, pay and benefits, and more.

Tired of being treated like a second-class citizen at the auto dealer or repair shop? The best defense is a strong offense. Get all the knowledge you need at automotive sites geared just for women. Woman Motorist (www.womanmotorist.com) is a supportive site with guides to buying a new or used car that make

car shopping easier and less stressful. It has articles on new auto products, racing, RVs, and safety. Head for HerAuto (www.herauto.com) for more car help.

WORK AND FAMILY

Balancing work and children is no easy feat. Get advice from sites dedicated to making this juggling act easier. Canadian Parents Online (www.canadianparents.com) is the online version of a magazine that covers such topics as child health, family finances, and working mothers. The site has chat and bulletin boards.

Keep track of your own financial health with sites designed just for women. MsMoney (www.msmoney.com) is focused on providing women with the tools and resources necessary for learning about and managing their finances. Moneyminded (www.moneyminded.com) is a personalized and

practical online guide to saving, investing, borrowing, and spending your cash.

Put together an "old girls" network to compete with the boys in the business world. The Canadian Women's Business Network (www.cdnbizwomen.com) is a business skills-training website dedicated to helping the entrepreneurial. The site offers the information and expertise needed to plan economic independence through working for yourself.

WOMEN'S WISDOM

Good role models are important in building self-esteem. Find female role models at Distinguished Women of Past and Present (www.distinguishedwomen.com). This site offers a comprehensive and searchable list of notable women, divided by field of activity. The Garden (www.doenetwork.com/garden) features profiles of women of African descent.

For all you toastmasters out there, gain inspiration from Gifts of Speech: Women's Speeches from Around the World (http://gos.sbc.edu). The site contains speeches by influential contemporary women, such as Christiane Amanpour, Gloria Steinem, and Maya Angelou, and the speeches can be searched by speaker or chronologically.

Women are telling their stories, discussing issues that affect them, and sharing their hard-won wisdom online. CoolWomen (www.coolwomen.org) celebrates Canadian women who have a story to tell, in a wide variety of fields. She-Net (www.she-net.com) is a virtual community where open-minded women share feelings and views. Swan Story (www.swanstory.com) offers support and inspiration for developing and reaching goals in life.

TRAVEL AND ENTERTAINMENT

If you enjoy traveling, but don't have anyone to travel with, there are websites that can help you hook up with a group. Journeywoman (www.journeywoman.com) is an online magazine for women who love to travel. Travelgrrl (www.travelgrrl.com) contains

links and a forum to exchange tips and find a traveling companion.

All kinds of adventurous urges are catered to on the Web, whether you like mountain-climbing or white water rafting. If you like cold climates, go dog-sledding and skiing with Wild Women Expeditions (www.wildwomenexp.com). They also offer wilderness canoe trips and getaways during the non-winter part of the year. Las Olas Surf Adventures (www.surflasolas.com), on the other hand, offers all-female surf adventures in Mexico. For a more complete women's travel directory, try WomenExploring (www.womenexploring.com); this website offers an extensive directory of outdoor adventure tour operators.

Find a culture buddy. Love the opera, art galleries, fine wine? Or are you more at home singing along to popular show tunes? Simply type your interest into a search engine and join an online discussion group.

Have kids but love to travel? Don't worry, you can take them with you. For information on cruises, camping, car trips, travel tips, and much more, visit Family Adventure Travel (www.familyadventuretravel.com) or Family Travel Forum (www.familytravelforum.com).

⇨ See also **Internet: Children, Health, Shopping Online, Travel Planning,** and **Wedding Planning.**

WORK OFFLINE

Connected to the Web through your phone line? Keep it free for the rest of the family by browsing offline.

Internet Explorer 5 allows offline browsing in several different ways. Found the web page you want? Save it for viewing offline later by going to the File menu, selecting Save as, and saving the page to a folder on your hard disk.

Each time you type a URL in Explorer's Address bar and hit Enter, the page at this address is stored in the cache—where downloaded pages from the Internet are stored. To read offline the last 25 pages accessed, click the down arrow by the end of the Address bar and click on a URL.

View the web pages you've already visited. The History button on the Explorer toolbar lets you review pages visited within a set period of time. Set the time scale by going to Tools ➔ Internet options ➔ History. Need to review a page you looked at earlier? Click on History while you're offline and click on the listed links. Remember that to connect to listed web links, you'll need to go back online.

Every Windows user needs Copernic 2000. This program trawls through 11 of the Net's top

search engines to collect search results. But the true beauty of Copernic 2000 is that it lets you download all of these search results to scan through when you're offline. To get the program, just hit the Download button at Copernic (www.copernic.com). Best of all, it's free!

WebZIP from Spidersoft (www.spidersoft.com) lets you download web pages or entire websites, including images and sounds, to your computer

while you're surfing elsewhere (see how to, opposite). You can then browse the web pages offline. Download and try out the program free.

Do you download lots of pages for offline reading? Organizing them can be a real chore. Enter SurfSaver (www.surfsaver.com), a browser add-on from askSam, which lets you store web pages directly from your browser into nicely organized folders. You can relax, knowing that you've got a permanent record of your research that can be browsed at leisure even if the original web page becomes defunct.

WORLD WIDE WEB

A vast amount of data can be found on the World Wide Web, so now the world is literally at your fingertips.

To use the Web, you need an application called a web browser. These translate the HTML code of web designers into viewable web pages. Wherever you go on the Net, your web browser—and all its familiar controls—are there with you. The two most popular browsers are Netscape Navigator and Microsoft's Internet Explorer.

Navigator and Internet Explorer offer similar features. These include Bookmarks (Navigator) or Favorites (Internet Explorer), a customizable toolbar, built-in or linked e-mail program, and newsgroup software.

OFFLINE BROWSING SOFTWARE
Save time and money by trying an offline browsing program.

Sierra Complete Web Studio 2.0 (www.sierrahome.com/software/catalog/web)
Includes the iCollect offline-browsing tool that rounds up text, graphics, and even entire websites for offline surfing.

Copernic 2000 (www.copernic.com)
Take advantage of search engine technology to speed your online searches and download relevant results for offline browsing.

SurfSaver (www.surfsaver.com)
Download and collate web pages with ease.

Webcelerator (www.webcelerator.com)
Speeds up your online browsing as well as letting you review visited pages offline.

WebZIP (www.spidersoft.com)
Download web pages and entire websites to your hard drive to surf the Web at leisure.

Your choice of browser may be reliant upon which one is supplied by your Internet Service Provider (ISP) as part of its starter kit. The ISP may be preconfigured and it may even be the only browser for which they'll provide telephone support if something goes wrong.

Each page on the Web has a unique address known as a URL (Uniform Resource Locator), which identifies its location on the server. To visit a website simply type the URL in the Address bar of your browser.

To move through the web quickly, try to connect at off-peak hours—usually in the morning or late at night. Midday and after-school hours offer the slowest connection rates because that's when the next generation of web surfers practice their stuff at school.

YAHOO!

Yahoo! is one of the Web's foremost search engines and provides a way to search the contents of millions of web pages simultaneously.

Yahoo! differs from most of its rivals in that the searching is done by predefined categories, although you can still do a keyword search. To begin your detective work, just click on one of these categories to receive a list of websites.

Take a look at the Yahoo! home page to see a handy directory of services—from cool cinema links to online shopping in department stores, and more. Whatever you want, you'll find it here.

Want to focus on what's happening locally? Or maybe you want to visit another country? Look

at the various national versions of Yahoo! to get a round-up of news stories, what's going on, and so on.

Yahoo! Canada mail users can sign up for an e-mail address for free. This has the usual features—addresss book, spell check, attachments, and you can send an invitation or greeting card from the same window. Yahoo! Canada also has instant messaging, with easily downloaded software.

Create and keep your own bit of cyberspace. Set up a website for free at Yahoo! Canada Geocities (http://ca.geocities.yahoo.com/home). Geocities, the "publishing community," provides you with all the necessary tools. If you're a beginner, try Yahoo! PageWizards. For more confident web creators, there's the Yahoo! PageBuilder.

ZINES

A zine is an online magazine published on the Web containing news, features, tips, and advice.

Like a website, in its purest form a zine is an electronic publication that Net users can access. They range from CanadaOne Magazine (www.canadaone.com/ezine/index.html), a free online magazine for small business, to Silicon Valley North's (www.silvan.com) up-to-the-minute technology news, to Chick Click (www.chickclick.com) a girl-powered zine that takes a feisty look at issues affecting modern women, to Failure Magazine (www.failuremag.com), an offbeat zine dedicated to glorious failures through the ages in the arts, entertainment, science and technology, and history.

To start reading online zines, simply type in the words "zines" or "ezines" in a search engine and see what you come up with!

Don't believe everything you read in zines and never be tempted to pass on personal details through them. Also check financial or health advice with an expert before you act upon it.

One of the longest established zines on the Net is The Onion (www.theonion.com). When the real news gets you down, try The Onion's spoof take on the world.

Want to keep an eye on the latest fitness news? LentilHealth.com (www.lentilhealth.com/fitness/html) puts fitness first. FitRec helps you achieve your personal goals. It includes sports training guides, from baseball to skiing, and a section on sports events for the disabled. Still on the subject of sport, try Greenside (www.golfball.com/green/greenmag.htm), which offers course listings, tips for the low, high, and medium handicapper, chat forum, and more.

For the latest in travel news, visit Trips (www.tripsmag.com/travelmag.html) for a listing of travel magazines. Or go to Babylon Travel Mag (www.babylontravel.net) for travel stories and photos from travelers around the globe.

HOW TO: BROWSE OFFLINE WITH WEBZIP

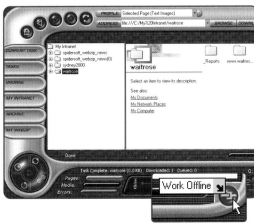

① With WebZIP installed on your PC, go to Start → Programs → WebZIP → WebZIP, and click Continue. Type in a website address, then choose how much you want to download by selecting an option from the Profile drop-down menu. Click the Download button.

② Watch the progress of the download at the bottom of the screen. When the task is complete, click the Work Offline button to disconnect from the Internet. Click on the My Intranet button and locate and open the downloaded file you want to browse.

Hardware

Get physical with the building blocks of your PC. Learn to tell your modem from your MIDI, and your palmtop from your printer, and find out what they can do for you.

BATTERIES

Make the most of your portable PC's power pack when you're on the go.

Batteries are included. Many laptops come prepackaged with a battery, but that does not mean you have to stick with that particular one. Technology is constantly changing and improving, so keep your eye on the market to see if better products are becoming available. While the latest battery design may cost you, it could be worth it for the extra time you gain, particularly if you are on the move a lot.

Be a conservationist. Optimize the settings on your portable PC when it is idle. This will conserve power and give you more time when you really need it. If you go to My Computer → Control Panel → Power Options you can adjust the amount of time the computer spends idle before it shuts down non-essential functions, such as the screen. Not only do you

save power, but you can also keep work in memory, allowing you to pick up where you left off each time.

There are three main types of battery for laptop PCs: nickel-cadmium (nicad); lithium; and nickel metal hydride. The nicad battery was the first to be produced and is the cheapest. A lithium battery is the longest lasting of all three options. It is more expensive as a result, but can normally provide around 4 to 5 hours of laptop computing time, as opposed to the 2 to 3 hours for other types. The nickel metal hydride battery usually lasts around 2 to 3 hours when fully charged. It is less toxic than the nicad and is reputed to be less prone to the "memory effect," while nicad batteries need to be fully discharged before they are capable of being fully recharged.

Save your work before shutting down. Although laptop batteries are highly reliable, you should always save your work before switching to standby. When the machine goes into standby, the data you have entered into the memory is not saved to the hard disk. If the power supply is cut off for any reason—you

drop the PC accidentally and dislodge the battery, for example—you may find that you've lost all your work when your restart your laptop.

If you need to save power only occasionally, you can set your laptop to standby (powered down but not shut down completely) manually in a few easy steps. The easiest way is to go to Start → Shut Down → Stand by. This powers the PC down, and it will restart when you press the power key again. Alternatively, you can go to Control Panel → Power Options → Advanced.

There will be a number of options available, depending on the model of the machine. These include the ability to switch to standby when you close the lid of the laptop.

Your laptop will have a power meter or battery scope, which you can configure to appear on the Taskbar as you work. This feature allows you to keep an eye on the amount of working time available. It can be customized to set off an

---

HOW TO: MAKE A CUSTOMIZED AUDIO CD

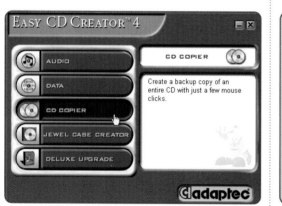

1 Insert a blank, writable CD-R in the recorder. Insert the audio CD you want to record from in the CD-ROM drive. Click on the CD recorder program to activate it. Open the File menu and click on New. If this isn't shown, consult your owner's manual.

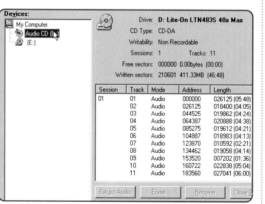

2 Open the Window listing the audio CD tracks. Click on the tracks you want to copy. Hold down the Shift button to highlight multiple tracks, or Ctrl to select non-consecutive tracks. If your software permits, you can also select the speed of recording.

3 A command, such as Save, Record, or Extract to File, will appear to prompt recording. Click this command and recording will begin.

alarm when power is running low. If your notebook PC doesn't show a power meter, bring up the Power Options window from the Control Panel, and use the Power Meter tab to switch it on.

CABLE MODEM

The days of slow Internet and e-mail access are a thing of the past thanks to cable technology.

What is a cable modem? Instead of sending and receiving data across a standard telephone line, a cable modem connects to your PC through the same coaxial cable used for your cable TV service. Contact your cable provider to see if they offer Internet service. A company that does will typically install a network card in your PC and split your cable signal. You then decide whether you want to lease or buy your cable modem. Cable companies generally charge a set monthly fee for unlimited Internet access.

Cable modems receive data 50–100 times faster than an average phone modem, at a speed of around 2–3Mbps. However, the speed drops as more local people subscribe. Also, receiving speed is greater than sending speed, so don't expect the same speed when uploading files.

Ask what your cable company can do for you. Have a good look at the package offered by your cable company. Like many Internet service providers, your cable company will probably offer a choice of user names and free web space where you can host your own web pages.

Check cable modem coverage in your locality. Canad currently boasts 1.7 million residential broadband Internet subscribers, representing 15 percent of Canadian households, and this figure is growing all the time. The Cable Datacom site (www.cabledatacomnews.com) gives up-to-date news on the coverage in your area.

Make sure your PC is powerful enough. It needs at least 32Mb of RAM and a 166Mhz processor, or preferably double this, to benefit from a high-speed link. If not, you need to upgrade your PC.

Keep prying eyes away. Because the cable modem connections tap into a single cable—which may serve any number of homes in your area—there have been incidents of neighbors being able to read files on other PCs. To guard against this security risk, go to Control Panel → Network → Configuration and make sure the File Sharing options are turned off.

An alternative to cable modems is DSL. This service allows your connection to be constantly available, although the connection speed will probably be less than advertised and, at present, some of the DSL technologies are incompatible with each other.

⇨ See also **Internet: DSL; Hardware: Upgrading Hardware.**

CD-BURNER

Creating your own CDs at home can save you time, money, and space.

Choose the writable CD disc that's right for you. There are two types of discs, commonly referred to as the CD-R (CD-Recordable) and the CD-RW (CD-ReWritable). CD-R discs can only be written to or "burned" once—their contents are then permanent. The CD-RW disks can be written to and erased over and over again. CD-R discs are more reliable for audio recordings than the CD-RW version, and much cheaper.

Decide whether you need CD technology. If you use a lot of floppy or even Zip disks to back up or archive your data, then a writable CD drive may be a good investment. A recordable CD holds about 640Mb of information, or 75 minutes of audio. That is approximately 444 floppy disks of 1.44Mb each, or 6-plus 100Mb Zip disks.

CABLE MODEM PROVIDER SITES
Where to developing Internet access on the Web

Cable Modem Info Center (www.cabledatacomnews. com/cmic.htm)
A cable modem hub site with FAQs, comparisons, and reviews of cable technology and providers throughout North America.

CATV.Cyberlab (www.catv.org)
Another cable hub site, but with more technical information.

Motorola CableComm Products (www.gi.com/index2.html)
Visit Motorola's broadband site to catch up with the latest technology.

**Cogeco Cable (www.cogeco.ca)
Rogers@Home (www.rogers.ca)
Shaw Cable (www.shaw.ca)
Videotron (Videon) (www.videotron.ca)**
Canada's major Canadian cable providers of Internet access.

Create your own original audio CDs. Once you've installed your CD burner, it's not just useful for storage. To burn your favorite music onto a CD, all you need is a standard CD-ROM drive as well as a CD burner attached to the PC. The software you need should come with the burner.

CD-ROM

Access huge amounts of information on these handy high-capacity discs.

Create a library of information. CD-ROMs have become much less expensive in recent years and have opened up a massive number of channels for information storage and retrieval. Good choices for a CD-ROM library include reference titles, such as encyclopedias, along

DVD HARDWARE AND DISK SITES

Discover how to be versatile with your video discs.

DVD City (www.dvdcity.com)
A useful site to compare both prices and performance of DVD players.

DVD.Com (www.dvd.com)
Up-to-date reviews and advice, news, and a significant online help section.

DVD Review (www.dvdreview.com)
The URL says it all—this site previews all imminent releases and reviews the latest ones, features hardware reviews, a hefty FAQ section, and offers downloads.

DVD Verdict (www.dvdverdict.com)
Features DVD movie and player reviews, peripherals, news, resources, and a user forum to post questions.

with special interest titles, such as music, art, wildlife, or history.

Do you really need that CD-ROM? Whether you need to purchase a CD-ROM rests on the amount of use you will get from it. For example, if you need to find out the capital cities of all the countries in the world, a quick Internet search will give you that information. However, if you need more detail, such as maps and other statistics, buying an atlas on CD-ROM is the answer. Also try the free sample copies of CD-ROMs that are available from many magazines.

Use the search facility of the CD-ROM. Most reference CD-ROMs use search facilities similar to those on the Internet to find information, which can cut down on your research time.

DEVICE DRIVER

Device drivers are essential for keeping your computer hardware up to date and running smoothly.

Device drivers are small programs that allow pieces of hardware, such as printers, keyboards, and disk drives, to run correctly on the PC. Many are preinstalled, but if you add new hardware, you will have to install its driver before it will work. Regularly updating the device drivers can optimize the all-round performance of your computer.

Download the latest drivers for free. The company that made your hardware will usually post the latest drivers on a website. Check the site to see if there have been any updates. Other sites such as DriversHQ (www.drivershq.com/) and Mister Driver (www.mrdriver.com) act as hubs from which you can search for hundreds of driver types. Keep a note of the device's model type and number and make sure you download the correct version. (To update or replace a driver, see the How To opposite.)

Beware of beta versions of drivers. If your PC is working well already, don't rush to download beta versions, which are a pre-release version of the program. As such, they are often not fully tested and can contain glitches and errors. The frustration caused when one crashes in your system far outweighs any possible benefits. Only get new drivers if you really need them.

Make sure that you fully uninstall old drivers before replacing them with new versions. Go to Start → Programs, open the folder for your hardware, and click on the Uninstall icon to remove the driver. Alternatively, you may be able to go to the Control Panel in My Computer and use the Add/Remove Software option. Device Manager can also be used by right-clicking My Computer, selecting Properties, highlighting the old device, and then clicking Remove.

Don't change your mind during installation. Always let a new driver finish downloading completely without interruption. Stopping an installation halfway through can badly damage the system files and put your PC out of business until a professional repairs it.

To eliminate any installation doubts, make use of the free software available on the Internet to

help you. One example is the Driver Detective, available free from PC DriversHQ (www.drivershq.com) The site has it's own driver installation wizard.

DRAWING PAD

Replace your mouse with a faster pen-and-pad alternative.

Speed up your work. Drawing pads use a digital pen and screen to create items on your Desktop, In certain situations, such as on-screen design, you'll find it's faster to use them than the standard mouse. They also sit in the palm of your hand, allowing you to move more freely.

strain injury. So, remember to take regular breaks and flex your hand and wrist muscles. For more advice visit www.rsiprogram.com.

Drawing pads are more expensive than a standard mouse because they are not yet in mainstream use. Before you buy, weigh how much you will use one and ask to try one in your local PC store.

If you have ever tried to draw a detailed picture or artwork using a standard mouse, you know how frustrating the process can be. Some pad providers, such as Wacom (www.wacom.com), offer pressure-sensitive software bundles to accompany their standard mouse, making the process easier and more intuitive.

Mouse and pad in perfect harmony. Finding a drawing pad that happily co-exists with your standard mouse gives you flexibility when using different programs or functions. But if you prefer a drawing pad, then use it as your main mouse.

Using a digital pen for long periods may give you writers' cramp, just as a normal pen might, and a mouse can sometimes cause repetitive

DVDS

Join the sound and vision revolution with DVD technology.

DVD stands for Digital Video Disc or Digital Versatile Disc and is fast replacing CD-ROMs. A DVD has up to 28 times the storage capacity of a CD. With DVD, you can look forward to

crystal-clear digital sound and images, extras such as freeze-frame options, and special content, such as documentaries on the making of feature films, and more.

DVD technology will transform your PC into a multimedia station. DVD software includes more and much better detailed graphics than ordinary CD-ROMs. You can also watch DVD movies on your PC screen. Many movie DVDs also have subtitles, allowing you to watch the film in several languages, and often contain previously unreleased scenes and biographies.

Don't throw away your old CD-ROMs. DVD drives are backward compatible, which means you can play all your existing CDs on the system as well as any new DVDs.

Replace and upgrade. DVD upgrade kits are simple to install and mainly consist of a DVD drive and a decoder card that slots inside your PC's main unit. The card translates digital data into stunning full-motion video and surround-sound audio. For more information on upgrading your computer, visit the Creative Labs website (www.creative.com/pcdvd).

HOW TO: UPDATE OR REPLACE A DEVICE DRIVER

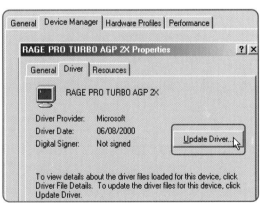

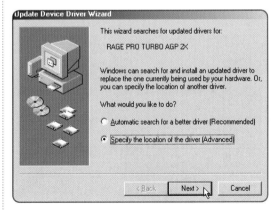

1 After downloading your driver update from the Web, go to My Computer → Control Panel → System → Device Manager to find the description of the hardware you want to update or replace. Click on the + next to the name to show the associated devices.

2 Double-click on the icon of the hardware whose driver you want to update, for example, the videocard. A dialog box shows a brief history of the devices. Select the Driver tab and click on Update Driver. The Update Device Driver Wizard appears.

3 The easiest way to proceed is to choose the Specify the Location option. You will then be asked to give a location where the PC can find the drivers. Once this step is complete, your PC will update the driver automatically.

DIGITAL CAMERAS

M ost of us already have a traditional camera that uses film, so why should we bother with a digital camera? Well, digital photography has lots of advantages over the traditional kind, including editable pictures and almost instant results, which make it an appealing option.

DIGITAL CAMERA FEATURES

Normally, you take pictures and then get the film developed by a store or mail-order firm. But this can take time. And it might be weeks or months before you finish a roll of film, especially if it's for 36 pictures. With a digital camera you

DIGITAL CAMERA SITES
Before you buy, you can learn a lot from these websites.

MANUFACTURERS
Agfa (www.agfa.ca)
Canon (www.usa.canon.ca)
Casio (www.casio.com)
Epson (www.epson.com)
Fuji (www.fujifilm.com)
Hewlett Packard (http://welcome.hp.com/country/ca/eng/wel.htm)
Kodak (www.kodak.ca)
Olympus (www.olympusamerica.com)
Ricoh (www.ricoh.ca)
Samsung (www.samsung.ca)
Sanyo (www.sanyo.ca)
Sony (www.sonystyle.ca)
Toshiba (www.toshiba.ca)

REVIEWS AND INFORMATION
These sites offer general buying advice, reviews, and information about specific digital cameras.

CNET (www.cnet.com)
PC Photo Review (www.pcphotoreview.com)
Short Courses (www.shortcourses.com)

can print an image as soon as you get back to your computer, so everything remains fresh. Better still, you can e-mail images to friends.

Most digital cameras allow you to view an image immediately and retake the shot if it isn't right. You can edit images on your computer, creating artistic or humorous effects. Equally important, digital cameras tend to be small and light, so they are easy to carry.

All the standard extra features you expect on a traditional camera are available on a digital camera, such as a flash unit, red-eye reduction capability (to avoid those ghoulish red-eye centers caused by harsh flash light), and a self-timer so that you can get yourself in the picture. You might find a digital camera that also offers sound-recording features, so that you can add a commentary or voice note to an image, and date and time stamping onto the picture itself. Some digital cameras can even be used for video conferencing.

Extra! Extra! You can buy optional extras for digital cameras just as you can for conventional ones, but it's also worth considering additional batteries for long trips.

Going to the movies. Continuing up the scale of additional features are digital cameras that can capture short movies. Imagine, for example, capturing a short sequence of a grandchild blowing out candles on a birthday cake, and then sending it to friends and family over the Internet on the same day.

IMAGE RESOLUTION
Most digital cameras can take pictures at different image resolutions. The image

resolution is a measure of the number of dots (called pixels) that are used to make up a photograph. The more dots in an image, the sharper it will be, but also the more space will be required to store digitally. Image resolution is presented either as the number of dots on both the horizontal and vertical lines or as a grand total. So an image taken at 1280 x 960 pixels (or 1.3 megapixels) will be less clear than one taken at 1800 x 1200 pixels (or 2.3 megapixels). If you intend to print an image, use the highest resolution your camera can manage. If you just want to put an image on the Web, the lowest resolution your camera supports will usually be fine, because the higher the resolution, the longer it will take to download on your webpage.

IMAGE STORAGE
Most digital cameras support removable storage media of some sort, though some budget models only have built-in memory. The larger the capacity of the storage media, the

more pictures you can store. Some digital cameras support CompactFlash cards, which can come in very high capacities. When one memory card becomes full, you can simply take it out of the camera and replace it with an empty memory card.

GETTING IMAGES ONTO YOUR PC

Most modern digital cameras come with a USB cable for getting their images into your computer. It is far faster than the older serial cable and makes transferring images relatively fast. If you are a serious user of digital cameras, though, you might want to invest in a memory card reader. For a few dollars you can have a reader that is permanently plugged into your computer. Then whenever you want to transfer data, you take the memory card from your camera and put it into the reader. You can also

plug some digital cameras directly into a printer or even into your TV for an instant slide show.

Because digital cameras don't use film but storage media, you can use the same storage device over and over again—but you have to empty it before you can re-use it, and you will need a system for storing and organizing your digital images. One method is to download the images to your computer and from there onto a storage device, such as Zip disk or a CD-R. This allows you to carry your photo collection around to show pictures to others and keeps photos securely separate from your PC. It also means you will always know where to go to find a picture, no matter how long ago you took it.

USING A DIGITAL CAMERA

All those extra features your digital camera includes are usually accessed through buttons on a panel next to the LCD (liquid crystal display), but sometimes they are located

elsewhere on the camera. When buying a digital camera, make sure these buttons are easy to operate and their functions are clear. On some digital cameras you have to go through long sequences of button presses to gain access to some of the features. This can be tedious and the sequences can be difficult to remember, making using the camera unnecessarily complicated.

 HOW TO: DOWNLOAD DIGITAL PHOTOS ONTO YOUR PC

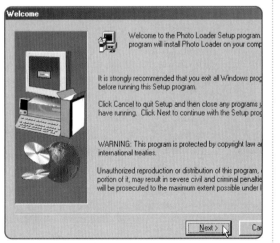

1 Install any special software your camera requires for the downloading of images onto your PC. The manual that came with your camera will explain how to do this.

2 Connect your digital camera to your computer. Again, the camera manual will explain how to use the connection wires that came with the camera. Now you can begin the download process.

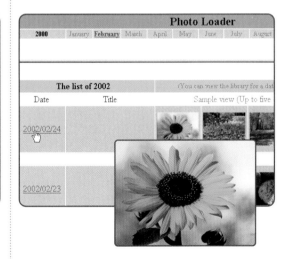

3 Your camera will probably have come with some software into which you can download images. Open the software and then select the Acquire image option. Once the images are on your computer, you can delete them from your camera.

ERGONOMICS

A safe and comfortable working environment will boost your energy and help you to avoid fatigue.

Ergonomics is the study of workspace design. If your working area is well designed, you'll be able to work comfortably and efficiently in one position with no adverse side effects to your health. It's all too easy to spend hours working at your computer so, before you get started, make sure you pay particular attention to how your work station is set up.

Choose the right chair for you. If you spend a lot of time in front of your computer screen, then a well-designed chair will help you to avoid backaches and tiredness. Back support and height-adjustment features will let you adopt an upright posture while remaining properly supported. For the most full-featured chairs, try an office supply store.

Sit directly facing your monitor and keyboard. To avoid back strain, sit in an upright position, with your arms roughly horizontal and your eyes level with the top of the monitor's screen. Body joints should be at right angles to each other and your feet placed firmly on the floor.

Make sure you have unobstructed access to your keyboard, monitor, and mouse. Avoid Repetitive Strain Injury (RSI) in your wrists—

work with a computer desk that provides space for the keyboard and mouse, and a separate shelf that keeps your monitor at eye level.

Don't rest the heels of your hands on the desk while typing. Instead, keep the hands parallel with the desk surface. Although a wrist support may look useful, if it's positioned incorrectly it can actually increase strain.

A good-quality monitor will reduce eye strain and help you to avoid headaches. There are many factors that affect the impact a monitor can have on your health and well-being. These include the amount of ambient light in the room, your monitor's refresh rate (which determines the amount your screen flickers), glare, reflectiveness, and dot pitch (the distance between identically colored dots on the monitor). The lower the dot pitch, the clearer the image. Go for a 0.26mm or lower dot pitch monitor for greater clarity—ask your computer store about this before buying.

Avoid sitting with your back to a window or other light source, because your eyes' ability to read the screen is hampered by reflections. Reduce eye strain further by maintaining a distance of 20 inches or more between your eyes and your monitor.

There are several keyboard shapes and layouts to make typing easier. A contoured keyboard, for instance, provides a more natural position for your hands. If your desk is cluttered, try a wireless keyboard. This uses a built-in radio transmitter to send signals to a receiver plugged into your PC. Some keyboards have extra control buttons, to launch your favorite software. Whatever keyboard you use, keep it perpendicular to your body, with the rear edge of the keyboard raised.

Give yourself a break from your PC, every 20 minutes or so. This reduces wear and tear on both body and mind. Keep yourself fresh by

stretching, walking around, and drinking water. If you're a workaholic, you can get software that prompts you to take a break and suggests anti-RSI exercises—try Ergosense by Omniquad (www.omniquad.com).

EXPANSION SLOTS AND BAYS

Every PC motherboard has several slots and bays to let you upgrade or add new components at any time.

There are two types of PC connection slots. Industry Standard Architecture (ISA) connections have been in use since 1984 and

HINTS FOR INSTALLING HARDWARE

Find out how to become an expansion-slot expert.

Open sesame
If you're purchasing a new PC, buy one with a hinged side panel on the system unit for easy access to your expansion slots.

Divide and rule
If you play games a lot on your PC, consider partitioning your hard disk in two parts with Partition Magic software (www.powerquest.com), and dedicating one part to games.

Down to earth
During installation, be careful to avoid static discharge from the computer's components. Do not use magnetic screwdrivers, and use an antistatic wrist strap attached to a grounded metal object.

AGP or PCI?
AGP (Accelerated Graphics Port) cards are faster than otehwise identical PCI cards. For details visit SysOpt.com (www.sysopt.com/agp.html).

are still a very common PC connector. But this format is considerably slower than the second type of connection—Peripheral Component Interconnect (PCI)—and is being phased out gradually. ISA doesn't support Plug and Play devices, which are pieces of hardware you can simply connect to your PC and start using without complicated installation procedures.

Upgrading your hardware? Check that the items are compatible with PCI expansion slots. Most modern PCs are built with these.

A PC usually has four to six expansion slots inside. These are parallel sockets on the motherboard, corresponding to removable panels in the rear of the PC case. You can attach a wide range of devices to these, such as modems and video capture cards. To do this, remove the

corresponding panel in the case and make sure the card is firmly in the PCI slot before finally screwing it into place (see How To: Install a Graphics Card, p.310).

You can attach up to four IDE devices. IDE stands for Intelligent, or Integrated, Drive Electronics. Normally, your motherboard will have two IDE interfaces, to each of which you can attach two mass storage devices (such as your hard disk or CD-ROM)—one as a master controlling the other, known as the slave. The cables each have a mid-connector and an end-connector. Follow the instructions to set each device as either the master or slave during installation, using jumpers (metal bridges that complete electrical circuits) on the back.

Add more hard disks to expand your storage. If you have one hard disk and one CD-ROM, your computer case usually has internal space for one or more extra hard disks. You can insert them beside the existing hard disk slot. Adding an extra hard disk gives you space to keep large

graphics, video, or music files, or you can keep your data separate from your Windows system files. If you are installing an extra drive yourself, make sure you set the jumpers on the back before you slide it in; it's difficult to see them once in place. Also, check that the power and IDE cables are seated properly in their sockets to make sure there is a proper connection.

⇨ See also **Hardware: Monitors.**

FLAT PANEL SCREENS

See the difference a flat panel screen provides, and enjoy a sharper resolution and a clearer image.

For the best resolution and clarity on a flat panel display, choose a Thin Film Transistor (TFT), or active matrix, screen. Each pixel is controlled by transistors within the screen, which produces a bright and clear light. Often, the surface is nonreflective as well as flat. TFT screens can help you to avoid eye strain, and they emit virtually no radiation. But they are currently more expensive than a standard monitor.

A passive matrix screen is cheaper and uses less power than a TFT flat panel, but bear in mind that the display will not be as bright or clear, and is not as easy to read from an angle. The screen works well on a portable device such as a laptop and is useful to have when you can't recharge your battery frequently. But it is tiring on the eyes during long periods of use.

Look out for a plasma display. This new flat screen technology gives a 160-degree viewing angle that is bright and clear. But they are very expensive, use more power, and are heavier than active or passive matrix screens. Plasma displays work very well as flat television screens, so they are good for combining TV and computer functions in one screen, and can be wall-mounted.

Handle with care! Laptop screens and flat panel screens in general are more easily damaged than conventional monitors. While it's normal

HOW TO: INSTALL A CD BURNER

① Push out the front panel on the PC casing to reveal the empty slot for your CD burner. Set the jumpers on the back of the burner to master, if connecting to a free IDE socket, or to slave, if connecting to a cable with another device attached. Slide the burner into the slot.

② Now Attach the power and IDE cables, but make sure you do so correctly. The red edge of the IDE cable goes next to the power socket. Screw the device in securely, then close the case and restart your machine.

for one or two pixels to be dark, even on a new TFT screen, you should check the guarantee if more than that number of pixels stop working. Try not to touch the surface of the screen and remember to dust it regularly with a dry cloth.

↪ See also **Hardware: Laptops and Monitors.**

FLOPPY DISKS

The faithful floppy disk has been around for a long time, and it's still a great way to transfer small files from one PC to another.

Use a compression program, such as WinZip (www.winzip.com), to get more onto a floppy disk. Word processor or spreadsheet files will give you the best compression at around 85

percent. Graphics files, such as JPEGs and executable files (.exe) downloaded from the Internet are already compressed and you won't be able to squash them much more.

Compress several files into one. If you select a group of files at once you can compress them into one file to save space on your floppy. This works well if you are creating backups.

If a file is too big for one floppy, even when compressed using WinZip, you can split the file up over several floppies. The data can then be recombined on another PC, as long as it has WinZip installed. This method is called "spanning," because one file spans several disks. Make sure you have enough blank floppy disks and number them carefully, since you will have to insert them in the correct order when uncompressing the file.

Keep floppy disks in a cool, dry place, preferably in a real floppy disk box. Since floppy disks are magnetic media, exposure to

magnetism is particularly damaging. Keep them away from loudspeakers, magnetic tools, and even automatic gearboxes. Unfortunately, although generally reliable, all magnetic media will deteriorate over time.

If you get a disk error when reading a floppy, run ScanDisk to find and repair file errors. Go to Start → Programs → Accessories → System Tools → ScanDisk. If the scan of the A: drive is successful, copy the data to a new disk as an extra precaution.

Replace your floppy drive with SuperDisk. This is an identically sized drive, which is "backward compatible," meaning it will still read all your old floppies. But it can store up to 120Mb on its special floppy disks—over eight times more data. If you're reluctant to open up your computer's case to install a new drive, get an external USB version. This is easy to install and portable, too, so you can copy files onto a super floppy and then take the SuperDisk to another computer.

HOW TO: INSTALL A GRAPHICS CARD

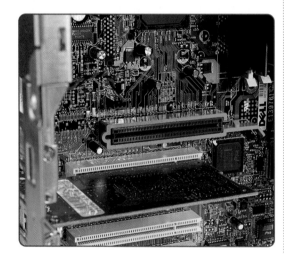

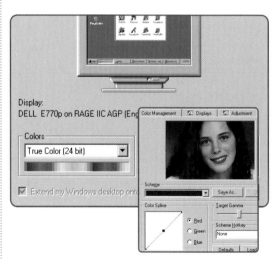

① Disconnect the monitor and power cables, open the case and remove the old graphics card. If your new card is AGP, locate the AGP slot—usually a single brown slot next to the row of white PCI slots. See your PC manual for further details if you're unsure about this.

② Gently, but firmly, press in the new adapter. Close the case and reattach the monitor and power cables. Turn on your PC. Windows detects new hardware and prompts you to insert the graphics card disk and install the card's driver from it. Now restart your PC.

③ When the PC restarts, readjust your color-depth, resolution, and refresh rate to your personal choices. Most graphic cards come with extra software to allow you to fine-tune the settings. Check the manuals for help on how to optimize the card and game play.

Take care of your disks. Never pull back the guard and touch the disk surface because any dirt or dust can cause the data to be misread. Don't bend a floppy disk, or put it in your pocket where it can get distorted—this will almost certainly destroy the data. If you want to send a disk though the mail, wrap it in aluminum foil and use a cardboard envelope.

⇨ See also **Windows: Disk Drives.**

GRAPHICS CARDS

Upgrading your PC's graphics card can dramatically improve screen display and 3-D game play.

All PCs are fitted with graphics cards, also called adapters, capable of displaying millions of colors at resolutions greater than 1,024x768 dots per inch (dpi). If you work with graphics software or have a digital camera, you will need a good adapter to get the best from your pictures. Also, a good graphics card can generate refresh rates of 75Hz or more. Higher refresh rates reduce screen flicker, making prolonged viewing less hard on your eyes.

Choose the right graphics card for your games. Special graphics cards are required to play 3D-accelerated games. Three main standards of card are available: 3Dfx, OpenGL, and Direct3D. The 3Dfx cards will play games

designed for OpenGL or Direct3D cards, and many gamers opt for these, with Direct 3D cards a close second favorite. Open GL-only cards are rare, and most Direct 3D cards can run in Open GL mode.

From PCI to AGP. Originally, graphics cards plugged into the Peripheral Component Interconnect (PCI) slot inside the PC, also used for sound cards and modems. The Accelerated Graphics Port (AGP) was then developed to cope with the huge amounts of data processed in modern 3-D games. Not all PCs have an AGP port, so check your motherboard's manual to see whether you have the right slot.

The final conflict! Having problems in a certain game or graphics program? There may be a conflict between that software and your graphics adapter. A patch—a piece of bug-fixing computer code to insert or "patch" into a program—can be downloaded from sites like VersionTracker.com (www.versiontracker.com). Or you may get a message saying you need to update your graphics adapter. Visit PC Drivers HQ (www.drivershq.com), or try the website of the graphics adapter manufacturer.

HARD DRIVE

Your computer's hard drive is its most important component and needs regular maintenance.

Beware of fragmentation. This means that a single file, for example, may not occupy a continuous area of the drive surface, but dispersed areas instead. The result is slow performance and the risk of data disruption.

Reorganize regularly with Disk Defragmenter. This handy program defragments your hard disk so that each file and program occupies a continuous area. Go to Start → Programs → Accessories → System Tools and select Disk Defragmenter. Under Select Drive, enter the

hard drive, usually C:. Defragmentation takes a little while and you should leave the PC alone while this process is in progress—overnight, for example.

System Tools also contains ScanDisk, a powerful tool that checks and repairs disk errors. Regularly running ScanDisk in Thorough mode can help avoid data loss. It checks the drive's surface and file structure for problems, marks damaged sectors of the drive so that they are avoided by the operating system, and reclaims space lost by damaged sections.

Don't knock the computer when its hard drive is reading or writing data because this could cause the heads to crash into the disk surface.

Windows includes a Task Scheduler, which can be set to run Defragmenter and ScanDisk for you at fixed times. Go to Programs → Accessories → System Tools and select Scheduled Tasks. Alternatively, double-click the Task Scheduler icon in the System Tray, next to the clock on the Taskbar. Double-click Add Scheduled Task to start the Scheduled Task Wizard, which will take you step-by-step through setting up the tasks and the times.

The more programs you use, the slower your PC gets. Windows starts to run slower the more programs you add, because it is scanning a huge database, or list, called the Registry during start-up and operation. This grows each time you add a new program.

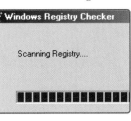

Reformat and restore. Periodically reformatting a hard drive can restore the PC to smooth running condition, but this process requires some planning and a complete system backup, because all your data and applications will be deleted during reformatting.

⇨ See also **Windows: Backing Up, Hard Drive,** and **Optimize Your PC.**

With advances in technology, the minicomputer or PDA (personal desktop assistants) is now a reality. Deciding which PDA is for you can be tricky with so much choice, but each has distinct strengths and weaknesses, making it a matter of determining your needs and finding a handheld computer to match.

MAKING YOUR CHOICE

If you simply want a replacement for your calendar and address book, take a look at any basic monochrome handheld that runs the Palm Operating Sytem. They are compact, easy to use, and the batteries last for months. Information is entered by drawing characters with a stylus on a screen area—a system called "Graffiti." The software instantly recognizes each character and shows the letter on the screen. Some characters are slightly different from the letters they represent, but the alphabet is easy to learn, and soon becomes second nature.

A PDA without a keyboard is called a palm PC and several manufacturers make full-color, multimedia-enabled versions. Although they are virtually a Windows laptop in the palm of your hand, the battery life suffers as a result. While a monochrome Palm OS PC may last up to 3 months on one charge or one set of batteries, a color-display palmtop may only last for 6 to10 hours of continuous use.

Connecting all PDAs to Windows is straightforward. Almost all PDAs come with software that needs to be installed on your PC to allow it to communicate with the handheld device. This software handles backups, synchronization, and file conversion to and from the PDAs. Most units come with a cradle that is plugged permanently into the PC's serial port or USB port. USB is much quicker and speeds up the copy and transfer data, especially large files like MP3s or images.

THE RIGHT SYSTEM

Even though the Pocket PC is a Microsoft Windows operating system, the Palm operating system links equally well to Windows. All allow you to synchronize your diary with Outlook or a similar PC organizer, convert text files to Word, spreadsheets to Excel, and databases to Access. It can be done automatically using the PDA software on your PC, or you can drag the PDA file into the appropriate PC program.

If you want to record sounds, play MPEG videos and MP3s, and view images in full color, you need a Pocket PC or Palm operating system PC. Pocket PCs include the Windows Media Player, which you can also download from

Microsoft (www.microsoft.com/windows/windowsmedia/en/download). It can play back MP3s through stereo headphones, even while you are using other functions on the PDA. You can play graphics-based games on both Palm OS and Pocket PC handhelds, although they will run

THE MAIN PDA MANUFACTURERS

Get the lowdown on the latest advances in portable computers at these sites.

**Casio
(www.casio.com/personalpcs)**
A wide choice of color PDAs, scanners, wrist PCs, and business-oriented handhelds.

**Compaq
(www5.compaq.com/products/handhelds)**
Compaq's iPaq and Aero handheld computers have color display on the top models.

**Hewlett Packard
(www.hp.com/jornada)**
Known mainly for home computers, HP's new Jornada range of PDAs takes on the world.

**Palm
(www.palm.com)**
Slimline PDAs with a range of capabilities and styles, plus a host of Palm applications.

**Handspring
(www.handspring.com)**
Palm OS computers with numerous add-ons, all in one slimline unit.

**Sony
(www.sonystyle.ca)**
The Clié is Sony's Palm OS-based contender in the handheld computers competition.

fairly slowly because of the number of resources they require. Some models let you plug in a digital camera and store photos on your PDA.

MP3s, MPEGs, and high resolution images use a lot of memory. Although most modern Palm OS PCs have 32Mb RAM, this is also used for software and all your data. For more memory, you can plug in memory cards to certain handhelds—available in 64, 128 and 192Mb versions. Sony's Clié supports the Memory Stick, Palm OS PDAs use the Secure digital card, and the Handspring Visors range use the Flash Springboard module. If you are using them to store music, keep in mind that you'll need at least 64Mb free to store an MP3 album.

Transferring files onto your PDA can be a lengthy process, especially if it's plugged into

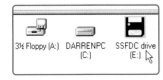

your PC's serial port. If you have a Pocket PC, it's far quicker to get a USB card reader

and plug your CompactFlash card into that. It then appears in My Computer and Windows Explorer as another drive to which you can drag your MP3 album.

SOFTWARE UPDATES

If you already have a PDA, check the Web for additional software. You can download some powerful and extremely useful software that can greatly enhance your PDA's functionality. Some add-ins allow you to store e-books and dictionaries and create presentation flip charts. Some are complete applications, such as fully functional spreadsheets and even global positioning system software so that you will never get lost again. All programs are first downloaded onto your PC from websites such as Handango (www.handango.com) and Palm (www.palm.com/ resources/shareware.html) for the Palm OS models. You then install them using the PDA's software.

Some PDAs with touch sensitive screens will run third party software capable of translating

handwriting into text. Only a few systems can read cursive handwriting— CalliGrapher for the Pocket PC platform is one of them. This speeds up data entry as you write normally on the screen, and every word is turned into text as it is completed.

If you have a compatible cellphone, you may be able to use it as a modem to connect your PDA to the Internet—although currently it's somewhat slow and awkward with connections speeds of around 14Kbps. Check with your PDAs manufacturer about which phones work with your device. You have to set up your dial-up account in a similar way to Windows, but then you can connect anywhere that your cellphone can get a signal.

HOW TO: DOWNLOAD AND INSTALL A PALM SPREADSHEET PROGRAM

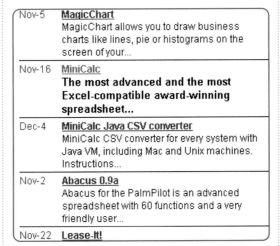

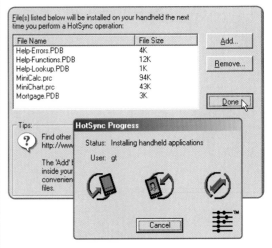

1 Make sure your Palm Desktop software is installed on your PC. Log on to the Internet and go to the Palm website (www.palm.com/ resources/shareware.html). Click on the Business & Productivity link, and then on Spreadsheet.

2 Choose a spreadsheet program that is compatible with your Palm PDA. Either click on the title to see more information or click on the .zip icon. The file will start to download. When the download is finished close your browser. Unzip the file if necessary.

3 Double-click your Palm Desktop icon. Click the Install button. In the Install Tool window, click on Add and locate the Palm files. Double-click each file and click Add to include more. Click Done and OK. When you HotSync your Palm, the program will be installed.

HELPLINES

Sometimes—no matter how much you know about computers—it's useful to call a helpline when you come across a problem.

Before you call a helpline, first dig out all the relevant information you can about your computer. The person on the other end will want to know precisely what version of the software you are having a problem with and what version of Windows you are using. Your helper will also want accurate details about your PC, such as the CPU, amount of RAM, hard drive space, and so on.

Try to call the hotline number from in front of your PC. It's likely that you can quickly work

PROTOCOLS
Computer protocols enable PCs to communicate across networks.

After installing networking hardware, you need to make sure each Windows PC knows how to communicate with the others. The different languages used are called protocols. There are three common network protocols that you need to be aware of:

IPX/SPX is the fastest of the three common protocols, and it is used for many networkable games.

NetBEUI is an IBM protocol, and it is easy to setup. It is a very fast protocol when used on small LANs and is ideal for a small home network.

TCP/IP is the Internet protocol, available on a variety of networks. It's fast becoming the protocol of home LANs, because modern messaging software and many online games require an assigned IP address to operate.

through the problem in a few simple steps as the helpline assistant talks you through. Make sure your computer is only running essential programs so nothing slows it down, and—if appropriate—is set up to recreate the problem.

Write down the exact text of any error messages that constantly recur. Have this text handy when you phone the helpline. Make sure you have details of the precise version number of your software, and details about your operating system and hardware too.

Record the conversation using your answering machine or a cassette recorder with a simple suction-cup attachment on your phone. This will leave you free to concentrate on the problem without worrying about taking down complex notes for future reference. Remember you might be paying a premium for the helpline call and want to extract the maximum value from it.

If you have to reboot your computer to effect any changes that the helpline has talked you through, hold down the Shift key while you click on

Restart. This saves a few seconds, because just Windows restarts, and your PC doesn't switch off completely.

Software and hardware manufacturers should have comprehensive websites that deal with common problems. Can't locate a specific troubleshooting part of a site? Look for a frequently asked questions (FAQ) page. The helpline staff might refer you to the website anyway, especially if you need to download a software "patch" to fix your program or accessory.

HOME NETWORKING

For any home with more than one PC, a home network is a great idea.

A home network also gives older equipment a whole new lease of life. If you have a PC without a CD-ROM drive, for instance, it's hard to install new software easily. With a home network, you can log on to the PC that does have a CD-ROM drive and use that.

Networking introduces a new range of jargon into the world of computers! A home network is known as a LAN, which means Local Area Network. If you connect two or more PCs together—and share files and peripherals— it's called a peer-to-peer network.

Offices usually have a client-server network, which uses one or more big, fast computers called servers—for keeping files, handling printing, e-mail, and so on—while the client machines are where people sit and work.

Each computer on the network needs a network card. These are rarely included on home PCs, and you need to open your computer up to install one. The cost of a network card varies from a few dollars to hundreds of dollars, and so does its performance and features. The least expensive require directly cabling each PC. However, there are other, more flexible options available: some use radio waves, some use your phone lines, and others your home power lines.

Network cards are available in different speeds. You can purchase them in either 10Mbps or 100Mbps, or you can purchase cards that can operate at both speeds—sold as 10/100 cards—which are the best value.

Before you buy a card or other hardware to go inside your PC make sure you have a spare PCI or ISA slot. To tell the difference between a PCI and an ISA slot on your motherboard is easy. The PCI slots are white, and ISA slots are black.

If you have more than just two computers to network, plug all the cables into a hub. Hubs are generally placed in a centralized location and cables are run from each computer to the hub in a star shape. When using a hub, a big advantage is that a problem with one of the PCs or network cards will not affect the other users on the network.

Get hold of a home network kit. Prices for these—which include a hub, two Ethernet cards, and a cable—are under a $100 for a 10Mbps kit. Dual-speed 10/100Mbps kits are available for only a little more.

Terk LeapFrog Audio/Video Distribution System
LF-10S
1 Qty
Add $139.95
Click here to view a printable brochure
Complete System Includes
(1) Transmitter, (1) Receiver, (3) A/V dubbing cables, (2) AC adapters, (2) phone cords,

HOME CONTROL

With home control devices attached to your PC, you can use it to control your lights, heating, TV, video, and many other things.

You can start controlling your home with a special kit that includes a module that you plug into your computer and smaller satellite units that plug directly into your electrical outlets. You then plug each item you want to control into a wall outlet unit.

Home control is modular, so you can buy a command unit and build up additional equipment as you need it. Start off by using it to operate a few features in your rooms, perhaps the lighting and drapes. When appropriate, add monitoring equipment so you can use your PC to monitor pool and aquarium temparatures, and other aspects of your home. Home Controls (www.homecontrols.com) is a useful website, offering this type of computer automation for monitoring home and property.

Security is often a worry, especially when you're away from home. Add some Closed Circuit TV cameras (CCTV) to your security system, and with PC-based home control you can see what's happening in your house from any other Internet-connected PC. Home Controls supply video surveillance cameras of this kind as part of their home security merchandise.

If you already have some home automation, you might want to try HAI Web-Link software (www.homeauto.com). Add space-age voice control using HAL2000 speech recognition software. Now you'll be able to call your computer and say "lights on" for example, so the house looks occupied, or "heating on" to warm it up.

Some control systems have a complex user interface that makes you feel as though you're a NASA scientist if you've managed to even turn the lights on without any problems! To avoid this unwelcome scenario, it's a good idea to spend some time looking for a model with a friendly, Windows-style interface.

HOW TO: SHARE A SINGLE INTERNET CONNECTION

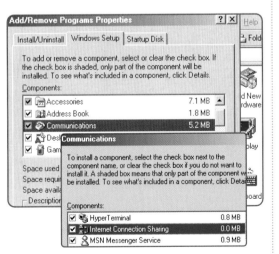

1 Any PC on your home network can access the Internet through a shared PC with direct Internet access. On all the PCs involved, click Start → Settings → Control Panel, and double-click on the Add/Remove Programs icon.

2 On the Windows Setup tab, select Communications, then click on the Details button below. In the Communications dialog box, check the Internet Connection Sharing box, and then click OK twice.

3 The Home Networking Wizard guides you through configuring your computers. Select the appropriate Internet connection option for each PC: connect through another PC on your home network or directly from that PC.

JOYSTICKS

The keyboard—usually with over 100 keys and a delicate mouse—can take some fun out of action games, but a joystick is the perfect tool.

If a cheap and cheerful joystick came with your PC, consider buying a new one with the latest features because it will work better with your games. If your current joystick is so lightweight that you can't adjust its sensitivity or alter its performance, consider getting a new one.

For real fun, try a force-feedback joystick. Imagine if you had to make a hard landing with a real aircraft on a bumpy runway without feeling the pull and tug of the controls! That's the kind of lifeless response you get with a normal joystick, but a force-feedback version behaves like a real joystick in a real aircraft.

SITES FOR JOYSTICK MANUFACTURERS
Here's a selection of the best-selling joysticks on the market.

Gravis (www.gravis.com)
Check out the Xtermiator, Eliminator, and Destroyer joysticks and gamepads listed at this site.

Logitech (www.logitech.com)
Lists many different controllers, including Logitech's Wingmaster joysticks.

Quickshot (www.quickshot.com)
Offers a wide range of game controllers for you to browse through.

**Sidewinder
(www.microsoft.com/products/hardware/sidewinder/newsw.htm)**
Microsoft claims the Sidewinder will take your favorite flight, combat, and action games to another level.

To make your joystick work more effectively, go to Start → Settings → Control Panel and click on the Gaming Options icon. Click on the joystick you want to adjust and select Calibrate. Follow the on-screen prompts to set up the joystick correctly. If you use your joystick everyday, it's best to do this every few months.

Some joysticks use motion-sensing technology. This means that you only have to move your hand in the air, while holding onto the gamepadlike joystick, for the roll-and-pitch commands to take effect. The joystick gives you the opportunity to become more physically involved in the action of the game.

Voice control for games is possible using Microsoft's Game Voice controller. You can operate your favorite games by telling your PC what you want to operate, while also using the control to chat to other players over a network or Internet connection.

If you are serious about being a computer pilot, replace your joystick with a yoke. These are designed to look and feel as if you are at the controls of a real aircraft, from a Cessna 152 to a Boeing 747. You can also add foot pedals, used to operate the rudder and the nosewheel steering in most light aircraft. Remember, though, that most military combat aircraft use a joystick, and the fly-by-wire Aerospatiale Airbus A340 has replaced its yoke with a left-hand joystick that is very similar to the average home PC device.

CH Products FlightSim Yoke USB

⇨ See also **Software: Games.**

KEYBOARDS

More options than you might think possible are available with the humble keyboard.

Often the keyboard supplied with your PC is a budget model, but upgrading to a good-quality version is an inexpensive and worthwhile consideration. Check out the dozen or more replacement models in computer stores to find one you like.

Don't forget to prop your keyboard up! Keyboards usually have two folding legs at the back or underneath, which places the keys in the optimum position for your hands. It's surprising how often this stand goes unnoticed.

The Num Lock key can be a constant source of confusion. The numerical keypad—the 17 keys on the right side of the keyboard—won't work if the Num Lock light is not on. To operate the Num Lock, press the Num Lock key once and the keypad is operative again!

Pressing the Print Screen key makes a copy of whatever is open on-screen on the Windows Clipboard. To use it, open a graphics-capable program, such as Paint or Paint Shop Pro, and click on Edit → Paste.

When you add words to previous sentences, do you find that you end up typing over them instead of just inserting them? This means that you have accidentally pressed the Insert key. To correct this, simply press the Insert key again but make sure that the letters "OVR" at the bottom in your word-processing software are no longer in bold.

Do you hate all the wires snaking round your desk? Then use a wireless keyboard. Some work using line-of-sight infrared light, while others use radio waves. The latter are superior if you want to try typing in bed, although this would be an ergonomically poor position! Wireless keyboards are useful in those situations where you want to be farther away from the computer than an extension cord would reach. They are ideal for hyperactive students who like to move around a work area.

If you allow your kids to use the PC, then a cheap "emergency" keyboard is a great idea. In the event of an accident, the spare keyboard could save you from a keyboard-less holiday period— and maybe a couple of missed deadlines, too.

Do you tend to dribble your double-decaf? Try a spill-proof keyboard, such as the Memorex TS1000 (available from www.memorex.com or www.saleonall.com). Alternatively, spill-proof your existing keyboard by using an inexpensive plastic membrane, available from your PC dealer. A much better idea altogether, though, would be to make the area around your computer into a "No Drinks" zone.

Try a Microsoft Natural keyboard. This type of keyboard is fitted with the traditional QWERTY key layout (originally designed to slow down typists so old-fashioned typewriters could cope), but splits the area that's covered by your left and right hands into two, so that your fingers are allowed to fall more naturally on the keys. The keyboard has no special requirements—you just have to acclimatize yourself to the new layout.

Do away with your mouse! Instead, look for a keyboard that incorporates a touchpad or rollerball, like the ones found on laptops. If the keyboard is also wireless, then it will make hiding all the unattractive hardware clutter that always comes with a computer so much easier.

LABEL PRINTERS

This dedicated second printer speeds up the label-making process.

Special label printers are ideal for printing multiple sets of labels. Label printers operate alongside your existing printer and they are connected to your computer via a data cord. You can print labels in quantity for business packages or for large mailings, and you can also use a label printer for envelopes, disks, CDs, and 35mm slides.

Most dedicated label printers use thermal technology and require a special thermal paper that reacts to heat to produce a black-and-white output. With this advanced thermal technology, label printers can print out a label in just a few seconds, and you won't ever need to purchase ink or toner.

There are two different types of thermal printers: the direct thermal printer and the thermal transfer printer. Direct thermal printers use paper that is treated and turns black with heat. The advantage of this type of printer is that it needs no ribbon. The thermal transfer printer takes untreated paper and needs a thermal transfer ribbon. This printer is designed to print at a lower temperature, which will give your print head a longer life.

Microsoft Word makes printing onto sheets of ready-made labels a practical proposition. Even though the software might be configured to work with a particular brand of labels—such

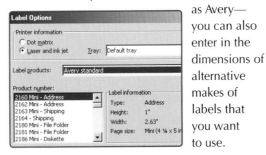

as Avery— you can also enter in the dimensions of alternative makes of labels that you want to use.

Some label printers can be used to print commemorative stickers or even real stamps. The U.S. Postal Service can use a barcode, such

as Information Based Indicia (IBI), to process your mail extra-efficiently. You can log onto E-stamp (www.e-stamp.com) to learn more about this and printing commemorative stickers or real stamps.

Use a shortcut in Microsoft Word to print an address on a label. To do this, simply highlight the address in the Word document and click on Tools → Envelopes and Labels. From Labels, click on Options to get a list of available label products. Alternatively, you can create your own label just by clicking on the Details button and entering in the measurements.

⇨ See also **Software: Labels.**

LABEL PRINTER SITES
Here's some information about where to buy your label printer.

**AArmedia
(www.aarmedia.com)**
Displays printers from Zebra, Datamax, Eltron, and many more models—plus a toll-free number.

**Dynascan
(www.dynascan.com/
label_printers.html)**
Offers links to major manufacturers for printers and label design software.

**Graphic Products
(www.graphicproducts.com)**
Information and specifications for label printers, plus labeling systems. Graphic Products supplies and service for discontinued models, too.

**Seiko smart
(www.seikosmart.com)**
Information and specifications on Seiko's Smart label printers, including where to buy, and all about buying labels online.

LAPTOPS

Recent technological advances in hard drive and processor miniaturization have made laptops as powerful as desktop computers, yet they are small enough to fit inside a briefcase. Improvements in battery capacity have increased longevity, making the modern laptop a truly portable device.

LAPTOP ADVANCES

Need a computer on the go? Displays that were previously tiny and unclear and could not display high-resolution graphics are now razor sharp and capable of rendering 3D accelerated graphics in 32-bit color. And there's a huge range of peripherals designed to make the laptop PC as versatile and functional as its bigger desktop brother. You can put together a multimedia presentation, with video and sound, connect to the Internet using an infrared link to your mobile phone, or just sit and watch a DVD movie wherever and whenever you like. Pick up your e-mails anywhere there's a phone connection, and take your vacation photos to show relatives and let them choose which ones they would like printed.

Today's laptops have a much greater battery capacity which makes them better travelers, although they don't like to be away from a connector for too long. A laptop (also known as a notebook) can be stowed away on a shelf or under a chair rather than taking up an entire desktop, which is often the case with a PC.

CHOOSING A PORTABLE PC

Buying a laptop can be tricky. There is a wide selection of configurations and options available. The choice depends on what you intend using your laptop for. Modern screens can easily display a Word document or spreadsheet, and a 400MHz processor with 64Mb RAM and a 6Gb hard drive is adequate for everyday use. However, if you want to create multimedia presentations, play games that require 3D acceleration, or run several applications at one time, you'll need a TFT (Thin Film Transfer) screen, a faster processor, and at least 128Mb RAM and a 3D accelerated graphics adaptor.

Construction quality is crucial in a laptop because all the components are so highly engineered. Unlike a desktop PC, most of the hardware on a laptop is built in to the system and therefore can't be easily replaced if it fails. It is best to avoid unnecessary extra features because each one brings with it an increased chance of something going wrong.

Making the right connections. For ease of connecting peripheral devices, make sure any laptop you consider has at least one USB (Universal Serial Bus) port and one Type II PC card slot as well as a serial and a parallel port. Without these, you won't be able to expand your laptop with extra PC card devices or easily connect it to networks, external drives, and printers. USB gives you fast access to all sorts of peripheral devices, from external CD drives to printers and scanners. A PC card slot allows you

to insert or connect miniaturized versions of hardware that you would normally install inside a desktop PC—such as a modem, network card, and additional hard drive storage.

Handle with care. Laptops require more care than standard PCs. The screen is especially fragile and should be closed gently and slowly. Always hold the unit firmly, plug in devices carefully, and never jar or handle a laptop roughly. Keep your laptop away from heat sources; never leave it in the sun or by a sunny window. Don't lock it in the trunk of your car even on a moderately warm day.

Even with the most advanced 3D graphics card in your laptop, you will be restricted to less sophisticated, non-3D accelerated games because most 3D games are optimized for a 16Mb graphics card. However, some top-of-the-line laptops now include a DVD drive and DVD decoder chips. This means that you can watch a DVD movie wherever you are.

ON THE ROAD

If you're planning to use your laptop on the road, there are several adjustments you can make to maximize its battery life. Windows lets you adjust the power options settings to reduce power consumption while you're not using your laptop. To access these settings, go to Start ➔ Settings ➔ Control Panel and select Power Options. Choose the Advanced tab and then select either Hibernate or Standby. Hibernation shuts down the computer but keeps a record of all the programs and documents you have open, so that when you press a key, your Desktop is restored, with programs and data intact. Standby is a basic power-saving mode where your hard drive and monitor are shut down. Set separate Hibernation and Standby times for when your laptop is

When I press the power button on my com
Hibernate

When I press the sleep button on my comp
Stand By

running on batteries or when it's plugged in. By carefully adjusting these settings, it's possible to significantly prolong your laptop's battery life.

Set up your dial-up accounts so that you can use them when you're at home or away. Include the dial-out digit, often 9, so that you don't have to modify your ISP's access number when you leave home. If you stay in accommodation with no access to telephone sockets, you can use an infrared or cable link to a cellphone—as long as it's compatible with your system.

You'll need to install the correct drivers and software to be able to use your PC with a cellphone, so that, in effect, Windows will see it as a modem. They are usually downloadable from the phone manufacturer's website. Data transfer speeds will be limited to 9,600Kb per second, adequate for e-mails and basic Internet access, but browsing the Web will take a lot longer, and you may run up high calling charges.

TALKING WITH YOUR DESKTOP

Getting your data from your laptop to your primary PC is simple if it all fits onto one floppy disk. With the increasing demands made by sophisticated software such as Office and graphics and multimedia programs, files often exceed the floppy's 1.44Mb capacity. Other options for data transfer are to use a Zip drive—available in 100Mb or 250Mb formats—or another removable media device, such as a CD recorder. Make sure any you get is a USB model.

If you need to regularly move data back and forth between your laptop and desktop PC, a PC card network adaptor will allow you to connect to a small home network. Copying or moving files is then a simple matter of dragging and dropping the files using Windows Explorer. If you buy a wireless network card, you don't even need to plug in cables to make a connection.

Windows also allows a direct PC-to-PC connection without having a home network. To do this, you need a serial or parallel cable to

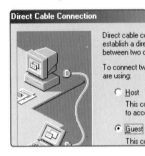

connect the PCs and Direct Cable Connection (DCC) Software— which is part of the Windows program.

Direct Cable Connection

Direct cable co
establish a dire
between two c

To connect tw
are using:

○ Host
This co
to acce

⦿ Guest
This co

However, the direct connection is much slower than a PC card network, so you won't be able to use either PC to its full capacity while files are being copied across.

Windows' My Briefcase can keep files on your laptop and desktop PC in sync. Drag the files you want into the Briefcase and copy it to your laptop. When you've worked on the files, click on the Update button in the Briefcase toolbar to synchronize the files. If the My Briefcase icon isn't on your Desktop, install it from your Windows CD-ROM.

YOUR AGING LAPTOP

If you have an older laptop without a built-in CD-ROM drive, your Windows installation files will be stored on your hard drive. When you install a new device, you won't need to insert the Windows CD. However, this can be a disadvantage if you want to upgrade Windows or create an emergency startup floppy disk (see Windows: Startup Disk). To do either, you'll need to attach an external CD-ROM drive to access the Windows operating system files.

➭ See also **Windows: Networks; Hardware: Batteries, Home Networking, Telephone Connections, USB,** and **Zip Drives.**

ADDITIONAL SUPPORT FOR YOUR LAPTOP
Extras you can get for your laptop.

- External USB or PC Card CD-ROM for laptops without built-in CD-ROM drives.

- A solid carrying case with extra storage for the power cord with adaptor.

- An external mouse because some people find the touch pad or wiggle stick included with laptops awkward to use. First check what type of connector your laptop has, either PS2 or USB.

- A wireless network PC card, coupled with a matching transceiver in your PC allowing you to connect anywhere without cables.

- If you have more than one USB device and only one slot, you can get a USB hub. It allows you to attach more than one USB device at a time, which is a great advantage.

MEMORY

Decide how much memory you need and assign or add more.

Don't confuse memory with hard drive space. Hard drive space is where your programs and files are stored all the time, while RAM memory is where your PC works with programs and data. The more memory you have, the better your computer will perform.

If anything is certain about computer memory, it's that no matter how much memory your computer already has, there never seems to be enough once you really start using it.

The amount of memory you need for your PC depends on the kind of tasks you are performing and the sort of software you are using. A modern spreadsheet program would be comfortable with 12Mb, but remember that the Windows program itself requires plenty of memory. You need to choose memory that matches the speed of your PC's motherboard. This is difficult to tell from inspection, so it's best to contact your PC supplier and ask them about the right speed to buy for your upgrade. Many applications—especially those handling graphics—require at least 64Mb, but are happier with 128Mb. Consider adding more memory if you have less

than 128Mb on your machine and regularly work with graphics or use multimedia software.

Think you need more memory? If your PC is slow—and you are constantly closing programs to keep working—then you could probably use more memory. First, you need to know the type of memory you require. Most modern computers use SDRAM (Synchronous Dynamic Random Access Memory), a Dual In-line Memory Module (DIMM). Some old PCs, however, use Single In-line Memory Modules (SIMMs), a slower form of memory. To check what type your PC uses, go to Kingston's Memory Assessor (www.kingston.com/tools), where you can enter in your operating system and find out its specifications.

You need to choose memory that matches the speed of your PC's motherboard. This is difficult to tell from inspection, but you'll find the information in the documentation that came with your PC. Alternatively, ask your PC supplier about the right speed to buy for your upgrade.

Make sure you remember to save as you work. Anything that is in RAM memory when your PC freezes or crashes will probably be lost. However, the data saved on the hard drive will still be safe.

Some software can impair a PC's performance by causing a "memory leak." When a Windows application shuts down, it surrenders its resources, which means it should not leave anything in RAM. However, some programs might not release all the memory, leaving less available when another program starts. To recover lost memory, exit Windows and reboot.

To find a leaking program, check the amount of free RAM when you first start up the PC. To do this, go to Start ➔ Settings ➔ Control Panel, double-click on System, and then click the Performance tab. Look at the System Resources unit and write down the value. Now start a program, use it normally, then close it and check the resources again. Compare the amounts. If the resources don't

System Properties			
General	Device Manager	Hardware Profiles	Performance
Performance status			
Memory:	192.0 MB of RAM		
System Resources:	74% free		
File System:	32-bit		
Virtual Memory:	32-bit		
Disk Compression:	Not installed		
PC Cards (PCMCIA):	No PC Card sockets are installed.		

return to a figure close to the original value, the program you just closed is probably the culprit. To correct the leak, go to the software maker's website and download patches or updates.

MICROPHONES

Here are some tips on selecting and using a microphone.

Microphones are often bundled with soundcards or computer packages. And more interesting and useful programs to make the most of them are becoming available. For example, you can record spoken comments as a sound file and embed the file into a spreadsheet. You can also use your PC as an answering machine. Conferencing software can enable two people to call each other through their PCs, and simultaneously talk, share data, and see video images of each other. And if you use instant messaging and chat programs—such as Yahoo!, Chat, or ICQ—you can send voice messages as well as text.

There are programs that enable voice interaction with your computer. One of the most exciting is speech recognition, which allows for dictation into any Windows application, such as WordPerfect or Microsoft Word. Check Dragon products (www.dragonsys.com) or ZdNet (www.zdnet.com/products) online. You'll never have to type again!

Use a PC headset to add a microphone and earphones to your computer. A headset plugs into the speaker and the microphone jacks onto the back of PC cards. The connectors are marked with icons that match the icons on the PC sockets. Make sure you purchase a headset with a cord at least 10 feet long so you can work comfortably, especially if the system unit is under your desk.

Microsoft NetMeeting—included with Windows—enables users to communicate by voice over the Internet. Internet games that previously used text chat windows for communication now allow players to communicate with their voice in real time, just as if they were in the same room.

Windows' Sound Recorder can be used to make your own recordings. Go to Start → Programs → Accessories → Entertainment → Sound Recorder. Click the button with the red circle to start recording, and the black square button to stop.

⇨ See also **Software: Sound Recorder** and **Voice Recognition.**

MIDI

Musical Instrument Digital Interface (MIDI) lets your computer work just like any musical instrument.

MIDI lets you connect electronic musical instruments to your PC. You can use a MIDI keyboard to "play" the synthesizer chip that's built into your PC's sound card. You can also use PC software to make compositions and play sounds on the MIDI keyboard.

Press any key on a piano and a sound will occur; aim the tip of a drumstick firmly at a snare drum

and—bang! MIDI interprets any action like this as a "Note On" state. Most instruments will also allow a musician to stop the sound at any time. MIDI interprets this as a "Note Off" action.

Many piano-style keyboards that have their own built-in sounds can be controlled by a computer via MIDI. These keyboards vary in price from hundreds to thousands of dollars. A less expensive keyboard might have a more limited number of octaves available. And while a full, piano-sized keyboard consists of 88 keys, most inexpensive versions are made up of just 48 keys.

There are two main types of MIDI software. One of these is a notation program, which is designed to help musicians print out their finished work in manuscript form. The other type of program is sequencing software, which enables you to mix different segments of music. Some powerful sequencing programs are now available for use in conjunction with a MIDI keyboard.

Cakewalk produces a range of exciting programs to help you compose any kind of music, from the simplest of pop tunes to more ambitious pieces of classical music. You can

create audio for CDs, film or video soundtracks, multimedia games, live stage sound, and Internet music delivery. To find out more about the service and to download trial versions of software, visit their site (www.cakewalk.com).

If you have a keyboard with its own sounds, consider how compatible those sounds are with those of other keyboards. There is a standard set of sounds, known as General MIDI, which many home computers use. If your computer uses General MIDI, you will be able to share your MIDI files with others as well as download files and hear them correctly.

Your soundcard is the key. The quality of music varies greatly between soundcards. Although any soundcard can recognize a MIDI file, each will play it slightly differently—much like different musicians interpreting the same music each in his or her own way.

⇨ See also **Internet: Music.**

HOW TO: ADD A MIDI KEYBOARD TO YOUR PC

(1) You can add an inexpensive MIDI controller keyboard to your computer very easily. When you press the keys, MIDI signals are sent to your PC, and you'll be able to hear music from the PC's speakers.

(2) You'll need a MIDI soundcard adaptor cable to attach the keyboard to the PC. The end that fits into your keyboard will either have a 5 pin connector or be split into two connectors marked in and out. If you need to buy a cable, check your keyboard first.

(3) Plug the other end of the MIDI cable into the joystick socket at the back of your PC . When the keyboard has been securely connected, use the CD-ROM that came with your keyboard to install the appropriate MIDI software onto your computer.

MODEMS

The term "modem" comes from two words: MOdulator—DEModulator, which describes exactly what a modem does.

A modem transforms digital data from your PC into analog format so that it can be sent down your phone line, then converted back into digital data by another modem at the other end.

The speed of a modem is measured in bits per second (bps) and refers to the number of bits (digital data that makes up, for example, a web page) that it can pass down a phone line in one second. The faster the speed, the quicker you can send and receive data. Most home PCs now come equipped with modems that work at up to 56Kbps (56,000 bits per second), which is the minimum you should consider buying.

In practice, modems will usually operate at slightly less than full speed due to blips on your phone line and "traffic jams" on the Internet. You can't receive data any quicker than it is being sent, but in order to use the Internet efficiently your modem should run at a speed of at least 33Kbps. To see your connection speed, hover your mouse over the dial-up icon in the System Tray on your Windows Taskbar.

Internal modems come in the form of a small circuit board that fits into an expansion slot in your PC's main unit in the same way as a sound or graphics card. The advantage of this type of modem is that they take up less space than an

external model. But don't forget this means using up one of your expansion slots, for which you may have other uses later on.

External modems are small boxes that plug into your computer via a serial or USB port. An external modem has the advantage of

portability—you can disconnect it easily from one PC to use on another but, obviously, it takes up more desk space and adds to your cord tangles. External modems have indicator lights to tell you that they're working properly, and many people prefer them for this reason.

Voice modems come with a built-in speaker and microphone, allowing you to use your PC as a phone very easily. With cheap international calls now available on the Internet, this could save you money on your phone bill. You can even set up your modem to act as an answering machine, to take calls in your absence. A switch allows you to choose between data and voice mode.

WinModem is an unusual type of modem because it is software driven and only works with Windows. If you're considering one of these: DON'T! Because they work off your Windows operating system, they can slow down your PC dramatically and are much harder to fix if something goes wrong.

 HOW TO: USE TWO MONITORS AT THE SAME TIME

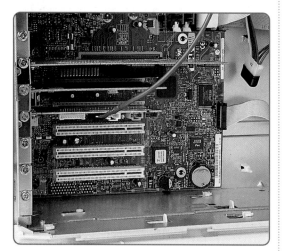

1 Before buying a second graphics card and monitor, you need to find out what type of slot is available. Most modern PCs have their first graphics card in the AGP slot, and the second must be a PCI card to fit in a PCI slot. Ask your PC supplier if you're not sure.

2 Switch off the PC, open it up and plug in the the second graphics card. Connect your second monitor and then switch on the second monitor and your PC. Windows Me will detect the new device. Begin the Installation Wizard to install your new graphics card.

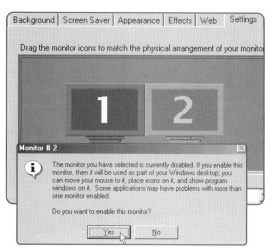

3 Adjust the settings for your new monitor. Right-click on the Desktop, select Properties and click on the Settings tab. Click on the picture of the second monitor and click Yes when asked to include the second monitor as part of your Desktop. Finally, click Apply.

MONITORS

Buying the right monitor is vital to enhance your enjoyment and the efficient use of your PC.

The first consideration when choosing a monitor is the screen size. This is measured in inches—across the diagonal—like a TV screen. Some of the screen is hidden behind the casing, so stating the actual screen size would be misleading. Manufacturers are required to quote the visible screen size, and this is the measurement to look for. A typical viewable screen size is 14 inches but the largest ones reach the size of an 11x17 inch sheet of paper. But size comes at a cost—a few extra inches can push the price up by a few hundred dollars. If you're going to be using graphics programs or multiple applications at once, however, a larger screen is worth considering.

Resolution indicates how many "pixels" or dots make up the screen image—the higher the number the better the image. Most of today's monitors can display at least 1,024x768 pixels and this is the minimum that you should consider buying.

The refresh rate tells you how many times the screen is redrawn every second. Poorer quality

monitors often have a low refresh rate, causing the screen to flicker annoyingly as it redraws itself. To avoid this, look for a refresh rate of at least 72Hz.

Many LCD screens employ a technology called Thin Film Transistor (TFT) screens. The result is a completely flat screen (as opposed to the curved edges of a standard tube). A flat panel takes up about 80 percent less space, is anti-glare, and more energy- and radiation-efficient.

If you want to hook up two monitors, you need to find out what type of slot is available before you go ahead and buy a second graphics card and monitor (see How To opposite). Most modern PCs have their first graphics card in the AGP slot, and the second must be a PCI card to fit in a PCI slot. Ask your PC supplier if you are not sure which one to get.

⇨ See also **Hardware: Flat Panel Screens.**

MOUSE

This small device is the interface between human and computer.

If you're forever getting your mouse-tail tangled up, it's worth considering a cordless option. A radio signal between the mouse and a base unit replaces the need for a cord. These models are more expensive, however.

If you don't have a lot of room on your desk to maneuver your mouse, try using a model with a scroll wheel. This will allow you to work your way up and down a document while keeping the mouse stationary. Similarly, a trackball mouse—with a large ball on top spun by your fingertip—eliminates the need to move your mouse around. Some mice even have extra buttons on the side that allow you to navigate quickly back and forth between web pages.

It's a good idea to clean the dust and dirt from the rollers of your mouse about once a month to ensure smooth operation. First, turn your mouse upside down and wipe over the

base with a clean cloth. Now twist the cover off the base of the mouse (usually counterclockwise) so that the ball falls out into your hand. Clean the ball with the cloth. Cellophane tape is also good for carefully removing dust or dirt. Use a cotton swab to clean the mouse ball socket, and then replace the ball. Twist the cover back into place. Never use sharp tools when cleaning; they could damage your mouse.

If you need to adjust the way your mouse works, go to Start ➔ Settings ➔ Control Panel, and double-click the Mouse icon. Use the Buttons, Pointer, and Pointer Options tabs to alter the mouse functions. If you're left-handed, switch the left and right mouse buttons.

⇨ See also **Software: Scroll Bars.**

NEWS AND REVIEWS
Keep up with what's hot and what's not for mice, modems, and monitors.

Maximum PC (www.maximumpc.com)
News and reviews on a wide variety of PC products, and the chance to subscribe to *Maximum PC* magazine.

PC Guide (www.pcguide.com)
A host of great PC reference material plus buyer's guides, discussion forums, and invaluable tips and tricks.

Tech TV (www.techtv.com/techtv/)
A great site for computer tips and tricks as well as reviews of the latest technology.

ZDNet (www.zdnet.com)
The website of *PC Magazine* offers reviews of the latest PC products and its own guide to the best PC sites around.

MP3 PLAYERS

If you love music on the move, try a portable MP3 player. You can select tracks in an instant, re-record as often as you like, with no moving parts.

Buy an MP3 player with a USB connection. All MP3 players link to a PC in one way or another to transfer the music files; however, the data will be transferred much faster using USB rather than a serial communications or COM port. A USB connection also means that you can plug in the player while Windows is running; the player will be instantly detected and the correct driver loaded.

Transferring files is as simple as copying from one folder to another on your PC. In Windows Explorer, drag and drop your recorded MP3s onto your connected MP3 player.

When buying an MP3 player you have a choice of built-in memory, a removable memory card, or a combination of both. It's usually best to purchase one with a built-in memory of 64Mb that you can add to using one of the standard memory-card formats, such as CompactFlash or SmartMedia.

Use good-quality MP3 software to record your MP3s. You can use Windows' own Media Player

or download another program. RealJukebox (at www.real.com) is a full-featured Windows multimedia player that will convert your music CDs to MP3 files, and to save time, can do it at up to five times the normal playing speed. Each of the tracks on the CD becomes a separate MP3 file, and—if the CD is by a popular artist—you will be able to automatically download the track names.

Choose the rate at which you want your MP3 tracks recorded. In Media Player go to Tools → Options, and click the CD Audio tab. The adjustment is in the Copying Settings section. The data rates can range from 32Kbps to 256Kbps. A 256Kbps rate records at the highest quality, but the resulting MP3 files will be eight times the size of those recorded at 32Kbps because there will be eight times the amount of data converted.

Experiment with the rate settings to get the balance between quality and file size that is best for you. If a typical CD takes up 44Mb at medium quality, it will easily fit onto a 64Mb memory card. However, at around 90Mb per CD—a higher setting—you will need more memory to fit the whole album onto your MP3 player.

If your MP3 player has a removable memory card, such as CompactFlash, SmartMedia, or a Sony Memory Stick, you can buy a card reader to plug into your PC's USB port. Rather than plugging in your MP3 player every time you want to transfer files, you can just slot the card into the reader, and it'll appear in My Computer or Windows Explorer as another drive letter. If you have two cards, you can still use your player while copying files onto the other memory card in the card reader.

If your PC has a CD burner installed, burn your MP3s onto recordable CDs. That way you

keep your hard drive free from hundreds of MP3 files, and your data will be safe if the PC breaks down. Some CD players can now decode MP3 files directly—giving you approximately 6–8 hours of play on a single CD. Keep track of your MP3 files by labelling your CDs carefully and keeping all your original MP3 tracks in clearly labelled folders on your computer's hard drive.

Each CD can store around 650Mb of data. This means you can store as much as ten albums of MP3 music on one CD. Even though recordable CDs are fairly robust, you should treat them like any other CDs and keep them in a cool, dark place, and handle them with care to avoid scratches and finger marks.

➪ See also **Software: MP3 Players.**

PALMTOP REQUIREMENTS
Palmtops vary in performance, functions, and capacity, so it's essential to map out your requirements before you buy.

Batteries: Batteries for palmtops can last from a few hours to two or more months. Some use AAA alkaline while others have built-in rechargables.

Screen: A palmtop can have a color screen or a black-and-white display. However, the color screens use batteries more quickly.

Sound: Some, but not all, palmtops have sound support which lets you record your own sounds through a built-in microphone.

Handwriting: Most palmtops use the Graffiti handwriting recognition program. You enter individual characters using a pointer on a touch-sensitive pad.

E-mail: If you want to collect your mail on the road, make sure you buy a palmtop with e-mail support and a modem.

PALMTOPS

A palmtop is a small computer, usually without a keyboard, that sits comfortably in your hand.

If you want a simple-to-use, yet powerful device with incredible battery life, try out the Palm OS series of palmtop computers. They have an intuitive interface, far-reaching performance, and a compact size, although at the cost of a little sophistication.

Palmtops link to your PC by a cradle attached to either the serial communications or the USB port. Some models use an infrared link. All let you back up and synchronize the palmtop with files on your PC at the touch of a button.

Palm OS computers use handwriting recognition software called Graffiti. You write, one character at a time, on a special area at

the bottom of the screen. Some of the characters, especially those that normally require you to lift your pen—such as T and F—look a little different. Although this might seem unnatural at first, the technique soon becomes second nature.

Need to enter lots of data on the road? Get an add-on keyboard for your palmtop. Most are lightweight and fold up to a compact, easy-to-carry size, although you can also get nonfolding models with the solid feel of a full-size keyboard. Just make sure it is compatible with your brand and model of palmtop. Try Palm.com (www.palm.com), Handango (www.handango.com), or Handspring (www.handspring.com).

Need to get hundreds of addresses onto your palmtop? No problem. All palmtops coordinate with your desk PC through a program called Palm Desktop, which you install on your PC. Palm Desktop is a calendar/address book/to-do program that you use on your PC much like Outlook. When you sync your palmtop with your desk PC, all the new information on each

one is copied onto the other, including appointments noted on your palmtop and the addresses on your PC. If you use the Outlook or Lotus Organizer manager, you can set your palmtop to sync with it instead of Palm Desktop.

Even if the built-in calendar, contact, and memo software are adequate on your palmtop, the Internet has lots of extra software to download and try out. The vast range of add-on programs include games, database, communications, and spreadsheet programs. Try Palm.com (www.palm.com), Palm Gear (www.palmgear.com), and Tucows (http://pda.tucows/palmsoft.html).

PLUG-AND- PLAY

Abbreviated as PnP, Plug-and-Play was developed by Microsoft and Intel to allow Windows to automatically set up hardware resources.

If you're buying a second-hand graphics adaptor, sound card, or other hardware, make

---

HOW TO: SEARCH FOR PLUG-AND-PLAY AND NON-PLUG-AND-PLAY DEVICES

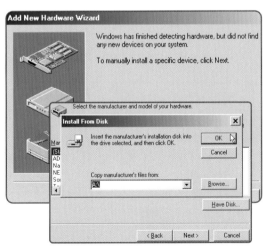

(1) Go to Start → Settings → Control Panel and double-click the Add New Hardware icon. Click on Next to start Windows searching for new Plug-and-Play devices on your system. If no device is found, manually specify a device from the generic list of products supplied.

(2) If the new device is non-Plug-and-Play, you can still install the drivers from the manufacturer's disc. Once the Plug-and-Play search is done, click on Next to start the non-Plug-and-Play search. Or select No, I want to select the hardware from a list and click Next.

(3) If you are manually specifying a device, or have completed Step 2, choose your hardware from the list shown. If you can't find it on the list, select Other devices and click the Have Disk button. Finally click OK to start the driver installation.

sure it is Plug-and-Play compatible. Otherwise, you may find you have to configure it by hand—by using tiny switches or jumpers on the card or by using special configuration software. It is also more difficult for Windows to actively manage non-Plug-and-Play hardware.

Each time Windows starts, it looks for new devices and should detect any new Plug-and-Play hardware attached. However, this sometimes goes wrong. If so, use the how to on the previous page to locate the device.

If your computer keeps crashing, or the Windows Desktop appears in only 16 colors and the icons are large, right-click on My Computer and choose Properties. Take a look in the Device Manager for any yellow exclamation marks on the list. Any device with such a mark has a "hardware conflict."

If you still have problems, use Help's useful Hardware Troubleshooter, selecting "I need to resolve a hardware conflict on my computer" to run through a series of possible solutions. If this fails, make sure you have the latest drivers for all your hardware. Take a look at the manufacturers' websites and make sure you get the latest driver for your version of Windows.

POWER FAILURES

Careful planning, in addition to software and hardware tools, will help you survive a blackout or brownout.

To minimize the chances of data loss and damage to your computer in the unfortunate event of a failure or "spike" in your electrical supply, regularly backup your applications, save your files, and use a surge protector or uninterruptible power supply. To correct loss of data from a power cut, use a disk-repair utility.

Surge protectors are the most basic line of defense when it comes to protecting your computer from fluctuations in the power supply. High-voltage spikes are not uncommon with domestic electricity, and they can fry your

computer, causing irreparable damage. A surge protector maintains a constant flow of electricity into your computer and its peripherals. Windows Me includes a System Restore program, which enables you to return your computer to its original state before the problem occurred.

Uninterruptible Power Supplies, known as UPSs, provide a more extensive form of protection. In the case of a brownout or blackout they not only incorporate surge and spike protectors but they also contain batteries that will power your computer and connected peripherals for a short period. This allows your PC to keep going long enough for you to save your work and shut down correctly, avoiding data loss and disk corruption.

Some UPSs come with software that lets your computer respond to a power failure by automatically saving your work and shutting down. This solution is popular for computers used as file servers in office networks.

Use Window's ScanDisk to restore your computer after a power failure. If files were being written to your hard disk when the power failed, the hard disk may have become corrupted. Fortunately, Windows' built-in ScanDisk program (see page 28), will fix some problems. ScanDisk automatically runs when Windows starts up if it has detected that Windows was not shut down properly.

Alternatively, run a disk-repair utility, such as Norton SystemWorks 2001 (www.norton.com) or McAfee Utilities (www.mcafee.com). Like ScanDisk, this type of program will scan your hard drive, looking for errors and inconsistencies, and will make repairs where possible. Although the utility cannot replace missing data, it can

often fix a damaged drive that, otherwise, would stop the computer from booting up.

Many applications have an AutoSave or AutoRecover option, which automatically saves open documents at specified intervals. You can

usually set the time in the program's Preferences dialog box. In Microsoft Word, for example, go to Tools ➔ Options and click on the Save tab. Set AutoRecover to save every 10 minutes. Now, no matter what happens to your power supply, you'll never lose more than 10 minutes of work.

If you are running a laptop computer from your main electrical supply, it will automatically switch to its rechargeable battery if a power failure occurs. Because laptops, like PCs, can be damaged by power surges, always connect them to the electrical supply via a surge protector. There are compact surge protectors available so that you don't have to lug around a lot of extra weight, and these even have phone line sockets. If you travel often to Mexico or the Caribbean, where brownouts, blackouts, and spike damage are a problem, you'd be wise to invest in a compact surge protector.

RSI DOS AND DON'TS
Increase your chances of avoiding Repetitive Strain Injury.

- **Do** sit up straight with your feet on the floor and your legs uncrossed.
- **Do** make sure your seat is at the correct height (forearms and thighs parallel to the floor) and your lower back is supported.
- **Do** make sure you have enough elbow room around you.
- **Do** take frequent breaks for stretching.
- **Do** pay attention to your body: If your wrists or neck aches, stop, get up from your desk, and stretch.
- **Do** use keyboard shortcuts.
- **Do** investigate voice-recognition software, particularly if you tend to get RSI.
- **Don't** crane your neck forward or to one side to view your monitor.
- **Don't** work in inadequate lighting or poorly ventilated rooms.
- **Don't** work for prolonged periods in the same position.
- **Don't** hammer on the keyboard.

Take preventative action by making regular backups of your hard drive. While hardware is replaceable, your data is probably not, so backup to a removable device like a Zip disk or a recordable CD. Store the backups somewhere safe, away from your computer.

➡ See also **Windows: Hard Drive.**

REPETITIVE STRAIN INJURY

Learn to change the way you work to reduce the chances of getting this hand-disabling condition.

Repetitive strain injury (RSI) occurs when a particular tendon or muscle is overused while being forced into an unnatural position. It is not only due to computer use; writers cramp and tennis elbow are also RSIs. But if you use a computer keyboard and mouse regularly, it's a good idea to minimize the risk of this painful condition. Remember that it is easier to prevent RSI than to cure it.

Adopt a good posture when you work. It is not just the way you use your hands and arms that causes problems, but anything that creates awkward angles in the body. Sit up straight with your feet flat on the floor slightly in front of your knees. Your chair and keyboard should be set at an ideal height where both your thighs and forearms are parallel with the floor.

If Windows is configured to display small fonts onscreen, you may find yourself hunched forward to see them clearly, increasing your chances of suffering with RSI. To avoid this, configure Windows to display larger fonts. Larger fonts can be displayed by right-clicking any empty area of the Desktop. In the pop-up menu select Properties ➡ Settings. Next click on the Advanced button

and choose Large Fonts from the drop-down menu in the Font Size section. Click OK to apply.

Don't rest your wrists on your desk while typing. Rather than resting your wrists in front of the keyboard and stretching your hands to reach the keys, use your arms to position your hands over the keyboard. Your wrists and hands should lie in a straight line with your arms; don't twist the wrists at an awkward angle.

Learn to use both hands, even if you have no ambition to become a touch typist. When pressing combinations of keys, use both hands rather than twisting one hand over the required keys.

Be gentle. Computer keyboards, unlike the typewriters that preceded them, do not need pressure or velocity to be applied to the keys. Similarly, when using a mouse, hold it gently and apply light pressure to the buttons. If your mouse has become difficult to control, debris has probably collected on the rollers. If so, remove the ball and clean off the dirt. Better still, get one of the new breed of optical mice, which have no moving parts.

Learn keyboard shortcuts. Rather than constantly losing your keyboard position by

moving your hand back and forth to the mouse, learn the shortcuts for the commands you use most often. Keyboard shortcuts are indicated next to the commands in the menus.

➡See also **Software: Keyboard Shortcuts; Hardware: Ergonomics** and **Mouse.**

RESET BUTTON

When should you use the Reset button to reboot your computer?

Don't use the reset button unless you are sure that your computer has stopped responding, and there is no other way to continue working. If a program has crashed or your computer does not respond to the mouse and keyboard, you may be able to recover from the situation without performing the "hard reset" that the reset button will perform.

Before you push the reset button, try the Ctrl+Alt+Delete key combination in Windows. You'll be prompted to terminate a program or perform a "soft reset." This, however, does not reinitialize your computer's hardware—which is sometimes necessary in the case of a serious crash.

Do use the reset button as an alternative to switching the computer on and off with the power switch. The advantage of the reset button is that it resets the computer's hardware without putting physical and electrical stress on the components within your computer. The reset button is also faster than using the power switch.

Remember—as soon as the reset button is pressed, any unsaved work will be lost. After a reset, Windows will also need to perform a scan of your hard drive to check for errors while Windows is running. For this reason, the button is often recessed slightly to avoid it being pressed accidently.

PRINTERS

Probably the most important peripheral to buy for your computer is a printer, and many models are available. Making the right choice depends on assessing your needs. For instance, will you use the printer for work, or just for home computing? Always try out the printers in the store before you buy.

TYPES OF PRINTERS

Color inkjet printers are by far the most common printers for the home. They are good for printing photos and web pages, as well as letters and other text. The printers work by pushing tiny droplets of ink onto the page. Inkjet printers can be quite slow at times and are often relatively noisy, especially when compared to laser printers. Ink cartridge prices vary between manufacturers but can be costly if you do a lot of printing.

How many cartridges? When buying a color inkjet printer you may face a choice between a one, two, or four-cartridge system. Beware of a printer that has only one cartridge; you will have to constantly swap color and black cartridges while printing. Two-cartridge printers cost very little more and include one black and

one color cartridge. But the best are four-cartridge printers. They produce the best colors and are most economical on ink over the long term.

Laser printers are ideal for high-quality printing. They use LEDs or a laser to mark out each page as a positive electrical charge on a rotating drum. Negatively charged toner (the ink) is put onto the drum and placed on the paper. A heated roller ensures that the toner sticks to the paper. Laser printers are fast and produce sharply detailed output. Although they can be cheaper to run than inkjets, they are more expensive and normally take up more space.

A toner cartridge on a laser printer lasts a long time, but when you need to replace it, it can be expensive. Check the price of replacement cartridges before you buy a printer.

Portable printers are powered by an internal battery and can be carried around with a laptop. However, the print quality is usually limited and, compared to other printers, they are expensive.

Other types of printers are available. Photo printers use special photographic paper, and are excellent for printing from digital cameras. Multifunction devices can fax, scan, photocopy, and print. These devices are useful if you spend time working from home or have relatively little space. But while they can do all these functions, they can't do any of them as well as a dedicated one-function device.

Don't forget your cable! Most printers don't come with a cable to connect them to your PC, so be prepared to pay out another $20 for one. USB versions are the most versatile but parallel port cables give a more secure connection. IEEE1284 is the industry standard in parellel port cables, and most new printers support both USB and parallel ports.

PRINTER PROBLEMS

If your printer does not seem to be connected, or it isn't printing, go to Start → Settings → Control Panel and look in Printers to see if the printer icon is displayed. If it isn't, check that all your printer cables are plugged in. Restart the computer. If Windows still doesn't recognize the printer, you may have faulty hardware. If the printer itself seems in working order, the cable may need replacing. Alternatively, you may need to reinstall your printer driver software (see How To: update or replace a driver, p. 305).

If the text prints in wrong place on a page, you may need to change the paper size or margins. Your printer software might have paper size

PRINTER PLACES
Most printer manufacturers have an established online presence.

Brother (www.brother.ca)
Featuring an ample array of printers.

Canon (www.canon.ca)
Can and do provide printers for all sorts of jobs and tasks for the home and office.

Epson (www.epson.com)
Supplies a wide range of models for the demanding home computer market.

Hewlett Packard (www.canada.hp.com)
Pick and purchase a printer online.

IBM (www.printers.ibm.com)
A good bet if you plan on printing a heavy workload at home.

Lexmark (www.lexmark.com/canada)
Just click on the Home Printing Center link or the Lexmark Store.

options, but check your software as well. For example, in Microsoft Word 2000, go to File → Page Setup to change the document's paper-size or margin settings, and other features.

Many modern printers issue a warning when the ink cartridge gets low, and they also often have an ink status gauge that shows how full a cartridge is. You can usually continue using a cartridge for a while after the printer warns you to replace it—just have a new one on hand.

One common printer problem is a paper feed error, where a sheet gets stuck in the printer's rollers. If this happens, you should see an on-screen warning, telling you what to do. Usually it is just a matter of removing the paper.

If your printer's software becomes out-of-date, you could have problems getting the printer to work with the latest applications. All the

Download Drivers

main printer manufacturers have websites (see box opposite) with updated drivers available for downloading free, so keep a regular check on your manufacturer's website.

SPECIAL PRINTING

Most printers can print labels on standard letter-sized sheets, and there are dozens of label sizes to choose from. Always print a test sheet on plain paper to check that your software is printing correctly. If you have an inkjet printer you can use labels sold for either inkjet or laser printers, but if you have a laser printer you should use only laser labels.

Use your printer's manual feed for tasks such as a printing on special paper or card, labels, a letterhead, or a transparency. Many printers also have a slot for envelopes.

Use the right paper for the job. Although you can print on standard letter-quality or copier paper from any stationery store, specialty paper

can really help. If you are designing greeting cards, for example, look for higher quality paper meant for printing color images and photos.

⇨ See also **Software: Labels** and **Printing; Hardware: Label printers.**

 HOW TO: SET UP THE PRINTER

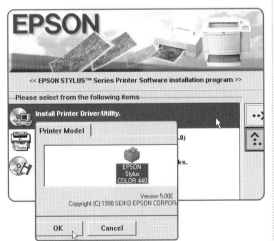

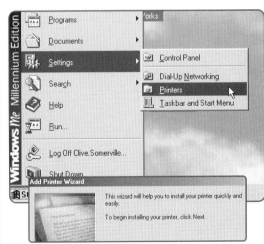

(1) Following the manufacturer's instructions provided with your computer, connect your printer to the PC's printer port using the cable recommended. Depending on the printer, this may be a parallel port (requiring a 1284 bidirectional cable) or a USB cable port.

(2) Install the printer drivers—the software that came with your printer. With most modern printers this is pretty straightforward—you just insert the CD that came with the printer and follow the on-screen instructions.

(3) If no instructions appear, go to Start → Settings → Printers, double-click on the Add Printer icon, then follow the Printer Wizard's on screen instructions for installing the driver. Your PC will now automatically detect that a new hardware device has been attached.

SCANNERS

N ot so long ago, scanners were a very expensive computer peripheral, but they are now substantially lower in price. As a result, scanners have become a very popular computer add-on. With a scanner by your side, you can send photos to friends and family around the world via e-mail.

TYPES OF SCANNERS

Flatbed scanners are the most common type. They can scan a single sheet at a time, but are large. Even slim, streamlined models take up a fair amount of desk space. Although many can't cope with any item larger than legal-sized paper, this type of scanner is usually fine for personal use in the home.

Business card scanners are small and have optical character recognition (text-recording) software built in. They are expensive but can send business card information to your personal organizer software so you don't have to type it in.

High-resolution flatbed scanners with a transparency attachment are ideal for designers and photographers who want to scan slides or negatives. Smaller versions, which can handle originals up to 4x5 inches, are considerably less expensive than full-sized models.

Handheld scanners are good for use on the move but are tricky to operate.

If your PC has a USB port, get a scanner with a USB connector to take advantage of the speed it offers. You cannot chain-link a USB scanner to a printer, however, so if you want to be able to do

HOW TO: SCAN AN IMAGE

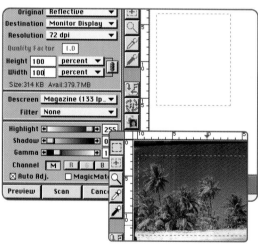

① Place the original image you want to scan on the scanner and close the lid. Start the scanner's software (many scanners have a simple one-touch button to do this) and the image will start to scan.

② You may get a previewed image first. If you are not happy with the image, change the image resolution and any other settings. You may be able to alter the colors scanned, the actual size of scan, the crop of the image, or to apply filters to sharpen or blur the image.

③ Get a second preview with your new settings. When you are satisfied with the preview, complete the scan. You can then use photo-editing software for the final touches to an image. You might want to change the size of the picture to fit or edit the colors.

this, you will need a parallel port scanner. These are becoming less popular, so you might be able to find a real bargain.

TERMINOLOGY AND SPECS

Scanners quote their image resolution as a key feature, so it is worth understanding what this means. The abbreviation used to describe image resolution is dpi, which stands for dots per inch. In an image scanned at 300x300dpi every square inch is made up of 90,000 dots.

Some scanners quote an interpolated resolution as well as an optical one. The optical resolution is the true resolution at which a scanner scans. Interpolated resolution is a higher resolution, achieved by software producing more dots in an image than were actually scanned in. Interpolated resolutions can go to 9600dpi, or higher. Generally, it's best to use the optical resolution as a buying guide.

Is more better? When it comes to image resolution the answer is probably "no." Most people do not need images scanned at the very highest resolution. The ultra-high quality that, for example, 1200x1200dpi delivers is great for printing—if your printer is up to it—but not necessary for viewing on a computer.

Files scanned at high resolution can be very large, so your friends might not appreciate you e-mailing such files to them. The larger the file, the longer it takes to download. For general computer use, 300x300dpi is enough. Many websites use images scanned at just 72x72dpi to speed up their download time. This does not mean that you should buy a lower resolution scanner to save money. With scanners so affordable, go for the highest resolution you can afford, even if you don't intend to use it often.

All scanners quote their color capability in bits. A 24-bit scanner can scan about 16.7 million different colors in an image. Scanners can pick out more colors than this, but in reality this is the highest number that most people are ever likely to need.

USING SCANNER SOFTWARE

Get to know your software. Scanner software

offers a range of settings, depending on the kind of image you want to scan, such as a photograph, text, printed material, or a web image. Making the right choice will improve the quality of your scan.

Almost all scanners come with a software bundle. Often simplified "lite" versions of full-priced software are included and are adequate for general use. Look for image-editing, image-organizing, and filing software as well as an optical character recognition program. You may also get graphics software, such as printed-card or e-card creation tools.

Use optical character recognition software to turn text on a printed page into text you can edit on your computer. This has more potential than you might think. Imagine you are a student and want to quote heavily from a book, or you want to get text into your computer for easy searching. Or perhaps you just need to edit a document someone has sent you in printed form.

If you intend to e-mail a scanned image, keep the image file as small as possible. A low image resolution helps, but so does reducing the actual area being scanned. If your scanner software does not allow you to do this, use a graphics editing application, such as Paint Shop Pro, to crop off uninteresting parts of the image.

⇨ See also **Software: Graphics** and **Photo Editing.**

SPEAKERS

With the right speakers, you can listen to five channels of Dolby Digital surround sound while playing a movie or game.

Although most modern PC sound systems are compatible with current software, it is best to stick with well-known, and trusted, manufacturers. Not only does this ensure that you'll get consistent and high-quality sound from games and multimedia software, but, if there is a problem, help will be readily available and driver updates can be easily found and installed from the manufacturer's website. This applies to both the soundcard and speakers, since having a good soundcard is pointless if the speakers aren't up to the job.

Using a decent soundcard will let you play back surround sound through four speakers. Yet, this will only emulate the effect of 3D sound. To get full Dolby Digital surround sound from your PC,

you need a soundcard with digital output. You also need a decoder/amplifier, to turn the digital signal into five discreet channels of sound: two at the front, two at the back, and a central channel for speech.

Many manufacturers, such as Creative Labs, sell complete systems, with speakers and stands included. The speakers are relatively small, but powerful and of high quality. It is a good idea to check out a few different speaker systems in the store before you buy, because sound quality is really a matter of personal taste.

If you have a home sound system situated near your PC, you don't necessarily need to have separate speakers for your computer. The PC's sound can be rerouted into a spare input on your stereo system—an auxiliary input, for example—to play back the sounds. The disadvantage with this is that your sound system will need to be on all the time if you want to hear the Windows system and Office alert sounds while you work.

A subwoofer speaker does not need a separate sound channel. A special filter separates the lowest frequency sounds—those that cannot be adequately projected by small speakers—and plays them back through a much larger sub-woofer speaker, which is usually placed on the floor. The subwoofer doesn't need to be positioned as carefully as the other speakers because the human ear is less sensitive to the direction of low-frequency sounds.

⇨ See also **Software: Games.**

SURGE PROTECTOR

Learn how to use a surge protector to help prevent computer damage.

Surge protectors are small adaptors which fit between your PC and your electrical outlet. Some protectors come with a guarantee against problems caused by electrical surges while using the device. Always turn off all devices before plugging and unplugging connections.

 HOW TO: ADD DOLBY DIGITAL SURROUND SOUND

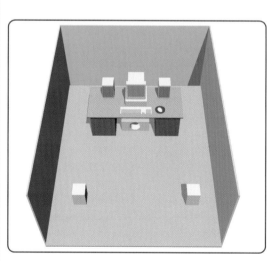

1 To be able to listen to Dolby Digital sound from your PC, you need a soundcard that has a digital output. The SoundBlaster Live! Platinum has a special input/output panel, which uses up a spare drive bay and has the appropriate output.

2 After installing the soundcard, connect the digital output to the input of the Dolby Digital decoder box. Rather than the PC handling the conversion of sound from digital data to analog waves, the task is handled by the decoder box.

3 Position all speakers away from the walls. Place the two front speakers equidistant in front of you, with the speech speaker in the middle. Place the rear speakers behind you. Put the subwoofer on the floor, between the front two speakers, and plug in the cables.

A **large percentage of data loss** and computer hardware failures are the result of power problems. Even a single surge protector between your computer and the electrical outlet will provide you with protection against voltage fluctuations and surges in your power supply.

Because an electrical surge can also affect your PC through connected drives—such as the monitor, printer, modem, or telephone connections—try to get a multioutlet surge protector with telephone cable sockets. Plug all

your computer devices and peripherals into it, and connect the phone line. The multisocket version will protect against surges that can damage your PC through the serial, USB, or monitor connections.

Not sure exactly what you want or where to get it? There are many manufacturers to choose from and many different types of surge protection device. For more advice and products try the American Power Conversion site (www.advanced power.com) or Panamax (www.panamax-dist. com). Or visit the BuyBuddy website (www. buybuddy.com/sleuth/27/1/1030402/0/) to see comparisons between the most popular devices

on the market. Alternatively, try FirstSource.com (www.firstsource.com), click on Computer Hardware and then the Power Equipment link on the left-hand side. On the next page, click on Surge Suppressors to view This Week's Specials, including suppressors for home PCs, laptops, and notebooks.

TELEPHONE CONNECTIONS

Make the most of your modem and get the ultimate Internet conection for your particular device.

Problems with you Internet connection? Make sure that the telephone number for your Internet service provider's dial-up is correct. Start Internet Explorer and click on Tools → Internet Options. Select the Connections tab and then click the Settings button in the Dial-up settings panel. In the next dialog box, click on Properties. Check the Internet service provider's dial-up number and area code, and adjust if necessary. You may need to confirm your Internet service provider's dial-up number by phoning their helpline.

Not sure whether you are actually connected to the Internet? Even if you are not connected you may still see your homepage if it's has been cached. So try loading another web page and take a look at the System Tray in the bottom right-hand corner of your Desktop for the Dial-up icon—two green computers. Watch them for a few seconds, and if the small screens flash, then your computer is receiving data over your Internet connection.

You still can't get connected? Check that the telephone cable is securely attached to your modem, and if you share a phone line with other telephones in your home, make sure that no one else is on the line and that all handsets are properly replaced; otherwise, they will cause your connection to fail.

How old is your telephone cable? Old or your Internet surfing. If you can hear crackling when you listen to your phone receiver and you use the same line for your Internet

connection, that noise can be enough to cause your connection to falter or fail completely. The only way to remedy this is to replace the cable.

Telephone charges can vary to a minor extent, depending on where you live in Canada. But most major Canadian telephone companies, such as Manitoba's MTS (www.mts.mb.ca), have extensive websites to provide you with information about the quality and the cost of

the full variety of Internet-connection services they are able to supply to their customers.

Avoid missing phone calls when you're online. Many modern modems—both internal and external—are capable of notifying you when a phone call is trying to get through while you're surfing the Net—some even act as answering machines with a message playback facility. To use such modems, however, you must subscribe to your phone company's call waiting service.

DSL (Digital Subscriber Line) technology is the fastest Internet connection medium currently available at an affordable price. DSL (www.dsl. com) can transmit up to 6Mbps to a subscriber and 832Kbps to subscriber and sender at the

same time. A DSL circuit connects a DSL modem on each end of the sender and receiver's regular phone line. Since the signal is digital, it can transmit signals simultaneously.

DSL does have its drawbacks. The quality of your connection is dependent on the number of people using the DSL line through your local telephone exchange. It can also be affected by how far away the local exchange is from your home—generally, problems may occur if it's over four miles—because the digital signal weakens the further it has to travel along standard telephone cable. As a result, the older the cabling, the greater the possibility of signal deterioration.

TROUBLESHOOTING

Even the most reliable PCs can have a few operating problems from time to time. Here are a some helpful tips to solve some computer glitches.

Some hardware problems are easily solved by simply checking the connections. If a message tells you that the printer is not connected, for example, then check that the cable from your PC to your printer is secure. Also check that the power cord is securely connected to your printer and plugged into the wall outlet.

Before or after? Many hardware devices require you to install the driver software that runs them on your PC before you physically connect the device to your computer. But other devices may need connecting before the drivers are installed.

Check the manual before you start; otherwise you may find you've installed items in the wrong order and your computer will not recognize the new device.

If you've installed new hardware, it might be causing conflicts with existing devices. Right-click on My Computer and select Properties. Click on the Device Manager tab in the System Properties window. If there are any devices causing problems, they will either have a yellow question mark next to them, meaning the system is having problems resolving the function of the device, or a red cross, meaning that the device is actively tagged as being disruptive to the system.

Having hardware problems? Click on Help in the Start menu. In the Help and Support window type "hardware" in the Search panel and click on Go. When the search results appear, click on the Hardware Troubleshooter link In the right-hand panel a series of questions will help locate the problem and take you through the repair process.

TROUBLESHOOTING SITES
Want to know what the online experts advise? Here's where to look.

PC Hell (www.pchell.com)
A helpful site offering support for online hardware, software, problems, and more.

Host Club (www.hostclub.net)
Provides free membership in a hardware troubleshooting site composed of literally hundreds of computer users.

Smart Computing (www.smartcomputing.com)
An invaluable site offering troubleshooting, tutorials, and general advice on a wide range of PC topics.

PC Guide (www.pcguide.com)
An all-round PC reference site, including a dedicated troubleshooting and repair guide

ZDNet (www.zdnet.com)
Don't be put off by the techy content of the homepage—the site contains a very useful Help and How -To section for PC users.

HOW TO: REINSTALL YOUR PRINTER SOFTWARE

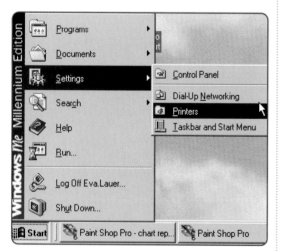

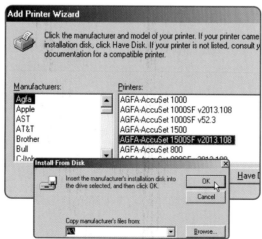

① Remove your printer from the Windows setup. Go to Start → Settings, and select Printers. In the Printers window, click the icon representing your printer, and then press the Delete key on your keyboard.

② Click the Add Printer icon. In the Wizard that pops up, click Next. Select Local printer, click Next, and then select your printer from the Manufacturers and Printers lists. Then, click Have Disk and follow the Wizard's on-screen instructions to reinstall your printer.

Printing problems can be caused by your printer software. First make sure that your computer recognizes your printer. Go to Start → Settings → Printers. In the Printers dialog box, select the printer you want to use by clicking the appropriate icon. Make this your default printer by going to File → Set as Default.

Is your hard disk causing the problem? Errors do occur on your hard disk, and they happen for a variety of reasons. Sometimes errors can't be repaired, but more often running the ScanDisk program will sort them out. Go to Start → Programs → Accessories → System Tools → ScanDisk. Select the hard drive, click on Thorough in the Type of test section, and make sure there's a checkmark in the Automatically fix errors box. Click Start. It is likely to take a little while to scan and repair the whole disk.

Does your PC freeze whenever you run a specific program? If so, it will be either a problem with the program itself or a conflict with another program you are running. When you get a freeze, press the Ctrl+Alt+Delete keys together. The Close Program window shows all the programs currently running, and highlights the program with the problem. To close the program, click the End Task button.

Keep your computer trouble free with diagnostic software such as Dr. Watson in your System Tools menu or your Windows folder, and Norton Utilities, available online from Symantec (www.symantec.com/product/home-ps.html).

TV ON YOUR PC

Watch your favorite TV shows on your PC by installing a TV tuner card.

A TV tuner card is hardware that converts the digital signal of your PC into a television signal and vice versa, letting you watch TV on your computer or use your TV screen as a monitor. Make sure that the monitor and TV display are the same number of pixels in size and have the same color settings. Go to Start → Settings → Control Panel and double-click the Display icon. Adjust the Screen area and Colors settings and finally Click OK.

Tuner cards come with suitable software. For example, the Pinnacle Studio PCTV comes with a Pinnacle Systems TV viewer and a Video Editor, so that you can save your video clips as .mpeg files. You will need a free PCI slot in your computer, and a graphics card that supports Windows 95 DirectDraw. Your soundcard must also be Direct X compatible. Some graphics cards, like the Photon Torpedo 3DMTV (www.photonweb.com), incorporate a TV tuner as well as an FM radio and camera and VCR input. So you don't need any other hardware to watch TV on your PC.

Check your external connections. First locate the PC graphics card, and then check whether it features a TV-out socket. This socket connects to your TV via a cable. One common connection is a DS-Video to Scart adaptor cable. If your

graphics card does not support TV-out, you will need to upgrade it for one that does.

Receive cable and over-the-air TV channels. Most tuner cards are compatible with both cable and over-the-air TV channels, but be sure to choose the right TV region (for example U.S.A.) when scanning for cable channels.

Tune in to Internet transmissions. Some tuner cards let you watch transmissions from the Net. Tuner cards offer a variety of features, so it's worth checking exactly what's offered before you purchase a particular type.

⇨ See also **Hardware: Video Capture Cards.**

USB

Most modern PCs come with two USB (Universal Serial Bus) ports, found on the back of the case.

The need for speed. If you are considering buying a digital camera, or other devices that

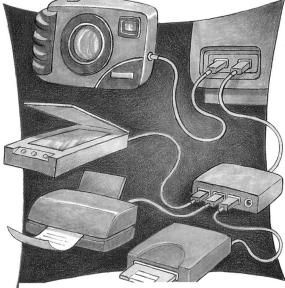

require data to be transferred quickly to and from your PC, take a look at the USB version rather than serial- or parallel-port versions. USB is considerably faster than either of the other methods of connection, and you can plug in and unplug a USB device without having to switch off your PC.

HOW TO: CONNECT YOUR TV TUNER CARD

1 Turn off the PC and remove the cover. Plug the tuner card into a free PCI slot on your motherboard—it is a long connector into which your tuner card will fit neatly. Replace the cover.

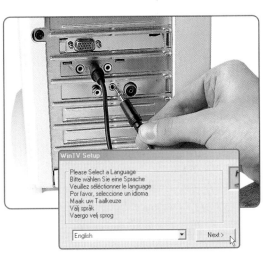

2 To get sound, connect the audio loop-back cord from the Audio Jack-Out socket on the tuner card to the Audio Jack-In socket on your soundcard. Restart your PC. Insert the installation CD and follow the instructions.

Computer crossover. USB allows you to use the same devices, such as printers, Zip drives, scanners, and CD-R writers, with either a PC or a Mac. This allows you to buy a printer that can work with both your PC and your kid's iMac.

A PC usually has two USB ports. If you have more than two USB devices, such as a digital camera, mouse, and modem, use a USB hub, which lets you attach four or more devices. These are unobtrusive and inexpensive, and require no installation. You can even connect hubs together and have up to 127 USB devices connected at one time.

If your PC doesn't have USB ports, you can buy a USB card, which fits into a spare slot inside your PC. You can also get a USB port adapter that fits into the card slot on a laptop. Installation is easy and once installed, the connection will operate

USB DEVICES
Hardware that works better using a USB connection.

Scanners
USB enables a fast transfer of large amounts of data to your PC.

Handheld computers
These need fast connections to regularly backup and send data to your PC.

Digital cameras
Cameras are similar to scanners and the image files can be large (up to 3Mb), so they need a fast connection.

CompactFlash and SmartCard readers
These plug into a USB port and allow you to read your cards directly from your PC.

A USB hard drive
This is a useful portable option for keeping data safe and secure, and it lets you transfer information quickly and efficiently.

just as well as a standard USB port. Before you buy, check that you have a spare PCI slot on your motherboard—these are the white blocks.

UPGRADING HARDWARE

Upgrading your hardware can breathe new life into an older PC, and delay the expense of having to buy a new computer.

Expanding your computer's RAM from 16Mb or 32Mb to 64Mb or 128Mb can drastically improve your computer's performance, especially if you want to run more than one application at a time. Windows Me needs at least 64Mb RAM to run correctly, and if you run applications such as MS Access, Word, and Excel, you should consider 128Mb of RAM.

Recent graphics cards have more built-in memory than many new PCs had only a few years ago. If your display updates slowly, you won't be able to play 3D-accelerated games or achieve the resolution, or color depth you need. You need to install a more recent graphics card. Make sure your card is capable of displaying 3D graphics and has at least 16Mb RAM.

Modern soundcards can not only reproduce 3D sound, but also have wavetable synthesizers built in, allowing you to make your own music and play the latest computer games with surround sound. Installing a new soundcard is simply a matter of sliding the hardware into place on the motherboard and restarting your PC. Coupled with new speakers, it makes your PC sound like a home cinema and synthesizer in one.

Whether you can upgrade your processor to a higher speed depends on the processor socket on your motherboard. If you currently have a Pentium III 450MHz, you can almost double the speed just by slotting in a new processor. However, if your PC is old or if you want a processor faster than 850MHz, you'd be better

off buying a new PC because the cost of the fastest computer processors can be several hundred dollars.

Speed up your CD access and data transfer. Changing your CD-ROM for a later, faster version can speed up your data access times considerably. Alternatively, keep your old drive and add a CD burner so you can backup important data and create MP3 CDs. Because CD burning is always much slower than reading, aim for a 6 or 8x speed burner. How fast the burner can read a CD depends on the quality of the CD-Rom drive you are using and the performance of your PC. However, as a general rule, go for a read speed of at least 24x.

VIDEO CAPTURE CARDS

A video capture card is used to convert analog data from a video tape into digital information, which is then stored on your hard drive.

A video capture card fits into a PCI slot inside your PC and has connections for your camera or VCR outputs. You can even get a USB version of the card if you don't have any PCI slots left, or if you don't want to open your PC case. You'll need a reasonably fast PC to get the best results, because converting full screen video to digital data is a processor-intensive process. Try lowering the resolution if the frame rate is erratic.

Video takes up a lot of hard drive space and will require a lot of memory to run. If you are thinking of editing your videos on your PC, consider adding a large second hard drive, greater than 15Gb, to store your video data.

Some video capture cards also have built-in TV tuners. You can use these to watch TV on your computer screen, but you'll have to plug an antenna or cable in the back of the card. You can watch TV in a small window on the computer screen and can capture the video—like a video recorder—from the tuner. Most TV tuners let you capture standard broadcast and cable channels, but it's best to check this before buying the card.

If you have a digital video camera, then you don't need a video capture card because the signal is already stored in a digital format. These cameras use FireWire (a special high speed data

transfer connector) to send the data to your PC. You'll need to install a FireWire card in your PC to connect the digital video camera.

ZIP DRIVES

Zip drives are a simple and economical way to store data. You can get a parallel or USB port version, or install one internally.

Zip drives come in 100Mb or 250Mb versions, and the disks are barely larger than a standard floppy disk. The external drive unit is compact, and especially in the USB format, the transfer of data is also much faster than copying data onto

a floppy disk. The 250Mb drive version is "backwards compatible," meaning that it will also take the 100Mb disks.

You can unplug a USB drive and plug it into another computer, even an iMac, without turning either off, so long as Zip drivers are installed on both machines. Windows recognizes the Zip drive and loads the necessary drivers.

If you need to send information to a Mac, use IBM-formatted Zip disks. These work in both machines, while Mac-formatted disks are only compatible with Macs.

Zip drives include software for backing up your data. You can set up a scheduled backup, select specific files and folders to be backed up, and set how frequently backups should occur. To save you time, set the automatic backup for a time when you're not using your PC.

If you want to speed up data transfer from a USB Zip 250 drive, you can get a FireWire adaptor, which plugs on the back of the drive and more than doubles the read speed. If you have a laptop without a USB port, you can get a PC card adaptor for the Zip 250.

HOW TO: INSTALL A ZIP DRIVE

(1) To install the USB Zip drive, insert the installation CD into the computer's CD-ROM drive. The program should run automatically. Follow the on-screen instructions to install the software. Choose a destination directory for the program files.

(2) Use the USB cord supplied with the drive to connect it to your PC. Each end is different, so it is easy to insert them correctly. If the plug doesn't fit, try it the other way round, because USB plugs only fit one way.

(3) Connect the power supply to the Zip drive. Insert a disk into the drive. The Zip250 icon, showing that it is installed, will appear in My Computer and Windows Explorer.

GLOSSARY

A

A: The floppy disk drive on a PC. In speech, it is referred to as the "A drive." See *Floppy disk*.

Accessories Mini-programs, such as Calculator or Notepad, built into Windows to perform simple tasks.

Active window The window you are working in. To activate a window, click on it, and it will jump to the front of your screen, in front of any other open windows. See *Window*.

Alt key A key on the keyboard that gives commands when pressed in combination with other keys.

Application A program that performs specific kinds of tasks. For example, Microsoft Word is a word-processing application that is used to create text-based documents.

Archive To transfer files to a separate storage system, such as a Zip disk.

Arrow keys The four keys at the bottom of the keyboard that move the cursor up, down, left, and right.

Attachment A file, such as a picture or spreadsheet, sent with an e-mail message.

Audio file A file containing a digital recording of sound. In Windows, audio files usually have ".wav" after their file name. See *Digital*.

B

Backup A duplicate copy of a file, made in case of accidental loss or damage to the original file.

BIOS Basic Input/Output System. Instructions that control the computer's hardware at the most basic level. The BIOS tells the operating system which hardware to expect to come into operation and how it is arranged.

Bit The smallest unit of computer memory, bit is a contraction of "binary digit." Its value can be only 1 or 0. All computers use the binary system to process data.

Bitmap An on-screen image made up of tiny dots or pixels. See *Pixel*.

Bits per second (bps) A measurement of the speed at which data can be sent to or from a computer via a modem.

Boot or boot up To switch on the computer.

Bug An accidental error or fault in a computer program. Bugs may cause programs to crash, which can lead to data loss.

Button An on-screen image that can be clicked on using the mouse. Clicking on a button performs a function, such as opening a dialog box or confirming an action.

Byte A unit of computer memory, made up of eight bits. It takes one byte of memory to store a single character, such as a letter of the alphabet. See *Bit*.

C

C: The hard disk of a PC, on which all programs and documents are stored. In speech, it is referred to as the "C drive."

Cache A section of high-speed memory that stores data recently used by the PC's processor, thereby increasing the speed at which that data can be accessed again.

Cell A small rectangular section of a spreadsheet or database, into which text or figures are entered. Click on a cell to make it active, ready for entering data.

CD-ROM Compact Disc Read Only Memory. A CD containing up to 650Mb of data. Most software programs now come on CD-ROM. CD-ROMs are usually inserted into and accessed from the "D drive" on the PC. See *Drive*.

Chip A device that processes information at the most basic level within a computer. A processor chip carries out calculations and a memory chip stores data.

Click To press and release the left mouse button once. This is how to select menu and dialog box options and toolbar buttons.

Clip art Graphic images that can be inserted into text-based documents and then resized and manipulated.

Clipboard When text or an image is cut or copied from a document, it is stored on the Clipboard. The Windows Clipboard stores only one piece of data at a time, regardless of its size—anything from a comma to this whole glossary and more. Each new cut or copy automatically overwrites the previous material on the Clipboard. You can put the current Clipboard material into as many documents as you like using the Paste command. See *Cut, Copy,* and *Paste*.

Close A command, usually found on the File menu, that shuts the active document, but not the program. A document can also be closed by clicking the close button in its top right-hand corner.

CMOS Complementary Metal Oxide Semiconductor. A memory chip that stores the computer's configuration settings and the date and time. See *Configuration*.

Compressed files Files that have been temporarily condensed so they use less memory and can be copied or downloaded in a fraction of the time it would otherwise take.

Configuration The settings used to make sure that hardware or software runs as the user wants.

Control Panel Any adjustments made to your system or its settings are made through the Control Panel. For example, you can change the way your Desktop looks, add new hardware, or alter your PC's sound output. To access the contents of the Control Panel, go to Start→Settings→Control Panel. Or click on the My Computer icon, then on the Control Panel icon.

Copy To make a duplicate of a file, image, or section of text.

CPU Central Processing Unit. The brain of your PC, which carries out millions of arithmetic and control functions every second. The power of a CPU is usually defined by its speed in MegaHertz (MHz), which is the number of times it "thinks" per second. For example, an 800 MHz CPU carries out 800 million calculations per second.

Crash Your PC has crashed if it has stopped working, the screen has "frozen," and there is no response to keyboard or mouse commands. A crash usually requires you to restart the computer.

Cursor A marker, usually a flashing vertical line, that indicates where the next letter or digit typed in will appear in the document.

Cursor keys See *Arrow keys*.

Cut To remove selected text and/or images to the Clipboard, where they are stored for later use.

D

Data Any information processed by, or stored on, a computer.

Database A program used for storing, organizing, and sorting information. Each entry is called a record, and each category in a record is called a field.

Default Settings and preferences automatically adopted by your PC for any program when none are specified by the user.

Defragmenter A program that "tidies" files on the hard disk. When a file is saved to the hard disk, Windows may not be able to save all parts of it in the same place, so the elements of the file become fragmented. This makes the retrieval of the file much slower. The Disk Defragmenter program solves this problem by regrouping all related data in the same place.

Delete To remove a selected file, folder, image, or piece of text completely. If you delete text or another item from a document, you can immediately undelete it using the Edit ➔ Undo function or the Undo toolbar button.

Desktop When Windows has finished starting up, it presents you with a set of icons on screen. The icons represent the items you would find in an office, such as files, folders, and a waste basket. These icons, together with the Taskbar and Start button are known collectively as the Desktop. See *Icon* and *Taskbar*.

Dial-up connection The process of accessing an ISP or another computer along a phone line.

Dialog box A window that appears on screen displaying a message from the program currently in use. This usually asks for preferences or information to be input by the user. See *Prompt*.

Digital Data that exists in binary number form as "zeros" and "ones." Computers process digital data.

Digital image An image stored in number format, which can be transferred to hard disks or removable storage disks, displayed on screen or printed.

Disk A device for storing digital information. A hard disk is composed of a stack of rigid disks; a floppy disk has just one flexible disk.

Disk tools Programs that manage and maintain the hard disk. They can make sure that data is stored efficiently and that the hard disk runs at optimum speed.

Document A single piece of work created in a program. Also referred to as a file. See *File*.

DOS Disk Operating System. The standard operating system for PCs before *Windows*.

Dots per inch (dpi) The number of dots that a printer can print on one square inch of paper. The more dots, the greater the detail and the better quality the printout.

Double-click To press and release the left mouse button twice in quick succession.

Download To copy a file or program from another computer to your own. For example, when you collect e-mail from an Internet service provider, you are downloading it.

Drag A mouse action used to highlight text, reshape objects, or move an object or file. To move an object, for instance, with the mouse pointer, click on it and keep the left mouse button held down. Move the mouse pointer and the object moves with it.

Drive A device that holds a disk. The drive has a motor that spins the disk, and a head that reads it—like the needle on a record player.

Driver Software that translates instructions from Windows into a form that can be understood by a hardware device such as a printer.

DVD Digital Versatile Disc or Digital Video Disc. A CD-like disc that can store 4.7Gb or more of information—several times more data than a CD-ROM. It can store an entire movie.

E

E-mail Electronic Mail. Messages sent from one computer to another through the Internet.

Error message A small window that appears on screen warning the user that a fault has occurred and, where appropriate, suggesting action to remedy it.

Expansion card An add-on piece of hardware that fits into a PC and expands its functions—for example, a soundcard.

External hardware Additional computer equipment, such as a printer or scanner, attached by cable to a PC.

F

Field A category of information in a database, such as Name, Address, or Telephone Number.

File Any item stored on a computer, for example a program, a document, or an image.

File extension A three-letter code that appears at the end of a file name to indicate what type of file it is.

File format The way in which files created by different programs are saved. This differs from program to program, so that one program may have difficulty reading files created by another. Common file format extensions are:

Text	.asc .doc .html .msg .txt .wpd
Image	.bmp .eps .gif .jpg .pict .png .tif
Sound	.au .mid .ra .snd .wav
Video	.avi .mov .mpg .qt
Compressed	.arc .arj .gz .hqx .sit .tar .z .zip
Program	.bat .com .exe

Find A program that searches a PC for a file, if given information such as the file name or creation date. Also, a similar command in a program that searches a file for specified information, such as a phrase.

Floppy disk A portable data storage device. Each disk can hold up to 1.44Mb of information. Often used to back up data from the hard disk. See *Hard disk*.

Folder An electronic storage compartment used to keep related files and relevant documents in the same place on the hard disk.

Font A specific point size, style, and set of characters for a typeface (e.g., 12 point Arial Bold.) A typeface is a particular type design.

Format To establish the appearance of a document—for example, its typography, layout, and so on.

Freeware Programs, usually produced by hobby programmers, for which users do not pay a fee. Freeware often can be downloaded from the Internet.

Function keys These are the 12 keys (labelled F1, F2 and so on) situated at the top of the keyboard. They perform special operations, depending on which program is being used. For instance, Shift+F7 in Word will call up the Thesaurus.

G

Gigabyte (Gb) A unit of memory capacity. A single gigabyte is 1,000 megabytes which is equivalent to almost 200 copies of the Bible.

.gif file Graphics Interchange Format. A common format extension, used for storing images and bitmapped color graphics, especially on the Internet.

Graphics Pictures, photographs, illustrations, clip art, and any other type of image.

H

Hard disk A computer's high-speed storage device. It contains the operating system, the programs and all created files. The hard disk is referred to as the C drive or hard drive.

Hard drive see *Hard disk.*

Hardware The physical parts of a computer, including the CPU, monitor, keyboard, and mouse.

Header The area at the top of a page in a document. Text entered in the header (such as a title) appears on every page of the document.

Help key Usually the F1 key. Pressed to access advice and information on how to perform the task the user is currently engaged in.

Highlight To select a word, a section of text or a group of cells, use the mouse to click and drag over them.

I

Icon A graphic representation of a file or a function, which is designed to be easily recognizable as the item it represents. For example, the printer icon on the toolbar accesses the print function.

Import To bring in and use an element, such as text, a picture or clip art image, from another file into the active document.

Inkjet printer A printer that works by squirting tiny drops of ink onto the surface of the paper. Inkjets are by far the most common type of home printer.

Install To copy a program onto the hard disk and then set it up so it is ready for use. Programs are usually installed from CD-ROMs, but can be downloaded from the Internet.

Internet Millions of computers throughout the world linked together by telephone and cable lines. Computer users can communicate with each other and exchange information over the Internet with a phone connection to their Internet service provider.

ISP Internet Service Provider. A company that provides a connection to the Internet (compare *OSP*).

J

Jaz disk A portable storage device that is capable of storing up to 2Gb of data. See also *Floppy disk, Zip disk.*

JPEG Joint Photographics Experts Group. A compressed format for storing images so that they use less storage space on a computer.

K

Keyboard shortcut A method of issuing a command using a combination of keystrokes. To the practiced user, this is quicker than manipulating the mouse.

Kilobyte (Kb) A unit of memory capacity. A single kilobyte is equivalent to 1,000 bytes. A short letter created in Word uses about 20Kb. See *Gigabyte, Megabyte.*

L

Landscape See *Orientation.*

Laptop A portable computer.

Laser printer A printer that uses a laser beam to etch images onto a drum and then transfers the image to paper. The reproduction quality is usually higher than with an inkjet printer. See *Inkjet printer.*

Launcher A window in some software suites, such as Microsoft Works, through which the suite's various programs are opened.

Logging on The process of accessing computers, files or websites using a password or other instructions.

M

Maximize To increase the size of a window so that it fills the entire screen. The Maximize button is the middle button in the set of three in the top right-hand corner of a window. Once used, this button becomes a Restore button. Click on it to restore the window to its original size.

Megabyte (Mb) A unit of memory capacity. A single megabyte is 1,000 kilobytes, which is equivalent to a 400-page novel.

Memory A computer's capacity for storing information. See also *RAM* and *ROM.*

Menu bar The line of menu options that runs along the top of a window. When a menu is selected, its entire list of options (a drop-down menu) is displayed.

MIDI Musical Instrument Digital Interface. A universal standard language that allows specially adapted musical instruments to communicate with computers. MIDI cables are required to connect the instrument to the computer.

Minimize To reduce a window to a button on the Taskbar. The Minimize button is the left button in the set of three in the top right-hand corner of a window. To restore the window to the screen, click on its button on the Taskbar.

Modem A device that converts digital signals from a computer into analog signals that can be transmitted by phone, then reconverted by another modem into the original digital data.

Monitor The viewing screen on which you see your computer's files. Images are made up of thousands of tiny dots.

Motherboard The circuit board that houses a PC's central processing unit (see *CPU*), some memory, and slots into which expansions cards can be installed. See *Chip, Memory,* and *Expansion card.*

Mouse pointer A small arrow on screen that moves when the mouse is moved. Other representations of the pointer—depending on the program being used and the type of action being carried out—include a pointing hand, a pen and a cross. When you click in a text document, the cursor will appear. See *Cursor*.

Multimedia Sound, images, animated graphics, text, and video are all different types of media—means of communicating. A single document using more than one of these can be said to be a multimedia document. A computer able to provide and handle different media is generally referred to as a multimedia computer.

My Computer An icon found on any PC Desktop running Windows. Click on the icon to open a window that gives access all the computer hardware present in the system. These might include the hard drive [C:], floppy drive [A:], CD-ROM drive [D:], printer, and tools for monitoring and adjusting the system set-up. See *Icon*.

My Documents An folder icon located on the Desktop of any PC running Windows. It represents a storage location for files that users have created themselves. Click on the icon to open the folder.

N

Network The connection of several computers and printers so that they can share files and messages.

O

Online The status of a computer that is actively connected to the Internet. Also used as a general term for people who are able to connect to the Internet. See *Internet*.

Open To look inside a file or folder to view its contents. To open a file or folder, either double-click on it, right-click on it and select Open from the pop-up menu, or select it and go to File ➔ Open.

Operating system The software that controls the running of a computer, allowing, for example, programs to communicate with hardware devices such as printers. Windows is now the most popular operating system for PCs.

Orientation An option available when creating a document. Users can choose to set up a page as either Landscape (of greater width than height) or Portrait (of greater height than width), depending on how they want the final version of the document to appear.

OSP Online Service Provider. A company that provides not only Internet access (compare *ISP*), but also additional content, such as shopping, entertainment and leisure channels, chatrooms, and newsgroups. OSPs include AOL, AT&T Canada, Rogers, and Videotron.

P

Page break The point at which one page ends and another begins. In Microsoft Word, a page break can be inserted by pressing the Ctrl and Enter keys at the same time.

Parallel port A socket at the rear of a computer that allows you to connect a printer.

Paste The insertion into a document of text or other data that has been cut or copied.

PC-compatible Software or hardware that will work on a standard PC.

PCI slot A spare space inside a PC for extra expansion cards, such as a soundcard or graphics card.

Peripheral A device, such as a scanner, that can be connected to a PC but is not vital to its function.

Pixel An individual dot on a computer screen. The number of pixels horizontally and vertically on the screen determines the level of detail and the quality of the image that can be displayed. This can be set and altered by the user.

Plug-ins Programs that are needed to open and run certain files, such as video clips or sound files. Websites often provide plug-ins for visitors to download, so that they are able to view the entire site. See *Download*.

Point size Measurement used for typefaces. For example, the type on this page is 9 point; newspaper headlines are usually between 36 and 72 point.

Port A socket at the rear of a computer that allows users to connect a monitor, printer or a peripheral device, such as a modem.

Portrait See *Orientation*.

Primary key In a database this is the main category by which you generally sort your database entries.

Printer driver A piece of software that enables Windows to communicate with the printer. See *Driver*.

Print Preview On-screen display that shows users exactly how the active document will look when printed.

Processor The central processing unit (CPU) of a PC. See *Chip, CPU*.

Program Software that allows the user to interact with the computer's hardware to perform a specific type of task. For instance, a word-processing program allows the user to direct the computer in all aspects of handling and presenting text.

Prompt A window that appears on screen to remind users that additional information is required. See *Dialog box*.

Properties The attributes of a file or folder, such as its creation date and format. Some properties, such as the author's name, can be altered. To access the Properties window, right-click on an item and select Properties from the pop-up menu.

R

RAM Random Access Memory. Memory chips used for the temporary storage of information, such as the currently active file.

Record An individual entry in a database comprising several categories of information. For example, an address book database comprises entries—or records—each of which has a name, address and telephone number.

Recycle Bin A Desktop feature that allows you to delete files. To delete a file completely, drag it onto the Recycle Bin, right-click, and select Empty Recycle Bin from the menu.

Registry This is Windows' own database of instructions and settings that is the operating system's main reference for the effective running of the computer.

Reset button A button on a PC that allows users to restart it if it "freezes" and refuses to respond to any commands. The Reset button should only be used as a last resort.

Resolution The degree of detail on a screen or a printed document. It is measured in dots per inch (dpi). The more dots per square inch, the greater the detail.

Right-click To press and release the right mouse button once. Most commonly used to display a pop-up context menu.

ROM Read Only Memory. Memory chips used by the computer for storing basic details about the PC, such as *BIOS*.

Run command A Windows feature that allows you to type in the name of the program you want to use, or the DOS command you want to execute. To use, go to Start ➔ Run.

S

Save To copy a document to the computer's hard disk for future use. To do this, press Ctrl+S on the keyboard, click on the Save toolbar button, or go to File ➔ Save.

Save As A way of saving a file under a different name or format. If the file was previously saved under a different name or format, that version will remain unchanged. This is useful for saving an edited file, while still keeping the original.

Scanner A device for converting images on paper into electronic images that can then be manipulated and reproduced by a PC. See *Digital, Digital Image.*

Screensaver A picture or animation that appears on screen when the PC is left idle for a specified time.

Scroll To move through the contents of a window or menu vertically or horizontally.

Search engines Huge databases on the Internet that are used to locate websites relevant to specified search criteria. They can look for either key words or phrases or for categories, then subcategories.

Select To choose a file, folder, image, text, or other item, by clicking on it or highlighting it, before manipulating it. For example, selecting some text before styling it.

Serial port A socket at the rear of a computer that allows one of a number of peripheral devices, including a modem, to be connected. Most PCs have two serial ports, identified as COM1 and COM2. See also *Parallel Port.*

Shareware Programs, or reduced versions of programs, that can be sampled for free for a limited period. Users must then purchase the program to continue to use it.

Shortcut An icon on the Desktop that links to a file, folder, or program stored on the hard disk. It is created to provide quicker access to the file and looks identical to the icon of the linked item, except that it has a small arrow in the bottom left-hand corner.

Software Programs that allow users to perform specific functions, such as to write a letter. Microsoft Excel and Microsoft Word are examples of software.

Software suite A collection of programs that come in a single package, often supplied when a PC is bought. For example, Microsoft Office is a software suite that includes word processing, database, and spreadsheet programs.

Soundcard A device that lets users record, play and edit sound files. It fits into an expansion slot on the motherboard. See *Sound file.*

Sound file A file containing audio data. To hear the sound, double-click on the file (you will need speakers and a *soundcard.*)

Spreadsheet A document for storing and calculating numerical data. Spreadsheets are used mainly for financial planning and accounting.

Start button The button on the left of the Taskbar through which users can access the Start menu and its options, which include Programs and Help. It is sometimes referred to as the Windows button.

Status bar A bar that appears along the bottom of program windows, giving users information about the document being worked on.

Styling Establishing the appearance of the contents of a file. For example, by making text bold (heavier-looking and more distinct) or italic (slanting to the right), or by changing its color and size. See *Format.*

Super disk A portable storage device similar in appearance to a floppy disk. Each disk can store up to 200Mb of data. A super-disk drive can also read floppy disks. See also *Floppy disk, Zip disk, Jaz disk.*

System software The software that operates the PC, managing its hardware and programs. Windows is the system software for PCs.

System unit The box-shaped part of the PC that contains the hard disk, the CPU, memory, and sockets for connections to peripheral devices.

T

Tab A function used for setting and presetting the position of text.

Tab key A key on the keyboard (next to the Q key) used to tabulate text, to move between cells in spreadsheets, or to move from one database field to the next.

Taskbar A bar usually situated along the bottom of the screen in Windows that displays the Start button and buttons for all the programs and documents that are currently open. The Taskbar can be moved to any of the four sides of the screen by clicking on it and dragging it to a new location.

Task Wizard See *Wizard.*

Template A format for saving a document, such as a letterhead, the basic elements of which you want to use in future documents. When you open a template, a copy of it appears for you to work on; the template itself remains unaltered for further use.

Tile To reduce in size a group of open windows and then arrange them so that they can all be seen on screen together at once.

Toolbar A bar or window containing clickable buttons used to issue commands or access functions. For example, spreadsheet programs have a toolbar containing buttons that are clicked on to perform calculations or add decimal places. Other toolbars let you make changes to pictures or drawing. See *Taskbar.*

Typeface See *Font.*

U

Undo A function in some programs that allows you to reverse the task (or last three tasks) most recently carried out. Go to Edit ➔ Undo or click on the Undo toolbar button.

Uninstall To remove programs from the PC's hard disk. Software is available for uninstalling programs that do not contain an inbuilt uninstall option.

Upgrade To improve the performance or specification of a PC by adding new hardware components such as a higher capacity disk drive. See *Hardware.*

URL Uniform Resource Locator. A standard style used for all website addresses on the Internet.

The first part of the URL, such as www.yahoo.com, indicates the location of a computer on the Internet. Anything that follows—such as /myhome/mypage.htm—gives a location of a particular file on the computer.

USB Universal Serial Bus. A hardware connector that allows users to add devices such as mouse, modems and keyboards to a computer without having to restart. See *Device, Hardware.*

Utilities Software that assists in certain housekeeping or troubleshooting computer functions, such as uninstalling and virus-scanning.

V

View A menu in many programs through which users can change the way a file is displayed on screen. For example, users can choose to see a Word document in Normal, Web Layout, Print Layout, or Outline View.

Virus A program designed to damage a computer system. Viruses can be spread through floppy disks or through programs downloaded from the Internet.

W

Wallpaper In Windows, an image or pattern used as the background on the Desktop.

Window Each program or file on your PC can be viewed and worked on in its own self-contained area of screen called a window. All windows have their own menu bar, through which users can issue commands. Several windows can be open at once on the Desktop.

Windows The most popular operating system for PCs, which allows users to run many programs at once and open files on screen enclosed by frames called "windows." See *Operating system.*

Windows Explorer A program that allows users to view the contents of a PC's hard disk in a single window. See *Hard disk.*

Wizard A tool within a program that guides users through customizing a predesigned document.

WordArt A graphic text image that can be customized and imported into a document for decorative effect.

Word processing Text-based operations on the PC, such as letter writing.

World Wide Web The part of the Internet, composed of millions of linked web pages, that can be viewed using web browsing software. Other functions of the Internet, such as e-mail, are not part of the World Wide Web. See *Internet.*

Z

Zip disk A portable storage device that is capable of storing up to 200Mb of information. Zip disks require a special Zip drive.

Zip file A file that has been compressed with WinZip or another compression program. The term is not related to Zip drives or disks.

Zoom To enlarge an area of a document for ease of viewing.

INDEX

Page references in **bold** indicate the page or pages where the main entries for the subject appear.

ACKNOWLEDGMENTS

We would like to thank the following individuals and
organizations for their assistance in producing this book.

Agfa, Casio, Epson, Fuji, Hewlett Packard, Logitech, Microsoft, Microtech,
Sony, Superhire, Texas Instruments, Twinhead, Yepp
Photography: Karl Adamson
Styling: Darren Jordan, Jo Harris
Illustrations: Richard Elson, Nigel Dobbyn, Ian Ward
Willian McLean Kerr, David Farris, Matt Drew
Web image (p. 288): Reproduced with the permission of
the Minister of Public Works and Government Services Canada, 2001